Cyber Security: Law and Guidance

Cyber Security: Law and Guidance

Second Edition

Helen Wong MBE

Bloomsbury Professional

LONDON • DUBLIN • EDINBURGH • NEW YORK • NEW DELHI • SYDNEY

BLOOMSBURY PROFESSIONAL

Bloomsbury Publishing Plc
50 Bedford Square, London, WC1B 3DP, UK
1385 Broadway, New York, 10018, USA
29 Earlsfort Terrace, Dublin 2, Ireland

British Library Cataloguing-in-Publication Data

A catalogue record for this book is available from the British Library.

ISBN: PB: 978-1-52652-810-0
Epdf: 978-1-52652-812-4
Epub: 978-1-52652-811-7

Typeset by Evolution Design & Digital Ltd (Kent)
Printed and bound by CPI Group (UK) Ltd, Croydon, CR0 4YY

About this book

In the current dynamic landscape, the world remains critically vulnerable to cyber-attacks, and the intricacies of cyber-security laws are often misunderstood. The complex matrix of data protection, privacy, and cyber-security laws, along with self-regulatory frameworks, best practices, and business contracts, continues to govern the processing and safeguarding of information globally, as well as the protection of critical industrial infrastructure. 'Cyber Security: Law and Guidance' remains an essential handbook for professionals, businesses, and entrepreneurs navigating these challenges.

The past few years have witnessed an escalation in cyber threats, underscored by incidents like the sophisticated ransomware attacks targeting healthcare systems, educational institutions, and critical infrastructure worldwide. These events highlight that cyber-security is an issue impacting everyone, yet many are unsure of what they are defending against. This topic intersects with criminal, corporate, IT, and international law. This book aims to demystify cyber-security, helping you understand the issues, devise strategies, and meet the dual challenges of the digital age – advancing and protecting your interests online.

In this era of unpredictability and insecurity, organisations are redefining their approach to security, balancing risk, innovation, and cost. The cyber-security domain is undergoing dramatic changes, necessitating that organisations adopt new practices and skillsets. Online security and the protection of freedom online are not only compatible but mutually reinforcing. A secure cyberspace fosters trust and confidence for individuals, businesses, and the public sector to share ideas and innovate.

The internet continues to transform how we socialise and conduct business in unprecedented ways. Cyber-security risk is now squarely a business risk – neglecting security can jeopardise an organisation's future. Despite this, many organisations still view cyber-security as an IT issue. This perspective must evolve.

An open, free, and secure internet is essential for ensuring public and financial accountability and strengthening democratic institutions. It underpins freedom of expression and reinforces vibrant communities. To fully realise the social, economic, and strategic benefits of being online, governance must remain with users, not be dominated by governments. However, cyberspace must not become a lawless domain. Both government and the private sector have vital roles to play. Governments can facilitate innovation and provide security, while businesses must ensure their cyber-security practices are robust and current.

All entities are targets for malicious actors, including organised criminal syndicates and foreign adversaries, who exploit cyberspace to further their aims. The scale of cyber threats affecting public and private sectors is unprecedented. The rate of compromise is increasing, and malicious methods are rapidly evolving. With technological advancements like generative AI and quantum computing on the horizon, the cyber landscape is becoming even more complex.

The rise of mobile device usage presents both challenges and opportunities. The trend of Bring Your Own Device (BYOD) continues to grow, complicating security management. These devices often contradict traditional security measures: they are mobile, data-rich, easy to lose, and connected to various systems lacking sufficient security measures.

Conversely, technology offers opportunities, such as big data analytics, which provide new insights for a proactive security approach, provided organisations can employ individuals who understand these technologies.

We all have a duty to protect our nations, organisations, businesses, and personal data from cyber-attacks and defend our interests in cyberspace. Safeguarding against criminality, espionage, sabotage, and unfair competition online is paramount.

This book brings together leading experts in the field to promote norms of behaviour consistent with a free, open, and secure internet. These norms include state commitments to abstain from cyber-enabled intellectual property theft for commercial advantage. Efforts must also intensify to counter the spread of online propaganda that incites extremist and terrorist violence.

The Snowden disclosures showed that often the most damaging risk to online security is not malware but 'warmware' – the trusted insider capable of causing massive disruption or leaking classified material. While technical solutions are vital, cultural change is most effective in mitigating insider threats.

Businesses and governments must better educate and empower employees to use sound online practices. This book aims to promote an improved institutional cyber culture and raise awareness of cyber practices across government and business, enabling all to be secure online. It is understood that with enough determination and skill, a persistent attacker can breach any defence. However, complicating this process reduces risk, extends response times, and enhances interception capabilities before significant impact.

To achieve security, it must be integrated into the organization's core, both in technology (by incorporating security into design) and in behaviour (by providing secure options that are preferable to less secure ones). Fear alone is no longer an effective motivator.

This book complements key elements of governmental economic plans, aiding the transition to a diverse economy driven by innovation, market expansion, and increased enterprise investment. The cyber-security industry, though still maturing, is experiencing rapid growth. The UK is poised to lead in cyber-security, leveraging technology to manage the risks of interconnectedness and realise its potential.

This book will guide you and provide a roadmap to ensure cyber-security is prioritised in an age where cyber-opportunities and threats coexist and must be proactively addressed. Organizations must adapt to remain competitive and influential in the ever-evolving technology landscape.

I am honoured by the contributions of so many experts to this book. Cyber-security is vast and all-encompassing, allowing you to explore each chapter independently and learn from the best. This book offers a glimpse into various areas, each with its nuances. Please feel free to contact me if my team and I can assist you. I look forward to collaborating with you and your business to strengthen trust online and better realise your digital potential. Now is the time to stay ahead in the cyber-security game.

Best wishes,
Helen Wong MBE
24 October 2024

Dedication from Helen Wong

I dedicate this book to God, my husband Colin, my parents Mabel and Eric, my twin sister Lisa, Janet, Jimmy, Kitty, Sam, Kimmy and Anson.

Contributors

Farid Abdelkader is a seasoned Cybersecurity Audit and Risk Executive with over 20 years of progressive experience. He currently serves as the Global Head of Technology Audit for a Fortune 100 Financial Services company and was previously the Managing Director leading Protiviti 's National Cybersecurity Audit Program. Farid is also the immediate past president of the ISACA Metropolitan New York Chapter (~5,000 members). Farid has successfully implemented numerous Fortune 500 cybersecurity and privacy programs, conducted technology audits, served as a virtual CISO, and performed extensive cybersecurity, vendor, IT risk, and privacy assessments across the financial services, insurance, and life sciences sectors.

LinkedIn:www.linkedin.com/in/faridkader/

Dr Reza Alavi, a seasoned Technology Risk specialist with over two decades of experience, thrives on guiding organisations through the intricate landscape of technology operations risk, cybersecurity, and digital trust programs. He is adept at achieving practical results within regulated environments, consistently supporting organisations in realising their technology transformation goals. As a cross-functional change agent, Reza fosters global collaboration and strengthens digital offerings, ensuring sustainable growth. His expertise lies in Information Security Risk Management, Data Governance, Digital Transformation Projects, Cloud Native technologies, Open Source Software, DevRiskOps, DevSecOps, and the development of robust security resilience and controls.

Email: Rezaalavi@me.com

Tel: +44 (0)7900 480039

LinkedIn:www.linkedin.com/in/reza-alavi/

Benjamin Ang is Senior Fellow and Head of the Centre of Excellence for National Security, Future Issues in Technology, and Digital Impact Research, at the S Rajaratnam School of International Studies, Nanyang Technological University in Singapore, leading public policy research in cybersecurity, international cyber conflict, hybrid threats, disinformation, foreign interference, and emerging technologies like artificial intelligence, space, quantum, and clean energy. He has testified as legal expert to the United Nations Open Ended Working Group on Cyber, and lectures at the UN-Singapore Cyber Fellowship.

Email: isbang@ntu.edu.sg

www.rsis.edu.sg/profile/benjamin-ang

Mark Blackhurst LLB (Hons) is co-founder of Digital Next an online search and web optimisation agency where he serves as its Chief of Operations. Mark has a wealth of business knowledge and brings great expertise to the Digital Next team. Digital Next has offices in Manchester, Melbourne and the UAE, servicing many thousands of web and online clients.

Mark has an extensive knowledge of International Marketing and web security. He lectures on the Staffordshire University MSc Digital Marketing course and has been involved most recently in many high profile panels and discussion including topics such as E-Commerce, Cryptocurrency, Blockchain and Brexit.

Mark has long recognised the rapid advancement of AI technologies and their role in enhancing business efficiencies. His foresight has allowed him to implement AI-driven strategies that streamline operations, reduce costs, and boost productivity, giving the organisations he works with a competitive edge. Over the last few years, he has worked on multiple AI projects across various types of businesses, from tech to e-commerce, which have streamlined efficiencies, built cost savings, and improved processes.

Email: mark@digitalnext.co.uk

https://digitalnext.co.uk/

Stefano Bracco is Knowledge Manager – Team Leader of the Security Office in the Director's Office at Agency for the Cooperation of Energy Regulators. He has been working in EU Institutions/Bodies for the past 20 years, focusing on implementation of policies in different areas. He has been a researcher and co-author of papers published in peer-reviewed international journals or presented at international scientific conferences, covering several topics (Energy, Nuclear Energy, Natural Language Processing and Bio-Informatics).

He has an extensive knowledge of energy cyber-security in Europe. He is chairman and co-chairman of Task Forces focusing on cyber-security for Energy from a Regulatory perspective and member of the Smart Grid Task Force of the European Commission.

Email: braccos@usa.net

William Christopher is a partner in Kingsley Napley's Dispute Resolution team, specialising in civil fraud cases. He leads the firm's Cybercrime Group.

Email: wchristopher@kingsleynapley.co.uk

www.kingsleynapley.co.uk

David Clarke is the founder of GDPR Technology Forum over 15,600 members https://www.linkedin.com/groups/12017677 and an internationally known GDPR and security advisor.

He is recognised as one of the top 10 influencers by Thompson Reuter's 'Top 30 most influential thought-leaders and thinkers on social media, in risk management, compliance and regtech in the UK' and is in the top 50 list of Global Experts by Kingston Technology.

In the past, David held multiple security management positions such as Global Head of Security Service Delivery and Head of Security Infrastructure for Global FTSE 100 companies.

His experience in both security and compliance including ISO27001, PCI-DSS, BS 10012 make him the professional authority on GDPR implementation.

Email: info@gdpruk.eu

LinkedIn: www.linkedin.com/in/1davidclarke

Twitter at @1DavidClarke

Kevin Curran is a Professor of Cyber Security at Ulster University. He is also a senior member of the IEEE. His expertise has been acknowledged by invitations to present his work at international conferences, overseas universities and research laboratories. He is a regular contributor on TV and radio and in trade and consumer IT magazines.

https://kevincurran.org/

Mark Deem is a partner at Wiggin LLP, where he leads the litigation team and technology sector. He is a commercial litigator, with considerable experience of complex domestic and cross-border litigation, international arbitration and regulatory matters. Mark focuses on technology, media and telecommunications (TMT) litigation, contentious privacy, data protection and cybersecurity issues and financial services disputes. He has particular experience in a variety of industry sectors, including aviation and aerospace, communications, digital, TMT and banking and finance. He is a regular speaker on the topic of data, cybersecurity and AI and is the author of "AI on Trial" (published Bloomsbury Professional, June 2022).

Email: mark.deem@wiggin.co.uk

https://wiggin.co.uk/people/mark-deem

Tan E-Reng is a Research Analyst at the Centre of Excellence for National Security (CENS), S. Rajaratnam School of International Studies (RSIS), Nanyang Technological University (NTU), Singapore.

Email: isereng.tan@ntu.edu.sg

www.rsis.edu.sg/profile/tan-e-reng/

Ffion Flockhart is Global Head of Cybersecurity at A&O Shearman. She has handled some of the largest cyber incidents for multinational clients across a range of sectors and has overseen hundreds of incident responses, some involving legal and regulatory issues in more than 100 jurisdictions and requiring notifications to millions of data subjects.

Email: ffion.flockhart@aoshearman.com

Simon Goldsmith CEng, has 17 years' experience in Intelligence, Security and Financial Crime with the UK government, BAE Systems Applied Intelligence and EY. He specialises in cyber-security and financial crime in National Security, Financial Services and Critical Infrastructure.

Email: cybergoldsmith@gmail.com LinkedIn: www.linkedin.com/in/smg-cyber/

Steven Hadwin is a counsel in A&O Sheaman's global cyber practice. He advises clients on the implications of cybersecurity incidents from a legal, regulatory and liability risk perspective, and has extensive experience of regulatory investigations and disputes following incidents.

Email: steven.hadwin@aoshearman.com

Ria Halme is a Group Data Protection Officer in the financial sector with expertise in creating and implementing scalable global privacy programmes. She has successfully integrated GDPR with local regulations across regions, including Singapore, Brazil, the U.S., and Dubai. Ria has led transformative initiatives, including launching a Data Loss Prevention programme, leasing data erasure projects and developing a privacy risk framework for acquisitions. Committed to inclusion and leadership development, she founded a women's network and mentors junior colleagues, equipping them with the skills to excel in their careers.

LinkedIn: www.linkedin.com/in/ria-halme-586a3993/

Gary Hibberd is the co-founder of Consultants Like Us who specialise in Information Security and Data Protection. Gary has over 30 years' experience in Information Security and Data Protection and Privacy, and is able to make these topics exciting and accessible to businesses large and small. He helps organisations implement security frameworks like NIST, SOC2, ISO27001, ISO27701, ISO22301 and ISO42001. Helping them to maximise on the benefits they bring.

Email: gary.hibberd@consultantslikeus.co.uk

www.ConsultantsLikeUs.co.uk

Dr Klaus Julisch is the Partner in charge of Deloitte's Cyber Risk Services in Switzerland. He has over 20 years of experience in designing, assessing, and transforming secure enterprise solutions. Klaus' work has been published internationally in over 25 articles and resulted in 15 patents. He holds a Ph.D. in Computer Science from the University of Dortmund, Germany, and an MBA from Warwick Business School, UK.

www2.deloitte.com/ch/en/profiles/kjulisch.html

Arthur Keleti is an expert on cyber-security, book author and a visionary in his field maintaining an interdisciplinary approach, researching the topic of secrets in cyber-space together with sociologists, psychologists, and IT professionals. Today he works for T-Systems Hungary, where he has served as IT security strategist since 1999. He is the founder of the long-running East-European cybersecurity grand conf-expo: ITBN (Infosec, Trends, Buzz, and Networking).

LinkedIn: www.linkedin.com/in/arthurkeleti

https://thecybersecretfuturist.com

https://arthurkeleti.com

Yazad Khandhadia is a cyber/information security professional with 20 years of experience in the industry and is currently the Head of Architecture at Emirates NBD, a leading financial institution in the UAE & Middle East. He ideates, runs and governs successful cyber security programs and was solely responsible for the implementation of key security controls for new technology implementations ,such as CI/CD pipelines, containers, blockchains & cloud-native environments during Emirates NBD's digital transformation program. As a cyber security leader he is also credited with fostering the 'security as an enabler' culture by introducing guard rails in the Agile development process that led to better agility & security for products and services used by customers. He holds multiple certifications in security & data privacy and is a certified Coach and Mentor at Emirates NBD.

Yazad is also the Lead Author to Cloud Security Alliance's (CSAs) Cloud Control Matrix (CCM) Implementation Guidelines v2 for the Data Security & Privacy (DSP) Management control and volunteers as Adjunct Faculty, at Middlesex University, Dubai, teaching the Masters in Cyber Security course to students.

Email: yazadk@EmiratesNBD.com

EmiratesNBD.com

Semen Kort is a security analyst at Kaspersky Lab's ICS-CERT and Critical Infrastructure Defense department specialising in the scope of modeling, intrusion detection and education. He contributes to IEEE and Industrial Internet Consortium cyber security recommendations and to national standards. Semen holds a Ph.D. in Computer Security.

Email: Semen.Kort@kaspersky.com

Rhiannon Lewis is a lawyer specialising in data protection and privacy law in the payments sector.

LinkedIn: https://uk.linkedin.com/in/rhilewis

Adelaide Lopez is a senior litigator at Wiggin LLP, specialising in data protection and commercial litigation in the technology, media and telecoms sectors. She is particularly interested in the intersection of law and technology, with a focus on cybersecurity and AI. Her practice also includes disputes in privacy, breach of confidence and defamation.

Email: Adelaide.Lopez@wiggin.co.uk

https://wiggin.co.uk/people/adelaide-lopez/

Jill Lorimer is a partner in the Criminal Litigation department at Kingsley Napley LLP. She specialises in advising individuals and corporates facing investigation or prosecution for cyber-related offences, including computer-enabled fraud, malicious communications, data protection breaches and other forms of computer misuse. Jill has written and spoken widely on this topic and has a particular interest in the regulatory and criminal aspects of crypto assets.

Email: jlorimer@kingsleynapley.co.uk

www.kingsleynapley.co.uk/our-people/jill-lorim

Ryan Mackie, Founder of AILegalCompliance.com, is a specialist in Artificial Intelligence (AI), Intellectual Property (IP), Commercial, Data Protection, Information, and Cyber Security Law. As a Subject Matter Expert (SME) in these fields, Ryan brings extensive expertise to the table. With several years of experience as an AI, Data Protection, Information, and Cyber Security Lawyer, he has served as a Data Protection SME and/or DPO, either directly or in an advisory capacity, for numerous multinational corporations. His notable clients include Honda, Schroders, Marks & Spencer, Pearson, Clydesdale Bank, and Credit Suisse. Recently, Ryan completed a project for Intel as an AI & Data Protection Legal Consultant and is currently helping clients with the implementation of the EU AI Act.

Email: rmackie@ailegalcompliance.com

LinkedIn: www.linkedin.com/in/ryanmackie

William J McBorrough is Co-Founder and CEO at MCGlobalTech, a Washington, DC-based Information Security Management Consulting Firm. For more than 19 years, Mr McBorrough has demonstrated success as an administrator, engineer, architect, consultant, manager and practice leader developing cost effective solutions to enable and support strategic and operational goals of client organisations in the areas of Enterprise Information Security Risk Management, IT Governance, Security Organisation Development and Management, and Government Information Assurance and Compliance. His experience spans the spectrum from small e-commerce start-ups to multi-campus state and federal agencies to global financial sector organisations.

Email: wjm4@mcglobaltech.com

linkedin.com/in/mcborrough

www.mcglobaltech.com

Kevin Murphy is an international award-winning cybersecurity professional. Current Director of ISACA (Scotland); and Chair of ISACA Scotland's Quantum Computing and Artificial Intelligence Working Groups. He is the former Vice-President of ISC2 (Scotland).

Previous Cybersecurity experience includes as a serving Police Officer, where he was awarded a Chief Constable's commendation. Founding member of KPMG's award-winning Cyber Security and Privacy Team within the UK. Former Global Head of Cyber Risk for an international bank.

Kevin has authored two books on training and development; and previously contributed to a number of industry leading technology publications. He is a renowned cybersecurity trainer and holds 25 technology qualifications including cloud architecture, data science, quantum computing, and ethical hacking.

Kevin currently works as a Director for Quantum Cybersecurity Consulting, and lead cybersecurity risk architect for a global bank. He is also a member of MIT's

Cybersecurity Research Council. His clients include Fortune 100 companies, leading venture capitalist firms, and international government agencies.

LinkedIn: www.linkedin.com/in/kevin-murphy-llb-dip-pslm-cipm-7b923b21/

Cosimo Pacciani is the Group Head of Research for Poste Italiane SpA. His area of expertise ranges from corporate and leverage finance to derivatives and to development of risk and compliance management functions, matured in nearly two decades of experience in the City of London. He holds a masters degree in economics from the University of Florence and a Ph.D. Degree in Economics from the University of Siena.

LinkedIn: www.linkedin.com/in/cpacciani/

Steven Peacock has over 25 years' experience within the financial services arena having held several senior executive level positions across a number of different types of organisations of scale and maturity. He is an industry recognised specialist in the areas of internal audit, compliance, risk management, governance and transformation. Steven also holds non-executive director and board advisor positions to financial service and non-financial service businesses.

Sally Penni MBE is a top ranked barrister by Chambers & Partners 2014. Called in 2000 with 24 years experience practicing law.

Recognised for the breadth of her practice across serious crime, mental health crime, regulatory crime, fraud and computer crime. Her practice combines criminal and employment work many cases of which concern cyber-security.

She has the distinction of being awarded two honorary doctorates in Law from Manchester Metropolitan University and University of Salford.

She is an Industry Advisor to University of Salford and Board Advisor to University of Durham Law School. Durham Law school advisory board is chaired by Sir Andrew McFarlane, President of the family division.

Sally sits as part time Judge in VTE Tribunal.

Sally is author of 16 books and is the recent winner of the WeAreTheCity Themis20 women trailblazers in law powered by Magical circle firm Norton Rose. Sally is also the founder of professional development organization Women In The Law and Business UK and the host of Talking Law podcast. A podcast listened to by over 7 million listeners globally and in the top 2 percent of all global podcasts.

Email: pa.sallypennibarrister@gmail.com

Email: sjpenni@yahoo.co.uk

www.kenworthysbarristers.co.uk/barristers/sally_penni

Podcasts: talkinglaw.buzzsprout.com/1614520/12022035-lord-david-pannick-kc; www.buzzsprout.com/1686745/8173162

LinkedIn: www.linkedin.com/in/sallypenni/

Vijay Rathour leads Grant Thornton's Cyber and Digital Investigations team, helping clients react to constantly evolving cyber threats and digital opportunities. He is a former barrister, solicitor, FCA regulator and he works at the interface of legal and technical teams, providing strategic guidance and crisis management, typically to Boards and management committees.

He leads Grant Thornton's Data Breach Response team, advising on information governance, forensic evidence collection, recovery and review protocols, regulatory reporting, and data analytics. He is an expert advisor to the United Nations on Cyber Crime and International Ransomware policies.

Vijay supports Grant Thornton's Digital Asset Investigations team and is an ethical hacker and a member of the ICAEW Digital Assets Working Party addressing developing cryptocurrency initiatives.

Email: Vijay.Rathour@uk.gt.com

www.grantthornton.co.uk/

Ekaterina Rudina is an analyst at Kaspersky Lab's ICS-CERT and Critical Infrastructure Defence department specialising in the scope of threat research, modelling, and risk assessment. She contributes to IEEE, ITU-T, and Industrial Internet Consortium cyber security recommendations and to national standards. Ekaterina holds a Ph.D. in Computer Security.

Email: Ekaterina.rudina@kaspersky.com

Madelaine Rugg law student at Royal Holloway, University of London.

Marcus Turner is an associate within A&O Shearman's AI advisory practice, specialising in legal and regulatory issues related to generative AI. He advises a syndicate of 80+ of the largest global businesses on safe AI development and deployment. He provides businesses with practical tools and methodologies to enable them to manage the legal risks associated with AI and comply with regulatory requirements. As a core member of the Markets Innovation Group (MIG), Marcus has been instrumental in the firm's groundbreaking deployment of generative. He also played a key role in developing the firm's AI-powered solutions, such as ContractMatrix, which was developed in partnership with Microsoft and Harvey in the first collaboration between a law firm and Microsoft to develop, and license, a software product. Marcus helps clients to make sense of the rapidly evolving AI policy and regulatory landscape, as well as to develop effective AI governance. Examples of his work include advising a sovereign wealth fund on the nation's approach to AI regulation and policy, a US G-SIFI to develop a global AI policy framework, and a UK-based G-SIFI to develop its generative AI strategy. Marcus is a legal advisor to the Partnership on AI (PAI), the non-profit dedicated to ensuring that AI adoption benefits humanity. His work has been featured in leading publications, including the *Financial Times*, and he has contributed to reports published by the Alan Turing Institute and European Intellectual Property Review.

Email: Marcus.Turner@AOShearman.com

David Wakeling is founder and Global Head of A&O Shearman's Markets Innovation Group (MIG), which is made up of lawyers, developers and technologists, who create innovative solutions that address clients' needs. Recognised as one of the world's leading AI lawyers, David advises some of the largest global companies and sovereigns on safe AI development and deployment. David also founded, and leads, the firm's global AI advisory practice, as well as its AI client working group. Through the latter, he is delivering a syndicated program of advice regarding AI adoption to 80+ of the largest global businesses. As Chair of the firm's AI Steering Committee, he has led on the development and implementation of A&O Shearman's AI strategy. Under David's leadership, in 2022 A&O Shearman became the first law firm in the world to deploy AI in its operating model. He also led MIG's development and launch of ContractMatrix, in partnership with Microsoft and Harvey. This marked the first collaboration between a law firm and Microsoft to develop, and license, a software product. David serves as a member of the Policy Steering Committee for, and legal adviser to, the Partnership on AI (PAI). His work has received widespread recognition; it has been featured in top-tier outlets, including the *Financial Times*, *The Wall Street Journal*, *Forbes*, *Wired*, *Fortune* and *POLITICO*, to name a few.

Email: David.Wakeling@AOshearman.com

Charlie Weston-Simons is a partner in A&O Shearman's global cyber practice. He has a particular focus on post-incident claims, regularly representing cyber-attack victims faced with data breach claims (including group litigation) and commercial disputes. He also advises on cyber insurance.

Email: charlie.weston-simons@aoshearman.com

Helen Wong MBE is a corporate solicitor specialising in mergers and acquisitions, private equity with a focus on the healthcare and education sectors. Her unrivalled legal experience includes Clifford Chance (London and Hong Kong), PricewaterhouseCoopers and Walkers in the Cayman Islands. Helen is highly sought after by high net worth entrepreneurs, family businesses and overseas clients to assist with their corporate and commercial transactions. Alongside her legal teams, Helen helps clients manage the risk of cyber security. She is instrumental in many of the dental, optician, pharmacy, GP, vet business sales and purchases which requires an in-depth review of the due diligence process with a growing focus on the cyber security risks. Helen is the author of six other books including the book Doing Business After Brexit. Helen was bestowed with the coveted MBE (Member of the British Empire) and is invited as a keynote speaker worldwide.

Email: helenthelawyer@gmail.com

Contents

Table of Statutes

Table of Statutory Instruments

Table of Cases

CHAPTER 1

THREATS

Helen Wong MBE

WHAT ARE CYBER SECURITY THREATS?

1.01 Computer networks, systems, and user data are the main targets of cyber security threats. Examples of these threats include malware, phishing attacks, and other malicious activities.

1.02 A cyber security threat specifically targets computer networks, systems, and user data. There are various forms of threats, such as malware, phishing, and other malicious activity.

1.03 Common cyber threats are:

1 Backdoor attacks

A backdoor attack is classified as a cyber attack. This approach enables the attacker to breach security protocols and gain entry into a system or network. After successfully accessing the system, the attacker can then proceed to install malicious software or execute other malicious activities.

2 Formjacking

Formjacking involves injecting malicious code into a form-using web page, constituting a cyber attack. Unsuspecting users who enter their information into the form inadvertently provide sensitive details, including credit card information. The attacker receives the stolen information and utilizes it for fraudulent activities.

3 Cryptojacking

Criminal hackers use cryptojacking to hijack computers and mine cryptocurrency. The hacker usually accomplishes this by implanting harmful code in a website or email, leading to the victim's computer mining cryptocurrency unknowingly or without permission. The victim's computer may experience decreased speed and increased electricity usage, potentially resulting in higher bills. Physical damage could also occur to the victim's computer.

4 DDoS attacks

DDoS attack is a cyber attack that disrupts service by overwhelming a system. A network is targeted by a malicious actor who aims to overload it with traffic from multiple origins. This can be accomplished by bombarding the target with fake requests or inundating its systems with a massive data load.

5 DNS poisoning attacks

DNS poisoning occurs when attackers manipulate the records used by a server to direct traffic to the correct websites. The name server's error can result in the redirection of traffic meant for a legitimate website to the attacker's site. DNS poisoning facilitates different types of attacks, including man-in-the-middle, phishing, and malware distribution.

6 Malware

Malware is software created to cause damage to computers, servers, or networks. It is capable of stealing information, deleting files, or causing equipment damage.

7 Botnet software

Botnet software is a malicious program that enables hackers to manipulate a network of compromised computers, known as 'bots'. The uses of botnets include launching attacks, stealing data, or sending spam.

8 Ransomware attack

A user's files are encrypted by ransomware, which demands a payment in exchange for decryption. The payment of a ransom does not guarantee the retrieval of encrypted data.

9 RATs

A remote-access Trojan, also known as a RAT, is a malicious program that enables unauthorized individuals to remotely control a user's computer. The victim's computer can be controlled by the attacker remotely, unbeknownst to the victim. The use of RATs is frequent in spying on victims or stealing their sensitive information.

10 Rootkits and bootkits

Attackers can obtain administrator-level access to a system using a rootkit, a type of malicious software. Other malicious software, like viruses, Trojans, and backdoors, can be secretly installed on a system using rootkits. Additionally, they can conceal the existence of other malicious software like botnets. Attackers frequently employ rootkits to preserve system access once they have initially gained it.

Start-up code, the software that loads before the operating system, is susceptible to infection by bootkits, a specific type of rootkit.

11 Spyware

Secretly installed on computers, spyware is a software that remains undetected by users. The intention is to acquire user data, like their web browsing behaviour, and forward it to the creator of the spyware.

12 Trojan

A Trojan is a specific kind of malware that uses camouflage to infiltrate a computer system, appearing as a legitimate file or program. Trojans are capable of stealing personal data, installing various malware, or commandeering a victim's device.

13 Viruses and worms

Without the user's knowledge, a computer virus is installed as a malicious code. By attaching to computer files, viruses are able to replicate and spread to other computers.

Worms, similar to viruses, have the ability to self-replicate. Nonetheless, there is no need for them to rely on another program to accomplish this.

14 Common cyber attacks

Cyber criminals utilise cyber attacks as a means to distribute malware and other threats. The following options may be utilised by them.

15 Drive-by downloads

Without the user's knowledge or permission, a drive-by download executes malicious code. Visiting a malicious website or clicking on a malicious link can lead to this outcome. Malware can be installed on the user's computer through drive-by downloads, allowing attackers to steal sensitive information or take control of the system.

16 Exploits and exploit kits

Exploits are malicious codes that have the ability to compromise security vulnerabilities. Developed by the security services, there are many of them. An example of this is the WannaCry ransomware, which used EternalBlue to propagate in 2017. The US National Security Agency is responsible for both creating and having this exploit stolen.

Collections of multiple exploits are known as exploit kits. Found on the dark web, these can be rented to help unskilled criminals automate attacks on vulnerabilities they already know.

17 MITM attacks

A hacker can execute a man-in-the-middle attack by positioning themselves between a device and a server to intercept communications.

Insecure public Wi-Fi networks are a common breeding ground for MITM attacks when users log on. A visitor's device and the network can be infiltrated by attackers inserting themselves in between. Without realising it, the user will transfer information through the attacker.

18 Phishing attacks

Phishing involves using social engineering techniques to deceive individuals into revealing sensitive or confidential information, commonly through email. Distinguishing these scams from authentic messages can be challenging and can result in significant harm to organisations.

19 Social engineering

Manipulating and deceiving victims is the main strategy of social engineering to gain computer access or acquire information.

Deception tactics, such as clicking on malicious links or gaining physical access, are employed to accomplish this.

20 SQL injection

When a user inserts SQL code into a web form, it is called an SQL injection and allows them to access restricted data. It enables users to see, delete, or alter data that is not typically visible.

WHO ARE THE PERPETRATORS?

States and state-sponsored threats

1.04 Efforts by states and state-sponsored groups to infiltrate UK networks are a regular occurrence, primarily targeting government, defence, finance, energy, and telecommunications sectors for political, diplomatic, technological, commercial, and strategic gains.

1.05 These state cyber programmes have different capacities and impacts. The advanced nations are constantly enhancing their capabilities.

1.06 They are incorporating encryption and anonymisation services into their tools for covert operations. Although they can execute complex attacks, they frequently succeed in their objectives by exploiting vulnerable targets with basic tools and techniques because of poor victim defences.

1.07 The UK's security and prosperity are only seriously threatened by a few states with technical capabilities. However, numerous states are currently developing advanced cyber programs that might endanger UK interests soon. States interested in cyber espionage can buy pre-existing tools and modify them for their espionage activities.

1.08 In addition to the threat of espionage, a handful of hostile foreign actors have advanced and utilized offensive cyber capabilities, including those with destructive effects.

1.09 The security of the UK's critical national infrastructure and industrial control systems is at risk due to these capabilities. In some cases, states may disregard international law and believe they can escape consequences, setting a precedent for others to do the same. Although rare, the number and impact of destructive attacks are increasing worldwide.

Terrorists

1.10 The UK and its interests remain targeted by terrorist groups seeking to carry out destructive cyber activities. Experts assess that terrorists currently have limited technical capabilities. Nonetheless, the effect of even minor attacks against the UK has been remarkably significant: basic website alterations and personal information leaks enable terrorist organisations and their followers to gain media coverage and instil fear in their targets.

1.11 According to the current assessment, terrorist groups will continue to prioritise physical attacks rather than cyber attacks in the foreseeable future. We predict that as the computer-savvy generation becomes more radicalised, there will be a rise in low-sophistication disruptive activities, such as defacement or DDoS attacks, targeting the UK. The emergence of skilled extremist lone actors may increase, along with the risk of terrorist organisations recruiting insiders. To maximise impact, experts expect terrorists to use any available cyber capabilities. Therefore, even a slight improvement in terrorist capability can pose a major danger to the UK and its interests.

Hackivists

1.12 Decentralised and focused on specific issues, hacktivist groups operate. Many of their acts take on a vigilante nature as they choose their targets based on perceived grievances. Although most hacktivist cyber activity involves disruption, such as defacing websites or launching DDoS attacks, more proficient hacktivists are capable of inflicting greater and more lasting damage on their targets.

1.13 UK organisations continue to face cyber risks from insider threats. The biggest danger comes from trusted employees within an organisation who have access to critical systems and data. The theft of sensitive data and intellectual property can result in financial and reputational harm. Trusted employees within an organisation can use their privileged knowledge and access to launch attacks that disrupt critical services or delete data from their organisation's network, turning it into a destructive cyber threat.

1.14 Equally worrisome are the insiders or employees who unintentionally cause cyber damage by clicking on a phishing email, inserting an infected USB, or disregarding security protocols and downloading unsafe content from the Internet. Their actions, despite no intention to harm, can be equally detrimental to the organisation because of their privileged system and data access.

1.15 Often, these individuals fall victim to social engineering tactics, unknowingly aiding fraudsters by granting access to their organisation's networks or following instructions in good faith.

1.16 Insider threats encompass more than just unauthorised access to information systems and their content, posing an overall cyber risk to organisations. It is equally important to have strong physical security controls in place to protect those systems from unauthorised access or data theft. An essential component of a comprehensive security strategy is a strong personnel security culture that acknowledges the dangers posed by disaffected employees, fraud in the workforce, and various forms of espionage.

'Script kiddies'

1.17 Script Kiddies who typically lack advanced skills and rely on others' scripts for cyber attacks, are not seen as posing a major threat to the overall economy or society. Yet, they can access hacking guides, resources, and tools online. The actions of 'script kiddies' can cause significant damage to organisations because of vulnerabilities in internet-facing systems.

Examples of Threats

1.18 A cyber attack on 21 October 2015 led TalkTalk, a UK telecommunications provider, to report a possible breach of customer data.

1.19 Further investigation revealed that a database containing customer information was accessed through publicly accessible internet servers. Approximately 157,000 customers are potentially affected, with their names, addresses, and bank account details at risk.

1.20 Multiple TalkTalk employees were sent an email on the same day, requesting a ransom payment in Bitcoins. The attackers revealed the database structure to show they had accessed it.

1.21 TalkTalk's report of the breach helped the police, supported by specialists at the National Crime Agency, to arrest the main suspects, all based in the UK, in October and November 2015.

1.22 The attack shows that vulnerabilities can still exist within even the most cyber-aware organisations. The impact of their exploitation can cause significant reputational damage and operational disruption, and this incident received a lot of media attention. TalkTalk's quick reporting of the breach allowed law enforcement to respond promptly, helping both the public and government prevent potential loss of sensitive data. TalkTalk's financial setback from the incident amounted to approximately £60 million, 95,000 lost customers, and a significant drop in their share price.

1.23 The SWIFT network facilitates secure communication among financial institutions worldwide regarding financial transactions.

1.24 The Bangladesh Bank experienced a cyber attack in early February 2016, resulting in the unauthorised transfer of funds from their account to accounts in the Philippines, as instructed by the attacker through the SWIFT payment system. An amount of $951 million was involved in the attempted fraud. The banking system prevented 30 transactions valued at $850 million. The recovered amount of $20 million can be linked back to Sri Lanka.

1.25 Casinos were used to launder the remaining $81 million that was transferred to the Philippines, with some of the funds later being forwarded to Hong Kong.

1.26 The forensic investigation conducted by Bangladesh Bank found that malware had infiltrated the bank's systems, collecting information on their international payment and fund transfer processes. BAE Systems' additional analysis of the malware connected to the attack revealed advanced capabilities for interacting with Bangladesh Bank's local SWIFT Alliance Access software. According to BAE, criminals are executing highly sophisticated attacks on victim organisations, with a particular focus on network intrusions.

1.27 The electricity distribution companies Prykarpattya Oblenergo and Kyiv Oblenergo were hit by a cyber attack in December 2015, causing a significant power outage in western Ukraine. More than 50 substations on the distribution networks were affected. According to reports, there was a blackout in the region for several hours, impacting over 220,000 consumers and causing some disruptions in other areas.

1.28 Some attribute the attack to the use of BlackEnergy3 malware, as samples were found on the network.

1.29 Malicious Microsoft Office documents were sent to power utility company offices in the Ukraine in phishing emails, at least six months before the attack. However, the malware is not believed to be the cause of the circuit breakers opening and causing the outage. The malware may have facilitated the attackers in acquiring credentials, which in turn allowed them to gain direct remote control of specific network components, ultimately resulting in the outage.

1.30 The Ukraine incident marks the first verified case of a disruptive cyber attack on an electricity grid. This incident emphasizes the significance of implementing robust cyber security measures in all Critical National Infrastructure (CNI) to prevent similar incidents in the UK.

CHAPTER 2

VULNERABILITIES

Helen Wong MBE

WHAT ARE CYBERSECURITY VULNERABILITIES?

2.01 Cybersecurity vulnerabilities refer to weaknesses in information systems, security procedures, or internal controls that can be exploited by threat actors. Unauthorised access to an organisation's confidential data can be achieved when threat actors exploit system vulnerabilities and steal the information. The stolen data is frequently sold by threat actors on the dark web or returned to the organisation for a ransom payment.

2.02 Vulnerabilities exist in every system. These can present as configuration issues for system administrators, software defects requiring vendor updates, or even unknown vulnerabilities without available mitigations.

2.03 Organisations must prioritise vulnerability management as a critical control.

2.04 Your organisation can gain insights into and regularly assess the vulnerabilities in your technical environment, identify areas with update failures, and actively minimise the impact of these vulnerabilities by establishing an effective vulnerability management process. It allows you to quickly respond to critical vulnerability disclosures by evaluating your organisation's exposure to them.

WHAT ARE FLAWS?

2.05 A flaw is an unintentional form of functionality. The cause could be either poor design or errors in the implementation process. Flaws might not be discovered for a considerable period of time. These types of vulnerabilities are commonly exploited in today's attacks.

CYBERSECURITY VULNERABILITY VS CYBER THREAT: WHAT'S THE DIFFERENCE?

2.06 There is a common misconception that cybersecurity vulnerabilities and cyber threats are the same, but they are actually different concepts. Weaknesses within a system's infrastructure are known as cybersecurity vulnerabilities. They are not introduced or created by cybercrime, but exist from the outset.

2.07 Conversely, a cyber threat refers to the danger of unauthorised access through exploiting cyber vulnerabilities. Threat actors introduce them into the system to exploit vulnerabilities. Cyber threats are a common outcome of unaddressed cybersecurity vulnerabilities.

Four Vulnerabilities

2.08 The four primary vulnerabilities in information security include network, operating system, process, and human vulnerabilities.

a. **Network vulnerabilities are weaknesses**

i. Cyber attackers can exploit weaknesses in an organisation's hardware or software infrastructure to infiltrate and cause harm. The areas of vulnerability can vary from unprotected wireless access to improperly configured firewalls that leave the network vulnerable.

ii. Zero-day vulnerabilities are software vulnerabilities that remain undiscovered by organisations and software vendors. Until someone uncovers them, zero-day vulnerabilities lack any form of defence. Advanced attackers with ample resources often utilise zero-days in targeted attacks. As soon as zero-days are made public, reusable attacks are created and become widely available. Computers or systems that haven't applied the patch or updated their antivirus software are at risk. The extent to which an attacker can discover and exploit software flaws or manipulate features is determined by the software's nature and their technical abilities. Web applications, for instance, have inherent connectivity to the Internet and can present an opportunity for attackers.

iii. Features: A feature is a designed capability that attackers can exploit to compromise a system. The user's experience, problem diagnosis, and management can benefit from features, but they can also pose a risk of exploitation by attackers.

iv. The introduction of macros by Microsoft in their Office suite during the late 1990s led to the rise of vulnerabilities, with the Melissa worm in 1999 being a notable instance. Even today, macros are vulnerable to exploitation.

v. Attackers continue to exploit JavaScript, widely used in dynamic web content. This entails redirecting the user's browser to a malicious site and discreetly downloading malware, while also evading basic web filtering by concealing harmful code.

vi. Vulnerable API: An Application Programming Interface (API) is a digital interface that enables applications to communicate with each other over the internet or a private network. Inadequately secured APIs with public IP addresses are vulnerable to targeting and exploitation by cybercriminals.

b. **Operating system (OS) vulnerabilities**

  i. Cyber attackers can exploit OS vulnerabilities to cause harm on any device running that OS. One type of attack that exploits OS vulnerabilities is a Denial of Service (DoS) attack, which overloads a system with fake requests.

  ii. Outdated software can expose the entire network to vulnerabilities, as the operating system running the application remains unprotected.

  iii. Cybercriminals can take advantage of the flaws and bugs in software where a programmer has overlooked these points. The software's failure to patch these bugs can lead to unauthorised access to the organisation's hardware, software, data, and resources by cybercriminals.

  iv. System complexity can lead to an organisation setting up its systems with misconfigurations, flaws, and unauthorised access points, which cybercriminals may exploit.

  v. Broad attack surface: Attack surface includes every conceivable entry point that cybercriminals can exploit to breach a system. The greater the number of connected devices and systems on an organisation's network, the more vulnerable it becomes to cybercriminal attacks.

  vi. When security measures are lacking, process vulnerabilities are formed. Weak passwords used by users, including IT administrators, contribute to one of the most common process vulnerabilities – authentication weakness.

  vii. Weak or compromised login information: Numerous individuals neglect to generate robust and distinct passwords for every account they own. Their tendency is to resort to ineffective password habits, like reusing passwords and creating weak ones for convenience. Weak login credentials provide an opportunity for cybercriminals to launch cyber attacks, such as brute force attacks, to steal passwords.

  viii. Insufficient encryption can lead to interception of data, unauthorised access, and potential malicious code deployment.

c. **Vulnerable settings or inconsistent security controls** on network assets lead to system misconfiguration. Incorrect manual configuration of the system can result in errors and gaps in the systems. These misconfigurations are sought after by cybercriminals to exploit and gain unauthorised entry.

  i. Cybercriminals exploit outdated software by searching for bugs and flaws. Unauthorised access and theft of sensitive data can occur by exploiting these flaws. Regularly updating software can patch most flaws or bugs, particularly the vulnerabilities that cybercriminals are most likely to exploit. Organisations running old software are vulnerable to cyber threats.

d. **Human vulnerabilities**

  i. User errors can inadvertently expose networks, hardware, and sensitive data to malicious actors. They are potentially the biggest threat, especially due to the rise of remote and mobile workers.

ii. Opening malware-infected email attachments or failing to update software on mobile devices are examples of human vulnerability in security.

iii. Cybercriminals can exploit human error, such as falling for phishing attacks or having weak password habits, to gain access to login credentials. By obtaining a user's login credentials, cybercriminals can enter an organisation's network without permission.

iv. Inadequate access control can make the network vulnerable to security breaches.

v. A system administrator who lacks experience and enables vulnerable features, fails to fix a known flaw, or does not change default passwords.

vi. Vulnerabilities can arise from users and pose a significant risk. Some mistakes they make include using a common or easily guessed password or leaving their laptop or mobile phone unattended. Users who are highly knowledgeable about cybersecurity can still fall victim to password theft, malware installation, or unintentional disclosure of sensitive information, including organisational roles and schedules. An attacker could use these details to target and time an attack effectively.

vii. Input sanitisation involves inspecting and purifying input data to prevent system damage from malicious code. Cybercriminals seek out systems lacking proper input sanitisation to inject malicious code and gain unauthorised access.

viii. Sensitive data and systems are at risk within organisations due to insider threats, which can be caused by employees, partners, contractors, or vendors. The result can be attributed to insiders who practice poor cyber hygiene or maliciously steal sensitive data.

ix. Organisations grant privileged access to employees for job-related resources. Yet, organisations may unintentionally grant excessive access and permissions to certain employees. Security risks may arise if an employee exploits these permissions or if a threat actor compromises their account.

HOW TO STAY PROTECTED AGAINST CYBERSECURITY VULNERABILITIES

2.09 Certain cybersecurity vulnerabilities will always be a challenge for organisations. Nevertheless, there are ways to minimise most vulnerabilities to hinder cybercriminals from exploiting them. Organisations can reduce cybersecurity vulnerabilities by doing the following.

a. Keep software up to date: Outdated or unpatched software is a common cybersecurity vulnerability that cybercriminals exploit. Nevertheless, software updates are frequently released by applications to fix security flaws and enhance device protection. Regular software updates are necessary for organisations to protect against security vulnerabilities that cybercriminals can exploit.

b. Practice cybersecurity best practices.

c. Human error can contribute to certain cybersecurity vulnerabilities. Encouraging employees to adopt cybersecurity best practices can help an organisation reduce the risk of security vulnerabilities.

d. Weak login credentials are frequently caused by human error and pose a common security vulnerability. Unauthorised access to a network can be obtained by cybercriminals through the cracking of weak credentials. To prevent compromise by cybercriminals, employees should create strong and unique passwords. To create a strong password, use at least 16 characters with a unique mix of letters, numbers, and special characters. It excludes personal details, consecutive alphanumeric characters, and frequently used words from the text.

e. To prevent unauthorised access, employees should enable Multi-Factor Authentication (MFA) for their accounts. Users must provide additional authentication as part of MFA, a security measure to confirm their identity. The additional authentication factor provides added security to user accounts, preventing cybercriminals from using compromised login credentials.

f. It's crucial to educate employees on social engineering attacks like phishing, which aim to deceive them into surrendering their login details. To prevent becoming targets of such attacks, employees must be wary of unsolicited messages and refrain from clicking on dubious attachments or links.

g. Implement least-privilege access: The principle of least privilege is effective in minimising security vulnerabilities resulting from insufficient access control. Users are only granted the necessary access to resources in the cybersecurity principle of least privilege. Implementing least-privilege access helps organisations limit the areas cybercriminals can exploit to infiltrate their systems. By implementing least privilege access, an organisation can impede lateral movement and minimise the access of a threat actor.

h. Secure WiFi networks: Inadequate or non-existent encryption is commonly exploited by cybercriminals, including on unencrypted WiFi networks. Organisations should safeguard their WiFi by using a strong password, updating router software, and enabling WPA3 or WPA2 encryption.

i. Run a penetration test: A penetration test mimics a cyber attack on a company's security systems to evaluate their effectiveness. It evaluates an organisation's security measures and detects any weaknesses that can be exploited by cybercriminals. An organisation can use a penetration test to evaluate the functionality of security protocols and identify vulnerabilities that require patching. Identifying security vulnerabilities, including human error and software bugs, is possible through a penetration test, which enables organisations to address these issues.

j. Invest in cybersecurity solutions: To decrease security vulnerabilities, an organisation should invest in cybersecurity solutions including antivirus software, a PAM solution, and a business password manager.

k. Antivirus software is a program that stops, identifies, and eliminates known malware from a device. Installing antivirus software can prevent malware and cybercriminals from accessing an organisation's systems.

l. PAM solution: A valuable tool that assists organisations in the management and security of privileged accounts with access to critical data. It determines who can access networks, applications, servers, and devices. By utilising a PAM solution, organisations can enforce least privilege access and minimise vulnerabilities in access control.

m. The business password manager is a tool that enables employees to securely store, track, share, and manage their login credentials. With the assistance of a business password manager, employees can securely store and access their login credentials in a cloud-based digital vault. By using a password manager, administrators can guarantee that employees have strong passwords and MFA enabled.

AN EXPANDING RANGE OF DEVICES (INTERNET OF THINGS)

2.10 Back in 2011, cyber security mainly revolved around safeguarding desktop computers and laptops. Over time, the Internet has become more and more intertwined with our daily lives, often without us even realising it. Exploitation and the impact of attacks are amplified by the 'Internet of Things', posing risks of physical damage, injury, and worst-case scenario, death.

2.11 Connectivity in critical systems across industries like energy, mining, agriculture, and aviation has led to the creation of the Industrial Internet of Things. The potential for hacking and tampering now extends to devices and processes that were previously considered safe, with potentially disastrous outcomes.

2.12 Therefore, our vulnerability to cyber harms extends beyond our own devices to include threats against interconnected systems crucial for society, health, and welfare.

POOR CYBER HYGIENE AND COMPLIANCE

2.13 Over the past five years, there has been a definite increase in the UK's recognition of technical vulnerabilities in software and networks, and the importance of cyber hygiene. One reason for this is the implementation of initiatives such as the Government's '10 Steps to Cyber Security'. Many cyber attacks can be avoided by fixing easily exploited vulnerabilities. The success of a cyber attack often hinges on the vulnerability of the victim, not the ingenuity of the attacker. When it comes to cyber security investments, businesses and organisations rely on cost-benefit evaluations, but they are ultimately accountable for protecting their data and systems.

2.14 By finding the right balance between safeguarding critical systems and sensitive data and investing in people, technology, and governance, businesses can minimise the risk of cyber harm.

INSUFFICIENT TRAINING AND SKILLS

2.15 There is a deficiency in skills and knowledge in meeting our cyber security needs, both in the public and private sector. Within businesses, numerous employees lack awareness of cyber security and fail to comprehend their responsibilities, partly due to inadequate formal training. The general population lacks sufficient cyber awareness.

2.16 In addition, we must focus on building specialised skills and capabilities to stay ahead of fast-changing technology and effectively manage cyber risks. The resolution of this skills gap is necessary to mitigate a national vulnerability.

LEGACY AND UNPATCHED SYSTEMS

2.17 Until their next IT upgrade, numerous UK organisations will still rely on vulnerable legacy systems. The software on these systems frequently depends on outdated, unpatched versions. Attackers actively seek vulnerabilities in older versions and possess the means to exploit them. Some organisations use unsupported software without patching solutions, which presents an additional problem.

2.18 With hacking information and user-friendly tools readily available online, individuals can now easily acquire hacking abilities.

2.19 Hackers can easily find and collect the information they need to successfully target victims. It's crucial for everyone, whether in the living room or the boardroom, to understand their level of online vulnerability and the potential for cyber exploitation.

2.20 The UK has implemented policies and institutions that improved our defences and reduced cyber threats.

2.21 Unfortunately, we still haven't surpassed the threat. The volume of malware and the number of malicious actors have grown rapidly, but the types and motivations of these cyber threats have remained largely the same. The abilities of our most skilled adversaries, including certain states and elite hackers, have increased. Our main goal is to strengthen our defences, making them more adaptable and capable of countering threats. Additionally, we need to minimise the attackers' ability to harm us and tackle the underlying causes of the vulnerabilities mentioned earlier.

A VALIDATION PROCESS

2.22 Organisations may find managing vulnerabilities challenging because it can be seen as a distraction from other important tasks. The purpose of vulnerability management is to evaluate and address the effectiveness of your organisation's software update process and security configuration controls.

2.23 We recognise that system and software updates may not currently be considered a routine control for many organisations, although we assume they are. Some organisations choose not to update by default due to concerns about potential system disruptions or the need for additional testing.

IMPLEMENTING THIS GUIDANCE

2.24 The purpose of this guidance is to assist organisations in focusing their vulnerability management efforts and establishing achievable goals.

2.25 The initial stages of implementing a vulnerability management process can feel overwhelming due to the multitude of issues uncovered, making prioritisation of actions essential. Starting small or with a specific focus is usually the best approach, gradually expanding the process to a larger scale. For instance, by concentrating solely on vulnerabilities in critical systems.

WIDER ORGANISATIONAL RELEVANCE

2.26 A vulnerability management process shouldn't exist in isolation. This effort involves not only IT operations, but also security and risk teams. Ensure that your organisation's risk register is comprehensive by adding time, budget, and risks, and consider engaging senior leaders, particularly if teams report to different board members.

2.27 Follow our best-practice timescales by applying updates promptly and preferably automatically.

2.28 To safeguard your estate, it is crucial to install the latest updates. It's advisable to establish a default policy for updating, ensuring that software updates are promptly and ideally automatically applied. Incorporate this into your update management process as the standard, with exceptions for safety-critical systems or operational technology.

DIFFERENT TYPES OF UPDATE

2.29 Software updates from different vendors can be confusing and bring their own set of challenges.

2.30 There are those who separate security updates and feature updates, and there are those who integrate them.

2.31 Occasionally, a previous update must be installed before you can install the latest one. Unintended side effects are more common with multi-version upgrades than with single updates.

2.32 Vendors may choose to publish advisories for certain vulnerabilities, while silently updating others without public acknowledgement. Overlooking an update could lead to missing these silent updates, which raises the risk for your organisation.

2.33 Installing updates immediately is strongly recommended by the NCSC for these reasons. To avoid being caught off guard and urgently needing to update to the latest version to address a new vulnerability, stay ahead of the game by giving yourself time for controlled updates.

2.34 Make sure to get updates from reliable sources, like the vendor support website.

ROLLING OUT TESTING

2.35 Once vendors release these updates, it's important for you to conduct your own testing on your systems. The rollout process can proceed smoothly by implementing a gradual approach, like a phased or staged rollout across all your platforms, or by using a canary deployment model for a selected group of users.

2.36 Implementing a phased rollout enables live testing of the estate with the security update. Conducting tests in the live system will help identify real-world problems. During live testing, the rollout can be halted or reverted if a problem is found.

2.37 Consider these factors to simplify update management and rollout.

2.38 Customise your communication preferences as the system owner to stay up-to-date with the latest available updates. Make sure to have the necessary licenses in place too.

2.39 Following the platform's application development rules is the best approach, rather than attempting to reinvent the wheel. The likelihood of experiencing issues is higher with specially packaged applications compared to those from a platform application store or using the platform's native installer.

2.40 Among the cloud services that support infrastructure as a service (IaaS), there are tools available to assist with vulnerability management and update implementation. To ensure compatibility, build your deployed IaaS on a supported OS variant with a cloud platform that has an auto-update service.

2.41 Implement infrastructure as code (IaC). The most reliable automation method involves replacing the running image or code with the updated version, instead of simply updating it. Ensure easy testing, updating, and rolling back by developing newly developed systems in a way that reduces the chance of issues.

2.42 Automation is crucial for alleviating the burden. For instance, you have the option to automate update deployment if scanning detects any missing updates.

2.43 Prior to installation, it is important to scan any removable media, like a USB stick, for viruses if it is being used to transfer updates from the internet to another system.

BEST-PRACTICE TIMESCALES

2.44 In order to aid in your rollout process planning, we have outlined our definitions of best practice below. Your organisation can use these timescales to improve contract development and achieve best practice. We have ensured that our timeframes align with vendor best-practice advice and our own Cyber Essentials certification. They are applicable to all updates, regardless of how severe the vulnerability is.

2.45 Aim to decrease the timeframe to the smallest window achievable. Attackers typically examine and seek to exploit a vulnerability after it has been fixed. This can result in a race between network defenders updating and attackers targeting those who haven't installed the update.

2.46 Maximise the benefits of vendor tools and services to meet the timeframe by enabling automatic updates and effectively managing rollouts. You can easily pause or undo an update if any issues arise. Keep in mind that a phased rollout may not be required if you're using default app or OS configurations.

2.47 When it comes to business-critical systems, consider the trade-off between timescales and system availability.

UPDATING WHEN EXPLOITATION IS RIFE

2.48 Although the timelines mentioned above are applicable to routine updates, there are occasions where attackers find a vulnerability and scan or attack the internet on a large scale to locate victims before completing the updates. The timelines provided are excessively long, making it essential to accelerate the update process.

2.49 The most effective approach is usually to use your existing internal procedures for managing internal IT incidents, such as outages. The rationale behind this is that the mandated governance processes, like on-call staff schedules, should already be set up. The seriousness of initiating an IT incident should not be underestimated, requiring collaboration between security teams and IT staff to determine the appropriate circumstances and procedures.

2.50 When this situation arises, make sure you are ready to install supplementary vendor updates immediately upon discovering a new vulnerability. The first update launch won't be hindered by this.

2.51 Before implementing any updates, make sure to look for signs of compromise if there is evidence of an ongoing exploitation of a vulnerability. Updates may not prevent compromise if exploitation took place during the exposure window.

2.52 Evaluate your assets by comprehending the systems, software, obligations, and susceptibilities in your technical inventory.

2.53 A successful vulnerability management strategy requires knowledge of the systems and software within your technical estate. Determining the person or entity responsible for each system or service is a critical step.

2.54 It is crucial to establish a common understanding of the tasks performed by security and IT system maintainers after identifying this. When reporting detected vulnerabilities, it's essential to provide details on cadence, nature, allocate time for fixes, and agree on priority, especially for critical vulnerabilities being exploited.

ASSET DISCOVERY

2.55 The main objective is to oversee and identify the systems, services, infrastructure, devices, and software in your estate. Properly addressing each category separately is essential in order to avoid confusion and effectively tackle all requirements and challenges.

2.56 The ongoing task is to continuously discover, catalogue, and manage your assets. By implementing automation, you can direct your attention towards the end results. Moreover, it has the ability to enhance incident response and other cyber security operations.

OUTDATED AND PRODUCTS WITH EXTENDED SUPPORT

2.57 When conducting asset discovery, it is usual to find products that are either obsolete or have extended support. It is important to categorise them correctly and provide a suitable response.

2.58 When discussing obsolete products, we're referring to ones that no longer receive updates and are no longer being developed. The suggested plan is to transition to a supported product before it becomes obsolete. If there's no way around it, you'll have to confront the potential risks of using outdated products.

2.59 You can receive ongoing software assistance by choosing an extended-support product and paying an extra fee. Nonetheless, not all known vulnerabilities will receive fixes, so manual updates may be mandatory. The NCSC advises moving to a supported version once a product is no longer supported.

CONFIGURATION MANAGEMENT

2.60 Maintaining secure and consistent configurations across all systems is crucial to protect your network from potential threats, as attackers can exploit vulnerabilities for unauthorised access.

2.61 For complete coverage of your entire estate, we recommend automating configuration audits. To simplify large-scale remediation and minimise misconfiguration risks, it is recommended to deploy new systems using infrastructure and configuration as code. By staying informed about the software and firmware versions installed on your assets, through the use of asset discovery and update management, and implementing a strong configuration management process, you can ensure better control.

CARRY OUT ASSESSMENTS BY TRIAGING AND PRIORITISING

2.62 If the reported vulnerability or misconfiguration persists despite updating to the latest software version or if there is no update, you must establish a process to triage and prioritise.

2.63 The goal of vulnerability assessments is to identify and address security, configuration, or update management issues. To ensure effective management of your attack surface, conduct monthly vulnerability assessments across your entire estate. If your organisation hasn't performed a vulnerability scan across the entire organisation, the initial report will likely reveal numerous vulnerabilities, possibly in the hundreds or thousands. The ability to differentiate between external and internal exposure is essential for understanding your attack surface.

2.64 It is advisable for mature organisations to enhance assessment frequency, specifically for services that can be accessed externally. When using the built-in tools of your cloud provider, it's important to stick to their recommended cadence.

2.65 Vendors usually adhere to a predetermined update schedule, but they can also release updates outside of that schedule, known as out-of-band updates. If a critical vulnerability is identified, this situation might arise. Having a procedure to analyse potential vulnerabilities in your organisation is absolutely necessary.

SCANNING

2.66 To comprehend potential risks your organisation may encounter, it is crucial to scan consistently. Special training for staff or involving external partners is unnecessary.

2.67 Issues that cannot be resolved with software updates or due to malfunctioning automatic updates may be brought to light by vulnerability and configuration scans, thus requiring manual remediation. When updates are not being installed, a vulnerability scan can effectively bring attention to this issue.

VULNERABILITY DISCLOSURE

2.68 For those involved in software development or system administration, it's important to establish a protocol for security researchers to report any discovered vulnerabilities.

2.69 Sorting vulnerabilities that are not immediately fixable or mitigated.

2.70 Updating the affected software may not always resolve the reported vulnerability or misconfiguration, and there might not be an available fix. It may be suitable to refrain from updating in certain situations, like when the system is about to be decommissioned and the vulnerability is both hard to reach and exploit. As long as decommissioning efforts are ongoing and sensible controls are in place, it's entirely reasonable to opt against updating.

2.71 However, organisations often find themselves unable to address the problem due to constraints like staff availability or compatibility concerns. It's crucial to grasp the potential consequences for your organisation.

2.72 While the vulnerability assessment software or vendor advisory may provide a severity rating for the finding (such as the Common Vulnerability Scoring System or CVSS), it's essential that you consider business impact and risk for your organisation.

CHOOSING NOT TO UPDATE

2.73 At times, an organisation may conclude that the risks associated with automatic updates are excessive. In situations like this, the system should be placed on an 'exception list' so that updates can be subject to safety testing as per your organisation's requirements. If availability is crucial and there is no safe recovery option, only perform additional testing on those systems due to the significant time it requires.

2.74 When there is no available update for any reason, you'll have to establish a triage process to prioritise fixes.

2.75 To manage issues effectively, consolidate them and implement a standardised triage and prioritisation process for system owners to have full visibility.

2.76 The first step in your triage process should involve grouping together related findings, such as merging all SSL issues into one. As an alternative, you may consider grouping them by category, such as organising externally exposed vulnerabilities separately.

2.77 Once grouped together, they should be separated into three categories: matters to address, acknowledge, or examine.

2.78 'Fix' is used in cases where you'll guarantee an automatic system update or implement a reconfiguration or mitigation. When creating a prioritised list, focus on vulnerabilities in internet-facing services or applications with high potential for negative impact if exploited. Additionally, record the scheduled fix date for each issue. The vendor may have provided a date for when the fix will be issued, or it could be an estimate for when the configuration change can be implemented. In the case of a temporary vendor workaround or mitigation, it needs to be time-limited and actively monitored for removal once the full vendor remediation is accessible and applied.

2.79 Acknowledge and accept unresolved issues that you decide not to resolve at the moment. Valid justifications for not immediately resolving a vulnerability should be noted, along with a planned review date. If the level of risk they bring is adequately high, make a note of the issue in a risk register. The decision to acknowledge an issue and not fix it can be justified if the vulnerability is exploited later. Additionally, it would be wise to have additional monitoring to notify of any exploitation of the known vulnerabilities.

2.80 Look into problems that cannot be categorised as either 'fix' or 'acknowledge' by the triage system. 'Investigate' should only be employed as a temporary status. The reason for this could be that the cost of resolving the issue is unknown, or further work is required to determine the most effective solution among several possibilities. Vulnerability assessment software is not immune to errors and can generate false positives. Prior to removing it as an issue, it is recommended to investigate in cases of suspicion. How long it takes to resolve issues in this category will be determined by the severity of the issue.

2.81 The responsibility of not updating lies with the organisation, as there may be valid reasons to refrain from doing so. The choice to abstain is a high-level risk decision that should be evaluated within the broader framework of organisational risk management policy and practice.

2.82 There's a good chance that you'll discover more problems than you have the means to resolve. At its core, the decision not to resolve an issue is a business risk decision made by senior-level management, rather than an IT problem, and every organisation has its own level of risk tolerance. Cost, resources, complexity, and operational risks are among the legitimate factors that need to be considered in this situation. The focus should be on default updates and minimising case-by-case decision-making. It is important for the organisation's risk management staff and structures to understand the risk that the organisation is currently willing to tolerate.

2.83 Prioritise based on your organisation's risk assessment and reference the CISA Known Exploited Vulnerabilities Catalogue or threat intelligence feeds. Making decisions solely based on a single severity score, like CVSS, is not advisable.

2.84 Evaluate the potential impact on the system or service. This includes backups and system recovery knowledge.

2.85 Potential for reputational damage to the system, service or your organisation.

2.86 Replacing outdated systems is an instance of a direct cost.

2.87 How accessible and affordable is a short-term remedy.

2.88 Availability and cost of skilled resources to carry out the work.

2.89 The overall cost of handling and recovering from an incident, including any potential fines in the worst-case scenario.

2.90 After making a decision, make sure to record the rationale behind it and factor in any remaining risks in your organisation's overall risk management framework. Consider this risk register as a way to categorise identical risks, such as 'High: Unpatched externally exposed vulnerabilities allow initial compromise'. The risk should rest with the business, not the security team, and be apparent to senior leaders.

2.91 Ensure the ongoing verification and review of your vulnerability management process: Regularly evaluate and adapt your vulnerability management process to stay current with changes in your organisation's environment, emerging threats, or new vulnerabilities.

2.92 Make sure to actively verify and continually develop your vulnerability management process. It would be beneficial to create a feedback loop to aid in resolving this. Possible improvements involve shortening update timescales and increasing the frequency of asset discovery and management scans.

VERIFICATION

2.93 To ensure a fixed vulnerability is truly gone, include a verification process after reconfiguration or mitigation. If the mitigation is only a temporary workaround, you'll have to stay vigilant and keep an eye on it. Installing a vendor update may replace the temporary workaround. Temporary measures should be overridden by all of these cases.

2.94 Third-party penetration tests are an effective method for validating the effectiveness of the vulnerability management process.

REGULARLY REVIEW

2.95 It's important to regularly review your vulnerability management process to stay updated with any changes in your organisation's infrastructure, such as an architectural change that exposes more services to the internet. Ongoing review is necessary to account for new threats and vulnerabilities that are being discovered. By subscribing to security alerts from vendors, suppliers, and services, you can stay informed about developments to incorporate into your vulnerability management process.

CHAPTER 3

THE LAW

Ria Halme

INTRODUCTION

3.01 This chapter is a general overview of the legal framework for privacy, data protection and the cyber-security on an International, EU and UK level. It is not legal advice, and nothing in this chapter will create a client relationship in any form. The chapter is an introduction, the law must always be applied on a case-by-case approach considering the context, and with the help of privacy and security professionals.

INTERNATIONAL INSTRUMENTS

Convention 108

3.02 The Convention for the Protection of Individuals with regard to Automatic Processing of Personal Data, also known as the Convention 108, first introduced in 1981 by the Council of Europe, was the first international data protection instrument, which is binding to its signatories. The Convention requires the signatory states to implement the Convention to their national legal framework with effective enforcement for breaches. As of today, the Convention has been signed and ratified by 55 states.[1]

3.03 The Convention serves as a legal instrument that provides the basis for regional and national data protection legislation when it's established or renewed. The 108 has served as a platform for several developments and key concepts in data privacy. For example, the Convention originally introduced Rights of the Data Subject (the person whose data is being processed) to access and correct their data. These rights have later on become more well known in regional and national privacy laws and regulations, such as the EU's General Data Protection Regulation (GDPR), Brazilia's Lei Geral de Proteção de Dados (LGPD) and Singapore's Personal Data Protection Act (PDPA). Similarly, several data protection principles, such as data minimisation, accuracy, fairness, lawfulness, and transparency, which have become the cornerstones of privacy laws around the world, were first laid out in the 108. The Convention also introduced the concept

1 Council of Europe Convention for the Protection of Individuals with regard to Automatic Processing of Personal Data, Treaty 108 Chart of Signatures and ratifications; https://www.coe.int/en/web/conventions/full-list?module=signatures-by-treaty&treatynum=108.

of scaled sensitivity of personal data, prohibiting the processing of sensitive data unless appropriate safeguards have been implemented to protect it.[2]

3.04 In 2004, an additional Protocol came into force, requiring the Signatory States to establish national authorities to enforce the national data protection laws. Emphasis was put on cross-border data transfers, and the Protocol prohibited personal data transfers to non-Signatory countries, which do not provide adequate levels of protection.[3]

Modernisation of the Convention

3.05 Following the developments in technology, increased cross-border data transfers, and the commercial use of personal data, the Convention went under review in 2010. A modernised 108 came into force in 2018 reflecting the global development in the regional and national privacy laws and regulations. Under the modern Convention, data breaches that may cause significant harm to the Data Subject must be reported to the national supervisory authority. The Data Subjects were also granted wider rights, such as the right to be consulted on being subjected to automated decisions and having the right to request rectification and erasure of their data. The conditions for the cross-border transfers became more elaborate and now follow the general principles of other existing legal instruments on cross-border transfers, such as ensuring a suitable legal basis and instrument govern the transfer. The modern Convention also applies to personal data, which is processed using non-automated means, and introduced new data protection principles limiting the purpose of use and fortifying transparency of processing. The scope of sensitive personal data expanded to include new categories such as criminal records, biometric and genetic data, and ethnic origin.[4]

3.06 The Council of Europe also published guidelines on the use of Artificial Intelligence (AI). The guidelines address expectations for how the Convention must be applied in the context of AI, but also directly address developers, manufacturers, and service providers on their responsibilities. The actors in the field must follow a 'privacy-by-design and default' approach, where data protection is built into the product or service from the start and strictest settings must apply to the use of the data. The guidance also addresses the legislators and policymakers instructing them to ensure laws consider human rights and the societal impact of AI, integrate risk assessments, and supervisory authority

2 Treaty 108, Arts 5-8; https://iapp.org/media/pdf/resource_center/Brazilia_General_Data_Protection_Law.pdf; https://sso.agc.gov.sg/Act/PDPA2012.

3 Additional Protocol to the Convention for the Protection of Individuals with regard to Automatic Processing of Personal Data, regarding supervisory authorities and transborder data flows www.coe.int/en/web/conventions/full-list/-/conventions/treaty/181.

4 https://rm.coe.int/cahdata-convention-108-table-e-april2018/16808ac958; https://rm.coe.int/modernised-conv-overview-of-the-novelties/16808accf8; https://www.coe.int/en/web/data-protection/convention108/modernised; https://rm.coe.int/cets-223-explanatory-report-to-the-protocol-amending-the-convention-fo/16808ac91a; https://search.coe.int/cm/Pages/result_details.aspx?ObjectId=09000016807c65bf.

consultations where 'the AI applications have the potential to significantly impact the human rights and fundamental freedoms of data subjects'. In its new form, the Convention is more closely aligned with other existing strict privacy laws and regulations, and can be expected to aid in the progressive development of data protection laws globally as we're at the verge of the next generation of technology emerging from WEB 3.0, the metaverse, the increasing sophistication of AI and smart technology.[5]

Council of Europe Convention on Cybercrime

3.07 The Council of Europe Convention on Cybercrime, also known as the Budapest Convention, is an international treaty on cybercrime and electronic evidence and is open for signatures by any State implementing the Convention on a national level. The Convention, binding to its signatories, was drafted by the Council of Europe and, as of September 2023, includes 68 States as Parties which have ratified the Convention and 21 States that are in the process of acceeding as they work towards implementation.[6] A Party to the Convention is required to implement a national legal framework that criminalises certain activity committed via the Internet and other computer network activity. The scope of activity is wide, including unauthorised access, child pornography, and computer-related fraud. The Party is also required to integrate procedural powers for investigating and securing evidence relating to any type of crime and to establish international co-operation.[7]

3.08 The signatories also form a Cybercrime Convention Committee (T-CY), which was established by the Convention itself.[8] The purpose of the Committee is to provide a forum for cooperation and information sharing to facilitate implementation.[9] To facilitate the practical work, the Committee has issued several high-level guidance notes[10] on different topics, such as identity theft and phishing in relation to fraud,[11] DDOS attacks,[12] and trans-border access.[13] The Cybercrime Programme Office of the Council of Europe (C-PROC) supports the work of the T-CY by aiding the Convention signatories draft and implement their legal frameworks on cybercrime, and electronic evidence. They also provide training for different office holders, such as judges, and law enforcement

5 https://rm.coe.int/guidelines-on-artificial-intelligence-and-data-protection/168091f9d8.
6 www.coe.int/en/web/cybercrime/parties-observers.
7 https://rm.coe.int/cyber-buda-benefits-19april2023-en/1680aafa3d.
8 Budapest Convention, Art 46.
9 www.coe.int/en/web/cybercrime/tcy.
10 www.coe.int/en/web/cybercrime/guidance-notes.
11 T-CY Guidance Note #4 Identity theft and phishing in relation to fraud, 2013, Available at: https://rm.coe.int/16802e7096.
12 T-CY Guidance Note #5 DDOS Attacks, 2013, Available at: https://rm.coe.int/16802e9c49.
13 T-CY Guidance Note #3 Transborder access to data, 2014, Available at: https://rm.coe.int/16802e726a https://www.coe.int/en/web/cybercrime/guidance-notes.

officers.[14] The supporting work is done through international capacity building projects.[15]

3.09 To further support the implementation and development, the Council of Europe holds Octopus Conferences to 'bring together academia, international organizations, non-governmental organizations, and private sector cyber-crime experts from over 80 countries to discuss and exchange information.' The cycle of the conferences is 12–18 months,[16] and each conference is built around a specific topic, such as gathering criminal evidence from the cloud[17], crime and jurisdiction in cyberspace,[18] safeguards and data protection: criminal justice versus national security[19] and securing and sharing electronic evidence.[20]

3.10 Several important countries, such as Russia, India, and China have not signed the Convention, and Russia has explicitly contested the Convention as violating State sovereignty. Similarly, there is a vast number of non-signatories in larger regions, such as Qatar, Saudi Arabia, and the United Arab Emirates in the Middle East. This weakens the Convention to some extent, as substantial amounts of population are excluded.[21] The Budapest Convention, however, remains an important legislative instrument to prepare and improve the global legal framework on cybercrime with its active community developing the tools and international cooperation to combat cyber threats.

EUROPEAN AND EUROPEAN UNION-LEVEL INSTRUMENTS

The Convention for the Protection of Human Rights and Fundamental Freedoms (ECHR)

3.11 The Convention for the Protection of Human Rights and Fundamental Freedoms, which is more widely known as the European Convention of Human Rights (ECHR) is an international Treaty, which makes specific rights of the Universal Declaration of Human Rights binding.[22] The ECHR is open for signatures for the Member States of the Council of Europe, of which all 47 have signed, and ratified the Treaty.[23]

14 www.coe.int/en/web/cybercrime/cybercrime-office-c-proc-.
15 https://rm.coe.int/cproc-about/1680762b41.
16 www.coe.int/en/web/cybercrime/octopus-conference.
17 www.coe.int/en/web/cybercrime/octopus2015 Octopus 2015.
18 www.coe.int/en/web/cybercrime/octopus-interface-2016 Octopus 2016.
19 www.coe.int/en/web/cybercrime/octopus-interface-2013 Octopus 2013.
20 www.coe.int/en/web/cybercrime/octopus-conference-2023
21 Drahos, *Regulatory Theory, Foundations and Applications* (Australian National University Press, 2017) p. 543; www.coe.int/en/web/conventions/full-list/-/conventions/treaty/185/signatures.
22 www.echr.coe.int/pages/home.aspx?p=basictexts.
23 ECHR, Art 59; www.coe.int/en/web/conventions/search-on-treaties/-/conventions/chartSignature/3 (s 005).

3.12 The parties to the Treaty are referred to as 'High Contracting Parties', who are responsible for ensuring the rights are effective in practice. This means, the States must enact national implementing legislation, and the application of the law must be done in accordance with the Convention and the decisions of the European Court of Human Rights (ECtHR).[24]

3.13 Therefore, even though the ECHR in itself is not applicable between private parties (no horizontal applicability), the State is liable for ensuring there are adequate measures in place to exercise the rights in practice.[25] Anyone, who considers their rights to have been violated, can bring a case to the ECtHR, after all the national level remedies have been exhausted nationally.[26] Also, even though the ECHR applies vertically, the ECtHR has underlined, that the State may be required by a positive obligation to ensure the law is also applicable between private parties.[27]

European Court of Human Rights (ECtHR) and the application of the ECHR to privacy and data protection

3.14 The judicial body enforcing the ECHR is the European Court of Human Rights (EctHR), which was created in the Treaty.[28] The EctHR's decisions are binding to the signatories[29] and enforcement is supervised by the Committee of Ministers, which comprises of the Foreign Ministers of the States, who are Parties to the Council of Europe.[30]

3.15 In relation to data protection and privacy, Article 8 of the ECHR provides 'a right to respect for one's private and family life, his home and his correspondence'.[31] The applicability of the right is wide, as it applies in all contexts, whether a person is at home or at work.[32] However, the right to privacy and the protection of it, is not an absolute right. Article 8 includes conditions for a legitimate interference, which means, a violation of the right must be based on an applicable law and be necessary for crime prevention or another legitimate reason. The ECtHR evaluates four aspects of an interference in its rulings: firstly, has there been an interference; secondly, is the interference in accordance with the law; thirdly, is there a legitimate aim; and lastly, is the interference necessary.[33] In

24 ECHR, Arts 1, 13, and 46; Chlebny, Seibert-Fohr and Villiger, *Judgments of the European Court of Human Rights – Effects and Implementation, 'How a National Judge Implements Judgments of the Strasbourg Court'* (Routledge, 2016).

25 Lynskey, *The Foundations of EU Data Protection Law* (Oxford University Press, 2015) p. 113.

26 ECHR, Arts 34-35.

27 eg, *Von Hannover v. Germany (No. 2)* (application nos. 40660/08 and 60641/08).

28 ECHR, Art 19.

29 ECHR, Art 46.

30 ECHR, Art 46.

31 ECHR, Art 8.

32 In *Niemetz v. Germany* (application no. 13710/88), the ECtHR held, that Art 8 ECHR also extends to business premises.

33 ECHR, Art 8(2).

addition, as per the case-law the interfering measures must be proportionate and intrusiveness must be minimised to what is necessary to achieve the aim.

Case law of the ECtHR (on privacy and security)

Public side

3.16 On the public side, application to modern technology and data protection has in several cases concerned the public sector's involvement in interception. The ECtHR has followed the above-mentioned formula closely in its rulings, evaluating whether there has been a proportional legal justification for a necessary intrusion of privacy. After this, the Court looks at whether the intrusion was done with the least intrusive measures available. For example, tracking a person's GPS for a limited time as a least intrusive measure to gather evidence to prevent bomb attacks, pursued to protect national security, public safety, and the prevention of crime, was acceptable for the Court. It was considered a necessary measure in a democratic society.[34] However, if the conditions are not met, the Court will consider the intrusion unlawful. For example, The ECtHR considered it an unlawful invasion of privacy to intercept phones in efforts to uncover suspected drug-traffickers, where the national law did not provide for safeguards. The Court confirmed that the national law must be clear and provide adequate safeguards against abuse.[35] In line with this, the ECtHR considers mass or blanket surveillance unlawful, as it provides too wide a discretion for gathering intelligence, lacks appropriate legal justification, authorisation, remedies, and checks and balances against possible abuse.[36]

Private side

3.17 On the private side, several of the cases relate to the monitoring of employees. Also, in this context, the Court holds on to its balancing test to evaluate whether monitoring is justified and within the boundaries of the national legislation. There also needs to be evidence on balancing the interests of both parties, and the employees must be informed of the surveillance. The monitoring must be proportional to the danger or possible threat and be managed with appropriate safeguards. For example, the ECtHR has held that video surveillance in a university, which otherwise is a public place, was unlawful, as the institution had not conducted a balancing test, evaluating the intrusion, the surveillance breached the national law, and it could not be justified.[37] On the other hand, a cashier, who was dismissed from work based on undercover surveillance material showing her manipulating accounts and stealing money, was considered justified, as there had been a due strike of balance of interest

34 *Uzun v Germany* (application no. 35623/05).

35 *Dragojević v Croatia* (application no. 68955/11).

36 *Roman Zakharov v Russia* (application no. 47143/06) and *Szabó and Vissy v Hungary* (application no. 37138/14).

37 *Antović and Mirković v Montenegro* (application no. 70838/13).

between the employee's right to privacy, and the employer's interest to protect his property and administer justice. The national court also consistently noted in their own judgment of the case, that there had been reasonable grounds to suspect a theft, and in such cases undercover surveillance was in accordance with the law. The ECtHR did note, however, that as technology develops, possibly enabling a more intrusive method of surveillance, the balancing of the parties' rights may look different in the future.[38] Lastly, the Court has in all its judgments underlined the importance of notifying the employee of the monitoring. The ECtHR has several times decided cases in favour of the applicant whose privacy rights had been violated as they had not been informed of the monitoring. The notification requirement applies to all methods of monitoring, such as video surveillance, using Data Loss Prevention software and recording and further processing the employee's communication data.[39]

3.18 To summarise, the ECtHR accepts an intrusion of privacy, if the conditions of its test are met. In broad terms, the same rules apply to both the public and the private side. What is important to the outcome of the case is the legality and proportionality of the intrusion. The intruding entity must evaluate the level of intrusion, justify it, and strike a balance between the Parties interests and rights. Therefore, the Court's four-step evaluation is a good model to use by the entities implementing measures that violate the right to privacy as defined in Article 8 of the ECHR.

Treaty of Lisbon and the EU Charter of Fundamental Rights and Freedoms

3.19 The Treaty of Lisbon[40] came into force in 2009 after the Treaty Establishing a Constitution for Europe was vetoed by the Dutch and French referendums and reconsideration to the proposed EU's legal framework was required. The Lisbon Treaty comprises of the two pre-existing amended Treaties, the Treaty on the European Union, and the Treaty on the Functioning of the European Union. The Treaty is a Primary law and has direct effect subject to the conditions of applicability being fulfilled. Therefore, the Articles can be invoked in court in a dispute between private parties and the State (vertical direct effect) and it can also be applied between private parties (horizontal direct effect).[41]

3.20 The EU Charter of Fundamental Rights and Freedoms (Charter) was drafted in 2000 to provide certain rights and freedoms to the EU-citizens and

38 *Köpke v Germany* (application no. 420/07).

39 *Bărbulescu v Romania* (application no. 61496/08) and *López Ribalda and Others v Spain* (application nos. 1874/13 and 8567/13).

40 Treaty of Lisbon amending the Treaty on European Union and the Treaty establishing the European Community, signed at Lisbon, OJ C 306 p. 1–271.

41 C-26/62 *Van Gend en Loos v Nederlandse Administratie der Belastingen* for vertical effect, and C-43/75 *Defrenne v Sabena (No 2)* for horizontal effect.

residents,[42] and the Lisbon Treaty changed the Charter's legal standing by providing it 'the same legal value as the other Treaties'.[43] The Charter provides that 'everyone has the right to respect for his or her private and family life, home, correspondence,[44] and data protection',[45] and further clarifies, that the rights have the same meaning, as in the ECHR, with a possibility of EU law providing for a more extensive protection.[46]

3.21 By the Lisbon Treaty, the Charter is binding to the EU-institutions, making the right to privacy and data protection a fundamental human right.[47] The Treaty also prevails over the national legislation of the Member States, binding the national courts to adhere to the Charter. Whether the Charter is applicable only when the Member States implement the EU-law or in all cases has been under discussion in several cases of the European Court of Justice, with a clear line still to be established.[48] On state level the Charter is not widely used, mainly due to the requirement of further clarity on when the Charter becomes applicable on national level. The Council of the EU has invited the States to share experiences on the use of the Charter to improve the application and support the development. [49]

The European Court of Justice (ECJ)

3.22 The highest judicial body enforcing EU-law, including the Lisbon Treaty, is the European Court of Justice (ECJ). The ECJ has a holistic approach to rulings, when applying EU-law, which means they consider not only the written law, but the aim of it, and the overall interest of the EU. The rulings of the ECJ have in the past resulted into notable changes, and establishment of legal doctrines, which have later on developed into legislation. For example, the direct effect of the EU Treaties[50] and the supremacy of EU-law and hence the requirement for the Member States courts to set aside a contradicting national law come from the case-law of the ECJ.[51]

3.23 On privacy and security, the ECJ's rulings have significantly shaped the legal landscape and set expectations on how the privacy law should be implemented in practice. For example, the ECJ has several times annulled legal instruments and schemes that aim to personal data transfers from the EU

42 The Charter of the Fundamental Rights of the European Union (2000/C 364/01), Preamble.
43 Lisbon Treaty, Art 16.
44 Charter, Art 7.
45 Charter, Art 8.
46 Charter, Art 52(3).
47 Charter, Arts 51-52.
48 Lazovski and Blockmans, *Research Handbook on EU Institutional Law* (Edwar Elgar Publishing, 2016) pp. 20-21.
49 https://fra.europa.eu/sites/default/files/fra_uploads/fra-2020-fundamental-rights-report-2020-focus_en.pdf.
50 *Van Gend en Loos (referenced above) and Defrenne (No. 2) (referenced above).*
51 *C- 6/64 Costa v ENEL;* Graic and de Burga, *EU-law, Text, cases and materials*, Sixth edition, (Oxford University Press, 2015) pp. 62-63.

to the US[52] and narrowed the scope of the acceptable data transfers as set in the Passenger Name Records Agreement between the EU and Canada.[53] In the US case, the ruling came on the basis of insufficient protection of personal data from governmental access under the then existing Safe Harbour mechanism. The framework was then replaced by a 'Privacy Shield', a similar scheme that too was deemed inadequate by the ECJ.[54] In Canada's case, the ECJ considered the requirement to obtain sensitive data to prevent terrorism too extensive and violated the fundamental rights and freedoms of the Data Subjects under the scope of the EU's Privacy laws. The Court therefore ordered a reduction in the scope of air passengers' data.[55]

3.24 Cases where the legal landscape was significantly impacted by the ECJ's rulings include that decisions that IP addresses are in certain circumstances personal data,[56] and that the Data Subject has a (qualified) 'right to be forgotten', which means, the data subject[57] has the right to have his data erased. This decision later became a Data Subject Right in the GDPR. In *Digital Rights Ireland (DRI)*, the Court declared the Data Retention Directive[58] invalid, and ordered the implementing national legislation to be revised to comply with the ruling. The ECJ said inter alia that personal data which the Directive sought to retain for an indefinite time should be retained only based on a suspicion of a serious crime, be established by sufficient checks and balances, and there must not be blanket retention, as it would mean every EU-citizen would fall under the scope. The ECJ also ruled that the Directive also failed to provide appropriate security for the retained data.[59]

3.25 As the rulings above show, the ECJ has a strict approach on applying the law concerning privacy and data protection. Their rulings indicate a direction which aims to ensure an effective right to privacy and data protection.

52 C-362/14 *Schrems 1.*

53 Opinion 1/15 of 26 July 2017.

54 T-670/16 *Digital Rights Ireland v Commission*; The CJEU Judgement in the Schrems II Case (europa.eu).

55 Opinion 1/15 of 26 July 2017.

56 Case 582/14 *Patrick Breyer v Germany.*

57 Data subject means the natural person whose personal data is in question, Reg (eu) 2016/679 of the European Parliament and of the Council on the protection of natural persons with regard to the processing of personal data and on the free movement of such data, and repealing Dir 95/46/ec (general data protection regulation), 2016, Art 4(1).

58 Dir 2006/24/EC of the European Parliament and of the Council of 15 March 2006 on the retention of data generated or processed in connection with the provision of publicly available electronic communications services or of public communications networks and amending Dir 2002/58/EC, OJ L 105, 13.4.2006, pp. 54–63.

59 Joined cases C-293/12 and C-594/12, *Digital Rights Ireland Ltd v Ireland.*

The EU's General Data Protection Regulation (GDPR)

3.26 With an aim to harmonise data processing practices and the level of provided data protection, the EU's General Data Protection Regulation (GDPR)[60] came into force in 2018. It replaced the Data Protection Directive,[61] that had been the EU's main legislative instrument for data protection since 1995. The Directive described the level of protection which must be provided for the Data Subjects (persons whose data is processed) but left the means of reaching the legislative aim to the Member States. As a Regulation, the GDPR is applicable to the EU Member States as it is, subject to certain margins of discretion that remain with the Member States. The GDPR also applies to entities which are established outside of the Union but are processing the data of the Data Subjects within the Union.[62] Therefore, an entity established, for example, in India, which processes the data of Data Subjects within the EU, will need to comply with the GDPR. Another key aim of the GDPR is to give control of the data back to the people. This was done by several new Data Subject rights in addition to better enforcing the legacy ones, and imposing stricter responsibilities on the Data Controller[63] and the Data Processor.[64] Accountability and added liabilities for compensating damages further aim to enforce compliant data processing practices.[65] The data processing of the EU-institutions, agencies, bodies and offices falls outside of the scope of the GDPR, and is instead regulated by Regulation 45/2001. The Regulation 45/2001 is currently under review to align it with the GDPR.[66][67]

3.27 The following key areas of the GDPR are further elaborated below: Data Subject rights, data life cycle management and accountability, vendor management, data transfers, national derogations in general and HR-data, IT/cyber security, training and awareness, Data Protection Officer, record keeping, accountability (BAU), and enforcement.

Data Subject Rights

3.28 Under the GDPR, the Data Subject is provided with certain rights, which include the right to rectify incorrect data and, where they have suffered substantial harm due to a decision made using incorrect data, to be compensated for the suffered loss. The Data Subject also has a right to know if their data is

60 Reg (EU) 2016/679 of the European Parliament and of the Council of 27 April 2016 on the protection of natural persons with regard to the processing of personal data and on the free movement of such data, and repealing Dir 95/46/EC (General Data Protection Reg).

61 Dir 95/46/EC of the European Parliament and of the Council of 24 October 1995 on the protection of individuals with regard to the processing of personal data and on the free movement of such data, OJ L 281, 23.11.1995, pp. 31–50.

62 GDPR, Art 3.

63 Data controller is the one, who decides the purposes and means for the data processing, GDPR, Art 4(7).

64 Processor is the one, who is processing the data on behalf of the controller, GDPR, Art 4(8).

65 GDPR, eg Arts 5, 28-29, 82.

66 https://edps.europa.eu/data-protection/our-work/subjects/regulation-452001_en.

67 GDPR, Recital 17, Arts 2(3) and 98.

processed and further access it by receiving a copy alongside certain information on how it's being processed, such as whom it has been shared with, how long it has been retained for, and what the purposes of use are. The right to data portability exists partly to prevent 'lock-in' situations, where the customer cannot change the service provider due to the difficulties in migrating the data. Under the Portability Right the Controller must provide a limited scope of the Data Subjects data to him in an easily readable and commonly used electronic form or send the same directly to another Controller. In certain situations, the Data Subject also has a right to be forgotten, which means deleting the data relating to the Data Subject from the Controller's and Processor's databases. However, the right to be erased (forgotten) is a qualified right, which means, that it only applies in certain cases, such as when the data subject withdraws a previously given consent to process the data, the processing has not been based on an appropriate legal basis, and there are no other overriding reasons the Controller must continue processing the data, such as a legal obligation to process certain data for fraud detection purposes.[68]

3.29 The Data Subject has always the right to object to his data being processed for direct marketing purposes, and to being subjected to profiling and automated decision-making. Where the right to refuse direct marketing applies with no exceptions, there are scenarios in which the controller may continue to profile and conduct automated decisions, in which case the Data Subject can require a human intervention and contest a reviewed decision.[69] In certain scenarios, the Data Subject can also have his data processing restricted.[70] Furthermore the Data Subject has a right to transparency. This means the Controller must provide the Data Subject adequate information, including how the personal data is obtained, the legal bases and purposes of use, where the personal data is transferred to, and how it is safeguarded. Information must also be given on data sharing practices and whom the data is shared with.[71] In practice, transparency is implemented via privacy notices, and alongside exercising the rights.

3.30 Data Subjects Right Requests must be responded to free of charge, within 30 days by either implementing the Request or providing legitimate reasons why the Request cannot be actioned upon. Further time extensions are possible where the law provides a ground for it.[72] Refusing to act on a request is justified only if the Controller can evidence it is excessive or manifestly unfounded, or if the Controller is not able to identify the Data Subject after attempts to do so.[73]

68 GDPR, Arts 12-23
69 GDPR, Arts 21-22.
70 GDPR, Art 18.
71 GDPR, Arts 13 and 14.
72 GDPR, Art 12.
73 GDPR, Art 12.

Data Privacy Principles and Accountability

3.31 The GDPR's data processing principles form the heart of the Regulation, as they apply to all personal data processing. These principles require the Controller to process the *minimum* amount of personal data required *fairly* and for a *legitimate purpose*, The data processing must be *transparent*, and the personal data must be *erased* after it's no longer needed for the communicated purpose. *Security* measures must be applied according to the level of risk. The Controller is also *accountable*, and therefore must be able to demonstrate compliance with the above.[74]

Vendor management

3.32 The Controller is responsible for the protection of personal data, including engaging Processors which comply with the GDPR. The Controller must conduct adequate due diligence of the Processor's privacy and security practices and engage them with suitable data protection clauses.[75] Third party risk management is further elaborated in **Chapter 5**.

Record keeping and Risk Assessments

3.33 The Controller is required to keep a Record of Processing Activity (RoPA) which must include information on the full data flows, such as categories of data, data sharing and transfers, security measures, and retention times. The Regulator may request the Record for an inspection.[76] The RoPA is also the starting point for conducting a Privacy Impact Assessment (PIA) and a Data Privacy Impact Assessment (DPIA). These risk assessments are mandatory for identifying and further evaluating and mitigating risks in high-risk processing activities. It is the Controller's responsibility to ensure no personal data is processed unless the high risks are mitigated and further managed, or if this cannot be achieved, they must consult the Regulator for further advice.[77]

National Derogations

3.34 The GDPR leaves a margin of discretion for the Member States, such as setting the age between 13–16 on when parental consent is required for providing the minor information society services.[78][79] Additionally, the GDPR applies alongside the national employment laws,[80] and hence will have a remarkable

74 GDPR, Art 5.

75 GDPR, Art 82; Art 29 Working Party, Opinion 1/2010 on the concepts of 'controller' and 'processor', February 2010.; GDPR Arts 28-29.

76 GDPR, Art 30.

77 GDPR, Arts 35-36.

78 GDPR, Art 8.

79 GDPR, i.a. Arts 6(3) and 23.

80 GDPR, Art 88.

impact on how the data is processed and protected in this context. Therefore, it is important for the multinational company to ensure they are considering the local employment legislation in parallel with the laws on data protection and privacy. Differences exist, for example, on what kind of and how extensive employee monitoring can be implemented and how investigations into the employee's emails can be conducted. The European Data Protection Board (EDPB)[81] Opinion on Data Processing at Work provides guidance on how to address privacy in the employment context[82], and **Chapter 5** of this book discusses privacy and cyber security at a workplace in more detail.

Data Protection Officer (DPO)

3.35 Where data processing is of certain scope or nature or scope, the Controller and the Processor must appoint a Data Protection Officer (DPO) who must be placed in an independent position to advise the entity on data protection related matters. The role of the DPO also includes training personnel and communicating with the Data Subjects and the national data protection authority, investigating and further managing personal data breaches and DPIAs. The background and the skills needed by the DPO differ according to the sector, size, and position within the entity, but generally they must have a strong understanding of the legal privacy framework, understand information security, IT, and the business processes. Outside of strict technical communication and cooperation skills are needed, as the DPO co-operates with all the departments on a daily basis and, where applicable, communicates with the supervisory authority and the Data Subjects.[83]

IT and cyber security

3.36 IT and security in the GDPR include several matters, such as incident and breach management, including breach notifications,[84] Data Subject's rights execution in practice, evaluating and implementing appropriate security levels,[8586] and ensuring privacy by design and default are implemented in application development.[87] The appropriate security measures depend on the context, such as the sensitivity of the data, industry practices, and identified risks in the data

81 An independent advisory body (ppreviously the 'Article 29 Working Party'), which comprises out of the representatives of the National Data Protection Authorities, the European Data Protection Supervisor (EDPS), and the Commission.

82 Art 29 Working Party, Opinion 2/2017 on data processing at work, Adopted 8 June 2017.

83 GDPR, Arts 37-39.

84 GDPR, Arts 33-34.

85 GDPR, Art 32.

86 GDPR, Arts 35-36.

87 GDPR, Art 25 Privacy by design means, that privacy will be considered from the beginning of the development of the new product or service, and according to the privacy by default requirement, the strictest privacy measures must apply when the product or service is provided to the end-user.

processing. [88] Appropriate Identity and Access Management (IAM), logging, penetration testing, anonymisation, and ensuring recovery capabilities are just a few examples of security measures that must be considered when implementing appropriate security measures.[89]

Training and awareness

3.37 However strong privacy controls have been implemented, when it comes to processing personal data, there is always a human element involved. To provide the employees with the right tools and skills to comply with the data protection principles, the Controller and Processor must provide adequate training. Where the company has appointed a Data Protection Officer, it is their responsibility to train the employees on data protection and how to apply appropriate security measures. The more knowledgeable the personnel are on when and how to process personal data, understand how to escalate and further manage incidents and breaches, the better equipped the entity is. It is in the everyday data processing where compliance is ensured.[90] Topics to train include managing Data Subject Right Requests, escalating breaches, vendor onboarding, phishing, social engineering, encryption, and appropriate access management, which are just some of the key points to train. The training materials must be regularly reviewed to ensure they address the key topics.[91] Training and awareness are further elaborated in more detail in **Chapter 6**.

Data Transfers

3.38 Outsourcing of data processing to Processors is a common practice, and multinational companies often share data globally within the Group or with affiliates. As a part of secure data governance, it is important to consider the tools for international data transfers. Data transfers are governed by specific legal instruments, such as Standard Contractual Clauses, Binding Corporate Rules (BCRs), and the Commission's Adequacy Decisions.[92] Standard Contractual Clauses are standardised clauses the Commission has drafted. Additionally, the exporter of the data must complete a Transfer Impact Assessment to evaluate the risks and ensure the protection of data is adequate to comply with the GDPR's

88 GDPR, Art 32.

89 GDPR, Art 32; i.a. Directive (EU) 2016/1148 of the European Parliament and of the Council of 6 July 2016 concerning measures for a high common level of security of network and information systems across the Union (NIS Directive) Recital 69.

90 GDPR, Art 39.

91 Managing an Information Security and Privacy Awareness and Training Program, Herold, CRC Press, 2010, p xix, 193, 330; ENISA, Obtaining support and funding from senior management while planning an awareness initiative.

92 Arts 44-49. Please note, that several of these tools are at the moment under review by the Commission and the ECJ. Until decisions are made, the existing tools are however applicable.

requirements.[93] The Adequacy Decision is a Commission's approval for a certain area, sector, or State outside the EEA, considering the protection for personal data to be sufficiently compliant with the GDPR and therefore data transfer is legitimate. As of August 2023, there are 15 Adequacy Decisions.[94]

3.39 The Binding Corporate Rules are a data transfer instrument, which multinationals can use for Intra-Group data transfers. These can also be used for data transfers between entities, which do not belong to the same Group but have shared economic interests.[95]

Enforcement

3.40 The GDPR is enforced via Member States' Data Protection Authorities (DPAs). The authorities have wide powers, including to investigate, ask for information in relation to personal data processing, issue fines and require defined mitigating actions from the Controllers and Processors. For multinational Controllers and Processors, a Lead Supervisory Authority can be named in the Member State where the main establishment of the entity is located.[96] As mentioned, Article 29 Working Party, was replaced by the European Data Protection Board (EDPB). The EDPB's composition is similar to the predating Article 29 Working Party's, consisting of the EU's national supervisory authorities, the European Data Protection Supervisor (EDPS) and the European Commission. The EDPB 'has the power to determine disputes between national supervisory authorities and to give guidance on the implementation of the Regulation and approve EU-wide codes and certification.'[97]

3.41 As the EU's GDPR came into force in 2018, the different national authorities have moved into issuing higher fines for data protection breaches, including €1.2 billion fine for Meta regarding EU-US data transfers,[98] €746 million fine to Amazon for failing to implement a suitable legal basis for marketing

93 2001/497/EC: Commission Decision of 15 June 2001 on standard contractual clauses for the transfer of personal data to third countries, under Dir 95/46/EC, OJ L 181, 4.7.2001, pp. 19–31; 2004/915/EC: Commission Decision of 27 December 2004 amending Decision 2001/497/EC as regards the introduction of an alternative set of standard contractual clauses for the transfer of personal data to third countries OJ L 306M, 15.11.2008, pp. 69–79 (MT); 2010/87/: Commission Decision of 5 February 2010 on standard contractual clauses for the transfer of personal data to processors established in third countries under Dir 95/46/EC of the European Parliament and of the Council, OJ L 39, 12.2.2010, pp. 5–18.

94 GDPR, Art 45; https://ec.europa.eu/info/law/law-topic/data-protection/data-transfers-outside-eu/adequacy-protection-personal-data-non-eu-countries_en; Art 29 Working Party, Adequacy Referential, 11/2017.

95 GDPR, Art 47; https://ec.europa.eu/info/law/law-topic/data-protection/data-transfers-outside-eu/binding-corporate-rules_en.

96 GDPR, Arts 51-63.

97 GDPR, Art 68.

98 www.computerweekly.com/news/366538116/Facebook-owner-Meta-fined-record-12-billion-over-EU-US-data-transfers#:~:text=Meta%2C%20the%20company%20which%20owns,for%20breaching%20data%20protection%20regulations.

purposes[99] and €90 million for Google for failing to provide easy refusal of non-mandatory cookies.[100]

GDPR in practice

3.42 However, despite the attempts for the GDPR to be applicable as it is, the entities conducting their GDPR-compliance programmes during the past two to three years, have needed substantial guidance from the EU-level. The GDPR sets out the requirements on data protection and information security, but the entities have been struggling with practicalities on how to achieve the required level of protection, or understanding what the requirements mean in detail. To answer this need, the EU-level data protection advisory body, the European Data Protection Board, has issued several Guidelines on the implementation and meaning of several topics of the GDPR. These include Guidelines on how to conduct a Data Protection Impact Assessment (DPIA)[101] and Guidelines on Data Protection Officers (DPOs)[102] In addition, the previously provided Guidelines of Article 29 provide useful information, such as how to define the roles of the controller, and processor, and hence the liabilities and rights of the parties.[103]

3.43 One of the key aspects in implementing the GDPR is to be able to base the data processing and made decisions on analysed and documented decisions, and to be able to document the compliance with the Regulation.[104] The GDPR leaves certain responsibilities to the controllers and processors to decide upon themselves, and the entities are well advised to acknowledge that there is no silver bullet for GDPR compliance, but it is a continuous team effort, which requires the engagement of the personnel, including the top management. It is essential to document the decision-making and data processing processes, and if requested on the reasons of certain data processing activities, to be able to provide a legitimate explanation based on the laws and best practices, including sector specific differences.

E-privacy Directive

3.44 The E-privacy Directive (Cookies Directive) has been in force since 2002. It regulates the protection of personal data and privacy in the context

99 www.simmons-simmons.com/en/publications/ckrus16301do70a28ptvwqy5t/amazon-faces-record-gdpr-fine.

100 www.cnil.fr/en/cookies-cnil-fines-google-total-150-million-euros-and-facebook-60-million-euros-non-compliance#:~:text=As%20a%20result%20of%20this,the%20company%20FACEBOOK%20IRELAND%20LIMITED.

101 Guidelines on Data Protection Impact Assessment (DPIA) and determining whether processing is 'likely to result in a high risk' for the purposes of the Reg 2016/679, Adopted on 4 April 2017.

102 Guidelines on Data Protection Officers (DPOs), Adopted on 13 December 2016, and Revised and Adopted on 5 April 2017.

103 Art 29 data protection working party, opinion 1/2010 on the concepts of 'controller' and 'processor', adopted on 16 February 2010.

104 GDPR, Art 5, recital 75-77.

of using public electronic communication service providers services, direct marketing and cookies. The Directive indicates the end-result the Member States are expected to achieve but leaves the specific methods for them to decide upon. As the GDPR emerged, and the communication methods further developed, the Commission published a proposal for an E-Privacy Regulation in 2017. The aim is to harmonise the regulations on electronic communications and direct marketing.[105]

3.45 The Regulation would also bring new actors within its scope, extending the applicability of the law from the more traditional communication methods, such as SMS and phone, to private communication networks, such as airport WiFi, internet-based messaging apps, and web-based e-mails. The proposed regulation also extends the scope of the law from the content of the communications to metadata and[106] machine-to-machine communications.[107] As one of the aims of the proposed regulation is to protect the people against unsolicited marketing, direct marketing will by default require an opt-in, subject to certain exceptions. Additionally, the cookie rules would become more stringent and user-friendly.[108]

3.46 The original aim was for the Regulation to apply alongside the GDPR in May 2018,[109] but several of the amendments are still under discussion as of August 2023, and the law can be expected to change before the final text has been agreed upon.[110]

Payment Service Directive 2 (PSD2)

3.47 The initial Payment Services Directive was passed in 2007, with an aim to develop a single market for payment services.[111] The technological development in the financial industry saw rapid growth after the adoption of the PSD, which led to a renewal of the law, and in January 2016 the PSD2[112] was adopted. The Member States were given a two year grace period to implement the Directive into

105 Proposal for a Regulation of the European Parliament and of the Council concerning the respect for private life and the protection of personal data in electronic communications and repealing Dir 2002/58/EC (Regulation on Privacy and Electronic Communications), January 2017.

106 Proposal for a Regulation, Arts 7-8; Dir 2002/58, Arts 5-6, 9.

107 Art 29 Working Party Opinion 01/2017 on the Proposed Regulation for the ePrivacy Regulation (2002/58/EC), adopted on 4 April 2017.

108 Proposal for a regulation, Arts 3.4-3.5; https://digital-strategy.ec.europa.eu/en/policies/eprivacy-regulation.

109 Proposal for a regulation, Art 29.

110 For more information, and following the legislative process: https://ec.europa.eu/digital-single-market/en/news/proposal-regulation-privacy-and-electronic-communications; e-privacy regulation train: www.europarl.europa.eu/legislative-train/theme-connected-digital-single-market/file-e-privacy-reform/03-2017; Art 29 Working Party Opinion 01/2017 on the Proposed Regulation for the ePrivacy Reg (2002/58/EC), Adopted on 4 April 2017.

111 Directive 2007/64EC of the European Parliament and of the Council, OJ L319/1, Recital 60.

112 Directive (EU) 2015/2366 of the European Parliament and of the Council, on payment services in the internal market, amending Dirs 2002/65/EC, 2009/110/EC and 2013/36/EU and Reg (EU) No 1093/2010, and repealing Dir 2007/64/EC, OJ L 337/35 (PSD2).

their national legislation, and in January 2018 the Directive became in force.[113] Extending the scope, the PSD2 aims to also protect competition, by making entry to the banking market easier for new kinds of service providers, while enhancing the security of the transactions.[114] The Directive also aims to protect consumers by regulating and monitoring the new financial service providers, creating more cross-border transactions and affordable payment methods, and facilitating the development of the Single Euro Payments Area (SEPA).[115]

3.48 The PSD2 also widened the scope of applicability to Payment Initiation Service Providers (PISPs), and Account Information Service Providers (AISPs), together referred as third-party service providers (TPPs). The PISPs initiate payments for a defined sum from the end-user's bank account online, also without a credit-card.[116] AISPs on the other hand provide the end-user information of his financials, such as accounts, transactions, funds, and investments.[117] These can be used for example to gain a comprehensive understanding of one's own finances.

Application Programming Interfaces (APIs) and access for the third-party service providers (TPPs)

3.49 The PSD2 requires the Account Servicing Payment Service Providers (ASPSPs), which are mainly banks, and some building societies) to build solutions, which will enable accordingly registered TPPs[118] to provide banking services, using the payment service user's existing bank's infrastructure. This means, that the banks will need to ensure that the duly registered PISs and AISPs will have cross-border access to the client's account and can conduct payment transactions in a secure manner. The TPPs must be able to 'use a software bridge to access the accounts.[119] In practice, the banks are required to build a secure Application Programming Interface (API), which the TPPs can use to access and process the end-user's funds, information, and initiate payments.[120]

Security

3.50 The PSD2 also requires the Member States to 'ensure that payment service providers establish a framework with appropriate mitigation measures and control mechanisms to manage the operational and security risks.'[121] To secure cross-border integration of the systems used by different actors, the Directive imposes certain security measures on the payment and account service providers. For example, the banks are required to ensure that opening

113 PSD2, Art 115.
114 PSD2, Recital 1-10, 27-33.
115 PSD2, Recital 75-76.
116 PSD2, Recital 29.
117 PSD2, Recital 28.
118 PSD2, Arts 5, 11-16, 28-29.
119 PSD2, Recital 27, Arts 35-36.
120 PSD2, Recital 28.
121 PSD2, Art 95.

their infrastructures for co-operation, the security and privacy of their customers is maintained. The AISPs and PISPs are required to demonstrate a level of appropriate security standards if they want to receive a license and be registered as approved service providers.[122] All of the actors must ensure their operational model includes implementing appropriate incident reporting,[123] authentication and secure communication processes.[124]

3.51 Each EU Member State has a national financial regulator, which imposes certain security standards on the entities functioning in the financial sector. These standards vary within the States.[125] As the national authorities are the ones evaluating the applications, including approving or rejecting the implemented security measures, certain differences in these exist.[126] To address the differences and harmonise, the PSD2 requires the European Banking Authority (EBA) to develop regulatory technical standards (RTS), which the EU Commission can then adopt.[127] The TPPs are then required to implement the agreed security measures. The RTS include measures such as implementing 2-factor authentication, and secure communication channels between the TPPs and the banks. Banks are also in certain cases required to provide access to the client's interface as a 'fall-back' mechanism, should the API fail.

3.52 There are also other RTSs, for example guidelines on the security measures for operational and security risks of payment services under Directive (EU) 2015/2366 (PSD2), which address the governance, operational and risk management framework, access control, physical security, and testing for security measures.[128] The RTS, despite their name, are however not highly technical but instead set out the overall framework and a high-level standard which the security solutions must comply with. On one hand this leaves room for technical development and adapting the security for the context. choices of the entity, and on the other, it may be too vague to be considered standards in its fullest meaning.[129]

122 PSD2, Art 5.

123 PSD2, Art 96.

124 PSD2, Art 65(1)(c).

125 www.fca.org.uk/firms/passporting/regulators-eu-eea, see, for example, Greece: Operational risk management principles for information systems in financial institutions, Bank of Greece, the governor; Estonia: REQUIREMENTS FOR THE ORGANISATION OF THE INFORMATION TECHNOLOGY AND INFORMATION SECURITY OF THE SUBJECT OF FINANCIAL SUPERVISION. The advisory guide was instated by decision no. 1.1-7/19 of the Management Board of the Financial Supervision Authority on 23 January 2017.

126 PSD2, Art 5.

127 PSD2, i.a. Recital 107, Arts 5, 95(3)-(4), 98(4).

128 Final Report on Guidelines on Security Measures for Operational and Security Risks under PSD2; www.eba.europa.eu/documents/10180/2060117/Final+report+on+EBA+Guidelines+on+the+security+measures+for+operational+and+security+risks+under+PSD2+%28EBA-GL-2017-17%29.pdf.

129 Final Report on Guidelines on Security Measures for Operational and Security Risks under PSD2, pp. 9, 121.

3.53 As there is no standardisation for the banks on how to implement their APIs, nor for the TPPs on how to build their services and business models to be compatible with the available APIs. The absence of harmonisation poses possible problems for the interoperability of the network. This is possibly also in relation to the competition, as the ones with the best APIs and the most suitable TPPs to match, will benefit the most, whereas the customer experience with lower APIs may affect negatively on the banks or TPPs position. To help promote the implementation of the PSD2's harmonising aim, there are different initiatives, such as the Berlin Group, which bring together several banks and TPPs to solve common issues, including the lack of standardisation.[130] The UK's Open Banking Implementation Entity, set up by the Competition and Markets Authority, works with the same aim as the Berlin Group.[131]

PSD 3 Proposal

3.54 In many ways, the implementation of PSD2 has been successful. Since its adoption in 2018, it has improved the levels of security and access to open banking and enhanced competition in the financial sector. The implementation has also reduced fraudulent activity. In 2022, the EBA responded to the Commission's call for advice on the revision of PSD2 by supporting the initiative. In specific, the EBA welcomed further development for the PSD in some key areas, including clarification on the scope of applicability, licensing, and supervision of payment service providers and rights and obligations related to blocking of funds, liability regime, and adjusting the legal framework to fit the specific nature of instant payments. EBA also called for further measures to enforce the PSD2.[132]

3.55 Acknowledging the responses and the changes the payment industry has seen in the past five years, in June 2023 the Commission set out key objectives for the PSD3. These include further measures to combat payment fraud by enhancing cooperation and information sharing between the actors, improving the functioning of open banking by removing further obstacles, and improving the availability of cash in retailer shops without having to make purchases and clarifying rules around ATMs. Other aims of the PSD3 include improved consumer rights, further improved non-bank payment service providers access to all EU payment systems, and improved enforcement of the law. The Commission is also working for customer data sharing between the actors, such as financial institutions and fintech service providers, clarifying data sharing practices, rights, and obligations. The development is aligned with the Commission's Strategies on European Data, Retail Payments, and Digital Finance.[133]

130 www.berlin-group.org/governance-and-structure.
131 www.openbanking.org.uk/about-us/.
132 www.eba.europa.eu/sites/default/documents/files/document_library/Publications/Opinions/2022/Opinion%20od%20PSD2%20review%20%28EBA-Op-2022-06%29/1036016/EBA%27s%20response%20to%20the%20Call%20for%20advice%20on%20the%20review%20of%20PSD2.pdf.
133 https://ec.europa.eu/commission/presscorner/detail/en/ip_23_3543.

Regulation on electronic identification and trust services for electronic transactions in the internal market (eIDAS)

3.56 E-identifications (eIDs) are a key to enabling e-governance to function. E-IDs are physical cards issued by a national authority and used for secure online services with the help of an eID-card reader and specific software.[134] The EU Member States have e-IDs for differing purposes. As a way of enabling the national e-ID cards to be recognised within the Digital Single Market, the eIDAS Regulation was passed in 2014, replacing the Electronic Signatures Directive. As a regulation, the eIDAS is applicable to the Member States as it is. The aim of the law is to enable identification and authentication by using an approved national e-ID when accessing public side services within the EU. Since September 2018, the Member States had to make sure officially issued and duly registered EU-citizens e-IDs are accepted cross-border for public services. The service providers had to integrate the national schemes as part of the eIDAS network. The purpose of the legal framework is to increase cross-border offering of services and enable authentication without meeting face-to-face.[135] This is made possible using several methods of identification, the most common one within the EU being a Public Key Infrastructure (PKI). PKI functions via public and private keys, of which the private is used to verify the identity of the person by tying the private key based verification to the public key's security certificate.[136]

3.57 EIDAS provide the Commission a mandate to adopt implementing acts and delegated acts, of which The Commission has adopted several. These include an interoperability framework on e-IDs and trust services for electronic transactions,[137] procedural arrangements for cooperation between Member States on electronic identification,[138] technical specifications and procedures for

134 Gomes de Andrade and others, *Electronic Identity* Springer 2014, p. 83.

135 Reg (EU) No 910/2014 of the European Parliament and of the Council of 23 July 2014 on electronic identification and trust services for electronic transactions in the internal market and repealing Dir 1999/93/EC, OJ L 257, 28.8.2014, pp. 73–114, Recital 1-20, Arts 1-2, 4, 6.

136 Naccache and Sauveron, *Information Security Theory and Practice: Securing the Internet of Things* Springer, 2014, p. 161.

137 Commission Implementing Reg (EU) 2015/1501 of 8 September 2015 on the interoperability framework pursuant to Art 12(8) of Reg (EU) No 910/2014 of the European Parliament and of the Council on electronic identification and trust services for electronic transactions in the internal market (Text with EEA relevance) http://eur-lex.europa.eu/legal-content/EN/TXT/?uri=CELEX%3A32015R1501.

138 Commission Implementing Decision (EU) 2015/296 of 24 February 2015 establishing procedural arrangements for cooperation between Member States on electronic identification pursuant to Art 12(7) of Reg (EU) No 910/2014 of the European Parliament and of the Council on electronic identification and trust services for electronic transactions in the internal market Text with EEA relevance http://eur-lex.europa.eu/legal-content/EN/TXT/?qid=1441782671426&uri=CELEX:32015D0296.

assurance levels for identification,[139] and on notification of the national electronic schemes to the Commission.[140] The Cooperation network allows the Member States to share information, best practices and co-work to create solutions, and discuss topics such as security and conduct peer-review for the notified schemes of the States, by communicating through a single point of contact.[141] An example on the implementation of eIDAS is German and Austrian citizens being able to access certain Dutch public services using their eIDs. The first privately led eIDAS scheme notification was made in December 2017 by Italy.[142]

3.58 In addition to IDs, the eIDAS deals also with other authentication and recognition methods, such as eSeals, which function confirming the document's origin and integrity,[143] 'or authenticate the legal person's digital asset, such as software code or servers'.[144] Other areas within eIDAS' scope are electronic signatures, electronic time stamps, electronic documents, electronic registered delivery services and certificate services for website authentication, and electronic trust services.[145]

EIDAS and the PSD2

3.59 The European Banking Authority EBA, which develops the above discussed Regulatory Technical Standards (RTSs) and opinions on the secure authentication and communication when implementing the PSD2, has also published a discussion paper on the interoperability of the PSD2 with EIDAS. The e-IDs have been considered as a way to comply with the 'know-Your-Customer' of anti-money laundering requirements, and to provide strong authentication, which is required under the PSD2. In addition to authenticating the end-users, the eIDAS has potential to be used for authenticating the website of the Payment

139 Commission Implementing Reg (EU) 2015/1502 of 8 September 2015 on setting out minimum technical specifications and procedures for assurance levels for electronic identification means pursuant to Art 8(3) of Reg (EU) No 910/2014 of the European Parliament and of the Council on electronic identification and trust services for electronic transactions in the internal market (Text with EEA relevance) http://eur-lex.europa.eu/legal-content/EN/TXT/?uri=OJ:JOL_2015_235_R_0002.

140 Commission Implementing Decision (EU) 2015/1984 of 3 November 2015 defining the circumstances, formats and procedures of notification pursuant to Art 9(5) of Reg (EU) No 910/2014 of the European Parliament and of the Council on electronic identification and trust services for electronic transactions in the internal market (notified under document C(2015) 7369) (Text with EEA relevance) http://eur-lex.europa.eu/legal-content/EN/TXT/?uri=OJ:JOL_2015_289_R_0007.

141 EIDAS, Arts 1(c), 8, 9, 12-14.

142 https://ec.europa.eu/digital-single-market/en/news/access-european-public-services-national-eid-becoming-possible; https://ec.europa.eu/digital-single-market/en/news/first-private-sector-eid-scheme-pre-notified-italy-under-eidas.

143 EIDAS, Art Recital 58-62, Art 24.

144 EIDAS, Recital 65.

145 Arts 1(b)-(c).

Service Provider (PSP), to prevent fraudulent websites from operating.[146] As a way to acquire consent, the electronic signatures will hold the same value as the traditional ones.[147]

Development of the EIDAS

3.60 The interoperability of the e-IDs has been previously difficult to create because of the varying capabilities and functionalities of the national e-IDs. E-IDs can come with certain difficulties, as a breach in a certain security certification can result into the e-ID being a security risk, instead of an enabler. However, if the Digital Single Market is to be developed further, requiring interoperability of the e-IDs on cross-border level is logical, and has the potential to help lower fraud. EIDAS may take off slowly, as security is balanced against the market needs, and before appropriate interoperability and technical integration is achieved widely, but via co-operation, the level of implementation may provide useful for several sectors.[148] The Commission has recognised the highest potential benefiters on the eIDAS as being insurance, the financial sector (consumer credit), and postal services.[149]

The Directive on security of network and information systems (NIS Directive) and NIS2

3.61 The NIS Directive was the first EU-level legal instrument addressing cyber security, as the aim of the NIS is to provide a generally elevated level of cyber security within the Internal Market. It was and entered into force in 2016, and it applies to all the Member States. As a Directive, NIS leaves Member States in charge of how to achieve the aim, but by May 2018, the States had to have implemented NIS into their national legislation. In practice, the Member States are responsible for creating a suitable level of cyber security measures on State level.[150]

3.62 For example, the MSs must establish or further develop a national strategy on the security of network and information systems, which will function as a high-level guideline. The Member States must also create a regulatory framework for cyber-security measures and mandate an official enforcing body.

146 European Banking Authority, discussion paper on future Draft Regulatory Technical Standards on stronger customer authentication and secure communication under the revised Payment Services Dir 2, 'Possible synergies with the regulation on electronic identification and trust services for electronic transactions in the internal market (e-IDAS)'.

147 EIDAS, Recital 49-52, Arts 25-27.

148 Identity theft: Breakthroughs in Research and Practice IGI Global, Information Resources Management Association, 2017, p. 168.

149 https://ec.europa.eu/digital-single-market/news/eidas-private-sector-engagement-high-level-event-boosting-line-trust-and-convenience-business.

150 Dir (EU) 2016/1148 of the European Parliament and of the Council of 6 July 2016, concerning measures for a high common level of security of network and information systems across the Union, OJ L 194/1, 9.7.2016, pp. 1–30, Arts 1, 25.

They must also establish a Computer Security Incident Response Team (CSIRT), which is tasked to manage risks and incidents and cooperate with the private sector to mitigate identified risks. Additionally, the Member States must be a part of a sufficient cooperation network to share information, create cyber security strategies and to promote implementation of cyber-security in the essential sectors.[151] Member States are encouraged to draft harmonised standards, in co-operation by the European Union Agency for Network and Information Security (ENISA), which is Europe's Centre of Excellence for cyber security.[152]

3.63 NIS is applicable to the 'operators of essential services'. Within the scope are services which are necessary in a modern society such as banks and other financial service providers, telephone companies or infrastructures, healthcare, transportation and electricity, and gas providers. Included in the scope are also 'essential digital services providers' (DSPs), of whom the client is many times dependable on conducting their everyday business. These include entities such as cloud service providers, online markets and search engines.[153] Software and hardware providers are excluded, 'as they are liable for their products under a different set of rules'.[154]

3.64 In January 2023, the NIS2 entered into force, adding further entities, security requirements, and cooperation models within the scope.[155] It created a cyber crisis management structure (CyCLONe), which is a cooperation network for Member States national authorities in charge of cyber crisis management. NIS2 also brought with it additional enhancements to cooperation between the Member States and an expectation to introduce new areas of interest into the scope, such as supply chain, vulnerability management, core internet and cyber hygiene their national cybersecurity strategies. The PSD also provided ENISA with more powers and tasks, such as the development and maintenance of a European vulnerability registry and support for the organisation of peer reviews between Member States.[156]

Mandatory security measures

3.65 The essential service providers are required to implement appropriate technical and organisational security measures to their network and information systems.[157] What is appropriate depends on the level of risk, which the entity must consider, and the existing state of the art of security products.[158] Due consideration must also be given to harmonise a level of security measures as

151 NIS Directive, Arts 1, 7-14, Annex I.
152 NIS Directive, Recital 66, Art 19.
153 NIS Directive, Recital 48, Arts 5-6, Annex II.
154 NIS Directive, Recital 50.
155 www.enisa.europa.eu/topics/cybersecurity-policy/nis-directive-new.
156 www.enisa.europa.eu/topics/cybersecurity-policy/nis-directive-new; www.enisa.europa.eu/topics/incident-response/cyclone.
157 NIS Directive, Recital 46, 52, Art 14.
158 NIS Directive, Recital 49, 51, 53, Art 16.

the provided essential services are often crossing borders. Member States must therefore cooperate to work towards a harmonised approach on cyber security.[159]

3.66 The essential service providers and the DSPSs must also implement an incident management model, which includes 'measures to identify any risks of incidents, to prevent, detect and handle incidents and to mitigate their impact'.[160] Computer incident Response Team (CSIRT) is a mandatory part of an effective incident management model. The essential service providers CSIRTs must have effective communication channels to the governmental CSIRT, and certain security incidents must be communicated to the State's CSIRT.[161]

3.67 The service provider is responsible for the security measures irrespective of whether these are in-house managed or outsourced, and therefore the same security and breach management requirements apply.[162] Possible risks lie especially when an entity uses shadow IT, which means purchased or implemented IT-solutions, that are not approved according to a centralised process. An effective vendor management model, including enforcing internal standards on vetting the vendor, is therefore essential.[163]

NIS and Privacy

3.68 When data is shared between the Cooperation Group and the CSIRTS, it is subject to the GDPR. The Member States can share data about risks and incidents via the cooperation network and the NIS encourages the essential service providers to report suspicions of serious criminal activities to the law enforcement authorities. Because of the nature of the cases, where data is shared, the personal data is likely to be categorised as sensitive (special categories) and criminal data, falling respectively under Articles 9 and10 of the GDPR.[164] The NIS encourages the coordination between competent authorities and law enforcement authorities to be facilitated by the European Cybercrime Centre (EC3) and ENISA. In addition, they are required to cooperate with the national Data Protection Authorities (DPAs), especially should there be any breaches of personal data.[165] The EU's Law Enforcement Directive and the national implementing legislations which establish certain levels of data protection while enforcing the laws, must also be adhered to as applicable.[166]

159 NIS Directive, Recital 49.
160 NIS Directive, Recital 46.
161 NIS Directive, Recital 47, Arts 14, 16.
162 NIS Directive, Recital 52.
163 Gonzalez, *Managing Online Risk: Apps, Mobile, and Social Media Security* (Elsevier, 2015) p. 27.
164 NIS Directive, Recital 62, 72, Art 2 GDPR, Arts 9-10.
165 NIS-Directive, Recital 62, Art 8(6).
166 Dir (EU) 2016/680 OF THE EUROPEAN PARLIAMENT AND OF THE COUNCIL of 27 April 2016 on the protection of natural persons with regard to the processing of personal data by competent authorities for the purposes of the prevention, investigation, detection or prosecution of criminal offences or the execution of criminal penalties, and on the free movement of such data, and repealing Council Framework Decision 2008/977/JHA.

NIS in practice

3.69 As NIS and NIS 2 are Directives, some level of differences exist between the Member States opinions, interpretations, and implementing measures.[167] A cooperation network and enhanced communications are necessary for harmonising implementation. The States infrastructures and security capabilities were and continue to be on differing levels, and investing in a new structure and implementing it in practice takes time. Most of the Member States have had a cyber security strategy in place for a longer time[168] and the same applies to the CSIRTS.[169] However, in practice, these function on differing levels, skills, and budgets. Directives will be reviewed periodically by the Commission to address changes in technological and market conditions, as well as political and societal changes.[170]

3.70 Timing for notifying of breaches is a matter of discretion, especially when the notification may cause more damage than provide protection until the breach has been mitigated and the issue effectively addressed.[171] Multinational entities operating within several Member States are well advised to create a harmonised guidance on the notification of incidents and breaches for the competent authorities.

3.71 For both the public and private sector, for having the NIS function in practice, adequate training is one of the keys for successful implementation. Also, having appropriate resources and budgets on both public and private side is essential to establish appropriate security solutions, breach management models and CSIRTS.

UK'S LEGISLATION

The UK's Human Rights Act 1998 (HRA)

3.72 As a signatory to the European Convention for the Protection of Human Rights and Fundamental Freedoms (ECHR), the UK has implemented the Convention into national law via the UK's Human Rights Act (HRA), providing UK nationals the same rights as in the ECHR. The law was passed in 1998 and came into force in 2000. By implementing the HRA the national courts became bound to apply the law in compliance with the ECHR, including the interpretation of the ECtHR, and made the rights enforceable in the UK's national courts.[172] In the context of privacy, the notable article to discuss is Article 8, which provides

167 Consolidated version of the Treaty on the Functioning of the European Union, OJ C 326, 26.10.2012, pp. 171–172, Art 288.

168 www.enisa.europa.eu/topics/national-cyber-security-strategies/ncss-map.

169 www.enisa.europa.eu/topics/csirts-in-europe/csirt-inventory/certs-by-country-interactive-map.

170 Recital 71, Arts 5(7), 23.

171 Recital 59.

172 Human Rights Act 1998, Arts 1-2.

that 'everyone has the right to respect for his private and family life, his home and his correspondence'.[173]

HRA in practice

3.73 The HRA gives rights against the public authorities (vertical effect), but it has also been applied in disputes between private parties (horizontal effect), and in *Campbell*, the Court explicitly recognised the need to do so.[174] The HRA makes the same principles as the ECHR to apply. If there is an interference with the right, it has to be justified by being done 'in accordance with the law, and necessary in a democratic society in the interest of national security, public safety or the economic well-being of the country, for the prevention of disorder or crime, for the protection of health or morals, or for the protection of the rights and freedoms of others.'[175]

3.74 Similarly, as with the ECHR, the interpretation of the law has developed via case-law. The HRA's Article 8 rights has been many times balanced against the other rights of the Act, especially Article 10, right to freedom of expression. 'Public interest justification' is also an exemption journalists could use under the Data Protection Act (1998)[176] to publish information and pictures on public figures in magazines, and also this exemption has been under review in relation to the HRA several times, with differing outcomes.

3.75 One of the groundbreaking cases in the application of the HRA is *Campbell,* where the right to privacy was balanced against the right to freedom of expression, after a magazine had published pictures classified sensitive of the applicant, who is famous. The Court balanced the merits of the case under the Act, concluding that the applicants right to privacy was stronger than the right to freedom of expression and the publisher had overstepped their 'public interest justification' by 'publishing too extensive material on the celebrity, where the mere facts of the situation would have sufficed for the public to know'. The case was however eventually won by the applicant on the merit of the magazine publishing the images and hence breaching the confidentiality and the Data Protection Act, instead of the violation of an explicit right in the HRA[177] The HRA requires the national courts to take into account the ECHR and its application including the rulings and opinions of the ECtHR[178], and generally the courts' approach on the application of the Act is a similar balancing test on the rights and interest of the parties such as the ECtHR takes. The approach is summarised here according to Lord Steyn in *RE S:* 'first, neither article has *as such* precedence over the other. Secondly, where the values under the two articles are in conflict, an intense focus on the comparative importance of the specific rights being claimed in the

173 Human Rights Act 1998, Art 8.
174 *Campbell v MGN*; Human Rights Act 1998, Arts 16-18.
175 Human Rights Act 1998, Art 8(2).
176 Data Protection Act 1998, s 32.
177 *Cambell v MGN Ltd* [2004] UKHL 22.
178 Human Rights Act 1998, Introduction 2 'interpretation of the Convention rights'.

individual case is necessary. Thirdly, the justifications for interfering with or restricting each right must be taken into account. Finally, the proportionality test must be applied to each.'[179]

3.76 The HRA is also applicable in the context of employment in the public side. In the employment context, the right to privacy is most obviously present in the context of employee monitoring which then again can be justified to a legitimate extent by the employer's interests. As the HRA is implementing the ECHR, the employee however must balance the interests of both parties and be able to indicate that monitoring is based on an appropriate and necessary legal ground implemented to the extent, that is necessary to achieve the purpose. The employees must also be informed of any monitoring, such as CCTV for the intrusion of the right to be justified. However, as has been seen in previously, the private side is not excluded from the scope of the HRA, and in particular, should a case go further to an employment tribunal they are required to take the HRA into consideration in their rulings.[180]

HRA and privacy in common law (tort of invasion of privacy and breach of confidence under the DPA)

3.77 Traditionally in English law, there has not been a common law tort of invasion of privacy. It has been argued several times that the HRA has had an impact on the development of the common law in England, as the courts have had to consider their rulings in the light of the Act against the absence of the tort of privacy, while acknowledging the need for it.[181] As late as in 2003 (the events of the case took place in 1997, before the HRA had been passed) the applicants in *Wainwright* lost their case after bringing charges for invasion of their privacy after being strip searched on their way to the jail to pay a visit to a family member. The County Court acknowledged there had been an unproportionable invasion to their right to privacy and awarded compensation, but as the case went forward all the way to the House of Lords, the Lords reversed the ruling, elaborating on the history and the absence of the tort of violation of privacy in English law.[182] In *Campbell*, the events of the case took place in 1998 after the passing of the HRA and despite that the ruling was awarded for the benefit of the applicant from the basis of the publication of the pictures violating the confidentiality breaching the Data Protection Act. This was more successful for the applicant than in the *Wainwright* case.[183]

179 Opinions of the Lords of Appeal for judgment in the cause *In re S (fc) (a child) (appellant)*, [2004] UKHL 47.

180 Bowers and others, *Blackstone's Employment Law Practice* (Oxford University Press, 2011) pp. 238-239; Gennard and Judge, *Employee Relations* (Chartered Institute of Personnel and Development, 2005) pp. 117-118.

181 *Vidal-Hall and others v Google*, Case No: A2/2014/0403.

182 *Wainwright and another v Home Office*, Opinions of the Lords of Appeal for judgment in the cause, [2003] UKHL 53.

183 The English law of privacy – an evolving human right, Walker, Supreme Court Speech, Available at: www.supremecourt.uk/docs/speech_100825.pdf.

3.78 The Court in *Campbell* also considered the development of the breach of confidentiality. They drew the reasoning from the common-law and the courts of equity having previously ruled there had been a breach of confidentiality, if the parties involved were in direct relationship, and the information was provided with a trust that it would stay private. The Court considered that the approach would not be sufficient anymore, and the approach would have to be extended, but continued explaining the case at hand had been brought under different grounds, and hence did not rule from the basis of the tort.[184] The breach of confidence dates back to nineteenth century,[185] but after *Cambell* and the HRA the breach of confidence has developed into a stronger doctrine, which is considered a breach of the Data Protection Act. The definitions of the tort of privacy and breach of confidentiality, and how the interplay, have been discussed in several cases[186], until in 2015 in *Vidal-Hall and others v Google*, the Court of Appeal recognised the existence of the tort of privacy in misusing private information. The Court based its reasoning on the development and definition of a 'tort' and found that misuse of private information fulfills the elements. The compensation the applicant was given was based on distress hence the tort is actionable also without pecuniary loss.[187]

UK GDPR and the Data Protection Act (2018)

3.79 After Brexit, the UK adopted a UK GDPR and alongside it the Data Protection Act 2018. The UK's GDPR is largely aligned with its EU counterpart, and the DP Act implements into the UK's legal framework the UK GDPR, the EU Law Enforcement Directive, and further areas of law. A notable part of the Act is following the line of the GDPR, integrating the main principles of data protection, Controller's and Processor's responsibilities, derogations, security, data transfers, Data Subject Rights and sanctions, including fines.[188]

The Act's structure

3.80 The Act needs to be read together with the GDPR, as instead of rephrasing, the Act makes direct references to the articles and requirements of it. The Act is structured to cover different processing activities in different ways, and there are seven parts, each comprising out of several Chapters. In addition, there are also 18 schedules, which further defines and clarifies the conditions and exemptions set out in the parts.[189]

184 *Campbell v MGN Ltd.* [2004] UKHL 22.

185 *Prince Albert v Strange.*

186 See, eg: *Douglas v Hello! Ltd (cases 1-3), McKennitt v Ash* [2006] EWCA Civ 1714, *Murray v Big Pictures (UK) Ltd* [2008] EWCA Civ 446.

187 *Vidal-Hall and others v Google, Case No: A2/2014/0403.*

188 Data Protection Act (2018); https://ico.org.uk/media/2614158/ico-introduction-to-the-data-protection-bill.pdf; www.legislation.gov.uk/ukpga/2018/12/schedule/2.

189 The Bill, Preliminary.

3.81 The first part of the Act provides an overview of the law and defines the used terms.[190]

3.82 The second part addresses the general terms of processing which apply to most situations of data processing and should be read together with the Schedules 1, 2 and 4, which set out the derogations and their conditions and clarifies the requirements set out in the parts. The second part is largely aligned with the GDPR, but there are however exceptions, as the part makes use of the national margin, which is left for the Member States to regulate upon. This includes for example the age when limit parental consent is required for the minor's us of an information service, and certain limits to the Data Subject Rights. The second part also further defines the exemptions for requiring consent to process sensitive or criminal data, and when an exemption to processing for archiving, research and statistical purposes applies. Several of the exemptions concern data processing for national security and defence and conditions for the same.[191]

3.83 The EU's new Law Enforcement Directive (LED)[192] requires certain data protection measures to be complied with in the context of processing data for law enforcement purposes, when the EU-law applies. The Member States had until May 2018 to implement the Directive into their national law. The part differs from the GDPR but is evidently written drawing from it the six 'data protection principles' applicable to processing for law enforcement. The Act requires the processing to be lawful and fair, and the processed data to be accurate and minimised to the predefined purpose. Retention times must reflect the necessity for the data, and appropriate security measures must be implemented.[193]

3.84 Part four sets out the requirements for intelligence services data processing. The Member States intelligence agencies actions fall outside of the competence of the EU, and the fourth part is drafted from the basis of the modernised Convention 108, instead of the GDPR. The modernised Convention is more in line with the GDPR than the original Convention, but is high-level and drafted to suit the need to find a common ground for all the Signatories. Intelligence services data processing is, and has traditionally been, under the competence of each State, and there are several exemptions to data protection and the right to privacy in this area especially in relation to national security and defence. The fourth part of the Bill reflects this, and while it applies the similar principles to intelligence agencies as for the law enforcement purposes, there are several exemptions to the requirements based on national security.[194] Intelligence

190 The Bill, Pt 1.

191 The Bill, Pt 2, Schs 1-2, 4.

192 Dir (EU) 2016/680 of the European Parliament and of the Council of 27 April 2016 on the protection of natural persons with regard to the processing of personal data by competent authorities for the purposes of the prevention, investigation, detection or prosecution of criminal offences or the execution of criminal penalties, and on the free movement of such data, and repealing Council Framework Decision, OJ L 119, 4.5.2016, pp. 89–13, Art 63.

193 The Bill, Pt 3.

194 The Bill, Pt 4.

services data processing is also regulated by the Investigatory Powers Act, which is discussed in more detail below.

3.85 Part five appoints the Information Commissioner as the enforcing body to the Act and equips them with additional powers such as issuing higher fines, conducting audits, and preparing several codes of practice, including concerning the children as Data Subjects. The Information Commissioner's Office has traditionally been a notable influencer amongst the EU's Data Protection Authorities, and the Act requires them to continue building international co-operation.[195]

3.86 The sixth part explains the enforcement of the law. In addition to being able to issue fines, and exercise the above-mentioned rights, the Commissioner can issue information, assessment enforcement and penalty notices. Information notices can be issued to the controller or processor requiring them to provide information the Commissioner needs to carry out his duties. Assessment notices are notices which the Commissioner can provide to a controller or processor to assess their compliance with the data protection laws, and enforcement notices require the controller or the processor to enforce certain data subject's rights or ensure the accuracy of the data, after having failed to do so. Penalty notices are enforcement actions should the previously mentioned notices not be complied with. The Commissioner must publish instructions on how these rights are intended to be used. The part also defines the maximum level of fines and how the data subjects can exercise their rights to complain. Certain exemptions are also covered, such as for journalism, academic, artistic and literature purposes. Altering or erasing data to prevent it being disclosed to the data subject is also offence, which means, that modifications aiming to restrict data, which otherwise would be under the data subject's access or portability request's scope, is illegal.[196]

3.87 Part seven includes supplementary and final provisions on the application of the Act. It requires the Secretary of State to make changes to align the law with the modernised Convention 108 and prohibits to force someone to use their right of access to gain access to that data. Data subjects can have a representation in relation to exercising their certain rights and seek compensation. The functioning of the Tribunal, from where to direct complaints and seek compensation is also described.[197]

3.88 The Act also criminalises reckless or knowingly conducted re-identification of anonymised data, unless the de-identifying controller has given consent, and no other justifications apply.[198] This has the potential to become a discussed topic in the context of big data. Despite implementing safeguards, conducting analysis using an additional anonymised database can link the once

195 The Bill, Pt 5.
196 The Bill, Pt 6.
197 The Bill, Pt 7.
198 The Bill, s 171.

anonymised data back to being identified to an individual.[199] It is thus advised to ensure the algorithms and safeguards exists to keep anonymised data as it is, and conduct appropriate DPIAs and mitigate risks.

The Privacy and Electronic Communications (EC Directive) Regulations (PECR)[200]

3.89 PECR implements the e-privacy Directive in the UK, its scope covering direct marketing, cookies, and telecommunication privacy. The PECR is applicable alongside the UK GDPR and the Act 2018, regulating the specific areas within its scope. Therefore, eg, the marketing and cookie practices of the companies will also need to consider PECR, not only the other laws.[201] However, the data processing must be aligned with all of these laws, hence, eg, acquiring consent for direct marketing must be compliant with both the GDPR and the PECR. As the e-Privacy Directive is being renewed, PECR can be expected to be replaced with the e-Privacy Regulation, once it becomes applicable. Until then, the ICO has a guide and other resources to help in the implementation of the law.[202]

3.90 PECR is one of the most enforced data privacy laws in the UK and the recent trends globally have concentrated on marketing practices. The enforcing body is the Information Commissioner's Office (ICO) and examples of fines include: £140 000 to EB Associated Group Limited for unsolicited marketing calls regarding pensions,[203] £70 000 to Ryan Hill Partners for unsolicited text message marketing[204] and £200,000 to Home2sense Limited for unsolicited marketing calls.[205]

Regulation of Investigatory Powers Act (RIPA, 2000), Data Retention and Regulation of Investigatory Powers Act (DRIPA, 2014), Investigatory Powers Act (IPA, 2016)

3.91 The Investigatory Powers Act is a legislative tool for the UK's public authorities to intercept communications from the basis of suspecting a serious crime, or otherwise protecting national security or defence.[206]

199 Hoffman, *Electronic Health Records and Medical Big Data, Law and Policy* (Cambridge University Press, 2016) p. 136.
200 The Privacy and Electronic Communications (EC Directive) Regulations 2003.
201 The Privacy and Electronic Communications (EC Directive) Regulations 2003, Section 4.
202 https://ico.org.uk/media/for-organisations/documents/2784/guide-to-ico-pecr-audits.pdf; https://ico.org.uk/media/for-organisations/guide-to-pecr-2-4.pdf; https://ico.org.uk/for-organisations/guide-to-pecr/what-are-pecr/.
203 https://ico.org.uk/media/action-weve-taken/mpns/4019111/eb-associates-mpn-20211129.pdf.
204 https://ico.org.uk/media/action-weve-taken/mpns/4023266/ryan-hill-partners-mpn.pdf.
205 https://ico.org.uk/media/action-weve-taken/mpns/4019530/home2sense-mpn-20220202.pdf.
206 Investigatory Powers Act 2016.

The history of the interception powers and retention of data, which led to the current Act

3.92 In 2014, in *Digital Rights Ireland (DRI)*, the ECJ declared the Data Retention Directive[207] invalid, the reason being that the Directive was enacted disregarding the principle of proportionality, allowing too intrusive measures in relation to one's privacy, and for retaining too much data for too long. As a result of invalidation, the Member States, which had implemented the Directive into their national legislation, were required to revise their existing legislation, which in UK was The Data Retention Regulations 2009.[208]

3.93 The Regulation of Investigatory Powers Act (RIPA) 2000 regulates the governmental interception powers.[209] To bring new powers for the government, and to comply with the requirement to renew the data retention regulation, in 2014 the Data Retention and Investigatory Powers Act (DRIPA) came into force. The Act regulates the 'governmental access, interception and use of electronic communications', amending the RIPA by extending several of the powers RIPA provided for governmental interception. DRIPA granted the interception services several methods to gain access to communication data, especially from the basis of national security.[210]

3.94 The Act was contested from several sources, including an English MP, on the ground of the legislation being too extensive and intrusive in relation to the right to privacy, and a Swedish telecommunications company Tele2 which contested a UK governmental order to retain data. As a result of the *DRI* case, the Swedish national law implementing the Data Retention Directive was changed, making data retention from too general grounds illegal. The ECJ declared DRIPA invalid, ruling that data retention and interception must be based on a suspicion of a serious crime, capping the bulk-interception possibilities, and requiring the permission to intercept to be provided by an independent body. [211]

3.95 The revision, which was ongoing already during the DRIPA being contested in the ECJ, resulted in the IPA being applicable since 2016. IPA amended DRIPA by providing interception permissions only for 'serious crimes', and establishing a separate body, which issues the permissions.[212]

207 Dir 2006/24/EC of the European Parliament and of the Council of 15 March 2006 on the retention of data generated or processed in connection with the provision of publicly available electronic communications services or of public communications networks and amending Dir 2002/58/EC.

208 C-293/12 Digital Rights Ireland; The Data Retention (EC Directive) Regs 2009 (Repealed).

209 Regulation of Investigatory Powers Act 2000.

210 Data Retention and Investigatory Powers Act 2014 www.legislation.gov.uk/ukpga/2014/27/crossheading/investigatory-powers/enacted s 3.

211 Joined Cases C-203/15 and C-698/15, *Tele2 Sverige AB v Post- och telestyrelsen* and *Secretary of State for the Home Department v Watson, Brice, Lewis.*

212 Investigatory Powers Act 2016.

Reflections on IPA

3.96 The IPA, similarly as its predecessors is under high criticism, which is evident from the law's commonly used nickname 'Snooper's Charter'.[213] The Act allows for example bulk hacking and interception of personal data, access to e-mails, internet history and phone calls. The grounds for intercepting are criticised for being too vague. The Human Rights Group Liberty launched a crowdfunding campaign to fund a law suit against the government, challenging the Act in Court.[214] The UK government has also admitted that the IPA needs to be amended to comply with EU-law. To remediate the situation, in November 2017, the draft regulations amending the IPA were passed, alongside a draft code of practice. Both of these were open for public consultation until January 2018. There are also a draft Impact Assessment, Draft Regulations for amending the Act and case-studies on the Vital Importance of Communications Data available on the government's website.[215]

Computer Misuse Act (CMA)

3.97 The Computer Misuse Act (CMA) was passed in 1990 after a failure to charge hackers who 'obtained, without the persons knowledge, the username and password of an I.T. engineer who worked for a large telephone communications company and used them to access the data of Prince Philip'.[216] The CMA criminalises using computers for criminal purposes, including any unauthorised access, and providing help to unlawfully accessed data, or computers. This means, for example, using a colleague's username and password to gain access to data you are not otherwise allowed to process. Similarly, social engineering, phishing or whaling would fall under the Act, as the purpose of these activities is to gain illegal access to data.[217] Actions that lead to a later unauthorised access to a computer or data are also within the scope.[218] To ensure the legislation follows the technical development, a computer covers a wide range of devices, as it's defined as 'a device for storing, processing and retrieving information.'[219]

213 www.ft.com/content/526bfd62-b3bf-11e5-8358-9a82b43f6b2f; http://www.bbc.co.uk/news/uk-38565083.

214 www.liberty-human-rights.org.uk/campaigning/people-vs-snoopers-charter.

215 www.gov.uk/government/consultations/investigatory-powers-act-2016.

216 Fafinski, *'Prestel hack' Computer Misuse: Response Regulation and the Law* (Routledge, 2014) pp. 43-44.; https://nationalcrimeagency.gov.uk/who-we-are/publications/523-cyber-choices-hacking-it-legal-computer-misuse-act-1990/file#:~:text=The%20Computer%20Misuse%20Act%201990,a%20large%20telephone%20communications%20company.

217 Where the person will try to get the one with legal access to certain data, to hand over their username and password by pretending to be that person, or someone else with a legitimate access right. Alternatively using hacking, keylogging, etc. to steal data or access, Fafinski, *Computer Misuse: Response, Reg and the Law* (Routledge, 2014), pp. 5, 60; www.techopedia.com/definition/28643/whaling.

218 Computer Misuse Act, s 2(3).

219 www.cps.gov.uk/legal-guidance/computer-misuse-act.

3.98 The CMA also criminalises malicious acts done on a computer or data, which may hinder the functioning of the computer, such as spreading viruses and other malware and hacking into a system and altering data. To be found guilty, the person should also be aware at the moment of accessing the data, or making the computer perform an action or function immediately or by assisting a future action, that it is illegal. Incitement, attempt, and conspiracy are within the scope in addition to the actual offence, therefore an unsuccessful attempt to hack or incitement to gain unauthorised access to data are offences under the Act. The CMA applies widely as it is triggered whenever an act has a significant link to the United Kingdom.[220] The sanctions for the breach depend on the offence, ranging from monetary sanctions to imprisonment.

3.99 Based on the Police and Justice Act 2006, the CMA was amended in 2006 bringing under the scope of criminal acts the 'making, supplying or obtaining articles for use in computer misuse offences'. The aim was understood to be aligning the law with the Budapest Convention, which has been discussed earlier in this chapter. The articles, such as packet analysers are however also used in the field of information security to detect vulnerabilities. The CMA does require to show intent and awareness that the act is criminal, malicious, or unlawful, but the fear of sanctions arose within IT-security professionals, as previous cases had made no proper distinction between whether the intent was malicious or not.[221] In 2015, the CMA was amended again aligning it with a new EU Directive, the Directive on Attacks Against Information.[222] The amendments aligned the CMA with EU-law, redefined the applicability, and provided the intelligence services an exemption to the applicability of the cybercrime legislation during their course of work.[223]

CMA in practice

3.100 The Computer Misuse Act has been used in a relatively small number of cases. This is understood to be due to the difficulty of proving the actions are illegal, as it requires technical skills, understanding, and being able to prove incitement and intent, which are open for interpretation. Also, companies that have had a breach may fear unwanted public attention should they litigate.[224] The cases have also been received with controversial feedback. While the aim of the law has been generally understood, the practicalities have led to many IT-professionals to criticise the vagueness and criminalisation of the tools that

220 Computer Misuse Act, ss 3, 4, 6, 9.

221 Fafinski, *Computer Misuse: Response, Regulation and the Law* (Routledge, 2014) pp. 68-76.

222 Directive 2013/40/EU of the European Parliament and of the Council of 12 August 2013 on attacks against information systems and replacing Council Framework Decision, OJ L 218, 14.8.2013, pp. 8–14.

223 Home Office, Policy Paper, Serious Crime Bill, 2014: Amendments to the Computer Misuse Act impact Assessment, Aggravated offence impact assessment, Fact sheet: computer misuse, available at: /www.gov.uk/government/publications/serious-crime-bill-computer-misuse.

224 Doyle, *Essential ICT A Level: AS Student Book for AQA* (Folens, 2008) p. 186; Parliamentary Office of Science and Technology Post note, 2006, Number 271.

can be used for security as well. The critique has been amplified by the Court's approach in certain cases where the intention might not have been malicious per se, and could have been justified by notifying the end-user of the actions the person or entity took. This was the case, for example, where a software company cancelled a subscription when it expected the bills would not be paid and was found guilty under the CMA. Whether the outcome of the case followed the CMA has been debated, as an intent for a malicious action is an integral part of the scope of the acts which are defined as criminal offences. Similar criticism sparked from a case where an employee who had installed encryption-decryption software on his work computer was fined after his employment ended after a disagreement, and the software later stopped working, rendering the computer unusable.[225] Several cases that are initiated under the scope of the CMA will often be further tried under a different legal framework, such as the Fraud Act 2006, as it becomes more suitable to the case. The young age of persons engaging in acts that may fall under the CMA may also be a contributing factor to a low number of enforcements, as persons under 18 years of age will be prosecuted under different rules than adults.[226]

A FOCUS ON THE COMPUTER MISUSE ACT

Gary Broadfield

3.101 In 1989 Intel released its 486 DX Processor, capable of clock speeds of up to 50 MHz and consisting of approximately 1.2 million transistors and a cache of 8kb.[227] In contrast, the Intel Core 'i9-7980XE Extreme Edition Processor' launched in the third quarter of 2017 has a maximum clock speed of 4.20 GHz, a cache of 24.75MB and about 7.2 billion transistors.[228][229] A modern processor's capabilities are vastly superior to that of their predecessors, which look almost prehistoric in comparison; the clock speed is 84 times more powerful, it has a cache 3,000 times larger and 6,000 times as many transistors. The pace of development has been phenomenal and seemingly unabated.

3.102 The vast increase in raw computing power has largely been accompanied by increases in connectivity and battery life. These developments have combined to fuel similarly huge changes in our lives and in our society. In 1990 there was no Social Media; the founding of Facebook (2004) was 14 years in the future; indeed, even Facebook's long dead ancestors Myspace (2003) and Friends Reunited (2000) were a decade away. So were YouTube (February 2005) and the iPod (2001), much less the iPhone (2007). Google (1998), Ebay (1995) and Amazon (1994) were more proximate, but each took time to achieve their pre-eminence and ubiquity.

225 Fafinski, *Computer Misuse: Response, Regulation and the Law* (Routledge, 2014) p. 227.
226 Jahankhani and others, *Global Security, Safety and Sustainability: The Security Challenges of the Connected World* (Springer, 2017) pp. 63-64.
227 www.intel.com/pressroom/kits/quickreffam.htm#i486.
228 https://ark.intel.com/products/series/123588/Intel-Core-X-series-Processors.
229 https://en.wikipedia.org/wiki/Transistor_count.

3.103 As late as 1998, only 9% of UK households were connected to the internet, rising to above 90% today.[230] That increased connectivity has not been 'static'. Mobile devices have ensured that we increasingly live our lives online; we interact with each other through email and social media accounts, we receive our news, fake or otherwise via the web, live and as events take place. We shop and bank online. We relax and game online, and advertise ourselves and our businesses online.

3.104 These opportunities and developments have carried with them additional risks; companies hold ever more and more personal and private data in respect of their customers; this can range from their financial and contact details to intimate photographs uploaded to private 'cloud' storage.

3.105 Of course, businesses also hold their own data online or, at the least, electronically. This may include sensitive commercial information such as the Research and Development (R&D) data on potential new product designs, or potential and planned mergers and acquisition as well as payroll and HR data on staff and employees. Even more straightforwardly, almost every business has a web presence which may well be its primary source of new business and sales.

3.106 In such a 'target rich environment' for those intent on doing harm through computer misuse, the need to ensure that the legislative landscape can deal with a range of complex and constantly developing challenges is clear.

3.107 The Computer Misuse Act legislates for five specific offences relating to computer misuse, ostensibly closing a gap in the law that had seen the first 'hackers' prosecuted under legislation that simply did not cover the acts complained of, as in the case of *R v Gold and Schifreen* [1988] 2 All ER 186. In that case, said to be one of the major factors behind the drafting of the Computer Misuse Act 1990 (CMA 1990), the two defendants had hacked into the BT Prestel system (a precursor to email) after one had 'shoulder surfed' a BT employee to observe the username and password details required to gain access to the system. The defendants were convicted at first instance of six counts of Forgery pursuant to section 1 of the Forgery and Counterfeiting Act 1981, but successfully appealed their convictions on the basis that no 'false instrument' had been created, a prerequisite of that offence.

3.108 The Act has received only two major upgrades in its lifetime, firstly by the Police and Justice Act 2006 and more recently by the amendments made by the Serious Crime Act 2015. These amendments incorporated and criminalised new developments in cybercrime that could not have been easily foreseen in 1990.

3.109 Equally, the amendments made in 2006 and 2015 have served to strengthen the penalties available to the courts in respect of those convicted of

230 www.statista.com/statistics/275999/household-internet-penetration-in-great-britain/.

computer misuse, reflecting the rising number of instances of computer crime, and the increasing seriousness of the consequences. Despite that, this short, 18 section statute has been remarkably robust and has survived the 28 years since inception largely intact, despite the technological revolution since 1990 ensuring that the Computer Misuse Act can perhaps claim to be the most antiquated statute in force in England and Wales.

3.110 Thus, the offences covered by the Computer Misuse Act 1990 are as follows.

(1) Section 1 dealing with Unauthorised Access to Computer Material.

(2) Section 2 deals with unauthorised access with the intent to commit or facilitate further offences.

(3) Section 3 deals with unauthorised acts with intent to impair (or with recklessness as to impairing the operation of a computer.

(4) Section 3 ZA, was added by the Serious Crime Act 2015 and deals with unauthorised acts causing or creating risk of serious damage.

(5) Section 3A, added by the Police and Justice Act 2006 and amended by the Serious Crime Act 2015, created an offence of making, supplying or obtaining articles for use in offences under section 1, 3 or 3ZA.

(1) Unauthorised Access to Computer Material.

3.111 The concept of 'unauthorised access' underpins not only section 1 of the Act, but the Act itself. It is therefore helpful to look first at section 17 which provides clarity as to both 'securing access' and 'unauthorised'

17 (2) A person secures access to any program or data held in a computer if by causing a computer to perform any function he—

(a) alters or erases the program or data;

(b) copies or moves it to any storage medium other than that in which it is held or to a different location in the storage medium in which it is held;

(c) uses it; or

(d) has it output from the computer in which it is held (whether by having it displayed or in any other manner);

and references to access to a program or data (and to an intent to secure such access or to enable such access to be secured) shall be read accordingly.

(3) For the purposes of subsection (2)(c) above a person uses a program if the function he causes the computer to perform—

(a) causes the program to be executed; or

(b) is itself a function of the program.

(4) For the purposes of subsection (2)(d) above—

(a) a program is output if the instructions of which it consists are output; and

(b) the form in which any such instructions or any other data is output (and in particular whether or not it represents a form in which, in the case of instructions, they are capable of being executed or, in the case of data, it is capable of being processed by a computer) is immaterial.

In respect of 'unauthorised' access, see ss 17 (5) and 17 (8):

(5) Access of any kind by any person to any program or data held in a computer is unauthorised if—

(a) he is not himself entitled to control access of the kind in question to the program or data; and

(b) he does not have consent to access by him of the kind in question to the program or data from any person who is so entitled but this subsection is subject to section 10].

(8) An act done in relation to a computer is unauthorised if the person doing the act (or causing it to be done)—

(a) is not himself a person who has responsibility for the computer and is entitled to determine whether the act may be done; and

(b) does not have consent to the act from any such person.

In this subsection 'act' includes a series of acts.

3.112 Finally, the interpretation provided by section 17 also clarifies at section 17(6) that the Act covers removable storage media such as hard drives or USB sticks temporarily connected to a computer:

(6) References to any program or data held in a computer include references to any program or data held in any removable storage medium which is for the time being in the computer; and a computer is to be regarded as containing any program or data held in any such medium.

And at 17(10) that 'References to a program include references to part of a program'.

3.113 Thus, it can be seen from the definitions provided at section 17 of the Act that the concept of unauthorised access to a computer is drawn about as widely as is possible; for a s 1 offence nothing further than access is required; no more is necessary. Any action such as deleting, copying, moving, downloading or displaying data or executing a program in any way would form the basis of an offence. A number of newsworthy and high-profile attacks against public figures, businesses and authorities are well known but real-world examples of potential section 1 offences could also include something relatively innocuous like reading a colleague's emails, or logging on to their social media accounts.

3.114 In this context, it is possible to criminalise a multitude of everyday transgressions under the statute. Whilst this flexibility and ability to cover a range of behaviour suggests that individuals risk criminal liability for trivial acts, in practice common sense and the limited resources of investigators and the CPS mitigate against that risk. Thus the flexibility of the Act has been a strength, allowing it to remain robust in the decades since it was enacted. In that context it is perhaps less surprising than it may seem at first sight that there is, and never has been, any definition within the Act of the meaning of the word 'computer,' and it is left for the courts of the day to determine what that term may or may not cover.

3.115 In relation to the section 1 offence, section1(1), A person is guilty of an offence if:

(a) he causes a computer to perform any function with intent to secure access to any program or data held in any computer or to enable any such access to be secured;

(b) the access he intends to secure or to enable to be secured, is unauthorised; and

(c) he knows at the time when he causes the computer to perform the function that that is the case.

3.116 Furthermore, section 1(2) further clarifies the position in respect of *mens rea:*

(2) The intent a person has to have to commit an offence under this section need not be directed at—

(a) any particular program or data;

(b) a program or data of any particular kind; or

(c) a program or data held in any particular computer.

3.117 As initially enacted in 1990 the section 1 offence was a summary only offence with a maximum sentence in the Magistrates Court of six months' imprisonment. Section 35(3) of the Police and Justice Act 2006 (PJA 2006) amended section 1 by making the offence triable either way. The PJA 2006 increased the maximum sentence on Summary conviction from six months' imprisonment to two years and stipulated that the maximum sentence available to a Crown Court Judge would be two years imprisonment.

(2) Section 2: Unauthorised access with the intent to commit or facilitate further offences.

3.118 The section 2 Offence builds on section 1 by providing that where an individual commits an offence under section 1 with intent to commit or facilitate the commission of further offences by another. Section 2(2) sets out that this section applies to offences:

(a) for which the sentence is fixed by law; or

(b) for which a person who has attained the age of twenty-one years (eighteen in relation to England and Wales) and has no previous convictions may be sentenced to imprisonment for a term of five years…

3.119 Again, the provision are widely drafted in order to catch a range of actions: section 2(3) confirms that the 'further offence' to be committed does not have to be committed on the same occasion as the unauthorised access offence, but can be committed 'on any future occasion'. Equally section 2(4) states that the section 2 offence can be made out even where 'the facts are such that the commission of the further offence is impossible'.

3.120 Again, the section 2 offence is triable either way and on summary conviction the maximum penalty is imprisonment for 12 months and a fine. However, in a reflection of the increased seriousness of the offence as compared with section 1, and the seriousness of the 'further offences', the maximum penalty available in the Crown Court is five years' imprisonment as well as a fine.

(3) Section 3: unauthorised acts with intent to impair (or with recklessness as to impairing the operation of a computer.

3.121 Section 3 was significantly amended from its original form by the PJA 2006. As originally enacted, to be guilty of a section 3 offence, an individual had to 'do any act which causes the unauthorised modification of the contents of any computer' with intent to impair the operation of a computer, program, the reliability of data or to prevent or hinder access to a program or data held in the computer. The offence carried a maximum penalty of five years' imprisonment on Indictment.

3.122 The amendment of section 3 was necessary; as originally enacted it covered the offences that were foreseen at the time; that is to say an individual who gained unauthorised access to a system and modified the data therein. Modification in this context meant the amendment or deletion of files, or through uploading a virus, malware or other malicious code to a system. Whilst the original section 3 anticipated those actions and was intended to criminalise them, it did not easily cover a newer generation of internet-enabled offences such as Distributed Denial of Service (DDOS) attacks which came to prominence long after 1990.

3.123 DDOS attacks work by overloading a webpage or ISP with 'spam' traffic from an attack server, or in more recent years a 'botnet' of malware infected internet enabled devices. The malicious spam traffic overwhelms the victim's system, causing it to slow significantly or perhaps to crash altogether. It is worth recording that in latter years, this type of attack has become readily available online where users can subscribe to DDOS-for-hire services where an existing infrastructure can be rented to attack a target of choice. Whilst these attacks are certainly capable of impairing the operation of a victim's computer systems, they do not necessarily *modify* them and thus did not fall squarely within section 3 as initially enacted.

3.124 Thus the amended section 3 was extended so that it covered 'any unauthorised act' in relation to a victim's computer rather than simply unauthorised modification. Furthermore in order to be convicted of an offence under section 3 as originally enacted, an individual had to have both the 'requisite intent and the requisite knowledge.' In short, he or she had to intend to cause a modification that would impair the computer etc and know that the modification was unauthorised. As amended, the Act additionally provides that the damage or impairment caused pursuant to section 3 (3) need not be intended but can also be a result of recklessness.

3.125 The widened scope of the section is clear:

3 (1) A person is guilty of an offence if—

(a) he does any unauthorised act in relation to a computer;

(b) at the time when he does the act he knows that it is unauthorised; and

(c) either subsection (2) or subsection (3) below applies.

(2) This subsection applies if the person intends by doing the act—

(a) to impair the operation of any computer;

(b) to prevent or hinder access to any program or data held in any computer; or

(c) to impair the operation of any such program or the reliability of any such data; or

(d) to enable any of the things mentioned in paragraphs (a) to (c) above to be done.

(3) This subsection applies if the person is reckless as to whether the act will do any of the things mentioned in paragraphs (a) to (d) of subsection (2) above.

(4) The intention referred to in subsection (2) above, or the recklessness referred to in subsection (3) above, need not relate to—

(a) any particular computer;

(b) any particular program or data; or

(c) a program or data of any particular kind.

(5) In this section—

(a) a reference to doing an act includes a reference to causing an act to be done;

(b) 'act' includes a series of acts;

(c) a reference to impairing, preventing or hindering something includes a reference to doing so temporarily.

3.126 The amended section 3 offence is also an either way offence, with the maximum penalty on Summary conviction being imprisonment for a term not exceeding 12 months and a fine. In the Crown Court, the PJA 2006 also increased the maximum penalty from five years' imprisonment to ten.

(4) Section 3 ZA, Unauthorised acts causing or creating risk of serious damage.

3.127 Section 3ZA was inserted into the Act by the Serious Crime Act 2015. The new offence was created as the existing provision under which such offending would previously have been prosecuted, section 3, did not carry sufficient penalties, even after the maximum penalty had been raised to 10 years imprisonment following the PJA 2006 where the object or result of a cyber-attack has been to cause damage to critical national infrastructure. Section 3ZA therefore creates such an offence, triable on indictment only, and allowing the Criminal Courts to impose their most severe punishments.

3.128 Again, a core element of the offence is the commission of any unauthorised act in relation to a computer (s 3ZA (1)(a)), which the individual knows, at the time of doing the act, is unauthorised (s 3ZA (1)(b)). However, in order to be guilty under section 3ZA, the act must also cause or create a significant risk of serious damage of a material kind and the person must intend to cause such damage (s 3ZA (1)(c)) or be reckless as to whether such damage is caused (s 3ZA (1)(d)).

3.129 Damage of a 'material kind' is defined in section 3ZA (2) as being:

(a) damage to human welfare in any place;

(b) damage to the environment of any place;

(c) damage to the economy of any country; or

(d) damage to the national security of any country.

3.130 And damage to human welfare is defined by section s3ZA (3) as being damage that causes:

(a) loss to human life;

(b) human illness or injury;

(c) disruption of a supply of money, food, water, energy or fuel;

(d) disruption of a system of communication;

(e) disruption of facilities for transport; or

(f) disruption of services relating to health.

3.131 Subsection (4) provides that it is immaterial for the purposes of subsection (2) whether or not an act causing damaged does so directly (s 3ZA (4)(2)(a)) or is the only or main cause of the damage (s 3ZA (4)(2)(b)).

3.132 Finally, subsection 5 ensures that the ambit of the act is kept as wide as possible, clarifying that for the purposes of section 3ZA:

(a) a reference to doing an act includes a reference to causing an act to be done;

(b) 'act' includes a series of acts;

(c) a reference to a country includes a reference to a territory, and to any place in, or part or region of, a country or territory.

3.133 Pursuant to section 3ZA (6) the offence is indictable only, reflecting its seriousness and will normally carry a maximum sentence of 14 years. However, subsection (7) allows that where a section 3ZA offence has been committed that causes or creates significant risk to human welfare as defined under subsections (3)(a) and (b), (loss to human life or human illness or injury) or serious damage to national security, the potential penalty is increased to life imprisonment.

3.134 The new section 3ZA therefore represents a significant uplift to the powers of law enforcement to deal with the emerging threat of cyber-terrorism and acts that put at risk vital national infrastructure.

3.135 It should be noted that the threat intended to be countered by section 3ZA is real and one that has already manifested itself within the UK. Perhaps the most high profile cyber-attack of 2017 was the WannaCry Ransomware. The scale of the infection was major; within 24 hours of the first infections on 12 May2017, WannaCry was reported to have infected more than 230,000 computers in over 150 countries, affecting a long list of companies and organisations as diverse as Telefonica, Renault, Deutsche Bahn FedEx, Nissan Hitachi, Sberbank, Petrobras and the Russian Central Bank. By the now familiar method of encrypting infected computers and demanding a ransom in Bitcoin in exchange for the decryption keys, the attack caused widespread disruption to systems around the world.

3.136 Crucially, a number of NHS trusts throughout the UK were also affected; according to the National Audit Office, the attack led to disruption in at least 34% of trusts in England (81 out of 236). A further 603 primary care and other NHS organisations were infected by WannaCry, including 595 GP practices. The effect was that thousands of appointments and operations were cancelled. In five areas accident and emergency departments were unable to treat some patients leading to them being diverted further afield.[231]

3.137 It is easy to see how the creators of the WannaCry pathogen would fall squarely within the new section 3ZA. Malware, and particularly Ransomware like WannaCry are indiscriminate in nature, they spread automatically and infect wherever possible. However, whilst the intention of the creators of WannaCry was more likely to be the harvesting of ransom monies rather than to deliberately cause disruption to critical infrastructure, the effect of WannaCry in practise

231 www.nao.org.uk/report/investigation-wannacry-cyber-attack-and-the-nhs/.

was certainly to cause the 'disruption of services relating to health' and 'risk of causing loss to human life, illness and injury'. In releasing code of this nature 'into the wild' the creators were certainly reckless as to the consequences.

3.138 However, although section 3ZA may put in place the legal framework to fully deal with this type of offending, it may well be the case that section 3ZA is only ever rarely used by the authorities; hacking threats of this nature would seem to largely derive from Nation States (WannaCry was suspected to be a tool created by North Korea)[232] or terrorist groups operating extraterritorially where practical difficulties in respect of investigation may preclude a prosecution. As yet, it is unclear whether any prosecutions have been brought under this provision.

3.139 Alternatively, it may be that as the provision is so widely drafted, in future years section 3ZA becomes used more regularly in cases not involving the above groups. One potential example where it might be considered would be in relation to hacking or computer misuse linked to 'swatting' which can cause widespread disruption and risk to life (in respect of which see **Chapter 1.17** 'Script Kiddies'), although that would seem to diverge somewhat from the original intention behind the provision.

(5) Section 3A: Making, supplying or obtaining articles for use in offences under section 1, 3 or 3ZA

3.140 Section 3A was added to the Act by the PJA 2006, in response to the growing market for 'hacking tools' that were becoming widely disseminated online.

3.141 The offence itself is relatively straightforward; a person is guilty of an offence if he makes, adapts, supplies or offers to supply any article intending it to be used to commit, or to assist in the commission of, an offence under section 1, 3 or 3Z, (s 3A (1)) or if he supplies or offers to supply any article believing that it is likely to be used to commit, or to assist in the commission of, an offence under section 1, 3 or 3ZA (s 3A (2)). Equally an offence is made out if an individual obtains any article intending to use it to commit, or to assist in the commission of, an offence under section 1, 3 or 3ZA, (s 3A (3)(a)) or with a view to its being supplied for use to commit, or to assist in the commission of, those offences (s 3A (3)(b)).

3.142 Section 3A (4) specifically confirms that an 'article' includes any program or data held in electronic form, thus ensuring that it encompasses software programs and tools commonly used for fraud and computer crime, such as Remote Access Trojans that, if uploaded to a victim's system (usually through a successful phishing scam) will allow the attacker to take control of it.

3.143 The section 3A offence is an either way offence, with a maximum penalty on indictment of two years imprisonment. That is surprising given that

232 www.wsj.com/Arts/its-official-north-korea-is-behind-wannacry-1513642537.

this section is also capable of applying to tools used for the most serious offending under the Act, pursuant to section 3ZA, for which the maximum penalty is life imprisonment. It may be therefore that in future this maximum penalty is revised upwards.

TERRITORIAL SCOPE

Sections 4 and 5

3.144 The Act originally provided for a degree of extra-territorial jurisdiction. As enacted, the Act ensured that a person could be prosecuted for an offence under section 1 or section 3 that had been committed abroad, provided that there was a 'significant link' to the UK.

3.145 The extra-territorial jurisdiction of the Act was widened by the Serious Crime Act 2015 (SCA 2015). It not only amended section 4 to extend extra territorial jurisdiction to section 3A and to the newly created section 3ZA offence, but also inserted the new sections 5(1A) and (1B), the effect of which was to increase the scope of the Act considerably; those sections allow the prosecution of UK nationals for Computer Misuse Act offences regardless of whether or not the conduct has any other link to the UK, as long as the conduct also amounts to an offence in the country in which it took place.

3.146 Section 5 of the Act was also amended by the SCA 2015 to define what constitutes a 'significant link' to the UK, in order to ensure that the ability to prosecute non-UK nationals under the Act was enhanced. In essence, as originally enacted, a significant link was established if the suspect was in the UK at the time of the alleged offence. The SCA 2015 extended this to catch scenarios where the *individual* was not present in the UK at the time of the offence, but that the *computer or data accessed* was.

3.147 In the case of section 3ZA an additional possibility exists to extend the extra-territorial jurisdiction of the Act. A section 3ZA offence is still committed If the suspect 'caused or created a risk of material damage' to the UK, even if neither he nor the computer or data accessed where not within the UK at the time of the access.

Sentences

3.148 As yet, there are no sentencing guidelines issued by the Sentencing Council in respect of the Computer Misuse Act. As a result, various precedents may be of assistance to practitioners in their submissions to a sentencing court.

3.149 In *R v Mangham* [2012] EWCA Crim 973, the Court of Appeal quashed a sentence of eight months' imprisonment imposed at first instance and substituted four months' imprisonment concurrent for a 26 year old defendant who had entered guilty pleas to three counts securing unauthorised access to computer material with intent, contrary section 1; and a further count of unauthorised modification of computer material, contrary to section 3.

3.150 The brief facts of the case were that the defendant, engaged in a sophisticated and persistent course of conduct to hack into Facebook servers and succeeded in downloading part of the Facebook source code onto his own devices. It was accepted that he had not acted for financial gain, albeit that his actions had cost Facebook some $200,000 in investigating and repairing the breach.

3.151 At paragraph 19 of the Judgment, the Court provided useful guidance as to the aggravating and mitigating factors that might be present in a Computer Misuse Act prosecution:

> 'From these authorities we would identify a number of aggravating factors which will bear on sentence in this type of case: firstly, whether the offence is planned and persistent and then the nature of the damage caused to the system itself and to the wider public interest such as national security, individual privacy, public confidence and commercial confidentiality. The other side of the coin to the damage caused will be the cost of remediation, although we do not regard that as a determining factor. Next, motive and benefit are also relevant. Revenge, which was a feature in Lindesay and Baker, is a serious aggravating factor. Further, the courts are likely to take a very dim view where a hacker attempts to reap financial benefit by the sale of information which has been accessed. Whether or not the information is passed onto others is another factor to be taken into account. The value of the intellectual property involved may also be relevant to sentencing. Among the mitigating factors the psychological profile of an offender will deserve close attention.'

3.152 As well as identifying a number of other factors, the Court gave particular regard to the psychology of the defendants in these matters; Mangham himself had been diagnosed with an Autism Spectrum Disorder and was described by the Court as 'relatively young in years but possibly emotionally younger, and that he had a psychological and a personal make up which had led to the behaviour' (Paragraph 11). The need to identify the presence of any relevant mental health condition became a key element to the defence preparation of such matters.

3.153 *Mangham* was reconsidered by the Court of Appeal the following year, in *R v Martyn* [2013] EWCA Crim 1420. In that case, the Court took the view that Mr Martyn's appeal against a first instance of two years' imprisonment could not succeed.

3.154 Like Mangham, Martyn had entered guilty pleas to a number of offences; five offences of unauthorised modification of computer material contrary to section 3(1) of the Act (two years' imprisonment), one offence of securing unauthorised access to computer material with intent contrary to section 2(1)(a) (12 months' imprisonment), one offence of securing unauthorised access to computer material contrary to section 1 (six months' imprisonment) and two offences of making, supplying or obtaining articles for use contrary to section 3(A) and (5) (four months' imprisonment). The sentences were to run concurrently, giving a total of two years' imprisonment.

3.155 Martyn's conduct had a number of aggravating factors that were not present in Mangahm. Those identified included the sophisticated planning behind the offending, the significant damage caused as a result of it, the potential consequences for the organisations targeted and the public interest in protecting them (Martyn's institutional targets were Universities' and Law Enforcement Agencies) and the invasion of privacy of Martyn's individual victims. Indeed the Court said that 'In our judgment, these offences fall into the highest level of culpability: they were carefully planned offences which did and were intended to cause harm both to the individuals and organisations targeted.' (Paragraph 36).

3.156 A further factor was the Defendant's lengthy criminal record of similar offences. The only significant mitigating factor taken into account was the fact that the offences had not been committed for personal gain.

3.157 Significantly, the Court took care to comment on the growing public interest in dealing harshly with cyber criminals:

> 39. The wider implications of such crimes for society cannot be ignored. Offences such as these, have the potential to cause great damage to the community at large and the public, as well as to the individuals more directly affected by them. Further, it is fortuitous and beyond the control of those who perpetrate them, whether they do so or not. This finds reflection in the maximum sentence which may be passed of ten years' imprisonment for an offence contrary to section3(1) of the Act and of five years' imprisonment for an offence contrary to section 2(1) of the Act. These offences are comparatively easy to commit by those with the relevant expertise, they are increasingly prevalent, and the public is entitled to be protected from them. In our view, it is appropriate for sentences for offences such as these to involve a real element of deterrence. Those who commit them must expect to be punished accordingly.

3.158 The Court also went on to specifically comment on the decision in Mangham, which had been heavily relied upon by the Defence in the Appeal, stating that:

> 43. Without seeking to undermine the mitigating features or the sentence in Mangham, in our judgment, it should not be considered a benchmark for such cases, which, in the ordinary course, are now likely to attract sentences that are very considerably longer: for offending of this scale, sentences will be measured in years rather than months. The prevalence of computer crime, its potential to cause enormous damage, both to the credibility of IT systems and the way in which our society now operates, and the apparent ease with which hackers, from the confines of their own homes, can damage important public institutions, not to say individuals, cannot be understated. The fact that organisations are compelled to spend substantial sums combating this type of crime, whether committed for gain or out of bravado, and the potential impact on individuals such

as those affected in this case only underlines the need for a deterrent sentence.

3.159 However, despite the failure of the appeal and the obvious hardening of the Court's position in respect of the sentences to be imposed in such cases, the position was not entirely bleak for defendants; no issue was raised in respect of Mr Martyn's psychology and thus the Court expressed no view that would contradict the ruling in *Mangham* that psychological conditions such as Asperger's Syndrome deserved careful consideration in a sentencing exercise.

3.160 Finally, the recent case of *Mudd* [2017] EWCA Crim 1395 highlights that the Court of Appeal has continued in the direction of travel identified in *Martyn.*

3.161 In *Mudd* the defendant admitted operating the DDOS for hire service 'Titanium Stresser'. He entered guilty pleas to and was sentenced on a single count contrary to section 3(1) and (6) (24 months' detention in a young offender institution); an offence under section 3A of the Act (nine months' detention concurrent); and a single count of concealing criminal property, contrary to section 327(1) of the Proceeds of Crime Act 2002 (24 months' detention concurrent).

The total sentence imposed was, therefore, 24 months' detention in a young offender institution.

3.162 The scope of the offending was severe; Titanium Stresser had 112,298 registered users and in total, 1,738,828 attacks were carried out, directed against 666,532 individual IP addresses or domain names. In total, the appellant received some £248,000 from Titanium Stresser and other DDoS tools that he supplied.

3.163 Like Mangham, Mudd suffered from Autism and a number of reports were commissioned into his psychological condition and how this potentially affected his motives. The Court's opinion was plain: 'that condition cannot and does not absolve him from criminal responsibility. The judge said, very fairly, that where a diagnosis of autism or Asperger's is established, as the judge accepted it was in this case, that must be taken into account in determining the appropriate sentence. The question remained as to whether it should be determinative of what the sentence must be.'

3.164 Again, the Court in *Mudd* was concerned with 'the scale of criminality' and the 'very considerable public interest in and concern about criminality of this kind.'

> '...Offending of this kind, which was both facilitated by and carried out by this [appellant] has the potential to cause great and lasting damage, not only to those directly targeted but also to the public at large. It is now impossible to imagine a world without the internet. There is no part of life that is not touched by it in some way. These offences may be relatively easy to commit but they are increasingly prevalent and the public is entitled to be protected

from them. It follows that any sentence passed in a case of this level of seriousness must involve a real element of deterrence'. (paragraph 35)

3.165 The sentencing Court indicated that had the defendant been an adult of good character, convicted after a trial, the starting point would have been a custodial sentence of six years' imprisonment. However, in the light of the defendant's youth, psychological condition, and the delay between arrest and charge the Court was able to reduce that period substantially to 32 months' custody. That figure was reduced further by the Judge at first instance by 25% for Mr Mudd's early guilty plea, giving the total sentence of 24 months. The Judge chose not to exercise his discretion to suspend the sentence.

3.166 The Court of Appeal agreed with the sentencing Judge in all aspects, save the relatively minor point that the defendant should have been awarded full credit of 33% for his plea, not merely 25%. Thus his sentence following appeal was set at 21 months' custody in a Young Offenders Institute. A harsh sentence indeed in comparison with that handed to Mangham just five years earlier, and one that is anchored in the need to deter widespread online criminality and to protect the general public.

3.167 Unfortunately for defence practitioners, the line of the authorities is clear; the sentences imposed by Courts and upheld on Appeal have become steadily more severe as the true impact of this offending has become more readily understood.

The Future

3.168 It is difficult to see the extent to which the Computer Misuse Act will need to be updated to cope with future technological changes. However, it is clear that both the Act itself as well as the amendments made by the PJA 2006 and the SCA 2015 take into account the pace of change and have been deliberately drafted in an attempt to be as 'future proof' as possible. The wide scope of the definitions within the Act as well as its vast territorial scope are an intentional effort to ensure that the Act can, to the fullest extent possible, move with the times.

3.169 However, whilst the Act may be said to cover the potential offences that might be committed by an individual or a hacking group, one area where it is arguably deficient is in respect of the defences available to those under suspicion by the Authorities.

3.170 There are two areas where thought might be given to amending the Act in this way. Firstly, there is, at present no concept of 'cyber self defence' or of retaliating against an attacker in order to protect oneself or one's business from outside interference. At present, any individual gaining unauthorised access to an attacker's system would themselves potentially be at risk of Criminal liability under the Act.

3.171 The concept of 'hacking back' is not new and is extremely controversial, giving rise to legitimate concerns of cyber vigilante-ism. However the idea received a recent and significant boost in October 2017 when the 'Active Cyber Defense Certainty Bill' was introduced to the US Congress. The Bill is in the earliest stages but would, if passed into law, seek to act as a deterrent to cyber criminals by giving authorised individuals and companies the legal authority to leave their network to 1) establish attribution of an attack, 2) disrupt cyber-attacks without damaging others' computers, 3) retrieve and destroy stolen files, 4) monitor the behaviour of an attacker, and 5) utilise beaconing technology.[233] The Bill may well not pass into law, and even if it did, similar legislation might never be introduced in this country, but were it to do so, it would be interesting to see how it operated in practice.

3.172 Indeed it may be the case that hacking back, although risky unless adequately safeguarded, is now something that should be considered by the UK authorities. In an ideal scenario, there would be adequate resources available to public law enforcement bodies to enable them to deal with cyber threats. Although in comparison to other branches of law enforcement the UK's cybercrime investigators are well trained and resourced, the overall scale of the problem is such that they simply cannot investigate all breaches fully. In such circumstances it is arguable that private bodies should be permitted to defend themselves more aggressively.

3.173 That said, it may well be that the counter arguments are more persuasive; that many companies which are breached are breached because of the inadequacy of their defences, not through the sophistication of the attacker, and would therefore be unlikely to be able to hack back in any safe or meaningful way. One might also argue that in any event, in practical terms the risk of prosecution for hacking back, if done in a limited and proportionate fashion is vanishingly small and thus any amendment would deal with a risk to businesses that is largely theoretical.

3.174 In a similar vein, the Act could be amended to provide a degree of protection to Hacktivists or individuals who believe that their unauthorised access to a computer was justified in the public interest. It could be thought surprising that the Act does not contain such a defence already. As an example, the Criminal offence created by section 55 of the Data Protection Act 1998 of obtaining or disclosing personal data unlawfully (ie without the consent of the Data Controller) provides for two defences that are not available to those charged under section 1 of the Computer Misuse Act. Those defences are:

- At 55 (2)(c) that the individual acted in the reasonable belief that he would have had the consent of the data controller if the data controller had known of the obtaining, disclosing or procuring and the circumstances of it, and
- At 55 (2)(d) that in the particular circumstances the obtaining, disclosing or procuring was justified as being in the public interest.

233 https://tomgraves.house.gov/news/documentsingle.aspx?DocumentID=398840.

3.175 Thus, if amended in line with the section 55 of the DPA 1998, the CMA would protect an individual from criminal liability in circumstances where they had gained access to a computer system without authorisation but where they held a belief that access would have been authorised by an individual capable of providing authorisation, had they known of the circumstances of the access.

3.176 Equally, providing protection for those engaged in hacking in the public interest would assist in clarifying the status of so called 'ethical hackers'. Whilst this suggestion might call to mind controversial whistle-blowers such as Wikileaks and difficult considerations of whether those actions are genuinely in the public interest, the position is that such a provision might genuinely improve cyber security for businesses by enabling individuals to safely test for and report vulnerabilities in a system without fear of prosecution.

3.177 The absence of those potential defences does not, of course mean that the public interest is not a consideration; the full code test for Crown Prosecutors requires that when considering whether or not to prosecute, the reviewing lawyer should be satisfied firstly whether or not there is sufficient evidence to give a realistic prospect of conviction. If so, they must then consider whether it is in the public interest to bring a prosecution. Thus whilst the safeguard may not be as strong as it might be if it were enshrined in the Act, it does exist.

3.178 The Computer Misuse Act has been remarkably successful in dealing with the evolution of online crime in an era that has seen technology change our lives in a way that was scarcely imaginable when the Act was first drafted. The key to that success has been the wide scope of the offences and the broad definitions that are applicable, ensuring that it can cover a range of behaviours without requiring much amendment. As amended, the Act seems well set to extend its useful life well into the future. There are caveats for the unforeseeable of course; the pace of change is accelerating, not slowing down. Perhaps public policy will demand specific offences to prosecute those who interfere with a self-driving car, although such activity could also fall squarely within the existing offences. Equally, it may be that debate over future prosecutions under the Act bring the lack of a 'public interest' defence under scrutiny.

CHAPTER 4A

THE RISK PRACTITIONER'S JOURNEY: RISK ALIGNED ASSURANCE AND THE THREE LINES OF DEFENCE

Farid Abdelkader

SECTION 1: AN INTRODUCTION TO RISK ALIGNED ASSURANCE AND MY JOURNEY ACROSS THE THREE LINES OF DEFENCE

4.01 As a risk practitioner, I have always been passionate about identifying, assessing, and mitigating risks that organisations face. My extensive experience of over 18 years in a top 20 Risk Management Consulting organisation and years as a Global Head of Technology Audit for a Top 4 Mutual Insurance Company have allowed me to work across all three lines of defence in various industries, with a particular focus on insurance and banking.

4.02 My journey began in the first line as a help desk and systems engineer, which provided me with invaluable hands-on experience. As I progressed, I moved to the second line as a Risk Practitioner and Virtual CISO (V-CISO), where I honed my skills in risk assessment and mitigation. Eventually, I reached the pinnacle of my career at the consulting organisation, becoming the Managing Director of Technology Risk and Global Head of the firm's Cybersecurity Audit Pillar. Now, I serve as the Global Head of Technology Audit (third line of defence) for a global Fortune 75 Insurance Organization and President of the ISACA Metropolitan New York Metropolitan Chapter.

4.03 Over the years, I have witnessed the evolution of risk management strategies and frameworks that help organisations better prepare for and respond to risks. One such framework is Risk Aligned Assurance, which is grounded in the principles of the Three Lines of Defence model. Initially introduced during the dot-com bubble burst (~2000), the Three Lines of Defence model was introduced by the Institute of Internal Auditors' (IIA) standards (2013) and has become a cornerstone of risk management practices. Its impact and relevance have also led to its widespread adoption into banking by the Office of the Comptroller of the Currency (OCC) as part of the Code of Federal Regulations (CFR) 12 Part 30. This widespread adoption impacted not just in banking, but various industries.

4.04 In this chapter, I will take you through my personal journey of Risk Aligned Assurance and its development through the Three Lines of Defence.

I will also delve into the importance of this approach across industries and explore real-life case studies that demonstrate the benefits of aligned assurance, including independence in risk coverage, comprehensive risk coverage, cost savings, and more. As we embark on this journey together, you will gain valuable insights into the world of risk management from my firsthand experiences and learn how Risk Aligned Assurance has become an essential part of modern risk management practices.

SECTION 2: THE BEGINNING – OCC'S CFR 12 PART 30, GLOBAL REGULATIONS, AND THE THREE LINES OF DEFENCE

4.05 The roots of formalised Risk Aligned Assurance can be traced back to the Three Lines of Defence model, introduced by the OCC in CFR 12 Part 30. The OCC, responsible for regulating and supervising national banks and federal savings associations in the United States, recognised the importance of a robust risk management framework, particularly in the aftermath of financial crises and increasing regulatory scrutiny.

4.06 CFR 12 Part 30, or the 'Safety and Soundness Standards' regulation, outlines guidelines and expectations for national banks and federal savings associations concerning risk management practices. It aims to ensure the safety and soundness of financial institutions and promote a more resilient financial system. The Three Lines of Defence model is central to these guidelines and has been incorporated into other global regulations and best practices, such as the Bermudian Code of Conduct for Corporate Governance (CCC), New York Department of Financial Services (NY DFS) 23 NYCRR 500, General Data Protection Regulation (GDPR), and other relevant international regulations.

4.07 The Three Lines of Defence model consists of:

1. **First Line of Defence:** Business operations and management, responsible for identifying, assessing, and managing risks within their day-to-day activities, implementing risk control measures, and ensuring compliance with policies and regulations.
2. **Second Line of Defence:** Risk management and compliance functions, tasked with providing oversight and support to the first line, developing risk management frameworks, policies, and procedures, and monitoring the effectiveness of risk controls.
3. **Third Line of Defence:** Internal audit functions, providing independent assurance on the effectiveness of risk management, internal controls, and governance processes while reporting directly to the board or audit committee to ensure objectivity and independence.

4.08 The model's simplicity and effectiveness in promoting clear roles and responsibilities for risk management made it appealing to organisations beyond the banking sector, with industries such as healthcare, manufacturing, and technology adopting it as a foundation for their risk management practices. Its widespread adoption also caught the attention of the IIA, which incorporated the model into its standards, further cementing its importance in the risk management landscape.

4.09 Global regulations and best practices, such as the Bermudian CCC, NY DFS 23 NYCRR 500, GDPR, and others, have contributed to the widespread adoption of the Three Lines of Defence model. These regulations emphasise a structured approach to managing risk across various lines of defence, including technology, privacy, and cybersecurity risks.

4.10 As organisations navigate the complexities of an increasingly interconnected and regulated world, the Three Lines of Defence model offers a structured approach to managing risk. This alignment of assurance across the three lines of defence enables organisations to be more resilient and better prepared for potential threats.

4.11 Risk Aligned Assurance has become a critical component of risk management for organisations worldwide, enabling them to better identify, assess, and mitigate risks while ensuring compliance with various global regulations. By embracing this approach and the principles of the Three Lines of Defence model, organisations can create a more robust risk management culture that supports their long-term success and resilience in the face of evolving challenges.

SECTION 3: RISK ALIGNED ASSURANCE – THE EVOLUTION OF THE THREE LINES OF DEFENCE AND THE EMERGENCE OF ALIGNED ASSURANCE

4.12 As the Three Lines of Defence model gained traction, organisations began to recognise the need for a more integrated approach to risk management. This realisation led to the development of Risk Aligned Assurance – an approach that builds upon the Three Lines of Defence model by emphasising the alignment of risk management activities across the organisation. This evolution was further reinforced by the Institute of Internal Auditors' (IIA) insights on the model, highlighting the importance of clarity, collaboration, and continuous improvement in risk management.

4.13 Risk Aligned Assurance enhances the Three Lines of Defence by:

- **Ensuring clear communication and collaboration between the three lines:** This fosters a shared understanding of risk and promotes a consistent approach to risk management across the organisation. For instance, the first line shares information about identified risks and control measures with the second line, which in turn provides oversight and guidance on risk mitigation strategies. The third line then independently evaluates the effectiveness of the risk management framework and provides feedback for improvement.

- **Encouraging the integration of risk management activities into the organisation's core processes and decision-making:** By embedding risk management into day-to-day operations, organisations can proactively address risks and improve overall performance. For example, integrating cybersecurity controls into application development processes can help prevent potential data breaches and protect sensitive information.
- **Focusing on the continuous improvement of risk management practices:** Risk Aligned Assurance encourages organisations to regularly assess and enhance their risk management processes, frameworks, and controls, ensuring they remain effective in a constantly changing risk environment. This might involve implementing new technologies, updating policies and procedures to address emerging risks, or refining risk assessment methodologies based on lessons learned.
- **Promoting a risk-aware culture:** A key aspect of Risk Aligned Assurance is cultivating a culture where all employees understand their role in managing risks and are empowered to take appropriate actions to mitigate them. For instance, organisations can invest in ongoing risk awareness training and communication initiatives and recognise and reward employees who proactively identify and address risks.

4.14 The evolution of the Three Lines of Defence model into Risk Aligned Assurance has allowed organisations to reap significant benefits from its structured approach. The alignment of risk management activities across the organisation enables more efficient and effective risk mitigation, leading to cost savings, better risk coverage, and enhanced independence in risk assessments.

4.15 Moreover, the incorporation of global regulations, such as the Bermudian Corporate Governance Code (CCC), New York Department of Financial Services (NY DFS) 23 NYCRR 500, and the General Data Protection Regulation (GDPR), into risk management frameworks has further emphasised the importance of a strong, aligned risk management structure. By adhering to the principles of Risk Aligned Assurance, organisations can better navigate the complexities of these regulations and ensure compliance while addressing various technology, privacy, and cybersecurity risks.

SECTION 4: RISK ALIGNED ASSURANCE AND ITS LEVERAGE ACROSS INDUSTRIES

4.16 While the Three Lines of Defence model and Risk Aligned Assurance originated in the banking sector, their principles have proven valuable across various industries. The need for effective risk management is universal, as all organisations face a range of risks that can impact their ability to achieve their objectives.

4.17 In the healthcare industry, for example, the alignment of risk management activities can help organisations better anticipate and address risks related to patient safety, data security, and regulatory compliance. By ensuring that all three lines of defence work together to manage these risks, healthcare providers can improve patient outcomes and reduce the likelihood of adverse events.

4.18 Similarly, manufacturing companies can benefit from Risk Aligned Assurance by identifying and managing risks related to product quality, supply chain disruptions, and workplace safety. By adopting a unified approach to risk management, manufacturers can improve the efficiency of their operations and minimise the impact of disruptions.

4.19 Technology companies, too, can leverage Risk Aligned Assurance to address risks related to cybersecurity, data privacy, and rapid technological changes. By aligning their risk management efforts, technology companies can better protect their assets and maintain their competitive edge in an increasingly digital world.

4.20 Moreover, even in industries that are not as heavily regulated, Risk Aligned Assurance has proven to be valuable. For instance, the Payment Card Industry Data Security Standard (PCI DSS) requires organisations that handle cardholder data to implement a comprehensive risk management framework. By applying the principles of Risk Aligned Assurance, organisations can ensure compliance with PCI DSS requirements while effectively managing risks associated with cardholder data security.

SECTION 5: CASE STUDIES – THE BENEFITS OF ALIGNED ASSURANCE

4.21 To fully understand the value of Risk Aligned Assurance, let's examine some case studies that demonstrate its benefits, including independence in risk coverage, comprehensive risk coverage, cost savings, and more.

> **Case Study 1: Independence in Risk Coverage – A Global Bank**
>
> A large global bank recognised the need to strengthen its risk management practices in the wake of increased regulatory scrutiny, such as Basel III standards and the Dodd-Frank Wall Street Reform and Consumer Protection Act. The bank implemented Risk Aligned Assurance, ensuring clear communication and collaboration between the three lines of defence. This alignment allowed the third line (internal audit) to maintain its independence while providing assurance on the effectiveness of risk management activities carried out by the first and second lines.
>
> As a result, the bank was able to identify gaps in its risk management processes and address them proactively, leading to a more robust risk management framework and increased confidence from regulators and stakeholders.
>
> **Case Study 2: Comprehensive Risk Coverage – A Healthcare Provider**
>
> A large healthcare provider faced numerous risks related to patient safety, data security, and regulatory compliance, such as the Health Insurance Portability and Accountability Act (HIPAA) and the European Union's General Data

Protection Regulation (GDPR). The organisation implemented Risk Aligned Assurance, focusing on aligning the three lines of defence and integrating risk management activities into its core processes.

This approach allowed the healthcare provider to have a comprehensive view of its risk landscape, enabling it to proactively identify and mitigate risks before they resulted in adverse events. The organisation was able to improve patient outcomes, reduce the likelihood of data breaches, and maintain compliance with regulatory requirements.

Case Study 3: Cost Savings – A Manufacturing Company

A manufacturing company was struggling with inefficiencies in its risk management processes, leading to duplicated efforts and increased costs. By implementing Risk Aligned Assurance, the company was able to streamline its risk management activities, ensuring that each line of defence focused on its core responsibilities and worked together to manage risks effectively, following the ISO 31000 risk management standard.

This alignment resulted in significant cost savings for the organisation, as it eliminated the need for redundant risk assessments and controls and allowed the company to allocate resources more efficiently.

Case Study 4: Improved Decision Making – A Technology Company

A technology company faced risks related to cybersecurity, data privacy, and rapid technological changes. The organisation adopted Risk Aligned Assurance to better address these risks and support informed decision-making, adhering to regulations such as the California Consumer Privacy Act (CCPA) and best practices like the NIST Cybersecurity Framework.

By aligning the three lines of defence and integrating risk management activities into the company's core processes, the technology company was able to make more informed decisions about investments in cybersecurity, data privacy initiatives, and technology development. This proactive approach to risk management allowed the company to protect its assets and maintain a competitive edge in a fast-paced, digital world.

Case Study 5: Enhanced Compliance – A Retail Organisation

A retail organisation faced challenges in complying with the Payment Card Industry Data Security Standard (PCI DSS) requirements, which aim to protect cardholder data. The organisation implemented Risk Aligned Assurance to align the three lines of defence and improve its risk management framework.

By adopting this approach, the retail organisation was able to better identify and address potential vulnerabilities in its cardholder data processing systems, ensuring compliance with PCI DSS requirements. In addition, Risk Aligned Assurance helped the organisation proactively manage risks associated with data breaches, reducing the likelihood of financial and reputational damage.

In conclusion, the principles of Risk Aligned Assurance, originating from the Three Lines of Defence model, have demonstrated their value across a variety of industries, including healthcare, manufacturing, technology, and retail. The implementation of Risk Aligned Assurance has led to significant benefits such as improved risk coverage, cost savings, and better decision-making. As organisations continue to face an increasingly complex risk environment, the adoption of Risk Aligned Assurance will likely become even more crucial in ensuring their success and resilience.

Case Study 6: Strengthened Supply Chain Management – An Automotive Company

An automotive company faced risks related to supply chain disruptions, such as supplier insolvencies and geopolitical events. The company implemented Risk Aligned Assurance to integrate the three lines of defence and strengthen its supply chain risk management framework, following best practices like the Supply Chain Operations Reference (SCOR) model.

By adopting this approach, the automotive company was able to proactively identify and mitigate supply chain risks, reducing the impact of disruptions on its operations. Furthermore, Risk Aligned Assurance enabled the company to make better-informed decisions regarding supplier selection, inventory management, and logistics planning, ultimately leading to increased operational efficiency.

Case Study 7: Enhanced Environmental, Social, and Governance (ESG) Management – An Energy Company

An energy company faced various risks related to environmental, social, and governance (ESG) factors, such as regulatory compliance, stakeholder expectations, and climate change impacts. The company implemented Risk Aligned Assurance to better manage these ESG risks, following guidelines such as the Global Reporting Initiative (GRI) and the Task Force on Climate-related Financial Disclosures (TCFD).

By aligning the three lines of defence and integrating ESG risk management activities into its core processes, the energy company was able to address potential ESG risks more effectively. This proactive approach to ESG management allowed the company to improve its sustainability performance, reduce regulatory risks, and enhance its reputation among stakeholders.

4.22 In summary, Risk Aligned Assurance has demonstrated its value in various industries and contexts, including automotive, energy, and ESG management. The implementation of Risk Aligned Assurance has resulted in tangible benefits such as strengthened supply chain management, enhanced ESG performance, and increased operational efficiency. As organisations navigate an ever-evolving risk landscape, the adoption of Risk Aligned Assurance will become increasingly important in ensuring their ongoing success and resilience.

SECTION 6: IMPLEMENTING RISK ALIGNED ASSURANCE – KEY CONSIDERATIONS AND BEST PRACTICES

4.23 Implementing Risk Aligned Assurance within an organisation requires careful planning, a commitment to fostering a risk-aware culture, and adherence to regulatory, compliance, and best practice guidelines. Here are some key considerations and best practices for organisations looking to implement this approach:

1. **Assess the current state of risk management:** Before implementing Risk Aligned Assurance, it is essential to assess the organisation's current risk management practices, identify gaps, and determine the areas that require improvement. This assessment will serve as a foundation for developing a tailored implementation plan. Utilise frameworks such as the COSO ERM or ISO 31000 to guide the assessment and establish a robust risk management foundation.

2. **Define roles and responsibilities:** Ensure that roles and responsibilities for risk management activities are clearly defined and communicated across the organisation. This clarity will help promote collaboration and coordination between the three lines of defence. Align these roles and responsibilities with regulatory requirements and industry-specific standards, such as Basel III for banks, HIPAA for healthcare providers, or GDPR for data privacy.

3. **Establish a common risk language:** To facilitate effective communication and collaboration, it is important to establish a common risk language that is understood by everyone within the organisation. This shared understanding of risk will help promote a risk-aware culture and improve the overall effectiveness of risk management activities. Adopting widely accepted risk taxonomies and frameworks, such as the FAIR methodology or NIST Cybersecurity Framework, can provide a strong foundation for a common risk language.

4. **Embed risk management into core processes:** Risk management should not be an afterthought or a separate activity. Instead, it should be embedded into the organisation's core processes and decision-making, allowing for proactive identification and management of risks. Adopt a risk-based approach to strategic planning, project management, and operational decision-making, integrating risk management best practices such as risk appetite statements, risk assessments, and risk mitigation strategies.

5. **Monitor and continuously improve risk management practices:** Implementing Risk Aligned Assurance is not a one-time event. Organisations should regularly monitor the effectiveness of their risk management practices, identify areas for improvement, and make necessary adjustments to ensure they remain effective in a constantly changing risk environment. Implement key performance indicators (KPIs) and key risk indicators (KRIs) to measure the effectiveness of risk management activities and drive continuous improvement.

6. **Foster a risk-aware culture:** Promote a culture where all employees understand their role in managing risks and are empowered to take appropriate actions to mitigate them. Provide training and awareness programs to ensure employees at all levels comprehend the organisation's risk management objectives, principles, and practices. Encourage open communication about risks and create an environment where reporting and learning from risk incidents is valued and supported.

4.24 By following these key considerations and best practices, organisations can effectively implement Risk Aligned Assurance, leading to improved risk management, increased operational efficiency, and enhanced compliance with relevant regulations and standards.

SECTION 7: MANAGING, MONITORING, AND REPORTING ON RISK ALIGNED ASSURANCE TO SENIOR MANAGEMENT AND THE BOARD OF DIRECTORS

4.25 Implementing and maintaining Risk Aligned Assurance requires clear lines of communication and accountability between risk practitioners, senior management, and the board. In this section, we'll explore the roles and responsibilities of each party, the importance of risk appetite, key metrics to monitor, and relevant best practices, regulatory requirements, and standards.

1. Roles and Responsibilities: The RACI Model

4.26 A useful way to understand the roles and responsibilities in Risk Aligned Assurance is by applying the RACI model, which stands for Responsible, Accountable, Consulted, and Informed:

- **Responsible**: Risk practitioners, such as risk managers and compliance officers, are responsible for day-to-day risk management activities, including identification, assessment, mitigation, and monitoring of risks.
- **Accountable**: Senior management is accountable for ensuring the effectiveness of the organisation's risk management practices, providing strategic direction, and making decisions based on risk information.
- **Consulted**: Subject matter experts and other stakeholders may be consulted to provide input on specific risks, controls, or mitigation strategies.
- **Informed**: The board of directors is informed about the organisation's risk profile, risk management performance, and any significant risk events or changes in the risk environment.

2. Risk Appetite

4.27 Risk appetite plays a crucial role in Risk Aligned Assurance by helping to align risk-taking activities with the organisation's strategic objectives. Senior management and the board should define the organisation's risk appetite, setting clear boundaries for acceptable levels of risk. This risk appetite should be communicated and embedded in the organisation's risk management processes, guiding decision-making and resource allocation.

3. Key Metrics

4.28 Monitoring and reporting on key metrics are essential for maintaining effective Risk Aligned Assurance. Some important metrics to track include:

- **Key Risk Indicators (KRIs):** Quantitative or qualitative measures that signal changes in risk levels, such as the number of data breaches, safety incidents, or regulatory violations.
- **Key Performance Indicators (KPIs):** Measures of the effectiveness of risk management activities, such as the percentage of risks mitigated within the defined risk appetite, or the timeliness of risk assessments and control testing.
- **Risk trends:** Analysing changes in risk levels over time can provide valuable insights into the organisation's risk environment and inform decision-making.
- **Best Practices, Regulatory Requirements, and Standards**

  Risk practitioners should ensure that Risk Aligned Assurance aligns with relevant best practices, regulatory requirements, and standards.

  Some examples include:

  - **COSO ERM and ISO 31000:** Widely recognised risk management frameworks that provide guidance on establishing and maintaining effective risk management processes.
  - **NIST Cybersecurity Framework:** A standard for managing and reducing cybersecurity risk, particularly relevant for organisations handling sensitive data.
  - **Basel III and other industry-specific regulations:** Depending on the organisation's sector, various regulatory requirements may apply to risk management practices, such as capital adequacy requirements for banks or data privacy regulations like GDPR.

4.29 Risk practitioners should regularly update senior management and the board on the organisation's risk profile, performance against risk appetite, and adherence to relevant best practices and regulations. By effectively managing, monitoring, and reporting on Risk Aligned Assurance, organisations can ensure that risk management remains a top priority, and that decision-making is informed by a comprehensive understanding of the organisation's risk landscape.

SECTION 8: THE CRUCIAL ROLE OF RISK ALIGNED ASSURANCE: THE EXECUTIVE STAKEHOLDERS, SHAREHOLDERS, AND POLICY HOLDERS LENS

4.30 Risk Aligned Assurance is a critical aspect of an organisation's risk management framework, playing a vital role in the interests of board directors, policyholders, shareholders, and senior management. These stakeholders depend on the organisation's success and resilience, making effective risk management crucial to achieving their objectives.

Board of Directors: Boards are accountable for setting the organisation's strategic direction, overseeing risk management, and ensuring compliance with regulatory requirements. The National Association of Corporate Directors (NACD) emphasises that boards should have a comprehensive understanding of the organisation's risk profile and actively participate in the risk management process (NACD, 2020). Risk Aligned Assurance offers boards increased visibility into risk management activities, ensuring that these activities align with the organisation's strategic objectives and risk appetite. This alignment promotes better decision-making and resource allocation at the highest levels of the organisation.

Policyholders: Policyholders, such as insurance clients or customers of financial institutions, rely on organisations to manage risk effectively to protect their investments and ensure the organisation's long-term stability. McKinsey & Company's research (2018) reveals that organisations with robust risk management capabilities demonstrate better financial performance and a reduced probability of experiencing a significant risk event. By implementing Risk Aligned Assurance, organisations can assure policyholders of their proactive risk management approach and commitment to increasing resilience, ultimately leading to increased customer trust and satisfaction.

Shareholders: Shareholders focus on the organisation's financial performance and long-term stability. A study by the Economist Intelligence Unit (EIU, 2015) found that 76% of surveyed executives believe that effective risk management positively impacts long-term shareholder value. Risk Aligned Assurance supports shareholder value by fostering proactive risk management, reducing the likelihood of significant risk events, and cultivating a risk-aware culture within the organisation. This risk-focused culture can translate into better financial results and more sustainable growth, ultimately benefiting shareholders.

Senior Management: Senior management is responsible for executing the organisation's strategy and managing its day-to-day operations. Effective risk management is essential for senior management to make informed decisions, allocate resources efficiently, and maintain a competitive advantage in the market. A study by PwC (2019) discovered that organisations with strong risk management practices had a 36% higher return on equity compared to their peers. Risk Aligned Assurance supports senior management in achieving these results by providing a comprehensive view of the organisation's risk landscape and enabling more effective risk management practices, leading to better decision-making and improved overall performance.

4.31 High-profile case studies, such as the collapses of Enron, Bear Stearns, and WorldCom, underscore the importance of robust risk management practices and the severe consequences when they are lacking. These organisations experienced massive losses and reputational damage due to inadequate risk management and governance. These examples highlight the critical role of Risk Aligned Assurance in promoting a risk-aware culture and protecting stakeholder interests.

4.32 Risk Aligned Assurance is essential for board directors, policyholders, shareholders, and senior management as it promotes more effective risk management practices, enhances the organisation's resilience, and supports long-term value creation. By adopting Risk Aligned Assurance, organisations can demonstrate their commitment to proactive risk management and secure the trust of these vital stakeholders, contributing to their long-term success and sustainability.

SECTION 9: THE FUTURE OF RISK ALIGNED ASSURANCE

4.33 As the world becomes more complex and interconnected, the importance of effective risk management grows. Organisations must adapt and evolve their risk management practices addressing emerging risks and shifting business landscapes. In this context, Risk Aligned Assurance will play a critical role in helping organisations achieve their objectives while mitigating risks.

4.34 Several trends are expected to shape the future of Risk Aligned Assurance, aligning with the best practices and forecasts of organisations such as the Institute of Internal Auditors (IIA), ISACA, and other relevant accounting and risk organisations:

Emphasis on resilience: Organisations must focus on building resilience to withstand shocks, disruptions, and adapt in the face of change. Risk Aligned Assurance, supported by IIA's guidance on resilience, will play a crucial role in identifying vulnerabilities and building the necessary resilience to manage emerging risks.

Integration of technology: As organisations increasingly rely on technology and data for decision-making, Risk Aligned Assurance must leverage these tools to enhance risk management practices. ISACA's COBIT framework promotes the use of advanced analytics, artificial intelligence, and machine learning to better understand the risk landscape, predict emerging risks, and optimise risk management activities.

Focus on sustainability and environmental, social, and governance (ESG) risks: With ESG risks becoming increasingly important, Risk Aligned Assurance must evolve to address these challenges. Organisations must ensure that their risk management frameworks and processes, as recommended by the IIA and other organisations, effectively identify, assess, and manage ESG risks.

Collaboration and information sharing: The interconnected nature of risks demands greater collaboration and information sharing between different lines of defence and external stakeholders, such as regulators, industry peers, and supply chain partners. Risk Aligned Assurance, in line with IIA and ISACA recommendations, will promote this collaboration and sharing.

Strengthening risk culture: As the risk landscape evolves, organisations must invest in strengthening their risk culture. Risk Aligned Assurance will play a key role in fostering a risk-aware culture and driving risk management maturity across the organisation, as emphasised by both IIA and ISACA.

4.35 Risk Aligned Assurance will remain an essential component of organisations' risk management strategies, adapting to the ever-changing risk landscape and supporting the achievement of strategic objectives. As a risk practitioner, it is important to stay informed about these trends and ensure that your organisation's risk management practices remain robust, effective, and aligned with the evolving business environment, guided by the best practices of the IIA, ISACA, and other relevant organisations.

SECTION 10: ESSENTIAL SKILLS FOR RISK PRACTITIONERS IN THE ERA OF RISK ALIGNED ASSURANCE

4.36 In the era of Risk Aligned Assurance, risk practitioners must adapt and develop their skills to remain effective.

4.37 Essential skills for risk practitioners include:

Analytical and critical thinking: Risk practitioners must analyse complex information, identify patterns, and make informed decisions. Critical thinking skills enable them to evaluate risk scenarios and develop appropriate strategies. Certifications like CRISC (Certified in Risk and Information Systems Control) can help build these skills.

Technological competency: Risk practitioners should be proficient in using technological tools, such as data analytics, artificial intelligence, and machine learning. Technological competency enhances risk management activities and helps identify emerging risks. Certifications like ISACA's CISA (Certified Information Systems Auditor) can enhance technological understanding.

Communication and collaboration: Effective communication and collaboration promote a risk-aware culture and ensure the three lines of defence work together effectively. Risk practitioners must convey risk-related information to stakeholders and collaborate to develop risk management strategies.

Adaptability and learning agility: Risk practitioners must adapt and learn quickly in a constantly changing risk landscape. Learning agility keeps practitioners current with industry trends, emerging risks, and risk management best practices. Continuous professional development and attending industry conferences can facilitate adaptability.

ESG and sustainability expertise: As ESG risks become increasingly important, risk practitioners must develop expertise in this area to effectively manage these risks. This expertise helps organisations integrate ESG considerations into their risk management frameworks and decision-making processes.

Leadership and influence: Risk practitioners must lead and influence others to promote a risk-aware culture and drive the adoption of Risk Aligned Assurance. This skill requires inspiring, motivating, and guiding others in managing risks effectively.

4.38 By developing these essential skills and acquiring relevant certifications and education, risk practitioners can better support their organisations in implementing Risk Aligned Assurance and navigating the complex risk landscape.

SECTION 11: EPILOGUE – THE ONGOING JOURNEY OF RISK ALIGNED ASSURANCE AND THE ROLE OF PROFESSIONAL ASSOCIATIONS AND STANDARD-SETTING BODIES

4.39 The continuous journey of Risk Aligned Assurance requires organisations and risk practitioners to adapt and evolve in response to the ever-changing risk landscape. Embracing the principles of Risk Aligned Assurance and fostering a risk-aware culture is essential for risk practitioners to effectively support their organisations in achieving strategic objectives.

4.40 Professional associations and standard-setting bodies play a critical role in the development and adoption of Risk Aligned Assurance. These organisations provide guidance, best practices, and resources to help risk practitioners implement effective risk management frameworks, such as the Three Lines of Defence model and Risk Aligned Assurance.

4.41 Key organisations in the field of risk management include:

The Institute of Internal Auditors (IIA): Provides standards for the internal audit profession, resources, guidance, and certifications for internal auditors to enhance their skills and contribute to risk management activities.

The Committee of Sponsoring Organizations of the Treadway Commission (COSO): Offers thought leadership and guidance on enterprise risk management, internal control, and fraud deterrence. COSO's ERM framework is widely used for developing effective risk management practices.

The International Organization for Standardization (ISO): Develops and publishes international standards, including the widely used ISO 31000 standard on risk management, which offers principles and guidelines for organisations to implement effective risk management practices.

The Global Risk Management Institute (GRMI): Offers the Certified in Risk Management Assurance (CRMA) designation and provides resources, guidance, and professional development opportunities for risk practitioners.

4.42 Risk practitioners should engage with these organisations to stay informed, enhance their skills, and contribute to the ongoing development of risk management practices. Joining professional associations, attending industry events and conferences, and pursuing certifications can help practitioners stay current with industry trends and best practices, ensuring their organisations' risk management practices remain effective in an ever-changing risk landscape.

4.43 Risk Aligned Assurance adoption across industries is influenced by professional associations and standard-setting bodies. Risk practitioners must stay connected with these organisations to support their organisations' risk management efforts and contribute to the continuous evolution of risk management practices.

SECTION 12: TRUST, COLLABORATION, TEAMING, AND TRANSPARENCY IN RISK ALIGNED ASSURANCE

4.44 Trust, collaboration, teaming, and transparency are essential components of an effective Risk Aligned Assurance structure. These elements are critical in fostering a strong risk culture and ensuring that the three lines of defence work together seamlessly to manage risks and protect the organisation.

4.45 When one or more of these elements are missing, organisations may face a range of issues, such as poor communication, ineffective risk management, and ultimately, the potential for catastrophic failures. Several high-profile cases highlight the consequences of a lack of trust, collaboration, or transparency:

1. **Enron**: The collapse of Enron in 2001 was driven by a combination of poor corporate governance, weak internal controls, and a lack of transparency in financial reporting. The company's complex financial structures and fraudulent accounting practices went undetected, ultimately leading to one of the largest corporate bankruptcies in history.
2. **Bear Stearns**: The failure of Bear Stearns in 2008 was due in part to inadequate risk management and a lack of collaboration among key stakeholders. The investment bank's overexposure to mortgage-backed securities and high leverage contributed to its collapse during the financial crisis.
3. **WorldCom**: The WorldCom accounting scandal in 2002 was the result of a lack of transparency and trust within the organisation. The company's top executives manipulated financial records to hide massive losses, eventually leading to bankruptcy and severe reputational damage.

4.46 In these cases, the absence of trust, collaboration, teaming, and transparency resulted in significant organisational failures. As risk practitioners, it's crucial to recognise the importance of these elements in creating a robust Risk Aligned Assurance structure.

4.47 It's essential to have the courage to engage in difficult discussions about risk, keeping the organisation's best interests at heart. These conversations might involve challenging assumptions, addressing potential conflicts of interest, or discussing unpopular risk mitigation strategies. However, fostering an open and transparent environment where stakeholders can engage in honest dialogue about risk is vital for the long-term success of the organisation.

4.48 Trust, collaboration, teaming, and transparency are indispensable components of a robust Risk Aligned Assurance structure. By prioritising these elements, organisations can develop effective risk management practices, learn from past failures, and ensure their resilience and success in an increasingly complex risk environment.

SECTION 13: CONCLUSION – EMBRACING THE FUTURE OF RISK ALIGNED ASSURANCE

4.49 Throughout this chapter, we have explored the concept of Risk Aligned Assurance and its importance in today's complex risk landscape. As we have seen, Risk Aligned Assurance is a powerful tool that enables organisations to manage risks proactively and effectively, ensuring resilience and success in an ever-changing business environment.

4.50 In summary, we have discussed:

1. The Three Lines of Defence model and its evolution to a more collaborative, integrated approach through Risk Aligned Assurance.
2. The importance of aligning risk management with strategic objectives and risk appetite.
3. The role of senior management and the board in overseeing Risk Aligned Assurance and fostering a risk-aware culture.
4. The key take aways of Risk Aligned Assurance through the lens of board directors, policyholders, shareholders, and senior management.
5. The future of Risk Aligned Assurance and its implications for risk practitioners, including the need to develop essential skills and embrace emerging trends.
6. The importance of trust, collaboration, teaming, and transparency in a robust Risk Aligned Assurance structure.

4.51 As risk practitioners, we must recognise that Risk Aligned Assurance is not merely a passing trend but a critical approach to risk management that is increasingly becoming a focal point for board directors and stakeholders. It is essential for organisations to embrace this approach or risk being left behind, facing potential regulatory action or negative consequences from policyholders and stockholders.

4.52 In closing, we encourage risk practitioners and organisations alike to consider the following key points when implementing Risk Aligned Assurance:

1. Develop a strong risk culture and ensure that risk management is aligned with strategic objectives and risk appetite.
2. Foster collaboration, trust, and transparency among the three lines of defence and throughout the organisation.
3. Continuously assess and enhance risk management practices, frameworks, and controls.
4. Stay current with industry trends, best practices, and guidance from professional associations and standard-setting bodies.
5. Invest in ongoing professional development for risk practitioners, including certifications, education, and training.

4.53 By embracing Risk Aligned Assurance and implementing its principles effectively, organisations can navigate the complexities of today's risk environment, protect their interests, and achieve their strategic objectives. As risk practitioners, we play a crucial role in this process and must continue to learn, adapt, and evolve to support our organisations in managing risks effectively and ensuring a resilient and successful future.

CHAPTER 4B

DEFEND BY NATIONAL CYBER SECURITY CENTRE

NCSC RESEARCH PROBLEM BOOK – HOW TO DEFEND

The NCSC research problem book

4.54 The most significant problems which the NCSC believes are in need of concerted and significant collaborative effort from multiple and diverse disciplines over the next decade.

Introducing the problem book

4.55 Cyber security is hard and it's unlikely to get easier over the next decade. The NCSC views research as the way we can meet our greatest cyber security challenges in the long term. The UK National Cyber Strategy 2022 asks the NCSC to provide leadership to find the solutions to these challenges. To this end, we have built a research 'problem book'.

4.56 Our aim is to guide cyber security research towards the most critical security challenges that we have identified as significant barriers to improving cyber security. The problem book starts by setting out the most significant 'cross-cutting' problems, where multiple and diverse disciplines need to collaborate to tackle the overarching problem. The newest problem book chapter covers hardware security. In future, we will add further chapters to the book which will cover other specific cyber disciplines, such as socio-technical or cyber physical.

4.57 The research book is intentionally not an exhaustive list of problems, but instead a set of focus points that we judge require coordinated and significant efforts over the next decade.

WHO IS IT FOR?

4.58 The problem book is primarily intended for academia, but it may also be useful to private sector companies carrying out research or identifying innovation gaps.

HOW SHOULD IT BE USED?

4.59 As outlined, the book describes the problems we believe need significant research activity over the next five to ten years. We have suggested some research strands of our own under the 'sub-problems' but also hope they will inspire you to think of your own research projects to help solve the overarching problems described.

4.60 For each problem, you will find:

a description of the problem;

the NCSC's view on some of the sub-problems within it, for specialist disciplines to work through;

a statement from an NCSC expert explaining why this problem is a priority.

THE CHAPTERS

The cross-cutting problems

4.61 The five cross-cutting problems span different disciplines and areas, looking at big questions like: how can we make phishing a thing of the past? How can we speed up the take-up of better security measures in OT? And the really hard question of how can we build systems we trust when there is a complex chain of individual components within them? Visit the cross-cutting problems chapter.

The hardware security problems

4.62 Processors and microelectronics are now such a common feature of everyday devices that how they behave is foundational to every aspect of our digital lives. This makes it crucial to understand the impact they have on the security of a wider system. This chapter sets out four problem areas that we think will benefit from increased focus. They build up from the physical properties of an electronic device, through designing devices with security in mind, up to integrating these devices into wider systems. Visit the hardware security chapter his section contains the five cross-cutting problems that span different disciplines and areas and looks at big questions.

Cross Cutting Problems

4.63

1. How can we build systems we can trust when we can't trust any of the individual components within them?

   An important question to address diminishing confidence in security of supply chains.

2. How do we make system security assessments more data driven?

   To help turn the art of security architecture review into a science.

3. How do we create and adopt meaningful measures of cyber security?

   To enable countries and organisations to make better decisions about which security initiatives will have the best return on investment.

4. How do we make phishing a thing of the past?

   To make phishing an ineffective infection vector for cyber attacks.

5. How can we accelerate the adoption of modern security mitigations into Operational Technology (OT)?

   To help the inherent security of OT catch up, or even overtake, IT.

6. How can we build systems we can trust when we can't trust any of the individual components within them?

4.64 Hardware is becoming more complex all the time and it's difficult to gain confidence in long global supply chains. This in turn means diminished confidence in individual computers, circuit boards and microchips. But to protect our critical national infrastructure (CNI), defence and intelligence systems and more besides, we need to build computer systems we can rely on.

4.65 Addressing this problem requires a combination of techniques that touch on many different aspects of cyber security, technology and risk.

Strands or sub-problems

Compute foundations

4.66 Researchers need to build a deep understanding of the security properties and trustworthiness of components at the hardware/firmware level and use it to identify or design 'safe places to stand' – that is, to run code or carry out a cryptographic function, with high confidence in its integrity. Are there certain compute element architectures in which we could have higher confidence? Are there new ways to gain confidence in the integrity of integrated circuits, both in design and manufacture? And for new classes of compute elements, such as artificial intelligence co-processors, how can we have equivalent or better forms of separation between tenants if we want to allow multiple users to share a single chip?

Security architecture

4.67 Using system security architectures to address the diminishing trust in underlying component supply chains, can we design system architecture patterns that are resilient to high degrees of failure or a high percentage of hostile components, while still functioning as an overall system with high integrity? Or can we design a system with high levels of redundancy and then seek to automatically detect and eradicate components that appear to be operating outside of the expected behaviour? Is it possible to build such architectures cost efficiently? Other research in this area could explore the concept of 'anti-fragility' and how it applies to system architecture design.

Security engineering

4.68 Through new engineering practices, standards, tools, languages, and architectures, can we find new ways to eliminate entire classes of vulnerabilities from software supply chains? CHERI2 and Rust are great examples of new developments that, if widely adopted, could eliminate classes of memory corruption vulnerabilities. So what equivalent innovations could eliminate other classes of vulnerability? If we apply security engineering in a different way, to improve how we understand the software that forms part of an overall computer system, can we also help solve the overarching problem by reducing complexity and increasing confidence in its quality and integrity?

Cryptography

4.69 Can we explore how cryptographic techniques, such as multi-party computation, can help design system security architectures that are tolerant to a level of component compromise?

Monitoring

4.70 Supporting the security architecture strand, can we explore whether there are new techniques which could detect compromised individual components or supply chains within an overall system architecture, or improve accuracy in existing techniques?

4.71 Why this is important

> 'Today's commodity hardware has a complex supply chain. A CPU that is 'designed in the UK' can incorporate IP from multiple sources in different countries. It could be manufactured in Taiwan, packaged somewhere else and assembled onto a server motherboard in yet another location, along with many other complex components. The motherboard may end up in a server installed in a rack in a shared data centre, operated by a managed services provider. It will then have software installed with a similarly complex supply chain of code from individuals and organisations.
>
> Gaining independent confidence that the result doesn't contain anything malicious is infeasible, and at the moment risk owners need to trust that manufacturers are managing supply chain security well. Top-tier threat actors have identified the complexity of supply chains as a prime attack vector for gaining access to high-value customers, and we need to counter the successes they're having. This research challenge directly addresses our ongoing ability to build resilient systems in future.'
>
> Paul W, NCSC Head of Technology Resilience

HOW DO WE MAKE SYSTEM SECURITY ASSESSMENTS MORE DATA DRIVEN?

4.72 Along with many private sector consultancy companies, the NCSC offers security architecture reviews as a service, by highlighting flaws in system designs so they can be corrected. The NCSC has a small number of highly skilled and experienced security architects who make professional judgements about whether a system design is secure enough to protect against certain threats. The demand for these architects will always be greater than their capacity. Another problem is that as threat-actor tradecraft is always evolving, it's not possible to have in-depth and current knowledge of all threats. So unless we evolve the approach, mistakes will be inevitable, and systems that could have been defended will be breached.

4.73 We need to apply more rigour to the approach to system security assessments, to improve efficacy and repeatability, while also enabling a larger workforce. We also need to be able to apply knowledge of threat actor tradecraft to guide these security assessments, or perhaps even automatically validate designs as being secure against known threats.

Strands or sub-problems

Data science and modelling

4.74 It's important that we can map system architectures, component properties and security mitigations in a way that is suitable for automated reasoning. We also need to validate if any given system can defend against threat actor TTPs (tactics, techniques and procedures). We need research and analysis on modelling techniques for this problem, along with real-world examples of their application.

Product assurance

4.75 Security products are designed to mitigate certain risks, but which ones do they mitigate, and how well? A codified model here would be another vital component necessary for automated reasoning on overall system security where multiple security products are in use. As well as security products, we also need to consider the security properties of other products or components when securing a wider system: how can we better understand the provenance and supply chains that make up the hardware and software bills of materials for a component in the architecture, and how that affects the confidence we can have in that component?

Socio-technical factors

4.76 People using or operating the system also pose or mitigate risks, and it's important to factor this into a model for system security – how can these risks be codified?

Security architecture

4.77 This sub-strand is about modelling architectural mitigations rather than security products or configurations: for example, an architecture with more independent layers of defence. This area is also a logical place to be able to apply the above models to consider the different mitigation options – what are the practical tools and assessment methodologies needed to do that?

Measuring software security quality

4.78 This is about developing a taxonomy and objective measures for how difficult it's likely to be for security researchers to find vulnerabilities in any given software project, to inform the level of confidence we then have when that software is present in a system architecture. In other words, lack of knowledge of specific vulnerabilities shouldn't be taken as a clean bill of health, as it may just be that no one has looked for vulnerabilities yet. So can we come up with an objective measure of how easy it might be to find vulnerabilities?

Attack simulation

4.79 Breach or attack simulation tools are another method to gain evidence of resilience to defend against an attack. How can we make tooling representative of real-world threat actors and their TTPs?

Risk

4.80 Finally, there is a need to bring together all of these strands to support a system owner's risk decision about whether the defences in place are sufficient. How can we help a system owner make that decision confidently? And how can this more data-driven approach combine with other risk assessment approaches such as system theoretic process analysis (STPA)?

4.81 Why this is important

> 'As one of the people responsible for defending the NCSC's own technology from cyber attacks, I grapple with making decisions that balance security, usability and cost. Much of this decision hinges on my own judgement and the advice from security advisors, as there is little good-quality data about whether the security mitigations in place on a given system are sufficient to defend against current threats. This research challenge represents the best chance we have to move security assessments from an art to science, helping people like me make more confident decisions that the defences in place are sufficient. Ideally, I'd have data and tooling telling me automatically when we need to take some action because threat actor tradecraft has changed, and my particular systems are now at risk.'
>
> Carolyn A, Chief Engineer, NCSC

HOW DO WE CREATE AND ADOPT MEANINGFUL MEASURES OF CYBER SECURITY?

4.82 Governments around the world are publishing their cyber security strategies, starting new initiatives to improve the cyber security of their citizens and businesses, or to minimise the harm in the wake of incidents. But as an industry, we have no means of measuring success or comparing results. Is the UK National Cyber Strategy living up to its objective to make the UK 'the safest place to work and do business online' – or is another country's cyber security strategy somewhere else making more of a difference?

4.83 Whether focussing at the country scale, or within an individual organisation, we can't understand which investments in cyber security will make the biggest difference without a meaningful set of metrics and measurements.

Strands or sub-problems

Modelling

4.84 This involves defining meaningful taxonomies and measures of vulnerability, threat, impact and risk that can be applied to a single organisation, an individual sector or a whole country. Would models like those used in healthcare measuring population health also be suitable for cyber security? And if so, what are the right indicators to be measuring?

Data science

4.85 This is important to define the methodologies for applying these models and running experiments to measure impact of cyber security interventions or policies. What are the ethical considerations and best approaches for running these experiments?

Socio-technical security

4.86 This incorporates the human element in measuring security, as well as making sure the measures in decision making are understandable and actionable.

Data and tooling

4.87 Collecting and analysing the data needed to make comparative assessments of sectors or countries over time is a crucial step. Is there a simple but meaningful way for individual organisations to measure their own cyber security by applying the research from the other strands?

4.88 Why this is important

> 'A couple of years ago, we started wrestling with the problem of whether the UK is getting more or less secure in cyber space. As my area of expertise

is vulnerabilities, I've focused on trying to understand this aspect of the problem – what do we mean by vulnerability, and how can we meaningfully measure it at country scale? In exploring this problem, we've identified some parallels with how population health is measured at country scale, using a set of domains and indicators, and we're looking at how we could apply this to cyber security. We think our results so far are promising, but we'd be keen to see much more research happening here across the community and internationally.'

Rob T, NCSC Technical Director for Vulnerability Research

HOW DO WE MAKE PHISHING A THING OF THE PAST?

4.89 For years, cyber security practitioners have been asking users to try and spot phishing emails and to not 'click the link' or open an attachment. But we know that with enough research, or a large enough sample size, an attacker will always succeed in tricking the user. This is not the user's fault – we shouldn't expect a user to be able to detect a suspicious message when a computer can't. We need to reduce the burden on users and make computers do the heavy lifting.

Strands or sub-problems

Keep phishing away from users

4.90 Although open messaging systems like email and SMS support innovation, interoperability and competition, they're also open to abuse. Developing new mitigations for open systems would result in fewer malicious messages reaching users. This could include reputation-scoring different properties in messages, and mechanisms to transfer intelligence between service providers. What other techniques can we develop to automatically detect malicious messages, so the user doesn't have to?

Mitigating successful phishing

4.91 Adopting technologies and standards like FIDO2, which enable authentication without using passwords should reduce phishing to steal credentials, but take-up of these new technologies is slow, so how can we accelerate and broaden this? For other types of phishing (to collect payment or financial details, for example), what equivalent approaches could be adopted? And more broadly, how can we make web browsers better at spotting when legitimate brands are impersonated, so we can better protect users?

User experience design

4.92 This strand relates to research in user interface design to understand which designs help users make better security decisions when they are about to take a significant risk. Is there scope for standardisation in this space to support users working across different applications, services or devices?

Security architecture

4.93 This is about developing infrastructure and application security patterns that assume users will be tricked, to limit the further impact of a breach. What are the effective mechanisms to do this and the operational impacts? What architectural patterns should organisations adopt to confidently mitigate the risk?

Mitigating misuse of technology advances

4.94 It's important that we understand the next generation of phishing attacks and that our current mitigation methodologies still apply. For example, how do we automatically detect AI-generated phishing emails or the use of 'deep fakes' in social engineering attacks? How do we develop new methodologies where current ones fail?

4.95 Why this is important

> 'Although phishing has been around for a long time, it's still one of the primary vectors used by threat actors of all capability levels. Users are either tricked into disclosing sensitive information, clicking a link, or opening an attachment, which then results in their device being exploited, and gives the attacker a foothold to build from. Even the savviest users can be duped by well-crafted phishing emails, which is why we need much more work to address this problem and make phishing a thing of the past.'
>
> Harry W, NCSC Technical Director for Incident Management

HOW CAN WE ACCELERATE THE ADOPTION OF MODERN SECURITY MITIGATIONS INTO OPERATIONAL TECHNOLOGY?

4.96 Operational Technology (OT), such as the Industrial Control Systems (ICS) that operate factories, smart cities, and our energy infrastructure, often lacks many of the security controls and mitigations that we take for granted in Information Technology (IT). This means that if threat actors manage to reach OT systems, they may then be able to use relatively simple techniques to have a physical real-world impact. Research in the areas below could contribute to significantly improvingthe security of OT systems.

Strands or sub-problems

Security architecture

4.97 There are security architecture interventions that could reduce the risk to OT, such as developing templates for risk reduction to help manage the hazard of living with legacy or known vulnerable equipment. Another area to explore is how we can use cross-domain solutions or software-defined networking to provide stronger separation between IT and OT systems. This would allow visibility of data/management information from the OT environment to be accessible to business users, without undermining security. Proven examples of architectures that reduce the risk to OT environments, as well as templates to aid adoption of good practices, would also be welcome additions to support improvements in this area.

Platform security

4.98 Modern IT systems have many security controls (such as authentication or access control) and exploit mitigations that are rarely found in OT. Even when security controls exist, they are missing exploit mitigations like data execution prevention (DEP) and address space layout randomisation (ASLR), that make it harder to turn software vulnerabilities into working exploits, meaning security controls are easier to bypass when vulnerabilities are found. Beyond the software, hardware-based mitigations like Secure Boot, which we also take for granted in modern end-user computing devices, are also rarely found in OT. Widespread take-up of hardware-backed security controls would help improve confidence in supply chain integrity, and more generally support the detection of tampering. How can we speed up the take-up of all of these modern security controls and exploit mitigations? How can we accelerate the removal of vulnerable legacy systems, or better protect them from harm?

Incentives

4.99 How can we incentivise vendors and operators to rapidly improve the security of OT? How can customers better assess the security properties of what they are buying and be influenced to choose more secure products and systems?

Operational security

4.100 It isn't common for OT environments to undergo the active security testing of IT environments. One reason often given is that OT equipment may be disrupted by common vulnerability scanning or penetration testing tools. Testing is instead carried out on reference environments, which may not always mirror production environments. Are the resilience concerns that prevent security testing of OT systems valid? If they are, how can we rapidly reach a position where they're not, so that operational security testing can become the norm? And if they're not valid, how do we quickly dispel this myth? Also, are there other options to explore for gaining assurance in OT environments?

4.101 Why this is important

> 'Although there has been a heightened focus on OT cyber security in the past decade, many modern OT components and systems still don't include even baseline security features and capabilities. And those which do rarely have these features enabled by default. Our understanding of vulnerability

and risk in these environments is rarely informed by testing to actually evidence the effectiveness of controls, and to gain confidence in overall security architecture. All of this often results in an illusion of security, where security capability is claimed, but not enabled, and the true vulnerability of a given system or architecture isn't accurately understood or reflected in the end approach to managing risk.'

Ben R, NCSC Technical Director for Cyber-Physical Systems

'Modern mobile phone handsets have more technology to ensure the integrity of the system and data than the current or near-future operational technology that we rely on to provide essential services such as power and water. To date we have only scratched the surface of why this position persists and how we might remedy it.'

Mat P, NCSC CTO for Private Sector Critical National Infrastructure

Introducing the hardware security problems

4.102 Processors and microelectronics are now such a common feature of everyday devices that how they behave is foundational to every aspect of our digital lives. This makes it crucial to understand the impact they have on the security of a wider system. This chapter in the problem book sets out to inspire the wider research community and highlight the areas where we think further research can make the most difference.

4.103 These problems are hard, and each one encompasses specific research questions, with a common thread of physical hardware. They are closely linked to most of the cross-cutting problems described in the cross-cutting chapter, but with a particular focus on the hardware angle.

4.104 We have identified the following four problems and justifications:

1 How do our devices physically behave, and how do we secure those behaviours?

To address physical attacks, and to establish the behaviour on which the rest of the system builds.

2 How do we know that we can trust our devices?

It's important to understand the amount of trust we have in a device, and the limits of that trust.

3 What device architectures help us to improve security further up the stack?

To build devices that meet our security goals by design.

4 How do we integrate secure devices, to ensure that the security still holds at the system level?

To make it easy to build a secure system without needing to be an expert in every device used.

4.105 *Defend by National Cyber Security Centre*

WHAT DO WE MEAN BY HARDWARE SECURITY?

4.105 It can be difficult to define hardware security. It's not always clear what the term 'hardware' includes, and so this follows through when it comes to its security. In cyber security, 'hardware' is commonly paired with 'embedded systems' or 'firmware'.

4.106 In the context of the problem book, when we say hardware, we mean everything physical that contributes to a computing end product. This includes everything from semiconductor physics up to the design and use of a multi-core processor. We also include the nuances of how software interacts with hardware – whether this is an interface definition, a configurable behaviour such as microcode, or low-level firmware like bootloaders and management engines.

4.107 This might seem like a slightly strange definition, since we're saying that 'hardware' actually includes some software. But this is important because 'software' here only makes sense in the context of the specific hardware, and it ensures that security in the hardware-software interface is properly considered.

4.108 To help consistency and clarity, we provide definitions below for some of the key words that appear frequently in this chapter:

> Device – a single entity that provides a specific function within a system. In most contexts this refers to a single integrated circuit, such as a central processing unit (CPU), graphics processing unit (GPU), or memory chip. This might be in the form of a microchip, or could be a chiplet within a multi-die package.
>
> System – a set of devices working together as part of a wider computing platform. This could be a PC, mobile, gateway, radio or other custom platform.
>
> Architecture – in this chapter we talk about both device architectures and system architectures.

4.109 Device architectures describe the way functional blocks within a device are logically laid down and connected together. These might include a multi-core CPU, the compute units in a GPU, or the digital blocks instantiated on a field programmable gate array (FPGA).

4.110 System architectures describe how these devices are connected, what function each device performs, what interfaces/protocols are used, and how the full system is built up.

4.111 How do our devices physically behave, and how do we monitor and secure those behaviours?

4.112 The physical behaviour of semiconductors and other materials leads to several classes of vulnerabilities and attacks. This problem focuses thinking on these attacks, and how to mitigate them. Most of these vulnerabilities are only a concern if an attacker is 'hands on' in a lab, but as an example, rowhammer demonstrated how the physical behaviour of a device (in this case DRAM) could be exploited remotely.

4.113 While these threats are out of scope for many systems, the NCSC is responsible for the security of some of the country's most sensitive systems, in which an adversary may attempt to exploit these types of vulnerabilities. There is already considerable research underway in the field, but there are some areas where we see value in more focused work.

Strands or sub-problems

Practical vulnerabilities and protections

4.114 There is a big difference between an attack that is possible, and one that is practical. Research into attacks will be more valuable if it includes an explanation of how practical the attack is. Similarly, understanding the protections that make an attack hard in practice is of more value than designing a perfect mitigation.

Resilient hardware security primitives

4.115 There is a lot of ongoing research into hardware security primitives such as physically unclonable functions (PUFs) and random number generators (RNGs). But many of these designs are missing evidence of long-term reliability and their resilience to faults and attacks. Practical evidence of this would be of significant value to help decide when it's appropriate to use them in a system.

Anti-tamper

4.116 In the face of physical attacks, we want to make it harder for an adversary to gain access to a sensitive device in the first place, and to ensure there is no sensitive data left in the system if they do manage to reach the device. We think of this through three lenses: resistance (making it hard to do), detection (making sure we know it's happening), and response (taking action to protect the system and/or data, and to recover if possible). A complete approach would therefore encompass both powered and unpowered anti-tamper solutions, so we're interested in novel approaches to designing and incorporating these solutions.

4.117 Why this is important

> 'Devices used in the most sensitive systems, including communications platforms for defence, intelligence and critical national infrastructure, need to be resistant to attack from our most sophisticated adversaries. A threat scenario might be an adversary getting access to a device and passing it for analysis to a well-equipped lab of highly capable experts. If this enables access to sensitive data held in the device or within the wider system, such

as long-term cryptographic keys, a compromise could be highly damaging to national security.'

Jeremy B, Principal Technical Director for Cryptography and High Threat Technologies, NCSC

HOW DO WE KNOW THAT WE CAN TRUST OUR DEVICES?

4.118 In the cross-cutting problems chapter we ask: How can we build systems we can trust when we can't trust any of the individual components within them? This problem requires an understanding of what trust we have in the hardware devices in a system, and what the limits of that trust are. With increasingly complex devices, more interconnection and global supply chains, this is becoming harder.

4.119 Much of this isn't specific to hardware, but the application to hardware provides some specific challenges that, if addressed, would help us understand the risk we take when we use a given product.

Strands or sub-problems

Mapping the supply chain

4.120 As a product manufacturer, I might know who designed the chip I have bought, but what about any third-party design IP used? Has the supplier of that IP also bought in further IP? To place more trust in a device, we need to know the full tree of IP in a device: an IP bill of materials (IPBoM). Equally, with manufacturing, packaging, and distribution covering multiple continents, it's valuable to understand the manufacturing chain. Putting these two elements together leads us to ask: how can we improve transparency in the semiconductor supply chain?

Assuring devices

4.121 This sub-problem is easy to describe, but incredibly hard to solve. How can I know a device does exactly what it says it does, nothing more and nothing less? Reducing risk in this space needs improvements to scalability in verification and inspection, whether that's manual, automated, or formal. For example, how does a developer measure and demonstrate the verification they have carried out? How can we use inspection or alternative methods to detect post-verification changes? Current state-of-the-art verification and inspection techniques are often expensive, and either not scalable, or they're invasive and destructive, or both, so there are many routes to improve the situation.

Demonstrating trust

4.122 As we start to develop our understanding of the supply chain and gain improved assurance, we need mechanisms to demonstrate the trust you can have in a device, which includes understanding the current state of the device. This would include, but also expand on, existing attestation techniques and could also consider mechanisms to automate key generation and enrolment. Availability of information about the levels of verification and assurance a device has, and its IPBoM, will help product developers make informed decisions about what they include in their products.

4.123 Why this is important

> 'It's not currently feasible to gain confidence that a device you haven't designed and manufactured yourself doesn't contain anything malicious, and meets your own standards of testing and verification. This means that a product manufacturer can't truly trust in the devices they include in their systems. But if we can improve our understanding and demonstrate the security and trust you get from any given device, we can begin to mitigate supply chain risks. This directly feeds into how we build trusted and resilient systems, for both commodity and high-assurance uses.'
>
> Máire O'Neill, Professor of Information Security, Queen's University Belfast

WHICH DEVICE ARCHITECTURES HELP US IMPROVE SECURITY FURTHER UP THE STACK?

4.124 Over recent years, the primary use cases for many devices have changed. The rise of cloud computing and edge computing, autonomous vehicles, and the digitisation of critical national infrastructure means that we need not just to understand the security of devices, but also improve the security that a device offers a system. These new use cases often need devices to be architected differently, which can open up new security concerns. So this problem is about how we secure these new device architectures, and whether they offer opportunities to improve security further up the technology stack.

Strands or sub-problems

Multi-domain devices

4.125 Sharing a processor among multiple users in a cloud environment is a fairly well understood problem, if not perfectly resolved. Less well understood is the use of other devices in a multi-tenant scenario. If a GPU or machine learning accelerator is used by multiple tenants in parallel, how much confidence do we have that a user's data will be protected? Alternatively, can we partition a device into multiple domains working at different security levels? What could it mean to use physical, logical or temporal separation of domains? In some of these contexts we want to prevent dataflow between domains (tenants in a cloud perhaps), but in others we want deliberate but controlled dataflow. This sub-problem covers both understanding the risks in these architectures, and developing new architectures to mitigate those risks.

Novel architectures

4.126 Sometimes using a new or alternative architecture can alleviate entire classes of vulnerability, improve the sociotechnical aspects of security (such as 'secure by design' and 'secure by default' concepts), or at the very least make it easier to achieve security goals. We are always interested in identifying and developing new architectures that achieve this, but particularly where there is an achievable route to adoption. This means that research into adoption, or into architectures that don't create significant incompatibilities with existing systems, is especially interesting. Another approach could be to deliberately engineer significant differences into our architectures, creating deliberate variability, to reduce the risks from any single attack.

4.127 Why this is important

> 'Computing devices are foundational to our increasingly connected lives. If we can improve security of our systems at the device level, this security can carry through and impact our entire society and economy. Where a new device architecture can close off an entire class of vulnerabilities, or secure new use cases, the impact could be profound. Because processors and similar devices are everywhere, improvements here strengthen the foundations of practically every system we rely on.'
>
> Charlie D, Technical Director for Hardware Security, NCSC

HOW DO WE INTEGRATE SECURE DEVICES SO THEY CONTRIBUTE TO SECURITY AT THE SYSTEM LEVEL?

4.128 In other problems in this chapter, we've outlined the challenges in developing trustable devices. We want the security properties that these devices enforce to add value to a wider system, but the security goals of a system are different from the security goals of a device, and the act of integrating these devices potentially changes the security behaviours. We're therefore interested in researching the composability of security, and how we can use devices to improve the security of a system.

Strands or sub-problems

Understanding the security properties of a device

4.129 As things currently stand, understanding what security a device does or doesn't offer requires wading through marketing material, datasheets or white papers, searching through academic archives, or engaging with device vendors. This doesn't scale, and is probably the reason behind many of the accidental misconfigurations and misuse of devices that lead to vulnerabilities. With this strand, we're asking if there is a better way to do this and whether one approach is to develop a standard mechanism to describe the security properties of (and the assumptions made by) a device.

Interfaces

4.130 In some respects, we can treat interfaces as another device in the system. If two devices each guarantees confidentiality of data, but communicate over an interface that doesn't, it undermines our confidence in the system. Understanding the security properties of an interface is just as important as understanding the devices themselves.

Emergent properties

4.131 Once we have a way to understand the properties of a device and an interface, we can start to understand the system's security properties. If we can describe the properties of the components of a system in a standard way, can we automatically report the properties of the system? And once we can do that, what does it show us about how these properties integrate? This problem becomes even more prevalent as the complexity of systems increases, and as heterogeneous integration makes devices even more tightly coupled than before.

Using hardware security primitives

4.132 As described above, there is a lot of research happening into hardware security primitives, but there is less of a focus on how many of them can be used practically in a system. Understanding the security needs of a system, and the security of the end-to-end protocol in which a primitive is used, could lead to more focused research into the use and design of primitives.

Working with the market

4.133 How do we incentivise adoption of better hardware security? This includes points already raised around simplifying integration, default behaviours, and providing evidence, but also requires understanding of the market. What will incentivise demand for these technologies? How do we design secure hardware to be cheaper and easier to use? An improved understanding of the requirements of particular markets, and the constraints on products within them, will focus hardware security research into areas where there is already demand for their outputs.

4.134 Why this is important

> 'Security analysis is a hard and manual process that often struggles to account for the business and practical requirements. This might never go away, but if we can automate any of the processes, if we can produce systems that can describe, or even maintain their own security, then we're in a much stronger position.
>
> If our devices and primitives are designed with the rest of the system in mind, or the system can be designed to cope with whatever security properties a

device includes, then as with previous problems, we will have a much better idea of what we're getting from a system, and that transparency will enable better decisions. This could take the form of hardware to enable zero-trust systems, or providing the agility to update security over time.'

Charles Brookson OBE, Chair of the Industry Advisory Board at the Research Institute for Secure Hardware and Embedded Systems

CHAPTER 5

PRIVACY AND SECURITY IN THE WORKPLACE

Ria Halme

INTRODUCTION

5.01 This chapter is an overview of some of the key areas of privacy and security-related matters at the workplace within the EU. The main emphasis is placed on addressing the matter from a data protection perspective, but as the fields are intertwined, security is also discussed. Please note, that this is not legal advice, and will not create any form of client relationship. The chapter is an introduction to the topic. Implementing privacy and security must be done considering the context, all applicable laws and regulations and with the help of privacy and security professionals.

5.02 The privacy and security in the workplace is twofold. On the one hand the employees are part of a Processor's or a Controller's entity,[1] and on the other, the employees are also Data Subjects and have certain privacy rights.[2] This chapter discusses key points of how privacy, security and business operations intertwine in the workplace. The main emphasis of the chapter is on the privacy and security measures considering the employee as a Data Subject, but certain aspects such as training, also touch upon the role of the employee as an actor in the Controller's or Processor's entity.

LEGAL INSTRUMENTS ON DATA PROTECTION AND SECURITY IN THE WORKPLACE

5.03 There are several legal instruments, which are applicable to the privacy and security in the workplace. On the international level, there is the European Convention of Human Right (ECHR)[3] and the European Court of Human Right's (ECtHR's) case-law, followed by the national level legislation and case-law

1 REGULATION (EU) 2016/679 OF THE EUROPEAN PARLIAMENT AND OF THE COUNCIL of 27 April 2016 on the protection of natural persons with regard to the processing of personal data and on the free movement of such data, and repealing Dir 95/46/EC (General Data Protection Regulation, GDPR), Art 39(1)(a).

2 Data subject is an identifiable natural person, whose personal data is being processed, GDPR, Art 1(1).

3 European Convention on Human Rights (ECHR).

within the signatory States.[4] While the ECHR does not explicitly have horizontal applicability (between private parties), it has in many cases been applied horizontally. The national implementing legislation can also become applied in court proceedings, where the court is by its public institution nature required to apply it.[5] On an EU-level there is the GDPR, which leaves the Member States a margin of discretion in relation to employee's privacy,[6] which is then regulated by the national level employment laws of the EU Member States. This means, that there are possibly multiple legal instruments on Member-State level regulating the data protection in relation to the employees. Additionally multiple sector specific laws may apply, such as related to financial or healthcare.

5.04 In relation to security, the GDPR requires to implement 'appropriate technical and organizational security measures to protect the personal data',[7] and obligates the privacy to be designed into a process, product or service from the beginning, with the strictest privacy measures in place by default.[8] Additionally, a Data Protection Impact Assessment to identify risks and implement suitable controls to close compliance gaps are required for high-risk processing activities before processing can begin. Evaluating the appropriate security in practice is a task left for the Controller and Processor which they must complete considering the level of risk and industry standards and practices. There are also additional security requirements for example for entities which fall under the scope of the NIS-Directive.[9]

Several EU Member States are also signatories to the Budapest Convention, which they have implementing into the national legislation enforcing rules on cyber security.[10] Additionally, there are several regulatory and sector specific regulations, requirements, best practices, and guidelines, which must be followed when implementing privacy and security.[11] For example, legally required background checks in the financial industry are extensive, as the employees process other people's financial and sensitive data.[12] Similarly, for a person holding a public office, certain background checks are required to prevent

4 European Court of Human Rights (EctHR), which rulings are binding to the signatories, Art 46. The Member States must implement the Convention into their national law, Art 59.

5 Gennard and Judge, *Employee Relations* (Chartered Institute of Personnel and Development, 2005) pp. 117–118.

6 GDPR, Art 88.

7 GDPR, Art 32.

8 GDPR, Recital 78, Art 25.

9 Dir (EU) 2016/1148 of the European Parliament and of the Council of 6 July 2016 concerning measures for a high common level of security of network and information systems across the Union (NIS-Directive), Arts 1, 14, and 16.

10 Council of Europe Convention on Cybercrime, Treaty No. 185 (Budapest Convention), Art 36; www.coe.int/en/web/conventions/full-list/-/conventions/treaty/185/signatures?desktop=false.

11 See, eg, the Information Commissioner's consolidated Employment Practices Code, Available at: https://ico.org.uk/media/for-organisations/documents/1064/the_employment_practices_code.pdf.

12 See, eg, Finnish Act on the Protection of Privacy in Working Life (759/2004), 5 a 1-3 §; UK, Financial Conduct Authority's Handbook, 'Fit and Proper' test.

criminal offences and compromising publicly important objectives, such as national security or a significant private financial or business interest.[13]

ROLE OF THE EMPLOYER

5.05 An 'entity's role in relation to the employee is that of a Controller, as the entity decides why and how the employees' personal data is processed.[14] In a Group of companies, the employee's data can also be transferred within the Group or with affiliates and the entities could therefore also be Joint Controllers. For compliance reasons, it is important that the role is defined in writing, as the role also defines the rights and liabilities.[15] The employer is responsible for implementing appropriate data protection practices and security standards to protect the employee's privacy and data.[16]

The definition of an employee

5.06 Despite the differences at the Member State level on how employees are defined, in this chapter employees are referred to as a broad concept, including also for example rented workers, interim contractors, or people doing secondments, alumni and job applicants.

CATEGORIES OF PERSONAL DATA PROCESSED IN THE EMPLOYMENT CONTEXT

5.07 The nature of the processed personal data in the context of employment often includes special categories and otherwise sensitive information. Ethnicity, trade union memberships, financial information, biometric and health related data may be processed for multiple purposes. This ranges from identification, complying with equal opportunity reporting, confirming a correct pay package, grievances, performance reviews and a general requirement to administrate the employment contract. Hence, the Controller must apply elevated levels of security.[17] In addition the personal data must be minimised to what is absolutely necessary and the purpose of use must be limited to what the Data Subject has been informed of and what can lawfully and fairly done with the data. The Controller must also implement suitable erasure controls once the data is no longer needed. Additionally, there are limitations to what kind of information

13 See, eg, the Act on Background Checks (177/2002), ss 1–2, Unofficial translation, Ministry of Justice, Finland, Available at: www.finlex.fi/en/laki/kaannokset/2002/en20020177.pdf.

14 Art 29 Working Party, Opinion 1/2010 on the concepts of 'controller' and 'processor', adopted on 16 February 2010.

15 GDPR, Recital 48, Arts 4(7)–(8), 26, and 28; Art 29 Working Party, Opinion 1/2010, cited above.

16 GDPR, Art 32.

17 GDPR, Arts 9, 32; Art 29 Working Party Opinion 2/2017 on data processing at work, adopted June 2017.

can be collected of the employee or a candidate, and these vary according to the State, sector and role.

Legal grounds for processing personal data

5.08 In the context of employment, it is difficult to fulfill the conditions for an explicit consent as defined by the GDPR, as it is difficult to prove that the employee is without any pressure to consent. Where the employee does not consent, it will likely be difficult to evidence it did not negatively impact the employee, such as for career advancement or other opportunities. The three main grounds for processing of personal data in the employment context are preparation and performance of a contract, legal obligation and legitimate interest. Of these, the preparation and performance of a contract and legal obligation are necessities, as the employer will in most cases need to form a contract and be able to administrate the employment, by for example paying salary. There are also several legal obligations for the employers to process personal data, such as for taxation purposes. Legitimate interest on the other hand is a balancing act, where the employer will need to show their interests overrides the employee's rights and freedoms.[18]

5.09 in addition to the GDPR and the national legislation, the employer will also need to consider the European Convention on Human Rights and the applicable case law. This is most prominent in the context of employee monitoring as the applied measures must comply with the all the legal instruments, be necessary, proportionate and balance the interests and rights of both parties.[19]

DATA PROTECTION AND SECURITY REQUIREMENTS EXTEND TO ALL MEDIAS

5.10 In this digital era, the right to privacy and data protection can easily be understood in the context of digital production data flowing through the systems, but it is noteworthy to keep in mind that the privacy requirements extend to all personal and personally identifiable data,[20] and all the medias. The personal data does not fall out of the scope of the definition just because the media it is processed in changes, hence, in addition to the digital production data, in the scope is also, for example, paper documents, USB-sticks, CDs, and external hard-drives.[21]

18 GDPR, Arts 6, 7; Art 29 Working Party Opinion 2/2017 on data processing at work, adopted June 2017, pp. 6–8.
19 European Convention on Human Rights, Art 8, *Niemetz v Germany* (application no. 13710/88).
20 C 582/14 *Breyer v Germany*; GDPR, Recital 30.
21 Morley and Parker, *Understanding Computers today and Tomorrow, Comprehensive*, 15th edn (Cengage Learning) p. 616; GDPR, Recital 26, Art 1(1).

5.11 The concept of personal data is also extensive, including the more obvious such as name and address but also categories of data which are not always considered personal data. For example, a log indicating who has made changes or looked at certain data, or a recorded call to customer services is personal data.[22] If a person's fingerprint or voice is used to recognise that person, it is classified as biometric data, and therefore specially categorised under the GDPR.[23] Therefore, in addition to having appropriate data life cycle management practices in place for the used applications and systems, other media must be managed according to the same scrutiny, and appropriate security measures.[24]

THE CONTROLLER IS RESPONSIBLE FOR CHOOSING A COMPLIANT DATA PROCESSOR

5.12 Outsourcing data processing is a common practice. It is also good for the employee to understand how much of the data is processed outside of the company, and it is the employer's responsibility to inform the employees of this.[25] The GDPR requires the Controller to choose Processors, entities which process data on behalf of the Controller, which are GDPR compliant. The Controller is also required to instruct the Processors in a sufficiently detailed manner on the purpose and means of processing, and the Processor may not deviate from the instructions.[26]

Roles of the Controller and the Processor

5.13 Defining the roles in writing in the beginning of the engagement is essential for compliance as the relationship must be governed by suitable privacy clauses. To assist in the definition of the roles and understanding the Parties rights and liabilities, the European Data Protection Board (EDPS)[27] has provided guidance on how to define the roles.[28] The Controller is the one 'who determines the purposes and means of processing' and this role comes with a responsibility to protect the personal data throughout its life-cycle. The processor on the other hand is 'the entity, which is processing personal data on behalf and under the instructions of the Controller'.[29]

5.14 According to the EDPS, the role of the entity as a Controller or a Processor is defined not according to what is contractually agreed, but what

22 GDPR, Recital 26, Art 1(1).
23 GDPR, Arts 4(14), 9.
24 GDPR, Art 32.
25 GDPR, Arts 13–14.
26 GDPR, Arts 5(f), 28, 32.
27 Pre-GDPR the Art 29 Working Party, an independent advisory body on data protection and privacy, GDPR, Arts 68–70.
28 Art 29 Working Party, Opinion 1/2010 on the concepts of 'controller' and 'processor', adopted on February 2010.
29 Opinion 1/2010, pp. 3–5; GDPR Art 4(7)(8).

kind of decisions the Parties make and how the processing happens in practice do in practice. The EDPB's guidance also elaborates where the margin of decision-making powers lie before a Processor will be considered a Controller. To define where the limit of decision-making goes, the entities involved can apply a test to evaluate who is making decisions on Why the data is processed – not disregarding the means. That Party is considered the Controller.[30] While both Parties have certain liabilities, such as implementing appropriate security measures, the Controller remains ultimately responsible for the protection of the personal data.[31]

5.15 Decision-making on the purpose includes the decision on why the personal data is processed and for what purpose, whereas the means is a broader concept. 'Means' includes essential elements, such as what data to process and for how long and defining access rights. Less substantial matters, such as which software to use fall on the side of non-essential elements.[32] The essential elements are for the Controller to decide, whereas in regard to the non-essential matters, the Processor can also make decisions without overstepping the margin of discretion. The overall responsibility placed on the Controller is 'to allocate responsibility', while remaining responsible for compliance.[33]

5.16 The Controller must instruct the processor in a sufficient manner to ensure they have complied with the obligation to decide upon the essentials matters of data processing. From a practical perspective 'this means The Controller must have an adequate third-party risk management process in place. This can further be divided into the engagement and onboarding processes, updating changes, and ending the vendor relationship.[34]

Practical approach to third party risk management

5.17 The initial stage is to evaluate which vendors will need to be reviewed for privacy, most often by the Data Protection Officer (DPO) or the Privacy Team. This requires an initial evaluation of the vendor's personal data processing practices, including categories of personal data, scope, etc. Where a personal data is processed as part of the outsourcing engagement, the vendor must go through a vetting process and be engaged with suitable contractual clauses before personal data can be shared with them.

5.18 The vetting process includes a Due Diligence which evaluates the data processing practices of the Processor by going through a set of differing levels of inspections, audits and/or questionnaires. To streamline the process, the Controller can create a model which includes a different set of questions

30 Opinion 1/2010 p. 13.
31 GDPR, Art 28–29.
32 Opinion 1/2010 p. 14.
33 Opinion 1/2010 p. 4.
34 GDPR, Recital 81, 83–84, Art 28.

used for different kinds of processors, for example payroll, recruitment, cloud-service, such as saas,[35] and paas,[36] providers and paper archiving. Alternatively, the Controller can create a Due Diligence questionnaire which can be sent or otherwise used to evaluate all the Processors they engage. The means are left for the Controller to define, the main aim is to ensure the Controller is familiar with the controls the Processor has in place to comply with the GDPR.

Once a decision to engage a Processor is made, the personal data flow must be documented, adding it to the Record of Processing Activities (RoPA). The Controller must also ensure they conduct a Privacy Impact Assessment, and where this indicates the processing is considered high risk, they must also complete a Data Privacy Impact Assessment (DPIA). These Impact assessments allow the Controller to identify risks and require the processor to remediate possible gaps in their processing by implementing agreed controls. This ensures the personal data is then processed with an adequate level of security and privacy measures in practice. A Processing activity which poses a low or a medium level risk must also be evaluated for its risks and required controls to ensure compliance with the GDPR's data protection principles.[37]

5.19 Models available for the controller to provide instructions for the processors vary. For example, a one-off instruction appendix for a continuous and simple service may be effective, whereas more granular instructions are likely needed to instruct a Processor who provides multiple or complex services, processing personal data of differing sensitivity and quantity. Data Processing Addendums, Controller-Processor Agreements and other types of contractual templates work well for the purpose. These Agreements must also include the mandatory contractual clauses which must govern the relationship of a Controller and Processor.

5.20 The Controller should also verify compliant implementation, which will depend on the Processor's systems, resources, nature of the data and the processor's ability to adapt the processing, which is often conducted under different controllers. Periodic re-evaluation of the Processor's compliance levels should be conducted as needed, for example when there are substantial changes to the processing of the data.[38] Similarly, the instructions will need to be amended accordingly. Ending the processing relationship needs to be considered at the

35 Software as a service.

36 Platform as a service.

37 GDPR, Recital 80–83, 116, Arts 28, 35; Art 29 Working Party Guidelines on Data Protection Impact Assessment (DPIA) and determining whether processing is 'likely to result in a high risk' for the purposes of Reg 2016/679, adopted April 2017.

38 GDPR, Arts 28–29, 32; Art 29 Working Party Guidelines on Data Protection Impact Assessment (DPIA) and determining whether processing is 'likely to result in a high risk' for the purposes of Reg 2016/679, adopted April 2017.

beginning. How data will be deleted, returned or otherwise processed when the contract ends, should be included in the instructions.[39]

5.21 The process should also consider a situation where the controller will engage a Joint Controller, instead of a Processor. The Joint Controllers must agree on the roles, responsibilities and liabilities. There can also be situations, where there is joint controllership in relation to a certain scope of data, but the other party is a processor in relation to another scope. Where there are multiple roles, it is important to separate the data in relation to, for example, access rights and discretion to the decision-making margin, as these influence liability. The Due Diligence and the contract must also reflect the relationships accordingly.[40]

5.22 The GDPR introduced new ways to indicate compliance with the privacy requirements, certifications, seals and marks. As of September 2023, there is still no guidance on how these can be acquired or will be implemented in practice. Once available, these compliance indicators can enhance the vendor engagement process for the benefit of both parties. A sign, certification or mark in itself does not guarantee GDPR-compliance and the implementation of appropriate security measures but it can however be expected to be seen as an indication that privacy and information security are taken seriously.[41] Purely from the security perspective, becoming ISO-certified is internationally recognised to indicate certain implemented standards.[42]

Training and Awareness

5.23 The Controller and the Processor are both required to ensure their staff are trained to process data according to the applicable legal requirements. The personnel are in a key position in terms of privacy and security, as compliance or an occasional breach happen on a day-to-day basis during the activities of data processing.[43] Providing training is also beneficial for the employees, as data processing is today a core activity for a large part of entities. Training and awareness also promote a less stressful working environment, as the employees understand what is expected from them. The managers will also be better equipped to make informed decisions on data processing.[44]

39 GDPR, Recital 81, Arts 28–29, 32; Art 29 Working Party Guidelines on Data Protection Impact Assessment (DPIA) and determining whether processing is 'likely to result in a high risk' for the purposes of Reg 2016/679, adopted April 2017; ICO GDPR guidance: Contracts and liabilities between controllers and processors.

40 GDPR, Art 26.

41 GDPR, Art 42.

42 www.iso.org/standards.html; Whitman and Mattord, *Readings & Cases in information Security: Law & Ethics* (Course Technology, Cengage Learning, 2011) pp. 119–120.

43 GDPR Arts 32 and 39, The Protection Officer Training Manual, International Foundation for Protection Officers, 2003, p. 106.

44 Obtaining support and funding from senior management While planning an awareness initiative, ENISA, 2008.

5.24 The purpose of providing training and increasing awareness is to make a permanent impact, which means that ideally training is more than providing materials to read or a video to watch. Change is an ongoing process and iteration and repetition are needed to ensure that personnel are provided with the necessary materials, tools and information they need to comply with data protection requirements.[45] Informing and advising personnel is named as one of the responsibilities of the Data Protection Officer (DPO), which is a new role introduced by the GDPR.[46] The engagement of senior management is however crucial, as they are in the end responsible for implementing adequate measures, and ensuring a sufficient budget for the purpose.[47]

Awareness

5.25 To develop a privacy aware culture which contributes to ensuring the data processing activities are compliant and in line with the internal data protection and security policies, increasing awareness is the first step. This can be done via internally developed campaigns, notes, screen savers, inductions and flyers. Investing into creating a network of privacy and security professionals, often referred to as Champions, who support the employees in their everyday activities are also one way to raise awareness on privacy and security.[48]

Training

5.26 It is advisable to implement the training from top to bottom, to ensure that the ones responsible for drafting and deciding on the policies are able to make informed decisions and understand risks and compliance. Similarly, the ones responsible for their team's practices, often Business Process Owners, are better equipped when there is adequate training in place so that they know what is expected of them.[49]

5.27 There are certain key topics which need to be trained to everyone to ensure internal and external processes are followed. All employees should know for example how to identify and further follow processes relating to Data Subjects' Rights, directing requests for the appropriate responsible persons or team to ensure timelines and processes are followed and adequately documented.[50] It's also important everyone knows how to engage vendors and identify, escalate and further manage data breaches and incidents. Training should be tailored towards the role, considering for example how much and how sensitive personal data the employee processes in their everyday activities. The

45 ibid.
46 GDPR, Art 39.
47 Obtaining support and funding from senior management While planning an awareness initiative, ENISA, 2008.
48 ibid.
49 ibid.
50 GDPR, Arts 15–22, 39.

C-suite and senior management are the ones ultimately making the high-level decisions, and providing adequate training also for them will help them make informed decisions in their everyday-activities and when sponsoring initiatives and setting strategic directions.[51]

5.28 It is also helpful to provide a centralised point of access for resources, so that the employees can find answers quickly to the most common data processing questions. Also, the Data Protection Office or Privacy Team and the Information Security Departments should have a designated contact point, such as an e-mail address, to which the operational personnel can send their questions and topics they seek guidance. The training should be timed so that it serves the purpose and is effective. This means training the new starters with inductions from the beginning of the employment or partnership relationship, and then periodically during the employment or co-operation.[52]

5.29 The Controller and the Processor need to be able to evidence they have taken appropriate measures to train their employees as a part of implementing appropriate security and privacy solutions. Therefore, maintaining training records, passing rates, and the type of training provided is essential.[53] When privacy and security measures are planned and implemented, it is important that the personnel responsible for making decisions on the security devices and activities are adequately trained on privacy and understand the requirements of the business to deliver practical solutions.

5.30 For example, HR-personnel need to be trained to understand what questions and hence what kind of personal, sensitive or specially categorised data can be collected, and in which circumstances. For example, to follow appropriate privacy and security standards, instead of sharing CVs between organisations via e-mail, they should be placed in a centralised application with suitable access rights which follow the company policies. After the CV is no longer required, it must be deleted and it is easier to do so from the centralised storage, than from people's e-mails. Also, e-mails cannot be monitored in relation to for example access management.[54]

PRIVACY MATTERS, EVEN IN DATA SECURITY

5.31 Cyber-security, privacy and data protection are intertwined, yet separate sectors. Privacy by design and default expectations require implementing appropriate security and privacy solutions from the start. From the privacy point

51 CISSP Guide to Essentials, Gregory, Course Technology, Cengage Learning, 2010, pp. 27, 32–34.

52 CISSP Guide to Essentials, Gregory, Course Technology, Cengage Learning, 2010, p. 25; GDPR, Arts 33, 37–39.

53 GDPR, Arts 5 and 39.

54 Gertz, Ludäscher, *Scientific and Statistical Database Management* (Springer, 2010) p. 407; GDPR, Art 5.

of view, employees are also Data Subjects and their right to privacy continues to exist at the workplace.[55] Therefore, it is important security, privacy and the business come together to find the appropriate level of controls, while ensuring the continuity of business operations.

5.32 The data needs to be protected with appropriate technical and organisational measures, including administrative information security.[56] The security level is set against the appropriate risk-level in relation to the data classification, processing, privacy requirements and business operations. From the security perspective, it is important that the security of the network is ensured and monitored as in this way, possible abuses of personal data, such as an employee downloading materials for themselves for personal purposes, such as selling them onwards to a competitor, will be detected.[57] As privacy is different between the jurisdictions it is of highlighted importance to understand the impact of privacy legislation to the practicalities of information security especially when implementing group-wide security policies. The differences in the national legislations have a direct effect on the allowed level of monitoring. For example, where in Finland there is a mandatory process for the employer to negotiate with the employee's representative about the necessity and measures for monitoring, in the UK, it is a more common practice to implement data loss prevention as a part of the security measures to a reasonable extent without discussing with the representatives of the employees. In more extreme cases in UK covert surveillance can be done at the discretion and approval of a manager should there be severe grounds to suspect criminal activity, and such covert monitoring was needed.[58] From the business operations perspective, it must be ensured that the security measures do not hinder the operational activities too much. For example, if all the external data is encrypted with the heaviest mechanisms, it can slow down the day-to-day operations too much by making the data transfers slow and hence hinder the business operations.[59] It is important to create a balance that implements security, while still protects the privacy.

5.33 Similarly, privacy needs to be taken into consideration in other situations when implementing security solutions in the workplace, such as CCTV and providing security passes. On an EU-level, there are guidelines on data processing at work, which also covers security and privacy via differing methods, such as data loss prevention and location tracking at the workplace.[60] These, in addition

55 *Niemietz v Germany* (application no. 13710/88).

56 Tipton, Krause, *Information Security Management Handbook* (Auerbach Publications, 2002) p. 60.

57 Hill, *Data Protection: Governance, Risk Management and Compliance* (CRC Press, 2010) pp. 130–131.

58 Finnish Act on the protection of privacy in working life 759/2004, s 21 Cooperation in organizing technical monitoring and data network use; ICO Employment practices code of practice, p. 74, s 3.4.

59 Hill, *Data Protection: Governance, Risk Management and Compliance* (CRC Press, 2010) pp. 130–131.

60 Art 29 Working Party, Opinion 2/2017 on data processing at work, June 2017.

to the application of the ECHR in the employment context,[61] are a good starting point to understanding the principles on a European and EU-level.

IDENTITY AND ACCESS MANAGEMENT (IAM) – LIMIT ACCESS TO DATA

5.34 All privacy laws set a requirement to keep personal data confidential, protected from unlawful access and processed according to the purpose it was gathered for. Therefore, data must be accessed only by those who have a legal ground to do so. The higher the sensitivity of the data the higher the potential of severe damage in a data breach. therefore, there needs to be a proper method for identifying the ones in positions to handle certain data, and ensuring access according to that need. For this, a suitable Identity and Access Management (IAM) model should be established.[62]

5.35 The more sensitive the data, the stricter privacy and security measures apply to it, including who should have access. Access should be provided on a role and need-to-know basis, restricting it to the least amount of people who need to process it. This is to comply with the purpose, lawful access and confidentiality requirements.[63] In addition to providing access, revoking the rights should be in-line with the employee's role and need to process certain data. Another important part of the IAM, is logging the actions of the person making changes to the data, to check on possible abuses, flag suspicious activity, and monitor compliance. The logs themselves should of course be appropriately protected from unlawful access, alteration and to protect the privacy of the data subjects themselves. When establishing the IAM model suitable for the purposes of the organisation, it should be considered that if the organisation is large, the global model may not be fit for the purposes of all the branches, which can have differing roles and responsibilities, especially if the branch is small and the roles can live more. It is also important to consider physical access in addition to digital, as server rooms and other archives are under the same scope of protection as data in other medias. Additional consideration for the model also depends on how the data is processed. For example, clouds present a more complex environment on access, than an in-house architecture.[64]

61 See, eg, *Antović and Mirković v Montenegro* (application no. 70838/13), *Köpke v Germany* (application no. 420/07), *Bărbulescu v Romania* (application no. 61496/08) and *López Ribalda and Others v Spain* (application nos. 1874/13 and 8567/13).

62 GDPR Arts 5, (6), 9 and 32: Cox, *Managing Information in Organizations: A Practical Guide to Implementing an Information Management Strategy* (Palgrave MacMillan, 2014) p. 132.

63 GDPR, Art 5.

64 Osmanoglu, *Identity and Access Management: Business Performance Through Connected Intelligence* (Elsevier Inc, 2014) pp. 187–189, 200–202.

REMOTE WORKERS

5.36 There is a growing trend in people working remotely either from home, the client's premises, cafeterias or other public places and working abroad is also nowadays becoming more common. While the flexibility in this model provides efficiencies, it is important to ensure that privacy and security are upheld to the same standard as when working from the office. From the security perspective, preventing data loss can mean, for example, enabling remote wiping of the laptop's and mobile phone's content,[65] and tracking these should they be lost or stolen. However, while implementing these controls, privacy should also be considered. The necessity of a measure must be evaluated against the employee's right to privacy. The employee must also be made aware of the measures that may impact their right to privacy. For example, wiping the phone clean may mean the person will also lose certain personal data and this should be a risk the employee takes willingly, if they are using their own phone for work purposes under a Bring Your Own Device (BYOD) Policy.[66]

5.37 The remote workers should be trained appropriately on security and privacy related responsibilities so they are aware what to do and not to do when working outside of the work premises. This means for example knowing what kind of a WiFi is appropriate to use to prevent personal and sensitive data being stolen by a third party from an unsecured public WiFi.[67] Encryption should be used whenever data is removed from the physical office to ensure the data cannot be easily accessed should the device, such as USB-stick be lost.[68] Regular backups also assist in preventing permanent data loss.[69] There are also security solutions to enable remote access to a company's intranet, shared drive and e-mails, via a VPN,[70] or virtual desktop infrastructure (VDI),[71]which do require investment and training, but will enable secure authentication and access and therefore more secure remote working.[72]

5.38 As employees may also have personal data at home, it is important to ensure the company specific materials are kept away from family members and visitors, and work calls are conducted in a way which do not expose personal data to people who are not allowed to access it.[73] Similarly, any printed papers must be disposed following the company policy and process which likely means

65 Hoog, *Android Forensics: Investigation, Analysis, and Mobile Security for Google Android* (Syngress, 2011) p. 179.

66 Art 29 Working Party, Opinion 2/2017 on data processing at work.

67 Smallwood, *Safeguarding Critical Documents* (Wiley & Sons, 2012) Ch 7.

68 Cox, *Managing Information in Organizations: A Practical Guide to Implementing an Information Management Strategy* (Palgrave MacMillan, 2014) p. 128.

69 Nelson, *Pro Data Backup and Recovery, Securing your information in the terabyte age* (Apress, 2011) p. 261.

70 Art 29 Working Party, Opinion 2/2017 on data processing at work.

71 See, eg: www.citrix.com/glossary/vdi.html.

72 Cox, *Managing Information in Organizations: A Practical Guide to Implementing an Information Management Strategy* (Palgrave MacMillan, 2014) pp. 358–359.

73 ibid, p. 358.

bringing the hard copies to the office for secure disposal.[74] Also while working remotely in public areas, it is important the employee considers and prevents unlawful access to the data. While it is convenient to work while in transit in a train or plane, video or telephone conversations while commuting or working without a proper privacy filter screen protector can expose the data to people who are legally not allowed to access it. Other people can see material they are not allowed to or for example steal passwords.[75]

5.39 In addition, there are also governmental access rights, which should be considered. Each State has their own derogations in relation to the level of protection of privacy, and each data protection instrument allows the derogation. Member States may make derogations to the privacy laws under a national security exemption, and the extent these activities is not public information. The checks and balances do need to exist and there need to be remedies to prevent abuse of the rights but regulating national security is under the competence of each State. Therefore, different governments have different rights and legal basis to access data. Several States may enter the device without a trace, taking vast amount of data, or tracking mobile phone usage. Hence, it is advised to check the laws and regulations, and especially exemptions to the data protection levels provided in each country before sending an employee abroad. In relation to governmental access, it is also good to look at the practice and the existing case-law if possible, as the implementation of the law depends on the interpretations and culture, and documents relating to this are not public. Understanding the political and practical atmosphere of the State is useful, as it indicates what to expect.[76]

5.40 Data breach management must be extended to remote workers. Losing a device or other materials, including sensitive data in a foreign country or otherwise away from the office premises should be handled according to the breach management process of the entity.[77] All the above refers back to the importance of the training and awareness the employer is responsible for providing to the employees, and the employees taking the training seriously. The best privacy and security standards will only be effective, when privacy and security are embedded into the every-day activities.

74 Bosworth et al, *Computer Security Handbook* (Wiley & Sons, 2009) 'Penetrating Computer systems and Networks'.

75 Bosworth et al, *Computer Security Handbook* (Wiley & Sons, 2009) 'Observe or Monitor', 3.4.2.10.

76 Cate, Dempsey, *Bulk Collection: Systematic Government Access to Private-Sector Data* (Oxford University Press, 2017) Sections: France and Italy.

77 Cox, *Managing Information in Organizations: A Practical Guide to Implementing an Information Management Strategy* (Palgrave MacMillan, 2014) p. 132.

DATA SUBJECT'S RIGHTS

5.41 Under the GDPR, the Data Subject is provided with certain rights, and these Rights are applicable also in the context of employment, as the employees are also Data Subjects in relation to the employer.[78]

The Data Subject has a right to rectify incorrect data, and where they have suffered substantial harm due to a decision made using incorrect data, be compensated for the suffered loss.[79] The Data Subject also has a right to know if their data is processed and further access it by receiving a copy alongside certain information on how it's being processed, such as whom it has been shared with, how long it has been retained for, and what the purposes of use are.[80] The right to data portability exists partly to prevent 'lock-in' situations, where the customer cannot change the service provider due to the difficulties in migrating the data. Under the Portability Right the Controller must provide a limited scope of the Data Subjects data to him in an easily readable and commonly used electronic form or send the same directly to another Controller.[81] In certain situations, the Data Subject also has a right to be forgotten, which means deleting the data relating to the Data Subject from the Controller's and Processor's databases. However, the right to be erased (forgotten) is a qualified right, which means, that it only applies in certain cases, such as when the data subject withdraws a previously given consent to process the data, the processing has not been based on an appropriate legal basis, and there are no other overriding reasons the Controller must continue processing the data, such as a legal obligation to process certain data for fraud detection purposes.[82]

5.42 The Data Subject has always the right to object to his data being processed for direct marketing purposes, and to being subjected to profiling and automated decision-making. Where the right to refuse direct marketing applies with no exceptions, there are scenarios in which the Controller may continue to profile and conduct automated decisions, in which case the Data Subject can require a human intervention and contest a reviewed decision.[83] In certain scenarios, the Data Subject can also have his data processing restricted.[84] Furthermore the Data Subject has a right to transparency. This means the Controller must provide the Data Subject adequate information, including how the personal data is obtained, the legal bases and purposes of use, where the personal data is transferred to and how it is safeguarded. Information must also be given on data sharing practices and whom the data is shared with.[85] In practice, the transparency is implemented via privacy notices, and alongside exercising the rights.

78 GDPR, Art 1(1).
79 GDPR, Art 16.
80 GDPR, Art 15.
81 GDPR, Art 20.
82 GDPR, Art 17.
83 GDPR, Arts 21–22.
84 GDPR, Art 18.
85 GDPR Arts 13 and 14.

5.43 Data Subjects Right Requests must be responded to free of charge, within 30 days by either implementing the Request or providing legitimate reasons why the Request cannot be actioned upon. Further time extensions are possible where the law provides a ground for it.[86] Refusing to act on a request is justified only if the Controller can evidence it is excessive or manifestly unfounded, or if the Controller is not able to identify the Data Subject after attempts to do so.[87]

86 GDPR, Art 12.
87 GDPR Art 12.

CHAPTER 6

CYBER SECURITY AND PHYSICAL BUILDINGS

Helen Wong MBE

INFORMATION TECHNOLOGY (IT) AND OPERATIONAL TECHNOLOGY (OT)

6.01 In a physical building or a built environment, a wide range of technologies are used across the lifecycle of a built asset.

6.02 The IT systems used in the built environment encompass personal devices like tablets, laptops, and desktop computers, as well as communication and networking infrastructure. They also include processing and storage systems, which can be local servers in data centres or cloud-based platforms. Operational Technology (OT) refers to the cyber-physical systems integrated into the built asset and its surroundings, providing services such as heating, ventilation, air conditioning (HVAC), lighting, access control, and the movement of people and goods via lifts and escalators. OT typically includes recognisable IT components, such as operator workstations running on a Windows operating system with built asset system applications, alongside more specialised elements like programmable logic controllers (PLCs), sensors, and actuators. The term OT is commonly associated with process, production, and engineering control systems, and depending on the specific built assets, it may be integral to the asset's business operations. Within this broader scope, OT components might consist of SCADA, IACS, and DCS systems.

6.03 Throughout the strategy, business case, and design stages of the built asset lifecycle, there is significant reliance on conventional IT. This includes office and design applications operated both locally and via cloud platforms. The IT technologies utilised are well-known to IT and cybersecurity professionals, and the security threats to these technologies are widely recognised.

6.04 The growing adoption of Building Information Modelling (BIM) has led to an increase in the use of 3D models and collaborative file and data storage environments, known as Common Data Environments (CDEs). The term 'digital twin' refers to a virtual representation of a physical asset. Understanding the nature and limitations of digital twins, along with potential threats and vulnerabilities, is crucial. These models can be simple graphical or computational representations of the asset, serving specific purposes like energy use and efficiency modelling. They can be utilised during the design phase of the built asset and throughout its operation to compare projected and actual performance using static data. More advanced models may allow for the evaluation of changes, 'what-if' analyses of modifications to the asset's operation and systems, based on static data. It is suggested that some digital twins should be connected to the built asset's systems, enabling live data exchange. In this case, the digital twin functions as a control system and should be managed as Operational Technology (OT), with proper testing, validation, and security measures.

6.05 Site-based design elements, such as surveying, are increasingly employing digitally enabled technologies like Light Detection and Ranging (LIDAR) scanning to capture point clouds, which are then used to develop 3D models of the surrounding assets. Topographical surveying may include the use of GPS-enabled tools and drone-mounted cameras to provide aerial views of the site.

6.06 The integration of new technologies can introduce novel risks, such as those stemming from the collection of sensitive data regarding existing and adjacent built assets, or from the inherent vulnerabilities of the technologies.

6.07 In the construction phase, a variety of IT and OT assets are utilised. The IT used is generally consistent with that described previously, but there is a notable increase in the use of mobile personal IT devices, like tablets and smartphones, for recording on-site data and updating construction details. Recently, there has been a trend towards employing OT in asset construction, including the use of robots and semi-autonomous machinery to augment construction workers' capabilities. Additionally, for enhanced safety and security, the implementation of electronic controls for site access and IoT devices worn by employees to track their location, health, and safety has become more prevalent.

6.08 The increased adoption of digital technologies on construction sites introduces new potential vulnerabilities that could be exploited. For instance, the use of near real-time reporting systems for built assets, which integrate various sensors and data reporting systems, could reveal access points to the systems recording as-built data. It is crucial for all disciplines involved in the project to understand how these automated systems are implemented and utilised. They should provide the necessary functionality for examining the collected data and detecting any anomalous or incorrect data. Recognising these vulnerabilities is key to ensuring the security and reliability of this dynamic data collection process, thereby preserving trust in the data's origin and quality throughout the project.

6.09 In the final phases of construction, the necessary Operational Technology (OT) systems for the built asset's operation will be installed, tested, and commissioned in preparation for handover to the asset owner or user. During this period, numerous contractors and suppliers will have access to the OT systems for testing and configuration purposes. This access can lead to various potential vulnerabilities concerning the authenticity of hardware and software components, the entities with on-site or remote access (authorised or otherwise), and the shift from testing and commissioning to operational status. Moreover, the increasing interconnectivity of OT systems with the internet (eg for remote monitoring or support) and the enterprise IT network of the asset's owner, operator, or occupier introduces additional vulnerabilities, especially since IT security managers often lack oversight of OT systems and their external connections.

6.10 Considering the relatively brief lifespan of most digital technologies in comparison to built assets, multiple technology updates are expected throughout the lifecycle of a built asset. Vulnerabilities associated with this include obsolete and unsupported systems/components, the merging of old and new technologies leading to hybrid systems, and the risk posed to previously isolated systems when connected to the internet. To mitigate security risks over the system's lifecycle, support arrangements must encompass the provision, installation, and testing of software and firmware patches. A crucial aspect of managing assets with software components involves understanding the duration of the supplier's support through updates, the methods of obtaining and implementing these updates, and strategies for dealing with software obsolescence once support ceases.

CONNECTED AND SMART BUILDINGS

6.11 In the ecosystem of the built environment, the connectivity level of buildings and the extent to which they are 'smart' can vary greatly. The usual goal is to provide various types of monitoring (such as energy, environmental, and occupancy) to inform and enhance the operation of systems. This aims to economically optimise the use of the built asset while ensuring a comfortable and healthy environment for occupants. A primary objective often includes achieving energy efficiency by minimizing energy use in unoccupied or sparsely occupied areas, leveraging environmental factors to lessen the need for energy-heavy heating or cooling, or implementing demand management to boost electricity grid efficiency.

6.12 The intelligent aspect of a building can include data collection, analytics, or machine learning to enhance the asset's performance. Meanwhile, demand-side electricity management will allow these assets and their devices to provide flexibility by adjusting demand levels, local production, or the release of stored electricity. Such innovations aim to foster a sustainable built environment, with intelligent features facilitating a cooperative management of limited resources. It is crucial to consider and mitigate cyber vulnerabilities during the design and construction phases of a smart building.

6.13 In theory, a connected building could feature devices that are networked and capable of communication, offering a remote monitoring data feed to organisations responsible for supporting or managing the plant and machinery essential for the building's operation. For instance, lift manufacturers might gather telemetry data from their installed lifts to detect early indications of malfunction, allowing them to send out spare parts and maintenance staff to address the issue before a service disruption occurs. Additionally, connectivity can facilitate new business models for plant and machinery, eg where a service provider maintains ownership of the heating system and provides heating services based on performance metrics.

6.14 The incorporation of technology and data sharing with external entities in smart, interconnected buildings can lead to numerous security risks. For instance, there's an increased danger that connections could be deliberately or accidentally connected to the occupant's corporate IT network, creating a potential backdoor. Additionally, the potential to use aggregated system data to discern patterns in the occupants' lifestyles or in the use of certain areas within the building could be misused for malicious purposes.

6.15 The recent breach of cyber security firm Crowdstrike's monitoring and management tools, which impacted physical buildings, banks, airports, the NHS, and numerous businesses, serves as a stark reminder of the risks inherent in placing trust in seemingly secure third parties. The problem was caused by an update to Crowdstrike's update to its antivirus software, which is designed to protect Microsoft Windows devices from malicious attacks.

DIGITAL ENGINEERING AND BUILT ASSET INFORMATION

6.16 The widespread adoption of digital engineering tools, such as 3D modelling and laser surveying, poses several risks for entities aiming to safeguard sensitive data related to their built assets. The deployment of these digital technologies should be complemented by robust information management and cybersecurity policies to mitigate the risk of compromising the security and safety of the asset and its users. Particularly for high-profile built assets, like those integral to defence, healthcare, or law enforcement and critical national infrastructure, unauthorised access to 3D models and asset data could facilitate hostile reconnaissance.

SECURITY OF ENDPOINTS

6.17 In the architecture, construction, and engineering sectors, extensive subcontracting is common, which increases the attack surface due to the integration of third-party devices. These devices can be organisation-owned or personal, as in the case of Bring Your Own Device (BYOD) policies, connecting to built asset systems. Cyber risks may emerge from compromised devices like laptops and tablets, as well as endpoint peripherals including mice, keyboards, printers, and barcode scanners. The risk from unauthorised devices is widely recognised and can be reduced through good cyber hygiene practices. However, the danger posed by malicious hardware or peripherals is often overlooked. This risk can be lessened by using specialised solutions to detect compromised hardware and by ensuring peripherals are purchased from trusted sources.

INFORMATION MANAGEMENT

6.18 In the realm of the physical building and built environment, information management is the method employed to uphold data quality throughout the lifecycle of a built asset. This quality pertains to the data's suitability for the decisions that are, or will be, based on it. Considering the information of a built asset, essential quality attributes include relevance, clarity (the meaning of the data), consistency (data having the same meaning across different parts of an organisation or among various stakeholders), accessibility, and security. Data and information possess inherent value, defined by characteristics such as accuracy, timeliness, completeness, and origin. Nevertheless, these characteristics carry associated costs and benefits. Therefore, if the data is already sufficiently accurate and timely for its intended use, incurring additional costs to enhance these aspects may offer little benefit.

6.19 From a security standpoint, recognising the data's value to the built asset owner, its users, and third parties –whether their intentions are benign or malicious – is crucial. With this knowledge, one can implement suitable and proportionate safeguards to defend the organisation against both current and potential threats in the future.

CYBER SECURITY

6.20 Cybersecurity encompasses a suite of tools, policies, concepts, safeguards, guidelines, risk management strategies, actions, training, best practices, assurance, and technologies designed to maintain control, ensure coherence, and support the reliable functioning of both organisational and user assets within the cyber environment. Where:

1. The 'cyber environment,' also known as 'cyberspace,' consists of interconnected networks of electronic and computer-based systems. This includes the internet, organisational intranets, telecommunication networks, computer systems, embedded processors, controllers, and an extensive range of sensors, storage, and control devices. Due to the interconnected nature of these systems, the cyber environment extends beyond just the elements controlled or owned by a single organisation. The term 'organisation and user's assets' encompasses personnel, applications, services, and social elements; and business functions that exist solely in cyberspace encompass the entirety of data and information that is transmitted, processed, or stored within the cyber environment.
2. Establishing digital trust involves symmetry, reciprocity, and transparency among various stakeholders within the digital realm, guided by the corporate or personal risk appetites and the ability to manage those risks. Within the built environment, it's crucial to consider in what, or whom, as a business or individual, you place your trust, given that security responsibilities and governance in cyber and physical spaces often lack alignment.

3. Recognising that the cyber environment encompasses critical supporting infrastructure is crucial. This includes utilities, uninterruptible power supplies, generators, and main power switchboards. Experience has demonstrated that even systems presumed to be standalone and isolated are vulnerable to risks from malicious user attacks and the introduction of malware via removable media. The absence of an apparent connection to the internet or other networks does not guarantee security. Often, there is built-in connectivity, such as cellular phone technology, which is installed for maintenance convenience or remote management. Users are typically unaware of these capabilities, which can be exploited to download and install patches and updates remotely or to facilitate automated diagnostic and fault reporting. While physical access by an intruder or insider is currently the most common vector for cyber incidents, the frequency and sophistication of remote attacks are on the rise as criminals exploit unprotected pathways to infiltrate critical systems.

SECURITY GOALS

6.21 Considering the varying lifespans of the physical structures of built assets, their control systems, and typical organisational IT systems and personal computing devices, cyber security management must be adhered to. Throughout the built asset lifecycle, one must accommodate changes in the asset and technology, usage patterns, and the nature and severity of potential threats. When assessing residual risk, it is important to consider how resilient the organisation and the built assets would be should the risk materialise.

1. Confidentiality. Built asset systems and their processes must be designed, implemented, operated, and maintained to block unauthorised access, such as to sensitive financial, medical, or commercial data. All personal data must be managed in compliance with the Data Protection Act 2018 (as amended), and further measures may be necessary to safeguard privacy when data aggregation could reveal individual patterns of life.

2. Control. Built asset systems and their processes must be designed, implemented, operated, and maintained to prevent unauthorised control, manipulation, or interference. For instance, an authorised user losing access to a built asset system does not compromise confidentiality, system availability, or integrity, yet the owner or user loses control over the system.

3. Integrity. Built asset systems and their processes must be designed, implemented, operated, and maintained to prevent unauthorised alterations to assets, processes, system states, or system configurations, and to automatically report such changes or attempts. System integrity loss could result from physical alterations, like an unauthorised Wi-Fi access point connection to a secure OT network, or from faults like database corruption due to ransomware.

4. Authenticity. The authenticity of inputs and outputs, the system's state, and associated processes of built asset systems should be verifiable. Additionally,

the authenticity of components, software, and data within the system and its processes should be confirmable. Authenticity concerns may involve data, such as a falsified security certificate, or hardware, like a cloned device or a counterfeit system.

5. Availability. Built asset systems and their associated processes must be consistently accessible when needed and in a suitable manner. Should a system or process experience disruption, impairment, or an outage, restoring normal operations promptly is essential. Availability loss may result from a system component failure, like a disc crash, or a malicious act, such as a denial-of-service attack, which blocks access to an internet-connected system.
6. Utility. Built asset systems and their associated processes must be designed, implemented, operated, and maintained to preserve the assets' utility throughout their lifecycle. For instance, utility loss could happen if system sensors are replaced with ones of differing technical specifications. Even if the system functions properly, the altered data quality can undermine its use in ongoing condition monitoring and trend analysis.
7. Resilience. Systems of built assets and their related processes must be designed, implemented, operated, and maintained to guarantee that data, information, systems, and any associated processes or services are capable of adapting, renewing, and recovering swiftly in the face of adverse events. For example, if a building's HVAC system depends on cloud-based processing for energy efficiency, it must retain a fundamental level of operation in the event of cloud connectivity failure. Consequently, the building stays habitable, though there may be potential economic and environmental consequences from reduced energy efficiency.
8. Safety is paramount in the design, implementation, operation, and maintenance of built asset systems and their processes, aiming to protect the health and safety of individuals, the environment, and related assets. Traditionally managed as separate disciplines, safety and security must now be jointly considered due to the interdependencies introduced by digital technology. For instance, malware can disrupt the functioning of critical alarm systems like smoke detectors, potentially causing property damage or loss of life. Safety and security are characterised by different initiating events – malicious or accidental – but both can result in similar detrimental effects. Malicious actors can undermine safety measures, while security can be jeopardised by unintentional user actions or system failures. Understanding the relationship between safety and security is essential to ensure that safety-related decisions in design or operation enhance, rather than undermine, security measures, and vice versa.

SECURITY PRINCIPLES

6.22 There are five top-level principles that should be applied to the application of digital technologies in the built environment:

1. Senior management accountability Senior board-level managers should be aware of and responsible for cybersecurity, implementing appropriate governance to mitigate threats and prevent harm to built assets and their environment.
2. Holistic approach to security; Adopting a holistic approach to cyber and cyber-physical security is essential, encompassing risk management and control measures across the four key domains: physical, personnel, procedural, and technical.

Security goals for cyber-physical systems

6.23 When developing and implementing security measures, it is essential to derive security goals from the business requirements of the built asset, its systems, and associated processes or services. These goals should maintain

1. Possession – designed, implemented, operated, and maintained in order to prevent any unauthorised control, manipulation, or interference with their intended function or usage.
2. To ensure confidentiality, it is important to control access to data and information, preventing unauthorised access in all situations.
3. Availability, including reliability, necessitates consistent discoverability, accessibility, usability, and, when necessary, appropriate and timely disclosure.
4. Safety measures must be incorporated into the design, implementation, operation, and maintenance of systems to prevent the occurrence of hazardous conditions. These conditions could potentially result in injury, loss of life, unintended environmental harm, or damage to assets.
5. Resilience is characterised by the capacity to adapt, rejuvenate, and bounce back promptly when faced with unfavourable circumstances.
6. Integrity refers to the commitment to preserve the qualities of completeness, accuracy, consistency, coherence, and configuration.
7. The utility of data and/or information should be maintained and preserved throughout its lifecycle, as well as that of any associated asset, individual, or organisation.

6.24 Authenticity – the provenance should be verifiable in respect of:

the input and output of data and/or information to systems;

the existing systems and their current status;

All data and information regarding the built asset and its environment.

6.25 Balanced approach to safety and security: When developing and operating the constructed asset, it is crucial to find a balance between safety and security on a case-by-case basis, ensuring that the measures implemented to achieve one objective do not compromise the other.

MANAGING CHANGE

6.26 The growing integration and interoperability of built environment systems offer both risks and benefits concerning the security of built assets. Security strategies should address and adapt to emerging threats stemming from the convergence and hybridisation of technologies, as well as those present in existing and legacy systems.

THE BUILT ASSET LIFECYCLE

6.27 Built assets usually have a lifecycle spanning decades, in contrast to most digital technologies that undergo refresh cycles in less than ten years. Besides software patches and updates that may bring new risks, the fundamental operational technologies within a built asset seldom change. Nonetheless, there are components linked to these operational systems that might change monthly or yearly, such as BYOD policies and equipment utilised by maintenance and facilities management staff.

6.28 Built assets can experience various changes throughout their lifecycle, including changes in ownership and operational shifts such as alterations in use, physical reconfigurations, and enhancements or renovations of the structure, fabric, infrastructure, and fixtures. Within the scope of this Code of Practice, the built asset is examined from the viewpoint of the asset owner and is assumed to possess a typical lifecycle.

6.29 The primary activities for the top-level elements in the asset lifecycle are outlined as follows:

1. The concept. The preliminary identification of a business or operational need for a constructed asset or for an operational alteration that could lead to a decision to divest it.
2. The preliminary phase leading up to implementation. This stage of the lifecycle encompasses critical decisions pertaining to the business or operational requirement, which may result in acquiring an established asset or undertaking the design (or redesign) and construction (or modification) of a new (or existing) asset. When viewed from the perspective of an asset owner, the lifecycle commences upon the recognition of a necessity for a new or altered built asset. From the perspective of a tenant or occupier of a built asset, the lifecycle commences upon acquiring the lease or the right to occupy the building.
3. In this phase, efforts will be made to not only develop the rationale or business case, but also to formulate the requirements or project brief. Furthermore, justifications for any alterations to the occupied site, its structure, services, internal layout, and/or use will be established. The level of formality, scope, and format for the strategy, business case, and project brief will be determined by the organisation and the magnitude of the investment or required changes.

6.30 Implementation phase. Following the decision to acquire an existing built asset or commence the construction of a new one (or modification of an existing asset), this phase encompasses the procurement and the majority of design activities. Typically, this process encompasses the progression of the project brief, commencing with the preliminary conceptual design of the constructed asset and advancing to the intricate technical design. The design process may consist of multiple stages, phases, or iterations, depending on the complexity of the requirements and the scale of the work. After the completion of the design work, the acquisition and/or implementation of build/changes are carried out in order to satisfy the strategic/business requirement for the asset and prepare it for operational use.

6.31 Operation phase. The operational and maintenance aspects of the constructed asset are encompassed in this phase, which is carried out by the owner or occupier. The current stage of the lifecycle commences once the constructed asset is utilised according to its intended purpose. In the course of this phase, the constructed asset may be susceptible to multiple operational alterations. Various factors, including changes in usage, fabric modifications, and system adjustments, may contribute to these transformations. The implementation of these operational changes gives rise to security risks due to alterations in personnel, responsibilities, and systems.

6.32 Disposal phase. An asset owner might determine that maintaining or using a built asset is no longer economically or commercially viable and opt to decommission or dispose of it. Similarly, a tenant or user of a built asset may decide that continued occupation or use of the asset is no longer necessary. For the asset owner, the lifecycle of the asset concludes once the asset is decommissioned and its disposal or demolition is finalised. For the tenant or user, the lifecycle ends upon lease termination or when they stop occupying the built asset.

APPLYING CYBER SECURITY THROUGH THE LIFECYCLE OF A BUILT ASSET

6.33 Built assets have intricate lifecycles and often go through numerous changes and updates in technology. The way built assets are used can also shift dramatically throughout their lifecycle, as can the potential vulnerabilities and threats they face. Swift advancements in technology or shifts in business needs can result in modifications to built asset systems and operations that were not anticipated during the design, refurbishment, or retrofitting stages.

6.34 An operational change that could introduce a new cybersecurity risk is the proposal by a new facilities management contractor to implement remote monitoring for cost savings, which could involve overseeing built asset systems, plants, and machinery. The possibility of such remote connectivity might not have been contemplated during the original system design, and adequate safeguards might not have been established to deter or mitigate damage from attacks through this remote access.

6.35 Cybersecurity affects both newly constructed assets, which are at the pre-implementation or implementation phase, and existing built assets that are undergoing acquisition or modification. This section explores the potential consequences of inadequate cybersecurity on built assets and their stakeholders.

WHO IS ACCOUNTABLE AND RESPONSIBLE FOR THE CYBER SECURITY OF BUILT ASSET SYSTEMS AND DATA?

6.36 Accountability and responsibility for the cybersecurity of a built asset, its systems, associated business processes, and the data should be managed in a cascading fashion, starting from strategic accountability at the senior management level down to the responsibility for daily operational activities.

Strategic level

6.37 The senior management of the built asset owner has the responsibility to ensure the existence of a cyber security strategy and accompanying security policies that encompass the built asset systems and data.

6.38 The built asset owner bears the responsibility of ensuring that contracts pertaining to the construction, operation, and maintenance of the built asset incorporate security requirements that facilitate the implementation of the security policies.

6.39 The senior management of the built asset occupier(s)/user(s) bears the responsibility of ensuring that its personnel adhere to the security policies of the built asset.

6.40 The entity or entities utilising the constructed asset are accountable for incorporating suitable measures into their security policies to meet their obligations to the asset owner.

Operational level

6.41 The operational managers in the asset owner and occupier/user organisations have the responsibility of ensuring the implementation of appropriate and proportionate processes and procedures to adhere to the built asset security policies.

6.42 It is the duty of the operational managers in the asset owner and occupier/user organisations to guarantee that all personnel, including contractors, strictly comply with the prescribed processes and procedures.

WHAT BUILT ASSET SYSTEMS AND INFORMATION ASSETS NEED TOBE PROTECTED?

6.43 The built asset owner and relevant stakeholders should evaluate the decision to protect any of the specified assets or items on a case-by-case basis.

When assessing specific cyber security risks, it is crucial for the built asset owner and relevant stakeholders to consider the value they attribute to an asset and the benefits it brings.

6.44 Protection may be necessary for the following types of assets or items, depending on the specific built asset, its intended use, and the needs of the stakeholders involved:

1. information assets (information or data) related to:

   (a) A site or built asset's business plans or strategy as formulated by its owner or investor.

   (b) The design and technical functioning of the constructed asset.

   (c) The contractual information related to the design, construction, operation, and alterations of the built asset.

   (d) The utilisation of the constructed asset and the operational activities associated with it.

6.45 Personally identifiable information (PII) pertaining to individuals occupying or using built assets systems, in order to:

1. prevent unauthorised changes to, or use of control and operation of, technical systems, including:
2. HVAC systems;
3. built asset management systems;
4. AACS;
5. CCTV and alarm systems; and
6. IACS;

6.46 Mitigate the risk of disclosing commercially or operationally sensitive information or data from built asset-related systems.

1. Mitigate the risk of information loss that could compromise an individual's privacy or security, including images captured by CCTV systems or personally identifiable information stored in systems.

6.47 Operational information pertaining to the utilisation of the constructed asset or its occupants, such as the location.

1. Sensitive operations are conducted or valuable items and dangerous materials are stored at this location.
2. When evaluating the necessity of safeguarding information assets, it is crucial to take into account the characteristics of the assets and their significance to authorised users (such as the owner, operator, or users) as well as potential adversaries or malevolent individuals. The unauthorised disclosure or use of various classes of information assets can have diverse consequences,

both in terms of economic impact and reputation, for the authorised users. When an organisation decides to disclose information assets publicly, it is crucial to prioritise secure communication practices. This can be achieved by consistently promoting security-oriented messages and refraining from sharing any information that could assist hostile reconnaissance or facilitate targeted phishing attacks.

WHAT COULD ADVERSELY AFFECT THE BUILT ASSET SYSTEMS AND DATA?

6.48 The growing dependence of organisations on information and communications technologies necessitates that any interference or failure of electronic and computer-based systems can result in significant consequences. In the realm of IT systems, the primary objective in terms of security is ensuring the confidentiality of information assets. In the context of operational technology systems, safeguarding the information assets is frequently imperative.

6.49 This entails the prevention of any delay, deletion, or alteration of data pertaining to the real-time functioning of physical components, such as sensor readings and actuator settings. It also involves safeguarding the master data from any modifications, including configuration settings, set points, and conversion tables.

6.50 The necessary level of protection is typically determined by evaluating the potential impact on asset owners and stakeholders, in relation to the cost of implementing suitable countermeasures. Instances that have the potential to impact these attributes include the following,

6.51 The disclosure of detailed business plans pertaining to the acquisition and redevelopment of a site by an unhappy employee without authorisation greatly impacts commercial negotiations regarding its acquisition and utilization. Additionally, it affects the disclosure of layouts or configurations of built assets or built asset systems, potentially assisting in hostile reconnaissance.

6.52 The infection of computers utilised by a design with encryption malware represents the acquisition or authority over them.

6.53 The team may face the risk of critical design information being held hostage, as they no longer have control over it and are unable to utilise it. A similar scenario may arise in an operational built asset if it becomes infected with ransomware, leading to a loss of control over the built asset system.

6.54 Wireless controllers are utilised to manage the lighting and ventilation in individual conference rooms, thereby upholding integrity. The operation experiences intermittent disruptions due to an electromagnetic interference issue caused by a nearby radio frequency (RF) source that interferes with and degrades the control signals.

6.55 The incident of purchasing heavily discounted software, only to discover that it is counterfeit, brings attention to the matter of authenticity.

6.56 As a result of malware being present on the source disks, it has been installed on both the users' organisation and built asset networks. This has subsequently spread to multiple clients and asset users, resulting in detrimental consequences to both reputation and finances.

6.57 The availability of cloud-based energy management services is severely disrupted as a result of a denial-of-service attack on the cloud service provider. This disruption leads to losses in energy savings and intermittent power outages.

6.58 The utility involves a process of converting files and data to facilitate the transfer of access control permissions.

6.59 The corruption of vital data occurred during the installation and commissioning process of a new access control system for the entire site. The manual recreation and entry of data into the new system disrupts site operations and results in substantial additional expenses.

6.60 The breach of remote support connections on fire alarm systems has resulted in the triggering of fire alarms on three successive days, prompting the fire and rescue service to respond on each occasion. Due to security breaches, the fire authorities have withdrawn the fire certificate, resulting in the built asset being deemed unusable for safety reasons. Modifications to the fire alarm system are required in order to reinstate its usability.

WHERE ARE THE BUILT ASSET SYSTEMS AND DATA LOCATED?

6.61 The geographic placement of systems plays a crucial role in the vulnerability of the systems, including their components and infrastructure, to a range of potential risks. An instance of unauthorised physical access to a workstation, such as the use of malware-infected removable storage media (eg, USB storage devices, SD cards, and optical discs), can compromise the system. The location of system components can also contribute to their vulnerability to physical damage or interference, whether unintentional, intentional, or natural in origin.

6.62 The systems utilised to create, process, manage, store, or display data for built assets may be situated:

1. within the built asset or site;
2. in other accommodation used by the owner, operator or occupier; or
3. with a third-party service provider, for example, the facilities manager or cloud service provider.

6.63 Understanding the location and criticality of a system's components to its ongoing operation allows for risk assessment and the adoption of suitable controls or countermeasures. The limited lifespan of digital systems, in contrast to the longevity of built assets, poses a significant risk. For instance, commercial operating systems typically receive support for no more than 10 years. Consequently, software updates or obsolescence over time may make accessing data from built assets increasingly challenging.

6.64 The identification of the location of built asset systems allows for the safeguarding of the generated, stored, and processed data pertaining to these systems, although it may not encompass all built asset data. To illustrate, it is improbable to encompass specific strategic information assets associated with the design and operation of the built asset, or BIM-related information produced within a design process, and so forth. Consequently, in addition to assessing the positioning of systems, the positioning of built asset data throughout the lifecycle of the built asset should be given due consideration. This allows for the evaluation of any risks associated with this information and the implementation of appropriate controls or countermeasures.

6.65 The data utilised by built asset systems, or necessary for the design, operation, and management of the built asset, may be stored on-site within the built asset, in an adjacent built asset, or it may be kept off-site by the parties responsible for the ownership, operation, or occupation of the built asset, or their designated advisers or representatives.

6.66 By a professional or supplier in the field of built assets, such as plans, detailed designs, configuration, and maintenance information.

6.67 Regulatory or statutory authorities, including those responsible for planning applications and building regulations, may necessitate the provision of this information by suppliers or providers of services.

6.68 For the purposes of archiving, backing up, or ensuring business continuity, by parties not directly involved.

6.69 It is probable that the location of built asset data will undergo changes during the lifecycle of the asset. The handling of this issue is crucial within the realm of data operational management, necessitating the establishment of offline backup systems to mitigate the risk of corruption resulting from cyber attacks. The creation of an appropriate environment for the handling and protection of BIM-related information should be taken into account during the entire lifespan of the built asset, which can be complicated by changes in ownership, occupancy, and operation.

HOW SHOULD BUILT ASSET SYSTEMS AND DATA BE PROTECTED?

6.70 The objective of managing Cyber Security is to maintain control, coherence, and ensure trusted operation of assets belonging to both the organisation and users within the cyber environment. The measures required to achieve this fall into one of four categories:

1. physical – to protect the built asset systems and data from damage, theft or interference;
2. technical – the electromagnetic, physical and logical design and implementation to enable and achieve trustworthy operation of built asset systems;
3. procedural – the process and procedures relating to the use of built asset systems and data throughout their lifecycle; and
4. personnel – the background checks, vetting, training and education of individuals who will have access to, or use of, the built asset systems and data.

6.71 The selection of measures will be contingent upon the cyber security context and the level of risk associated with identified threats and vulnerabilities of the constructed asset. Given the complexities of the physical building and built asset systems, when evaluating the measures to be implemented, it is important to consider the level of alignment that can realistically be achieved between the systems in place for enterprise systems and those utilised for built asset systems.

CHAPTER 7

CYBER BREACH PLAYBOOK

Helen Wong MBE

INTRODUCTION

Overview

7.01 In the event of a cyber incident, it is important that the organisation is able to respond, mobilise, and execute an appropriate level of response to limit the impact on the brand, value, service delivery, and the public, client, and customer confidence. Although all cyber incidents are different in their nature and technologies used, it is possible to group common cyber incident types and methodologies together. This is in order to provide an appropriate and timely response depending on the cyber incident type. Incident specific playbooks provide incident managers and stakeholders with a consistent approach to follow when remediating a cyber incident.

7.02 References are made to both a Core IT CIRT and a CIRT within this document. This is in recognition that the playbook will be used by organisations of different sizes. Some may initially manage an incident with a small response team within IT services, but where there is a confirmed compromise, this may be escalated to an extended level CIRT comprising members of the organisation outside the IT services who will deal with agreed categories of compromise. The Playbook, as with the Cyber Incident Response Plan CIRP, will require adjustment to reflect the organisational make up.

7.03 Playbooks describe the activities of those directly involved in managing specific cyber incidents. However, it is important to acknowledge the speed at which cyber incidents can escalate and become a significant business disruptor, requiring both business continuity and consequence management considerations. Early consideration should be given to engaging Business Continuity, Resilience and Policy Area Leads in order that the wider issues can be effectively managed. Business Continuity and Resilience leads within the organisation must therefore be familiar with the CIRP and Playbooks and how they link to wider Incident response and Exercising Playbooks and arrangements.

Purpose

7.04 The purpose of this Cyber Incident Response: Malware Playbook is to define activities that should be considered when detecting, analysing and remediating a malware incident. The playbook also identifies the key stakeholders that may be required to undertake these specific activities.

Malware Definition

7.05 Malware is any software intentionally designed to negatively impact a computer, server, client, or computer network. Malware must be implanted or introduced in some way into a target's computer. Malware can take the form of executable code, scripts, active content, and/or other software.

7.06 Malware can include: computer viruses, worms, trojan horses, spyware, rootkits, botnet software, keystroke loggers, ransomware, cryptominers, adware and malicious mobile code. Some types of malware (eg, spyware, rootkits, ransomware, cryptominers and botnet software) are often used during sophisticated cyber-attacks against organisations. In these cases, malware can be customised to target specific systems within an organisation's technical infrastructure and configured to avoid detection. Malware has a malicious intent, acting against the interest of the computer user thus does not include software that causes unintentional harm due to some deficiency, which is typically described as a software bug.

Scope

7.07 This document has been designed for the sole use of the first responders such as the Service Desk team when responding to a cyber incident. It is not standalone and must be used alongside the CIRP.

Review Cycle

7.08 This document is to be reviewed for continued relevancy by the Cyber Incident Response Team (CIRT) lead at least once every 12 months; following any major cyber security incidents, a change of vendor, or the acquisition of new security services.

PREPARATION PHASE

7.09

Preparation Phase	
Phase objectives	The preparation phase has the following objectives: • Prepare to respond to cyber security incident in a timely and effective manner; • Prepare organisational assets for malware outbreak; • Inform employees of their role in remediating a malware incident including reporting mechanisms.

Activity	Description	Stakeholders
Prepare to respond	Activities may include, but are not limited to:	
	Ensure that: • All desktop/laptop and server systems have an anti-malware solution deployed. • Gateway anti-malware solutions are in place. • Users are encouraged to store data on shared drives that are backed up and not on local device drives. • Local admin rights have been removed as far as currently practical.	• Information Security Manager • Head of IT
	Review and rehearse cyber incident response procedures including technical and business roles and responsibilities, escalation to major incident management where necessary.	• Head of Information Governance • Head of IT • Information Security Manager • Team Leader • Service Delivery Manager • Service Desk Analysts/ Technicians • Legal Team • Communications Team • Resilience Lead • Business Continuity Lead
	Review recent cyber security incidents and the outputs.	• Information Security Manager
	Review threat intelligence for threats to the organisation, brands and the sector, as well as common patterns and newly developing risks and vulnerabilities.	• Information Security Manager
	Ensure appropriate access to any necessary documentation and information, including out-of-hours access, for the following: • CIRP; • Network Architecture Diagrams; • Data Flow Diagrams.	• Information Security Manager
	Identify and obtain the services of a 3rd party Cyber Forensic provider.	• Information Security Manager
	Define Threat and Risk Indicators and Alerting pattern within the organisation's security information and event management (SIEM) solution.	• Information Security Manager

Activity	Description	Stakeholders
Inform employees	Activities may include, but are not limited to:	
	Conduct regular awareness campaigns to highlight information security risks faced by employees, including: • Phishing attacks and malicious emails; • Ransomware; • Reporting a suspected cyber incident.	• Head of IT • Information Security Manager • Resilience Lead • Business Continuity Lead
	Ensure regular security training is mandated for those employees managing personal, confidential or high risk data and systems.	• Head of IT • Information Security Manager • HR • L&D Department • Resilience Lead • Business Continuity Lead

DETECT

7.10

Detection Phase		
Phase objectives	The detection phase has the following objectives: • Detect and report a breach or compromise of the confidentiality, integrity or availability of organisational data; • Complete initial investigation of the malware; • Report the malware formally to the correct team as a cyber incident.	
Activity	**Description**	**Stakeholders**
Detect and report the incident	Activities may include, but are not limited to:	
	Monitor detection channels, both automatic and manual, customer and staff channels for the identification of a malware attack, including: • Anti-malware system notifications to the IT team; • User notification to the Service Desk; • Any other notification that raises suspicion of a malware incident. **Isolated malware infections are to be expected from time to time and will normally be dealt with automatically by the anti-malware technology implemented by the organisation. It is only if an outbreak is impacting on services that the cyber incident response process and this playbook will be engaged.*	• Information Security Manager • Core IT CIRT

	Report the cyber incident via the Service Desk. If a ticket does not exist already, raise a ticket containing minimum information. To report an incident, follow the process defined in the CIRP. Consider reporting to Police Scotland where criminal Investigation may be warranted	• Information Security Manager • Core IT CIRT
	Consider whether data loss or data breach has occurred and if so *refer to data breach playbook.*	• Information Security Manager • Information Governance Team • Core IT CIRT
	Classify the cyber security incident, based upon available information related to the malware attack the incident types **(see CIRP).**	• Information Security Manager • Core IT CIRT
	Report the cyber incident in accordance with the organisation's CIRP. Consider the Intelligence value to other organisations and share on the CiSP	• Information Security Manager • Core IT CIRT • CIRT
	Where appropriate consider reporting requirements to Information Commissioner's Office (ICO), relevant Regulator and or Competent Authority (NISD), National Cyber Security Centre (NCSC) and / or Police Scotland	• Information Security Manager • Core IT CIRT • CIRT
Activity	**Description**	**Stakeholders**
Initial investigation of the incident	Activities may include, but are not limited to:	
	Mobilise the CIRT to begin initial investigation of the cyber security incident **(see staff contact details within CIRP).**	• Information Security Manager • CIRT The following may also be included in the incident response team where appropriate for the incident: • Service Desk Analysts • Server Desk Technicians • Server Team • Mobile Device Team
	Identify likelihood of widespread malware infection.	• Head of IT • Information Security Manager • Core IT CIRT • CIRT

	Collate initial incident data including as a minimum for following; • A timeline of when the malware was first detected, and other significant events. • Whether the malware was detected by the anti-malware solution, or identified through other means. • The probable scope of the infection, in terms of the systems and/or applications affected. • Whether the malware appears to be spreading across the infrastructure. • The probable nature of the malware infection, if known. • Whether the anti-malware solution has successfully quarantined/cleansed the infection. • Likely containment options (eg, on the basis of publicly-available information, for known malware).	• Head of IT • Information Security Manager • Core IT CIRT • CIRT
	Secure artefacts, including copies of suspected malicious software and forensic copies of affected system(s) for future analysis.	• Information Security Manager • Core IT CIRT
	Research Threat Intelligence sources and consider Cyber Security Information Sharing Partnership (CiSP) submission to gain further intelligence and support mitigation by others.	• Information Security Manager • Core IT CIRT
	Review cyber incident categorisation to validate the cyber security incident type as a malware attack and assess the incident priority, based upon the initial investigation. **(See CIRP for Incident Severity Matrix)**	• Security Manager • Core IT CIRT
Activity	**Description**	**Stakeholders**
Incident reporting	Activities may include, but are not limited to:	
	Report the cyber incident in accordance with the organisation's CIRP.	• Information Security Manager • CIRT

Activity	Description	Stakeholders
	Report the Cyber incident in accordance with the organisation's CIRP. Consider the Intelligence value to other organisations and share on the Cisp.	• Information Security Manager • Core IT CIRT • CIRT
	Where appropriate consider reporting requirements to Information Commissioner's Office (ICO), relevant regulator and or Competent Authority (NISD), National Cyber Security Centre (NCSC) and / or Police Scotland.	• Information Security Manager • Core IT CIRT • CIRT
	Escalate in accordance with the CIRP.	• Information Security Manager • CIRT • Resilience Lead • Business Continuity Lead
Activity	**Description**	**Stakeholders**
Establish the requirement for a full forensic investigation	Activities may include, but are not limited to:	
	Consider conducting a full forensic investigation, on the advice of legal counsel. All evidence handling should be done in line with the Association of Chief Police Officers (ACPO) Good Practice Guide for Digital Evidence.	• Information Security Manager • Core IT CIRT • CIRT

ANALYSE

7.11

Analysis Phase		
Phase objectives	The analysis phase has the following key objectives: • Analyse the cyber incident to uncover the scope of the attack; • Identify and report potentially compromised data and the impact of such a compromise; • Establish the requirement for a full forensic investigation; • Develop a remediation plan based upon the scope and details of the cyber incident.	
Activity	**Description**	**Stakeholders**
Analyse the extent of the incident	Activities may include, but are not limited to:	
	Engage technical staff from resolver groups.	• Service Desk Technicians • Core IT CIRT
	Classify the malware by submission to multiple AV vendors and determine the family it belongs to.	• Information Security Manager • Core IT CIRT

	Scope the attack. • A timeline of when the malware was first detected, and other significant events. • Whether the malware was detected by the anti-malware solution, or identified through other means. • The probable scope of the infection, in terms of the systems and/or applications affected. • Whether the malware appears to be spreading across the infrastructure. • The probable nature of the malware infection, if known. • Whether the anti-malware solution has successfully quarantined/cleansed the infection. • Likely containment options (eg, on the basis of publicly-available information, for known malware).	• Information Security Manager • Core IT CIRT • CIRT
	Reverse-engineer the malware in a secure environment to understand its mechanisms, and the functionality it implements.	• Information Security Manager • Core IT CIRT • CIRT
	Execute the malware in a secure environment or sandbox, segregated from the business network, to determine its behaviour on a test system, including created files, launched services, modified registry keys and network communications.	• Information Security Manager • Core IT CIRT
	Review affected infrastructure for indicators of compromise derived from the malware analysis to identify any additional compromised system(s).	• Information Security Manager • Core IT CIRT
	Preserve all evidence to support attribution or anticipated legal action.	• Information Security Manager • Core IT CIRT • CIRT
	Examine threat intelligence feeds to determine if the malware attack is bespoke and targeted at specific accounts, infrastructure or systems.	• Information Security Manager • Core IT CIRT
	Verify all infected assets are in the process of being recalled and quarantined.	• Information Security Manager • Core IT CIRT • CIRT

REMEDIATION – CONTAIN, ERADICATE AND RECOVER

7.12

Remediation Phase		
Phase objectives	The remediation phase has the following objectives: • Contain the effects of the malware on the targeted systems; • Eradicate the malware from the network through agreed mitigation measures; • Recover affected systems and services back to a Business As Usual (BUA) state.	
Activity	**Description**	**Stakeholders**
Containment	Contain the technical mechanisms of the malware attack, including:	
	Monitor for any new infections which might suggest that the malware is spreading across the infrastructure, and alert the CIRT to any significant changes in the scope of the incident (eg, the infection of a previously unaffected business system or site).	• Information Security Manager • Core IT CIRT
	Ensure that the latest malware definitions have been deployed across the anti-malware solution.	• Information Security Manager • Core IT CIRT
	Initiate an estate-wide anti-malware scan.	• Information Security Manager • Core IT CIRT
	Identify the infected assets(s) and physically disconnect them from the network. Business continuity options for users affected by such disconnection include: • Replacing disconnected devices with fresh builds from IT, where stocks permit (ensuring they first have relevant updates applied). • Directing users whose devices are disconnected to work from an alternative location; such as another office, a Disaster Recovery facility or from home. Where necessary the corporate disaster recovery process will be followed.	• Information Security Manager • Core IT CIRT
	Determine whether the malware appears to be attempting to communicate with outside parties (eg, attempting to connect to botnet command and control servers on the public internet), and take steps to block any such communication.	• Information Security Manager • Core IT CIRT • CIRT

	Suspend the login credentials of suspected compromised accounts.	• Information Security Manager • Core IT CIRT • CIRT
	Secure copies of the malicious code, affected systems and any identified artefacts for further investigation (engaging with forensic support if forensic copies are required).	• Information Security Manager • Core IT CIRT
	Inform business data owner(s) and stakeholders of the progress of containment activities.	• Information Security Manager • CIRT • Resilience Lead • Business Continuity Lead • Policy Area Lead
Activity	**Description**	**Stakeholders**
Eradication	Activities may include, but are not limited to:	
	Identify removal methods from the results of the malicious code analysis and trusted sources (AV providers).	• Information Security Manager • Core IT CIRT
	Complete an automated or manual removal process to eradicate malware or compromised executables using appropriate tools.	• Information Security Manager • Core IT CIRT
	• Conduct a restoration of affected networked systems from a trusted back up.	• Information Security Manager • Core IT CIRT
	• Re-install any standalone systems from a clean OS back-up before updating with trusted data back-ups.	• Information Security Manager • Core IT CIRT
	• Change any compromised account details.	• Information Security Manager • Core IT CIRT
	• Continue to monitor for signatures and other indicators of compromise to prevent the malware attack from re-emerging.	• Information Security Manager • Core IT CIRT
	• Confirm policy compliance across the estate.	• Information Security Manager • Core IT CIRT
Activity	**Description**	**Stakeholders**
Recover to BAU	Activities may include, but are not limited to:	
	Recover systems based on business impact analysis and business criticality.	• Information Security Manager • Core IT CIRT
	Complete malware scanning of all systems, across the estate.	• Information Security Manager • Core IT CIRT
	Re-image systems.	• Information Security Manager • Core IT CIRT

	Re-set the credentials of all involved system(s) and users account details.	• Information Security Manager • Core IT CIRT
	Reintegrate previously compromised systems.	• Information Security Manager • Core IT CIRT
	Restore any corrupted or destroyed data.	• Information Security Manager • Core IT CIRT
	Restore any suspended services.	• Information Security Manager • Core IT CIRT
	Establish monitoring to detect further suspicious activity.	• Information Security Manager • Core IT CIRT
	Co-ordinate the implementation of any necessary patches or vulnerability remediation activities.	• Information Security Manager • Core IT CIRT

POST INCIDENT

7.13

Post-Incident Activities Phase		
Phase objectives	The post-incident activities phase has the following objectives: • Complete an incident report including all incident details and activities; • Complete the lessons identified and problem management process; • Publish appropriate internal and external communications.	
Activity	**Description**	**Stakeholders**
Incident reporting	Draft a post-incident report that includes the following details as a minimum: • Details of the cyber incident identified and remediated across the network to include timings, type and location of incident as well as the effect on users; • Activities that were undertaken by relevant resolver groups, service providers and business stakeholders that enabled normal business operations to be resumed; • Recommendations where any aspects of people, process or technology could be improved across the organisation to help prevent a similar cyber incident from reoccurring, as part of a formalised lessons identified process.	• Senior Stakeholders • Head of Information Governance • Head of IT • Audit Committee • Information Security Manager

Lessons Identified & Problem Management	Complete the formal lessons identified process to feedback into future preparation activities.	• Information Security Manager • CIRT • Resilience Lead
	Consider sharing lessons identified with the wider stakeholders where relevant.	• Information Security Manager • CIRT • Resilience Lead • Business Continuity Lead
	Conduct root cause analysis to identify and remediate underlying vulnerabilities.	• Information Security Manager • CIRT
Human Resources	Review staff welfare; working hours, over time, time off in lieu (TOIL) and expenses.	• Information Security Manager • HR
Communications	Activities may include, but are not limited to:	
	• Publish internal communications in line with the communications strategy to inform and educate employees on malware attacks and security awareness.	• Information Security Manager • CIRT • Communications • Resilience Lead • Business Continuity Lead
	• Publish external communications, if appropriate, in line with the communications strategy to provide advice to customers, engage with the market, and inform press of the cyber incident. These communications should provide key information of the cyber incident without leaving the organisation vulnerable or inciting further malware attacks.	• Head of IT • Information Security Manager • Communications Team

ANNEX A: FLOW DIAGRAM

7.14

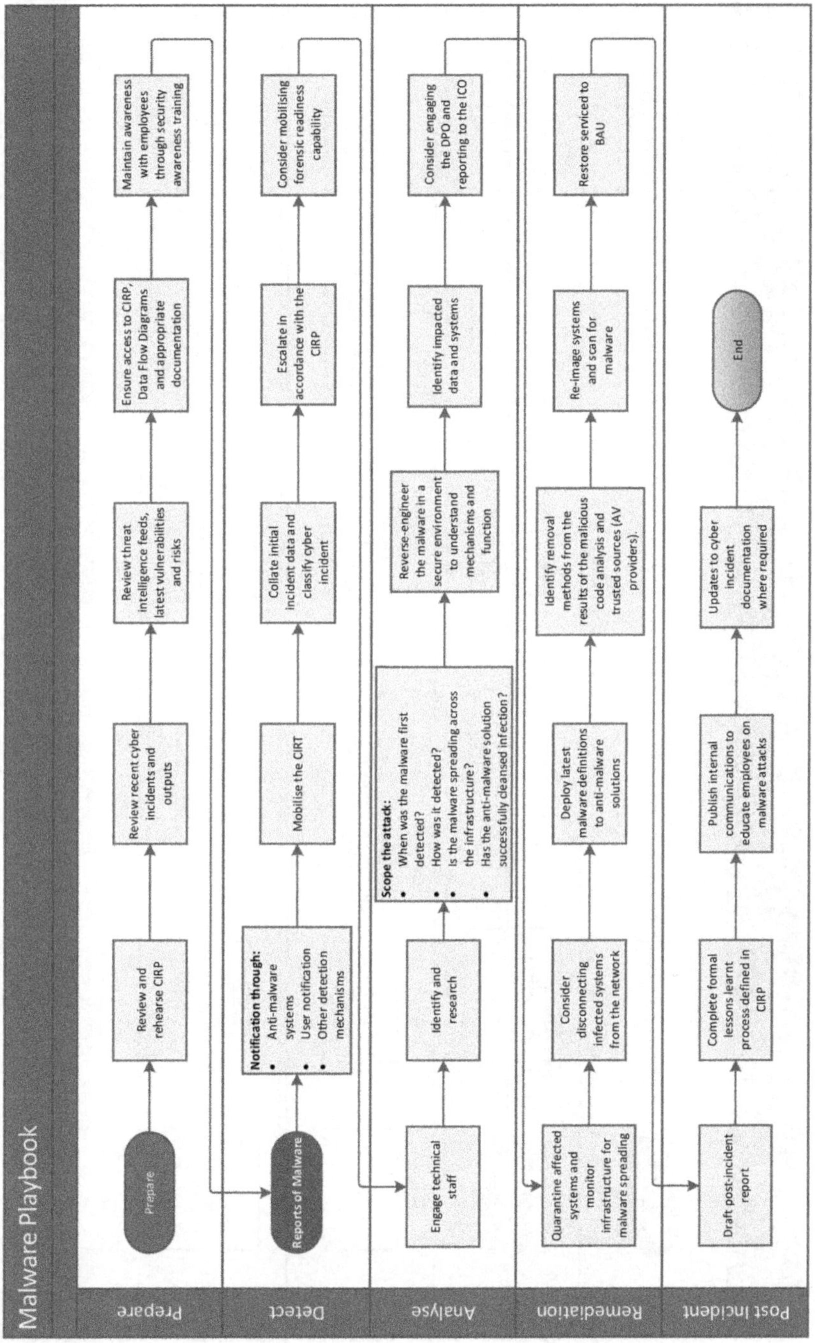

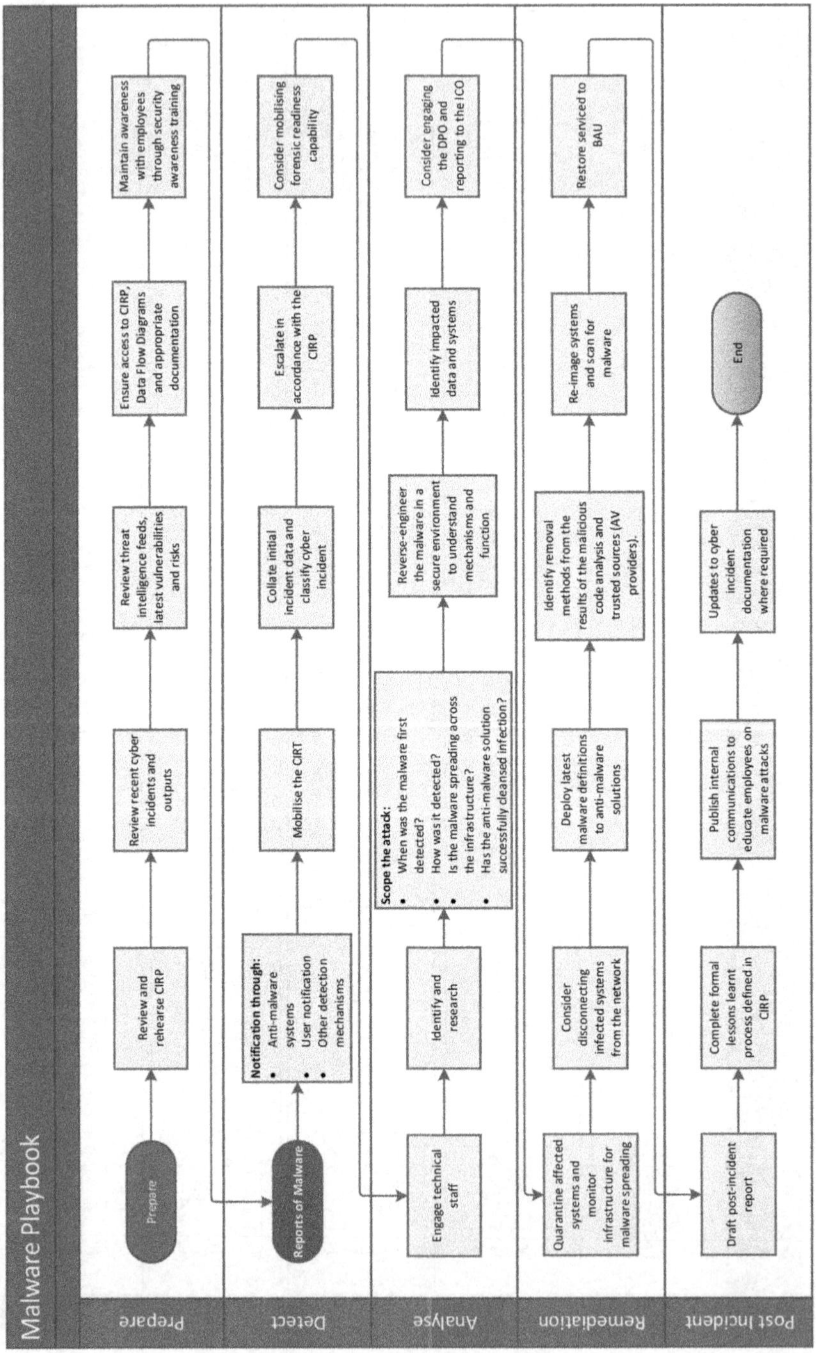
Malware Playbook
Prepare
Detect
Analyse
Remediation
Post Incident
Prepare
Review and rehearse CIRP
Review recent cyber incidents and outputs
Review threat intelligence feeds, latest vulnerabilities and risks
Ensure access to CIRP, Data Flow Diagrams and appropriate documentation
Maintain awareness with employees through security awareness training
Reports of Malware
Notification through:
• Anti-malware systems
• User notification
• Other detection mechanisms
Mobilise the CIRT
Collate initial incident data and classify cyber incident
Escalate in accordance with the CIRP
Consider mobilising forensic readiness capability
Engage technical staff
Identify and research
Scope the attack:
• When was the malware first detected?
• How was it detected?
• Is the malware spreading across the infrastructure?
• Has the anti-malware solution successfully cleansed infection?
Reverse-engineer the malware in a secure environment to understand mechanisms and function
Identify impacted data and systems
Consider engaging the DPO and reporting to the ICO
Quarantine affected systems and monitor infrastructure for malware spreading
Consider disconnecting infected systems from the network
Deploy latest malware definitions to anti-malware solutions
Identify removal methods from the results of the malicious code analysis and trusted sources (AV providers).
Re-image systems and scan for malware
Restore serviced to BAU
Draft post-incident report
Complete formal lessons learnt process defined in CIRP
Publish internal communications to educate employees on malware attacks
Updates to cyber incident documentation where required
End

CHAPTER 8

THE C SUITE PERSPECTIVE ON CYBER RISK

Klaus Julisch

ORGANISATIONAL RAMIFICATIONS OF CYBER RISK

8.01 The fact that many cyber-risks originate in technology should not detract from the fact that cyber-risks are business risks whose impact on the personal and commercial success of senior executives (CxOs) has continued to increase over recent years. This chapter explains how C-Suite executives are affected by cyber risk, what their role is, and how they can lead their organisations' approach to managing cyber risk.

8.02 Cyber-risks may begin as technology issues, but they typically extend well beyond the technology domain. Nowhere is this more apparent than in the event of a cyber-incident. Deloitte's research into the direct and intangible costs caused by cyberattacks[1] has produced telling findings. To begin with, it is noteworthy that the impact and associated cost of cyber-incidents play out over many years – up to five years in the case of major cyber-incidents.

8.03 A second important finding is that less than 10% of the total cost of incidents is incurred during the 'hot' *incident triage phase* where the attack is analysed and immediate steps are taken to stop the compromise, ensure business continuity, and manage relationships with external parties. Most of these triage-related costs are staff and technology costs, eg, for technical investigations, customer breach notification, public relations and stakeholder outreach, legal support, or cyber security improvements.

8.04 The remaining 90% of costs are incurred in the months and years after the attack. These costs tend to be of a more intangible nature and are aimed at recovering business assets rather than IT assets. Not surprisingly, these costs affect a diverse set of corporate functions, who are also involved in recovering the affected business assets:

- **Lost intellectual property** affects the Research and Development function, Corporate Strategy, Marketing, and Legal Counsel who have to collaborate to mitigate the impact of lost patents, designs, copyrights, trademarks, trade secrets or other proprietary and confidential information.

1 Mossburg, Gelinne & Calzada, *Beneath the surface of a cyberattack* (Deloitte, 2016), available online at https://www2.deloitte.com/us/en/pages/risk/articles/hidden-business-impact-of-cyberattack.html.

- **Devalued trade names** are the responsibility of Corporate Strategy, Marketing, and client-facing staff who work together to re-establish brands, logos, and symbols in the market place.
- **Lost contract revenue** includes revenue and ultimately income loss, as well as lost future opportunities associated with contracts that are terminated, delayed, or reduced as a result of cyber-incidents. Sales, Marketing and the affected business divisions must lead the recovery of this from of cost and business impact.
- **Increased cost of capital**, eg, higher borrowing costs due to a downgraded credit rating or a drop in share value, primarily affects CFOs and divisional business leaders.
- **Increased cyber insurance premiums** are typically the responsibility of CFOs and CROs with support of CIOs and CISOs.
- **Cyber security improvements** are technical improvements to the IT infrastructure, security controls, monitoring capabilities, or surrounding processes, specifically to recover business operations or to prevent similar occurrences in the future. They are the responsibility of CIOs, CISOs, and CTOs.

8.05 In summary, although cyber-attacks are conducted through technology-based means, the principal damage will usually be to business assets, rather than IT assets, and a multitude of corporate functions beyond IT have a crucial role to play in recovering said business value. Of course, these corporate functions' roles should start well before any incidents occur, and the following sections will further expand on this point.

ASSIGNING ACCOUNTABILITY

8.06 As with any other business risk, 'the buck stops at the top'. CxOs can delegate certain technical aspects of cyber-security to IT security or other specialist functions; furthermore, if the impact of a cyber-incident is contained, they can frequently assign accountability to certain individuals. For example, if some employees' access rights were not revoked after they left the organisation, this failure can be attributed to the owner of the so-called 'Joiner-Mover-Leaver' control process. More generally, however, the history of the past five years and specifically the cyber-related departures of a multitude of CEOs, CIOs, CFOs, and CSOs of major international organisations are proof that the C-Suite is held accountable if cyber-incidents have a major business impact, are handled poorly, or reveal significant shortcomings in an organisation's approach to cyber-security.

8.07 By way of illustration, Table 8.1 summarises how accountability for key business assets can be assigned to the C-Suite. The exact assignment is generally company-specific and is less important than the fact that accountability for key business assets should be assigned to C-Suite owners. Moreover, even if such an assignment is not done explicitly, past experience has shown that in the event of cyber-incidents, de-facto accountability will be assigned in a manner similar to Table 8.1.

8.08 Regarding the asset of 'Sensitive or proprietary data', a common alternative to the assignment shown in the table below is to assign accountability in a more granular manner to data owners, eg, the Head of Research and Development (R&D) would be made accountable for intellectual property, the Divisional CEO(s) for customer data, the CFO for financial information, etc. For the sake of simplicity, this chapter assigns all sensitive or proprietary data to the Divisional CEO(s).

8.09 Assigning C-Suite accountability for business assets is crucial to managing them effectively. For example, the *reported* costs of major cyber-incidents have been in the hundreds of millions of dollars. Insiders postulate that at least for some major incidents in recent years, *actual* costs exceeded $1 billion, and the cost of a major cyberattack on a systemically relevant bank is likely to also exceed $1 billion. These are very significant costs that no current cyber insurance policy will cover; accordingly, it takes a senior finance leader to develop a strategy for dealing with potential costs or losses of this magnitude.

Table 8.1: Sample assignment of accountability for business assets.

Business Asset	**Accountable Owner**
Regulatory license to operate	Head of Legal and Compliance
Brand and reputation	Head of Marketing
Design quality of products (incl. safety and security)	Head of Research and Development (R&D)
Actual quality of manufactured products	Head of Production & Manufacturing
Availability and security of technology infrastructure	CIO
Accuracy of financial reporting	CFO
Capital efficiency and preservation*)	
Sensitive or proprietary data	Divisional CEO(s)
Cyber culture and awareness	
Integrity of supplies and third-party inputs	Head of Vendor Management

* Includes cost of raising debt or equity capital, cost of cyber insurance premiums, cost of cyber-related operational risk reserves, provisions for and cost of responding to cyber-incidents.

8.10 The logic for the assignments in Table 8.1 is that accountability is with the executive who has the most to lose if any given business asset is impaired and who has the most direct influence to prevent or minimise such impairments. For example, poor 'cyber culture and awareness' frequently leads to data loss via unsafe work practices such as use of private email or unencrypted email attachments, which threatens 'sensitive or proprietary data' – a key business asset owned by Divisional CEOs. Conversely, Divisional CEOs have the most effective means to improve their organisation's cyber culture and awareness, eg via enforcement, sanctions, setting the tone at the top, and by providing secure technical solutions for bring your own device (BYOD), mobile, remote-working, cross-company collaboration, and other workplace situations that can expose sensitive or proprietary data. For these reasons, it can be suitable to assign accountability for 'cyber culture and awareness' to Divisional CEOs. Later sections of this chapter will further elaborate on why it is so crucial for CxOs to take ownership of key business assets.

SETTING BUDGETS

8.11 Senior executives have a duty to invest their organisations' resources wisely. As such, they have to determine how much to invest to improve cyber-security. Moreover, many organisations have spent a lot of money on cyber-security over the past five to eight years, and their executives ask what tangible benefits they have obtained and how much more they will have to invest.

8.12 A common approach to determining security budgets is using benchmarks that express security spending as a percent of total IT spending or as a multiplier to the number of employees.[2] [3] Despite their popularity, peer benchmarks can at most give an indication if one might spend too much or too little on security, but they should not be used as a sole basis for setting budgets. The limitations of benchmarks include that they insufficiently capture good practice, they use their own cost accounting that may not translate easily into how other organisations account for their costs,[4] and they fail to capture any organisation's circumstances, such as its current-state of maturity, its business assets, business and technology strategy, unique threats, organisational and technological complexities, and so on.

8.13 More importantly, however, tying security budgets to benchmarks reflects a compliance-based mindset that is no longer useful in today's threat environment. A compliance-based mindset asks: 'is it enough to spend X amount on cyber security?' – not realising that no amount of money will ever be big enough if the aim is to prevent every possible incident. As such, the question is less about the amount of money and more about what constitutes 'good enough' security. This question must be answered in the context of an organisation's business assets, how well they are already protected, what threats they face, and what risk appetite the organisation is comfortable with.

8.14 A compliance-based mindset also asks: 'when will I be done?' – not realising that for cyber-security, there is no 'finish line'. Note that for classic technology risks the notion of 'being done' makes sense, for example, in the case

2 Hall et al., *IT Key Metrics Data 2018: Key IT Security Measures: by Industry* (Gartner, 2017).
3 Pollard, *Security Budgets 2018: Uncertainty Trumps Normalcy* (Clingendael, 2018).
4 The biggest differences arise from the treatment of depreciation versus cash cost, run versus change cost, security versus infrastructure cost, and IT security versus information security costs. Also, there is no uniform treatment for related costs such as fraud or physical security.

when the fail-over disaster recovery facility goes into operation, when the legacy application is migrated, when anti-money laundering controls are established, or when independent testing has been mandated prior to all software releases into production. This logic, however, does not translate into the world of cyber-security, where threats constantly change and cyber defences have to be evolved in lockstep. For example, just over the past two years, ransomware, memory-based attacks, supply chain attacks, and attacks against connected devices have emerged as new threats, to which new or upgraded defences have to be deployed.

8.15 Lastly, looking at cyber-security budgets as one monolithic cost puts this cost into the wrong category on one's income statement and, more importantly, in one's mind. If cyber-security is a monolithic cost item then it is accounted for as a 'Selling, General, and Administrative (SG&A)' cost, ie, as an overhead that is to be managed down. In reality, however, cyber-costs are a cost of doing business and they should be factored in the 'Cost of Goods Sold' category (see Table 8.2 for a simplified illustration). The rationale is simple: In a digital world, cyber-strategy and business strategy go hand-in-hand. Although business objectives are paramount, it is no longer possible to develop effective business strategies and business models without thinking about how they will be affected – and in many cases enabled – by digital technologies, and how the organisation will protect itself from cyber-threats. Even the most brilliant business strategy is worthless if an organisation cannot secure the required technology from cyberattacks.

Table 8.2: Simplified model of accounting for the cost of cyber on the income statement.

Cyber as a monolithic cost	Cyber as a cost of doing business
Revenue	**Revenue**
– Cost of Goods Sold	– Cost of Goods Sold incl. Cost of Cyber
Gross Profit	**Gross Profit**
– SG&A incl. Cost of Cyber	– SG&A
– Deprecation & Amortisation	– Deprecation & Amortisation
– Interest and Taxes	– Interest and Taxes
Net Earnings	**Net Earnings**

8.16 In summary, cyber-budgets should be set based on the risk reduction that one seeks to achieve and while for the foreseeable future, there will remain a monolithic cost position to remediate vulnerabilities in legacy systems, it is important that cyber-security and associated costs become integral components of future business strategies.

BUILDING A CXO-LED CYBER STRATEGY

8.17 The **Deloitte Cyber Strategy Framework**, shown in Figure 8.1, is a business-driven and threat-based approach to managing cyber-risks. While the capability to secure assets is important, the framework emphasises that being vigilant and resilient in the face of cyber-attacks is imperative. As such, the framework defines four categories of cyber-capabilities:[5]

- '**Governance**' is the capability to maintain clear cyber-roles and responsibilities as well as a continuous process of assessing business assets, cyber-threats, and determining the resulting investment priorities.
- '**Security**' refers to an organisation's preventative capabilities. Like fences and door locks in the physical world, these are the mechanisms that actually keep bad guys out. In cyber terms, 'secure' includes capabilities such as infrastructure hardening, vulnerability management, identity and access management, and data leakage prevention.
- '**Vigilance**' is an organisation's early warning system. Like security cameras and a guard at the front desk, capabilities in this area help sense, detect, and predict threats before they become attacks, attacks before they become breaches, and breaches before they become crises.
- '**Resilience**' is an organisation's ability to manage cyber-incidents effectively, respond quickly to minimize the damage from incidents, and get its business and operations back to normal as quickly as possible.

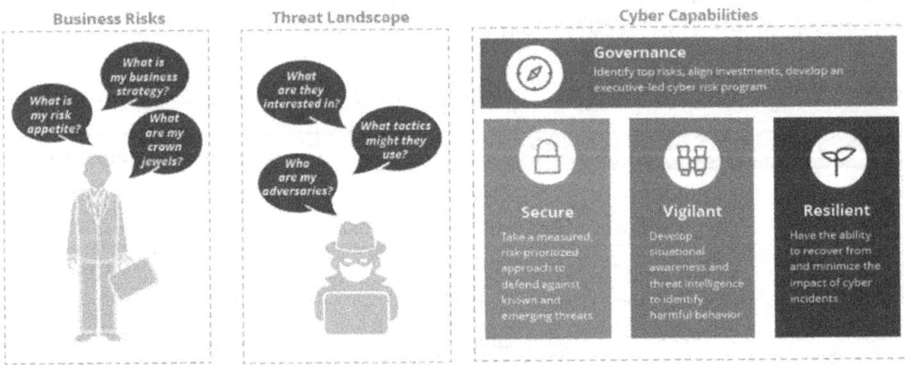

Figure 8.1: Deloitte cyber strategy framework.

8.18 This framework is used routinely to develop security strategies for technical security teams. When using this framework to help CxOs lead cyber-risk the only difference is that the discussion is more high-level and conceptual in terms of the assets, threats, and cyber-capabilities. Moreover, it is generally helpful to have a technical security expert, eg the CISO, facilitate the discussion to provide technical know-how and the latest insights on threats and state-of-the-art cyber-capabilities. The steps of developing a CxO-led cyber-strategy are then as follows:

5 Cyber capabilities are similar to security controls, but in addition to defining a control mechanism, they emphasise the organisational and procedural governance aspects needed to maintain and update the mechanism so as to keep it effective and 'capable' of producing desired security benefits in light of changing threats.

Step 1 – 'Assets': The first step is to identify the business assets that need to be protected and to assign C-level owners who are accountable for their security. Table 1 shows ten generic business assets and typical owners to illustrate the level of abstraction suitable for this step. Being one step more granular – eg distinguisihing types of sensitive or proprietary data rather than treating them all as one category – can also make sense in larger organisations. For the sake of this chapter, we will work with the example in Table 1.

Step 2 – 'Threats': Threats are best described by the *adverse impact* they create and how *credible* they are. A threat is *credible* if it is technically feasible to bring about the associated adverse impact despite an organisation's existing security controls and there is a *threat actor* who can be expected to have sufficient skill and motivation to do so. The *adverse impact* of a threat is the business impact it creates. Again, there are various ways to describe adverse impact and we will stick with a relatively straightforward classification:

- **Theft or loss** of sensitive or proprietary data;
- **Theft or loss** of money;[6]
- **Sabotage** of data or IT infrastructure, destroying its integrity, availability, or purposeful use;
- **Impairment** of reputation, brand, or regulatory approval or standing.

For example, thanks to WannaCry and NotPetya[7] the threat of losing all or large parts of one's IT infrastructure has become very credible, and its adverse impact is rated as devastating. As such, it is a threat that many organisations will want to consider.

Step 3 – 'Capabilities': The owner of each business asset is also responsible for the cyber-capabilities that mitigate the identified threats. For example, based on Table 8.1, we can conclude that the CIO owns the threat of a 'major cyber-sabotage of the IT infrastructure' as in the events of WannaCry and NotPetya. Other owners are possible, such as the CEO, because ransomware can change its blackmail tactics and, for example, threaten to publicly release stolen data rather than withhold or destroy it. Ultimately, the specific owner is less important than the fact that an executive owner is appointed. The owner is responsible for defining the cyber capabilities, or capability improvements, needed to defend against identified threats.

In general, identifying cyber capabilities is a highly interactive process where all C-Suite executives level-set their risk appetite and the technical

6 Note the difference to the first impact category: An amount of money, say $100, is not confidential by itself. It can, however, only be owned by one party at any given time, ie, two parties cannot have the same $100. Sensitive or proprietary data, by contrast, is confidential but it is possible to create as many replicas as one wants – at the expense of losing the data's confidentiality, that is.

7 Hern, *WannaCry, Petya, NotPetya: how ransomware hit the big time in 2017*, *The Guardian*, December 2017.

facilitator injects industry good practice and the art of the possible. Moreover, budgets must be discussed and investments must be staged, in many cases over years, in order to formulate viable investment plans. The outcome is cyber-investment priorities that are business-driven, threat-based, and genuinely owned by the C-Suite.

Step 4 – 'Monitoring': Leading cyber-security is a continuous responsibility, not a one-time planning task. In practice, this means that CxOs need a dashboard that keeps them abreast of the state of cyber-security within their organisations. While most organisations build their own tailor-made dashboards, emerging good practice suggests that the following information should be part of most dashboards:

- A summary of **cyberattacks and breaches** that the organisation experienced in the last reporting period. This information shows – to the extent that an organisation's monitoring systems could pick it up – what really happened.
- A summary of current and emerging **cyber threats**. Understanding threats is important to gage the risk to the organisation from cyber-threats and in order to decide if any tactical or strategic steps are needed outside the regular planning cycle.
- Statistics summarising the **operating effectiveness** of cyber-capabilities. For example, this could include the delay in patching systems or the percentage of endpoints that have malware protection. This information shows if the existing controls do what we designed them to do.
- The status of ongoing **cyber remediation projects**. This view shows whether ongoing efforts to improve cyber capabilities are on track to deliver the expected risk reduction.

Typically, Step 4 (monitoring) is repeated monthly or quarterly while Steps 1–3 follow an annual planning cycle.

SUMMARY AND OUTLOOK

8.19 This chapter provides a playbook for engaging CxOs in a very hands-on manner that nonetheless suites their seniority and the limited time budget they have for cyber-security. It requires executives to understand and own their business assets, the cyber-threats to those assets, and the solutions – or 'cyber-capabilities' – needed to defend those assets against the identified threats. As such, this chapter operationalises more abstract recommendations such as that executives should 'set the tone at the top', 'should understand cyber-risks', or 'should have regular cyber-discussions'.

8.20 This transition towards CxO-led security is crucial for several reasons. Firstly, some cyber-capabilities are cross-organisational and have no natural owner in today's organisations. For instance, and continuing the example from

8.17, the threat of a 'major cyber-sabotage of the IT infrastructure', tends to have no natural owner in many organisations. While there is agreement that criminals are attacking production systems and backups simultaneously in sophisticated ways designed to wreak havoc on businesses, there frequently is no natural solution owner, as the capability to address this threat fits neither the classic 'Disaster Recovery' nor the 'Cyber Security' definitions. Having C-suite leadership in this case has been crucial for several organisations to overcome such hurdles and mobilise around building a new capability that provides air-gapped tertiary storage onto which the most crucial organisational data is backed up so the organisation can recover from scratch should the primary and secondary IT systems be destroyed by a cyberattack.

8.21 CxO-led security is also crucial because it is transformative for corporate culture. As has been explained from **8.11**, cyber-strategy should be an integral part of business strategy, and no business strategy – no matter how brilliant – should go forward unless the organisation can secure the required IT infrastructure from cyber-attacks. These things are easy to say but hard to put into practice, and experience has shown that only organisations with a very strong and deeply embedded security culture manage to live up to this ideal. Most organisations find themselves somewhere on the cyber-cultural spectrum illustrated in Figure 8.2.

8.22 Having CxOs own cyber-security as described in this chapter can be transformative in advancing an organisation's cyber-culture. For example, while it would not be uncommon for IT and business managers to debate the benefits of two-factor authentication for finance-related applications, having the CFO own these applications, the cyber-threats to them, and the decision to implement two-factor authentication as a mitigating cyber capability resolves these debates very decisively.

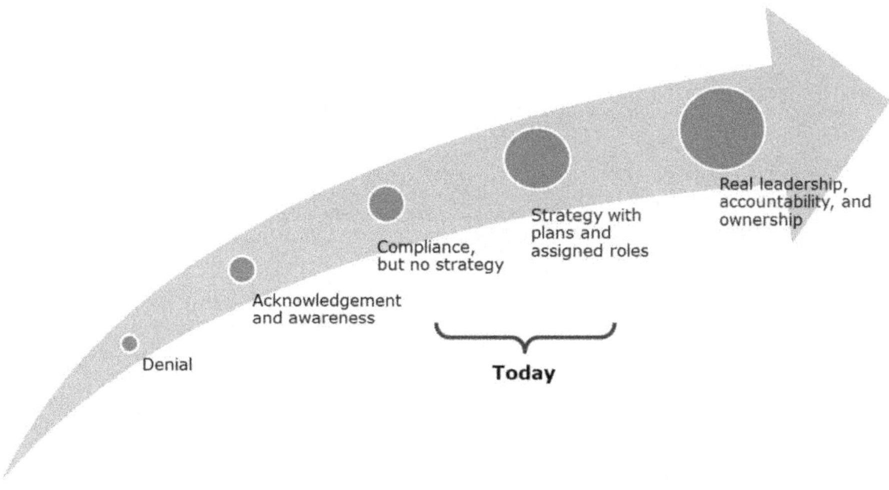

Figure 8.2: The cyber awareness journey from delial to true ownership and leadership.

8.23 Lastly, this chapter also provides guidance on the frequent issue of how much to spend on cyber-security. The recommendation provided is that cyber-budgets should be set based on the risk reduction sought rather than following a fixed budgeting formula such as 'percentage of IT spend' or 'percentage of last year's budget'. Moreover, to set the right incentives, the responsibility and cost for cyber security should be treated as a cost of doing business rather than a back-office cost item.

CHAPTER 9A

CHECKLIST FOR ADDRESSING AND PREPARING FOR CYBERSECURITY INCIDENTS

Helen Wong MBE

ACTION ITEMS

9.01

1. **Preparation**

   1.1. **Develop, Implement, and Rehearse Incident Response Plan (IRP)**

   - **Formulate an IRP:** Develop an Incident Response Plan (IRP) that aligns with the organisation's specific risk profile and exposure levels, ensuring it addresses potential threats, vulnerabilities, and impacts unique to the organisation.
   - **Engage Experts:** Enlist the assistance of cybersecurity specialists and external legal counsel to comprehensively cover all relevant areas, ensuring the IRP can withstand regulatory scrutiny and legal challenges in the event of an incident.
   - **Organisation-Wide Implementation:** Implement the IRP across all departments and levels of the organisation, ensuring that all relevant employees are trained and familiar with their specific roles, responsibilities, and the procedures outlined in the IRP.
   - **Regular Rehearsals and Updates:** Conduct regular rehearsals and simulations of the IRP to identify any deficiencies or areas needing improvement. Continuously update the IRP to adapt to evolving threats, regulatory changes, and organisational needs, ensuring stakeholders are proficient in executing the plan.

   1.2. **Establish Core Internal Incident Response Team**

   - **Assemble the Team:** Form a dedicated incident response team with a designated leader responsible for managing the incident response. Ensure the team possesses a clear mandate, the necessary authorities, and decision-making powers.
   - **Expertise and Skills:** Ensure the incident response team includes members with the required technical, legal, and commercial skills to address the incident comprehensively.

- **Conflict of Interest Management:** Identify and manage potential conflicts of interest within the team. Exclude individuals who may be at fault or responsible for causing the incident from the investigation to maintain impartiality.
- **Communication Protocols and Legal Privilege:** Ensure the incident response team adheres to approved communication protocols. Protect communications under legal privilege through the early engagement of external counsel to maintain confidentiality and privilege over sensitive information.
- **Access to IRP:** Provide the incident response team with full access to the IRP and ensure they are thoroughly briefed on its contents and procedures.
- **Review Triage Containment Measures:** Review existing or proposed triage containment measures to ensure they are effective and align with the IRP.

1.3. Engage External Advisors as Necessary

- **Retain External Advisors:** Engage external advisors, including cybersecurity consultants, legal counsel, and public relations experts, as needed. For incidents involving ransomware, consider engaging professional ransomware negotiators.
- **Utilize Outside Counsel:** Ensure the engagement of outside counsel to assert legal privilege where applicable and to provide specialised legal advice and representation.
- **Communication Protocols:** Ensure all relevant personnel within the organisation know the designated points of contact, their contact information, and the procedures for handling internal (eg, employee) and external (eg, media, customers) inquiries through established communication protocols.
- **Access to Policies and Procedures:** Ensure that relevant policies and procedures are accessible to the business despite the effects of the incident, such as email or intranet being unavailable.

1.4. Inform the Board of Directors

- **Initial Notification:** Provide a high-level initial notification to the board of directors and ensure the board is kept informed of new developments as the incident response progresses.
- **Regular Updates:** Establish a regular cadence for updates to the board and relevant board committees or chairs (eg, audit committee chair).
- **Preserve Legal Privilege:** Ensure legal privilege over advice provided to the board by instructing external counsel early in the incident response.

2. **Evidence Preservation and Activity Logging**

2.1. **Preserve All Relevant Logs**

- **Secure Logs:** Preserve all relevant logs (eg, authentication, remote access) with guidance from the forensic team to ensure retention of key materials, initiate forensic imaging if necessary, and maintain the chain of custody for evidentiary purposes.
- **Forensic Imaging:** Conduct forensic imaging of affected systems as needed to capture a snapshot of the compromised environment, aiding in the investigation and preservation of evidence.

2.2. **Maintain an Activity Log**

- **Document Activities:** Record all activities and decisions taken during the incident response, including the rationale and reasoning behind each action, in an activity log. This documentation ensures that actions can be explained to regulators or in subsequent litigation based on the knowledge available at the time, rather than with hindsight.

3. **Identify and Contain the Breach**

3.1. **Collaborate with Forensic and Cybersecurity Professionals**

- **Incident Identification:** Work with forensic and cybersecurity professionals to identify the nature and extent of the incident (eg, ransomware attack, data exfiltration, commercial espionage, nation-state actor, rogue employee).
- **Malware Assessment:** Forensic providers will determine the extent of malware infection, the type of malware (eg, encryption-only, exfiltration, or both), and the extent of any unauthorised access or acquisition of data.

3.2. **Conduct a Comprehensive Investigation**

- **Lead Investigation:** The response leader or a third-party forensic expert should lead the investigation, ensuring a structured and thorough approach.
- **Root Cause Analysis:** Identify the root cause(s) of the incident, commonly referred to as 'patient zero'.
- **Assess Impacted Assets:** Identify potentially affected equipment, data, systems, or infrastructure and assess whether their physical location in different jurisdictions impacts notification requirements.
- **Data Access and Exposure:** Identify any data that was accessed or exposed, and, if possible, determine all data elements that were copied or exfiltrated. Use forensic analysis and interviews with relevant custodians to identify affected data.

- **Workstreams and Team Members:** Establish various workstreams (eg, technical, legal, executive management, PR) and designate team members for each. Consider using mailing lists and project management software to track progress and manage tasks.
- **Regular Updates:** Set up regular stand-up calls with internal and external incident response team members (eg, forensic analysts, internal IT teams) and ensure external counsel is present to maintain privilege.
- **Additional Calls:** Schedule other necessary calls, such as regular briefings with the in-house legal team or management to update them on developments and seek their input.
- **Preliminary Reports and Daily Updates:** Obtain preliminary reports and request daily updates from stakeholders (eg, forensic analysts, internal IT teams).

3.3. Deploy Containment Measures

- **Business Continuity Plans:** Implement business continuity management plans to ensure operational continuity and resilience. Prepare for queries from employees and customers.
- **Technical Response Timeline:** Establish a timeline for technical responses, including containment, eradication, and recovery.
- **Containment Response Measures:** Initiate containment measures such as locking down external or VPN access, disabling access to affected databases, implementing dual-factor authentication, or forcing password resets.
- **Monitor and Reassess Containment:** Continuously monitor and reassess containment measures to ensure their effectiveness.

3.4. Analyse Impact on Personal Data

- **Data Sensitivity Analysis:** Conduct an analysis of the sensitivity of the impacted data, the identities and number of affected individuals, and the locations of the impacted individuals.
- **Potential Impact and Harm:** Assess the potential impact and harm on data subjects, including risks of identity theft or financial loss.
- **Data Status:** Determine the status of the data (eg, lost, stolen, damaged, inaccessible) and whether the incident constitutes a breach of confidentiality, integrity, or availability.
- **Controllers and Processors Identification:** Identify all relevant data controllers and processors involved in the incident.
- **External and Statutory Notifications:** Refer to the 'Key External Notifications' and 'Statutory Notification Requirements' sections for further obligations.

4. **Remediation**

4.1. Implement Countermeasures

- **Vulnerability Assessment:** Undertake a thorough vulnerability assessment of systems to understand how attackers gained access and prevent future similar attacks.
- **Appropriate Countermeasures:** Implement appropriate countermeasures based on the assessment, such as deploying advanced antivirus software, employing multi-factor authentication, and conducting regular penetration testing exercises.

4.2. Engage Law Enforcement as Necessary

- **Evaluate Engagement:** Assess the benefits of early engagement with law enforcement based on the context and jurisdiction, seeking advice from local counsel.
- **Facilitate Engagement:** Use external counsel to facilitate engagement with law enforcement, keeping in mind the potential for resource strain and delays due to regular updates and data access requirements.

4.3. Engage Government Cybersecurity Bodies

- **Government Bodies:** Engage with government cybersecurity bodies (eg, UK's National Cyber Security Centre) for valuable threat intelligence on specific threat actors, aiding in identifying indicators of compromise (IOCs) and strengthening the network.

5. **Key Internal Notifications**

5.1. Prepare Press Releases and Media Responses

- **Draft Press Releases:** Prepare press releases or responses to media inquiries, ensuring content is confirmed with legal and business stakeholders.
- **Consistency in Press Inquiries:** Ensure all press inquiries are consistent and directed to a designated individual or team.
- **Proactive and Reactive Statements:** Prepare both proactive and reactive statements in case the incident becomes public before an official announcement.

5.2. Prepare Customer Communication

- **FAQ Pages and Dedicated Website:** Develop FAQ pages or a dedicated website for the cyberattack to redirect customers and alleviate pressure on customer service staff.
- **Careful Phrasing:** Phrase FAQ content carefully to avoid disclosing excessive or incorrect information, maintaining control over the narrative and preventing future complications.

5.3. Brief Customer Service Staff

- **Response Protocols:** Ensure customer service staff, social media managers, and other outward-facing employees are briefed on how to respond to customer queries, following legal and business stakeholder guidelines. Stick to approved scripts and avoid speculation.
- **Limit Incident Confidentiality:** If the incident is confidential, limit knowledge to as few employees as possible.

5.4. Arrange Additional Customer Service Resources if Required

- **Third-Party Providers:** Engage third-party providers if internal capabilities cannot handle a surge in calls or emails.

5.5. Issue Internal Notifications

- **Internal Announcements:** Issue internal notifications or announcements through appropriate channels (eg, mailing lists, intranet).

6. Key External Notifications (Including Contractual)

6.1. Prepare Consistent Language for Notifications

- **Consistent Scripts:** Prepare consistent language for notifications to external parties and follow-up queries, ensuring uniformity in responses.

6.2. Inform Insurers

- **Notify Insurers:** Inform insurers as required by cyber insurance policies, providing necessary details and updates.

6.3. Inform Banks and Credit Card Companies

- **Fraud Risk Notification:** Notify affected banks and credit card companies of potential fraud risks, complying with Payment Card Industry Data Security Standard (PCI DSS) requirements.

6.4. Confirm Contractual Notification Obligations

- **Supplier and Customer Obligations:** Review and confirm any contractual obligations to notify suppliers and customers of cybersecurity incidents, considering the potential resource intensity of this task.

6.5. Notify Affected External Parties

- **Contractor Notification:** Inform contractors if the cybersecurity incident has affected their network, aiding in mitigation, containment, and maintaining contractor relations.

7. Statutory Notification Requirements

7.1. Determine Duty to Inform Regulators or Data Subjects

- **Regulatory Compliance:** Establish whether there is a statutory duty to inform regulators or data subjects about the incident, consulting relevant practice notes and local counsel to identify jurisdiction-specific requirements.

- **Notification Duties:** Fulfil notification duties within prescribed timeframes, preparing for a variety of correspondence from data subjects, consumers, and contractors. Anticipate potential legal claims from affected parties.

7.2. Solicitors' Notification Obligations

- **SRA Code Compliance:** Determine if the incident requires notifying clients or the Solicitors Regulation Authority (SRA) in accordance with the SRA Code of Conduct and Conditions of Authorization, particularly if client data is impacted.

7.3. Listed Companies' Regulatory Notice Requirements

- **Market Notice Obligations:** Ascertain if listed companies must provide regulatory notice to the market, referencing cybersecurity guidance and standards for public companies.

8. Follow-Up

8.1. Conduct Post-Incident Review and Implement Improvements

- **Structured Review:** Conduct a structured review and lessons learned exercise post-incident, implementing improvements to systems and procedures.
- **Follow-Up Timeline:** Establish a timeline for further follow-up with regulatory bodies or other entities (eg, credit card companies) as applicable.
- **Team Reviews:** Each team impacted by the incident should review findings and implement enhancements to prevent recurrence and improve incident response protocols.

8.2. Consider Incident Report Creation

- **Incident Report Awareness:** Be aware that incident reports requested by regulators, insurers, or claimants may not be covered by legal privilege, and prepare accordingly.

CHAPTER 9B

CYBER INCIDENT CHECKLIST

9.02 This checklist is to aid your organisation's initial assessment of its readiness to respond to a cyber security incident. This checklist is not an exhaustive list of all readiness activities.

Preparation	
☐	Your organisation has a cyber security policy or strategy that outlines your organisation's approach to prevention, preparedness, detection, response, recovery, review and improvement. • For example, does your organisation have a position on, for example, paying ransom, reporting incidents to government, publicly acknowledging cyber incidents, sharing information about incidents with trusted industry and government partners?
☐	A Cyber Incident Response Plan has been developed, which: • Aligns with your organisation's operating environment and other processes, including emergency management and business continuity processes. • Has been reviewed or tested in an exercise to ensure it remains current and responsible personnel are aware of their roles, responsibilities and processes. • Templates have been prepared, for example Situation Reports.
☐	Staff involved in managing an incident have received incident response training.
☐	Up-to-date hard copy versions of the Cyber Incident Response Plan and playbooks are stored in a secure location (in case of electronic or hardware failure) and are accessible to authorised staff members.
☐	Specific playbooks to supplement the Cyber Incident Response Plan have been developed, that define step-by-step guidance for response actions to common incidents, and roles and responsibilities.
☐	A Cyber Incident Response Team (CIRT) and a Senior Executive Management Team (SEMT) – or equivalents – have been formed to manage the response, with approved authorities.
☐	All relevant IT and OT Standard Operating Procedures (SOPs) are documented and have been reviewed or tested in an exercise to ensure they remain current and responsible personnel are aware of their roles, responsibilities and processes.
☐	Arrangements for service providers, including cloud and software as a service, to provide and retain logs have been established and tested to ensure these include useful data and can be provided in a timely manner.

☐	Log retention for critical systems have been configured adequately and tested to confirm that they capture useful data.
☐	Your organisation has internal or third party arrangements and capabilities to detect and analyse incidents. If these capabilities are outsourced, your organisation has an active service agreement/contract.
☐	Critical assets (data, applications and systems) have been identified and documented.
☐	Standard Operating Procedures (SOPs) have been developed, and roles and responsibilities assigned for use of facilities and communications technologies in response to cyber incidents, and these resources are confirmed as available. This includes for alternative/back-up ICT-based channels.
☐	Incident logging/records and tracking technologies used to manage a response are confirmed as available and have been tested.
☐	Role cards have been developed for each person involved in the CIRT and the SEMT. Individual actions will depend on the type and severity of the incident.
☐	Your organisation has internal or third party arrangements and capabilities to monitor threats. Situational awareness information is collected from internal and external data sources, including: • Local system and network traffic and activity logs • News feeds concerning ongoing political, social, or economic activities that might impact incident activity • External feeds on incident trends, new attack vectors, current attack indicators and new mitigation strategies and technologies.
Detection, Investigation, Analysis and Activation	
Standard Operating Procedures (SOPs) have been developed, and roles and responsibilities assigned for:	
☐	Detection mechanisms which can be used to identify potential information security incidents, such as scanning, senses and logging mechanisms. These mechanisms require monitoring processes to identify unusual or suspicious activity, for example behaviour and logging, commensurate with the impact of an incident. Common monitoring techniques include: a) network and user profiling that establishes a baseline of normal activity which, when combined with logging and alerting mechanisms, can enable detection of anomalous activity; b) scanning for unauthorised hardware, software and changes to configurations; c) sensors that provide an alert when a measure breaches a defined threshold(s) (e.g. device, server and network activity); d) logging and alerting of access to sensitive data or unsuccessful logon attempts to identify potential unauthorised access; and e) users with privileged access accounts subject to a greater level of monitoring in light of the heightened risks involved.

☐	Incident detection, including self-detected incidents, notifications received from service providers or vendors, and notifications received from trusted third parties
☐	Incident analysis, including how incidents are to be categorised, classified and prioritised, and controls related to how data is stored and transmitted (i.e. if out-of-band transmission is required).
☐	Activating a Cyber Incident Response Team (CIRT) to manage critical incidents, with roles and responsibilities assigned.
☐	Activating a Senior Executive Management Team (SEMT) to manage critical incidents, with roles and responsibilities assigned.
Containment, Evidence Collection and Remediation	
☐	Standard Operating Procedures (SOPs), playbooks and templates, have been developed, and roles and responsibilities assigned for containment, evidence collection and remediation. These can be included as appendices to the Cyber Incident Response Plan.
☐	A secure location is available for storing data captured during an incident, which could be used as evidence of the incident and the adversary's tradecraft, and ready to be provided to third-party stakeholders if needed.
Communications	
☐	Policy, plans, Standard Operating Procedures (SOPs) and templates have been developed to support communicating with: • Internal stakeholders (e.g. Board, staff) • External stakeholders (e.g. stakeholders to assist with the response and stakeholders with an interest in the response)
☐	Policy, plans, Standard Operating Procedures (SOPs) and templates for media and communications professionals have been developed, and roles and responsibilities assigned, to support public and media messaging.
☐	You organisation has assigned a public and media spokesperson, who is supported by subject matter experts.
☐	Staff have been trained to implement the communications processes and execute their roles and responsibilities.
☐	Staff who are not involved in managing incidents are cognisant of your organisation's policy and processes and their responsibilities when an incident occurs (e.g. exercising discretion, using approved talking points, referring enquiries to the designated officer).
Incident Notification and Reporting	
☐	Processes and contact details are documented to support the organisation to meet its legal and regulatory requirements on cyber incident notification, reporting and response, with roles and responsibilities within your organisation are assigned. This includes the processes for obtaining authority to release and share information.
☐	Processes are documented for insurance requirements.

Post Incident Review	
☐	A process is documented to conduct Post Incident Reviews (PIR) following conclusion of an incident and PIR reports with recommendations are submitted to management for endorsement.
☐	A process is documented to ensure actions following incidents and/or exercises are tracked and completed (e.g. Action Register).

APPENDIX

Triage Questions

9.03 Where applicable, personnel reporting cyber security incidents on behalf of their organisation should try to have information available to answer the following questions:

- Who is reporting the incident? (include their position e.g. CISO, ITSA, SOC Manager etc.)
- Who/what is the affected organisation/entity?
- What type of incident is being reported? (e.g. ransomware, denial of service, data exposure, malware)
- Is the incident still active?
- When was the incident first identified?
- Are you reporting for awareness or is assistance required?
    - If assistance is required, what assistance is needed?
- What type of system or network has been affected?
    - Information Technology (IT)
        - Corporate systems/networks, databases, servers, VOIP (voice) systems.
    - Operational Technology (OT)
        - Remote sensors, logic controllers.
- What was observed (the sequence of events)? E.g. was lateral movement observed?
    - Date/Time
    - Effect/Event
- Who or what identified the problem?
- Has a data breach occurred?
    - What type of information was exposed?
        - What impact will this have on the organisation?

        - What impact (if any) will the breach have on public safety or services?
    - What volume of records/data was exposed?
    - Was it a misconfiguration/error, or was a malicious exfiltration or theft of data identified?
- What actions have been taken to rectify the issue?
    - Does the organisation/entity have internal or external IT and/or cyber security incident response providers?
    - Are services/business as usual operations interrupted?
        - If so, how long do they expect before they are back at normal operating capability?
- Will you be communicating publicly about the incident and engaging with media?

CHAPTER 9C

SECURITY INCIDENT NOTIFICATION REQUIREMENTS (UK)

OVERVIEW

9.04 This guide summarises the notification obligations under UK cybersecurity laws that may apply if a cybersecurity incident occurs. The requirements vary based on the type of organisation and the nature and severity of the breach. This guide reflects the position after the UK left the EU and the end of the transition period on 31 December 2020.

TYPES OF INCIDENTS COVERED

UK cybersecurity laws cover:

1. Personal data breaches (as defined by the UK GDPR).
2. Cybersecurity incidents that do not involve personal data.

Some laws apply only to specific sectors like telecoms, energy, transport, health, water supply, and digital infrastructure.

NOTIFICATION OBLIGATIONS

The guide provides tables detailing:

- Who needs to notify whom.
- The required actions.
- Time frames to take action.
- Penalties for failing to report.

SPECIFIC NOTIFICATIONS

Personal Data Breaches (UK GDPR)

Who Notifies	Notified To	Required Action	Time Frame	Penalties
Controller	Information Commissioner (IC)	Notify the IC about the personal data breach unless it is unlikely to risk individuals' rights and freedoms. The notice should describe the breach, provide contact details, explain likely consequences, and outline measures taken or proposed to mitigate effects.	Without undue delay, and within 72 hours of awareness. Delays must be justified.	Fines up to £8.7 million or 2% of total worldwide turnover, whichever is higher.
Controller	Data Subjects	Inform data subjects if the breach is likely to result in a high risk to their rights and freedoms. The notice should describe the breach in clear language, provide contact details, explain likely consequences, and outline measures taken or proposed to mitigate effects.	Without undue delay.	Fines up to £8.7 million or 2% of total worldwide turnover, whichever is higher.
Processor	Controller	Notify the controller about the personal data breach.	Without undue delay after becoming aware of it.	Fines up to £8.7 million or 2% of total worldwide turnover, whichever is higher.

Telecommunication Networks and Service Providers (PECR & CA 2003)

Who Notifies	Notified To	Required Action	Time Frame	Penalties
Providers of public electronic communications networks (PECNs) and services (PECS)	Ofcom	Notify Ofcom about any significant security compromise affecting the network or service, including unauthorized access or exploitation that has a significant effect.	Urgent compromises: Initially as soon as reasonably practicable, ideally within 3 hours, with a full report within 72 hours. Non-urgent compromises: Within 72 hours.	Up to 10% of provider's relevant business turnover or £100,000 per day for ongoing contraventions.
Providers of public electronic communications networks (PECNs) and services (PECS)	Users who may be adversely affected	Take reasonable steps to inform users in clear language about the risk, nature of the security compromise, technical measures to prevent adverse effects, and provide contact details.	n/a	n/a
Providers of public electronic communications networks (PECNs) and services (PECS)	Ofcom may direct the provider to notify users.	Ofcom can direct the provider to inform past and current users about security compromises, the risk thereof, and technical measures users can take to prevent or mitigate adverse effects.	As Ofcom directs, within a reasonable period specified by Ofcom.	Up to 10% of provider's relevant business turnover or £100,000 per day for ongoing contraventions.
Providers of public electronic communications networks (PECNs) and services (PECS)	The public	Ofcom may direct the provider to inform the public about security compromises or the risk thereof and technical measures the public can take to prevent or mitigate adverse effects.	As Ofcom directs, within a reasonable period specified by Ofcom.	Up to 10% of provider's relevant business turnover or £100,000 per day for ongoing contraventions.

Who Notifies	Notified To	Required Action	Time Frame	Penalties
Providers of public electronic communications networks (PECNs) and services (PECS)	Secretary of State	Ofcom must inform the Secretary of State if a security compromise could result in a serious threat to public safety, health, national security, or cause serious economic or operational problems for users or providers of electronic communications services or networks.	n/a	n/a
Providers of public electronic communications networks (PECNs) and services (PECS)	Overseas regulatory authorities	Ofcom may inform overseas regulatory authorities and the European Network and Information Security Agency (ENISA) about the security compromise if deemed appropriate.	n/a	n/a
Providers of public electronic communications networks (PECNs) and services (PECS)	Communications providers	Ofcom may inform other communications providers or those who make associated facilities available about the security compromise if deemed appropriate.	n/a	n/a
Providers of public electronic communications networks (PECNs) and services (PECS)	Users and the public	If Ofcom thinks it is in the public interest, it may inform users and the public about security compromises and technical measures they can take to prevent or mitigate adverse effects.	n/a	n/a

Who Notifies	Notified To	Required Action	Time Frame	Penalties
Providers of public electronic communications services (PECS)	Information Commissioner (IC)	Notify the IC about a personal data breach. The notification must describe the breach, its consequences, and measures taken or proposed to address the breach.	Without undue delay and within 24 hours of detection. An initial notification can be made within 24 hours, with a subsequent notification providing further details within three days.	Fixed monetary penalty of £1,000 for failure to notify the IC.
Providers of public electronic communications services (PECS)	Individual subscribers and users	Notify subscribers and users if the personal data breach is likely to adversely affect their personal data or privacy. The notification must describe the breach, provide contact information, and recommend measures to mitigate possible adverse impacts.	Without undue delay.	Fixed monetary penalty of £1,000 for failure to notify.

Operators of Essential Services (NIS Regulations)

Who Notifies	Notified To	Required Action	Time Frame	Penalties
Operators of Essential Services (OES)	Designated competent authorities	Notify the designated competent authority in writing about any incident significantly impacting the continuity of essential services provided. The notification must include the operator's name, the essential services provided, the time and duration of the incident, the nature and impact of the incident, any cross-impact information, and any other helpful information.	Without undue delay and within 72 hours of becoming aware of the incident.	A maximum amount of £17 million for serious failures and £8.5 million for other failures.
Competent authority	Computer Security Incident Response Team (CSIRT)	Share the incident information with the CSIRT.	As soon as reasonably practicable after receipt of notification.	n/a
Competent authority	The public	Inform the public if necessary to handle the incident or prevent future incidents (following consultation with the OES and CSIRT).	As soon as reasonably practicable after receipt of notification.	n/a
CSIRT	Relevant authority in an EU member state	Inform the relevant authority in an EU member state if the incident significantly impacts essential services in that member state.	n/a	n/a

Who Notifies	Notified To	Required Action	Time Frame	Penalties
CSIRT	The public	Inform the public if necessary to handle the incident or prevent future incidents (following consultation with the OES and competent authority).	As soon as reasonably practicable.	n/a
Relevant Digital Services Providers (RDSP)	Information Commissioner (IC)	Notify the IC in writing about any incident with a substantial impact on the provision of digital services. The notification must include the same information as required for OES and additional details to determine the significance of any cross-border impact.	Without undue delay and within 72 hours of becoming aware of the incident.	A maximum amount of £17 million for serious failures and £8.5 million for other failures.
Information Commissioner (IC)	CSIRT	Share the incident information with the CSIRT unless it is confidential or may prejudice security or commercial interests.	As soon as reasonably practicable after receipt of notification.	n/a
Information Commissioner (IC)	The public	Require the RDSP to inform the public if necessary to prevent or manage the incident or if it is in the public interest (following consultation).	As directed by the IC.	A maximum amount of £17 million for serious failures and £8.5 million for other failures.

Who Notifies	Notified To	Required Action	Time Frame	Penalties
CSIRT	The public	Inform the public if necessary to prevent or manage the incident or if it is in the public interest (following consultation with the RDSP and IC).	n/a	n/a
Operators of Essential Services (OES) reliant on an RDSP	OES's competent authority	Notify the designated competent authority in writing about any significant impact on service continuity caused by an incident affecting the RDSP.	Without undue delay.	A maximum amount of £17 million for serious failures and £8.5 million for other failures.

Trust Service Providers (UK eIDAS)

Who Notifies	Notified To	Required Action	Time Frame	Penalties
Qualified and non-qualified trust service (TS) providers	Information Commissioner (IC)	Notify the IC about any breach of security or loss of integrity significantly impacting the TS provided or personal data maintained.	Without undue delay and within 24 hours of becoming aware of it.	Fixed monetary penalty of £1,000.
TS providers	Natural or legal persons to whom the TS has been provided	Notify affected persons if the breach of security or loss of integrity is likely to adversely affect them.	Without undue delay.	Fixed monetary penalty of £1,000.
Information Commissioner (IC)	The public	The IC may require the TS provider to inform the public if it is in the public interest.	As directed by the IC.	Fixed monetary penalty of £1,000.
Information Commissioner (IC)	The public	The IC may inform the public if it is in the public interest.	n/a	n/a

Law Enforcement and Intelligence Services (DPA 2018)

Who Notifies	Notified To	Required Action	Time Frame	Penalties
Controller (law enforcement processing)	Information Commissioner (IC)	Notify the IC about the personal data breach unless it is unlikely to risk individuals' rights and freedoms. The notice should describe the breach, provide contact details, explain likely consequences, and outline measures taken or proposed to mitigate effects.	Without undue delay and within 72 hours of becoming aware of it. Delays must be justified.	Fines up to £8.7 million or 2% of total annual turnover.
Controller (law enforcement processing)	Data subjects	Notify affected data subjects if the breach is likely to result in a high risk to their rights and freedoms. The notice should describe the breach, provide contact details, explain likely consequences, and outline measures taken or proposed to mitigate effects.	Without undue delay.	Fines up to £8.7 million or 2% of total annual turnover.
Controller (intelligence services processing)	Information Commissioner (IC)	Notify the IC about a serious personal data breach unless it is unlikely to seriously interfere with individuals' rights and freedoms. The notice should describe the breach, provide contact details, explain likely consequences, and outline measures taken or proposed to mitigate effects.	Without undue delay and within 72 hours of becoming aware of it. Delays must be justified.	Fines up to £8.7 million or 2% of total annual turnover.

Who Notifies	Notified To	Required Action	Time Frame	Penalties
Processor (law enforcement processing)	Controller (law enforcement processing)	Notify the controller about the personal data breach.	Without undue delay.	Fines up to £8.7 million or 2% of total annual turnover.
Processor (intelligence services processing)	Controller (intelligence services processing)	Notify the controller about the personal data breach.	Without undue delay.	Fines up to £8.7 million or 2% of total annual turnover.

Regulated Financial Institutions (FCA & PRA)

Who Notifies	Notified To	Required Action	Time Frame	Penalties
FCA-solo regulated firms (regulated by FCA only)	FCA and (where relevant) PRA	Notify the FCA (and PRA if applicable) about any matter that could have a serious regulatory impact, including issues affecting the firm's ability to continue providing adequate services.	Immediately upon becoming aware of the matter.	FCA can issue private warnings, public censure, vary or cancel authorisation, and impose fines. There is no limit on fines, but they must be proportionate. PRA has similar powers.

Pension Schemes (Pensions Act 2004)

Who Notifies	Notified To	Required Action	Time Frame	Penalties
Trustees, managers, scheme administrators, sponsoring employers, professional advisers	Pensions Regulator	Notify the Pensions Regulator of breaches where there is reasonable cause to believe that a duty relevant to the administration of the scheme has not been complied with and the failure is likely to be significant to the Regulator.	As soon as reasonably practicable.	Fine of up to £5,000 for individuals or up to £50,000 for others.

CHAPTER 10

INDUSTRY SPECIALIST IN-DEPTH REPORTS

10A MOBILE PAYMENTS

Rhiannon Lewis

10.01 As the payments industry continues to evolve, new mobile payment providers, such as online networks and telecom operators, are leveraging technologies, existing payment accounts and bank relationships, to create alternative payment mechanisms, such as mobile payments. Mobile payments are becoming increasingly more common, and are the way of the future, so it is important from a legal perspective to understand what the key information security risks associated with mobile payments are.

10.02 Authenticating payments to prevent fraudulent purchases tops the list of security concerns for financial institutions when implementing mobile payment technologies. Proper authentication of mobile payments to prevent fraudulent transactions is central to managing the information security risks associated with such payments. Yet, authentication concerns have not stopped financial institutions from moving rapidly to mobile centric interaction when providing services to consumers, including payment authentication.

10.03 Not surprisingly, the convergence of communications technologies and payments services inevitably challenges established regulatory boundaries and generates two key questions. First, how are information security risks associated with mobile payments currently being managed by regulation and industry standards? Second, how should responsibility for mitigating the potential information security risks of mobile payments be allocated? This chapter will consider these questions by focusing on the mobile payment sectors in the EU and the US.

Key technical and commercial characteristics of mobile payments

10.04 For the purpose of this chapter, a payment where a mobile device is used for authentication of a transaction is considered a mobile payment. The introduction of remote payments, such as, mobile payments, has added an extra layer of complexity where approaches from traditional face-to-face purchases and e-commerce environment may be used together with new transactional capabilities.

10.05 Not surprisingly, the mobile payment supply chain is complex. For example; the mobile manufacturer (eg, Nokia) supplies the hardware, such as a smartphone, to a payee. The mobile software company (eg, Android) supplies the payment software, such as an iOS or Android, on the smartphone. A payee can request for a payment instrument, normally a card, to be loaded on the smartphone. Broadly, there are two current methods available to consumers to do this:

1. the payee takes a photo of the card it wants to upload on the smartphone and the mobile software company extracts the card number and other details from the picture and will load the card onto the phone subject to authentication by it and/or the relevant card network; or
2. by default, a mobile software company will load card details that it already holds on a consumer to the phone subject to authentication by it and/or the relevant card network.

10.06 If the card is successfully loaded onto the smartphone, a secure token is created by the mobile software company, which is a substitute for the original card number. The secure token is only valid when used with the smartphone. When a payee makes a payment at a contactless reader, the secure token is read by the contactless reader and passed to the acquirer/payment processor, which then passes the secure token to the relevant card network. The card network then passes the associated card number to the payee's credit institution along with the transaction details to authenticate and/or authorise the transaction. The payee's credit institution will then authenticate and/or authorise the transaction and the payment is then authorised and settled by the card network in the usual way. Generally, more than one card may be loaded on any smartphone.

Complex regulatory landscape

10.07 The mobile payment supply chain, outlined above, leads to a complex regulatory landscape. Using the UK as an example, the regulation of mobile payment systems is carried out by a number of organisations whose remits derive from European and domestic UK law, which contain principles aimed at preventing fraud or reducing information security risks. For example, mobile manufacturers must comply with the Radio Equipment and Telecommunications Terminal Equipment Regulations 2000, which include a requirement that all apparatus and devices are constructed to support certain features that prevent fraud. Mobile networks must comply with the Privacy and Electronic Communications Regulations, which contain specific rules on marketing calls, emails, texts, faxes, cookies and requirements to keep communications services secure as well as notification obligations of personal data breaches. Financial institutions and payment services providers must comply with a number of regulations, namely the Money Laundering Regulations 2007 and the Payment Services Regulations 2009, that both aim to protect consumers and the resilience of the payments infrastructure. However, further critical elements of the mobile payment supply chain, like mobile wallet providers or mobile software companies, in essence the providers of the applications that enable the transfers of funds, are not currently captured under existing regulations. Given this, the convergence of communications technologies and payments services inevitably challenge established regulatory boundaries and generates key questions. First, how should responsibility for mitigating the potential information security risks of mobile payments be undertaken? Second, more generally, is it possible in practice to even design a framework to protect consumers from these risks because of the complexity in the supply chain?

Key technical characteristics of authentication

10.08 In its simplest sense, authentication is the process of verifying the validity of a payment instrument and ensuring its use is genuine. The authentication process for payments traditionally has been designed by card networks. Payment cards were first introduced in the 1940s and were embossed with details such as the card number and expiry date. The process was automated in the 1970s by giving cards a magnetic stripe. In the 1980s and 1990s chip cards, along with chip-based payment specifications, known as EMV, were introduced for payments. Today, in general, there are commonly three separate components in payment authentication, ie, device (eg, card, smartphone), payment (eg, regular transactions) or user (eg, identification of a customer by biometrics or passcode). However, authentication methods vary depending on the location and channel of payment. For example, where payments made in stores, the merchant verifies payment cards at the point of sale where a transaction is finalised or the moment where a consumer tenders payment in exchange for goods and services using a chip and pin machine. In remote purchases, the merchant, such as a call centre or website, is contacted by the consumer and facilitates payments, using card data provided by the consumer, without actually seeing the card. Card networks also now recognise mobiles as a card replacement. As mobile technology is rolled out, face-to-face transactions made at merchants using a mobile device are processed as online transactions, rather than chip and pin. That said, biometric authentication tools, such as fingerprints on mobile devices, could be used to authenticate every mobile payment. However, even though the technology to create strong consumer authentication of mobile payments already exists, the technology itself is designed to be used as part of the payment authentication as banks and card networks prefer to rely on their own risk based authentication of general payments, as they are ultimately responsible for the authentication process, rather than the mobile payment software provider.

10.09 For example, when Apple Pay first launched, consumers and banks saw an increase in fraud. The security problem had nothing to do with mobile payment technologies (eg, touch id, NFC, Apple's secure element) or stolen iPhones, rather the fraud was connected to the card issuers' consumer authentication process used to verify the payment instrument, in this case the card.

Key commercial characteristics of mobile payment authentication

10.10 The responsibility to authenticate the mobile payment is entirely on the bank/payment service provider. However, the bank does not have direct control over the technology used to register for the mobile payment tool and therefore cannot effectively mitigate the security risk (eg, the provision of cards on the mobile device, using the Apply Pay example). In addition, a number of industry commentators forecast financial institutions will move to device-based biometric authentication solutions, such as Apple's mobile biometric authentication platform, Touch ID fingerprint, to remove friction from the payment authentication and/or authorisation process and other account servicing activities, such as account log-in. Biometric technology is a powerful identity tool to promote reliable and secure authentication of consumers and one that consumers seem to want to use. That said, in the complex mobile payment supply chain, it is more common for biometrics to be introduced by new mobile payment providers, such as through handset manufacturers, rather than regulated financial institutions. Therefore, handset manufacturers are trusted to provide secure payment authentication technologies, which presents security and usability issues for the consumer and the payment account provider or issuer. Handset manufacturers are not likely to be subject to financial regulation or controls because their businesses operate outside the scope of financial regulators, which highlights a fundamental challenge with the current legal framework; established regulatory boundaries do not encapsulate the entire mobile payment supply chain.

Information security risks of mobile payments to consumers

10.11 The rapid growth in the volume of mobile payments over the last few years has prompted a number of studies on the risks involved with their use by consumers. The move to a single device, ie, the smartphone, to manage identity credentials used for financial authentication gives rise to particular concerns if the device is compromised or lost. Finally, many commentators have questioned the use of mobile technology to enable the collection of unprecedented amounts of data by banks, card networks and new mobile payment players at purchase and the potential privacy risks that such practices create. Besides possible concerns about consumers' privacy, poor authentication involved in the mobile payment process may increase the risk of unauthorised transactions.

10.12 Authentication is an important step to ensure transactions are genuine. Retailers and merchants are increasingly offering consumers the option to charge payments to their mobile phone accounts (known as direct carrier billing), as an alternative to paying with a credit or debit card. Direct carrier billing works much in the same way as premium rate services but purchases are applied directly to the consumer's mobile phone account. This payment option gives rise to increased risks of unauthorised transactions for consumers. In the US, enforcement action has been taken against four of the largest wireless mobile phone companies and smaller players for a practice known as mobile cramming: the unlawful practice of placing unauthorised charges of third parties on consumers' mobile phone accounts. These types of charges for goods and services were automatically charged to the consumer, without their consent and without them being able to question or prevent the charge from being applied to the account. Consumers were only about to dispute the transaction if they had checked their mobile statement carefully and were able to identify a fraudulent charge, as the charges were not authenticated or authorised by the consumer before they were applied to the mobile account. This practice is a significant concern for consumers as the FTC estimates that carrier billing is: 'the most popular mobile payment system in use in the world today'.

10.13 In the US, the Federal Trade Commission has also brought actions against companies that unfairly billed parents or the account holder for in-app purchases made by children, without informed consent, on mobile phones. Given this, proper authentication of payments is essential to prevent unauthorised or fraudulent transactions. In addition, the US actions highlight the issue that if consumers are not provided with the tools to properly authenticate charges/payments, a lack of authentication may lead to unfair and unreasonable practices by companies.

10.14 Many financial institutions see mobile as a profitable channel where biometrics technology is incorporated into online and mobile banking platforms as a way to limit, and in some cases remove, the need for username and password authentication. However, the move to mobile centric interaction, from application to servicing, gives rise to greater personal risks if the device is compromised or lost. First, common activities, such as making a transfer of money or checking your account balance, requires consumers to enter, send and/or store sensitive payment data on their mobile device. Second, the compromise of a mobile device may allow a fraudster to gain access to multiple authentication elements, such as passwords or biometrics, stored in/delivered to or accessed through the mobile device. This means consumers may unwittingly take on more risk, as it is their biometrics, such as face, fingerprint, iris pattern, that is used for payment authentication and/or shared between participants to facilitate such authentication. Now, more is at stake if the mobile device is lost or stolen.

10.15 Finally, mobile payments increase capabilities of mobile networks, payment platform providers and downstream payments participants, such as banks and card networks, to collect and use real time information about consumers' spending habits, locations, as examples, to sell such information for profits or predict and gain insight into consumer behaviour. This, in itself, is not a new problem. Zuboff is a critic of what she refers to as surveillance capitalism: '[the] accumulation [of free behavioral data] that produces hyperscale assemblages of objective and subjective data about individuals and their habitats for the purposes of knowing, controlling, and modifying behavior to produce new varieties of commodification, monetization, and control'.

10.16 In the case of mobile payments, banks, telecoms and other participants already work together to provide the mobile payment functionality, therefore it is likely that information sources are aggregated by participants in order to improve the shared commercial value of any mobile payment joint venture. For example, data collected from mobile payments gives mobile payment providers even more power to reason, predict and gain insight into new commercial prospects (eg, serving up advertisements when consumers are near a shop, offering discounts, coupons on purchases, profiling consumer, creating data segments from inferences about consumers). Second, gathering more data, including sensitive personal information such as biometric data, even if its use may create more secure authentication, could be seen to represent a shift of risk to the consumer in terms of a privacy compromise. Not surprisingly, the complex mobile payment supply chain may create privacy risks greater than privacy risks experienced in card transactions. The reason for this is that, whenever additional entities handle payment and consumer information, the processing risks, for example from the collection and improper use of such information, grow.

Information security risks of mobile payments to the payment system

10.17 In August 2013 the FCA launched a thematic review into mobile banking and payments to understand the potential risks to consumers and the market. It noted that mobile banking and payments present different challenges in relation to fraud and financial crime compared with established consumer servicing channels, such as internet banking. Fraud can happen in a variety of ways on mobile payments compared to other servicing channels. For example: mobile phones are easier to steal and/or lose and they are not designed for secure authentication (eg, multi-factor authentication tools that requires the consumer to use additional hardware, in addition to the mobile phone itself), as examples. That said, mobile money service providers, such as mobile payment platform providers, are not required to adhere to due diligence standards required by financial regulations. Financial institutions are required to thoroughly identify new consumers, in order to monitor the money flowing in and out of banks and financial institutions to prevent financial crime and promote financial stability. Some industry commentators argue that wholesale adoption of the consumer due diligence standards that financial institutions must comply with is unsuitable and may damage financial inclusion. That said, we should never lose sight of the fact criminals are always ready to exploit weaknesses in the payment system. For example, when the UK adopted EMV for face-to-face transactions, fraud shifted from face-to-face scenarios to online commerce. Financial security and financial accessibility are at the centre of every transaction, but it is important not to focus on one to the detriment of the other.

10.18 Finally, providers of mobile payment applications might have access to unprotected sensitive information (eg, biometric data) stored and processed on mobile phones, and both the owner of a mobile phone or a bank have virtually no control over handset hardware security. It is reported that attacks on mobile platforms through malicious links (eg, known phishing scams to access sensitive consumer data) and applications (eg, the danger of fake applications) could become one of the most common methods of stealing data and money. The United States National Institute of Standards and Technology's security guidance advises that the use of biometrics is not suitable for remote authentication, such as for payments made using mobile technology. Financial institutions are now reliant on a biometric implementation or tokenisation mechanisms that are not under their control or the oversight of financial regulators. It is arguable this may bring further problems in terms of security and control. The security of the authentication process is made harder or potentially not verified, and gives rise to increased risks when disputing transactions of the basis of technical evidence, which may not be accurate or reliable. This in turn could impact the legal enforceability of financial institutions' terms and conditions of service.

Legislative framework governing payment authentication in Europe

Law of payments in Europe

10.19 On 13 November 2007 the EU adopted Directive 2007/64/EC on payment services in the internal market ('the PSD'). The PSD provides a legal basis for the creation of a European-wide single market for payments and aims to harmonise the legal framework and remove any differences between Member States in respect of laws governing payment services. On 23 December 2015, the Revised Payment Services Directive (the 'PSD2') was published in the Official Journal, which Member States will be required to transpose into national law. This followed a long period of review, with the aim of ensuring the regulatory framework is able to respond to innovations in the payments sector, as well as improve standards with respect to security of online payments. The list of activities defined as payment services has been expanded under the PSD2 and is contained in Annex 1, as referred to in point (3) of Article 4, of the PSD2:

> '1. Services enabling cash to be placed on a payment account as well as all the operations required for operating a payment account.
>
> 2. Services enabling cash withdrawals from a payment account as well as all the operations required for operating a payment account.
>
> [3&4. Execution of payment transactions]
>
> 5. Issuing of payment instruments and/or acquiring of payment transactions.
>
> 6. Money remittance [...]'.

10.20 The activities of most new mobile payment providers are likely to fall outside the definition of a payment service in the PSD2. Despite the PSD2 attempts to reflect new types of payments services, it does not go far enough as some or all of the activities of new mobile payment providers appears to fall outside the scope of what is considered a payment service. First, this is because payments made by consumers are not generally directly made to new players and money is transmitted without any payment account being created. Second, payment platform providers, in providing software which may enable a card payment to be made, are not technically enabling cash to be placed on a payment account or withdrawn. Third, new mobile payment providers have no relationship with merchants, therefore there cannot be an argument that new participants acquire payment transactions. Fourth, PSD2 defines issuing payment instruments as: '[…] a payment service by a payment service provider contracting to provide a payer with a payment instrument to initiate and process the payer's payment transactions'.

10.21 New mobile payments providers in the payment system do not initiate and process transactions, as the acquirer will always process transactions. It may be possible to argue new players are part of the process that enables the execution of payment transactions. However, if these new mobile payment providers were deemed to be conducting a regulated activity, it is likely such participants may argue that they are exempt due to the technical service provider exemption provided under Article 3(j): '[…] technical service providers, which support the provision of payment services […]'.

10.22 The PSD2 introduces two new types of payment services; payment initiation services and account information services. Most new mobile payment providers do not carry out these types of payment services either. Recitals 27 and 29 of the PSD2 describe payment initiation services as: '[services] establishing a software bridge between the website of the merchant and the online banking platform of the payer's account servicing payment service provider in order to initiate internet payments on the basis of a credit transfer […] [services that] enable the payment initiation service provider to provide comfort to a payee that the payment has been initiated in order to provide an incentive to the payee to release the goods or to deliver the service without undue delay. Such services offer a low-cost solution for both merchants and consumers and provide consumers with a possibility to shop online even if they do not possess payment cards'.

10.23 New mobile payments providers do not do this. As a result of this, their activities would not be considered a payment initiation service. Recital 28 describes account information services as: 'those services provide the payment service user with aggregated online information on one or more payment accounts held with one or more other payment service providers and accessed via online interfaces of the account servicing payment service provider. The payment service user is thus able to have an overall view of its financial situation immediately at any given moment. Those services should also be covered by this Directive in order to provide consumers with adequate protection for their payment and account data as well as legal certainty about the status of account information service providers'.

10.24 However, most new mobile payments providers do not hold account information data, as consumers can only access their account information via its platform, therefore it is unlikely that their activities could be described as an account information service. Therefore, the activities of all new mobile payment providers do not or are unlikely to constitute payment services as defined under the PSD2.

10.25 In summary, the PSD2 seems to be defective when it comes to regulating mobile payments because most of the providers of these types of payments are not likely to be carrying out payment services and some parties to the supply chain for mobile payments will not be within the scope of the PSD2. Therefore, despite one of the PSD2's principal aims to reflect, and regulate, new types of payments services, it does not go far enough as it seems that some or all of the activities of the new mobile payment providers will be excluded from regulation, or they will likely be able to rely on an exemption. Therefore information security risks cannot be effectively managed by payment regulations that do not encapsulate the entire mobile payment supply chain, even with introduction of PSD2. Consequently, new mobile payment providers are likely to be able to continue to operate outside of the European payment services legal framework. That said, the PSD2 has not yet been transposed into national laws by Member States so there is a possibility that some European countries may look to find ways to bring these new mobile payment providers into scope.

10.26 Not surprisingly, new mobile payment providers, leveraging consumers' existing card accounts and bank relationships, have attempted to regulate the relationship between the mobile payment functionality they provide to consumers through contract. Unfortunately this means, in particular circumstances, consumers are not afforded the same level of protection when making payments via mobile devices. For example, under the PSD, payment service providers must only block the use of a payment instrument if it is reasonable to do so, and they give notice to the consumer. They must also unblock an instrument when reasons for blocking it have been removed. However, many new mobile payment providers, such as Apple Pay, have adopted the position that gives them extensive rights to withdraw or suspend such mobile payment platforms without reasons or giving notice. For example, typical terms are: '[] reserves the right to block, restrict, suspend, or terminate your use of the Digital Card and/or change the functionality of the services without reference to [the consumer's payment service provider]. You agree that in such circumstances [consumer's payment service provider] will not be liable to you or any third party'.

10.27 In the US, the mobile cramming problem explained earlier has been accompanied by divergent and inconsistent approaches taken with regard to carriers' dispute resolution policies for third-party charges. This has been combined with different approaches to the format and disclosures on mobile phone statements, leading to consumer confusion and a lack of understanding of what charges have been applied. Now, US consumers who use their mobiles to make payments, and such payments are then billed to their mobile phone account, do not appear to have the same level of protection in that they would otherwise enjoy if such payments were made via their bank or credit card accounts. In the UK, the body PhonepayPlus, supported by OfCom, is responsible for the day-to-day regulation of premium rate phone services and the underlying consumer issues associated with these practices, such as consumer control over spending levels and informed consent to charging (under the current UK Payment Services Regulations, payments made through a telecom operator or informational technology devices are exempt from being considered as regulated activities).

That said, under PSD2, the exclusion for payments through telecom operators or informational technology devices now limits the exemption to payments made through telecom operators or informational technology devices used to purchase digital services such as music and digital newspapers that are downloaded on a digital device or of electronic tickets or donations to charities, rather than the purchase of physical goods and services through a telecom operator or informational technology device.

10.28 However, the proposed framework under the PSD2 still provides an exemption for telecom operators or informational technology devices not only when they act as an intermediary for the delivery of digital services through the device in question, but also when they add value to those digital services. Given that one of the key aims of the PSD2 is to decrease the potential security risks in the payment chain, it seems inconsistent that the regulatory framework will continue to provide exemptions for new mobile payment providers and does not seem to give such operators any incentive to deploy or develop strong customer authentication of mobile payments.

Regulation of strong consumer authentication

10.29 Under PSD2, whenever a consumer logs into their payment account online or accesses it through a remote channel, such as mobile, the payment institution is required to apply strong consumer authentication. Where a payment service provider fails to use strong consumer authentication, when required, the consumer will not bear any financial loss unless they have acted fraudulently. Strong consumer authentication, commonly known as multi-factor authentication, must be based on the combination of two or more of the following elements categorised as: '[…] knowledge (something only the user knows), possession (something only the user possesses) and inherence (something the user is) that are independent, in that the breach of one does not compromise the reliability of the others, and is designed in such a way as to protect the confidentiality of the authentication data'.

10.30 In addition, if the consumer is initiating a transaction online or remotely, strong consumer authentication must also dynamically link the transaction to a specific amount and a specific payee. However, the PSD2 provides exemptions from using the above authentication standards for low value payments at the point of sale, such as low value contactless and mobile payments. This is because there is a provision in the PSD2 that exempts payment service providers from performing strong consumer authentication for a range of transactions where the risks have been properly assessed, such as: low value payments, outgoing payments to trusted beneficiaries, transfers between two accounts of the same payment service user held at the same payment service provider, low-risk transactions based on a transaction risk analysis, purely consultative services (with no display of sensitive payment data). Data compromise and other information security risks associated with mobile payments remain real, therefore providing an exemption for low value payments as an example, which would likely include mobile payments, is not an effective way to manage such risks. The PSD2 alone will not deal with information security risks of mobile payments because authentication, which is central to managing those risks, is not applied to a range of transactions.

Other sources of EU guidance

10.31 On 23 July 2014 the EU adopted the Regulation 910/2014/EC on electronic identification and trust services for electronic transactions in the internal market ('eIDAS Regulation'). The eIDAS Regulation establishes a new legal structure for electronic identification, signatures, seals and documents throughout the EU, including recognising multi-factor authentication as a method of authentication. Some commentators have suggested that the eIDAS Regulation could be considered as a possible solution for facilitating strong consumer authentication more widely. In a nutshell, the eIDAS Regulation does establish the recognition of electronic identification ('eID') and different level of eID assurance. That said, it is not clear how the eIDAS Regulation could facilitate strong consumer authentication more broadly than within Europe. In addition, no country outside Europe has yet indicated it would be willing to adopt identification services set out in the eIDAS Regulation. In addition, the scope and timeline of adoption of the eIDAS Regulation by the private sector and by different Member States is unclear. Therefore, any authentication framework established by the eIDAS Regulation would appear to not encourage a global authentication solution; rather it aims to provide an identity solution for the European internal market, which severely limits its appeal for its use in mobile payment authentication. The eIDAS Regulation alone will not deal with information security risks of mobile payments because any authentication solution, which is central to managing those risks, would only seem to be relevant for transactions carried out in Europe.

10.32 Finally, the Article 29 Data Protection Working Party ('Article 29 WP'), issued guidance regarding authentication in the context of online services in 2003. The Article 29 WP recommends four authentication solutions to help manage the challenges websites were facing at the date of writing the guidance. The guidance does not effectively deal with information security risks of mobile payments because the recommended solutions, which are central to managing those risks, do not appear to promote strong customer authentication, which may be expected given the context, ie, website registration, and the date of publication.

Legislative framework governing payment authentication in the United States

10.33 The EU has prescribed rules for payment service providers to promote the security of the European payments sector, including payment authentication requirements. In the US, some sources say there are rules that apply to mobile payments but other commentators suggest this is not the case. In a recent testimony to US Congress, Sarah Jane Hughes of the Maurer School of Law at Indiana University told the committee: 'Two federal statutes protect consumers with credit and debit payments – the Electronic Fund Transfer Act [Regulation E] and the – EFT and [Dodd-Frank Wall Street Reform and] Consumer Protection Act [...] those same protections for mobile do not exist, and that is a big issue for the underbanked'.

10.34 There is a wide range of guidance distributed by the Consumer Financial Protection Bureau, the Federal Trade Commission ('FTC'), the Office of the Comptroller of the Currency, the Federal Deposit Insurance Corp., the Federal Reserve Board and the Federal Financial Institutions Examination Council ('FFIEC'), relating to safeguarding of consumer information of financial institutions and oversight of third-party service providers to financial institutions. Broadly, this guidance, which is considered mandatory, establishes standards for safeguarding consumer information and utilising third-party service providers with the objective of protecting consumers from harm and protecting financial institutions from reputational, transactional, and compliance risks, and providers aim to comply with these standards.

10.35 When it comes to payment authentication in the US, there is current regulatory guidance. The FFIEC distributed updated guidance in 2009 that suggests financial institutions should implement authentication techniques appropriate to the risk of the transaction and concludes that single factor authentication is inadequate for high risk transactions involving access to consumer information or the movement of funds to other parties. However, the guidance provides no further information for financial institutions to assess when or how authentication should take place, including for mobile payments. In light of the above position and the lack of clear rules, the New York State Department of Financial Services recently issued a letter to all national bank regulators, calling for the use of multifactor authentication. The New York State Department of Financial Services' letter was followed by the Federal Trade Commission's issuance of orders to nine companies that serve as qualified security assessors, asking them to provide information about how they audit companies' compliance with the Payment Card Industry Data Security Standard. Perhaps this could be a sign that increased federal oversight of payments security is on the way in the US? That said, it is too premature to suggest the US is moving closer to the EU approach with regard to the regulation of payment authentication. However, what we can draw from this is that strong payment authentication is a key tool to manage the information security risks of mobile payments in both regions, but the legal frameworks in both the US and Europe do not currently operate as an effective tool to manage these risks.

Industry standards governing payment authentication do not exist in the context of mobile payments

10.36 Industry standards have been driven by card networks. Card networks have focused their efforts on improving only card-based authentication, and not authentication for other types of payment instruments, such as mobiles. There is no single industry standard for payment authentication in the area of mobile payments or biometrics. Security experts have expressed concerns that industry standards do not contain security requirements for authentication of mobile payments and raise the important issue that any standard ultimately has little enforcement action behind it. This is because compliance with industry standards is enforced by the card schemes, which have their own private enforcement processes and discretion to enforce penalties, which are generally never made public unless retailers challenge fines at court. As mentioned above, the Federal Trade Commission ('FTC') recently launched a probe into Payment Card Industry Data Security Standards ('PCI DSS') compliance auditing by nine companies and their roles in protecting consumers' information and privacy. The FTC investigation was followed by a request from the US National Retail Federation ('NRF'), which has asked the FTC to conduct an investigation into the PCI DSS. This highlights the limits of self regulation, ie, the lack of transparency of such assessments and legitimacy of standard setting bodies, which in the case of PCI DSS could be argued to be an inappropriate exercise of market power by payment card networks. Not surprisingly, even with the development of industry standards in the EU and the US, these have so far not been successful in managing information security risks because of they do not encapsulate the entire mobile payment supply chain nor do they deal with mobile payment authentication.

Competition law and mobile payments

10.37 The mobile payments sector is also subject to competition law. For example, there are clear principles in European law for identifying circumstances in which competition may be regarded as distorted. In exceptional cases, where competition is systemically weak, regulatory intervention going beyond the scope of the competition rules is possible. That may be appropriate where one or more undertakings have significant market power, and the competition rules are insufficient to address the problem. Mobile payments may introduce new challenges from a competition law perspective. Such challenges may not be answered by the status quo: (i) in the case of payments, the focus of authorities on interchange fee regulation over the past 20 years payments, and (ii) the European Commission's recent preliminary view that Google has, in breach of European competition rules, abused its dominant position by imposing restrictions on Android device manufacturers and mobile network operators. However, these actions are not relevant in this instance, as the issue is about ensuring safe and secure transactions to prevent fraudulent transactions. The mere fact that one group of operators is, for good pro-competitive reasons, subject to a different set of rules from another group of operators with much greater market power does not by itself give rise to a distortion of competition that requires correction through competition regulatory intervention. Such intervention is only justified where competition is restricted in such a way as to weaken the competitive structure of the market or where, without the intervention, competition might be foreclosed. General principles of European law also include the principle of non-discrimination, which prohibits both subjecting undertakings in similar economic situations to different rules, and treating differently situated undertakings in the same way. Given this, competition law provides a potential remedy if one part of the mobile payment supply chain becomes dominant, but this does not appear to be a current reality in the mobile payment sector.

Conclusion

10.38 The mobile payment supply chain contains numerous participants and leads to challenges for the regulatory landscape. Proper authentication of mobile payments to prevent fraudulent transactions is central to managing information security risks associated with mobile payments. Laws, regulations and industry standards are tools used to manage these types of risks. A review of the existing legal frameworks and industry standards in Europe and the Ud S have so far not been successful in managing such information security risks. One of the main challenges is that critical participants like mobile wallet providers or mobile software companies, in essence the providers of the applications that enable the transfers of funds, are not currently captured under existing regulations. As mobile payments are becoming increasingly more common, and are the way of the future, regulatory frameworks need to encapsulate more of the mobile payment supply chain. Also, importantly, regulation and industry standards alone are not sufficient to deal with information security risks because authentication, which is central to managing those risks, is not caught by regulation. So, how should responsibility for mitigating the potential information security risks of mobile payments be allocated? First, one of the major challenges seems to be the majority of the new mobile payment providers are opposed to accepting risk, eg, financial or regulatory, to be responsible to ensure the authentication process is secure. In addition, there is a lack of standardisation of approaches to authentication within the payments market, which means customer and payment authentication are seen more as competitive issues rather than risks that all participants must work together to resolve. Only a broader level of co-operation between parties in the mobile payment supply chain will result in the information security risks being appropriately managed. Such cooperation should focus on a number of key principles, which all participants should make every effort to produce and adhere to, to deliver an authentication framework to protect consumers from the information security risks of mobile payments.

10B ELECTRIC UTILITIES: CRITICAL INFRASTRUCTURE PROTECTION AND RELIABILITY STANDARDS

E Rudina and S Kort

10.39 An electrical grid is an interconnected network for delivering electricity from producers to consumers. It implements three main functions: electrical power generation, transmission over high voltage transmission lines from distance sources to demand centres, and energy distribution to the individual customers. Electrical grids vary in size from covering a single building through national grids to transnational grids that can cross the continents.

Electric Utilities as a part of critical infrastructure

10.40 The energy infrastructure provides the enabling function for all sectors of critical infrastructure. The significant risks in many critical infrastructure sectors arise due to their dependency from a power supply. The extended electric outage could trigger a domino effect resulting in communications failures, disruption to transportation, cuts to the water supply, and other impacts that may further complicate the situation. In today's world, without electricity, most of the systems that support the human being cannot work, health and welfare are threatened. Growing risks from cyber-attacks demonstrate how vulnerable the energy grids and dependent vitally important systems are to systemic failure.

10.41 To resist these risks and mitigate their effects it is important to analyse how electric utilities work and which reasons underlie possible threats to their reliable functioning. The processes of energy generation, transmission and supply are operated and automated by different types of control systems. Thus, at a glance, industrial automation and control systems comprise the core of the electric power industry. From this perspective, all cybersecurity issues and appropriate recommendations for industrial automation and control systems are applicable to the electric power facilities.

Electric utilities as a kind of industrial automation and control system

10.42 Industrial automation and control system (IACS) is the collection of personnel, hardware, software, procedures and policies involved in the operation of the industrial process and that can affect or influence its safe, secure and reliable operation.[1] Hardware and software components of an IACS comprise the control system.

10.43 Control systems may employ various technologies to communicate with each other, thus forming the technical layer of the integration and interoperation of in the electrical end-use, generation, transmission, and distribution industries. According to the GridWise®Interoperability Context-Setting Framework,[2] which is intended to provide the context for identifying and debating interoperability issues, two other layers are informational and organisational.

1 IEC 62443-3-3:2013 – Industrial communication networks – Network and system security – Part 3-3: System security requirements and security levels.

2 https://www.gridwiseac.org/pdfs/interopframework_v1_1.pdf.

Figure 10.1 – Interoperability Layered Categories, from GridWise®Interoperability Context-Setting Framework. Source: www.gridwiseac.org/pdfs/interopframework_v1_1.pdf.

10.44 Interoperability issues cut across all layers. Cyber-security issues affect those aspects that lie in the scope of information infrastructure (marked as 'I' on the figure). The most complicated issues arise on the edge of technical interoperability and semantic understanding where business needs meet technologies. New business challenges boost the implementation of new ways of applying the technological capabilities. These ways may also facilitate the unintended use of these capabilities. That is what usually happens when technical systems become 'smart'.

Current state and further evolution of electricity infrastructure – Smart Grid

10.45 The need for a smarter electric grid comes mainly from the demands of economy and society. The improvements in electronic communication technology aims at resolving the issues of the electrical grid that become apparent towards the end of the last century. These issues are the result of structural rigidities of the electric grid along with the lack of prompt delivery of data about current demand. The energy suppliers had to rely on electricity demand patterns established over the years compensating the daily peaks in demand with additional generating capacities. The relatively low utilisation of peaking generators, together with the necessary redundancy in the electricity grid, resulted in high costs to the electricity companies, and then – in increased tariffs for consumers. Eventually, technological limitations on metering made the power prices equally high for all consumers at the same location area.

10.46 The additional factors facilitating the development of a Smart Grid are growing concerns over environmental damage from fossil-fired power stations and the risk of terrorist attacks. Concern for the environment caused the shift to the renewable energy technologies. Dominant forms such as wind power and solar power are highly variable. Thus, the need for more sophisticated control systems became apparent, to facilitate the connection of energy sources to the flexibly controllable grid. The risk of potential attack on centralised power stations also led to calls for an energy grid that would be more resilient in the face of malicious impact.

10.47 Obtaining timely information about power demand may facilitate more efficient power generation due to the better control of the use and production of electric energy during the periods of peak and low consumption. The appropriate technology of automatically collecting consumption, diagnostic, and status data from energy metering devices – Automatic meter reading – was proposed in 1977. Another technology, Power line Technology Communication (PLC), uses electrical wiring to carry both data and electric power simultaneously. The data from meters are transferred over the existing power lines to the nearest electrical substation, and then relayed to a central computer in the utility's main office for processing and analysis. PLC technology may be also used by utilities for fraud detection, network management and support of advanced metering infrastructure, demand side management, load control, demand response, and other advanced energy management techniques. Other telecommunication technologies, including wireless communication, may be used together with PLC. Different topologies for these telecommunication networks may be in place thus making the overall infrastructure much more complex.

Sources of cybersecurity issues for electric power infrastructure

10.48 Computer and network technologies help to mitigate the complexity of managing the control systems at the power facilities and for connected infrastructure. They eventually permeate the whole process of power generation and distribution, make it much more effective, flexible, and smart, and much more vulnerable to cyberattacks.

10.49 Changing requirements to the electric power grid that are intended to make it more efficient and environmentally friendly create the new ways for affecting different aspects of its proper functioning. However, nowadays the known cyber-incidents in the energy sector are linked to the attacks on control systems that became possible due to the weak integration of these systems with information technologies.

10.50 Cyber-security challenges for the infrastructure of power generation, distribution, and supply are the result of exponentially growing use of information technologies at power facilities. For decades, the industrial control systems and corporate systems utilising computer technologies evolve independently. The security issues that appeared in corporate systems were not valid for the industrial environment due to the lack of channels for external impact.

10.51 As the demand for connectivity grows, the control processes incorporate information technologies. The additional communication and information exchange paths based on mostly ad-hoc solutions were the usual way for this integration. Some of these solutions may connect generally purposed computer systems with lower levels of control. Low attention to security matters in this case makes it possible to compromise the control processes via information channels.

10.52 Traditionally, cyber-security threats are considered as issues that arise in the information environment and target the data handling process. Information security is usually interpreted as the confidentiality, integrity, availability set of aspects. Software bugs, Trojan programs, backdoors, or any improper behaviour of IT systems is also considered as a source of problems that cause only data-related concerns. However, this is not so for the control systems where a cyber-attack may potentially cause unintended process failure. In power grid, such failure may cause to the outage and, in the worst case, have the physical impact on equipment.

Known cyberattacks on electric utilities

10.53 In the end of 2015, a wave of cyber-attacks hit several critical sectors in Ukraine. These incidents are mostly known because of an incident on 23 December 2015, when the Ukrainian Kyivoblenergo, a regional electricity distribution company, reported service outages to customers. The outages were originally thought to have affected approximately 80,000 customers. However, later it was revealed that three different distribution energy companies were attacked. Resulting outages caused approximately 225,000 customers to lose power across various areas.[3]

10.54 Illegal remote access of the company's computer and SCADA systems was the primary reason for these outages. The incident was thought to be due to a coordinated intentional attack. This was accompanied by the denial of view to system dispatchers and attempts to deny customer calls that would have reported the power out.

10.55 As a result of this attack, seven 110 kV and 23 35 kV substations were disconnected for about three hours. According to the later statements, the impact on additional portions of the distribution grid forced operators to switch to manual mode of control.

3 E-ISAC. Analysis of the Cyber Attack on the Ukrainian Power Grid Defense Use Case. March 18, 2016. https://ics.sans.org/media/E-ISAC_SANS_Ukraine_DUC_5.pdf.

10.56 The attack became possible because of the compromise of connected computer systems with malicious software (malware). It was BlackEnergy, a multi-purposed malware platform that ran several plugin modules some of which were specific for the industrial environment.[4] The platform was presumably deployed in a corporate environment as a result of the successful attack employing spear-phishing technique. Attacks of this kind are effective because they take advantage of the human factor, targeting the personnel, the weakest link in the cyber-security chain. Then attackers gained access to the ICS network by traversing the VPN connection with stolen credentials. Additionally, they showed expertise, not only in network connected infrastructure; such as uninterruptable power supplies, but also in operating the processes through the supervisory control system. Personnel performing routine operations of control from their workplaces could not even conceive of losing this control because of such a complicated attack.

10.57 The source of the attack is unknown. Attribution is not possible because of uncertainty on how, when, and under which circumstances the connected IT infrastructure was successfully attacked for the first time. The BlackEnergy platform used in this attack is used widely for conducting various attacks, and its victims are distributed geographically. Among victims, industrial, governmental, property holding, and technology organisations are identified.[5]

10.58 Another well-known attack on electric utilities is the compromise of the Ukrainian distribution grid that took place on 17 December 2016. The outage cut off power to the north part of Kiev just before midnight and lasted for about an hour due to the malfunction of an Ukrenergo substation. According to claims made by Ukrenergo, the failure at the substation was the result of an external impact on its SCADA systems.

10.59 Experts from some security companies, as well as a number of independent researchers, came to the conclusion that the outage may have been connected with the newly discovered malware, which they called CrashOverride or Industroyer.[6] [7] This malware was specifically designed to disrupt the operation of industrial control systems, particularly electrical substations. CrashOverride/ Industroyer is capable of directly controlling switches and circuit breakers in electrical substation circuits.

10.60 Similarly to BlackEnergy, CrashOverride/Industroyer is the malware platform that is capable of running plugin modules with various functionality. The difference in the second one is that is intended to attack industrial systems

4 https://securelist.com/blackenergy-apt-attacks-in-ukraine-employ-spearphishing-with-word-documents/73440/.

5 https://securelist.com/be2-custom-plugins-router-abuse-and-target-profiles/67353/.

6 Anton Cherepanov and Robert Lipovsky. Industroyer: Biggest threat to industrial control systems since Stuxnet. 12 of June 2017. https://www.welivesecurity.com/2017/06/12/industroyer-biggest-threat-industrial-control-systems-since-stuxnet/.

7 Dragos Inc. CRASHOVERRIDE. Analysis of the Threat to Electric Grid Operations. Version 2.20170613 https://dragos.com/blog/crashoverride/CrashOverride-01.pdf.

and may be reconfigured to target any industrial environment. The discovered version of malware works with four industrial protocols that are widely used in the power sector (IEC 60870-5-101, IEC 60870-5-104, IEC 61850, OLE for Process Control Data Access). It has to be mentioned that these protocols are specific to the energy infrastructure in Europe, while the majority of utilities in US employ DNP3 protocols. This fact gives an indication of planned geographical coverage for the attacks. However, CrashOverride/Industroyer was designed so it could be scaled for attacks against a variety of systems, rather than for a specific attack type.

10.61 Developers of the malware demonstrated thorough knowledge of how control systems work in electric power sector facilities. Another notable feature of CrashOverride/Industroyer is that it implements a tool for exploiting known vulnerabilities in protection relays. Devices can be forced to stop responding by sending them a specially crafted data packet; to re-enable a device then, it has to be manually rebooted. If the malware uses the tool, in the event of a critical situation in an electrical network, the damage may not be limited to a power failure; the attack could damage equipment due to relay protection and control systems failing to work properly. If overloads are planned in a certain way, an attack in one place can result in cascading power shutdowns at several substations.

10.62 The failure of the substation 'Severnaya' (literally, 'Northern') in Kiev was linked to CrashOverride/Industroyer because the activation timestamp was the date of the blackout – 17 December 2016 – and this malware implements the functionality to carry out such attacks. Nevertheless, there is no direct proof that this malware has been used in any known attacks against power sector facilities.

10.63 The malware examples described above provide insight into how sophisticated the specific targeted attack could be. However, even the unintended attack may cause the significant damage if the system is not protected enough. In most cases, industrial computer infection attempts are sporadic and the malicious functionality is not specific to attacks on the energy sector. This fact means that almost all threats and malware categories that affect non-industrial systems across the globe may be relevant to energy sector and smart grid. These threats include spyware and financial malware targeting corporate environments, ransomware which cyber-criminals extort money from victims, backdoors and wipers that put the computer out of operation and wipe the data on the hard drive. During the malware epidemic, even a chance infection can lead to dangerous consequences.

10.64 Ransomware has become a significant threat for companies, including industrial enterprises. It is particularly dangerous for enterprises that have critical infrastructure facilities, since malware activity can disrupt industrial processes. In the first half of 2017 the WannaCry outbreak and ExPetr attacks ensured this problem got widespread public attention.

10.65 During the period from 12 to 15 May 2017, numerous companies across the globe were attacked by a network cryptoworm called WannaCry. The worm's victims include various manufacturing companies, oil refineries, city infrastructure objects and electrical distribution network facilities.[8]

10.66 Energy sector facilities comprised 6.9% of that were affected by WannaCry industrial systems according to the statistics published by Kaspersky Lab.[9] Among confirmed incidents, a Spanish electric power company was affected by WannaCry as The Spanish newspaper El Mundo reported.[10]

10.67 It is not obvious how these infections became possible. As a rule either the industrial network is not directly connected to the internet or access is provided via the corporate network using network address translation, a firewall and a corporate proxy server, which should make it impossible to infect such systems via the internet. WannaCry infections probably got success because of industrial network configuration errors, alternative connections to the Internet through uncontrolled modems, including mobile phones, or due to the malware infiltration via connections intended for remote maintenance.

10.68 In the years since, and now, ransomware attacks on energy companies have only become more frequent, causing data leaks and corporate network problems more often than interruptions in power generation and supply. We'll consider just a few examples here.

10.69 Qulliq Energy Corporation (QEC), the territorial utility that provides power to Nunavut in Canada, announced[11] that its network was breached on 15 January 2023. It disclosed that the attack took down the systems at its Customer Care and administrative offices and didn't affect power plant operations, though customers were unable to pay their bills via credit card. The company enlisted external cybersecurity experts alongside QEC's and the Government of Nunavut's IT teams to investigate the scope of the attack and determine which data were accessed.

10.70 The Peruvian electricity supply company Sociedad Eléctrica del Sur Oeste (SEAL) suffered a cyberattack on 17 April 2023. The company reported in a press release sent to local news outlets that some services and user data were not available until further notice. The expiration dates of electric service payments and other services were also suspended. According to SEAL's General Manager, the attackers were seeking to steal information, however, the company had a security system that prevented it. The only thing they managed to obtain was access to the commercial part. The company reported that specialists were solving the problem in order to restore the service system.

8 Kaspersky Lab ICS-CERT. Wannacry On Industrial Networks: Error Correction. https://ics-cert.kaspersky.com/reports/2017/06/22/wannacry-on-industrial-networks/.

9 https://ics-cert.kaspersky.com/reports/2017/09/28/threat-landscape-for-industrial-automation-systems-in-h1-2017/.

10 http://www.elmundo.es/tecnologia/2017/05/12/5915e99646163fd8228b4578.html.

11 https://www.qec.nu.ca/qulliq-energy-corporation-impacted-cybersecurity-incident.

10.71 In May 2023, Madhya Pradesh Power Management Company Limited, based in Jabalpur, India, fell victim to a ransomware attack. The Jabalpur state Cyber Cell's superintendent of police said that an investigation was underway in response to a complaint. MPPMC chief general manager said those behind the ransomware attack had provided email IDs to contact them. MPPMC scanned the servers as per the guidelines of the government and tried to restore them with precaution. No further technical details were released at the time of the announcement.

10.72 We have also seen the impact of supply chain attacks on energy companies over the last few years, both in terms of products and services. The most remarkable case was the SolarWinds supply chain attack. On 13 December 2020, FireEye, Microsoft, and SolarWinds[12] announced the discovery of a large, sophisticated supply chain attack leveraging Orion IT, an infrastructure monitoring and management platform by SolarWinds. The SolarWinds supply chain attack was designed very professionally, with a clear focus on staying undetected for as long as possible. The Sunburst malware used in the attack includes a complex victim reporting, validation and upgrading scheme. It has been officially confirmed that about 18,000 users, including the electricity industry, may have installed backdoored versions of SolarWinds. Though, there is limited information on the number of organisations where the attack has evolved, and second-stage tools may have been deployed.

10.73 Since December 2020, the government authorities and cyber security vendors have continue to investigate and share new findings, threat vectors, and remediation tips for the SolarWinds attack. On December 14, 2020, the Electricity Information Sharing and Analysis Center (E-ISAC)[13] operated by North American Electric Reliability Corporation (NERC) published an allpoints bulletin to highlight the SolarWinds compromise and its potential impact, as well as several defence and detection tools produced by FireEye to aid industry in its response. In addition, on 17 December 2020, the E-ISAC hosted a Critical Broadcast Program call. In an effort to better understand the extent of the condition of the SolarWinds Orion compromise impact on BPS security and reliability, NERC issued a private Level 2 NERC alert on 22 December 2020. To support the ongoing and resource intensive industry response, the E-ISAC and the Electricity Subsector Coordinating Council (ESCC) produced additional resources to aid utilities in their response and hosted a series of restricted webinars to provide additional insights to electric utilities with key vendors involved in the response. Lessons learnt for the North American Electricity Industry, including the key recommended activities, were provided in a paper issued by NERC.[14]

10.74 The attack occurred on 22 February 2022 was targeting Viasat systems, belonging to one of the largest commercial satellite operators. The company

12 https://www.solarwinds.com/securityadvisory.

13 https://www.nerc.com/pa/CI/ESISAC/Pages/default.aspx.

14 https://www.nerc.com/pa/CI/ESISAC/Documents/SolarWinds%20and%20Related%20Supply%20Chain%20Compromise%20White%20Paper.pdf.

statement revealed that the attack caused a partial outage in their system which affected internet access in Ukraine and other European countries served by the KA-SAT network. The attack had an unexpected side effect – the downtime in the KA-SAT systems resulted in Enecron, a German wind power company, losing remote access to the controls of 5,800 wind turbines producing 11 GW of power. Company representatives stated[15] that the systems were not endangered, as the turbines work automatically and shut down in case of any issues. However, Enercon was forced to replace their IT equipment as a result of this cybersecurity incident.

10.75 Siemens Energy, a Munich-based energy technology company, officially confirmed a MOVEit data-theft attack to several news outlets on 27 June 2023[16] after the Clop ransomware group added the company to its data leak website. The attackers exploited a zero-day vulnerability found in the MOVEit Transfer platform to gain unauthorised access to sensitive information. However, Siemens Energy said that no critical data was stolen, and business operations were not impacted, according to a company spokesperson. The company took immediate action upon learning about the incident. Siemens Energy did not respond to follow-up questions from news outlets about what systems or devices were affected and what data was stolen.

10.76 A distinctive feature of recent attacks on the IT infrastructure of energy companies is their focus on employees, their personal data. A targeted attack on an employee can serve as an entry vector into the infrastructure. This is specifically dangerous when it comes to nuclear industry and nuclear energy.

10.77 The interesting case relates to the campaign attributed to the Lazarus APT group beginning in 2023 that targeted the defence industry and nuclear engineers. In this campaign, Lazarus tricks job seekers on social media into opening malicious apps for fake job interviews. To avoid detection by behaviour-based security solutions, this backdoored application operates discreetly, activating only when the user selects a server from the Trojanized VNC[17] client's drop-down menu. Numerous instances of compromised companies were confirmed. The majority of affected entities are directly involved in defence manufacturing, encompassing radar systems, unmanned aerial vehicles, military vehicles, vessels, weaponry, and companies related to the navy. Furthermore, in one of the cases, the username associated with the initial infection vector was identified. Through conversations with the victim, the researchers found out that this individual was a nuclear engineer based in Hungary who received the malicious file after getting into contact with a suspicious account via Telegram and WhatsApp.[18]

15 https://www.energate-messenger.com/news/220432/enercon-turbines-without-remote-control.
16 https://www.scmagazine.com/news/siemens-ucla-victims-moveit.
17 Remote access software for desktop or mobile device.
18 https://ics-cert.kaspersky.com/publications/reports/2024/04/02/apt-and-financial-attacks-on-industrial-organizations-in-h2-2023/.

10.78 On 14 October 2022, the largest Indian energy company, Tata Power Company Limited, confirmed[19] that it was targeted by a cyberattack, which affected its IT infrastructure. The company said that all necessary steps had been taken to restore its systems, adding that all critical operational systems were functioning. As a precaution, limited access and preventive checks were introduced for employees and customers when interacting with portals in order to prevent unauthorised access. The Hive ransomware group claimed responsibility for the attacks. Hive hackers claimed to have encrypted Tata Power systems on 3 October, revealing the attack on 24 October in a message on their DarkWeb website. The hackers uploaded a sample of the stolen files, including employment contracts, supplier contracts, files on various employees, documents detailing executive compensation packages, and more.

10.79 Hacktivists group SiegedSec hacked the Idaho National Nuclear Laboratory (INL), a US Department of Energy nuclear research center, and stole confidential data. This became known after SiegedSec published proof on the dark web on 20 November. INL has 50 experimental nuclear reactors and specializes in nuclear energy and national security. INL's current activities include the development of next-generation nuclear power plants, light water reactors, control system cybersecurity, advanced vehicle testing, bioenergy, robotics, and nuclear waste reprocessing.

10.80 SiegedSec hackers leaked detailed information on 45,047 former and current employees, spouses, and dependents on hacker forums and Telegram, including email and phone numbers, Social Security Numbers (SSNs), residential addresses, and employment information including bank information and salary details. SiegedSec also rolled out screenshots of the Oracle HCM system interfaces in INL, also simultaneously posting a message about the hack inside the corporate network. An INL representative confirmed the violation, noting that an investigation was underway with the participation of intelligence services and law enforcement agencies, which would have to establish the scale of the incident and the possible leak of scientific data.

Why guidelines and standards for the protection of electric utilities matter

10.81 The common factor facilitating both the highly sophisticated targeted attacks and accident malware infections is that both take advantage of the vulnerabilities and exposures at industrial network boundaries and exploit lack of awareness of probable ways by which the system components may be impacted. These vulnerabilities, exposures, and the appropriate ways are generally similar and mostly may be addressed in a standardised way.

19 https://archives.nseindia.com/corporate/TATAPOWER_14102022190039_SELetter.pdf.

10.82 This is why the approaches to hardening of control systems at electric utilities should be approved as official and voluntary recommendations: standards and guidelines.

10.83 Here we consider the most known of the standards and guidelines that are relevant to the power grid cyber-security. Most of the standards and guidelines that we focus on are adopted in the US That fact doesn't mean the recommendations from other countries don't exist or not mature enough. There are two reasons for which the standards and voluntary recommendations for North America are in the focus of our attention. The first reason is that these standards and recommendations are the result of long collaborative efforts of the state authorities, public and private partners and thus reflect the current realities of the energy sector, its needs, and concerns. The second one is that these standards and recommendations of any kind are mostly consistent with each other and refer to each other thus creating the transparent framework.

What comprises the core of these recommendations is considered below.

10.84 The following IT resources are usually referred to as potential targets of a cyberattack: SCADA servers, historians, human-machine interfaces (HMI), field devices, and network devices including gateways. These attacks exploit weaknesses, vulnerabilities, and exposures of the network protocols intended both for data transfer and control, routing protocols, physical environment, and organisation of control. Electric grid components that may be affected due to the successful attack relate to generation, transmission, and distribution of electric power.

10.85 To determine which informational and operational assets are critical, the stakeholders have to list potential goals of attacks that may lead to instability and unwanted behaviour of the power grid systems. These goals include denial of service of control and protection components, reconfiguration of protection relays, tampering with or disabling of alarm signals, generation of fake signals, wrong control of protection relay, manipulation with sensor readings, denial of vision for the system operator. The material consequences of attacks aimed at pursuing these goals include the instability of the electric power supply including power outages, insufficient transmission capacity for the power demand, transmission congestion.

10.86 These goals generally comprise the main risks linked to cyber-attacks. To avoid these risks it is recommended to put in place so-called Defence-in-Depth.

The recommended practice: improving industrial control system cybersecurity with defence-in-depth strategies by ICS-CERT of the US Department of Homeland Security

10.87 To avoid the damage, it is recommended to both harden the external perimeter to prevent the malicious impact and enhance the resilience of internal technologies to such impact. The set of comprehensive measures covering both informational and operational components puts into practice the Defense in Depth protection strategy.

10.88 The essential guide on how to implement this strategy and appropriately deploy cyber-security in an industrial environment is the Recommended Practice: Improving Industrial Control System Cybersecurity with Defence-in-Depth Strategies, the document, issued by the US Department of Homeland Security National Cybersecurity and Communications Integration Center (NCCIC) and Industrial Control Systems Cyber Emergency Response Team (ICS-CERT).[20]

10.89 The document lists the following key security features for information environment to significantly reduce the risk to operational systems:

1. Identify, minimise, and secure all network connections to the ICS.
2. Harden the ICS and supporting systems by disabling unnecessary services, ports, and protocols; enable available security features; and implement robust configuration management practices.
3. Continually monitor and assess the security of the ICS, networks, and interconnections.
4. Implement a risk-based defence-in-depth approach to securing ICS systems and networks.
5. Manage the human – clearly identify requirements for ICS; establish expectations for performance; hold individuals accountable for their performance; establish policies; and provide ICS security training for all operators and administrators.

10.90 These features provide the minimal base for security. However, the main idea is that they are not separate and must comprise the continuous process according to Defence-in-Depth strategy.

10.91 The Recommended Practice underlines that 'a holistic approach – one that uses specific countermeasures implemented in layers to create an aggregated, risk-based security posture – helps to defend against cybersecurity threats and vulnerabilities that could affect these systems. This approach, often referred to as Defense-in-Depth, provides a flexible and useable framework for improving cybersecurity protection when applied to control systems.'

10.92 Thus, the main principle originating from military strategy consists in the implementation of multiple barriers to impede the adversary activities. The attack containment process is supplemented with monitoring of the system and attacker's actions, developing and implementing responses to these actions.

20 Recommended Practice: Improving Industrial Control System Cybersecurity with Defense-in-Depth Strategies. September 2016. https://ics-cert.us-cert.gov/sites/default/files/recommended_practices/NCCIC_ICS-CERT_Defense_in_Depth_2016_S508C.pdf.

Defence-in-Depth implements both detective and protective cybersecurity measures and enables an appropriate response and recovery to reduce the consequences of a breach.

10.93 At the same time, not all threats require the same attention because of the different level of posed risks. Implementation of multiple countermeasures for a minor risk is not cost-effective.

10.94 The first step of planning the measures is threat modelling and risk assessment. As was discussed before, evaluation of threats, the probability of their implementation, and assessment of their possible impact is not an easy task. That is why the standards and guidelines for cyber-security pay quite a lot of attention to risk management process.

The electricity subsector cyber-security risk management process by the US Department of Energy

10.95 The US Department of Energy (DoE) developed the Electricity Subsector Cybersecurity Risk Management Process guideline in collaboration with the US National Institute of Standards and Technology (NIST), the North American Electric Reliability Corporation (NERC), and broad industry participation. The document is intended to enable applying of effective and efficient risk management processes in electric companies, regardless of their size or governance structure. Electric utilities can use this guideline to implement a new program meeting their organisational requirements or to enhance existing internal policies, standard guidelines, and procedures.

10.96 The guideline does not confine the approach of threats and vulnerabilities identification to review of information and operation technologies. Governance structures, mission and business processes, enterprise and cyber-security architectures, facilities, equipment, supply chain activities, and external service providers are all considered as a subject for risk management.

Risk management cycle includes risk framing, risk assessment, risk response, and risk monitoring.

10.97 Risk framing describes the environment in which risk-based decisions are made. This environment defines assumptions about threats, vulnerabilities, impacts, and likelihood of occurrence; constraints imposed by legislation, regulation, resource constraints (time, money, and people) and others; risk tolerance, or the level of acceptable risk; mission and business priorities and trade-offs between different types of risk; and trust relationships, such as physical interconnections, third-party service providers, reciprocity agreements, or device vendors.

10.98 To support the risk assessment element, electric companies identify tools, techniques, and methodologies that are used to assess risk; assumptions related to risk assessments; constraints that may affect risk assessments; roles and responsibilities related to risk assessment; risk assessment information to be collected, processed, and communicated; and threat information to be obtained.

10.99 The risk response provides an organisation-wide response to risk consistent with the organisation's risk exposure, including development of alternative courses of action for responding to risk; evaluation of these courses; determining the appropriate courses of action consistent with the defined risk tolerance level; and implementation of the courses of action.

10.100 The risk monitoring determines how risks are monitored and communicated over time by verifying that risk response measures are implemented and that the cyber-security requirements are satisfied; evaluating the ongoing effectiveness of risk response measures; identifying changes that may impact risk; and defining the process to assess how change impacts the effectiveness of risk responses.[21]

10.101 The risk management model[22] presented in this document uses a three-tiered structure to provide a comprehensive view of an electricity subsector organisation. The first tier is Organisation, the second is Mission and Business Processes, and the third is Information technology and Industrial Control System.

10.102 The stakeholders can build and implement the risk management program according to this tiered model, increasing the level of details up to the consideration of risks connected to technologies. At this level, the requirements to the particular technical design come into play. Thus, the standards and guidelines referring the countermeasures represent the next step in a consistent approach to creating a power grid infrastructure resilient to cyber-attacks.

The NERC critical infrastructure protection cybersecurity standards

10.103 The North American Electric Reliability Corporation (NERC) is a not-for-profit international regulatory authority whose mission is to assure the reliability and security of the bulk power system[23] in North America. Among

21 US Department of Energy. Electricity Subsector Cybersecurity Risk Management Process. May 2012. https://energy.gov/sites/prod/files/Cybersecurity%20Risk%20Management%20Process%20Guideline%20-%20Final%20-%20May%202012.pdf.

22 NIST Special Publication (SP) 800-39, Managing Information Security Risk, provides the foundational methodology used in the guideline. It is available by the link http://nvlpubs.nist.gov/nistpubs/Legacy/SP/nistspecialpublication800-39.pdf.

23 The meaning of the term 'bulk power system' covers facilities and control systems necessary for operating an interconnected electric energy supply and transmission network (or any portion thereof), and electric energy from generating facilities needed to maintain transmission system reliability. The term does not cover facilities used in the local energy distribution. Source: Memorandum by NERC Legal and Standards Departments on April 10, 2012, 'Use of 'Bulk Power System' versus 'Bulk Electric System' in Reliability Standards', http://www.nerc.com/files/final_bes_vs%20_bps_memo_20120410.pdf.

other activities, NERC develops and enforces Reliability Standards. NERC is also committed to protecting the bulk power system against cybersecurity incidents that could lead to mis operation or instability.

10.104 NERC's area of responsibility spans the continental US, Canada, and the northern portion of Baja California, Mexico. NERC is the electric reliability organization (ERO) for North America, subject to oversight by the Federal Energy Regulatory Commission (FERC) and governmental authorities in Canada. NERC's jurisdiction includes users, owners, and operators of the bulk power system, which serves more than 334 million people.[24]

10.105 On 22 November 2013, FERC approved Version 5 of the critical infrastructure protection cyber-security standards (NERC CIP standards Version 5). To ensure a smooth transition to this version from the previous version NERC later initiated a program intended to improve industry's understanding of the technical security requirements for the new standards, as well as the expectations for compliance and enforcement.

10.106 In the second half of 2017, the NERC Board of Trustees adopted three proposed standards, addressing cybersecurity supply chain risk management issues, and approved the associated implementation plans. These standards have since continued to evolve. In 2024, there are 12 documents that regulate the reliability and security of the North American power grid infrastructure. Although the NERC CIP standards are officially adopted and enforced for the bulk power system in the territory of North America, this set of standards is often referred as preferable to conform by stakeholders of electric utilities from other countries.

10.107 The standards prescribe the best practices for mitigating cyber risks to the bulk power system and focus on performance, risk management, and entity capabilities. They describe the required actions for security and reliability enhancement or results of this enhancement and not necessarily the methods by which to accomplish those actions or results.

10.108 The structure of all NERC CIP standards Version 5 is the same.

Introduction that contains the title, number, description of purpose, clarification regarding applicability of the standard, and some optional background information. Standards define applicability criteria with appropriate detail both for the functional entities, such as generator operator, balancing authority, distribution provider, and others and for facilities, systems, equipment, and cyber assets.

Requirements and Measures that list in a directive way the expected accomplishments and indicators for further evidence-based compliance

24 More information about NERC is available by the link http://www.nerc.com/AboutNERC/Pages/default.aspx.

monitoring. Some requirements set by the NERC CIP version 5 standards define a particular reliability objective or outcome to be achieved. Some others set up the measures to reduce the risks of failure caused by cyber-attack to acceptable tolerance levels. The last type of requirements defines a minimum set of capabilities an entity needs to have to demonstrate it is able to perform its designated reliability functions. Measures provide examples of evidence like documents describing implementation of the requirements.

Compliance section sets up the process for compliance monitoring including the definition of compliance enforcement authority, evidence retention requirements, processes for assessment and monitoring, and compliance elements.

10.109 Supplemental material may contain guidelines and technical basis for the implementation of requirements and measures clarifying how to apply technical controls to obtain the results referred by the main body of the standard.

10.110 The foundational definition for the NERC CIP version 5 is cyber assets. When cyber assets meet a threshold of impact on bulk energy system (BES),[25] they become BES Cyber Assets (BCA), which may comprise BES Cyber Systems (BCS). Stakeholders who, according to their competence, group BCA into BCS may further use the well-developed concept of a security plan for each BCS to document the programs, processes, and plans in place to comply with security requirements.

10.111 The purpose of the CIP-002-5.1a – Cyber Security – BES Cyber System Categorisation standard is to identify and categorise BES Cyber Systems and their associated BES Cyber Assets for the application of cyber-security requirements commensurate with the adverse impact that loss, compromise, or misuse of those BES Cyber Systems could have on the reliable operation of the BES. The criteria defined by the standard categorise BES Cyber Systems into impact categories.

10.112 According to this standard, the scope of the NERC CIP version 5 is restricted to BES Cyber Systems that would impact the reliable operation of the BES. Another defining characteristic for the BES Cyber Asset is a real-time scoping characteristic. 'Real-time,' BES Cyber Assets are those Cyber Assets that, if rendered unavailable, degraded, or misused, would adversely impact the reliable operation of the BES within 15 minutes of the activation or exercise of the compromise. This time window must not include in its consideration the activation of redundant BES Cyber Assets or BES Cyber Systems: from the cyber-security standpoint, redundancy does not mitigate cybersecurity vulnerabilities.

25 The 'bulk electric system' is a term commonly applied to the portion of an electric utility system that integrates the electrical generation resources, transmission lines, interconnections with neighbouring systems, and associated equipment, generally operated at voltages of 100 kV or higher. Radial transmission facilities serving only load with one transmission source are generally not included in this definition. Source: the NERC Glossary of Terms Used in NERC Reliability Standards, www.nerc.com/files/glossary_of_terms.pdf.

Almost all requirements set by NERC CIP version 5 are specific for the particular impact categories of BES Cyber Assets. Thus, the definition of High Impact BES Cyber Systems, Medium Impact BES Cyber Systems, and Low Impact BES Cyber Systems play a significant role for choosing the appropriate security measures and providing compliance to NERC CIP version 5.

10.113 First, the assignment of the impact category depends on where the BES Cyber System is used. High Impact BES Cyber Systems include those BES Cyber Systems, used by and at control centres that perform the functional obligations of the reliability coordinator, balancing authority, transmission operator, or generator operator. Additionally, if a transmission operator delegates some of the functional obligations to a transmission owner, BES Cyber Systems performing these functional obligations at the transmission owner's control centres would be subject to categorisation as high impact as well. The criteria for medium impact category generally apply to generation owners and operators, transmission owners and operators, and to the control centres of balancing authorities.

10.114 Second, for the definition of impact rating are used the relevant characteristic threshold values that reasonably well determine how important is the stable work of the appropriate functional entities. Thus, BES Cyber Systems' impact rating may be associated with generation facilities operating above a prescribed capacity, transmission facilities at specific voltage levels, or special protection systems. For example, high impact BES Cyber Systems include control centres used to perform the functional obligations of the balancing authority for generation equal to or greater than an aggregate of 3000 MW in a single Interconnection, while medium impact BES Cyber Systems cover balancing authorities control centres that 'control' 1500 MW of generation or more in a single Interconnection. Among the entities, medium impact BES Cyber Systems with external routable connectivity are distinguished from those cannot be directly accessed.

BES Cyber Systems not categorised in high impact or medium impact are assigned to low impact rating.

10.115 Additionally, standard defines the types of cyber assets associated to BES Cyber Systems. These cyber assets in case of their compromise pose a threat to the BES Cyber System. They include Electronic Access Control or Monitoring Systems (EACMS), Physical Access Control Systems (PACS) and Protected Cyber Assets (PCA). EACMS applies to each electronic access control or monitoring system associated with a referenced high impact BES Cyber System or medium impact BES Cyber System. Examples for EACMS may include, but are not limited to, firewalls, authentication servers, and log monitoring and alerting systems. PACS applies to each physical access control system associated with a referenced high impact BES Cyber System or medium impact BES Cyber System with External Routable Connectivity. Examples of PACS include authentication servers, card systems, and badge control systems. Examples of PCA may include: file servers, ftp servers, time servers, LAN switches, networked printers, digital fault recorders, and emission monitoring systems.

10.116 Responsible Entities can implement common controls that meet requirements for multiple high, medium, and low impact BES Cyber Systems. For example, a single cybersecurity awareness program could meet the requirements across multiple BES Cyber Systems.

10.117 Definition of controls starts with organisational measures. The standard CIP-003-8 specifies consistent and sustainable security management controls. These controls establish responsibility and accountability to protect BCS against compromise that could lead to mis operation or instability in the BES. The standard CIP-004-6 aims at nurturing the security awareness of the personnel to mitigate the role of human factor in cyber-attacks.

10.118 The standard CIP-005-6 regulates how to manage electronic access to BES Cyber Systems by specifying a controlled electronic security perimeter (ESP). All applicable BES Cyber Systems that are connected to a network via a routable protocol must have a defined ESP. Even standalone networks that have no external connectivity to other networks must have a defined ESP. The ESP defines a zone of protection around the BES Cyber System, and it also provides clarity for entities to determine what systems or cyber assets are in scope and what requirements they must meet. It must be mentioned that NERC CIP version 5 standards do not require network segmentation of BES Cyber Systems by impact classification. Many different impact classifications can be mixed within an ESP. However, all of the Cyber Assets and BES Cyber Systems within the ESP must be protected at the level of the highest impact BES Cyber System present in the ESP (ie, the 'high water mark') where the term 'Protected Cyber Assets' is used.

10.119 Two standards, CIP-006-6 and CIP-014-2, cover the aspects of physical security. The first is specifically for the BES Cyber Systems, and the second one is for transmission stations and transmission substations, and their associated primary control centres.

10.120 The standard CIP-007-6 – Cyber Security – Systems Security Management specifies technical, operational, and procedural requirements in support of protecting BES Cyber Systems against compromise. The requirements contain control of network ports and services, security patch management, malicious code prevention, security event monitoring, system access control. Thus, mostly these requirements are intended to reduce attack surface and compensate existing risks of cyber-attacks by monitoring of allowed data flows.

10.121 The standard CIP-008-6 – Cyber Security – Incident Reporting and Response Planning mitigates the risk of the reliable operation of the BES by specifying incident response requirements. In 2021 NERC introduces new requirements within this standard that mandate the reporting not only actual compromises but also attempted compromises of their systems to national security entities. This change was done due to previously mentioned SolarWinds attack.

10.122 The standard CIP-009-6 – Cyber Security – Recovery Plans for BES Cyber Systems helps to recover reliability functions performed by BES Cyber Systems by specifying recovery plan requirements in support of the continued stability, operability and reliability of the BES.

10.123 The standard CIP-010-3 – Cyber Security – Configuration Change Management and Vulnerability Assessments describes measures that prevent and detect unauthorised changes to BES Cyber Systems from compromise that could lead to misoperation or instability of BES.

10.124 The standard CIP-011-2 – Cyber Security – Information Protection defines, mostly in common terms, which requirements and measures are applicable to identification and protection of Cyber Assets containing BES Cyber System Information. It is not clarified which types of information may require protection, and this standard probably is the most abstract from the series.

10.125 The standard CIP-013-1 – Cyber Security – Supply Chain Risk Management addresses cyber threats to BES that come from the supply chain. Security controls implement both preventive and detective measures requiring technology-based monitoring solutions.

10.126 The latest updates coming out from FERC and NERC relate exactly to monitoring controls existence, which is implied by the mentioned standards. On 19 January 2023, FERC issued a rule instructing NERC to create new or modified CIP reliability standards covering the requirements for internal network security monitoring (INSM), particularly for high-impact Bulk Electric System (BES) cyber systems, irrespective of external routable connectivity, and medium-impact BES cyber systems with such connectivity. INSM operates within a trusted zone like an Electronic Security Perimeter (ESP), implementing defence-in-depth concepts even when perimeter network defences are breached.

10.127 The approval of NERC CIP-003-9 in March 2023 further evolves the approach to managing supply chain risks associated with low-impact BES. This measure is intended to supersede CIP-003-8, which was restricted to addressing high- and medium-impact systems. This rule prescribes for organisations to incorporate vendor electronic remote access security controls into their cybersecurity policies. This change addresses the risks from vendors' employees that could bring harm within their authorisation, eg, introduce a malicious code.

10.128 It also needs to be mentioned that many low-impact assets within BES cyber systems lack the proper level of protection. The compromise of multiple low-impact assets may have a serious impact compared to the attack on the single asset. Access to higher-impact assets may be obtained through low-impact systems. These issues should be addressed through an overall enhancement of the security posture of organisations maintaining BES cyber assets.

10.129 It can be concluded that NERC CIP standards are steadily addressing the risks of cyber-attacks on electric utilities as these risks become apparent. These standards put the result-driven requirements and describe measures to demonstrate evidences of their achievement. The requirements are improved over the time according to the shifting attack landscape.

10.130 However, this prudent approach to the cyber-security regulation of energy infrastructure has some drawbacks. First, the guidance on how the activities for improving current cyber-security indicators is considered supplementary. Mostly it is included as the technical background in endnotes. In some cases the third-party guidelines are referred as capable to assist the implementation of requirements. Second, the situation-based approach may end up in the appearance of so-called 'black swans', attacks that come suddenly from an unexpected perspective.

10.131 Thus, except the result-driven requirements that are binding on particular electric utilities according to the impact rating of BES cyber systems at these facilities, the industry needs non-obligatory documents accumulating more broad expertise that may help in seeing the whole thing. The type of these document include cyber-security improvement guidelines, descriptions of best cyber-security practices, typical threat models, functional frameworks for the integrated and consolidated cybersecurity activities, maturity models for measuring the effectiveness of cybersecurity controls.

The ISA99/IEC 62443 series of standards for industrial automation and control systems security

10.132 The 62443 series of standards are a joint development by the ISA99 committee[26] and IEC Technical Committee 65 Working Group 10.[27] They are intended to address the need to design cyber-security robustness and resilience into industrial automation control systems (IACS). These exist as the ISA versions of the standards and reports in the series that are named in the form ISA-99-*-* and the IEC versions that have the name starting with IEC 62443-*-*. The ISA and IEC versions of each document are released as closely together as possible.

10.133 The translations of the standards from this series are adopted in some countries as national standards, or the appropriate process of adoption is in progress.

10.134 The wide-ranging structure of the ISA99 and IEC 62443 series of standards and reports currently includes 13 standards and technical reports, each addressing a specific aspect of the subject. The figure below shows the current structure.

26 International Society of Automaton, Industrial Automation and Control Systems Security Standards Development Committee. http://isa99.isa.org/ISA99%20Wiki/WP_List.aspx.
27 http://www.iec.ch/dyn/www/f?p=103:14:0::::FSP_ORG_ID,FSP_LANG_ID:2612,25.

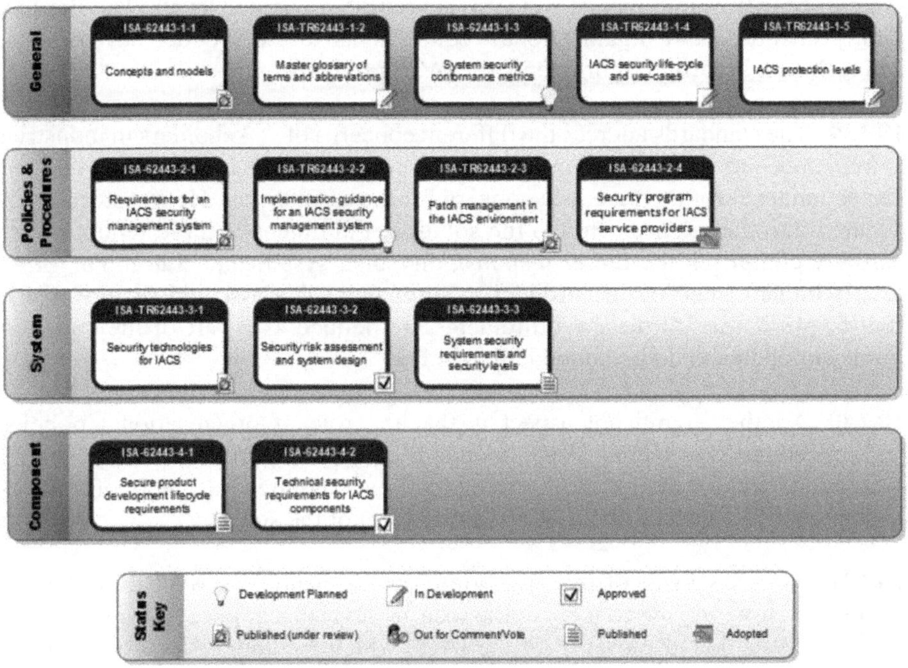

Figure 10.2 – The status of the various work products in the ISA/IEC 62443 series of IACS standards and technical reports. Source: ISA99 Wiki Home Page, http://isa99.isa.org/ISA99%20Wiki/Home.aspx

10.135 The Work Product List at ISA99 Wiki Home Page provides detailed information about the various work products, including their present development status, workgroup assignment, and relationship to equivalent IEC documents.[28]

10.136 Several of these documents have been completed and are now available from either ISA or IEC. Others are currently in development. Some documents are published but under revision to ensure their compatibility with other standards applicable in the area or for other reasons.

10.137 The standards are grouped into families. The General family of the standards contains definitions and metrics, but doesn't have any requirements nor provide guidance. The Policies and Procedures family contains four standards that provide the requirements for the security organisation and processes of the plant, its owner, and suppliers.

10.138 Both organisational and technical requirements are important for the implementation of the Defence-in-Depth concept. The System family contains the definitive standard regarding security technologies for IACS and two standards with particular provisions about security assurance levels for zones and conduits,

28 http://isa99.isa.org/ISA99%20Wiki/WP_List.aspx

system security requirements, and system security assurance levels. The Product family includes both organisational requirements to the product development and technical security requirements for IACS products.

10.139 The standards address the different concerns of stakeholders in industrial automation and cover different sources for the security issues. The required protection level for the asset is a concern for the asset owner. He transforms this concern into the requirements to the solution. Fulfilment of these requirements partially comprises the direct responsibility of a system integrator. The other part is implemented by the product requirements. The essential feature of the IEC 62443 is that all these requirements are defined as a part of the common framework and should be applied all together.

10.140 Another significant aspect is that the role of organisational policies and procedures and technical solutions are equally important for the resulting protection level for the IACS. A Protection Level requires fulfilment of policies and procedures and fulfilment of a security level of the solution.

10.141 An assessment of the protection level is mainly relevant to a plant in operation. However, the concept of the security level that applies to a solution and a control system is also useful for the IACS which are under development or in process of modernisation. Security levels defined in a way allowing formulating the assumptions regarding possible source of expected violations and their type. For example, the lowest security level SL 1 implies the protection against casual or coincidental violation, while the highest SL 4 means protection against intentional violation using sophisticated means with extended resources. Such an approach provides the possibility for the definition of requirements according to the results of threat modelling and risk assessment. The foundation for the system protection is compiled of the security mechanisms with appropriate security levels. The standard IEC 62443 3-3 sets security levels from 1 to 4 to the following controls: identification and authentication control; use control; system integrity; data confidentiality; restricted data flow; timely response to events; resource availability.

10.142 Security levels are applicable not only to the particular controls for the systems but also to the whole security zones and conduits. A security zone is a group of physical or logical assets that share common security requirements. A zone clearly delineates a unit by defining a physical or logical border, which separates the internal components from the external ones. A conduit is a communication path between two security zones. It provides security functions that allow two areas to safely communicate with each other; all communication between different zones must be carried out via a conduit.

10.143 Security zone notion in IEC 62443 set of standards is close to the BES Cyber System defined by NERC CIP version 5. On that understanding, this series of standards may be used to supplement the requirements of NERC CIP for the computer systems and networks at electric utilities and validate their protection.

Cyber-security capability maturity model (C2M2) by the US Department of Energy

10.144 While the notion of security level in regard to IACS is a measure of confidence that the IACS is free of vulnerabilities and functions in an intended manner, the security maturity addresses the concerns of consistency of this level with the real needs; assurance on the implementation of controls supporting security level; and confidence in assurance cases.

10.145 The Cybersecurity Capability Maturity Model (C2M2) program is a public-private partnership effort that was initially established as a result of the US Administration's efforts to improve electricity subsector cybersecurity capabilities and to understand the cyber-security posture of the grid. The Cybersecurity Capability Maturity Model (C2M2) version 2.1 issued in 2022 is intended to address only the implementation and management of cybersecurity practices associated with information technology (IT) and operations technology (OT) assets and the environments in which they operate.[29]

10.146 The C2M2 includes 356 cybersecurity practices, which are grouped into 10 domains. These practices represent the activities an organisation can perform to establish and mature capability in the domain. The practices within each domain are organised into objectives, which represent achievements that support the domain. Each of the objectives in a domain comprises a set of practices, which are ordered by MIL.

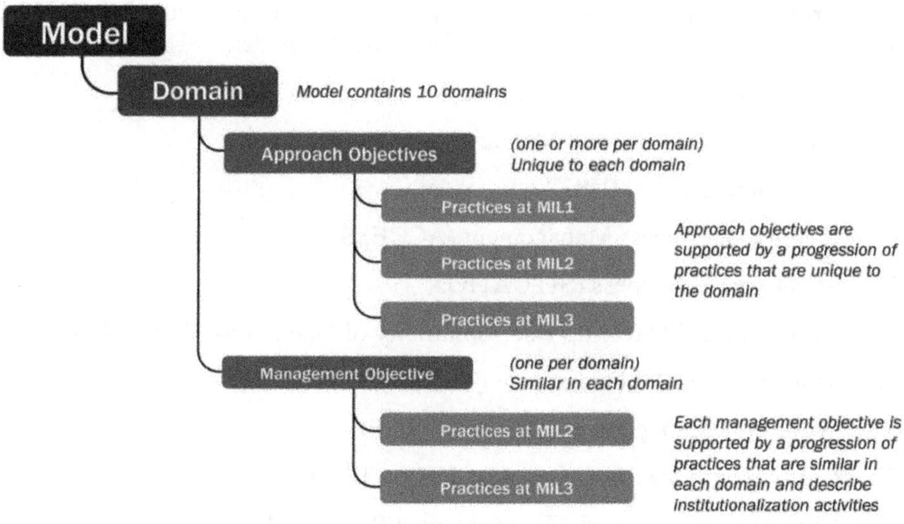

10.147 Within each objective, the practices are ordered by maturity indicator levels (MILs). The model defines four maturity indicator levels (MILs), MIL0

29 https://c2m2.doe.gov/C2M2%20Version%202.1%20June%202022.pdf.

through MIL3, which apply independently to each domain in the model. The MILs define a dual progression of maturity: an approach progression and a management progression. MIL0 level means that practices are not performed; MIL1 means that initial practices are performed but may be ad hoc. MIL2 for the management characteristic requires the practices to be documented and the process to be supported with adequate resources. For the approach characteristic MIL2 means that practices are more complete or advanced than at MIL1. MIL3 requires the management characteristic to guide the activities by policies, assign the responsibility, accountability, and authority for performing the practices, and require adequate skills and knowledge from personnel implementing practices, evaluate and track the effectiveness of activities. For the approach characteristic MIL3, it means that practices are more complete or advanced than at MIL2.

10.148 The maturity indicator levels apply independently to each domain. As a result, an organisation using the model may be operating at different MIL ratings in different domains. The domain-specific objectives and practices describe the progression of the approach to cybersecurity for each domain in the model. Approach refers to the completeness, thoroughness, or level of development of an activity in a domain. As an organisation progresses from one MIL to the next, it will have more complete or more advanced implementations of the core activities in the domain. At MIL1, while only the initial set of practices for a domain is expected, an organisation is not precluded from performing additional practices at higher MILs.

10.149 The set of domains almost exactly repeat the domains listed by the previous version of the maturity model applied in electricity sector, ES-C2M2.[30] The following domains are currently referred by the model:

1. Asset, Change, and Configuration Management (ASSET).
2. Threat and Vulnerability Management (THREAT).
3. Risk Management (RISK).
4. Identity and Access Management (ACCESS).
5. Situational Awareness (SITUATION).
6. Event and Incident Response, Continuity of Operations (RESPONSE).
7. Third-Party Risk Management (THIRD-PARTIES).
8. Workforce Management (WORKFORCE).
9. Cybersecurity Architecture (ARCHITECTURE).
10. Cybersecurity Program Management (PROGRAM).

30 https://energy.gov/sites/prod/files/Electricity%20Subsector%20Cybersecurity%20Capabilities%20Maturity%20Model%20%28ES-C2M2%29%20-%20May%202012.pdf.

10.150 The essential content of the model defining document comprises the descriptions of activities related to different MILs of objectives and practices. Practitioners may use these descriptions to evaluate the current level of security maturity and plan further evolvement.

10.151 Comparing to the previous one, version 2.1 of the model has been enhanced to improve alignment with the NIST Cybersecurity Framework (CSF) Version 1.1, released in April 2018. This Framework in considered further.

Critical infrastructure cybersecurity framework by the US NIST and implementation guidance for the energy sector

10.152 The voluntary Framework for Improving Critical Infrastructure Cybersecurity issued by the US National Institute of Standards and Technology (NIST) consists of standards, guidelines, and best practices to manage cyber-security-related risk. The Framework's prioritised and flexible approach helps to promote the protection and resilience of critical infrastructure and other sectors important to the economy and national security.[31]

10.153 The first version of the Framework was version 1.0 issued in 2014. At the time of writing, the most actual version of the Cybersecurity Framework (CSF) is version 2.0. Before version 2.0, the Cybersecurity Framework was called the 'Framework for Improving Critical Infrastructure Cybersecurity.' This title is not used for CSF 2.0. Portuguese translation and Spanish translation are officially available for this version (while for version 1.1 much more translations were available).[32] This fact demonstrates the positioning of the Cybersecurity Framework, issued by US NIST, as the document for international use.

10.154 The Framework is initially designed to complement, and not replace or limit, an organisation's risk management process and cyber-security program. Each sector and individual organisation can use the Framework in a tailored manner to address its cybersecurity objectives. This document describes what desirable outcomes an organisation can aspire to achieve. It does not prescribe outcomes or how they may be achieved. Descriptions of how an organisation can achieve those outcomes are provided in a suite of online resources that complement the CSF and are available through the NIST CSF website. These resources, including informative references, implementation examples, quick-start guides and templates, offer additional guidance on practices and controls that could be used to achieve outcomes and are intended to help an organisation understand, adopt, and use the CSF.[33]

10.155 CSF 2.0 includes the following components: CSF Core, CSF Organisational Profiles and CSF Tiers.

31 https://www.nist.gov/cyberframework.
32 https://www.nist.gov/cyberframework/csf-11-archive/translations#csf-20.
33 https://www.nist.gov/cyberframework.

10.156 CSF Core is a taxonomy of high-level cybersecurity outcomes that can help any organisation manage its cybersecurity risks. The CSF Core components are a hierarchy of Functions, Categories, and Subcategories that detail each outcome.

10.157 CSF Organisational Profile is a mechanism for describing an organisation's current and/or target cybersecurity posture in terms of the CSF Core's outcomes.

10.158 CSF Tiers can be applied to CSF Organisational Profiles to characterise the rigour of an organisation's cybersecurity risk governance and management practices. Tiers can also provide context for how an organisation views cybersecurity risks and the processes in place to manage those risks.

10.159 Energy sector organisations have a strong track record of working together to develop cyber-security standards, tools, and processes that ensure uninterrupted service. Almost immediately after the version 1.0 Cybersecurity Framework was released, the Office of Electricity Delivery and Energy Reliability of the US Department of Energy along with private sector stakeholders through the Electricity Subsector Coordinating Council and the Oil & Natural Gas Subsector Coordinating Council, and with other Sector Specific Agency representatives and interested government stakeholders, elaborated on how to develop such profile on the basis of industry experience.

10.160 On 8 January 2015, the US Department of Energy released guidance to help the energy sector establish or align existing cyber-security risk management programs to meet the objectives of the Cybersecurity Framework.[34] This Framework Implementation Guidance is designed to assist energy sector organisations to:

- Characterise their current and target cybersecurity posture.
- Identify gaps in their existing cyber-security risk management programs, using the Framework as a guide, and identify areas where current practices may exceed the Framework.
- Recognise that existing sector tools, standards, and guidelines may support Framework implementation.
- Effectively demonstrate and communicate their risk management approach and use of the Framework to both internal and external stakeholders.[35]

34 https://energy.gov/oe/downloads/energy-sector-cybersecurity-framework-implementation-guidance.

35 US Department of Energy Office of Electricity Delivery And Energy Reliability. Energy Sector Cybersecurity Framework Implementation Guidance. January 2015. https://energy.gov/sites/prod/files/2015/01/f19/Energy%20Sector%20Cybersecurity%20Framework%20Implementation%20Guidance_FINAL_01-05-15.pdf.

10.161 The Guidance discusses in detail how the Cybersecurity Capability Maturity Model (C2M2), which helps organisations evaluate, prioritise, and improve their own cyber-security capabilities, maps to the framework. The guidance also recognises that there are a number of other risk management tools, processes, standards, and guidelines already widely used by energy sector organisations that align well with the Cybersecurity Framework. Although the version of Cybersecurity Framework was updated while the Guidance remains unchanged, they still can be applied together with a proper consideration of major changes to the five existing CSF Functions from version 1.1.[36]

10.162 Section 2 of the Guidance provides key Framework terminology and concepts for its application, and Section 3 identifies example resources that may support Framework use. Section 4 outlines a general approach to Framework implementation, followed in Section 5 by an example of a tool-specific approach to implementing the Framework. The tool selected for this example is the DOE- and industry-developed Cybersecurity Capability Maturity Model (C2M2), both Electricity Subsector and Oil and Natural Gas Subsector specific versions.

10.163 As the Cybersecurity Framework is voluntary and cannot be implemented in a right or wrong way, it is reasonable to build the profile for the energy sector organisations during the establishment of organisational measures but conduct the gap analysis once the basic security controls and measures are in place. The maturity matters should be considered after the implementation of the minimal cyber-security baseline, eg, set by NERC CIP version 5 Standards.

UK National Cyber Security Centre guidance documents

10.164 In the UK, there are no adopted standards specifically for the cyber-security of the industrial automation and control systems in the energy sector. In practice, the companies that provide consulting on cyber-security of industrial control systems at electric facilities often refer the NERC CIP as a base for the compliance assessment.

10.165 That does not mean there are no relevant recommendations on cyber-security improvement for the OT environments forming the part of Critical National Infrastructure and requiring appropriate protection. Protecting the cyber security of the UK's CNI is a collaborative effort, and the National Cyber Security Centre (NCSC) therefore works with a wide range of partners towards this goal, consistent with the National Cyber Security Strategy 2016/21.[37]

10.166 The NCSC brings together and replaces three cyber-security organisations – the Centre for Cyber Assessment (CCA), Computer Emergency Response Team UK (CERT UK) and CESG (Communications-Electronic

36 https://energy.gov/oe/cybersecurity-critical-energy-infrastructure/reducing-cyber-risk-critical-infrastructure-nist.

37 https://www.gov.uk/government/publications/national-cyber-security-strategy-2016-to-2021.

Security Group, GCHQ's information security arm) – and includes the cyber-related responsibilities of the Centre for the Protection of National Infrastructure (CPNI). The authority was conceived as a bridge between industry and government, providing a unified source of advice, guidance, and support on cyber-security, including the management of cyber-security incidents.

10.167 Within the existing regulatory environment, the NCSC's aim is to operate as a trusted, expert, and impartial advisor to all interested parties. The NCSC does not have any regulatory responsibilities for cyber security itself.

10.168 The NCSC helps regulators in all CNI sectors build their internal cyber security expertise through accessing suitable training and provides threat intelligence information that supports regulators' cyber security work. The NCSC works with regulators with responsibilities under NIS and with other cyber security regulators, to support the security of the UK's CNI. The regulatory frameworks are not identical across England, Northern Ireland, Scotland, and Wales but the nature of support the NCSC provides to regulators across the UK is similar.

10.169 As part of the collaborative work to deliver improvements to the cyber security of the UK's CNI, the NCSC supports key cyber security regulators in a number of specific ways. For example, the NCSCs assist by helping develop and maintain cyber security standards, including the Cyber Assessment Framework guidance (CAF).

10.170 The NCSC Cyber Assessment Framework (CAF) is a valuable resource for organisations that form part of UK CNI to assess their cyber security strategy and to identify areas for improvement.

10.171 The CAF was developed for organisations responsible for services and activities that are of vital importance to us all. It is therefore most relevant to organisations identified as CNI or in support of CNI; including those within the scope of NIS, as well as both small and large enterprises.

10.172 There are several regulatory bodies responsible for cyber security standards across the different UK CNI sectors. Therefore, Regulators can use the NCSC's CAF resources within their sectors in support of a consistent approach to moderating and upholding UK cyber security standards. At the time of writing, the most recent version of NCSC's CAF is 15 April 2024.[38]

10.173 The Cyber Assessment Framework (CAF) provides a systematic and comprehensive approach to assessing the extent to which cyber risks to essential function(s) are being managed by the organisation responsible. CAF-based assessments can be carried out either by the responsible organisation itself (self-assessment) or by an independent external entity, possibly a regulator / cyber

38 https://www.ncsc.gov.uk/static-assets/documents/cyber-assessment-framework-v3.2.pdf.

oversight body or a suitably qualified organisation acting on behalf of a regulator, such as an NCSC assured commercial service provider.

10.174 An assessment of the extent to which an organisation is meeting a particular principle is accomplished by assessing all the contributing outcomes for that principle. In order to inform assessments at the level of contributing outcomes:

1. each contributing outcome is associated with a set of indicators of good practice (IGPs), and
2. using the relevant IGPs, the circumstances under which the contributing outcome is judged 'achieved', 'not achieved' or (in some cases) 'partially achieved' are described.

The result of applying the CAF is 39 individual assessments, each one derived from making a judgement on the extent to which a set of IGPs reflects the circumstances of the organisation being assessed.

10.175 A cyber oversight body will need to set target levels of cyber resilience for organisations within their sector. One way of setting these target levels is in relation to the ability to withstand specified categories of cyber attacks (eg, resilience to basic capability attacks, moderate capability attacks etc) and the CAF has been designed to support this approach via the idea of CAF profiles.

10.176 In practice a CAF profile consists of a mixture of some contributing outcomes to be met at 'achieved', some at 'partially achieved' and perhaps some (representing cyber security capabilities not appropriate at the level of the profile) identified as 'not applicable'.

10.177 The set of indicators (IGPs) to be assessed, the target levels and approach through profiling the organizations make CAF quite similar to a maturity model, like previously considered C2M2.

10.178 Similarly to C2M2, the CAF guidance provides the set of tables indicating which activities conform the particular level of principle (practice, in terms of C2M2) implementation. The levels are defined simply as 'Not achieved', 'Partially achieved' and 'Achieved'.

10.179 The NCSC issues other useful guidance which may be applied to CNI sectors, especially energy sector, including electricity. Many of them help in implementation of requirements of NIS2 Directive considered further.

10.180 Operational Technology Guidance issued on 18 March 2024, supports cyber security professionals in their work with OT environments.[39] Mainly it refers other NCSC documents and resources but also covers some specific issues like cloud-hosted SCADA systems.

39 https://www.ncsc.gov.uk/collection/operational-technology.

10.181 Building a Security Operations Centre (SOC) is guidance to help organisations design a SOC and security monitoring capability proportionate to the threat they face, their resources, and their assets.[40] This guidance, published in May 2022, is aimed at organisations that are considering investing in a SOC, or are looking at evolving a current SOC, as part of a wider approach to managing cyber risks. It describes the operating model, onboarding systems and log sources, detection, threat intelligence and incident management issues within a SOC.

10.182 Other guidance documents and resources covering cyber security principles, technology assurance and similar topics which only indirectly relate to electricity sector cybersecurity may be found on the NCSC official web page.[41]

NIS2 Directive

10.183 Directive on measures for a high common level of cybersecurity across the Union (NIS2 Directive) is the EU-wide legislation on cybersecurity. It provides legal measures to boost the overall level of cybersecurity in the EU.[42]

10.184 The EU cybersecurity rules introduced in 2016 were updated by the NIS2 Directive that came into force in 2023. It modernised the existing legal framework to keep up with increased digitisation and an evolving cybersecurity threat landscape. By expanding the scope of the cybersecurity rules to new sectors and entities, it further improves the resilience and incident response capacities of public and private entities, competent authorities and the EU as a whole.

10.185 Businesses identified by the Member States as operators of essential services in the above sectors will have to take appropriate security measures and notify relevant national authorities of serious incidents. Key digital service providers, such as search engines, cloud computing services and online marketplaces, will have to comply with the security and notification requirements under the Directive. Energy sector

10.186 The NIS2 Directive imposes specific obligations on certain companies, including operators of essential services (OES) and digital service providers (DSPs), to implement robust cybersecurity measures and report incidents to national authorities. It clearly lists all the sectors and subsectors (industries) that need to comply with this European cybersecurity Directive.

10.187 Due to its critical infrastructure status, the energy sector (including electricity) is particularly susceptible to the NIS2 Directive, as it provides essential services to the public and is a prime target for cyberattacks. As such, the Directive imposes specific requirements on energy companies to safeguard

40 https://www.ncsc.gov.uk/collection/building-a-security-operations-centre.
41 https://www.ncsc.gov.uk/section/advice-guidance/all-topics.
42 https://digital-strategy.ec.europa.eu/en/policies/nis2-directive/

their networks and information systems. It is important for energy companies to understand and implement its provisions and requirements.

10.188 The NIS2 Directive requires energy companies to implement appropriate technical and organisational measures to prevent, detect and respond to incidents that could impact the security and continuity of energy supply. This includes measures to protect critical infrastructure, data protection and privacy, and the availability of energy services. The complete list of cybersecurity risk-management measures is provided in Article 21 of the Directive, as follows:

(a) policies on risk analysis and information system security;

(b) incident handling;

(c) business continuity, such as backup management and disaster recovery, and crisis management;

(d) supply chain security, including security-related aspects concerning the relationships between each entity and its direct suppliers or service providers;

(e) security in network and information systems acquisition, development and maintenance, including vulnerability handling and disclosure;

(f) policies and procedures to assess the effectiveness of cybersecurity risk-management measures;

(g) basic cyber hygiene practices and cybersecurity training;

(h) policies and procedures regarding the use of cryptography and, where appropriate, encryption;

(i) human resources security, access control policies and asset management;

(j) the use of multi-factor authentication or continuous authentication solutions, secured voice, video and text communications and secured emergency communication systems within the entity, where appropriate.

NIS2 does not apply directly to UK businesses. However, the requirements coming into force in October 2024 include adding managed service providers to the scope. That means the NIS2 Directive applies to organisations operating or carrying out activities for EU businesses.

Specific cybersecurity considerations for the Nuclear Power Plants

10.189 Nuclear power plants usually considered separately from other types of electricity facilities due to their special status and possible damage in case of safety or security incident.

10.190 Usually the separate state regulating authority is responsible for nuclear energy, and following the national and international standards may be obligatory even it is not in other industries.

10.191 The International Atomic Energy Agency (IAEA) is an intergovernmental organisation that seeks to promote the peaceful use of nuclear energy and to inhibit its use for any military purpose, including nuclear weapons. The IAEA provides the basis for the state regulation regarding the protection of nuclear power plants against any hazards, including, especially in latest decade, cyberthreats.

10.192 According to the Objective and Essential Elements of a State's Nuclear Security Regime (NSS No. 20) and other publications in the IAEA Nuclear Security Series, including Nuclear Security Recommendations on Radioactive Material and Associated Facilities (NSS No. 14) Nuclear Security Recommendations on Physical Protection of Nuclear Material and Nuclear Facilities (INFCIRC/225/Revision 5) (NSS No. 13), states should define nuclear security requirements for nuclear or other radioactive material and associated facilities based on a threat assessment or a Design Basis Threat (DBT).

10.193 A DBT describes the capabilities of potential insiders and external adversaries who might attempt unauthorised removal of nuclear and other radioactive material or sabotage. The operator's physical protection system is designed and evaluated on the basis of the DBT. This means that, among other regulations on the state level, the nuclear security and cybersecurity of nuclear power plants are regulated according to the definition of DBT. This statement (which is usually restricted) defines the state's responsibility for the protection of nuclear power plants against any adversaries.

10.194 Potential external adversaries include terrorists and other criminals who might seek to use nuclear or other radioactive material for malicious purposes, or to sabotage a facility. Insiders are individuals with authorised access to facilities, activities or sensitive information who could commit malicious acts or help external adversaries to do so.

10.195 The state defines the roles and responsibilities of the regulatory body, other competent authorities and operators in the development of DBTs.

10.196 General guidance on computer security for nuclear security is provided in IAEA Nuclear Security Series No. 42G, Computer Security for Nuclear Security,[43] and more specific guidance on computer security of instrumentation and control (I&C) systems in nuclear facilities is provided in IAEA Nuclear Security Series No. 33T, Computer Security of Instrumentation and Control Systems at Nuclear Facilities.[44]

10.197 The most comprehensive technical guidance is the publication called IAEA Nuclear Security Series No. 17-T (Rev. 1) – Computer Security Techniques for Nuclear Facilities issued in 2021.[45] The objective of this publication is to assist Member States in implementing computer security at nuclear facilities with

43 https://www-pub.iaea.org/MTCD/publications/PDF/PUB1918_web.pdf.
44 https://www-pub.iaea.org/MTCD/publications/PDF/P1787_web.pdf.
45 https://www-pub.iaea.org/MTCD/publications/PDF/PUB1921_web.pdf.

the aim of preventing and protecting against unauthorised removal of nuclear material, sabotage of nuclear facilities, and unauthorised access to sensitive nuclear information. This publication addresses computer security for supporting activities and organisations such as vendors, contractors, and suppliers. While the focus of this publication is on the security of nuclear facilities, application of this guidance may also benefit facility safety and operational performance.

10.198 The recommendation IAEA Nuclear Security Series No. 8-G (Rev. 1) – Implementing Guide:2020, Preventive and Protective Measures against Insider Threats[46] provides updated guidance to States, their competent authorities and operators, shippers, and carriers on selecting, implementing, and evaluating measures for addressing insider threats. Threats (including but not limited to cyber threats) to nuclear facilities can involve external or insider adversaries or both together in collusion (cooperation for an illegal or malicious purpose with another insider adversary or with an external adversary).

10.199 Among other recommendations the most detailed approach to computer security for nuclear power plants demonstrate the recently issued standards of International Electronic Commission (IEC), including:

- IEC 62645:2019, Nuclear power plants – Instrumentation and control systems – Requirements for security programmes for computer-based systems;
- IEC 62859:2016 Nuclear power plants – Instrumentation and control systems – Requirements for coordinating safety and cybersecurity; and
- IEC 63096:2020 Nuclear power plants – Instrumentation, control and electrical power systems – Security controls.

10C SECURING CRITICAL MANUFACTURING SECTORS FROM MODERN CYBER THREATS

Helen Wong MBE

Introduction to Critical Manufacturing

10.200 The manufacturing industry, a cornerstone of the global economy, is characterised by its vast diversity and rapid evolution. This sector, encompassing everything from automotive production to pharmaceuticals, is a prime target for cyber threats. The integration of advanced technologies such as robotics, automation, machinery, IoT/IIoT, and smart devices makes it imperative to implement robust cybersecurity measures to safeguard this critical sector.

46 https://www-pub.iaea.org/MTCD/publications/PDF/PUB1858_web.pdf.

Defining Critical Manufacturing and Its Future Trajectory

10.201 Many segments within the manufacturing industry are designated as critical infrastructure, reflecting their essential role in supporting other economic sectors. Manufacturing is foundational, providing the infrastructure necessary for various industries to thrive. A robust manufacturing base is frequently seen as a key indicator of national strength and vitality.

10.202 The manufacturing sector encompasses a wide array of industries, including aerospace and defence, automotive, chemicals, computer hardware, electronics, construction, consumer packaged goods (CPG), food and beverage, transportation, pharmaceuticals, and industrial manufacturing. Currently, we are in the midst of a fourth Industrial Revolution, which is reshaping best practices in operations, supply chain management, cybersecurity, and disaster recovery. This revolution, known as Industry 4.0, emphasises the integration of cybersecurity as a fundamental element.

Industry 4.0: Evolution and Components

10.203 Industry 4.0, driven by innovation and investment from countries like Germany, Japan, and China, is about modernising manufacturing infrastructure with advanced technologies. These technologies include robotics, sensor technology, additive manufacturing (3-D printing), augmented and virtual reality, wearables, artificial intelligence, machine learning, big data analytics, and cloud computing. The goal is to create smart factories that are more efficient, responsive, and resilient while promoting a safer work environment.

Robotics

10.204 The journey of robotics in manufacturing began in 1961 with the deployment of the first industrial robot. Over the decades, the use of robots has expanded significantly, especially in automotive manufacturing, where they now account for more than half of the labour required to build automobiles and trucks. Robotics technology has advanced to the point where fully automated 'lights-out' factories have been operational for several decades, particularly in sectors like computer manufacturing.

10.205 Robotics in modern manufacturing is not just about automation but also about precision, efficiency, and flexibility. These machines can perform complex tasks with high accuracy, reducing the margin of error and increasing production speed. Moreover, advancements in robotics are making them more accessible to small and medium-sized enterprises (SMEs), which traditionally could not afford high-end automation solutions.

Wearables

10.206 Wearable computing and sensor devices are increasingly finding their place in manufacturing environments. These devices fall into several categories, many of which focus on employee safety. For example, wearables can help prevent falls, monitor sleep patterns, reduce noise exposure, and improve respiration. Additionally, wearables enhance communication between employees and machinery, providing easier access to information through various delivery mechanisms.

10.207 The integration of wearables in manufacturing also extends to augmented reality (AR) devices, which can overlay digital information onto the real world. This can assist workers in performing tasks more efficiently by providing them with real-time data and instructions. For instance, maintenance personnel can use AR glasses to view repair manuals while working on machinery, significantly reducing downtime and improving operational efficiency.

3-D Printing

10.208 Additive manufacturing, commonly known as 3-D printing, enables the creation of three-dimensional objects directly from CAD drawings by building up an object one layer of material at a time. While 3-D printing is particularly useful in the prototyping phase of product development, its capabilities have expanded significantly. Today, the size, speed, and quality of 3-D printing have improved to the degree that the technique is used in space, aerospace, wind turbines, and many other critical manufacturing sectors.

10.209 In the context of Industry 4.0, 3-D printing offers unparalleled flexibility in manufacturing. It allows for the creation of complex geometries that would be impossible or cost-prohibitive with traditional manufacturing methods. This technology is also conducive to on-demand manufacturing, reducing the need for large inventories and enabling more responsive supply chains.

Internet of Things/Industrial Internet of Things (IoT/IIoT)

10.210 The Internet of Things (IoT) and its industrial counterpart, the Industrial Internet of Things (IIoT), refer to a broad set of physical devices that combine embedded sensors, processing power, software, and often analytic capabilities to communicate real-time information about aspects of the physical world, such as temperature, pressure, motion, etc. Consumer applications of IoT include smart home devices, among many others. A subcategory of more hardened devices, generally termed IIoT, has also developed and found its way into manufacturing plants. IIoT devices can include an actuation component and, therefore, can function as industrial control system (ICS) devices. The manufacturing applications of IIoT are almost limitless.

10.211 IIoT is revolutionising manufacturing by enabling real-time monitoring and control of production processes. These devices can collect vast amounts of data, providing insights that can be used to optimise operations, improve product quality, and reduce downtime. For example, sensors on production lines can detect anomalies and alert maintenance teams before equipment fails, preventing costly disruptions.

Virtual Reality/Augmented Reality (VR/AR)

10.212 Virtual reality (VR) describes a self-contained, computer-simulated environment and is another technology with broad applications in product development for manufacturers. It is also an important tool for worker training. Augmented reality (AR) is a less immersive experience, involving the superimposition of digital information onto the real world. This information can be as simple as a heads-up display of written material, such as repair manuals, or it can be much more immersive and include other senses such as hearing and touch.

10.213 In manufacturing, VR can be used to create virtual prototypes, allowing designers and engineers to test and refine products before they are physically produced. This can significantly reduce development time and costs. AR, on the other hand, can enhance the capabilities of workers by providing them with real-time information and guidance. For instance, AR can be used to assist in assembly tasks, ensuring that components are correctly installed and reducing the likelihood of errors.

Machine Learning/Artificial Intelligence (ML/AI)

10.214 Machine learning (ML) is a subset of artificial intelligence (AI). ML involves training computer algorithms to improve through experience. AI and ML can enhance manufacturing techniques in numerous ways, including general process improvements, accelerated product development, and improved quality control. Manufacturers today use AI/ML to improve manufacturing yields, optimise asset management, manage supply chain and inventory, improve predictive maintenance, and forecast demand among many other applications.

10.215 AI and ML are transforming manufacturing by enabling more intelligent and autonomous operations. For example, AI algorithms can analyse production data to identify patterns and trends that can be used to optimise processes. ML models can predict equipment failures and schedule maintenance proactively, reducing downtime and extending the lifespan of machinery. Additionally, AI-powered robots can adapt to changing conditions and perform tasks with greater precision and efficiency.

Big Data Analytics

10.216 Many technologies, particularly IIoT, are driving the need for better analysis of large data sets. Big data analytics is a field of research that addresses techniques for analysing data sets that are too large to be dealt with using traditional data processing application software. Big data and IIoT work in tandem to monitor, analyse, and react to environmental data in manufacturing environments. Predictive maintenance is an early use case, but the applications are almost unlimited.

10.217 Big data analytics enables manufacturers to gain deeper insights into their operations by analysing vast amounts of data from various sources. This can include data from sensors, machines, supply chains, and customer feedback. By applying advanced analytics techniques, manufacturers can identify inefficiencies, optimise processes, and make data-driven decisions. For example, predictive analytics can help manufacturers forecast demand more accurately, enabling them to adjust production schedules and inventory levels accordingly.

5G

10.218 5G, the fifth-generation technology standard for broadband cellular networks, began rolling out in 2019. It is designed to deliver massive bandwidth improvements over its predecessor, 4G, with maximum download speeds of 10 Gbps. This should allow the networks to not only act as traditional networks for cellular calls but also to become general-purpose networks for internet service providers. This ubiquitous, global, wireless bandwidth is expected to further enable a multitude of IIoT use cases, as well as traditional industrial control system (ICS) applications.

10.219 The deployment of 5G networks is expected to revolutionise manufacturing by providing ultra-fast and reliable connectivity. This will enable real-time data transmission and communication between devices, facilitating the implementation of advanced technologies such as IoT, AI, and robotics. For example, 5G can support the seamless integration of IIoT devices, allowing manufacturers to monitor and control production processes in real time. It can also enable remote monitoring and maintenance, reducing the need for on-site visits and improving operational efficiency.

Framework for Industry 4.0

10.220 There is a concerted effort to provide a comprehensive framework for the technological changes currently underway in manufacturing. For instance, the German Electrical and Electronic Manufacturers' Association published the Reference Architecture Model for Industry 4.0 (RAMI 4.0) in July 2015. The RAMI 4.0 model maps hierarchical levels (eg, the Purdue model) against functional communication levels that run from high-level business concerns to individual assets. The model also considers the life cycle of a product under development or in manufacturing.

10.221 The big-picture approaches are welcome, and organisations should consider the strategic implications of each new technology purchase and how those technologies can best be deployed, integrated, and leveraged. Investments in these new technologies are typically made piecemeal, but by adhering to a common reference architecture, these incremental investments can provide more holistic benefits.

Deploying Industry 4.0 Technologies

10.222 Manufacturers can benefit from these technologies across multiple deployment scenarios. Broadly, they can be seen as affecting the supply chain, smart factories, and connected objects. The application of each technology can be found across this value chain, but these categories are useful when thinking about common use cases as well as compliance requirements associated with manufacturing activities, which are too broad a sector to have an overarching regulatory framework.

Cybersecurity in Manufacturing

10.223 The integration of IT and OT (Operational Technology) infrastructure in Industry 4.0 introduces new cybersecurity challenges. The increased connectivity and data generation necessitate a reevaluation of traditional disaster recovery and resiliency planning. Legacy OT systems, often unpatchable and lacking basic security features, must be secured despite their long life cycles.

10.224 Legacy OT systems are burdened with a long list of cybersecurity concerns, including equipment with decades-long life cycles, an inability to patch systems due to stability concerns, and a lack of basic cybersecurity features such as user authentication or encryption. Historically, OT security personnel could at least credibly claim that such systems were 'air-gapped' to ensure isolation from the rest of the world. However, complete isolation, if it ever existed, has become impossible today. No manufacturing organisation can embrace an Industry 4.0 strategy without addressing the severe cybersecurity risks that accompany it. This strategy requires a recognition of the almost complete integration of IT with OT in modern Industry 4.0 deployments.

10.225 OT cybersecurity has traditionally been its own discipline. OT cybersecurity is defined as: 'The practices and technologies used to protect people, assets, and information involved in the monitoring and/or control of physical devices, processes, and events, particularly in production and operations.' Over the years, as IT has been incorporated into OT systems, the approaches to cyber protection have also merged, but the primary goals of the two disciplines remain distinct.

IT vs. OT Cybersecurity

10.226 IT cybersecurity focusses on the confidentiality, integrity, and availability (CIA) of digital assets. Enterprise data is considered proprietary intellectual property, and therefore keeping digital assets under lock and key has been the primary objective of IT cybersecurity strategies. This is followed by the need to ensure the integrity of digital assets. Organisations must not only keep their data out of competitors' hands, but they must also ensure that data is not corrupted, either intentionally or otherwise. Finally, that data should be available internally to appropriate employees and partners, and potentially, customers.

10.227 The standard for OT cybersecurity, however, requires a broader and reordered set of priorities: control, availability, integrity, and confidentiality (CAIC). Maintaining control of all physical assets to ensure their safe operation at all times is the primary objective of OT cybersecurity and overrides all other concerns. The next most important goal for OT cybersecurity is availability. OT is present in all critical infrastructure facilities, and critical infrastructure typically needs to be available 24/7/365. Integrity is also essential, particularly to the degree it ensures safety and availability. The confidentiality of OT data is the least important concern.

Rising Cyber Threats in Manufacturing

10.228 The 2020 IBM X-Force Threat Intelligence Index reported an unprecedented 2,000% year-over-year increase in incidents targeting OT environments, such as critical infrastructure manufacturing. Attackers are taking advantage of the larger attack surface of these systems and, unfortunately, often are not finding them difficult to penetrate. Typical attacks include brute-force password attacks against legacy OT hardware and software, as well as targeted attacks against known vulnerabilities in legacy equipment.

10.229 While that extraordinary growth in attacks might astonish even close industry watchers, it should shock no one that attacks are on the rise. Juniper Research has forecast that globally there will be 83 billion connected IoT devices by 2024, and 70% of these will be in the industrial sector. This level of connectedness completely changes the relationship between IT and OT. And unfortunately, many new connected devices are built with just enough processing power and bandwidth to create vulnerabilities but not enough headroom either to support a firmware update if a vulnerability is discovered or to support an agent to provide protection in the event of an attack. This, of course, necessitates the need for a comprehensive OT protection strategy that reassesses the level of connectivity to and interdependency with traditionally OT assets.

Main OT Threat Actors and Attack Examples

10.230 According to a report by the cyber insurance company Allianz, cyberattacks against critical infrastructure are more likely to target ICS than attempt to steal data. A survey of critical infrastructure suppliers showed that 54% reported attempts to control systems, and 40% had experienced attempts to shut down systems. While manufacturers are particularly vulnerable to attacks designed to cause extended operational downtime, they are also highly sensitive to the loss of trade secrets and customer data. This is true across the board but particularly for manufacturers working in the Defence Industrial Base (DIB) sector.

10.231 Manufacturers face threats from both criminal and nation-state actors. Notable attacks include:

- **Honda Manufacturing Plant (2020):** The Ekans/Snake ransomware disrupted production in multiple countries. The attack temporarily halted production in Honda plants in North America, Brazil, India, and Turkey. The attack tool was suspected to be a new variant of ransomware designed to disrupt industrial systems. It is unusual in that in addition to encrypting data files, Ekans also includes functionality designed to stop a number of processes related to ICS operations. Argentinian energy company Edesur S.A. was also attacked with Ekans in June 2020.
- **Mondelez (2017):** The NotPetya malware caused significant damage. Mondelez was hit by the encrypting malware NotPetya in 2017, disrupting its operations and causing substantial financial losses. The attack resulted in the encryption of critical data and systems, rendering them unusable until a ransom was paid.
- **Renault-Nissan (2017):** The WannaCry ransomware halted production. Renault-Nissan had to stop production in five plants when the WannaCry ransomware struck, causing significant operational disruptions and financial losses.
- **Norsk Hydro (2020):** The LockerGoga ransomware forced plant closures. The aluminum manufacturer Norsk Hydro was forced to temporarily close many of its plants due to the LockerGoga ransomware attack, which encrypted critical systems and disrupted production.
- **Visser Precision (2019):** The DoppelPaymer ransomware targeted this space and defense manufacturer. Visser Precision, a company operating in the space and defense sector, was hit with the DoppelPaymer ransomware, resulting in the encryption of critical data and systems.

10.232 These attacks highlight the vulnerability of manufacturers to cyber threats and the potential impact on their operations. Manufacturers must develop robust cybersecurity strategies to protect their systems and data from such attacks.

Enhancing OT Cybersecurity

10.233 Manufacturers must develop a comprehensive OT cybersecurity plan, integrate IT and OT security efforts, and incorporate OT cybersecurity into broader risk management strategies. Key measures include:

- **Disconnecting unnecessary internet-connected systems:** Immediately disconnect any systems from the internet that do not need internet connectivity for safe and reliable operations. Additionally, implement compensating controls for systems where connectivity cannot be safely removed.

- **Preparing for manual operations:** Be prepared to operate processes manually should ICS infrastructure become unavailable or should it need to be deactivated due to a cyberattack.
- **Removing additional functionalities:** Remove any additional functionality that could induce risk and increase the attack surface area.
- **Understanding system and operational dependencies:** Identify and understand system and operational dependencies to ensure the safe operation of critical systems.
- **Restoring OT devices and services promptly:** Restore OT devices and services in a timely manner to minimise operational disruptions.
- **Maintaining and testing data backups:** Create and safely store gold-copy backup resources, such as firmware, software, ladder logic, service contracts, product licenses, product keys, and configuration information. Periodically test and validate data backups and processes in the event of data loss due to malicious cyber activity.
- **Creating an accurate map of OT connectivity:** For manufacturers, creating and understanding an accurate "as-operated" map of OT connectivity is critical to initiating a risk reduction cybersecurity plan.

Conclusion

10.234 The good news for critical manufacturers is that there is a large and growing set of resources designed to improve cybersecurity in this sector. Manufacturers globally should expect more cybersecurity oversight as Industry 4.0 technologies increasingly become commonplace and expand traditional attack surfaces. It is critical that manufacturers remain engaged with public and private organisations that are driving cybersecurity regulation and determining best practices in this sector. The expectation should be that additional regulation is coming, but it is likely to continue to be applied piecemeal.

10.235 Manufacturers should focus on creating a specific OT cybersecurity plan, integrating OT and IT cybersecurity efforts as much as possible, and looking to bundle OT cybersecurity more fully into broader enterprise risk management strategies. Business considerations are driving a wholesale revolution in manufacturing technology deployment, and OT cybersecurity strategy needs to be viewed as a foundational core competency within manufacturing organisations.

10.236 In conclusion, securing the manufacturing sector from modern cyber threats requires a comprehensive and proactive approach. The integration of advanced technologies in Industry 4.0 brings numerous benefits but also introduces new cybersecurity challenges. By developing robust cybersecurity strategies, manufacturers can protect their systems and data, ensure the safe operation of critical infrastructure, and maintain their competitive edge in the global market.

10D UK FINANCIAL SERVICES
Steven Peacock

Introduction

10.237 Advances in technology change the way people live their lives, financial services is no different and not immune from this. Indeed quite the opposite is true. During the first decade or so of the new millennium we have seen another step change in the way consumers expect to interact with their financial service providers and the basis on which they expect to interact. While many of the traditional ways such as branch networks, ATMs, telephone and online banking remain and continue to be very much part of a multi-channel offering; consumers continue to demand more immediacy in how they interact. The evolution of mobile phones to smart phones over the last ten years along with the use of tablets now being common place has seen the relatively new innovation of online banking being updated by app technology to enable even quicker access to customer accounts.

10.238 In addition to the traditional banks investing to keep up with consumer demand by delivering new and enhanced service, product and platforms; we are also seeing technology as an enabler to change how financial services are offered and provided. New technology, a loss of consumer confidence in the traditional banking product providers following the financial crisis and a government encouraged need for greater competition to challenge and break up monopoly positions has seen a raft of new entrants into predominantly the retail banking arena. These new entrants under the banner of 'challenger banks' are actively and aggressively driving new approaches and changing decades of practice.

10.239 Regardless of how or by whom financial services are offered, the same generic risk and threats remain to all; that of significant data theft and/or systems crippled by ransomware. Indeed, in just the last three years we have seen high profile and well documented examples on firms such as Sony, Talk Talk, Wannacry and Equifax. While none of these are retail banks, they all hold significant amounts of personal data which could include passwords and payment information.

10.240 To perhaps quantify the risk faced, the Financial Conduct Authority (FCA) in a speech in January 2017 highlighted that in the past twelve months the Nation Cyber Security Centre recorded over 1,100 reported attacks, with 590 seen as significant. Of these, 30 required action by government bodies and that the UK deals with more than 10 significant cyber-attacks each week. The FCA further commented that it had 69 material attacks reported to them during 2017. Moreover, the Office of National Statistics illustrated that in the region of 1.9 million incidents of fraud reported were cyber related.

10.241 It is fair to say the risk is real and increasing. With consumer confidence still largely fragile with banks following the financial crisis and significant choice available recognition, prevention and management of cyber-related risks needs to be considered with the same focus as financial risks at senior management level.

How severe could the impact of a cyber-attack be?

10.242 Unsurprisingly the answer is very! Indeed, one of the focuses of the regulatory and government bodies is the resilience of banks and financial institutions more broadly to withstand and recover from a cyber-attack.

10.243 It would seem that those who wish to undertake an attack are doing so to not only exploit vulnerabilities that may exist in an organisation's systems and network, but also utilise data processing speed and network connectivity that exist. To put this into context the June 2017 NotPetya attack was designed to spread fast and cause damage to companies of all sises using a strong malware code. The NotPetya malware's aim was to infect machines and travel through a firm's network as quickly as possible. One report on the attack put the time of failure of one of the largest victims with over 10,000 connected systems at 19 minutes. Clearly if there are less than 10,000 connected systems the time is likely to be less! One interesting final aside to the NotPetya attack in June 2017 is that the National Cyber Security Centre concluded that the Russian military was 'almost certainly' responsible, indicating that as well as criminal gangs and individuals state sponsored attacks are also an increasing source of cyber-attacks.

How Should Organisations Tackle the Challenge of Cyber Attacks?

10.244 In many ways the principles of good risk management apply:

- **Culture and Awareness:** Recognition, attention and severity of the issue needs to be recognised at Board level, through to senior managers and in turn to all staff. This should not be seen as purely and solely as an IT issue or problem to solve.
- **Governance:** Closely linked to the above. In particular, ensuring responsibility and accountability is in place at senior management level with board visibility of risks and issues to allow for challenge and oversight. Furthermore, governance arrangements should regularly review that staff possess the correct skills and knowledge to perform their roles and adequately discharge their responsibilities.
- **Risk Assessment**: A fully documented and regular assessment of the risks faced and their threats. Risks and controls should have nominated owners

and the risk assessment should be regularly reviewed by senior management committees and/or boards on a regular basis. Indeed, it would be good or even considered normal practice to have this as a mandatory agenda item at board and/or risk committee meetings.

In helping to set the context for boards and committee the setting or an appropriate risk appetite with risk targets and tolerances should be agreed. It is very likely that boards will naturally have a low appetite for any risk in this area due to the potential for the catastrophic impact a cyber-attack can have on the firm and its reputation, along with the obvious regulatory expectations from a particularly strong conduct regulator in the UK. Achievement of low to almost zero residual risk exposure is always costly and requires multiple tools and techniques to achieve. Furthermore, expectation should be set at board and senior management levels that the risk is never static and can increase quickly should and when new cyber approaches emerge. In many ways defences and safeguards are designed based upon history and not on future needs.

Central to the success of any risk assessment should be the identification of a firm's key assets and how they are protected.

- **Defences and Detection:** Are sufficient alerts and warning indicators in place to know whether a firm has been attacked, and as importantly do they operate on a timely basis to allow for any further action to be taken? Aligned to this is how strong is a firm's cyber-threat intelligence to help inform strengthening defences? On this point, it is no surprise that many innovations have taken place in the field of cyber-defences. Examples include website rescripting and using artificial intelligence to scour networks and automatically patch them. However, like the management of most risks no one solution will ever address all the risks complete and a multi solution approach is required. The challenge again reverts back to the firm's risk appetite and cost to manage within this appetite.

  Aside from the technology and the solutions available, it should be recognised that people can also be a firm's strength and weakness. Staff awareness and accountability as mentioned earlier is key. In many ways staff form the first line of defence for firms, therefore ensuring password disciplines are followed, ability to spot potential and actual phishing emails and having appropriate system and data access are as critical as technology solutions to prevent of highlight attacks.

- **Outsourced Relationships/Third Parties:** Over recent years there has been an increase in firms partnering with specialist business process outsourcing companies. These specialist firms offer a number of attractive options that can include: the performance of core and non-core processes for the firm's customers; the hosting and provision of IT services especially within the cloud; and, data storage.

  Outsourcing is an attractive option for many firms, particularly within the financial services arena as it brings both cost and efficiency savings. Having said that, it is important for a firm's senior management to ensure that they have and continue to consider the risks such arrangements introduce to their organisations and in turn their customers. Key to this is having a close and well-defined relationship with outsource/third party partners and understand how their data assets are protected.

As per the firm's own internal risk management activities the following should be seen as the type of mandatory activity for outsource/third party relationships:

- Comprehensive due diligence on the prospective outsourcer before entering into an arrangement. As part of this, themes such as policies, financial resilience, operational resilience including IT resilience and maintenance, other clients serviced and how their data and operations are segregated, who will have access to the firm's data, skill and ability of the employees and in particular management to provide the service and strongly defined measures and reporting agreed within the overall contract should be established.
- Regular relationship meetings and the provision of key performance metrics. Relationship meetings should focus not just on commercial performance but on how cyber-threats are identified, assessed and managed within the outsourcing firm's own risk appetite as set out by its Board.
- Adequate business continuity and disaster recovery arrangements that are subject to regular and frequent testing.
- Visibility and review of outsource provider resilience testing.
- Visibility of staff training.
- Industry recognised accreditations such as ISO27001.
- Reporting to the main board and/or risk committee.
- Regular independent review or internal audit.

- **Getting the basics right:** There is clearly a lot to be gained from having the appropriate framework to review and assess risk along with investing in leading edge or state of the art technological solutions, even though they can be costly. However, before committing to some of the more costly solutions available management should consider that some of the fundamental hygiene options are being performed well and regularly.

  A number of lessons can be learned from some of the higher profile cyber-attacks to demonstrate the value of ensuring the basics are performed well and on time. For example, the Investigations Report into the 2016 data loss suffered by the US telecommunications firm Verizon found that ten vulnerabilities covered 85% of successful breaches. The majority of the vulnerabilities used in these attacks were well known and fixes available. Indeed, some of the fixes had been available for over a decade. One of the basics therefore to get right is ensuring patching is up to date and remains up to date.

Initiatives such as Cyber Essentials or the 10 Steps to Cyber Security set out good practice as seen by the UK government and in turn the regulatory authorities that cover the financial services business that operate within the UK. It is widely felt that the adoption of these basic standards would significantly reduce a firm's cyber-risk exposure. Appendix 1 is a useful checklist that forms part of the Cyber Essentials thinking for firms.

The vast majority of financial services firms in the UK have Non-Executive Directors (NEDs) on their Boards. Often these individuals hold similar positions with other firms, therefore as well as providing challenge to the management of risks faced they are well placed to offer insight and share experiences. Indeed, post the financial crisis in the UK the role and expectation of the NED(s) has taken on increased importance not just with the UK Financial Authorities through the Approved Person regime and its successor the Senior Managers Regime; but also with bodies such as the Institute of Directors.

In a similar vein to that of NEDs, and with the emergence of a number of so called 'challenger banks' post the financial crisis many of which are investor backed it is likely and should be encouraged for investors to question the Boards they sit on on how these risks are being managed. Indeed, given the potential impact on reputation of any cyber-attack as well as the operation and customer impact could also lead to share price or balance sheet damage.

Another recommended activity is sharing information and learnings. The FCA has established a number of Cyber Coordination Group's (CCG's) to better understand risk profiles and how these risks could crystallise. Given the FCA regulates over 50,000 firms in the UK across a wide range of different types of financial service offerings the FCA has become ideally placed to better identify generic and specific sector threats.

10.245 To summarise effective cyber-security essentials:

- **Governance:** Ensure there is board awareness and regularly reviewed. Also, ensure appropriate ownership and accountability is in place. Define risk appetite and ensure annual budget is sufficient to achieve Board desired state.
- **Data Risk Management**: Understand what information is held and why? Is it classified to reflect its importance and use? Setting and reviewing access levels to data for new starters, movers and leavers.
- **Protection**: protect data with the use of encryption and password protection. In the case of data transfer use tools such as Secure File Transfer Protocol (SFTP).
- **Business Continuity and Recovery:** back up of key and critical systems and data, regular testing of data recovery, penetration testing and testing to recover should there be an attack.
- **Network and System Security:** Ensure software and applications are up to date along with patching. Ensure network configuration prevents unauthorised access and regularly test to confirm.

- **Logon and Access Credentials:** Use strong password protocol and ensure passwords are automatically enforced to change at least every 90 days. Where there is critical, sensitive or confidential information use two factor authentication.
- **Training and Awareness:** Ensure awareness is high and staff regularly trained. Use examples to bring common cyber-threats and risks to life so colleagues at all levels can spot suspicious behaviour. Share experiences via cyber forums and user groups.
- **Accreditations**: obtaining accreditation of Cyber Essentials or ISO 27001 can improve security levels.
- **Testing Defences**: Consider using external industry professionals to test defence capabilities.

Regulator Focus within the UK

10.246 As mentioned already the FCA is the regulator focused on conduct related matters in the UK and has a broad remit in terms of the size, number (circa 50,000 firms) and different product offerings provided by the firms it regulates. The FCA has a strong and very visible approach to regulation. Key stone to its basis of regulation are its statutory objectives as set out in the Financial Services and Markets Act 2000, which are:

- Protection for consumers.
- Protect financial services.
- Promote competition.

10.247 The FCA is a consumer outcomes focused regulator and its regulatory handbook is aimed at ensuring this either by way of specific rules and guidance or by applying the spirit if its thinking. The FCA, due to the size and breadth of firms it regulates can't be totally prescriptive, however it does require all firms to have appropriate systems and controls in operation commensurate to the size and complexity of their operations. The FCA supplements its specific rules and guidance with regular varied publications and speeches recognising new, existing or emerging risks.

10.248 As well rules and guidance, the central approach to how the FCA regulate is to ensure senior management roles that have the ability to cause significant harm require approval by the regulator. These are known as Approved Persons and cover roles such as Chief Executive and Compliance Officer. The FCA has commenced a programme to replace this scheme with a new more encompassing scheme known as the Senior Managers and Certification Regime. This revised approach will still see the basic principles of the Approved Person scheme remain, however it will have fewer Senior Manager classified functions, but will bring in those staff that can cause harm at more of an operational level, which traditionally would not have been covered by the Approved Person regime. Also under the new arrangements all staff, with the exception of ancillary workers will be bound by specific conduct rules. What this means is that in theory at least more accountability and recognition of responsibility permeates deeper into an organisation than under the previous Approved Person arrangements. Under the Senior Manager's Regime it will be likely in the bigger organisations that the chief operations role will have specific responsibilities covering cyber. Further, and especially in the larger organisation, it can be expected the roles of Chief Risk Officer, Chief Information Officer, Chief Information Security Officer and Chief Operating Officer will require structural clarity on the role they perform as part of their cyber accountability.

10.249 In addition to the underpinning spirit of the Approved Person regime the FCA's 11 Principles of Business still remain. In effect these underpin all aspects of the FCA's rules and guidance and how firms should operate. Principle 11 (PRIN 11) requires firms to have an open and close relationship with the regulator, and in the case of any cyber-attacks a firm is obliged and expected to notify the FCA of this as part of its PRIN 11 responsibilities. A breach of any of the Principles of Business and rules can lead to the FCA fining and/or taking other action against a firm and/or the accountable individual.

10.250 More broadly, outside of the expected way the FCA regulates, it also plays an international role in linking with other organisations and through bodies such as the G7 to help ensure the UK financial services industry both informs and reacts to emerging developments and threats particularly recently in the case of cyber security.

10.251 As mentioned earlier regulators and governments not just in the UK, but across the world are increasingly focusing on the complex subject of cyber-security. Particularly since the Wannacry attack in June 2017, there has been further increased focus on the resilience of organisations to withstand and attack and/or recover. It is safe to assume that regulators such as the FCA will increasingly challenge, question and expect the firms it regulates to have cyber-security as a high profile focus at senior management levels and throughout the organisation. A clear strategy and articulation of risks, threats and contingency plans will be the bear minimum expected at boards. Perhaps as important will be the intelligence firms have gathered and accessed to inform their thinking and provide confidence.

Other Threats and Challenges Facing Retail Banking

10.252 The pace of technological advancement and change is unlikely to slow and the retail banking sector will continue to develop bringing with it new cyber-threats. It is likely new entrants will continue to enter the sector, and it is likely some of these will be from non-traditional banking backgrounds with a focus on technology firms to provide financial solutions rather financial products provided using technology.

10.253 Two immediate initiatives, which on the face of it could appear to work against each other are now starting to come into effect. The General Data Protection Regulation (GDPR) and Open Banking.

10.254 GDPR came into effect on 25 May 2018. In many ways it is an evolution of the Data Protection Act that exists in the UK, but puts far more greater emphasis on firms to protect customers' data, only hold what is required and seek consent to use where there is not a legitimate interest. GDPR introduces a potential fairly hefty fine to firms who have a data breach where they have insufficient safeguards in place to protect consumers' data; up to 4% of worldwide revenue or EUR20 million. In many ways compliance with GDPR relies on getting the basics referred to earlier right and operating as expected, so should go some way to helping firms defend and protect themselves for any cyber-attack. Also, the required appointment of a Data Protection Officer at a senior level should drive improved ownership and board visibility. It is also a focus for firms to have timely and effective processes to allow for breach reporting as part of GDPR requirements.

10.255 At the opposite end of the spectrum and perhaps to add more challenge to financial services firms to meet customer demand is the introduction of the Open Banking proposition in the UK. Open Banking allows consumers to aggregate all their account holding with different financial services business in one place via an app. While in theory providing consumers with greater and easier access to their financial data, there are obvious challenges to firms with regard to securing consumer's data and also educating consumers to be confident that app providers are legitimate and not fraudulent. Open Banking does, at the outset at least, heighten the risk of fraudulent activity and also impacts the customer more as all their account holdings are in one place. Therefore we can expect firms to be naturally cautious in meeting consumer demand to ensure that their defences are suitably robust and they don't breach any of the data protection requirements that both the DPA and its successor the GDPR bring.

Appendix I

10.256 Cyber Essentials – Checklist:

1. Use a firewall to secure your internet connection:
   - Understand what a firewall is.
   - Understand the difference between a personal and a boundary firewall.
   - Locate the firewall which comes with your operating system and turn it on.
   - Find out if your router has a boundary firewall function. Turn it on if it does.
2. Choose the most secure settings for your devices and software:
   - Know what 'configuration' means.

- Find the Settings of your device and try to find a function that you don't need. Turn it off.
- Find the Settings of a piece of software you regularly use.
- In the settings, try to find a a function that you don't need. Turn it off.
- Read the NCSC guidance on passwords.
- Make sure you're still happy with your passwords.
- Read up about two-factor authentication.

3. Control who has access to your data and services:
   - Read up on accounts and permissions.
   - Understand the concept of 'least privilege'.
   - Know who has administrative privileges on your machine.
   - Know what counts as an administrative task.
   - Set up a minimal user account on one of your devices.
4. Protect yourself from viruses and other malware:
   - Know what malware is and how it can get onto your devices.
   - Identify three ways to protect against malware.
   - Read up about anti-virus applications.
   - Install an anti-virus application on one of your devices and test for viruses.
   - Research secure places to buy apps, such as Google Play and Apple App Store.
   - Understand what a 'sandbox' is.
5. Keep your devices and software up to date:
   - Know what 'patching' is.
   - Verify that the operating systems on all of your devices are set to 'Automatic Update'.
   - Try to set a piece of software that you regularly use to 'Automatic update'.
   - List all the software you have which is no longer supported.

References

- Building Cyber Resilience. Robin Jones, Head of Technology, Resilience & Cyber at the FCA. Speech delivered to PIMFA Financial Crime Conference, London 25/1/2018

- Cyber Resilience. FCA website. Published 18/5/2017
- Good Cyber Security – The Foundations. FCA website June 2017
- Our approach to cyber security in financial services firms. Speech by Nausicaa Delfas, Director of Specialist Supervision at the FCA. Delivered at FT Cyber Security Summit 21/9/2016
- Expect the Unexpected: Cyber Security in 2017 and beyond. Speech by Nausicaa Delfas, Executive Director at the FC A. Delivered at Financial Information Security Network 24/4/2017
- National Cyber Security Centre website – Cyber Essentials
- Cyber Risk and Regulation in Europe. Deloitte LLP. Published February 2018

10E CYBERSECURITY FOR THE ENERGY SECTOR: TOWARD ENERGY 4.0

Stefano Bracco

The Energy Sector: moving to the age of Smart and Digitalised Markets

10.257 The energy sector has been for a long time in its own isolated and anaesthetised world. In the year 2000, there was a first wave for digitalisation. Many people may argue why this was happening at that stage and with those later.

10.258 Well, we have to consider that most of the energy world has been involved in the general research for efficiency just at a later stage, when ecological feelings and movement started to look for new ways to optimise the use of the grid.

10.259 On the other side, a highly structured sector had the need to find ways to optimise, staying still within the boundaries of long-term investments. By a made of fact, some of the huge investments were already started and finalised between the 60s and the 80s, and they were done with an idea to keep them running for 40 to 50 years.

10.260 The digital age came announced, but at a speed and with an impact that was not predictable at the days when the investments were foreseen. This first element on the threats is then linked to the presence of legacy equipment that composes the electricity grids and gas pipelines, and that works together with others in a complex system called the 'energy system' (or an ecosystem, as it seems to work more as a biologically unpredictable body than as a system that will develop with fixed rules).

10.261 As anticipated, this system is still subject to a wave of innovation that for historical reasons, started from the bottom, and not from the top of the sector. A simple example is the new concept of 'prosumer': a consumer who is able to consume energy as well as, on an intermittent basis, to produce, and who is as well able to consume a good (electricity), but also to gain from the production and re-distribution of the same good, after paying necessary costs to the involved third parties. As the market changed, there was a need to introduce into the energy system new ways (mostly technological) to promote an inclusive policy. Those systems, even quite recent, had to be simple and user friendly, and sometimes were without any sign of security by design. Those systems, which started in 2010 and are still on their way to be deployed (think solar panel house systems, smart meters, and wind generators for small farms), became an additional threat, especially for the electricity network.

10.262 While the first concept is wide and applicable to the entire energy system, this wave of innovation and the absence of clear security instructions, are mostly applicable to the electricity subsector.

10.263 Finally, for years the energy sector has been thinking to be immune from cyber security risks and contaminations from cyber threats; this false feeling, became evident after a number of attacks. In this chapter we will talk of the main attack, but it shall be considered that the energy sector is, at the moment, among the most attacked.

10.264 Trying to simply at the extent possible, the threats against the energy system are many, and vectors can be a number. Moreover, it shall be considered that the energy system, as a body, can suffer not only from diseases but also from disturbances that may alter the status and make the grids and pipelines unusable. Concepts like calancing, frequency, and voltage, are essential to keep an electricity grid working properly, as is the concept of pressure, which is part of the basics for gas and oil. An alteration or disturbance that would alter the normal working conditions through a cyber attack, may have the same (or even worse) effect of a physical attack to the underlying critical infrastructure of the Energy Sector, as it may hit more points and more functions at the same time.

10.265 Also, being the sector highly automated and with a number of potential vectors, the same attacks may hit different functions.

10.266 On this must also be concretely understood that some of the past regulation took into consideration in a very comprehensive way all the operational needs, with the exception of those operations that were heavily depending on vulnerable IT or OT Systems.

10.267 The challenge for the future is exactly to promote smartification, having in mind the importance of the infrastructure and the changes in the threat landscape. On this, the cooperation of governments, regulators, operators, industry, and research, shall play a major role.

10.268 It is quite important to understand that a market like the energy market, needs to be resilient to cyber attacks, but the resilience must start from its core and essence. It may take years to bring the energy system to an acceptable level of resilience, but this all starts with an understanding of the problem.

10.269 Finally, we have to consider that the digitalisation dynamics may have a positive outcome for the entire sector. In a recent study, McKinsey & Company[47] outlined that the level of digitisation is still low compared to the potential. Having in mind that it may create a gain in the order of 20-40%, we may wonder why the sector does not invest in cybersecurity with the purpose of having a secure digitalisation phase, which may bring additional profits.

Critical Infrastructures in Energy and their key role for the civil society

10.270 Among the full set of the critical infrastructures, the energy infrastructures have been playing a core role since their establishment and their further development: energy was one of the biggest concerns for sustainable world growth prior the 2010 economic crises; moreover, its core role was testified by the attention of the political community in preserving and boosting its efficiency. Use of more inclusive markets and of digitalisation was seen as a viable option also to achieve urgent environmental targets.

10.271 Its role in the energy civil society is undeniable; also, the risks linked to Cybersecurity and cyber attacks are huge if put in the context of energy, and the consequences can be partially predictable, as shown in the context of the rare but highly impacting outages.

10.272 Civil society has seen several huge blackouts and several crises linked to shortages of gas and/or oil supply. Some of which had serious adverse effects from issues related to security and public order to more serious effects as diplomatic crises in certain critical areas. Most of the energy policies at the national and international level were focussing on guaranteeing security of supply in a number of adverse events; almost none were tailored to guarantee that supplies would reach the end point, even when a stack of production, generation, distribution, and transportation systems would have disrupted or prevented from executing its own function.

10.273 The energy system is extremely pervasive, and in fact it is an indispensable requirement to perform other functions; as an example, all the communication and processing functions would be extremely limited in the absence of the energy sector.

47 https://www.mckinsey.com/business-functions/digital-mckinsey/our-insights/accelerating-digital-transformations-a-playbook-for-utilities.

10.274 From an attacker perspective, the energy system can be seen as an ambitious, spread, but easy-to-attack sector. The possibility to convey political messages, to leverage citizens fears, and to use non-invasive methods to obtain a specific purpose, may provide a flavour of the many reasons why, among critical infrastructures, the energy sector has been the one on which most of the governments have concentrated regulation and policy efforts.

10.275 While we are still at an early stage in many countries, operators had to warn governments on the need to settle frameworks to increase preparedness of all involved actors. Many of the operators have strict links with local communities, and while they fully understand their critical role, they have limited visibility on the potential of a spread cyber attack. For this reason, many operators have started to look, sometimes with good results, to possible frameworks that may have been helping in mitigating their own risks. Unfortunately, they were partially aware of issues related to systemic failures as well as to attacks that may have hidden but relevant portions of cyber attacks.

10.276 In this complex landscape, all actors have to play a role, as the behaviour of the energy sector can be compared to a biological entity that is dependent on a number of external factors and, at the same time, is subject to the advent of new and unpredictable trends resulting from natural evolution. This entity can be easily destabilised by evolving adverse viruses. In the same way, the energy sector was destabilised in its equilibrium by a cyber security threat, and governments took conscience of this.

The IT-OT dilemma

10.277 The energy sector is unique in one way: while many other sectors, and especially the manufacturing industrial sector, are linked to the OT world, the energy sector is the only critical sector that has components of OT.

10.278 Operational technology is essential in the energy sector, especially to promote and implement safety in the design of the infrastructure. It is quite interesting how the concept of safety constitutes one of the pillars and problems resulting in security issues.

10.279 Safety and security are linked in essence, and they both have the same objective: the protection of the humans, of their assets, and of their activities.

10.280 Safety has been one of the most important achievements in the energy sectors, which would not be achieved without machines and a certain level of automation. This level of automation was not possible without putting humans in danger, and without using alternative ways to create safety. Those machines, which had to keep humans safe are performing very simple operations but are extremely critical, with a high number of inputs coming from different sensors. As we know, in the human world the number of inputs we can process is still limited, while a machine has a limited but higher capacity to process. Also, this processing capability can be

10.281 Those machines, unfortunately, had the need to communicate with all the rest of the system in a fast and efficient way. Years ago, it was not a huge concern the absence of security; also, some protocols were simple and had to serve simple purposes.

Obviously, cybersecurity and cyber threats were far from the industry.

10.282 Those simple OT systems still today perform critical operations within a reasonable high number of inputs coming from sensors. Lately, those OT had to start to communicate with a more complex IT world. The complexity of the IT world starts with communication protocols, but also with a number of controls that would need to be performed before an operation could be authorised and then performed. Here the gap started to be evident:

> 'the OT was well placed to implement an high level of safety, but was still a step behind from a security perspective. In fact it had to assure mainly safety using and acting fast to a number of inputs.'

10.283 IT, on the contrary, which is starting to have increasing computational power, has anyway some issues: delays due to very complex protocols, with some part of security, were not acceptable by the OT world.

10.284 Some compromises were then necessary, and it is obvious that those compromises were done in the direction of the OT world, which is more mission critical.

10.285 This problem is now reflected even in the organisations: in the same facilities, departments and staff working on OT are somehow far, or even in competition with those people working in IT, using different narratives and languages.

10.286 This cultural barrier is one of the core issues, but we must note the remarkable work of some governments through the appointed authorities. As an example, the UK National Cyber Security Centre is actually on the way to prepare specific guidance on the topic.[48] On the linked topic of Industrial Control Systems, which may cover a wider spectrum than the lonely energy sector, they already released a guidance in late 2016.[49]

10.287 In conclusion, OT and IT are one of the core, unique problems of the Energy Sector. They both want to achieve safety and security, but from different perspectives.

48 https://www.ncsc.gov.uk/guidance/operational-technologies.

49 https://www.ncsc.gov.uk/guidance/security-industrial-control-systems.

The legal efforts in the US

10.288 The legal efforts in order to tackle cyber security in the energy sector are quite complex and articulated, but looking at the United States example, sometimes are unpredictable.

10.289 In the US, the topic was tackled from two main angles, but at an already early stage. The Critical Infrastructure Information (CII) Act of 2002[50] provided to the Department of Homeland Security the legal means to enhance the voluntary sharing of critical infrastructure information between infrastructure owners and operators and the government by giving homeland security partners confidence that sharing their information with the government will not expose sensitive or proprietary data.

10.290 Even many people may question the importance of a similar tool; instead, the US provided to all the operators, including energy operators, to freely and confidently share information on potential threats, including but not limited to, cyber security.

10.291 The building of trust and the positive support of the federal government was most probably one of the most important steps to build awareness in the sector; we will see later that it was also a key element to further develop a mature market at state level.

10.292 The importance of the act is also testified by some other important documents: first, the Energy Sector Specific Plan,[51] first published in 2010 and then revised in 2015, shows the critical role of energy and its importance in the context of homeland security.

10.293 Secondly, the creation of effective tools such as the ICS-CERT[52] provided and still provides the operators with tangible tools to share information, assess risks, and take guidance, independently from their role within the energy sector.

10.294 The results of the the CII Act are visible to most people, and even some experts may argue that they did not exploit the full potential of information sharing; on the other side, it provided a first and essential step to build a secure and trustworthy cyber security related community, close to the energy sector.

10.295 The actions of DHS were complemented in 2005 by the Energy Policy Act.[53] The Energy Policy Act, being a 13-year-old document, provides a comprehensive vision on the energy sector, but it already gave a clear address to issues such as cyber security protection and handling of cyber security incidents in electricity in the bulk power system. The fact that this was already in a law

50 https://www.dhs.gov/publication/cii-act-2002.
51 https://www.dhs.gov/publication/nipp-ssp-energy-2015
52 https://ics-cert.us-cert.gov/.
53 https://energy.gov/downloads/energy-policy-act-2005.

10 years before the Ukrainian cyber attack could materialise may show how visionary this law may be.

10.296 On the basis of the Energy Policy Act of 2005, it was created the role of Electric Reliability Organization (ERO) to develop and enforce mandatory cybersecurity standards.

10.297 Also, in the Energy Policy Act, the Federal Energy Regulatory Commission (FERC) was provided with the authority to approve mandatory cyber security reliability standards.

10.298 NERC (North American Electric Reliability Corporation) applied for and was designated and certified as the ERO in 2006 by the FERC. NERC started fast to work, together with research laboratories and the electric power industry experts, to develop NERC CIP.[54]

10.299 The main objective of the NERC CIP standards is to protect the critical infrastructure elements necessary for the reliable operation of this system. This includes also protection from cyber threats. Being a standard, and being auditable and enforceable, it proved to be a good regulatory tool that allowed the Federal Government, FERC, and DoE, to keep control of the cyber security posture of the entire sector, with some exceptions.

10.300 Since 2008, the CIP standards have been updated as the threat landscape continues to evolve; this has created some tension on the cost of implementing cyber security, which is a continuously moving target. Also, the very high penalties[55] discouraged a late adoption of the standards.

10.301 To address other concerns that were emerging in the meantime in relation to Smart Grids, the Energy Independence and Security Act[56] of 2007 (EISA) gave FERC and the National Institute of Standards and Technology (NIST) responsibilities related to coordinating the development and adoption of smart grid guidelines and standards.[57]

10.302 Once again, and as we will see later in this chapter, Smart Grids emerged as an unpredictable source of risks and had to be tackled with unconventional means, basically guidelines.

10.303 In addition to the standards, DoE, in a public-private partnership, developed the Cybersecurity Capability Maturity Model (C2M2) Program.[58] The

54 http://www.nerc.com/pa/Stand/Pages/CIPStandards.aspx.

55 http://www.nerc.com/pa/comp/CE/Enforcement%20Actions%20DL/NOC-2547%20Non-CIP%20Full%20Notice%20of%20Penalty.pdf.

56 https://www.gpo.gov/fdsys/pkg/PLAW-110publ140/html/PLAW-110publ140.htm.

57 https://www.nist.gov/programs-projects/cybersecurity-smart-grid-systems.

58 https://www.energy.gov/oe/cybersecurity-critical-energy-infrastructure/cybersecurity-capability-maturity-model-c2m2-program.

C2M2, tailored for the energy sector, is a soft tool to improve electricity subsector cybersecurity capabilities and to understand the cybersecurity posture of the grid, as well as to evaluate, prioritise, and improve the cybersecurity capabilities of operators. Being a general tool, not enforceable, it was the perfect tool to allow operators not subject to a strict regulatory framework to check their posture and aim for substantial voluntary improvement.

10.304 In parallel, the Atomic Energy Act and Nuclear Regulatory Commission also created mandatory standards for nuclear power plants, which are constantly monitored and frequently reported.

10.305 Looking to cross-law collaborations, DoE and DHS collaborated with industry cybersecurity and control system subject matter experts to publish Cyber Security Procurement Language for Control Systems[59] in 2009. This document summarises security principles and controls to consider when designing and procuring control system products and services (eg, software, systems, maintenance, and networks), and provides example language that could be incorporated into procurement specifications.

10.306 In 2014, DoE issued procurement guidelines for building cybersecurity protections into the design and manufacturing of energy delivery systems. The Cybersecurity Procurement Language for Energy Delivery Systems focusses on perceived vulnerabilities in the industry's procurement process, including in software use and the account management of energy delivery systems.

10.307 Trying not to forget distribution operators and in addition to the effort done by the DoE through the C2M2, State Utility Regulators have been extremely active in providing guidance to State Utility Regulators in order to improve the resilience of the electricity system. The 'Cybersecurity – A Primer for State Utility Regulators'[60] of 2017, provides the readers with an easy but effective way in order to guide Energy Regulators in steering efforts in establishing, maintaining, and enforcing the desired cyber security posture at the state level in the US. As in the case of the European Union, having each state their own independence, the NARUC paper served as a guideline: different states took different decisions and tried to apply in different ways.

10.308 Finally, in the energy cyber security, the role of the National Labs[61] and of research, more in general, has been crucial and essential for the development of technical cyber security standards and for aligning expectations with the market needs and possibilities. Also, as a unique capability, the US can have the possibility to simulate real incidents through this network of Laboratories.

59 https://ics-cert.us-cert.gov/sites/default/files/documents/Procurement_Language_Rev4_100809_S508C.pdf.

60 https://pubs.naruc.org/pub/66D17AE4-A46F-B543-58EF-68B04E8B180F.

61 http://energy.sandia.gov/energy/ssrei/gridmod/cyber-security-for-electric-infrastructure/scada-systems/ and https://www.inl.gov/research-programs/control-systems-cyber-security/.

The Ukrainian case

10.309 The Ukrainian case is most probably one of the most intriguing and well-known facts about cyber security in the past decade.

10.310 But let us start assessing the facts. There were a number of reports and information on this case, but it can be summarised in a few lines. The main source for this has been SANS, and the report[62] is well known.

10.311 The attack has been focussing on three distributors in Ukraine. It was started two days before Christmas in 2015. The choice of the dates and the time of the attack are rarely a pure coincidence. As already told in other parts of this book, the cyber security threats are not depending on the availability of humans, and especially in the past 10 years, they have been enriched with precise tactical choices, and especially they have been performed as a result of consistent intelligence campaigns. In this case, the interesting fact is that, as reported in the report, the attack started with a phishing attack, which enabled the hackers to enter into a secure perimeter and to alter the distribution system in the subsequent days. The attack was focussing on a total of 30 substations, with a general direct impact resulting in a blackout for around 250.000 customers.

10.312 Compared to other non-cyber related blackouts (as an example, the blackout in 2006, which affected 15 million customers[63]), this may be considered a minor event; nevertheless, it was one of the first cases in human history where a cyber attack on IT means was able to impact OT means, having a direct consequence on the lives of a number of citizens.

10.313 The same attack also had some interesting side events: one of the objectives of the attack was to stop the ability of the customers to report an outage. In a catastrophic event of this size, with several operators involved and trying to analyse, react, and recover with a limited access to on-field information, the absence of communication with the lower layers became an additional issue that delayed the possible corrective actions.

10.314 More interesting, reading carefully the report, you may easily notice that the operation that allowed to escape an uncontrolled situation (and to expand further the effect) was the possibility to switch to manual all the systems, and to operate manually operations as a consequence of the loss of control by the facility owners.

10.315 As reported in the first paragraph, this may not be an option in modern economies where, for efficiency reasons, the possibility to move from automatic to manual has already been removed years ago and not contemplated in the original design.

62 https://www.dhs.gov/sites/default/files/publications/isc-risk-management-process-2016-508.pdf.
63 http://europa.eu/rapid/press-release_IP-07-110_en.htm?locale=en.

10.316 Today this event is correctly classified as a low impact event, as the number of the affected customers, in respect to the entire population, was rather small, and the same report highlights that the outage was lasting a few hours (maximum 6 hours).

10.317 Nevertheless, as told before, this attack had impressive media coverage, and it is still widely used to underpin the importance of cybersecurity in the energy sector, especially for the electricity sector, which was not fully automated in Ukraine at that time.

10.318 This was the first-of-a kind attack that was emerging from an undercover virtual world and that materialised an impact on a real human community, creating real problems, tangible damages, and exposing the population to serious risks.

10.319 To use an easy understandable metaphor, as in a military war, the use of stealth technologies is not only a tactical need, but it is also a huge advantage in complex scenarios; in this case, cybersecurity was a way to show the capabilities of a cyber attack which will harm the critical infrastructures as pillars of modern and advanced nation states. Analysing further, cybersecurity detection is often a problematic topic, but in the specific case, the attackers demonstrated how easy and effective the way was, which allowed them to enter the IT systems, moving then to mission-critical systems poorly protected and poorly designed systems.

10.320 The absence of in-time detection (which for energy infrastructures was at a very early stage due to the tendency of the sector to use very often proprietary or even undocumented standards) allowed criminal minds, with the use of cyber tactical means, to emerge and hit a real democracy. Looking from this angle and having in mind that this was just the materialisation of a presage of many democracies, but as a matter of fact, the raising of a new future trend, and the need to consciously review and effectively protect critical infrastructures.

10.321 We should also not forget that the attack and the following reports gave a flavour to the entire world of the opportunities that the digitalisation trends were opening in terms of the possibility to adapt strategies and tactics of the classical war to the less known cyberwarfare.

10.322 It was interesting to note that, as in field missions, the attackers tried to affect all critical infrastructures in a precise order, most probably trying to create disorientation and confusion and trying to reduce trust in the local government while damaging existing systems.

10.323 The real result was an immediate reaction of the Ukrainian Government and the adoption of a Cyber Security Strategy[64] in March 2016. Ukraine,

64 http://www.dsszzi.gov.ua/dsszzi/control/en/publish/article;jsessionid=6C8F470ED18D63FDC2E55CAE77EB1FC6.app2?art_id=273149&cat_id=35317.

following a subsequent attack in 2016, which likely had no impact on the grid, reacted with a very stringent regulation on cyber security.[65] Many analysts tend to say that this regulation is among the most stringent in Europe.

10.324 Ukraine is now an active actor, and together with other nation states, as well as, with the support of external entities, they have actively participated in awareness campaigns and thematic cyber security workshops dedicated to the energy and especially to the electricity sector.[66] Even Ukraine had to learn the 'hard-way'; they provided good ground to all nation-states on the possibility to act fast and in an effective way and to move from the role of the cyber victims, to the role of the cyber-influencers. In this respect, the pure fact that the attack was against electricity utilities and their processes, provided tangible evidence of the real risks that modern governments shall take into consideration in the age of digital markets.

The legal developments in the European Union

10.325 If we compare to the amount of laws and regulations in the US strictly related to the energy sector, Europe has shown less interest than others in cyber security matters, at least until 2013. A shy attempt to look into the matters was done in 2006 with the European Programme for Critical Infrastructure Protection (EPCIP) Communication[67] followed by the European Critical Infrastructure (ECI) Directive.[68] In the two documents, there is no mention of the cyber security for the energy sector, but it was a first attempt to identify Critical Infrastructures at the European Union level.

10.326 Another relevant point has been the general and horizontal approach that the European Union gave to all cyber security matters, which was very rarely sector-specific. While the energy markets were evolving through the implementation of what was called the 'Third Energy Package',[69] the European Union was more concentrated on setting clear technical and market rules than providing a resilient and secure cyber landscape as a background to the energy markets. In this respect, the European Union was creating a number of rules to set energy markets and run smooth and integrated operations: but among the rules there was no rule concerning cyber security. With the advent of the digital markets, instead, Europe found itself in the need to give a broader look to the cyber security issue, and to tackle in particular all cyber security aspects of the critical infrastructures at the same time. If we simply compare the dates and also the content, the first coordinated action from Europe that may have had an impact on cybersecurity for energy came in 2013 with the 'JOINT COMMUNICATION

65 http://www.golos.com.ua/article/295722.
66 https://www.naruc.org/bulletin/the-bulletin-122116/naruc-conducts-cybersecurity-workshop-for-black-sea-regulators/.
67 http://eur-lex.europa.eu/legal-content/EN/ALL/?uri=CELEX:52006DC0786.
68 https://eur-lex.europa.eu/legal-content/EN/TXT/?uri=celex:32008L0114.
69 http://europa.eu/rapid/press-release_MEMO-11-125_en.htm?locale=en.

TO THE EUROPEAN PARLIAMENT, THE COUNCIL, THE EUROPEAN ECONOMIC AND SOCIAL COMMITTEE AND THE COMMITTEE OF THE REGIONS Cybersecurity Strategy of the European Union: An Open, Safe and Secure Cyberspace.'[70]This document is considered to be among the most important pillars, and the legal basis for the further development of the Network Information Security Directive and the General Data Protection Regulation.

10.327 The use of the legislative means of the 'Directive', which sets just the principles but leaves to the European Union Member States the possibility to select means and ways, opened several discussions, in particular on the opportunity to have a specific and unified regulation for critical sectors as the energy sector: while the European Union was trying to harmonise and unify the energy markets, from a cyber security perspective (seen as part of the resilience feature), the same states may follow different paths, while they will still be all interdependent.

10.328 Moreover, in 2017, it was clear that there was an urgency to set and further develop concepts like resilience, but also to set clear milestones for both deterrence and defence of the European Single Digital Markets. This is one of the main reasons why Europe issued a new communication, which is more an updated strategy clarifying cybersecurity targets for the European Union. The 'JOINT COMMUNICATION TO THE EUROPEAN PARLIAMENT AND THE COUNCIL Resilience, Deterrence and Defence: Building strong cybersecurity for the EU'[71] was released in November 2017.

10.329 The real novel for Energy was the possibility to set, for specific sectors, cyber security strategies specific for the sector, in partial contradiction with the wider approach. The contradiction was just an apparent one; in fact, some critical infrastructures, including energy, through expert groups came to the conclusion that was advisable to have specific strategies and specific ways to tackle aspects of cyber security.

10.330 This review of the initial strategy in 2017 comes with a number of proposals; among the most important is simply called the 'Cybersecurity Act'. While the cybersecurity act doesn't have a direct and immediate impact on energy, it was not unnoticed the introduction of 'Cyber Security Certification Schemes', which, as in the case of the energy sector, were seen as an indispensable tool to help and support, for example, the energy regulators, when approving huge investments that have to be designed with minimum security capabilities.

The NIS Directive and Energy

10.331 Europe didn't show the same interest as the United States in cyber security for energy. The main issue relates to the need for the European Union to

70 https://eeas.europa.eu/archives/docs/policies/eu-cyber-security/cybsec_comm_en.pdf.
71 http://eur-lex.europa.eu/legal-content/EN/TXT/?uri=CELEX:52017JC0450.

complete all the efforts to unify and harmonise the energy markets. Nevertheless, the Directive on Security of Network and Information Systems (NIS Directive[72]) was a pillar of cyber security for the energy sector at the European level. It sets rules on cybersecurity. Being a Directive, the legislators were only able to set principles and common objectives and could not describe the means to be used. The objective of the Directive is to achieve a high common level of security of networks and information systems within the EU by means of:

1. Improved cybersecurity capabilities at national level by the EU countries.
2. Increased EU-level cooperation among all countries, with a role also for the European for the Network and Information Security Agency (ENISA).
3. Risk management and incident reporting obligations for operators of essential services and digital service providers.
4. Improved cybersecurity capabilities at national level.

10.332 In Annex II, the legislators describe the sectors and sub-sectors to be included. Energy, once again, is listed as first due to its central role, and sub-sectors like Electricity Transmission, Distribution, as well as oil and gas, are included. No reference is made to nuclear, as it is regulated by treaties and other more general Regulations.

10.333 If the aim was to harmonise and to make the cyberspace of the energy sector more homogenous, we may argue, as many other experts did, that this may be hardly achievable. The reason is very simple: setting standards and requirements for sectors very different in the way they operate and in the way they achieve their goals with respect to cyber security threats. Also, setting a reporting obligation without having a clear obligation of coordinated cross-border incident handling, for energy was extremely difficult to justify and understand. Moreover, it shall be considered that in a highly competitive market where market participants compete in trying to convince their customers to switch, cyber incidents and the reporting obligation became a sensitive issue.

10.334 The implementation is now in its core phase: while each Member State will have to adopt a national strategy on the security of networks and information systems, defining the strategic objectives and appropriate policy and regulatory measures, at the same time they should transpose the text of the Directive in National Legislation. For the energy sector the list of actors involved in the strategy implementation, will be a crucial point. In this respect, the Member States will designate one or more national competent authorities for the NIS Directive, to monitor the application of the Directive at the national level, but it is not clear if the use of the option to appoint one or more authorities will cause more problems than benefits. Also, the obligation for the Member States to designate a single point of contact, which will exercise a liaison function to ensure cross-border cooperation with the relevant authorities in other Member States and with the

72 https://ec.europa.eu/digital-single-market/en/network-and-information-security-nis-directive.

cooperation mechanisms created by the Directive itself, in the energy sector may pose strong limitations.

10.335 A very interesting aspect was the obligation to Member States to designate one or more Computer Security Incident Response Teams (CSIRTs).

10.336 The option to have one or more created quite some anxiety: the energy sector, as an example, tried in some cases to promote specific CSIRTs, which in the future will be responsible for monitoring incidents at a national level, providing early warnings, alerts, announcements, and dissemination of information to relevant stakeholders within the sector. An additional, and essential work of the CSIRTs, will be to provide a clear and firm response to incidents. In this context, we may argue that the choice to have just one, may be a huge limitation, and the creation of a dynamic network, as envisaged, is a necessity more than an option, especially for a highly interconnected and cross-border market, as the energy markets are. The NIS Directive established as well a Cooperation Group, to support and facilitate strategic cooperation and the exchange of information among Member States and to develop trust and confidence. In this context, the energy sector was among the first to promote the creation of thematic sub-groups, focussing on specific needs of the sector, and on specific problems that were not shared with the entire set of critical service providers and with the providers of essential services. While this further segmentation is still under discussion, the energy sector, as shown in the next paragraphs, started to mobilise to try to compensate for the mail gaps of the NIS Directive.

10.337 The envisaged network of the national CSIRTs was established, but having different implementations, and potentially more CSIRTs for the same Member State caused some doubts. The solution, which has been seen frequently, was the creation of a hierarchy of CSIRTs coordinated under a central CSIRT at the national level.

10.338 For the energy sector there were some other important factors to consider: the Directive does not define thresholds for what is a substantial incident requiring notification to the relevant national authority. It defines five parameters that should be taken into consideration: the number of users affected, the duration of the incident, the geographic spread, the extent of the disruption of the service, and the impact on economic and societal activities. Those parameters, in a complex energy sector, are extremely hard to assess, which created doubts on the real applicability of the Directive. Moreover, reading the list of services, we may argue that for electricity, as an example, generation was not included in the list: being the first stage and a core component of the grid, this was seen as an arguable decentralised approach, which would have requested quite soon a revision and/or being supplemented by additional regulation. This was exactly the purpose of the few articles introduced in the 'Clean Energy for all Europeans', also known as the 'Winter package'.

10.339 The need for minimum security standards most probably took the Member States a bit unprepared, especially having in mind the criticality of the sector. But on this ISO/EIC made a timely effort, which was completed by October 2017: ISO/IEC 27019:2017 Information technology – Security techniques – Information security controls for the energy utility industry[73] provided general guidance for energy utilities which may eventually be applicable also in the context of the implementation of the NIS Directive with a specific eye on the energy sector.

10.340 Finally, we should not forget the need of the European Union, still under a competitive market, to guarantee the General Data Protection Regulation,[74] which will enter into force in May 2017, provides additional constraints and sets additional requirements for the operators to follow. On this, the European Commission was already prepared to provide support and guidance: the Data Protection Impact Assessment of the Directorate General for Energy of the European Commission. The DPIA[75] is a privacy-related impact assessment whose objective is to identify and analyse how data privacy might be affected by certain actions, activities, and processes within the boundaries of the Energy Sector. Being tailored for the energy sector, but still rather generic, and with a precise attached guideline, it is the perfect tool to guide utilities to compliance with the new Data Protection Requirements, having an eye to the existing cyber security regulation.

10.341 The document, being still in the test phase, may be further developed in the future; nevertheless, it was a needed step to assure alignment between the on going efforts in cyber security and the citizens rights with respect to the protection of their personal data.

The Clean Energy for all Europeans

10.342 Following the adoption of the Network Information Security Directive (NIS) and of the General Data Protection Regulation (GDPR), many analysts were tempted to say that with the two new pieces of legislation (in reality, only the NIS Directive was brand new, the GDPR can be seen as a review of already existing legislation) the European Commission intended to close easily and smoothly the problem of cybersecurity for critical infrastructures, and in particular for energy. The NIS directive was touching just a few aspects of the cybersecurity problem, and on a limited number of assets of the electricity grids and of the gas and oil pipelines.

10.343 Another important issue was that the NIS Directive was the result of a very long negotiation process that was based on a cybersecurity strategy of the EU, which was already three years old at the time of the discussion and was not

73 https://www.iso.org/standard/68091.html.

74 http://eur-lex.europa.eu/legal-content/EN/ALL/?uri=CELEX%3A32016R0679http://eur-lex.europa.eu/legal-content/EN/TXT/?uri=uriserv:OJ.L_.2016.119.01.0001.01.ENG&toc=OJ:L:2016:119:TOC.

75 https://ec.europa.eu/energy/en/test-phase-data-protection-impact-assessment-dpia-template-smart-grid-and-smart-metering-systems.

updated with the new threats in the cyber security world. To better explain this concept; while in the real world there is space to evaluate the results of a strategy on a five-year' time frame, cybersecurity strategies and tactics can be obsolete in a shorter time. This is all linked to the technological advancements and to the research cycles which are moving at an unexpected speed, making most of the strategy papers for energy already obsolete at the date of their release.

10.344 The European Commission and its Task Forces and Expert Groups understood immediately the importance of this factor, especially in the energy sector: the NIS Directive, which is intended to be a cross-sectorial set of rules, didn't have the ambition to create several sets of rules that would have better served the needs of some (or all) the industrial sectors.

10.345 In this context, the European Commission had to use the existing Task Forces or had the possibility to set up new specific expert groups that may address issues at the strategic level or simply provide recommendations to the European Commission. This was the meaning and the aim of the Energy Expert Cyber Security Platform Expert Group Report (The EECSP Report[76]), which, running in parallel to the preparatory work for the new proposal on the 'Clean Energy for All Europeans',[77] was able to anticipate and provide inputs on topics that may have been introduced in several legal proposals.

10.346 The Clean Energy For All Europeans is the only legal text in the European Union that includes Cyber Security norms and is solely intended for the energy sector. For the first time, the proposed regulations and Directive were laying down provisions on cybersecurity for electricity, excluding all the other sub sectors of the Energy sector. The choice to have rules set only for electricity was dictated as a matter of urgency. It was obvious that while the Smart Grids were moving fast, the grid, as intended in the 70s and 80s, was evolving to unpredictable speed. There was also a general feeling that a number of non-considered risks that would have affected electricity before gas, where the technological changes are a bit slower. For this reason, the proposed package of measures to tackle cybersecurity for smart meters, putting under the spots especially Distribution System Operators (DSOs) and Transport System Operators (TSOs), recognising their key role in keeping the cyberspace a secure environment when performing standard market operations. The European Commission wanted to also ensure that the market (Regulators, Associations, TSOs and DSOs) would have been able to regulate those aspects that didn't find space in the NIS and GDPR Directive: it would have been hard to describe those rules needed to have access to and operate on the energy market in a cross-sectorial Directive. In order to delegate this hard task to the markets, a Network Code 'on cybersecurity rules' was introduced as a further step, which will only materialise after the package has been adopted, but which opened the ground for a long discussion among the operators, the regulators, and the cybersecurity experts, the industry, on the specific needs that must be

76 https://ec.europa.eu/energy/sites/ener/files/documents/eecsp_report_final.pdf.

77 https://ec.europa.eu/energy/en/topics/energy-strategy-and-energy-union/clean-energy-all-europeans.

imposed on access to the market participants and operators in order to operate in such a critical sector. The central role of ENTSO-E (European Network of Transmission System Operators for Electricity) and EU-DSO is crucial: in fact, all the implementation of cyber security in energy is subject to the agreement among hundreds of different operators. Also, being all responsible in an equal way, they all know of the critical role that all of them, with different shades, may play in the case of a large scale adverse event related to a cyber security attack. The proposal also sets obligations for electricity operators to contribute to the development of resilience in the energy sector with respect to the risk of cyber security malicious attacks, or incidents related to the information and operational technologies widely used in the electricity sector. The final purpose is to monitor and operate the grid effectively and efficiently with the new technological means and to provide services at the lowest market price possible to the end consumers.

10.347 The result is a proposal, still under discussion by the legislative bodies of the European Union, that would touch on some (but not all) aspects of cybersecurity for energy, and in particular, risk preparedness plans to be kept consistent and updated at the national and regional level, and which must also work on scenarios related to potential cybersecurity attacks, and hybrid attacks.

10.348 A peculiar aspect is the introduction of mandatory minimum security requirements to be used in Smart Metering Infrastructures, possibly already in the design phase, in order to avoid that emerging technologies would be deployed without minimum cybersecurity standards, and to preserve long term investments.

10.349 The proposal, at this stage in time, doesn't include the generation which is still crucial, and without which the distribution and transport system operators may not operate.

10.350 The legislative package was also criticised by some: the NIS Directive gave the competence to a central body designated for cyber security for all cyber security matters by the Member States, on the other side, the proposal in the clean energy package harmonises centrally some aspects, such as risk preparedness, with the option to select a specific body, and as in the case of the 'Network code for cybersecurity rules', delegates the drafting role to the Energy Regulators, while it leaves to the Member States the option to select a different role for the decisional aspects. By a matter of fact, this creates several issues, and will require a stronger coordination by all the bodies in the Member States that may be responsible for or may play a role in the daily management of energy critical infrastructures.

10.351 Directorate General of the European Commission – Joint Research Centre, developed BAT[78] and BREF[79] documents in the context of the deliverables of the European Commission Smart Grid Task force.

78 https://ec.europa.eu/energy/sites/ener/files/documents/bat_wp3_bat_analysis.pdf.

79 https://ec.europa.eu/energy/sites/ener/files/documents/bat_wp4_bref_smart-metering_systems_final_deliverable.pdf.

10.352 Going back to the Network Code, it is not completely clear to which extent cybersecurity should be covered by a secondary regulation, and which are the boundaries that are imposed on the topics that shall be part of the Network Code. The new Network Code, due to its critical role and to the speed of changes related to the technological evolution, depending on the level of the topics, may require frequent revisions, and may require unconventional ways to monitor its implementation. It is left to the European Commission to define the scope of the network code, and to the Agency for the Cooperation of Energy Regulators, together with the National Regulators to provide inputs through the Framework Guidelines. Also, it must be understood that the Network Code, as such, can only complement existing rules set by the NIS Directive, GDPR Regulation, any other existing EU Regulation, Directive, and proposal that were made by the European Commission, including and not limited to, the 'Clean energy for all Europeans'.

10.353 A final consideration has to be done on timing: the European Commission aimed to have the full or partial adoption of the proposal through a standard co-decision process, which would imply the agreement of both the European Parliament and the European Council, by the end of 2017. We should not forge that this topic would touch principles like national security and sovereignty which are sensitive matters, especially in times of political change.

10.354 Also, in the scenario in which the proposal and the aspects of cybersecurity will be substantially changed, the EU may have the need to find a strategy to mitigate imminent risks. In this scenario, the decision to update already in 2017 the cyber security strategy of the European Union, and to put forward a proposal for what we usually call the 'Cybersecurity Act' was a timely reaction to needs in specific sectors, such as the energy sector.

10.355 Looking at the work done in the context of 'Clean Energy for All Europeans', and having in mind that part of the sector is subject to a lower level of risk, it is already expected that similar measures will be extended to gas, and most probably to oil. Nuclear, due to the specific needs and to the need to cover the full fuel lifecycle and not only the generation phase, may be regulated on different grounds and will require a more complex process.

10.356 The Clean Energy for All Europeans seems to introduce a number of aspects on cybersecurity that are in favour of establishing a minimum level of cybersecurity, especially in the electricity sector, but still have the need to review frequently the risk scenario and the legislative landscape with slow legislative processes.

10.357 It doesn't address all other energy systems (eg,. gas) and the depending sectors (eg, water and telecommunications), which shall anyway be tackled by adopting coordinated policies in the scope of the NIS Directive.

10.358 Unfortunately this effort is limited to the electricity sector which, in any case, may be still seen as the most exposed to the risk of cyber attacks.

10.359 The work done until now will anyway continue: Smart Grids Task Force Expert Group 2[80] is in fact still operating under the European Commission, and in charge of advising the European Commission on Cyber Security matters since 2018. This effort will most probably provide the grounds to set a more flexible and agile governance for cyber security in the energy sector, with the need to constantly adapt to the new threat scenarios.

Beyond the US and the EU

10.360 Looking at the US and EU trends, it is undoubtable that the energy sector has been a pioneer in the field of strong regulation in cyber security. The two approaches described before show from a side a vertical approach, with a strong industrial connotation, in contrast to a wider approach, which requires and will require fast adaptations.

10.361 The energy sector brings to a number of reflections: first of all, cyber security in the sectors is heavily influenced by the way the markets where it shall be used operate. In the case of energy, there is no single way to adapt cyber security strategies to a member state, for a number of reasons. The energy mix, as an example, is very dependent on the available resources and on the markets. The increasing use of technologies which aim to improve efficiency, add additional complexity to a fast-changing market, and create a fluctuating risk for the entire sector. The political dimension and the growth, which are influenced and influence the energy in all nation states, are an additional factor of uncertainty for the strategies and for the measures applicable now and in the future. This has to be considered, especially when policies are rolled out. In the following paragraphs, we present a few cases: all of them show different aspects, and different trends, as well as, the general tendency to make different decisions depending on the needs.

10.362 South Korea, on the reverse, moved its first steps already in 2001[81] a centralised approach, supplemented by contacts with energy actors, provides a good level of control on cyber threats, and an overview that goes beyond the scope of this chapter.

10.363 The Kingdom of Saudi Arabia, playing a key role in energy worldwide, through the production of crude oil, following a well-known attack reported in this chapter, reacted with a cyber security strategy[82] that is still in draft.

10.364 At the same time, it established a National Cyber Security Centre in charge to set the vision for 2030, and to overcome immediate operational needs.

80 https://ec.europa.eu/energy/en/topics/markets-and-consumers/smart-grids-and-meters/smart-grids-task-force.

81 http://www.oecd.org/going-digital/digital-security-in-critical-infrastructure/digital-security-workshop-february-2018-%20Im.pdf.

82 http://www.mcit.gov.sa/Ar/MediaCenter/PubReqDocuments/NISS_Draft_7_EN.pdf.

10.365 Compared to the Qatar approach, which was subject to a well-known attack following the one to Saudi Aramco, seems to show a clearer picture. The small state in the Arab peninsula, issued a cyber security strategy[83] following the events of the RasGas hack/attack. Reading the strategy carefully, we may easily find that Qatar has established Information Risk Expert Committees (IREC), showing a level of maturity that is driving the state toward a risk-based approach, together with the establishment of Q-CERT[84] which provides the capability to report cyber security related information, and the possibility to seek for help. For the energy sector, Qatar intends to boost awareness and specific cyber security technologies through the financing of strategic projects. A cyber security exercise was performed already in 2013.

10.366 The Chinese example followed, partially, the European trend. The cybersecurity law, which entered into force in February 2017, provided a certain level of protection also to the energy sector through Article 31.[85] The Article seems not to clarify how this will be further organised. In this respect, it is difficult to assess the entire approach.

10.367 Singapore deserves a special mention: their Cyber Security capabilities, through their Cyber Security Agency, are undeniable While many still struggle to regulate cyber security in the energy sector, Singapore, already in 2016, managed to organise a cyber security exercise that included the 11 critical infrastructures, including energy.[86] Looking at the efforts of others, it seems that they have reached a good level of maturity, independently from the sector, understanding that all sectors are in a way interdependent.

The sectorial and silos strategies versus the multi-sector horizontal approach

10.368 As we have seen in the previous chapters, there is no single way to adapt broader policies and regulations to the energy sector. Exactly for this reason, many governments have been struggling trying to find the right balance. Also, as the technology and level of maturity are completely different, the approach may vary depending on the technological advancements.

10.369 Moreover, there is a general issue related to how the markets are designed and operate in the countries: in the EU, where there is a single market, there is the necessity to flatten the rules, and to provide a general guideline sector specific. Many people have been arguing on the opportunity to have strategies that are applicable to a single sector and which sometimes do not.

83 http://www.ictqatar.qa/en/cyber-security/national-cyber-security-strategy.
84 http://www.qcert.org/.
85 https://assets.kpmg.com/content/dam/kpmg/cn/pdf/en/2017/02/overview-of-cybersecurity-law.pdf.
86 http://www.straitstimes.com/singapore/cyber-security-exercise-involves-all-11-critical-information-infrastructure-sectors.

10.370 A multi-sector approach has the advantage to reduce in general the risk for the entire nation, while it may not reduce the risk in those sectors that are more exposed, or, worse, which are more prone to risks and on which the civil society is more depending. In this respect, while a strategy for the energy sector, as in the case of the EU, may be seen as an overkill and an unnecessary complication, on the other side if we consider the key role played by the energy markets, it may be argued that this legal over complication may bring in future good results and avoid major disruptions to the energy system which may easily propagate along the entire continent.

10.371 But in this context we also need to consider the position of the markets, and maybe we will look to some lessons learned. The possibility to have silos of cyber security where the risk level is constant, and to avoid having a common baseline for critical services, where the achieved risk level at the end of the exercise may vary depending on the field, may also affect the markets.

10.372 Looking to the energy sector, and looking to the experiences in Europe and abroad, consumers have always provided the right value to the quality of service. If we consider this factor, we may easily justify that a consistent expenditure on cybersecurity may have, in the medium and short run, a return for the operators, as they will continue to keep high the actual quality level, setting the right risk profile with respect to cybersecurity. The horizontal approach, on the other side, may impose higher standards in respect to the real needs (which is unlikely if we look at the different sectors), with the result of eroding the profits of operators, or may impose lower standards in respect to the real needs, which may endanger the operators, and cause, if the frequency of incidents linked to cyber security will eventually increase, instability on the markets, distrust on consumers, and a general reduction in quality levels. Obviously, at this stage, this cannot be substantiated by real facts and statistics, but as cyber security is still considered a part of the reliance, security and safety concepts applied to energy, the markets are extremely careful in monitoring the trends, as well as their governments.

10.373 If we judge from the participation of expert groups and task forces, operators are extremely careful and cautious on the topic, and rarely take a firm position on the need for the specific energy actions. Also, regulatory authorities recognise the importance of cybersecurity in the energy sector: some of them, having already taken an active role in this, and understanding in depth all the matters, may in the future also provide more inputs and analysis on how the cyber security needs are changing the markets, and how future markets may be designed to further develop, and exploit the efficiency potential.

10.374 For now, looking to the preliminary assessment, if we look to both the US and the EU, on wider markets a sectoral approach, organised in coordinated silos with other depending critical infrastructures, may still provide better results.

10.375 This must also be analysed in the context of the maturity of those markets and their openness toward better and higher cyber security standards in comparison to the existing. Both in the EU and in the US, the markets were already in a heavy digitisation phase. Adherence to the cybersecurity standards and guidelines (and thanks to the availability of good tools to evaluate risks, and address improvements), in order to continue to meet market specific quality requirements, was a need and not an option for most of the operators, with the exclusion of the smaller: customers are more and more sensible and aware of the quality service levels that can and shall be provided to them, especially in highly competitive markets where quality is a leverage to convince a customer to switch. The cyber security threat, because of its press coverage and because it became part of our everyday lives already years ago, appeared immediately as a factor when considering an energy operator, and its ability to provide the right service with the expected price and expected quality level.

10.376 On other international energy markets, where there is still a low level of unbundling, where monopolists and states play a crucial role, and where quality is not a concern as no possibility of switching is present, we may argue that the cross sector approach may still be the best option, even if it is suboptimal.

10.377 Indeed, this last statement may be argued looking also to the political and economical medium-long term objectives: in countries with high development rates, where energy demand and stability are again a need, and not an option, it may be advisable to have specific policies or specific guidelines for the energy sector, with stringent controls and close supervision.

10.378 We may indeed affirm that poor attention to the cyber security matters in the energy sector may be in the future a huge risk for the development of growing countries, but also for the development of healthy and digitalised democracies.

An analysis of the energy sub sectors: strengths, weaknesses and law

10.379 Moving far from economic and political analysis and considerations, and moving back to the cyber security in the energy sector, we shall recognise that the energy sector is not only electricity: and that not all the constituents of the sector suffer of the same risks and of the same issues.

10.380 Among the sub-sectors, some are heavily regulated, and act in a well-controlled market: if we take the example of the nuclear sub sector, we may expect that some work is already done. The nuclear subsector poses more risks, as it is intrinsically linked to the Nuclear Fuel Life Cycle. Indeed we may say that it is just a side risk, but the management of nuclear fuel and nuclear waste is somehow done with digital means. Those means should be subject to cyber security measures as well.

10.381 As reported before, the electricity sector, because of the possibility to affect human lives, is the most riskful, and the most impacting, but it is also the most known, which provides a competitive advantage.

10.382 We should not forget about gas: electricity in some areas of the EU and of the entire world, is heavily dependent on gas. While the gas sector is less heavily digitised, it is in an initial phase of digitalisation. Smart meters and smart metering infrastructures are starting to appear in many cities. In this context, we have to consider risks linked to some facilities: LNGs, as an example, are important, as are the ships that allow LNGs in many areas. As an example, many companies offering security services for gas facilities provide the same services for maritime fleets.

10.383 Oil, on the other hand, even though it is part of the energy supply chain but does not play a key role in the energy mix of some of the world countries, has a completely different connotation. We may bring a number of attacks to the oil companies, but until now they had the potential to create problems only to the ancillary activities (accounting and billing systems) and they were never focused on the disruption of the oil pipelines and of their facilities. Even in the future this may change. We have to consider that the industrial systems work by analogy like in gas, with a lower grade of complexity and distribution. By a matter of fact, we do not have a door-to-door distribution for oil, and most probably this is not planned in the future, while we have this for gas. Other issues are present, such as the necessity to have refineries which, on the contrary, are *complex* systems with complex IT/OT systems and with a certain degree of automation.

10.384 A special chapter is dedicated to renewables and more in general to distributed generation: even they may be included in the electricity chapter, there are some topics which may be better discussed separately. For example, the need to heavily use IoTs and the concept of prosumers, merit particular attention.

Electricity

10.385 The electricity sector, as reported before, is most probably the one that creates in all Nation States most of the concerns. Especially in areas where investments were done long years ago, the concerns may be supported by the materialisation of real attacks, and Ukraine, which is here reported as a case scenario, is a tangible proof, with limited consequences, of the risk.

10.386 The electricity sector is also central for all other sub sectors within the energy family, and all other energy sub- sectors, at the same time, are depending on the availability of electricity (think to the need to have electricity to activate gas compressors in some cases), which creates a special security profile for all electricity infrastructures and facilities. Electricity has a high potential impact on the economy and society. And, at the same time, has strong constraints to operate which may impact the availability of the resources. Under this framework, all governments have been acting, putting electricity at the very core of the cyber security legislation, but in some cases, and in some areas around the world, there are still urgent cyber security related problems that may not be easily resolved: the need to be interconnected to operate, to exchange information frequently, and in close to real-time, together with the use of operational technology means, which are somehow cyber security agnostic, creates the conditions for having big risks.

10.387 The electricity sector is one of the few sectors where problems cannot be simply solved at a sectoral, national, or regional level: operators in every area of the world are depending on other areas, as equipment used is unique.

Gas

10.388 The gas subsector is generally speaking exposed to a lower level of complexity. The main difference stands in the use of pipelines for transport distribution of natural gas, using very similar concepts as in the energy grids, but somehow with lower complexity and with less need to exchange real time information. The gas subsector, until now, didn't see events like the one in Ukraine for electricity, but there is the potential to have similar or even more disruptive events. The recent case of the Triton Malware[87] has shown the potential that, together with an effect on the sector, and a long-lasting crises, certain attacks may put in danger safety features of the systems deployed on the field. Also, the gas sector has the potential to be better resilient to cyber security crisis. We should not forget that the gas markets may benefit from storages and Liquified Natural Gas Hubs which may, in case of a cyber security crisis, provide the resources and means to overcome an ongoing crisis. The electricity sector, even in the United States starts to have the same capability, may not provide the same level of flexibility. As in the electricity sector, the gas subsector is prone to attacks to the interconnection network, and equipment is usually part of long-term investments. The need to embed cyber security capabilities, while meeting real time needs is, in some stages less stringent than in electricity, but still important as gas has a strong impact on the security and safety of the people surrounding the facilities.

10.389 Also, the gas subsector plays a crucial role in the energy mix in the energy mix of many states: the risk to cause an energy crises spreading to the electricity sector in some countries around the globe, is not only a remote event, but is taken into serious consideration as it is most probably the most probable start of a massive cyber attack on the energy critical infrastructures in some countries.

Nuclear

10.390 Cyber security in the nuclear energy sector has been perceived as a very sensitive topic, due to the potential devastating impact of incidents with nuclear.

87 https://www.fireeye.com/blog/threat-research/2017/12/attackers-deploy-new-ics-attack-framework-triton.html.

10.391 Nuclear and energy have one of the longer-lasting relationships. Also, when considering nuclear, we should not forget that special attention shall be paid to the nuclear fuel life cycle: the nuclear fuel cycle is composed of several processes, from mines, to enrichment, from energy production in nuclear power plants, to the storage and reprocessing facilities.

10.392 Looking back at the history, one of the most well-known cases, Stuxnet malware[88] was exactly attacking an enrichment facility. The nuclear sector has been, in comparison to smart grids and electricity networks, very stable since the eighties. Also, the level of control and protection in nuclear facilities and nuclear power plants is regulated both by national and internationally recognised standards. In the EU, as an example, under the EURATOM treaty, specific safeguards were established in order to prevent that nuclear material meant to be used in nuclear facilities, or the result of a nuclear reaction, would be used for military purposes. In this respect both EURATOM organisation and IAEA (the International Atomic Energy Agency), have provided clear guidance[89] to all operators on cyber security in nuclear facilities. Nevertheless, cyber security in the nuclear energy is perceived as a priority, and most of the operators autonomously started internal projects on the topic following the Stuxnet attack in Iran.

10.393 From a legal perspective, we may argue that establishing cyber security for nuclear related to the energy sector may be a difficult but necessary step ahead. Also, the trend of some states to avoid using nuclear in their energy mix, may be an easy solution: we should not forget that the waste cycle, managed by IT means, will still be prone to cyber attacks, and that the material that will be stored in safe locations, will still be active and potentially dangerous for centuries in some cases. In this respect, there is still a need to set clear rules for IT systems used in similar operations.

10.394 Nevertheless, as stressed before, the IAEA has played a crucial role in issuing non-binding guidance papers which may allow operators to autonomously design and implement protection concepts without the need to be subject to hard regulation.

10.395 If a similar approach will be successful, it will be most probably the only example in Energy of soft regulation applied to the energy sector

Oil

10.396 The oil subsector can be considered rather distributed with limited or without interconnection; in Europe no major oil pipelines are used for transport of oil, and no door-to-door concept is used to deliver oil: the distribution system for oil works on completely different models. Anyway, oil has other peculiarities that can be interesting for an attacker: the refineries, which are essential to

88 https://www.symantec.com/connect/blogs/stuxnet-breakthrough.
89 https://www.iaea.org/topics/computer-and-information-security.

deliver final products, are generally very rare and highly automated. The level of physical protection (very high fences, and multi layered physical security, with strict police and law enforcement control) may give the feeling to a non-expert of the importance of similar facilities. Many of them are operated locally, so they do not need access from remote locations, nevertheless the risk that malware may be used as an access point to then inject specific malware targeting Industrial Control Systems, is real. Oil is particularly delicate as it has a direct influence on the mobility of the citizens, as well as being unique facilities, in case of damages which may hit the physical dimension of a facility, which is usually built in several years, may require several weeks to recover. As in the gas subsector, the existence of storage facilities for oil and all its derivatives and the existence of storage strategies by the states that shall prevent similar crises as well, provide a general sense of comfort that even an attack lasting several weeks may eventually have a limited impact on the populations, but an impact on the affected company. An example in this case, with no consequences on the facilities, is the Saudi Aramco case:[90] the hack/attack was in this case linked to the Shamoon virus, so relatively common. It did not affect Industrial Control Systems, but a massive amount of IT devices (mainly servers and clients). The interesting outcome of this hack/attack was the amount of damages reported, or supposedly, which was estimated in thousands of devices to be fixed. While the on field operations were not affected, the loss of reputation, and the collateral damages to the internal processes were enormous. Keeping aside the political dimension, it shall be understood that a similar attack on small market participants in more competitive markets such as the European Union, may have created enough damages to push a market participant out of the market competition in a short time.

10.397 A few days after, a similar hack/attack, apparently on smaller scale, was hitting RasGas in Qatar, with negligible consequences.

10.398 Nevertheless, this supports the general understanding of a close link and a lot of similarities between the gas and oil subsectors, especially when approaching the cyber security matters.

Renewables and others

10.399 Distributed Energy Resources and renewables are the new frontier of cyber security for energy: while they continue expanding, and while they continue improving the diversification of the energy mix, at the same time increase the risks for the grid, and especially for the generation and distribution of electricity.

10.400 Solar panels and wind factories are not far in time, and many of them have been boosted through a number of incentives at the national and international level. Their key role in safeguarding the environment while providing indispensable resources for the growth of our economies, cannot be denied: having consumers

90 https://pjournals.com/index.php/ijmit/article/view/5613

more and more conscious of their active role, provides the basis for cooperative generation.

10.401 But as with all new technologies, there is a general need to communicate and coordinate efforts: most of this continuous and hidden cooperation is done through IT and OT means. While we can expect big operators to understand and manage properly cyber security, we cannot expect the same from small producers linked to virtual power plants. Unfortunately, those small producers may have, in the long run, the same destructive effect as big operators.

10.402 Law and Regulation has to take into consideration also those needs: while on the financial markets a small quantity of energy demanded/offered may be irrelevant to the entire system. In the cyber security environment, a number of actors with small quantities and subject to an identical attack may heavily destabilise large portions of the grid. What we generally call, the cascade effect, can be achieved in several ways: from a side targeting and attacking big operators, from the other side attacking a massive number of small operators. In both cases, the effects are unpredictable. Luckily there is no precedent on this, as told, the Ukraine case showed the effect on a number of operators. In this specific case it will require an attack of a large scale on a number of consumers in the same region.

10.403 Nevertheless, there are big concerns about the use of renewables and distributed energy resources and cyber security: the case of the photovoltaic inverters in Germany[91] created quite some anxiety. While the vulnerability was openly admitted by the company producing the Smart System,[92] and the extent of the potential was re-assessed as being negligible for the European and German grids, it should not be forgotten that clear regulation may also address and impose clear minimum cyber security standards for use of renewables and distributed energy resources in the energy grid. Moreover, it must be considered that intermediaries, as aggregators and virtual power plants, shall be part of the same requirements, and shall be considered in the future regulation. At this stage, it is very difficult to analyse and assess what governments and regulatory authorities may do in that direction, as renewables and DERs are an essential part of the transition to a more green economy. There is also a general concern that the use and abuse of regulation in cybersecurity for small actors may sound like a barrier to real and fair competition. This competition is anyway needed if we want to meet the ambitious environmental and economical targets: cyber security threats can then be perceived as an obstacle, to which only the solution is to have a strong defensive and/or offensive approach against criminal actors, which in the virtual space is extremely difficult.

10.404 Finally, one additional concern in the completely uncontrolled use of the Internet of Things: the IoT has been reported as a huge opportunity for a number

91 https://nakedsecurity.sophos.com/2017/08/22/smart-solar-power-inverters-raise-risk-of-energy-grid-attacks/.

92 https://www.sma.de/en/statement-on-cyber-security.html.

of companies, but has also been an uncontrolled flow of innovation. A number of simple functions can now be performed on the energy system by a plethora of simple IoT or Industrial Internet of Things devices: most of them play just the role of performing a simple assigned task, with no security design. Even though some of them perform complex functions, on the other side, many people doubt that the innovation flow should really pass through the IoT especially in the case of Industrial Control Systems. It is anyway important to highlight the existence of a number of small alliances that are now focussing on the design of reliable IoT for industrial use.

Conclusions and the way forward

10.405 The dependencies and interdependencies on and of the energy sector, and the need for the energy sector to sustain a fast growth, justifies the important social role of energy, and the number of laws specifically dedicated to cyber security in the sector (think what the world would be now without cyber media).

10.406 The differentiation between what can be critical for the functioning of civil society and what is perceived as critical but is marginal to the well functioning, justifies the central role provided by all the advanced governments.

10.407 In the case of energy, most probably there is a need for new dedicated legislation and technical standards which, on the other side, may just be a blocker to the current innovation of the energy sector. The Nation States have seen, through the example of Ukraine, that the threat of cyber security on the energy system is real and may hit more countries at the same time. Also, the number of technical standards proposing effective solutions to this threat, sufficient to allow operators and nation states to select those that may better fit with their medium-and-long term objectives. Many of the technical standards, on the contrary, may not be aligned with emerging new threats, for which information sharing and international cooperation are the only viable solutions, at least at this stage.

10.408 The interesting aspect of the energy sector, due to its criticality, is the need that regulation will move together and at the same speed with the development of technical standards and enforcement. While the US, through a very expensive but effective process, managed to partially implement a similar circle and achieve a number of ambitious targets, others are struggling to start this process with a considerable delay. Historically, the establishment of a similar virtuous process, as from the US experience, may take 10 to 15 years, but if we consider the level of obsolescence of the technologies used in the specific sector, this may not be an immediate concern for those nation states with a low degree of innovation in the energy sector.

10.409 For the legacy equipment, which is more than a simple concern, the solution will be the replacement of existing equipment with new equipment, with a partial protection of the boundaries surrounding those facilities. Where those cyber boundaries do not exist, they will need to be created, and this may have a direct impact on the digitalisation of the sector, which may require a slowdown, while the technology markets are actually pushing for a fast and progressive digitalisation. This may also have an impact at the political level and on the development of inclusive energy regional policies.

10.410 Finally, recent cases of attacks touching the safety of complex systems, opened a question on the need, in the future, to find ways to design IT and OT systems in a way that, even in case of malfunctioning, they may still avoid harming humans and their activities. Unfortunately, this is the hardest part, as this is an undiscovered field both for hackers and for researchers, for which research and further innovation seem to be the only solution in the medium and long term.

10F AEROSPACE, DEFENCE AND SECURITY SECTOR
Simon Goldsmith

Introduction

10.411 In January 2018, the World Economic Forum in Davos, Switzerland, announced that cyber-security threats were outpacing the abilities of governments and companies to overcome them. According to the Global Risks Report 2018[93] released at the time of the forum, cyber-attacks were perceived as the global risk of highest concern to business leaders in advanced economies – exceeding terrorist attacks, fiscal crises and asset bubbles. Cyber-crime was also viewed by the wider risk-community as the risk most likely to intensify in 2018, according to the risk perception survey that underpinned the Global Risks Report.

10.412 And the stakes in the Aerospace, Defence, and Security (ADS) sector are higher than in many other sectors. These companies must firstly defend themselves (including their customers, their employees and their shareholders), as a part of 'Critical National Infrastructure': they provide civilian aircraft, military platforms and intelligence capabilities and are often large employers and economic entities in their own right. However, they also have a key role in either directly defending other critical sectors or, at the very least, developing the technologies and techniques which these sectors urgently require. There are two main reasons why other sectors may come to be reliant on ADS companies for solutions.

10.413 Firstly, most other parts of Critical National Infrastructure such as Banking, IT and Energy and Utilities tend to be more focused on the benefits and disruptive opportunities of new technology. Technology risks to them are often programmatic or regulatory in nature, they are less familiar with the adversarial

93 www.weforum.org/reports/the-global-risks-report-2018.

risks posed by the scale and highly adaptive nature of Nation States, who are looking to exploit the increased digitisation of their targets. In the non-digital (ie physical) world, governments through military and law enforcement, have historically provided much of this protection on their behalf. In cyber-space, economic and technical practicalities, along with the speed of response required, demand that the obligation for self-defence increases tremendously.

10.414 Secondly, while many commercial organisations are accustomed to facing risks associated with fraud and systemic financial crime, such as money laundering and sanctions, their historic approaches are proving less effective against modern threats. Many companies have treated these risks as indirect threats to their business, only acting on money laundering and sanctions as a result of regulation and the threat of large fines in their industry. Moreover, they have often tolerated a certain level of fraud and theft as a 'cost of doing business'.

10.415 Many of the responsibilities for detection and disruption of more serious and organised criminal activities have traditionally sat with law enforcement. Corporations have not been prepared for the proliferation of advanced malware exploits, let alone the access, reach and scale that internet-based technologies and illicit online marketplaces provide to international criminal enterprises and other organised attackers. These threats emerge and evolve at a pace which law enforcement and regulatory action alone cannot match, and lead to a situation where a 'cost of doing business' mindset can pose an existential threat to a company's growth and profits.

10.416 It is this wide spectrum of threats, and attitudes to the risk of cyber-attacks, which have contributed to the level of concern expressed by the World Economic Forum. Solutions require closer partnership between government and industry, and a dramatic change in mindset from compliance and 'do the minimum' to more adversarial attack versus defence risk models and controls. These are both areas where the ADS sector has had a head start, and so potentially has much to offer.

Comparing Civilian and Military Cyber Security Sectors

10.417 State espionage has always presented a threat to the ADS sector because of the role it plays in developing National Defence and Security capabilities and the financial, military and 'state secrets' value of the Intellectual Property developed by their technology departments. Historically spies risked arrest or even execution if they tried to infiltrate organisations and smuggle out copies of documents. But those in cyber-space face little of that risk. Whereas a spy might once have been able to take out a few design blueprints or a file of material, now they take the whole library. Moreover, public declarations and published military doctrine since the 1990s show that governments and their militaries have been extending their thinking from the traditional physical theatres of war in air, land and sea into cyber-space.

10.418 There are two key drivers behind developments in cyber-security in the ADS sector, the first is common to most sectors, the digital age; the second, offensive cyber-security operations, is more specific to national military and intelligence operations.

The Digital Age and the Digital Battlespace

10.419 There are overwhelming benefits of connectivity through IP-based technologies and the increased information sharing and exploitation this enables. There are military advantages offered by doctrines such as Network Centric Warfare coined by the US Department of Defense (DoD), and what the UK called Network Enabled Capability – essentially giving Armed Forces personnel and equipment a 'force-multiplier' through better exploitation of information and connectivity in this 'Digital Battlespace'.

Offensive Cyber Capability

10.420 By conducting offensive operations in cyber-space, governments and their militaries see the opportunity to disrupt enemy military operations and civil infrastructure, undertake intelligence missions and deliver kinetic effect remotely; each of these cases offer the potential of lower chances of discovery and attribution. While it is relevant that the tradecraft and mindset vital to successfully defend computer networks share many traits with those needed to conduct offensive operations, the doctrinal, legal, political and security implications of non-military personnel involvement in offensive cyber-operations is beyond the scope of this chapter. It is therefore sufficient to state that offensive cyber-operations are a key element of modern military doctrine, and that governments, including the UK, have acknowledged this publicly.[94] Some examples of offensive cyber-security operations are covered later in this chapter.

10.421 The figures below provide a current summary of global threat actors and their capabilities. The data has been reproduced from security company Flashpoint's 2017 end-of-year update.[95] There is a note of recommended caution when interpreting this table and other cyber-threat intelligence reporting. There is an unfortunate degree of 'balkanisation' within the cyber-security industry whereby intelligence on threats can be skewed by national perspectives. While many organisations and security researchers strive to deliver independent analysis, it would be wise to exercise caution when reading their reports.

94 www.ft.com/content/9ac6ede6-28fd-11e3-ab62-00144feab7de.

95 Business Risk Intelligence Decision Report – 2017 End of Year Update, Flashpoint. https://go.flashpoint-intel.com/docs/BRI-Decision-Report-2017-End-of-Year-Update, February 2018.

	VERTICALS									RISK RANKINGS	
THREAT ACTORS	FINANCIAL SERVICES	RETAIL	LEGAL	ENERGY	HEALTHCARE	TECH / ENTERTAINMENT	TELECOM	GOV'T / MILITARY	NGO'S / CIVIL SOCIETY	CAPABILITY	POTENTIAL IMPACT
CHINA	×		×	×	×	×	×	×	×	TIER 6	CATASTROPHIC
FIVE EYES*	×			×			×	×		TIER 6	CATASTROPHIC
IRAN	×			×			×	×	×	TIER 4	MODERATE/SEVERE
NORTH KOREA	×			×		×	×	×	×	TIER 4**	SEVERE
RUSSIA	×		×	×		×	×	×	×	TIER 6	CATASTROPHIC
DISRUPTIVE/ATTENTION-SEEKING ACTORS						×		×		TIER 3	MODERATE
CYBERCRIMINALS	×	×	×		×	×	×			TIER 4	SEVERE
HACKTIVISTS	×	×		×		×	×	×	×	TIER 3	MODERATE
JIHADI HACKERS	×					×		×		TIER 2	NEGLIGIBLE

* Non-threat nation-states, to include the U.S. and its allies, represent the high-water mark for top-tier nation-state cyber capabilities. Risk assessments should measure adversarial nation-states against these top-tier actors when estimating cyber capability.
** Although assessed as a Tier 4 actor, North Korea is a unique case because the state is able to marshal state resources as necessary, which may enable capabilities that are generally ascribed to higher tier actors. North Korea in particular is likely capable of using destructive and highly disruptive attacks in kinetic conflict scenarios to support military objectives — a key differentiator of Tier 6 actors.

FLASHPOINT CAPABILITY SCALE

TIER 1	The cyber actor(s) possess extremely limited technical capabilities and largely makes use of publicly available attack tools and malware. Sensitive data supposedly leaked by the attackers are often linked back to previous breaches and publicly available data.
TIER 2	Attackers can develop rudimentary tools and scripts to achieve desired ends in combination with the use of publicly available resources. They may make use of known vulnerabilities and exploits.
TIER 3	Actors maintain a moderate degree of technical sophistication and can carry out moderately damaging attacks on target systems using a combination of custom and publicly available resources. They may be capable of authoring rudimentary custom malware.
TIER 4	Attackers are part of a larger and well-resourced syndicate with a moderate-to-high level of technical sophistication. The actors are capable of writing custom tools and malware and can conduct targeted reconnaissance and staging prior to conducting attack campaigns. Tier 4 attackers and above will attempt to make use of publicly available tools prior to deploying more sophisticated and valuable toolkits.
TIER 5	Actors are part of a larger and well-resourced organization with high levels of technical capabilities such as those exhibited by Tier 4 actor sets. In addition, Tier 5 actors have the capability of introducing vulnerabilities in target products and systems, or the supply chain, to facilitate subsequent exploitation.
TIER 6	Nation-state supported actors possessing the highest levels of technical sophistication reserved for only a select set of countries. The actors can engage in full-spectrum operations, utilizing the breadth of capabilities available in cyber operations in concert with other elements of state power, including conventional military force and foreign intelligence services with global reach.

[1] This scale is borrowed heavily and adapted from the U.S. Department of Defense Science Board's "Resilient Military Systems" report. The full report can be found at http://www.acq.osd.mil/dsb/reports/ResilientMilitarySystems.CyberThreat.pdf.

FLASHPOINT POTENTIAL IMPACT SCALE

NEGLIGIBLE	Damage from these attacks is highly unlikely or is unable to adversely affect the targeted systems and infrastructure. Such incidents may result in minor reputational damage. Sensitive systems and data remain intact, confidential, and available.
LOW	Attacks have the capacity to disrupt some non-critical business functions, and the impact is likely intermittent and non-uniform across the user base. User data and sensitive information remain protected.
MODERATE	Attacks have the potential to disrupt some core business functions, although the impact may be intermittent and non-uniform across the user base. Critical assets and infrastructure remain functional, even if they suffer from moderate disruption. Some non-sensitive data may be exposed. Actors at this level might also expose sensitive data.
SEVERE	Cyber attacks at this level have the capacity to disrupt regular business operations and governmental functions severely. Such incidents may result in the temporary outage of critical services and the compromise of sensitive data.
CATASTROPHIC	Kinetic and cyber attacks conducted by the threat actor(s) have the potential to cause complete paralysis and/or destruction of critical systems and infrastructure. Such attacks have the capacity to result in significant destruction of property and/or loss of life. Under such circumstances, regular business operations and/or government functions cease and data confidentiality, integrity, and availability are completely compromised for extended periods.

CRIMINAL MALWARE DEVELOPMENT

10.422 Design features of prominent State developed malware such as Stuxnet have appeared in criminal malware. One such feature is modular design. Modern criminal malware often has a modular design to enable actors to send upgraded parts as necessary, for example to perform particular actions or attacks.

10.423 It is an attractive way for malware authors to sell their work to others. Much like many software vendors it's an opportunity for upsell – providing the ability to offer upgrade kits to improve the software after the initial sale. Modularity also makes the malware more adaptable for different targets and harder for security solution vendors to detect and track – by only uploading modules tailored to specific targets it is a lot harder for security researchers and solutions to get all the components and see and know all of it.

10.424 Modern criminals also operate in an industrial, almost professional enterprise. Like businesses, they consume and provide digital services and use online marketplaces. They set up in difficult-to-track locations such as on the dark web and optimise for profit by only buying the components or services they need for their operation, or becoming a specialist provider in a supply chain. Developing the code from start to finish is a heavy investment and almost certainly unlikely to be profitable. So, while they do invest in their own code, profits dictate that they can't dedicate the resources on the same scale as governments, who are much more concerned about operational security, and so it is usually the minimum necessary to achieve their aim.

Benefit and Threat

10.425 Whereas the two trends of 'the Digital Battlespace' and Offensive Cyber Operations are highly complementary in military doctrine, and have become a significant element of military and National Security budgets, they also act as opposing forces as other Nations adopt similar strategies and polices. The greater the connectivity and integration of internet Protocol-based information technology, the greater the risk to civilian and military platforms and critical national infrastructure; our modern way of life is increasingly comprised of this technology. There are also clear national security implications as non-Nation State actors (eg terrorist organisations) seek offensive hacking capabilities.

10.426 For over 25 years, these two opposing forces have raised new requirements for ADS companies. Whether it is defending themselves and the classified information they hold (often on behalf of defence departments and law enforcement) against the rapidly evolving capabilities of State-sponsored espionage actors, or defending their customers by ensuring the systems they deliver are robust and resilient in the face of a cyber-attack. These new risks also introduce very large opportunities for those able to develop a competitive advantage in defending themselves and their customers in this new battlespace.

Opportunities for the ADS Sector

10.427 The first opportunity is an extension of existing business: continuing to compete with national and international industry rivals to build and sell 'better' cyber-security capabilities and infusing their existing military and commercial platform businesses with those capabilities. However, the potentially much larger opportunity is to use the unique insight they have gained on the frontline of cyber-security, facing the most advanced adversaries in cyber-space, to deliver 'military-grade' capabilities to the commercial sector. At least that was a conclusion of the market analysis conducted by strategy departments in the ADS sector in the mid-2000s.

10.428 The technology rationale for competing against traditional IT providers and the myriad of start-ups in the burgeoning cyber-security market was and remains twofold. Firstly, threats are adopting new tools and techniques at an accelerated rate. Secondly, other sectors are coming under attack from new threats as Nation States test their abilities to achieve military and political aims through cyber-attacks on non-military targets. The financial rationale also remains strong. Gartner estimated that the cyber security market will be worth $96 billion in 2018, up 8% from 2017,[96] and in a survey by McKinsey conducted in 2014, 70% of defence industry executives predicted a fall in traditional defence spending in Europe and North America over the following three years.[97]

Evolution of the Threat

10.429 The threat of a cyber-security attack is one that has been hanging over many civilian sectors such as financial services, legal, energy and transport for years; consequently this has been a key focus of the marketing departments in security product vendors. 'Advanced Persistent Threats' and doomsday scenarios have filled advertising space and unfortunately led to a situation where boards and risk decision makers find it next to impossible to discern facts from hype. However, there are two key trends which have become clear to those in the ADS cyber-security sector over recent years. The first is the level of industrialisation and professionalism which new technologies are providing to criminals as they look to cyber-space to increase the scale and financial reward of their activities. As Europol reports in its Internet Organised Crime Threat Assessment (IOCTA)

96 www.gartner.com/newsroom/id/3836563, December 2017.

97 www.mckinsey.com/industries/aerospace-and-defense/our-insights/defense-outlook-2017-a-global-survey-of-defense-industry-executives, April 2015.

2017 report,[98] Darknet markets are a key crosscutting enabler for other crime areas, providing access to, amongst other things, cyber-crime tools and services, compromised financial data to commit various types of payment fraud, and fraudulent documents to facilitate fraud, trafficking in human beings and illegal immigration. Mimicking the features of Amazon on the 'surface' internet, these markets offer features such as reviews and ratings systems and provide ready access to a sophisticated criminal supply chain.

10.430 The second trend is that the capabilities developed by governments are making their way into the hands of the threat actors which more often target commercial enterprises, for example criminals and activists. For one thing, sharing of programme code is a much harder to solve issue than proliferation of weapons of mass destruction. This was evident in 2010, when elements of the Stuxnet code started being copied and re-used in attacks in 2011. And in 2017, in code released by the 'Shadowbrokers' group, an exploit believed to be Nation State developed and codenamed Eternal Blue was re-used in the WannaCry and NotPetya attacks in the same year.

10.431 An official blog by security firm Symantec[99] detailed how the tools and infrastructure used in the WannaCry ransomware attacks bore strong links to a threat group called Lazarus, a group believed to be affiliated with the North Korean State and who some hold responsible for the destructive attacks on Sony Pictures in 2014 and the theft of US$81 million from the Bangladesh Central Bank in 2016.[100] Despite the links to Lazarus, the WannaCry attacks did not bear the typical hallmarks of Nation-State intent but were more typical of a cyber-crime campaign. However, it is also important to note that the Symantec analysis only attributed these attacks to the Lazarus group (or a close affiliate). The technical details did not enable them to attribute the motivations of the attacks to a specific Nation State or individuals. This disparity between technical attribution and the evidential processes required under current legal frameworks is a key focus area for policy-makers.

10.432 In addition, the often blurred lines between Nation States, criminals, political and social activists and terrorists in the physical world are even more difficult to discern in cyber-space. This should not be a surprise – for example, mercenary criminal hackers may be highly organised and professional and will often seek the biggest payday. Whether for financial reward, or political ideology, one source of income may be to become a deniable asset in a nation's intelligence apparatus. This can lead to a mix of espionage work for their country and criminal activity for personal gain, which in turn leads to techniques crossing over from espionage to financial crime. There are also strong similarities between Nation State and criminal

98 www.europol.europa.eu/sites/default/files/documents/iocta2017.pdf, European Union Agency for Law Enforcement Cooperation (Europol), 2017.

99 www.symantec.com/connect/blogs/wannacry-ransomware-attacks-show-strong-links-lazarus-group, Symantec, May 2017.

100 https://foreignpolicy.com/2017/03/21/nsa-official-suggests-north-korea-was-culprit-in-bangladesh-bank-heist/, FP, March 2017.

activities with respect to the assessment of risk and reward. Just as the deniability and removal of geographic constraints makes the cyber battlespace appealing to military forces and intelligence agencies, the low risk and high reward of robbing a bank or its customers through an online connection appeals to criminals.

10.433 ADS companies can see that the challenge they have faced for over 25 years of balancing the appeal of new technology with the opportunities it also provides to threat actors is playing out in multiple sectors. The risks multiply and potentially become more systemic as each sector adopts new highly disruptive and beneficial digital technologies and services. Meanwhile corporations encounter threats whose pace of development is both unpredictable and incredibly difficult for law enforcement to detect, deter and disrupt. These threats are outpacing the ability of corporations of all sizes to forecast or react due to the nature of criminal innovation and low barriers to proliferation. There is an opportunity for ADS companies to deploy their know-how, and help other industries face a bewildering array of threats as they increasingly realise they are both outnumbered and outmatched.

Corporations on the Frontline

10.434 The second technology rationale for ADS companies to move into the commercial cyber-security sector is that it appears several nations are 'preparing the battlespace' in case of future conflict. They are doing this by targeting corporations performing critical functions within a nation's economy and infrastructure, for example banking, energy and utilities and transport. While there is a significant role for governments to play in protecting their commercial sectors, it will be incumbent on these organisations to protect themselves to a greater extent than they have to date. Indeed, as the global attacks on the SWIFT alliance global payments network and the Ukrainian power network in 2015 and 2016 show, with evidence pointing to Nation-State actors, the threat is real. In the latter case, the physical effects should at the very least cause a re-think of the probability and impact elements of the risk assessments conducted by those corporations responsible for critical national infrastructure. Both in terms of the safety and wellbeing of their staff and the critical services they provide a country and its population. These are adversaries that ADS companies have faced for a longer time than most, and so have developed a culture and have designed approaches, platforms and systems that are harder to disrupt and damage.

Example of Proliferation – Stuxnet

10.435 Most, if not all, of those in cyber-security have heard of Stuxnet. Interestingly, so have most in the Defence sector. This is because it is probably the best-known 'real world' example of a cyber-weapon. It is also a good example of the differences presented by cyber-weapons as distinct to Nuclear, Biological and Chemical weapons due to the difficulties in deterring retaliation and stopping proliferation of such a weapon.

10.436 Stuxnet was a computer virus that was uncovered in 2010, after it shut down computers at offices in Iran. A Belarussian security company was notified of the technical problems with their clients in Iran, and discovered that a virus was responsible. They quickly realised that they had a special event on their hands, and it is fair to say that the entire cyber-security industry was astonished at what they found.

10.437 A team of programmers at US cyber-security company Symantec started unravelling the code line-by-line, and found that they were dealing with something which, in their view, had not been seen outside of classified government circles before. Most malware is made quickly and imperfectly, to swipe financial information from people, to hold information to ransom or in some cases to wreak havoc for bragging rights within the hacker community. The average worm is usually a small program that is simple in its execution. Stuxnet was twenty to thirty times larger than the average virus, and written as proficient code. It was James Bond 007 (or perhaps more accurately for film buffs – Q) level sabotage; the level of sophistication and professionalism and costs involved along with the intended target meant the evidence pointed to it having been sponsored by a State.

10.438 Two things that made Stuxnet so unique were its delivery system and the payload. A computer virus has a couple of parallels to a conventional missile. It needs both a delivery system (the rockets that get it to the destination), and it needs the actual warhead, or 'payload'. In this case, rather than a kinetic 'bang', the cyber-payload steals, corrupts, encrypts or destroys data.

Delivery System

10.439 In the Stuxnet virus, the delivery system was a rare exploit called a zero-day vulnerability. A zero-day vulnerability is an undisclosed security vulnerability (in this case in the Windows Operating System, although they can affect systems, browsers, or other programs); they sell for hundreds of thousands of dollars in the black and grey markets, because as soon as they are discovered they can be patched. There are also bounty programmes operated by many of the large computer and developer companies, so if a bug is discovered, the person who sends it to the company can get paid. Not only did Stuxnet use one zero-day, it had four. Just paying for the exploits alone could cost nearly a million dollars on the black market. Clearly this attack was beyond the average teenage hacker sitting in his parents' basement. To blow all four exploits simultaneously was another curious event; clearly wherever the creators wanted to attack, they were willing to pay very high stakes to get there.

Payload

10.440 The second part of a virus after the delivery system, is the payload. In this case, there was another first-time situation. After lots of research and work, researchers discovered that Stuxnet was targeting a very specific set of machines made by Siemens. They are a type of industrial computer called a 'Programmable Logic Controller', or PLC. PLCs are used to control industrial processes, and are used in applications from energy production, to assembly line manufacturing, water purification, and power plants. Further analysis revealed that Stuxnet was specifically targeting PLCs that were in nuclear sites in Iran. The virus was a type of 'logic bomb' and was discovered on millions of machines around the world. It spread itself and then lay dormant until it hit the uranium enrichment facilities in Iran.

10.441 So what happened once it was there? Well, this special piece of software engineering, after establishing it was on the exact machines it needed to be, compromised the controls for the centrifuges to make nuclear material. Stuxnet performed its attack by running the centrifuge rotors at too-low and too high frequencies (as low as 2 Hz and high as 1410 Hz). The periods in which they commanded the centrifuges to spin at these inappropriate speeds were quite short (50 and 15 minutes, respectively), and were separated by about 27 days between attacks, possibly indicating the designers wanted Stuxnet to operate very stealthily over long periods of time. Although the time spans during which the centrifuges were slowed down or sped up were probably too short for them to actually reach the minimum and maximum values, they still resulted in significant slow-downs and speed-ups. The slow speeds were sufficient to result in inefficiently processed uranium, and the high speeds were probably sufficient to result in centrifuges actually being destroyed, as they were at or near the centrifuges' maximum speed limit.

10.442 Stuxnet covered its tracks well so that it was difficult to find it at first. It hid itself from programmers, and spread its attack thin enough so that no one was quite sure what was responsible. However, the four zero day vulnerabilities indicate that a speedier infiltration was required which in turn led to widespread dissemination, and therefore a high likelihood of discovery. And then discovery happened.

10.443 When it was discovered, it was discovered on PLCs all over the world, and the cyber-security industry worked itself into a frenzy as they tried to figure out what it was for. Software engineers have since compared the level of sophistication to an SR-71 doing a flyby on the Wright Brothers at Kitty Hawk. But once it was out there, and known, the theories that made it work were in the hands of the worldwide community.

10.444 Unfortunately, unlike a conventional weapon that destroys itself upon detonation, the entire blueprint of a virus is retained in its full form wherever it goes. Especially when it's made for wide dissemination. So the worldwide cyber-community had a blueprint for a cyber-weapon. And in fact, several of the features have been used in attacks since then. So what are the lessons to be learned?

A new weapon

10.445 Cyber-weapons have similarities to nuclear, biological and chemical weapons: they can affect human populations on a large scale. A city or country can be devastated by sabotage or ransoming of critical systems like the power grid, communications, water systems and transport. But, the difference between a cyber-weapon and nuclear, biological or chemical weapons is that a cyber-weapon is both more deniable and more readily obtained by so-called rogue States and terrorist organisations alike. Admittedly, terrorist organisations are still more likely to go for the 'low tech' approach; after all their main aim tends to be to generate fear and provoke a response that greatly exceeds the actual risk they pose. But tactics change and threat capabilities are evolving; and evidence to date is that industrial systems lag even further behind IT systems in their approaches to security. Stuxnet and subsequent attacks all point to a clear risk that an individual with technical acumen, time and murderous or criminal intent could one day in the near future act with the power of a State. It's coming close to the point where an individual (or handful of individuals) can affect the same amount of people as a conventional weapon, thereby having State-level power with just a laptop and internet connection.

10.446 As we increasingly embed more and more devices in the fabric of our lives through the Internet of Things (IoT), corporations seek increased productivity, safety and efficiency through the same combination of connectivity and actions performed by machines. We are at a tipping point between progress, and an embedded risk caused by a combination of poor security and malicious intent. The solution is increased security, of course, but no one likes to pay more for security, and the security industry has done itself no favours by failing to communicate effectively. The benefits of building security in from the start have been drowned out by the money to be made from penetration testing and vulnerability research. Chief Information Security Officers have been stigmatised as policemen holding up flashing red scorecards filled with unquantifiable vulnerability and risk which only becomes 'real' once the organisation experiences an attack. So security gets left behind. The more our lives and technology intertwine, the more vulnerable we are to this sort of attack.

10.447 PLCs and the IoT are great things, but we need to close the gap as quickly as possible between security and vulnerability, before the worst happens in our own countries. It is fortunate that Stuxnet was so well created and resulted in no collateral damage in its first attacks. Unfortunately, the code is now out there for those with malicious intentions to hone and redeploy. 'This has a whiff of August 1945,' Michael Hayden, former director of the NSA and the CIA, said in a speech.[101] 'Somebody just used a new weapon, and this weapon will not be put back in the box.'

101 www.usnews.com/news/articles/2013/02/20/former-cia-director-cyber-attack-game-changers-comparable-to-hiroshima, US News, February 2013.

Example of Civilian Infrastructure under attack – Ukraine Power Grid

10.449 The US Department of Defense published a technical paper[102] in 2017 on the conflict in Ukraine, in which it analysed the combined threat environment stemming from the use of cyber, electronic warfare and information operations across the conventional, economic, and political sectors of conflict. The report found evidence to substantiate Ukrainian reports indicating the targeting of mobile networks, Wifi, mobile phones and other communications networks within military force structures both during the initial stages of conflict and continuing during current hostilities.

10.440 So far, so typical for a conflict in which one might expect a hybrid of military capabilities to be deployed. However, repeated power outages that have been attributed to cyber-attacks against the energy infrastructure may provide the best evidence that a new wave of Stuxnet-like operations against industrial systems is a cause for more immediate concern. In January 2017 the BBC reported that attacks against the power grid may be part of a cyber-war being waged against Ukraine.[103]

Cyber attack against a transmission station

10.451 According to researchers investigating the incident, the blackout in December 2016, which lasted just over an hour and started just before midnight was connected to similar outages in 2015 attacks, along with a series of hacks on other state institutions.

10.452 The 2016 power cut amounted to a loss of about one-fifth of Kiev's power consumption and left people in part of the city and a surrounding area without electricity. The signs first appeared in Ukrenergo's transmission station north of the city when multiple transmission systems' circuits inexplicably switched to off. The transmission station, normally a vast, buzzing electrical installation stretching over 20 acres, went eerily quiet. The three large transformers, responsible for about a fifth of the capital's electrical capacity, had gone entirely silent. Unlike the 2015 attack which hit distribution stations, this attack was more surgical targeting the transmission 'artery'. Luckily, the system was down for just an hour and Ukrenergo's engineers, used to manual recovery procedures from frequent blackouts, closed the circuits and brought the systems back online.

10.453 Cyber-security firms analysing the attack have concluded that it was far more evolved than the one in 2015: it was executed by a highly sophisticated, adaptable piece of malware now known as CrashOverride, an automated and targeted programme.

102 Defending the Borderland, www.dtic.mil/dtic/tr/fulltext/u2/1046052.pdf, US DoD, December 2017.

103 www.bbc.co.uk/news/technology-38573074, BBC, January 2017.

10.454 Researchers found that during the attack, CrashOverride was able to communicate the specific control system protocols of Ukrenergo's systems, and send commands directly to grid equipment. This meant the software could be programmed to scan the network to map out targets, then launch at a pre-set time, opening circuits on cue without having an internet connection back to the hackers. This bears a striking similarity to Stuxnet's design to independently sabotage physical infrastructure.

Wider concerns

10.455 Worryingly, researchers also claim the malware is reusable and highly adaptable. It has a modular structure, in which Ukrenergo's control system protocols could easily be swapped out and replaced with ones used in other parts of the world. While security in Western energy firms may be more advanced, they are also more automated and modern than those in Ukraine, which means they could present more of a digital attack surface.

10.456 There are conflicting views from security researchers whether this example is evidence of Nation-State actors 'preparing the battlespace' or testing techniques that could be used elsewhere in the world for sabotage. However, they are tangible examples of the 'art of the possible' and should serve as reminders of the threat to Industrial Control Systems and a dark side to the digitisation of our physical world through the Internet of Things.

Example of Criminal Attacks at Scale – SWIFT Payment Network

10.457 In February 2016 an attack against the Bangladesh central bank triggered an alert by payments network SWIFT, after it was found the attackers had used malware to cover up evidence of $1 billion in fraudulent transfers and had successfully stolen $81 million in this spectacularly audacious heist. SWIFT then issued a further warning, saying that it had found evidence of malware being used against another bank in a similar fashion. SWIFT concluded that the second attack indicated that a 'wider and highly adaptive campaign' was underway targeting banks.

10.458 The February 2016 attack was a defining moment for the payments industry. It was not the first case of fraud against a bank's payment endpoint, but the scale and sophistication of the attack shook the global financial community and has led to a global Customer Security Programme to better protect the SWIFT Alliance and its customers. The perpetrators had a detailed knowledge of the business processes involved in payment messaging between banks, leading in part to many early reports focusing on this being an 'inside job'. However, the attackers had also reverse-engineered the specific interface software running in the victim bank. With this knowledge they built custom malware both to aid sending fraudulent messages and to cover-up the evidence to enable their getaway. This was all co-ordinated with military precision, taking advantage of the extended weekend offered by the Friday and Saturday weekend in Bangladesh, and the Chinese New Year public holiday on the Monday celebrated in the destination banks and casinos used to launder the money.

10.459 SWIFT have reported[104] that the attack has also led to a raft of criminal groups ramping up copy-cat style attacks. Software updates were released to mitigate specific attack vectors – such as improved integrity checks to hamper the attackers' ability to modify the software and database. However, the attackers continue their reverse-engineering efforts and update their malware too. This game of security measure, countermeasure and counter-countermeasure has developed through successive attacks. In all significant cases, security weaknesses in the compromised banks have led to the attackers gaining Administrator access to their payment environments. With this they could not only monitor the victim banks' operations undetected over extended periods, but they could also modify victims' security defences and the operation of their software to enable their attacks – updating firewall rules, and bypassing security features in the interface software.

10.460 Since then, the attacks have continued to evolve with attackers adopting techniques one might have previously only expected from those adept in sophisticated espionage operations. The use of these techniques has been mastered through successive attacks, leading to a range of advanced toolkits and techniques and many security researchers expect the sophistication to continue to rise. Some of these techniques are described below.

Protection

10.461 Developers of commercial software are often required to protect the intellectual property contained in the software that they have built. To prevent their software from being analysed they sometimes rely on commercial software protectors. Cyber-attackers also want to protect their malware, and they choose the same commercial protection software – protection that is notoriously difficult to break.

Stealthiness

10.462 Attackers often need time to search and gain additional access privileges with their targets' environments without being detected, and therefore need to be stealthy in their operations. Malware has been seen using file less modules that were loaded into memory from the registry. Alternatively, when files were written to the hard drive, they have been encrypted and camouflaged in order to blend with other legitimate system files. As a result, the Administrators of

104 The Evolving Cyber Threat to the Banking Community, SWIFT and BAE Systems, November 2017.

systems were unable to distinguish the malicious components from the parts of the operating system.

Wipe-Out Techniques

10.463 The attackers have used a number of effective anti-forensic techniques to reliably erase all traces of their own activity making retracing and understanding their actions difficult. While this can make detection and response difficult, it also has the effect of making it extremely problematic for investigators when they examine the crime scene.

Hijacking

10.464 The attackers have been discovered attempting to hijack legitimate software in order to manipulate its logic. One malicious module recovered from a crime scene was programmed to always return 'success' result, even if the software attempted to throw an alert.

10.465 Hijacking system calls allow the attackers to monitor data in transit. Additionally, intercepted data can also be changed, so that the end parties receive modified information without even knowing that the data has been changed.

Surveillance

10.466 The attackers have deployed malicious modules that take screen shots (frames) along with the typed keystrokes. The intercepted frames are encoded in a way that resembles a video format, potentially allowing them to be reassembled into viewable recordings. The reconstructed surveillance videos can then be watched by a group of attackers, with an ability to stop, rewind, take notes, questioning every step taken by an administrator in order to fully understand how the system works before an attempt is made to subvert it.

10.467 Fully understanding the legitimate business process is not a quick task, in some cases the attackers spent more than a year studying the process. However, attackers do not always have the best operational security processes themselves and one SWIFT report tells of a group which left the recording running while they interacted with the system, thereby capturing their own activity.

False Flags

10.468 As has become popular parlance with stories of 'fake news' and election hacking, attackers have been discovered placing fictitious evidence into their malware code as false flags. Among these 'false flags' are diversionary language codes and various incorrectly transliterated words to mislead research into the true identity of the attackers.

Anonymity

10.469 In order to hide their tracks, the attackers set up a number of the 'hops' or proxies between themselves and the end target, making a long chain for investigators to trace in order to understand what is going on. This is similar in concept to controlling a puppet via another puppet. At any given moment, this keeps the attackers out of direct line of sight. If the number of such 'puppets' is large, such as more than three, it may be very difficult to establish who the real mastermind is behind the attack.

Watering Holes

10.470 In order to target the victims, the attackers do not need to target them directly. Instead, they 'bait' a legitimate website first. BAE Systems reported in 2017[105] that there had been a series of watering hole attacks on bank supervisor websites in Poland and Mexico, and a State-owned bank in Uruguay. These leverage exploits in commonly used website programmes to deliver malware. The exploits lie in wait for victims to visit that website. If the visitor is of interest, say a bank employee, then the malware attempts to infect the machine of that victim.

Exploits

10.471 The attackers are constantly searching for weaknesses in the 'defence in depth' most financial institutions have at least begun to adopt. Once they find a weakness, they penetrate the system, compromising nodes one after another. This creates a classic asymmetric situation familiar to those used to anti-terrorism operations, where the attacker only needs to find one weakness to get in, but the defender needs to fix all holes to be secure.

10.472 The attack against the Bank of Bangladesh reads like a Hollywood blockbuster. Ocean's 11-style, the Lazarus group plotted for over a year the perfect time to complete their attack: a weekend when the casinos would be full. Rather than a big money fight, it was Chinese New Year; rather than $160 million it was $1 billion. It seems, Hollywood for once, just didn't think big enough.

10.473 SWIFT has repeatedly emphasised that it was the banks' connection points to its network (and internal bank system interfaces) that attackers have been able to breach. And SWIFT's chief executive, Gottfried Leibbrandt was reported by the *New York Times* as saying that the recent attacks could do far more damage than breaches on retailers and telephone companies, which largely suffer loss of reputation and legal hits.

> 'Banks that are compromised like this can be put out of business.'[106]

105 http://baesystemsai.blogspot.com.es/2017/02/lazarus-watering-hole-attacks.html, BAE Systems, February 2017.

106 www.nytimes.com/2016/05/27/business/dealbook/north-korea-linked-to-digital-thefts-from-global-banks.html?_r=0, *New York Times*, May 2016.

SWIFT concluded their 2017 update report with the following statement:

> 'While each individual customer has to be responsible for its own security, a community-based approach is the best way to solve the security issues facing the industry.... The security of the community requires everyone's participation – starting with each individual participant's own security.'

Performance of the ADS Sector in Cyber Security

10.474 The combination of threat to their own systems, and opportunity to expand into commercial sectors, has led to a string of strategic acquisitions and investments by the top global Defence and Security players. To what extent have Defence contractors taken advantage of their experiences and insight and have they succeeded in their existing and new cyber security markets?

Lockheed Martin

10.475

Leadership: Marillyn Hewson, Chairman, President and CEO

2016 Defence Revenue (in billions):	$43.5[107]
2016 Total Revenue (in billions):	$47.2

Background

10.476 Lockheed Martin is the leading global Defence and Security contractor by revenues – albeit behind Boeing and Airbus in overall revenues when their commercial airliner businesses are included.

A quote from their website states: 'Cyber is ingrained in all aspects of the modern battlespace, and our Cyber Solutions team has the expertise to help defend and exploit enterprise IT networks, radio-frequency spectrums, and military platforms on land, sea and air.'[108]

Key Acquisitions

10.477

2013 – acquired Amor Group, a UK-based company specialising in information technology, civil government services, and the energy market.

107 Figures for Lockheed Martin and subsequent companies have been derived from multiple sources and should be considered estimates rather than reported earnings.

108 www.lockheedmartin.com/us/what-we-do/aerospace-defense/cyber.html, February 2018.

2014 – acquired Industrial Defender, a provider of cyber-security solutions for control systems in the oil and gas, utility and chemical industries.

Current commercial market status

10.478 Lockheed Martin announced in 2016 that it was withdrawing from the commercial cyber-security market. It had previously raised the prospect of selling or spinning off its roughly $4 billion government information technology business since early in 2015, including its cyber-security unit.

Lockheed Martin's Vice President for corporation communications was quoted by Forbes as saying: 'The cyber programs that will remain with the company are mostly focused on defence and intelligence customers and will be realigned into the corporation's other four business segments.'

> 'The main factors driving the spin-off or sale of our IT and technical services businesses (which include cyber security) are changing market dynamics, shifting government priorities, increased competition and industry trends that have led us to believe that these businesses may achieve greater growth, and create more value for our customers by operating outside of Lockheed Martin.'[109]

Boeing

10.479

Leadership: Dennis Muilenburg, President and CEO

2016 Defence Revenue (in billions):	$29.5
2016 Total Revenue (in billions):	$94.6

Background

10.490 Since 2015 Boeing's cyber-security and information management offerings have focused almost exclusively on their US Department of Defence and intelligence community customers. The company's offerings are slated as critical infrastructure protection network surveillance and data analytics, information security, mission assurance, and information operations capabilities. Internationally their website[110] cites success stories in Japan, UAE, Italy and Singapore.

109 www.forbes.com/sites/stevemorgan/2015/12/04/lockheed-martin-corp-to-exit-cybersecurity-double-down-on-helicopters-and-combat-jets/#4186de2710db, December 2015.

110 www.boeing.com/defense/cybersecurity-information-management/.

Key Acquisitions

10.481

2009 – acquired eXMeritus, a technology designed to connect systems at different levels of classification.

2010 – acquired Narus, which provided security, intercept and traffic management software solutions to protect and manage internet protocol networks.

Current commercial market status

10.482 Boeing exited the commercial cyber-security market in 2015, according to a story in *The Wall Street Journal*[111] which reported that Symantec was acquiring staff and technology licenses from Boeing's Narus subsidiary. Boeing apparently hoped to use Narus's internet-filtering technology to win commercial deals.

'That just didn't materialise the way we thought it was going to,' a Boeing vice president and general manager of their Electronic & Information Solutions division was quoted at the time.

BAE Systems

10.483

Leadership: Charles Woodburn, CEO

2016 Defence Revenue (in billions):	£14.5
2016 Total Revenue (in billions):	£19.0

Background

10.484 BAE Systems has sought to position itself as a Defence and Security company taking the techniques, analytics and intelligence used to defend nations to the commercial arena. They describe bringing experience at military-class levels to the protection of corporate assets, calling it 'business defence.'

Following their acquisition of Detica in 2008 they lay claim to helping to defend nations and businesses in the world for over forty years against a wide range threats. Their heritage in National Security, helping collect and analyse vast quantities of data combined with their cyber security managed services portfolio and financial crime software used by many of the world's largest banks for anti-money laundering and combatting fraud provides a combination of government and commercial capabilities.

111 www.wsj.com/articles/boeing-to-exit-commercial-cybersecurity-business-1421085602, *Wall Street Journal*, January 2015.

Key Acquisitions

10.485

2008 – acquired Detica, a consulting, software and electronic solutions business providing intelligence and analytical systems for commercial and government bodies. The majority of its sales were to the security industry, primarily in Britain but with a growing presence in the US.

2010 – acquired Stratsec, an information security consulting and testing firm in Australia.

2010 – acquired ETI, an intelligence company providing advanced technology products and services to government clients worldwide.

2010 – acquired Norkom Technologies which delivered software to combat fraud, money laundering, and other types of financial crime, used in many of the world's largest financial institutions.

2014 – acquired Silversky providing cloud-based security solutions including email and network security managed services to mainly US customers.

Current commercial cyber security status

10.486 BAE Systems has claimed some notable successes in the commercial cyber-security sector, in particular with some strong online brand sentiment following blog content with it findings on the Bangladesh central bank cyber-attack in 2016. Moreover, the company received extensive positive coverage from international media sources emphasising how its cyber-security solutions safeguard the global financial system.

Raytheon

10.487

Leadership: Thomas Kennedy, Chairman and CEO

2016 Defence Revenue (in billions):	$22.4
2016 Total Revenue (in billions):	$24.1

Background

10.488 In a similar fashion to BAE Systems, Raytheon positions itself as bringing military-level capabilities to the commercial arena. They claim an ability 'to build the most advanced cyber defences into operational systems to safeguard what matters most. From hardening defence systems against intruders to protecting critical infrastructure and data, we offer the most effective shields against cyber threats.'[112]

112 www.raytheon.com/cyber/, Raytheon, February 2018.

Key Acquisitions

10.489

2007 – Oakley Networks, a security services company that specialised in threat detection and prevention.

2008 – SI Government Solutions, delivering vulnerability assessment capabilities that protect complex and critical information technology assets of government customers

2008 – Telemus Solutions, a provider of information security, intelligence and technical services to defence, intelligence and other federal customers.

2009 – BBN Technologies, an R&D company with expertise spanning information security, speech and language processing, networking, distributed systems, and sensing and control systems.

2010 – Trusted Computer Solutions developing cross-domain solutions for secure access and transfer of data and information

2011 – Pikewerks Corporation, research, development, training, and consulting of a range of information security solutions.

2013 – Visual Analytics providing information sharing and visual data mining products.

2015 – Foreground Security providing security engineering, assessment, customised security training, and advanced incident response and forensics services.

2015 – Forcepoint providing a unified, cloud-centric platform that safeguards users, networks and data.

Current commercial cyber security status

10.490 In May 2015 Raytheon Company and Vista Equity Partners completed a joint venture to create a new company that combined Websense, a Vista Equity portfolio company, and Raytheon Cyber Products, a product line of Raytheon's Intelligence, Information and Services business. This new company was later renamed Forcepoint. The aim of this was to carve out its cyber security products and relocate them in a new business rather than continuing as a unit inside of Raytheon. It serves as evidence that Raytheon perceived a struggle to execute in the commercial cyber-security market.

More recent communications have focused around regional partnerships and sponsorships emphasising their alignment with governments' objectives and general notions of global safety, especially in the Middle East which is often at the centre of the global security discussion.

Northrup Grumman

10.491

Leadership: Wes Bush, Chairman, President and CEO

2016 Defence Revenue (in billions):	$20.2
2016 Total Revenue (in billions):	$24.5

Background

10.492 Northrop Grumman is positioned as a provider of military cyber-security solutions. Listed competencies include cyber-mission management; large scale cyber-solutions for national security applications; advanced defence and security services including cyber, network operations and security; analysis of network traffic, identification of malicious and unauthorised activity, and response to intrusion incidents.

Key Acquisitions

10.493

2012 – M5 Network Security Pty an Australian company providing cyber security services to military, government and large corporations.

Current commercial cyber security status

10.494 Northrop Grumman created a new business unit in 2015 Acuity Solutions – to pursue the commercial cyber-security market. Acuity pitches its flagship product, The BlueVector Cyber Intelligence Platform, on its own website. The BlueVector homepage cites research around the amount of money large corporations spend to combat cyber breaches, and related figures. Like Raytheon, it seems that Northrop has decided that the challenges around its brand competing in the commercial cyber security market are too great and have decided that a separate entity and brand building approach is required.

General Dynamics

10.495

Leadership: Phebe Novakovic, Chairman and CEO

2016 Defence Revenue (in billions):	$19.7
2016 Total Revenue (in billions):	$31.4

Background

10.496 Cyber-security falls under the remit of General Dynamics IT which in turn targets solutions at the US federal market.

Key Acquisitions

10.497

2012 – Fidelis focusing on automated threat detection and response and improvements in the effectiveness and efficiency of security operations.

Current commercial cyber security status

10.498 General Dynamics sold off its Fidelis cyber-security business in 2015 to US private equity firm Marlin Equity Partners. A GD spokesperson was quoted at the time as saying that Fidelis 'serves a commercial customer base, not in our core, and is better served with a commercially focused owner.' General Dynamics, for its part, 'will continue to focus on our comprehensive and robust cyber business, serving the US intelligence community; Department of Defence; Department of Homeland Security; and federal/civilian and law enforcement agencies.'

Thales

10.499

Leadership: Patrice Caine, Chairman and CEO

2016 Defence Revenue (in billions):	€7.4
2016 Total Revenue (in billions):	€14.9

Background

10.500 Thales have a strong international reputation in cryptographic security products and work across multiple sectors including government and military infrastructures, satellite networks, energy and utilities, banking and insurance, technology and transportation. They claim 19 of the 20 largest global banks, 4 of the 5 largest oil companies and 27 NATO country members as customers.

Key Acquisitions

10.501

2017 – Gemalto a digital security company, offers mobile connectivity, payment technology and data protection solutions to manage services.

Current commercial cyber security status

10.502 Thales has rebranded Gemalto as Thales e-Security providing 'everything an organization needs to protect and manage its data, identities and intellectual property and meet regulatory compliance – through encryption, advanced key management, tokenization, privileged user control and meeting the highest standards of certification for high assurance solutions.'

BT

10.503

Leadership: Gavin Patterson CEO

2016 Defence Revenue (in billions):	Not reported
2016 Total Revenue (in billions):	£24.1

Background

10.504 BT are included in this chapter due to their strategic position providing the 'backbone' infrastructure in the UK and as a strategically important information infrastructure provider to the UK government and Armed Forces. BT's origins date back to the establishment of the first telecommunications companies in Britain.

BT's website states: 'We help our Defence customers achieve information superiority, at home, on the move, and on the front line by securely getting the right information to the right place at the right time.'

Key Acquisitions

None to note.

Current commercial cyber security status

10.505 Better known publicly as a provider of phone and TV packages, BT, as with many multi-national telecoms companies, also addresses a very wide range of consumer, business and governmental security needs. It markets an ability to deliver simple antivirus products through to complex managed security solutions used by multinational companies and governments.

Cyber-security is still a relatively small segment of the BT Group in terms of revenue but it is listed as one of six core offerings for its range of customers and BT has regularly expressed its plans to expand this sector.

Notable cyber security events in the ADS sector

Lockheed Martin

10.506 In 2009, a number of publications including the US *Wall Street Journal*, UK *Guardian* and Germany's Der *Spiegel* reported on a tranche of documents provided by the former US National Security Agency contractor, Edward Snowden. The documents supported claims made in 2007 that hackers had been able to breach Defence contractor cyber-defences and steal data on Lockheed Martin's F-35 Lightning II joint strike fighter jet including data on the plane's design and electronics systems.

10.507 In 2011, Lockheed Martin published the best known product in their cyber-security portfolio – the company's Cyber Kill Chain framework.[113] The Cyber Kill Chain forms part of the approach they and subsequently many others use for the identification and prevention of cyber intrusions and by providing a means to understand and describe an adversary's tactics, techniques and procedures.

Also in 2011, the firm confirmed reports of a 'significant and tenacious attack' which was linked to an earlier breach at security firm RSA.

Boeing

10.508 In July 2016, a Chinese national who conspired to hack into US defence contractors' systems was sentenced to forty-six months in a federal prison.[114] The criminal complaint filed in June 2014 was that three Chinese nationals broke into the computers of Boeing and other military contractors, stealing trade secrets on transport aircraft. The criminal complaint describes in some detail how the alleged conspirators patiently observed Boeing and its computer network for a year, and then breached the contractor's systems to steal intellectual property on the C-17 military transport. It also cast light on the free-enterprise nature of the espionage, as the co-conspirators allegedly exchanged e-mails about profiting from their enterprise.

BAE Systems

10.509 BAE Systems is sub-contractor to Lockheed Martin on the US F-35 programme. While the hacks against Lockheed Martin made headlines, a hack against BAE Systems' components of the programme only surfaced in the press in 2012 when it was allegedly disclosed by a senior BAE executive during a private dinner in London for cyber-security experts in 2011.

113 Lockheed-Martin Corporation: Hutchins, Cloppert, and Amin, Intelligence-Driven Computer Network Defense Informed by Analysis of Adversary Campaigns and Intrusion Kill Chains, 2011.

114 www.justice.gov/opa/pr/chinese-national-who-conspired-hack-us-defense-contractors-systems-sentenced-46-months, US Department of Justice, July 2016.

10.510 In 2014 US media corporation CNBC reported a claim from BAE Systems that hackers had penetrated a large hedge fund in order to slow their high-speed trading strategy and send details of the trades outside the firm[115]. BAE Systems Applied Intelligence Global Product Director was interviewed on CNBC saying that it was the first time they had seen someone design a piece of software that was explicitly designed to attack an order-entry trading system. However, it became clear two weeks later that the attack was an illustrative example inaccurately presented by BAE Systems as a client case study. This was an embarrassing mistake for BAE Systems, particularly on such a public stage; protecting reputation and trust are key business objectives which security firms are seeking to deliver for their clients.

BT

10.511 In 2003, BT notified the UK government of Chinese electronics firm Huawei's interest in a £10 billion network upgrade contract. There has been public criticism levelled at BT that they did not satisfactorily raise the security implications and/or failed to explain the full extent of the Chinese company's access to critical infrastructure.

10.512 In 2012, the UK's '*The Independent*' newspaper reported that the UK's signals intelligence centre at GCHQ in Cheltenham had a technical laboratory which had been vetting and monitoring new Huawei equipment for over two years.[116]

10.513 In 2012, ZTE, another Chinese company that supplies extensive network equipment and subscriber hardware to BT 'Infinity', was also scrutinised by Parliament's Intelligence and Security Committee after the US, Canada, Australia and the EU declared the company a security risk.[117]

10.514 On 7 June 2013, the UK's Intelligence and Security Committee concluded that BT should not have allowed Huawei access to the UK's communications network without ministerial oversight,[118] saying they were 'deeply shocked' that BT did not inform government that they were allowing Huawei and ZTE, both with ties to the Chinese military, unfettered access to critical national systems. Subsequently, the committee reported that in case of an attack on the UK there was nothing that could be done to stop Chinese infiltration.

115 www.cnbc.com/2014/06/19/cybersecurity-firm-says-large-hedge-fund-attacked.html, CNBC, June 2014.

116 www.independent.co.uk/news/uk/politics/china-telecoms-giant-could-be-cyber-security-risk-to-britain-8420432.html, December 2012.

117 https://uk.reuters.com/article/uk-eu-china-telecoms/eu-report-urges-action-against-chinese-telecom-firms-idUKBRE8BB18420121212, December 2012.

118 Foreign involvement in the Critical National Infrastructure – The implications for national security, Intelligence and Security Committee, June 2013.

Cyber Security in non-Government sectors: Missed Opportunity?

10.515 While many of these ADS giants have claimed notable successes in their traditional markets, their track record in commercial sectors is not one of awesome success. It was perhaps to be expected that it would take time for the evidence to build that the threat was overwhelming the capabilities of traditional IT security providers. And it may take even longer for changes to be adopted by big business, however, the consensus among the large defence primes appears to be that either their brands do not translate well in commercial sectors or their capabilities are not suitable for the blue chip companies they were targeting. Most have taken actions to cut their losses and focus their efforts on more traditional markets.

10.516 In analysing the reasons for this, one clue may lie in the comfort and attraction of cyber-security in the US federal sector. With a market valued at $65.5 billion (2015–2020), the US Federal Cyber security market will grow steadily at about 6.2% CAGR, according to a report from Market Research Media. The report states 'the annual cyber security spending of the US Federal government is bigger than any national cyber security market, exceeding at least twofold the largest cyber security spending countries.'

10.517 However, at the root of this consensus (at least among US Defence prime contractors), there appears to be a more systemic failure to make the case to fund the requirement to build defences against more advanced threat actors in commercial sectors. While these threats have been widely publicised and governments and security specialists have been vocal in urging more action for nearly a decade, these recommendations have not translated into the levels of funding in the commercial sector that either may have hoped for. Among the corporations that deliver the critical functions that modern economies depend on, many appear to be falling short or are already victims of attacks (in public or in private). As with most system failures, there are likely to be multiple causes. These could include:

1. Governments failing to develop legal and regulatory frameworks that reflect the pace of digital change and match the scale, efficiency and resourcefulness of cyber-threats.

2. Governments being slow to pass legislation that promotes threat awareness for example compelling corporations to improve detection and share information.

3. Security specialists failing to make the case for better security in a way that goes beyond awareness and changes the behaviours of both business leaders and those engineering new technologies.

4. Security specialists prioritising and even glamorising hacking, testing and finding interesting exploits at the expense of helping developers design better security from the outset and helping to engineer better defences.

5. Security vendors undermining their case through exaggerated claims of effectiveness for technical solutions and falling victim themselves to attack.

6. Corporations sticking to risk management approaches that may have served them well in the past but are not sufficient now; particularly in a more directly adversarial threat environment created by greater connectivity and the Internet of Things.

7. Corporations miscalculating the human and engineering challenge and failing to prioritise security within the complex struggle of balancing advantages and costs of new technology.

10.518 After a year which recorded the most expensive cyber-attacks ever reported in WannaCry and NotPetya and as new attacks emerged on SWIFT payment systems worldwide, all eyes have again turned to the commercial cyber security community to markedly improve. It would be a missed opportunity on all sides if the ADS industry did not play a leading role in developing the solution.

10G BANKING IN THE EMIRATES – THE NBD WAY

'The Journey towards a better and healthier Information Security posture'

Yazad Khandhadia

10.519 We began our cyber security very slowly, akin to taking baby steps, in the year 2012. The vision started from there, and after almost six years of our existence, we have had so many valuable learnings and lessons, that we, as individuals have grown beyond imagination and have tried to make information security bigger than the sum of its parts. The brainchild behind this journey, started with selecting the right mix of team members, and maybe it was fate, but somehow it was meant to be, that all of us have this 'telepathic vision' of how our information security should look and feel like. And we realised, time and again, that it's 'The Team' that becomes the catalyst for better security; it's always the 'People' that are the most important.

10.520 So when we formulated this vision, we knew that all 3 components – People, Process and Technology would play a role but somehow we knew deep down that if passionate people who don't 'Eat, Sleep & Dream' security would not join us, we would not be as successful. And here is the short story of how we went about bringing in, what we think, is a change that was and still is better for the organisation that is so forward thinking, innovative and solid, all at once.

The People: Building a solid team

10.521 The key to building a successful information security team is like choosing the right mix of ingredients that complement each other, when one creates wholesome food. First, we need 'The Techie' – master of technology and deep knowledge of its security. Due to late nights spent on prior jobs and a thirst for learning, that exists even today, this individual's exposure to technology is so varied, that its breadth is commendable; and not just that – so is its depth. There is a very common saying in information security circles – 'The God is in the Details' – and it is absolutely 'spot-on'. 'The Techie' role loves details, and they know every parameter inside a technology standard, are passionate about how tech works and find ways to defend it and break it. Their analytical ability is also superior to most, and that is why are often labelled 'Chief Troubleshooting Officers (CTO)'. It is vital that someone can conduct containment, response and remediation with a calm mind and then come back and do a root cause analysis and 'The Techie/CTO' is just that. So in essence, one techie who is the 'go-to' individual for all technical solution help is a mandatory inclusion in a team.

10.522 Next in line, is the role of the 'The Executioner' – pun intended. They are individuals who run the program and ensure its completion. When you have challenges with processes and with people, you approach The Executioner. They have the ability to make a case, convince stakeholders, push hard, follow up, and then get it done. They are also very good at social skills and maintain very good relationships. This is another key team member required for any team. Executioners are also masters at budgeting and planning, so it would be prudent to let them create the first draft of how the information security budget will be requested (business case) and then spent.

10.523 With any information security function, there is always a need to ensure structure, to bring the team back in line with the required direction and the need to build and plan a program. 'The Processor' is just that person; they are individuals who bring structure, plan well in advance, see roadblocks earlier than others, and remind the team that there is a direction that needs to be followed. They are also policy guides and security architects who like to build frameworks, designs and programs – something very fundamentally important for structure. In its literal sense, the role of 'The Processor' is like a CPU in a computer, ensuring, via process, organisation and direction, that everything is flowing smoothly between all the roles in the team.

10.524 Finally, 'The Visionaries' enter the scene; they are master delegators who have one primary skill and ability – they have the knack of choosing the right mix of people for the team, trusting them, giving them autonomy and eventually, honing their skills and capabilities to become future visionaries. Visionaries often provide that '1%' outside view of a scenario that no other team member has thought of and that is why they are brilliant at playing 'Devils Advocate'. They teach team members how to think differently, how to empathise with stakeholders, how to stretch and persist beyond their own comfort zones and how to build confidence to build future teams.

10.525 All examples above are characteristics that the Cyber Security team at Emirates NBD was very fortunate to have, and the reason why we gelled so well as a team is because we learnt qualities, skills and capabilities that we did not have, from others who did. One very important learning during our people journey was that no matter how many information security certifications someone had, it was never more valuable than other very simple attributes like positive attitude, analytical ability, persistence, common sense and most importantly, passion. We always selected people based on scenario-based interviews to gauge many different aspects of how they fit the information security culture that we wanted to build and promote. The ability to handle pressure, to respond to stakeholders, to maintain relationships, and to communicate security risks effectively play an extremely important role in how cyber security is viewed from the outside by stakeholders. In today's world, people label this 'expectation management' or sometimes 'perception management'. All cyber security team members have to be technically good at security concepts, but one lesson we also learnt, is that concepts can be learnt and honed over time if you have all the other important ingredients. At the time when this team was setup, most members were not from cyber security backgrounds but what they had was this 'thirst for knowledge and this passion for everything cyber security', that we all recognised and promoted via methods like Coaching, Mentoring and the like.

10.526 A vital element that needs to be considered when talking about people is the concept of 'augmented resources'. When the team was stretched and we needed help, we sought it from cyber security companies that provide specialised resources. The key learning here is that when we treated cyber security companies like 'partners' and not just 'vendors', we realised larger benefits. We were able to convince them to become flexible in their approach, agree to more 'fixed bid' style delivery-based engagements (rather than 'Time & Material' – which have the potential of becoming very rigid) and also be reasonable with their pricing. The UAE cyber security services market, at the time, was not very large – it was big on cyber security products – but not as much on services – and feedback from customers on the performance of cyber security companies was always discussed in networking circles. It hence became extremely important that cyber security companies perform well, meet their commitments and be more flexible. We, as Emirates NBD, received queries many a time, from our cyber security counterparts, on specific companies we were using and how they performed, and it was always a contributing factor to that company being selected for future engagements with other banks. A lot of times we gave such feedback based on our collaborative 'team gut feel' and it usually turned out to be the right feedback. It's important to feel a 'good vibe' from a business partner; is makes things easier in the long run.

10.527 We also believed that 'honest feedback' on cyber security companies was important, without any gloss added on their performance. It's a fair deal because cyber security companies that do not perform well or typically are less flexible, are not healthy for the market and country in general. It's also important that such companies who wish to venture into this space in the UAE, understand its culture, way of working, and processes and respect them to the fullest in order to be successful in the long run.

10.528 Another thing we have learnt and experienced is how some cyber security companies always want to present their latest solutions to us and how we, as Emirates NBD, always practiced caution at such times. Our philosophy has been and will always be 'We want to see it working in our environment! Period!'; no matter who or what is being presented, this is a rule of thumb that we feel, worked best for us.

10.529 In essence, Cyber Security companies are deeply embedded within the ecosystem of the UAE and are a large contributing factor that influence the quality of products and services they provide to organisations in the UAE and hence has an indirect impact on their security posture. I say 'indirect' because, usually prudent and mature organisations assess the capabilities of such companies before they enter into long term engagements with them, and hence 'direct' impacts are considerably mitigated.

10.530 Cyber Security services and product contracts and their details are pivotal to ensuring that impacts to all parties are reduced. Basic hygiene like 'background checks' on employees, confidentiality of data, non-disclosure and assurance of malware free products are some of the important questions that should be asked of any cyber security vendor selling products or services. At Emirates NBD, as we operate in multiple geographies, this required collaboration from Cyber Security with other important internal stakeholders to ensure that we included required clauses into contracts to ensure compliance with laws in respective geographies.

The Process: Building a program

10.531 Cyber Security program management really boils down to figuring out what you currently have that can leverage gaps and how much more you need to fill those gaps in a cost effective manner. The first thing that we did when we began this journey, was a quick Cyber Security Maturity Assessment. We really were not into fancy numbers with respect to maturity (eg, CMMI Level 2 vs. Level 3) and although that was important from the perspective of measurement, more important were the conversations we had with various stakeholders and industry experts and asking the question 'what can we do better to improve maturity' or 'what are other organisations doing that we can learn from'. This is an important consideration because if controls are not effectively implemented and managed in a cost-effective manner, organisations end up being labelled 'box buyers'; you heard me right – 'box buyers'.

10.532 Within our Cyber Security program, we made a conscious decision to not just go out and buy 'the latest thing in the market' that will meet the requirement. Oh no Sir! We always endeavoured to re-use and leverage any existing security technology we had.

10.533 Post our maturity assessment, it finally came down to building the 'Big Picture View' and that is what we did as a team. We laid down all the building blocks we required to build, run, and sustain a futuristic Cyber Security Program and then joined those pieces together harmoniously – just like building Lego.

10.534 As is very obvious, Cyber Security professionals should understand that areas that are Red require the most priority while those in Amber, were important but could wait another budgeting cycle in order to be completed.

10.535 Cost effective Cyber Security Program Management, was, in our experience, all about common sense and financial prudence[119] – spend the money on the most important things and leave the rest for later. In fact, what we felt was, that if we managed the organisation's money using our own personal financial prudence habits, we could relate to it and plan much better for future expenses, we think might occur. Budgeting cycles were hence always very busy, but prior planning on which piece of the puzzle to always tackle first, made it relatively less difficult to assign a budget item to.

10.536 So – now that we have built the team and created the program, it was time for us to execute. When that time came, we again had a new realisation – 'Preventative controls' around various industries were being broken more often and hence, 'Detective Controls' were now being given more importance and relevance. After attending various short talks and conferences, along with some interesting webinars (in the wee hours post midnight), we started hearing the phrase 'Assumed Breach' and because we always kept our ears on the ground listening for something like a 'Threat Pulse' we knew we had to change our strategy, process and program often.

10.537 With the advent of 'Assumed Breach' – which basically means 'assume the attacker is already in the environment, lying low and watching your every move', we started marking Detective Controls as our 'Red Boxes' – the ones we needed to prioritise and spend money on to strengthen that control. There are many different ways to do this, but the most basic tenet is getting a mix of people, process and technology that enable some kind of monitoring in the environment. Some very simple use cases come to mind:

- Look at alerts from Workstation (Desktop) and Server protection technologies (eg, Anti-Virus, Host Intrusion Prevention/Detection, Application Whitelisting, Certain kinds of Native Logging, etc).
- Examine alerts on Privileged Access.
- Monitor traffic coming in and going out through infrastructure that enable Email and Internet Access for employees and systems.

10.538 Such basic hygiene practices went a long way in setting up our initial baselines of what we wanted to see and how we wanted to advance our monitoring for the future.

119 It would be of importance to note here, hence, that if an individual is planning a career path to become a Chief Information Security Officer (CISO) or Cyber Security Head, skills such as budgeting, financial planning and program management are key for success along with the mix of technical expertise and other skills.

10.539 When we realised that detection was becoming a key indicator of our strategy, we decided to create a dedicated unit only for it, and we then ensured that all Cyber Security architecture and design decisions always included a detection capability check before a system went live. This is basically what we call 'a holistic process' and we believed so strongly in 'the Big Picture' that we knew we had to always look at every business requirement, every architecture and design document, and every likelihood and impact or Risk, holistically.

10.540 As a team, we did not want to socialise this concept of 'stage gates' so explicitly in the entire process of security systems, so we kind of baked it into every stage of our portfolio (business demand) execution process. We baked it into business requirement documents, high-level design, low-level design, functional specifications, development, testing, Change Approval Boards (CAB) and eventually pre-production – that penultimate step before any solution that met business demand that went live.[120]

10.541 Stage gating is an important part of Cyber Security culture, but if stage gating makes Cyber Security look like a 'blocker' it is not helping its image. Cyber Security units have to become 'enablers' – cut the red tape, make the process easier for other units and show 'empathy'. We did that – in fact we did all of that and we taught newcomers in our team to do just that. We had to promote and build a collaborative culture where 'email exchange is minimised' and 'face to face interactions to understand problems and work out solutions are preferred'. That said, basic security principles should never be flouted and there is no compromise on that front; especially if compromises of any sort have the potential to impact regulatory requirements or cause critical/ high risk.

10.542 Coming back to our process, we learnt some very important lessons;

- Cyber Security Strategies cannot last the normal '3-5 Year Plans' that other typical business strategies are made up of. There is so much 'flux' in this domain and the 'rate of threat change' is so high, that it's best that a strategy be created for an 18-month period; we did just that. 18 months is a long time in Cyber Security because attacks are evolving so quickly, that 3-5 year strategies will become obsolete. All decisions we made, were always based on an 18-month plan, and there is widespread evidence to support this. If we do a simple Google search on the 'evolution of malware', for instance, we will see results that point us to how malware has evolved from 'viruses to worms to sandbox detection malware to file less malware' in just a few years! And now with the advent of 'machine learning' and 'Artificial Intelligence' there are new trends in Cyber Security that are taking centre stage. Primary among them is 'Security Data Science' which is the advent of ingesting data and making intelligent decisions based on them.

120 I personally really enjoyed doing all of this. It made me, as a Cyber Security professional, realise that this what 'application' of 'knowledge' really means. We study Preventative, Detective and Corrective controls as part of theoretical curriculum within books, but there is no better form of fulfilment when you sit down and actually apply these concepts within an organisation.

- Agility is key to making Cyber Security popular. Business & Technology units are under immense pressure to deliver and in an organisation like Emirates NBD where innovation is our primary differentiator, things move fast: really fast! We were clocking in a huge amount of business and IT portfolio initiatives year on year because we wanted to excel, be first-to-market and stand out. It is hence vital, that internal Cyber Security teams understand how the business wants to function, what is their revenue generation plan is, how they want to gain a competitive advantage, why they are pushing so hard, and why technology stakeholders like Project Managers, Solution Architects and others are also being pushed beyond their boundaries. When we put ourselves in the shoes of our stakeholders, we truly begun to understand their challenges and that is when we decided, that as Cyber Security we needed to be very Agile. The phrase 'Adapt or Die' is very true in Cyber Security; here we adapt to speed; the speed of change & speed of delivery and that requires a combination of hard and smart work. There is reason why we adapted the mantra of 'Leaning In' vs. 'Saying No'. And 'leaning in' requires sacrifices – it requires teams to go beyond their limits and help people but also deliver quality. Quality requires hard work in security; specially when it comes to Cyber Security – because you will always be torn between 'following a security principle' and 'providing Agility' – but being able to do both and still lower risk and ensure the least amount of exceptions requires hard work and going into detail. This is the kind of challenge we faced everyday but with practice, we got better at it.
- Periodic Assessments became a primary factor in our process to maintain adequate security. We built a custom framework around the very popular 'Plan-Do-Check-Act' cycle and that served us well. Cyber Security is NOT a 'Secure It Once and Forget It' activity; it has to be cyclic. If we missed one Change Approval Board (CAB) meeting for instance, where changes about to 'go live' are discussed, we had to ensure a backup plan for assessing those systems and Periodic Assessment was that plan. We created an Operations Charter of sorts that basically was a 'calendar of security checks' for the entire year and ensured that we assessed systems as part of this activity based on a set frequency.

The Technology: Oh! The Gadgets!

10.543 As a team, we loved playing with new technology. When we look back now at the number of Proof Of Concepts (POCs) we have done, it's just crazy! Tinkering with technology, understanding how it works, trying to break it and then learning how to secure it became part of our DNA; in fact, I say this as part of every other Cyber Security professional out there – 'it's part of every Cyber Security passionistas DNA'!

10.544 We strongly believed that 'no one control was ever going to be a silver bullet' in our security technology arsenal and we also ensured we communicated that back to senior stakeholders. The 'Defense in Depth (DiD)' concept was hence socialised at all levels, and we kept replaying that concept in every discussion or meeting we had so that technology and business stakeholders understood how we designed protection or detection mechanisms.

10.545 Defense in Depth is a very basic security principle that we endeavoured to build (and still do) in everything we do; without hampering Agility of course. If you build too much security, you tend to stifle 'Agility and Innovation', so 'Keeping it Simple and Lean' is a mantra we tried to follow as often as possible.

10.546 Every company has two core areas that they need to concentrate their security technologies on – The Outer Core (also called 'Perimeter' in security speak) and The Inner Shell (also called the 'The Core' in security speak). Traditional security strategies always focused on the 'Perimeter' via the usage of technologies like Internet Firewalls, Intrusion Prevention Systems (IPS), De-Militarized Zone (DMZ) Firewalls, Virtual Private Network (VPN) Gateways, Internet Proxies & Email Proxies. As threats began advancing, protecting the Inner Shell' or 'The Core' became more and more relevant. We hence began moving our focus, over the years, towards technologies like Network Access Control (NAC), segregating testing and production environments and monitoring malware that attacked credentials – especially privileged ones. Over time, we fine-tuned our use cases for alerting and response and because the attack surface is changing so rapidly, we have to keep fine tuning it further to better our containment, response and remediation capabilities in the long run.

10.547 We have also realised that the perimeter is now slowly eroding and that securing the end point and data has become more important. This concept has already been well publicised via a special project called the Jericho Forum[121] that talks about erosion of traditional secure boundaries, also commonly termed 'De-Perimiterization.'

10.548 An important thing to note here is that there are specific types of systems that apply to Financial Industries, like Banking, that require special mention and attention from a security perspective. I have listed them below for quick reference:

- Automated Teller Machine (ATM), Cash/Cheque Deposit Machines (CDM) or a combination of both, sometimes also called Smart Deposit Machines (SDM).
- Payment Systems like SWIFT, Direct Debit, Funds Transfer or similar.
- Switching Technologies that validate your PIN when you withdraw money or transfer control to a Central switch that allows you to use your ATM Card on any ATM in the world.

121 https://ccskguideen.org/jericho-forum-commandments/.

- Card Systems that authorize your transactions when you swipe your credit or debit card at a terminal in a shop where you buy merchandise.
- Treasury systems that allow banks to trade in currencies and the like.
- Trading systems that allow customers to buy shares and other instruments of their choice.
- Interactive Voice Recording (IVR) systems that authenticate customers and guide them, via a 'Call Tree' or 'a myriad set of options' to do a variety of transactions via their telephone or cell phones.
- Core Banking & Lending Systems.

10.549 The threat landscape, the attack scenarios, the risks, the impacts, and the effectiveness of controls differ drastically when technologies like the above are involved and that is why securing them alone, apart from the other innovative solutions we offer customers, is a massive challenge. This is where structure plays an important role and so does Enterprise Architecture. Cyber Security professionals need a 'blue print' of sorts to understand standardised technologies and then work with other stakeholders to secure them.

10.550 An interesting story comes to mind, when we talk about securing unique solutions. Emirates NBD launched the friendly robot named 'Pepper' as part of its 'Branch of the Future' initiative which received a lot of applause. Securing a technology like a 'robot' is amazingly interesting, but when faced with this challenge – we followed the approach of studying what it did, how it worked – down to the detail. A few weekends were spent on trying to understand it and then securing it:) and its experiences like these, that help us and the organisation grow. It also helps Cyber Security grow. Is there risk here? Yes – definitely! But as Cyber Security, we were also bold enough to embrace the challenge and then work towards mitigating it. Cyber Security units should take risks and always tell themselves 'The business should be able to go and choose whatever solution they want; we are confident that we can secure anything'! We followed this philosophy, primarily because we believed in the values of the organisation itself – Innovation, Service Excellence and the like. You cannot be innovative, if you don't take risks! The learning here is that if you fail, you fail fast, recover, fix it and move on! Get ready for that next challenge!

10.551 Another interesting technology that is becoming a challenge to secure nowadays is Containers. Containers are the next level of evolution after Virtual Machines and they are very unique in their own ways. When we embarked on the 'digital transformation' journey, we began experimenting with Containers and we realised that it had its own set of challenges. For instance, Containers are nimble and lean and can scale very well depending on business needs, but the underlying layer on which it runs, is still basically an Operating System (like Linux). If the underlying layer is not secure, the Container can be attacked and compromised. This is when, apart from training our people on Container technology and following the process of understanding its details, we also had to look at choosing technologies that secure and assess the security of Containers.

10.552 With all these new technologies at the helm, Cyber Security requires an 'out-of-the-box' approach to designing them securely. And it's not just securing technologies like these that matter here, the specific Cyber Security solutions also need to mature over time.

10.553 We were thrilled when we looked at demos of technologies like Security Orchestration – which basically automates entire incident run books, Container Vulnerability Management & Network Behavioural/Anomaly detection systems.

10.554 A revolutionary technology that is helping deter Cyber Security threats is Behavioural Authentication. With the advent of 'the digital bank', customers are now going mobile with everything and with sophisticated identity theft frauds such as Sim Swap,[122] which lead to 'Account Takeover', banks are losing a lot of money. Behavioural Authentication systems have really broken the innovation barrier by creating a 'bio footprint' of sorts for every customer in order for banks to ensure that 'A customer is indeed the same genuine customer' and not someone else who is trying to make a transaction or log in to the system. This works by collecting data on how a customer holds the mobile phone, button tapping pressure, swiping actions and many other sensors that a phone has. If an adversary, were to gain access to the customer's credentials or even to the customer's phone, they would not be allowed to authenticate to the banking system, since their behaviour (holding the phone, button tapping, swiping, etc) would not match that of the customer's. This is now going beyond the realm of Biometric Authentication where a fingerprint, voice print, face or even heartbeat are used to authenticate customers to a banking system.

10.555 Open APIs are another very interesting technology. Application Programming Interfaces (APIs) are like the waiters that bring food to your table when you go and dine at the restaurant. They are the key to delivering food back and forth from the kitchen, akin to what an API does with data and messages between applications. API Gateways do this job very often in corporate environments and they use interesting technologies that need to be studied and researched in order to be made secure. For instance, some Open API technologies today use different kinds of databases, like Cassandra[123] that are unique in nature and very atypical. Apart from the challenges of securing such technologies, general API security health checks also apply including using authentication best practices like OAuth 2.0.[124]

10.556 Last but not least, is the security beast that every security professional loves tackling – The Cloud. Assessing cloud deployments that are 'off-premise' (outside the physical location of where the organisation's servers are located) is indeed an amazing challenge.

122 http://www.infosecurityeurope.com/__novadocuments/86670?v=635672843150630000.
123 http://cassandra.apache.org/.
124 https://oauth.net/2/.

10.557 What we learnt over time, was that, sometimes, securing a cloud also came down to sharpening negotiation skills. Negotiation skills are extremely important when talking to cloud vendors because you have to convince them to align to your level of security, your risk management methodologies, and your incident response security remediation timelines – and this is no mean feat. In our experience, it served us well to nail down and decide – first and foremost – what kind of data can or cannot sit on an 'off-premise' cloud. With various regulatory frameworks that apply to us, considering we operate in many geographies, it's always important to first ask the Cloud Service Provider (CSP) the question – 'In which country are your data centers located?' Once we decided, that a certain kind of data was feasible for placing and using in the cloud, we learnt over time that 'Contracts' play a massive role in deciding the course of deployment. Clauses such as 'Right to Audit' and others are extremely important for inclusion in cloud contracts. Other factors such as 'Data Portability' – which ensures that you get your data back intact, in case the CSP goes 'out of business' or you terminate your contract with the CSP are also important considerations. CSPs are extremely hesitant to allow other organisations to conduct security assessments on their infrastructure – and that to some extent is fair, considering potential impacts to other customers in a multi-tenant environment – but we had to try and ask; and we always do. Sometimes, with a lot of convincing via data, facts and business cases, we were able to conduct tests while for others, we relied on independent reports as verification mechanisms. Today's cloud service offerings have matured from the time we started dabbling with it, and now it's great that services and products like Cloud Access Security Brokers (CASB) – who offer APIs for Data Leakage Prevention (DLP), Auditing and other security requirements – exist for us to explore and apply to our specific use case in an off-premise cloud.

In Closing

10.558 In summary, Cyber Security is growing at an exponential rate and so are threats. We, at Emirates NBD, will always strive to adapt to that rate of change and at the same time be agile towards business requirements fulfilment. Cyber Security is not a revenue generation unit in any organisation but it is a very big contributor to 'loss avoidance'. This is the kind of value that Cyber Security needs to show business stakeholders and 'leaning in vs. saying no' is a great start. Cyber Security at the highest level of engagement with 'C-Level' executives is only about keeping is simple and depicting relevant risks that affect the business. Senior Management only wants to know what the risks are and what amount of time and money is needed to mitigate this. Technical personnel on the other hand need support and guidance from Cyber Security, not fear or 'ivory tower approaches'. Cyber Security also needs to embed itself deeply into Innovation initiatives that the entire organisation undertakes. At Emirates NBD, we have participated in every Innovation Day event and always helped our colleagues show case some great solutions to our employees. When stakeholders see this level of engagement, they realise the good Cyber Security teams contribute to their way of working and align very well with organisational values.

10.559 In closing, I would like to say that a perfect blend of people, process and technology along with a healthy balance of technical (IQ) and soft skills (EQ) and limitless passion are what contribute to Cyber Security success stories.

10H HEALTHCARE
Helen Wong MBE

Introduction

10.560 Information, whether in paper or digital form, is critical to NHS patient care. The reason NHS organisations need to gather and hold information is to use it – both to treat and care for patients, and to improve the quality and efficiency of services. Using information so that patients get the best care possible means sharing it with staff and with other providers of care (for example, an ambulance crew, a local GP, a care home or a specialist in another hospital). When patient information, such as medical history, is not available to healthcare professionals, delays in treatment can occur. It is, therefore, vital that information systems ensure that patient information can be shared quickly, reliably and securely. The use of technology for managing patient data is growing. But without robust processes and adequate IT systems, the integrity of information will be at risk of being compromised by unauthorised parties, it may not be accessible where or when needed, and it may not be kept confidential. The financial cost of data breaches can be substantial and often more costly than prevention. While some financial institutions set aside money to recover from data breaches, the NHS covers such incidents with funds intended for patient care and healthcare improvements.

10.561 Healthcare has been an area that has been badly affected by cyber-security attacks. There is a fine balancing act for such decision-makers to embrace the digitisation of healthcare and defend against cyber-risks.

10.562 It is essential to ask the following questions:

1. How do I balance the central access to information initiative and data protection?
2. Do I have a 'good' cyber-security strategy in place?
3. What went wrong with the NHS and lessons to be learned.
4. How can I prevent or mitigate the disruption of a cyber event – How do I ensure that our business returns to normal as quickly as possible?
5. If I want to sell my healthcare business what cyber security aspects do I need to consider in the process?

10.563 The 'Wannacry' cyber-security attack put a halt to the NHS in May 2017 resulting in 6,900 NHS appointments being cancelled. All NHS trusts were left vulnerable in a major ransomware attack because cyber-security recommendations were not followed, a UK government report [125]has said.

What is Wannacry?

10.564 Wannacry began on 12 May 2017 and was the biggest cyber-attack to have hit the NHS to date. The malware encrypted data on infected computers and demanded a ransom roughly equivalent to £230 ($300).

10.565 The National Audit Office report said there was no evidence that any NHS organisation paid the ransom – but the financial cost of the incident remained unknown.

10.566 An assessment of 88 out of 236 trusts by NHS Digital before the attack found that none passed the required cyber-security standards. The report said NHS trusts had not acted on critical alerts from NHS Digital and a warning from the Department of Health and the Cabinet Office in 2014 to patch or migrate away from vulnerable older software.

What is ransomware?

10.567 Ransomware like Wannacry is a type of malware that blocks access to a computer or its data and demands money to release it. The malicious software from cryptovirology threatens to publish the victim's data or perpetually block access to it unless a ransom is paid. While some simple ransomware may lock the system in a way which is not difficult for a knowledgeable person to reverse, more advanced malware uses a technique called cryptoviral extortion, in which it encrypts the victim's files, making them inaccessible, and demands a ransom payment to decrypt them. In a properly implemented cryptoviral extortion attack, recovering the files without the decryption key is an intractable problem – and difficult to trace digital currencies such as Ukash and Bitcoin are used for the ransoms, making tracing and prosecuting the perpetrators difficult.

How does it work?

10.568 When a computer is infected, the ransomware typically contacts a central server for the information it needs to activate, and then begins encrypting files on the infected computer with that information. Once all the files are encrypted, it posts a message asking for payment to decrypt the files – and threatens to destroy the information if it doesn't get paid, often with a timer attached to ramp up the pressure.

125 Publication details: ISBN: 9781786041470 HC: 414, 2017-19 Published date: 27 October 2017 www.nao.org.uk/report/investigation-wannacry-cyber-attack-and-the-nhs/.

How does it spread?

10.569 Most ransomware is spread hidden within Word documents, PDFs and other files normally sent via email, or through a secondary infection on computers already affected by viruses that offer a back door for further attacks.

What can you do to protect your business?

10.570 Malware, patches and worms defined. Organisations could also have better managed their computers' firewalls – but in many cases they did not, it said.[126]

How did WannaCry end?

10.571 The National Audit Office credited the cyber-security researcher Marcus Hutchins, who accidentally helped to stop the spread of WannaCry. His 'kill switch' involved registering a domain name linked to the malware, which deactivated the program's ability to spread automatically.

Who was behind WannaCry?

10.572 Home Office Minister Ben Wallace told BBC Radio 4's Today programme that the government was 'as sure as possible' that North Korea was behind the attack. 'This attack, we believe quite strongly that it came from a foreign state,' he said. 'It is widely believed in the community and across a number of countries that North Korea [took on] this role'.

Lessons Learned

10.573 Healthcare providers were not prepared at all for a cyber-attack. Since WannaCry there have been significant moves to upskill the management teams and put systems and procedures in place.

10.574 Secondly the operating systems have been updated and patched so that even though they are connected to networks, the malware protection should prevent a repeat of such a widespread problem.

10.575 However, the weakest link is not appreciating that the IT aspect is the responsibility of all and not just the IT manager.

126 Publication details: ISBN: 9781786041470 HC: 414, 2017-19 Published date: 27 October 2017 www.nao.org.uk/report/investigation-wannacry-cyber-attack-and-the-nhs/.

10.576 Medical records, especially but not exclusively in the US, by dint of their comprehensive nature, sell for hundreds of dollars on the Dark Web and there is no shortage of them. However, for those compromised, many don't realise that their records can be sold repeatedly by the criminal networks operating in the Dark Web and that this could cause long term problems. Information that is contained in medical records can be used for many different types of identity fraud and phishing attacks and because of its comprehensive nature, the threat from these can persist for many years.

10.577 In the UK, the attack vector seems to be different to the US and attacks are mainly via ransomware – trying to extort money from vulnerable hospital trusts rather than individuals.

10.578 Common to all sectors and sizes of organisation was the range of human behaviours that could inadvertently lead to data breaches. As an example, a large hospital with diverse systems faced more difficulties than single-handed GPs or dentists, who were only working with a single system and were therefore less likely to have to log in and out of different systems to complete a single task. As a result, such a GP or dental practice was less likely to invent in the kind of insecure workarounds that we found in emergency care in large hospitals. However, some small primary care practices were working with outdated, unsupported technology, and did invent their own insecure workarounds in response to the challenges they faced, for example, taking home a system back-up in their bag, instead of backing up to a secure cloud (network of servers) or other secure mechanism.

How the Department and the NHS responded[127]

Devolved responsibility for cyber-security

10.579 The Department of Health (the Department) has overall national responsibility for cyber-security resilience and responding to incidents in the health sector. However, the Department devolves responsibility for managing cyber-security to local organisations – NHS trusts, GPs, clinical commissioning groups and social care providers. Regulators and other national bodies oversee and support local NHS organisations. While NHS foundation trusts are directly accountable to Parliament for delivering healthcare services, they are held to account by the same regulators as NHS trusts. Roles and responsibilities for cyber-security as at September 2017 are set out in the diagram below.

127 National Audit Office Investigation: WannaCry cyber attack and the NHS 25 October 2017.

Roles and responsibilities for cyber-security in the NHS as at September 2017

National and local bodies share responsibility for cyber-security in the health sector

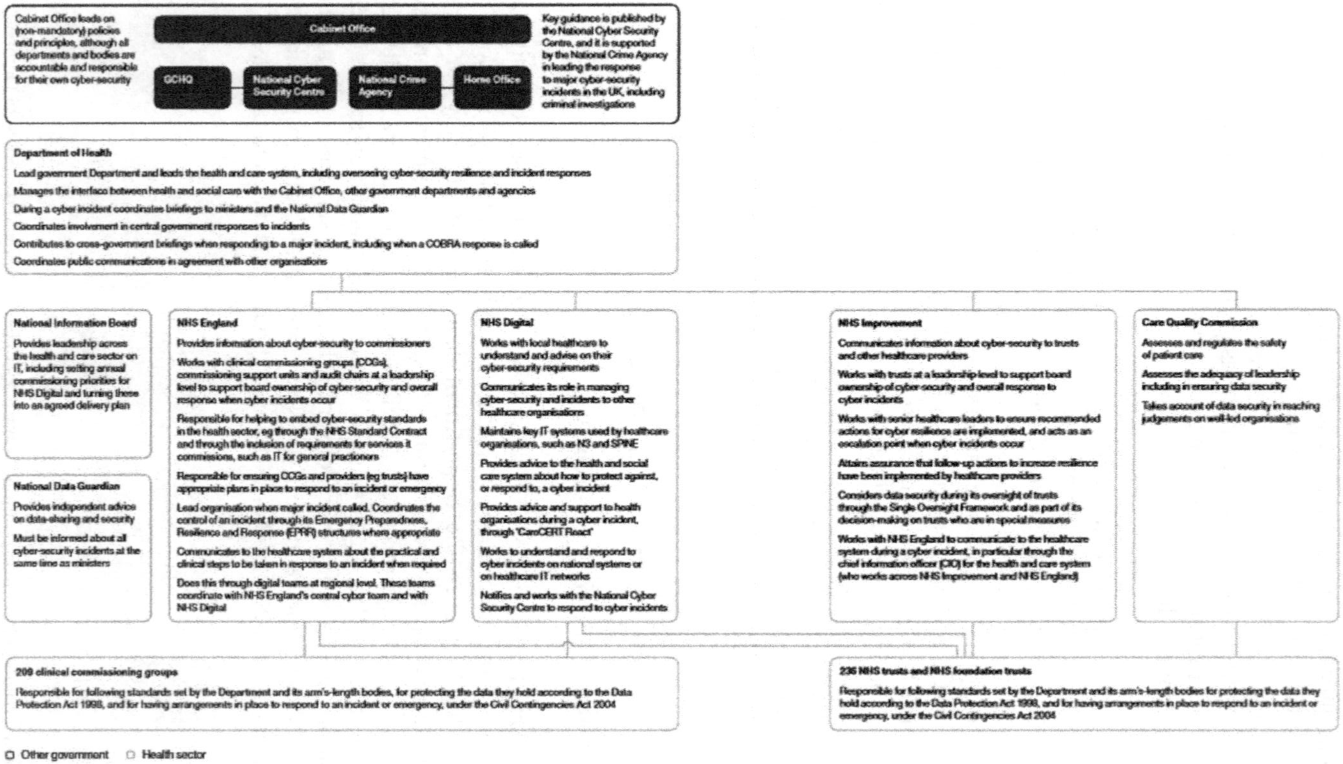

Source: National Audit Office analysis of Department of Health and NHS England data

Reproduced with kind permission from the National Audit Office. For further information visit www.nao.org.uk/

10.580 In particular:

- NHS Improvement holds trusts and NHS foundation trusts to account for delivering value for money; and
- the Care Quality Commission (CQC) regulates health and social care providers for safety and quality of their services.

10.581 Both bodies can mandate local NHS organisations to improve their performance. They also have a role in ensuring that local bodies have appropriate cyber-security arrangements, but neither are primarily concerned with cyber or information technology issues. NHS Digital provides guidance, alerts and support to local organisations on cyber-security, and can visit organisations to evaluate cyber-security arrangements if asked to do so, as part of CareCERT Assure.4 However, NHS Digital cannot mandate a local body to take remedial action even if it has concerns about the vulnerability of that organisation.

How the cyber-attack was managed

10.582 Before the WannaCry attack the Department had developed a plan for responding to a cyber-attack, which included roles and responsibilities of national and local organisations. However, the Department had not tested the plan at a local level. This meant the NHS was not clear what actions it should take when affected by WannaCry, including how it should respond at a local level. On 12 May 2017, NHS England determined that it should declare a national major incident and decided that it would lead the response, coordinating with NHS Digital and NHS Improvement. NHS England treated the attack as a major operational incident through its existing Emergency Preparedness, Resilience and Response (EPRR) processes. However, as NHS England had not rehearsed its response to a cyber-attack it faced a number of challenges. The cyber-attack was less visible than other types of incident and not confined to local areas or regions in the way a major transport accident would have been, for example. This meant that it took more time to determine the cause of the problem, the scale of the problem and the number of people and organisations affected.

10.583 Without clear guidelines on responding to a national cyber-attack, organisations reported the attack to different sources including the local police, NHS England and NHS Digital. For the same reason communications to patients and local organisations also came from a number of sources. These included the National Cyber Security Centre, which was providing support to all UK organisations affected by the attack, NHS England and NHS Digital.

10.584 In addition, the use of email for communication was limited, although NHS Improvement did communicate with trusts' chief executive officers by telephone. Affected trusts shut down IT systems, including some trusts disconnecting from NHS email and the N3 network as a precautionary measure.[128]

128 N3 is the broadband network connecting all NHS sites in England.

The Department coordinated the response with the centre of government, briefing ministers, liaising with the National Cyber Security Centre and National Crime Agency, and overseeing NHS England's and NHS Digital's operational response.

10.585 Affected trusts were triaged through the EPRR route and, where necessary, received assistance from national bodies, including advice and physical technical support from NHS Digital, which sent 54 staff out to hospitals to provide direct support.

10.586 Staff at the Department, NHS England, NHS Improvement and NHS Digital, as well as large numbers of staff in other organisations across the NHS, worked through the weekend to resolve the problem and avoid further problems on Monday. NHS England's IT team did not have on-call arrangements in place, but staff came in voluntarily to help resolve the issue. Front-line NHS staff adapted to communication challenges and shared information through personal mobile devices, including using the encrypted WhatsApp application. NHS national bodies and trusts told us that this worked well on the day although is not an official communication channel

The risk of a cyber-attack had been identified before WannaCry

10.587 The Secretary of State for Health asked the National Data Guardian and CQC to undertake reviews of data security. These reports were published in July 2016 and warned the Department about the cyber-threat and the need for the Department to respond to it[129]. They noted the threat of cyber-attacks not only put patient information at risk of loss or compromise but also jeopardised access to critical patient record systems by clinicians. They recommended that all health and care organisations needed to provide evidence that they were taking action to improve cyber-security, such as through the 'Cyber Essentials' scheme.[130]

10.588 Although WannaCry was the largest cyber-security incident to affect the NHS, individual NHS organisations had been victims of other attacks in recent years. WannaCry infected one of England's biggest trusts, Barts Health NHS Trust. This was the second cyber-attack to affect the trust in six months. A ransomware attack had also affected Northern Lincolnshire and Goole NHS Foundation Trust in October 2016, which had led to it cancelling 2,800 appointments.

Key findings

10.589 In the NHS organisations we reviewed, we found: There was evident widespread commitment to data security, but staff at all levels faced significant

129 National Data Guardian for Health and Care, 'Review of Data Security, Consent and Opt-Outs,' National Data Guardian, 2016

130 Cyber Essentials is a government-designed cyber-security certification scheme that sets out a baseline of cyber-security and can be used by any organisation in any sector, see: www.cyberaware.gov.uk/cyberessentials/.

challenges in translating their commitment into reliable practice. Where patient data incidents occurred they were taken seriously. However, staff did not feel that lessons were always learned or shared across their organisations.

Report into how data is safely and securely managed in the NHS

10.590 The quality of staff training on data security was very varied at all levels, right up to Senior Information Risk Owners (SIROs) and Caldicott Guardians.

10.591 Data security policies and procedures were in place at many sites, but day-to-day practice did not necessarily reflect them.

10.592 Benchmarking with other organisations was all but absent. There was no consistent culture of learning from others, and there was little evidence of external checking or validation of data security arrangements. The use of technology for recording and storing patient information away from paper-based records is growing. This is solving many data security issues but, if left unimproved, increases the risk of more serious, large-scale data losses.

10.593 Data security systems and protocols were not always designed around the needs of frontline staff. This leads to staff developing potentially insecure workarounds in order to deliver good timely care to patients – this issue was especially evident in emergency medicine settings.

10.594 As integrated patient care develops, improvements must be made to the ease and safety of sharing data between services. Successful data security demands engaged leadership and a culture of learning and sharing. Senior leadership teams must take data security seriously and ensure clear responsibilities for all members of staff.

Practical Points: Prevention and Protection

10.595 The standard ransomware process follows three common steps: infection, execution and payoff. Although one option is paying the ransom, it is far better not to be attacked in the first place, especially with new ransomware versions that just delete your data regardless of payment.

10.596 Prevention is the key! To implement an effective prevention and protection strategy, you should:

- Train users about the risk.
- Implement consistent data backups.
- Block executable attachments.
- Keep systems patched (especially J-Boss web servers, which are common in health care).
- Keep antivirus solutions updated.

Dentists

10.597 Dentists have so much to juggle with – from dealing with the local authorities, staff, patients and now technology. Providing dental care is changing at a rapid pace with a race to maintain maximum efficiency while utilising technology and digital records. As a result of the reliance on electronic data, dental practices have become vulnerable to cyber-security threats. However, many dentists are wondering how will a cyber-attacker even find me – wouldn't they rather go for the big boys? Well in actual fact, cyber-attackers focus on individual practitioners because often their defence is usually not as sophisticated and such persons may not be as vigilant against threats. Imagine an attack being effective – it can freeze an entire practice costing significant expenses, both financial and reputational, which can wreak havoc on a dental practice.

10.598 The key lesson is don't undermine the cyber-criminals and hackers. Choose a strong firewall and malware protection. Whilst you may be juggling a lot in a dental practice, you must allocate resources for IT security and time to train your team on security policies.

10.599 One of the key reasons why dental practices are at risk is because such patients who are NHS must visit their dentist regularly and therefore dentists hold huge amounts of relevant and up-to-date patient information – names, addresses, birthdates, national insurance numbers, and even banking information. A cyber-breach is a potential legal nightmare for the dental practice.

10.600 The most common causes of data breaches in a dental practice are theft, hacking, unauthorised access or disclosure, lost records and devices, and improper disposal of records. With the move of staff using laptops, this adds another security breach if that gets stolen.

10.601 Dentists are under a legal duty to maintain the privacy of patient health information and to take security measures to protect this information from abuse by staff members, hackers, and thieves. The penalties imposed upon health care providers such violations are an expensive cost especially with the introduction of GDPR.

10.602 Data security breaches occur when staff members do not follow office procedures or exercise poor judgment. Dentists should ensure computers are placed in areas where the computer screens are not visible to patients and visitors, are preferably a desktop so it is harder to steal and all computers should have a complex password which is not easy to guess. Human error often can be the cause, for example someone writing down the password and pinning on the notice board for other members of staff to use. Sometimes temporary staff or newer members might not realise how important it is to maintain the privacy of patient information.

10.603 There is the trend for dental practices to include a free Wifi option for patients. This can potentially be a threat. Likewise, staff on personal email sites or social media also introduce potential viruses and malware affecting the dental practice's firewalls, operating systems, hardware and software devices. The other way to keep good housekeeping is to regularly update the antivirus software.

10.604 Dentists have mainly digitised their practices but some still use paper. For the latter, it is imperative that documents are shredded and not just thrown in the bin. Finally it is definitely worth checking that your insurance policy covers cyber security breaches, theft, related legal action and legal fees.

Selling or buying your healthcare practice – things to look out for in the due diligence

10.605 There is a huge demand for medical practices – whether they are dental, doctors, vets, opticians, pharmacies or care homes. As part of the purchase and sale process, due diligence is key and usually includes looking at the financials, legal and intellectual property. Now, cyber-security practices and technologies are at the forefront of these same conversations.

10.606 If you are buying – knowing what you are buying is key because if you buy the shares in the business you also buy the liabilities and once disclosed are essentially put on the footing of 'buyers beware'. There is some consolidation in the healthcare sector to grow market presence, and branch into new regions. Or an acquisition can help diversify a portfolio.

So how does cyber security impact the purchase?

10.607 Looking at just the financials is one aspect of the due diligence. Irrespective of whether the financials are strong, if the purchaser doesn't look at the cyber security risk this is one area that can significantly impact the financial gains. Therefore the purchase should expand their due diligence process to include a cyber security assessment. With technology and IT, such issues can unravel years later but it might have originated from a security breach prior to sale.

How do you value the purchase?

10.608 Often companies are valued based on their financial reports but often if an IT breach has been discovered, the purchaser can request either a reduction in the purchase price, request an indemnity or if extremely serious not purchase the target in question. If it is revealed that client data is being sold on the Dark Web or intellectual property is being copied and produced overseas this could have significant criminal and civil legal implications for the potential buyer. It will depend on the severity of the risk and often such a discovery occurs post the purchase. That is why a cyber-security assessment is imperative as part of the due diligence process.

IT Due Diligence Assessment

10.609 An IT assessment will consist of assessing the controls and operational effectiveness and efficiency. It is important to perform an internal assessment of

IT infrastructure to assess the confidentiality, integrity and availability capabilities of connected systems. The specific areas tested should include the following:

- Software – Network and server.
- Hardware and device security.
- What is the back up plan for the practice?
- How are passwords protected?
- How are the staff trained re cyber-security?
- Are there physical security controls?

10.610 The other area to look at is risk management policies, controls, checks and balances. Request to see the policies for:

- Technology.
- IT Risk Management Program.
- Employees, Consultants, Contractors and Temporary Staff.
- Breach and Incident Response Plans.
- Know Your Client policies.
- Know Your Employee policies.

10.611 If you are considering acquiring a company, make sure you consider all of the factors that impact valuation, including cyber-security practices and technologies. And, if you are looking to sell your company, make sure to have your own IT Due Diligence assessment performed. This will enable you to take appropriate steps to 10.463reduce your company's IT risk and improve the valuation of your business prior to negotiations with a potential buyer.

Please also refer to the **Chapter 26** on M&A Due Diligence.

101 MEDICAL DEVICES

Helen Wong MBE

Introduction

10.612 Medical devices are the latest victim to cyber-attacks. KPMG's 2015 cyber-security survey reported 81% of healthcare organisations had been attacked in the past two years and only half felt adequately prepared.[131] Given such devices hold significant personal data which is transferrable to computers and to other devices, they've become a target for cyber-attackers. Healthcare organisations and manufacturers of such devices need to focus on this threat to patient safety. With the

131 KPMG, 'Health care and cyber security – increasing threats require increased capabilities,' KMPG, 2015.

integral use of software and hardware within healthcare the medical device such as heart monitors, wearable technology, medicine dispensers are all at risk. The use of technology, mobiles, wireless and the Internet of Things have exacerbated the risk. Criminals are using malware to infect the medical device to either extract sensitive information or demand a ransom to restore the operation of the device.

What is a medical device?

10.613 According to the World Health Organisation: 'medical device' means any instrument, apparatus, implement, machine, appliance, implant, reagent for in vitro use, software, material or other similar or related article, intended by the manufacturer to be used, alone or in combination, for human beings, for one or more of the specific medical purpose(s) of:

- diagnosis, prevention, monitoring, treatment or alleviation of disease;
- diagnosis, monitoring, treatment, alleviation of or compensation for an injury;
- investigation, replacement, modification, or support of the anatomy or of a physiological process;
- supporting or sustaining life;
- control of conception;
- disinfection of medical devices;
- providing information by means of in vitro examination of specimens derived from the human body;
- and does not achieve its primary intended action by pharmacological, immunological or metabolic means, in or on the human body, but which may be assisted in its intended function by such means.

10.614 Note: Products which may be considered to be medical devices in some jurisdictions but not in others include:

- disinfection substances;
- aids for persons with disabilities;
- devices incorporating animal and/or human tissues;
- devices for in-vitro fertilisation or assisted reproduction technologies.

10.615 The EU and FDA have stated that a device is not a medical device if it purely assists in fitness, lifestyle and well-being.[132] A medical device needs to do more such as connecting to a mobile network to run health applications.

132 FDA, 'MAUDE Adverse Event Report: Merge Healthcare Merge Hemo Programmable Diagnostic Computer February 201,' 2 August 2016. [Online]. Available: www.accessdata.fda.gov/scripts/cdrh/cfdocs/cfmaude/detail.cfm?mdrfoi id=5487204.

Lack of Staff Knowledge

10.616 Many medical practitioners and nurses may not be au fait with technology and inadvertently compromise patient information, records and their safety. For example, the staff may accidently download a virus, or insert an infected device into the network or share passwords to perpetrators.

10.617 Yet patient confidentiality remains absolutely a priority especially for patients who may not be in any fit state to look after their welfare. Whilst such medical devices may be an advance in the medical world, it brings with it a whole host of unexpected problems and threat. Here are some of the ways the medical device can be attacked.

Table 1 – Medical device example adversarial incidents – based upon NIST SP 800-82 Revision 2[133]

Event	**Description/risk**
Malware on device/ systems	Malicious software (eg Virus, Worm, Trojan, Ransomware) introduced onto the device or system
Denial of control action	Device operation disrupted by delaying or blocking the flow of information, denying device availability or networks used to control the device or system to healthcare staff
Device, application, configuration or software manipulation	Device, software or configuration settings modified producing unpredictable results
Spoofed device/ system status information	False information sent to operators either to disguise unauthorised changes or to initiate inappropriate actions by medical staff
Device functionality manipulation	Unauthorised changes made to embedded software, programmable instructions in medical devices, alarm thresholds changed, or unauthorised commands issued to devices, which could potentially result in damage to equipment (if tolerances are exceeded), premature shutdown of devices and functions, or even disabling medical equipment
Safety functionality modified	Safety-related functionality manipulated such that they do not operate when needed; or perform incorrect control actions, potentially leading to patient harm or damage to medical equipment

133 K. Stouffer, V. Pillitteri, S. Lightman, M. Abrams and A. Hahn, 'NIST SP 800-82R2 Guide to Industrial Control Systems (ICS) Security,' National Institute of Standards and Technology, 2015.

Event	Description/risk
Courtesy of the National Institute of Standards and Technology, U.S. Department of Commerce.[134]	

Medical Device Failures

10.618 Irrespective of whether a medical device experiences a cyber-attack, there may also be incidents where the medical device fails due to a technical flaw. For example, the monitor failed to recognise the patient's pathological data wasn't right until the computer was restarted. This delay could have caused serious harm. Other situations could be a cardiac device which when read shows a normal heart beat. However, a technical fault in the software or in the hardware meant the transmitter wasn't working and in actual fact the patient was at risk of a heart attack. In that instance a comparison of checking the pulse via the wrist exposed this error in the medical device. The final example would be a medical device dispensing medicine to prevent overdosing. There is a risk in this last example of the drug dose being maliciously altered with very dangerous results.

How can medical device manufacturers manage risk?

10.619 The examples above sound frightful but aren't unheard of. So all medical device manufacturers need to always test the following:

- the exploitability of the cyber-security vulnerability; and
- the severity of the health impact to patients if the vulnerability were to be exploited.

Table 2 shows the test used to assess whether the product passes clinical performances or not.

Table 2 – Qualitative severity levels – US Food and Drug Administration Postmarket Management of Cyber-security in Medical Devices Guidance

Common Term	Possible Description
Negligible	Inconvenience or temporary discomfort
Minor	Results in temporary injury or impairment not requiring professional medical intervention

134 K. Stouffer, V. Pillitteri, S. Lightman and M. Abrams, 'NIST SP 800-82R1 Guide to Industrial Control Systems (ICS) Security,' National Institute of Standards and Technology (NIST), 2013.

Common Term	Possible Description
Serious	Results in injury or impairment requiring professional medical intervention
Critical	Results in permanent impairment or life-threatening injury
Catastrophic	Results in patient death

Tensions in safety and security convergence[135]

10.620 A generic safety assessment considers the likelihood that a hazardous event will occur (frequency or duration) and the severity of the resulting incident or harm. Safety-related devices or systems are generally concerned with non-malicious faults, and how these can be avoided or mitigated. Safety-related systems and applications implement safety functions that act on the process under control to prevent identified hazardous events from occurring. The calculated probability that an undetected fault will lead to the loss of a safety function, when required is probabilistic, quantitative and seldom changes.

10.621 Conversely, security addresses the intelligent malicious attacks to a system by identifying the adversaries (otherwise known as threat actors), their capabilities, intent and resources, compromise methods and the vulnerabilities that may be exploited. This considers the likelihood that a threat will exploit a vulnerability leading to a (business) impact/ consequence. The result is qualitative and changes dynamically as potential adversaries, intent or capability change and as vulnerabilities are discovered and exploits are developed.

10.622 Several challenges arise in convergence and implementation. Not least, the separation of the safety and security engineering disciplines. However, tension is illustrated in the static and probabilistic nature of safety engineering versus the dynamic qualitative security assessment and treatment. There are implications for the management of safety certification and security of devices or systems in operation and therefore the need to proactively manage security incidents. Also, the approach of an intelligent adversary could consider the range of highly improbable events and use those as goal-based outcomes. Thus, undermining safety protection measures or intentionally triggering known safety functions (eg fail safe or safe motion) to create apparent failures and potentially denying use.

Controlling systems and data

10.623 The innovative thing with medical devices is that it talks to a computer and shares data, so it is imperative that such systems and data are controlled. Therefore it hopefully creates a second line of defence in the event the medical device hardware is maliciously compromised. One hopes the computer will

135 Permission to reproduce extracts from BSI publications is granted by BSI.

alert the user if things aren't quite right. There also has to be regular checks and training for all staff undertaking the usage of such medical devices. The biggest risk are the older systems which may not support the new technology or still working on an operating system which isn't protected by malware.

10.624 This according to the FDA may lead to the following that could affect medical devices and hospital networks:[136]

- network-connected/configured medical devices infected or disabled by malware;
- the presence of malware on hospital computers, smartphones and tablets, targeting mobile devices using wireless technology to access patient data, monitoring systems, and implanted patient devices;
- uncontrolled distribution of passwords, disabled passwords, hard-coded passwords for software intended for privileged device access (eg, to administrative, technical, and maintenance personnel);
- failure to provide timely security software updates and patches to medical devices and networks and to address related vulnerabilities in older medical device models (legacy devices);
- security vulnerabilities in off-the-shelf software designed to prevent unauthorised device or network access, such as plain-text or no authentication, hard-coded passwords, documented service accounts in service manuals, and
- poor coding/SQL injection.

European Union Regulation

10.625 The Medical Devices Regulations (MDR) published in 2017 significantly enlarges the scope of applicable devices, and will define more stringent post-market surveillance, as will the draft Regulation on in vitro diagnostic medical devices. The draft plans have provisions for vigilance, market surveillance and reporting in respect of serious incidents and implementing safety corrective actions. Member States will be required to analyse and risk assess incidents, the adequacy of corrective actions, and any further corrective action that may be required. Member States will also monitor the manufacturer's incident investigation. General safety and performance requirements prohibit the compromise of patient safety and include the application safety principles; taking account of state of the art security and identifying known or foreseeable hazards and risks from intended and foreseeable misuse. Any remaining risks are to be reduced as far as possible by taking adequate protection measures.

136 FDA, 'Cybersecurity Vulnerabilities Identified in St. Jude Medical's Implantable Cardiac Devices and Merlin@home Transmitter: FDA Safety Communication,' 09 January 2017. [Online]. Available: www.fda.gov/MedicalDevices/Safety/AlertsandNotices/ucm535843.htm.

10.626 The regulations do specifically stipulate devices incorporating software and the requirement to implement 'state of the art' (albeit at a high level, referring to information) security, protection against unauthorised access and ensure intended operation. The regulations also highlight risks from external influence (including electrical and radio) and negative interaction of software and its operating environment. As such the draft regulations seek to address the consequences of cyber-incidents and the foreseeable safety hazards. Confidentiality of personal data is to be undertaken in accordance with the EU Data Protection Directive for both implementations. Member States will implement 'effective, proportionate, and dissuasive' penalties for infringement.

10.627 The current EU Medical Devices Directive does not explicitly reference cyber-security, focusing upon safety risk assessment. The European-harmonised ISO standard BS EN ISO 62304 *Medical device software — Software life-cycle processes* includes security provisions. The European standard for the application of risk management to medical devices BS EN ISO 14971:2012 highlights that probabilities are very difficult to estimate for software failure, sabotage or tampering.

10.628 Medical device incidence reporting to regulators focuses on safety, not security. Obtaining suitable data to support estimations is therefore highly likely to be problematic. The international standard used by regulators for medical device surveillance in the post-market phase (DD ISO/TS 19218-1:2011+A1:2013) for sharing and reporting adverse incidents by users or manufacturers, does not offer cyber specific categorisation. Arguably, a cyber-incident could be identified with any of the following categories: computer hardware, computer software, electrical/electronic, external conditions, incompatibility issues, non-mechanical, loss of communications, incorrect device display function, installation, configuration, performance deviation, output issue, protective alarm or fail-safe issue, unintended function – resulting in malfunction, misdiagnosis or mistreatment, or simply as 'other device issue'.

Procurement

10.629 It is imperative that hospitals control their procurement and only buy such devices from manufacturers who have successfully completed robust testing. Healthcare organisations need to set out specifications, covering all aspects of cyber-security, including acceptance testing, verification, integration, maintenance guidance and any supporting references (guidelines, regulation or standards). Anticipate the development of the 'intelligent customer' as a management function that fully understands cyber-security requirements, having specified the requirements, supervised the procurement and integration and has the ability to technically review all facets of the security lifecycle. Healthcare procurement will increasingly focus upon security, given high profile incidents, and the launch of assurance services, which seek to offer third party validation and verification.

10.630 Manufacturers and suppliers should view cyber-security as a business enabler and potentially as an opportunity to differentiate in the medium term. The poor handling of security incidents can rapidly become public knowledge and damaging to corporate reputation, with predictable downsides. Therefore, developing incident response strategies, processes and support mechanisms to deal with inevitable security issues is an absolute requirement.

Information sharing

10.631 Data sharing is essential for high quality healthcare and care services. Mandatory reporting is already a requirement for some, as noted earlier. However, collaborative sharing between all stakeholders is recommended to facilitate early mitigation. Timely sharing of information can provide actionable threat intelligence, enhancing situational awareness and permit pre-emptive activities to address cyber-security vulnerabilities.

10.632 In the UK CareCERT has been analysing threat intelligence and broadcasting advisories to health and care organisations since late 2015. It also provides national cyber-security incident management. In September 2016, CareCERT launched Assure, React and Knowledge services to support implementation of the new Data Security Standards for Health. These added risk assessment, mitigation and incident response advice, along with cyber-security eLearning services. Organisations and individuals can also participate in information sharing. In the UK, the NCSC operate the Cyber- security Information Sharing Partnership (CiSP), formerly a CERT UK function. It is a joint industry and government initiative to exchange cyber-threat information in real time, in a secure and confidential environment. The US National Health Information Sharing and Analysis Center (NH-ISAC) operates in collaboration with the FDA, and is a non-profit organisation that provides members with actionable information on cyber-security and coordinates cyber-security incidence response. The organisation also provides cyber-security tools, guidance via members, events and access to special interest groups.

Conclusions and recommendations

10.633 Whilst medical devices are a welcome introduction to improve the dispensation of medicine and assist the medics, it brings with it risks. Cyber-security is no longer just something for the IT department to deal with but all have to be alert and involved. A medical professional will be expected to be proficient not just in medicine, healthcare but also in tech. The procurement process needs to be robust and onus placed on the manufacturer to prove the testing has been done to the highest standard This should include product lifecycle security, stipulated in emerging assessment schemes, which will be articulated in healthcare procurement. Mature incident response plans and processes are essential for all healthcare entities, in anticipation of the inevitable cyber-security event.

CHAPTER 11

SOCIAL MEDIA AND CYBER SECURITY

Helen Wong MBE

INTRODUCTION

11.01 The field of social media law encompasses criminal and civil elements and is continuously evolving. It deals with legal matters concerning user-generated content and the hosting or transmission of such content by online platforms. It is important for both companies and employees to exercise caution on social media. Privacy is a major legal concern in social media, involving the rights of users and third parties. Intellectual property rights, such as copyright and trademark, can be infringed upon by content shared on social media.

11.02 With the implementation of the Online Safety Act on 26 October 2023, social media platforms are now held accountable for ensuring internet safety and providing choice. The new laws are designed to safeguard children from online harm and grant adults increased agency in their online browsing. After intense scrutiny and debate in both the House of Commons and the House of Lords, this Act imposes legal obligations on tech companies to prevent and swiftly remove illegal content, such as terrorism and revenge pornography. Additionally, they must prevent children from accessing harmful content like bullying, self-harm promotion, eating disorders, and pornography. Significant fines, potentially reaching billions of pounds, await those who fail to adhere to the rules. Moreover, if they neglect to protect children as mandated by Ofcom, their bosses may face imprisonment. While it's a positive step, social media continues to be plagued by cyber breaches.

WHY SOCIAL MEDIA IS VULNERABLE TO CYBERCRIME

11.03 Over 59% of the global population, or nearly 4.8 billion people, use one or more social media platforms. Although social media platforms have their benefits, they also expose users and businesses to cyber threats in the following ways.

Increased Risk of Social Engineering Attacks

11.04 Social media is a valuable marketing tool, but it also raises the risk of social engineering attacks for businesses. By showcasing internal information and employee contacts, social media channels can expose businesses to a wider attack surface, allowing cybercriminals to execute phishing attacks, steal credentials, data, or perpetrate other scams.

11.05 This also applies to employees' personal social media accounts. The content posted on a business's social media profiles could enable cybercriminals to exploit their systems and data using social engineering techniques or other means. The public can usually see information once a digital profile is made. The greater the amount of information uploaded by the user, the higher the risk of cybercrime.

11.06 Cybercriminals use fake accounts on social media to deceive users into sharing personal information, access credentials, or downloading malicious software.

Oversharing

11.07 There is a specific threat to businesses posed by people who post personal information frequently on social networking sites. They not only jeopardise themselves by sharing confidential information – such as travel plans, business data, or patient records – but also give cybercriminals a treasure trove of leverage.

11.08 Spear phishing tries to deceive individuals with greater accuracy and depth compared to regular phishing, utilising up-to-date news or important financial records.

11.09 In whaling attacks, senior executives are targeted and manipulated into performing a secondary action, often involving the transfer of funds.

11.10 Cybercriminals use spoofing to pretend to be someone else and gain access to private data.

11.11 Cybercriminals can exploit social media connections to carry out fraudulent activities like phishing, spoofing, and impersonation, as user engagement reveals useful relationships.

11.12 Cybercriminals can leverage a user's social media relationships to increase cyber risk through inference. Analysing a user's profile can reveal potential identity fraud or theft, even if they hide their interests, location, and other information.

Data Aggregation

11.13 Respondents' accounts can be compromised by cybercriminals through quizzes and puzzles on social networking sites.

11.14 Though not intentionally harmful, even fun or psychological online tests gather personal information, including maiden names and first pet names. Even personal preferences can be used as common security questions for password and account recovery.

11.15 Having profiles on multiple social networking sites can enable cybercriminals to create a comprehensive profile of a user, allowing them to launch targeted attacks against the individual or their associated business.

Unsecured Portable Devices

11.16 People can conveniently access social media while on the move thanks to social networking apps. Most users spend around 2.5 hours each day on social media, primarily on mobile devices. Roughly one-third of the US population solely relies on mobile apps for social media.

11.17 When devices are lost or stolen, there is a potential for information to be stolen. While connecting to social media with a single tap is convenient for many users, it also presents an opportunity for cybercriminals or opportunists to gain unauthorised access to other people's accounts.

11.18 Personal data, such as credit card information, confidential business data, customer lists, or more sensitive information, can be accessed by the bad actor. They have the ability to pose as individuals or businesses to carry out additional criminal activities, like spreading harmful links to the user's contacts, launching realistic phishing attacks on everyone in their friend lists, organising scam campaigns, and leading other cyber assaults.

BUSINESS CYBER RISKS ASSOCIATED WITH SOCIAL MEDIA

11.19 Hackers and other cybercriminals are experts in mining private data from social media sites and manipulating users.

11.20 Users often underestimate how much information can be exposed through posting on social media.

1. Contact information.
2. Date of birth.
3. Gender.
4. The post's timestamp can provide insights about the person behind it.
5. The place where the post originated.
6. Places that can be identified through visual media.
7. Providing links to friends and other users.

8. Follow the links to find the people who have been tagged in the post.
9. The social media network or other users can identify and recognise faces.

SOCIAL MEDIA POSES SIGNIFICANT CYBERSECURITY RISKS FOR BUSINESSES, SUCH AS SOCIAL ENGINEERING, IDENTITY THEFT, AND THE SPREAD OF MALWARE

11.21 The impact of AI technology attacks should be considered by users, as attackers can use gathered information to create a detailed profile of their targets. AI advancements now enable the creation of highly sophisticated phishing attacks that closely resemble legitimate companies or domains. Impersonation attacks deceive customers by pretending to be an online business, leading to fraudulent transactions.

HOW TO REDUCE THE CYBER RISKS OF SOCIAL MEDIA USE

11.22 Businesses are now expected by modern consumers to have an online presence, including on at least one social media platform. Trust, visibility, customer reviews, research, comparisons, and direct contact with businesses are all reasons why social media is a necessary tool. Businesses have the ability to minimise cyber risk related to social media.

Social Media Access Control

11.23 Teams are commonly employed by big businesses to handle all aspects of their social media presence, including post creation, messaging, and customer interactions. A smaller number of individuals with social media access simplifies the identification, containment, and resolution of data breaches.

11.24 To mitigate security risks, it is beneficial to assign one person with oversight responsibility for social media. Furthermore, it is essential for the person to be educated in social media security, encompassing the protection of business information and the ability to identify risky fake accounts.

11.25 Furthermore, companies need to remove account access when it is no longer needed, like when the social media manager switches positions or quits the organisation.

11.26 Besides maintaining consistent branding and messaging across platforms, this person should also communicate effectively with the IT department to manage and reduce risks.

11.27 It is crucial to regularly review social media security controls and threats as cybercriminals are constantly evolving their scams, strategies, and malware.

Tracking brand mentions through social monitoring tools enables organisations to detect any suspicious account activity.

Social Media Policy Implementation

11.28 It is essential for the organisation to have a readily-available social media policy that outlines recommendations for safeguarding sensitive information and clearly states what is strictly prohibited, including for executives at the highest level.

11.29 The policy document should include information on the brand's official social media channels and provide guidelines for employees on how to effectively utilise social media as part of a broader social media strategy. Both personal and professional social media use should be included in the guidelines.

11.30 By implementing a social media policy, firms can safeguard their brand voice, uphold regulatory compliance, and promote inclusive and secure communication.

A CHECKLIST FOR COMPANIES USING SOCIAL MEDIA

Establish terms of use and privacy policies

11.31 Set guidelines for using online platforms, services, and apps. These should:

1. Increase the likelihood of enforceability by obtaining users' explicit consent through methods like an 'I Agree' button.
2. Add safeguards to prevent misuse, infringement, and misappropriation of the company's intellectual property and unauthorised disclosure of confidential information.
3. Ensure that there are provisions in place to limit liability for third-party intellectual property infringement, defamation, privacy breaches, employment-related harassment, and the conduct of third-party users, particularly regarding any content they post or upload.
4. Ensure that there is a website terms of service on the company's website.
5. Implement an online privacy policy to ensure the company's compliance with privacy and non-disclosure obligations to third parties. The privacy policy needs to cover data collection, usage, disclosure, and maintenance for users.
6. Confirm that the terms of use and privacy policies encompass any tailored pages or channels provided by the company on external social media platforms.
7. Mitigate legal liability resulting from user-generated content.

8. Allowing users to contribute content on a website presents legal issues for the site owner, including the risk of being held accountable for copyright infringement, privacy breaches, defamation, and unlawful material. Implement measures to reduce liability for user-generated content, such as:

Determining the applicability of defences under

11.32 As per the EC Directive Regulations of 2002, ISPs are granted immunity from liability if they function as a mere conduit, cache, or host for the material and promptly take action to remove or block access to it once they are informed about it.

11.33 The Defamation Act 1996, specifically section 1, grants intermediaries such as ISPs a defence against liability if they unknowingly distribute defamatory content in certain circumstances.

11.34 According to section 5 of the Defamation Act 2013, website operators can claim a defence by following the procedure detailed in the Defamation (Operators of Websites) Regulations 2013 (SI 2013/3028).

Prepare take down policies and procedures

11.35 Putting into effect all-encompassing terms for website use that:

1. Prohibit the upload of content that is infringing, defamatory, obscene, or otherwise unlawful or offensive.
2. The company is not responsible for any liability regarding that content.
3. Content removal is at the discretion of the site operator.
4. Before using users' content, make sure it complies with laws and obtain necessary rights. For more information on advertising-related issues.

Incorporating third-party websites for business purposes

11.36 Familiarise yourself with the terms of use and privacy policies of third-party providers.

11.37 It's important to ensure that the company's use aligns with the terms of each site, as these terms can vary greatly and include crucial limitations. Be especially attentive to terms connected to:

1. There are limitations on using social media sites for commercial purposes, such as advertising and marketing.
2. Ownership of intellectual property used on the site, including copyright material, trademarks, and customer information collected through the site.

3. Licensing requirements for the site owner and third parties to use the company's trademarks and intellectual property.
4. If other users misuse the company's intellectual property rights, what steps can the company take?
5. Make sure the site owner has appropriate and sufficient privacy practices for data disclosed or collected from site users.
6. Be vigilant about monitoring site terms and privacy policies for changes.
7. Make sure social media use is in accordance with legal requirements.
8. There is a risk of liability and reputational harm associated with certain activities for the company.
9. Laws against defamation and false advertising exist to prevent unfair and deceptive practices. Specifically, avoid participating in or allowing unethical marketing tactics, such as creating false blogs, posting fake positive or negative reviews about competitors.

The rules governing promotions and competitions

11.38 Restrictions on insider trading and other instances of market abuse.

11.39 Additionally, ensure adherence to industry-specific rules and regulations.

11.40 Provide clear guidance that includes provisions to protect:

1. Assets like trademarks, copyrights, and patents owned by the company.
2. Sensitive data belonging to the company.
3. Confidentiality and privacy of third-party information, including employee, customer, supplier, and other personal data protection.
4. Employee statements, particularly those made by senior management, can impact the company's reputation and relationships with customers, clients, and other third parties.

11.41 Include in this guidance provisions to prevent:

1. discrimination;
2. issues of harassment and bullying;
3. whistle-blowing or union activities can lead to victimisation and other forms of unlawful harm;
4. misrepresentation; and
5. defamation.

11.42 Ensure clear communication of this guidance, monitor compliance, and maintain consistent enforcement throughout the organisation. Discrimination or unfair dismissal claims could arise from inconsistent enforcement.

CONSIDER USING SOCIAL MEDIA AS A LEGAL TOOL

11.43 Take into account the use of social media websites.

11.44 This involves actions such as searching for conflicting trademark use and patent prior art, as well as monitoring for potential third-party infringement.

11.45 To share legal information and get referrals to legal advisors, this is an effective method.

11.46 How social media affects litigation.

11.47 Litigators have the ability to leverage social media sites to:

1. Lay claim to jurisdiction based on the international availability of social media websites.
2. Identify potential experts and other witnesses.
3. Seek disclosure of online communications and profiles to undermine the testimony of opposing parties and witnesses.
4. When a party discloses social media communications, it should focus on specific defence, claims, and witnesses. Even if a party can't get the requested disclosure from the other party or the relevant social media site, they may still be able to obtain it if the online information is publicly accessible (eg, publicly available YouTube videos, tweets, or Facebook profiles).
5. Content published on social media platforms could be subject to disclosure. The company's legal privilege protection could be jeopardised if information is disclosed on social media.

POSSIBILITY OF MARKET MANIPULATION

11.48 To communicate with investors, market professionals, and the public on social media sites, a company should:

1. Keep track of employee statements to prevent prohibited behaviour under the UK Market Abuse Regulation. This behaviour encompasses revealing non-public information outside of normal job duties and spreading false information about securities.
2. Monitor employee statements for accuracy, transparency, and compliance with securities regulations. Making these statements could be against the Financial Services Act 2012. Furthermore, make sure to monitor any links to third-party sites or content. Utilizing the links may give the impression that the company endorses this information.
3. To ensure compliance with Article 17 of the UK Market Abuse Regulation, which mandates prompt public disclosure of inside information that

directly concerns a company, selective disclosure of such information via social media should be prohibited, mirroring the company's regulation of disclosures through other media channels. This is except in specific situations where disclosure may be lawfully delayed.

4. To comply with the Financial Services and Markets Act 2000, make sure that social media posts do not encourage unlawful investment activity or offer securities.
5. Monitor connections to third-party sites or content. There are situations where sharing a link to another website may result in the communication of a financial promotion on that site.
6. Avoid making 'forward-looking statements' on social media without including necessary cautionary language, written risk factors, and disclaimers.
7. Before using names, images, or information of employees or third parties on social media for commercial purposes, make sure to obtain consent.
8. Before using an employee's or third party's name, image, or information, communicate the purpose and extent of the company's intended use and obtain written consent, especially for photographs.
9. If unauthorised use occurs, the company could face claims due to public disclosure or misuse of personal information, violating data protection laws.

REFLECT ON THE LEGAL RISKS INVOLVED IN USING SOCIAL MEDIA FOR SCREENING PURPOSES

11.49 It is important to disregard any protected characteristic disclosed on social media when making employment decisions.

11.50 To avoid potential discrimination claims, ensure that the same screening protocols are used for social media assessment of applicants or employees, regardless of their protected characteristics.

11.51 To prevent the creation of a prohibited blacklist, do not collect information on trade union membership or activities, and ensure there is no discrimination based on union membership, non-membership, or activities.

11.52 Follow UK data protection laws to guarantee that all data is obtained and processed fairly and lawfully. It's necessary to let the individual know how you conduct background checks.

11.53 Unauthorised access to password-protected electronic resources violates website terms of use and is unlikely to be fair and lawful handling of personal data.

11.54 Make sure the company follows social media website 'terms of use' policies during background checks.

11.55 Prioritise reliable and accurate information when making employment decisions, being mindful of the possibility of false or misleading information on social media platforms.

MENTIONS OF THE COMPANY ON RELATED SOCIAL MEDIA PLATFORMS

11.56 Provide information about any connections with third-party social media accounts.

11.57 The CPRs, also known as the Consumer Protection from Unfair Trading Regulations 2008, require fair trading. Specifically, the CPRs state that:

1. Unfair commercial practices include intentionally leaving out relevant information (regulation 4(b) and regulation 6).

2. It is inequitable to feature editorial content in the media to market a product without making it clear that the promotion was paid for by the trader (regulation 4(4)(d) and Schedule 1).

11.58 Since 1 April 2014, the Competition and Markets Authority has been enforcing these rules.

11.59 If the company decides to remunerate an influencer or give free products for reviewing, the company should:

1. Make sure the influencer understands their responsibility to disclose any form of compensation given to them.

2. Make sure the social media account is in compliance by monitoring it.

3. Keep an eye on the influencer's social media account to make sure they are not making false or misleading claims about the company's offerings.

INSURANCE

11.60 Liability from specific online activities may not fall under the coverage of commercial general liability insurance policies. Check existing insurance policies for proper coverage and determine if additional insurance is necessary and suitable. As an example, additional insurance might involve:

1. Coverage for cyber-liability, including data breaches and privacy breaches.

2. Interruption in business operations.

3. The issue of liability regarding website content.

IN SUMMARY

11.61 Do:

a. Ensure that there are clear, written terms of use and privacy policies for all the social media platforms, services, and apps offered by the company.

b. Familiarise yourself with the legal challenges of enabling users to post content and proactively manage the risks involved.

c. Before using any third-party social media sites, services, or applications, be sure to review their terms of use and privacy policies.

d. Make sure the company follows all relevant laws when using social media.

e. Give all staff explicit instructions on how to use social media in relation to the company.

f. Take into account the potential of social media as a legal instrument.

g. Realise the potential impact of social media on the way legal cases are handled.

h. Be transparent about any relationships with third-party social media personalities.

i. Examine the insurance policies of the organisation to make sure they offer the right coverage.

11.62 Do not:

a. Place unrealistic limitations on employees' social media usage.

b. Violate stock market regulations by utilising social media.

c. Without obtaining consent, do not use names, images, or information of employees or third parties for promotional or commercial purposes on social media.

d. Conducting background checks on job applicants and promotion candidates via social media without considering legal risks is not advisable.

SOCIAL MEDIA CHECKLIST FOR EMPLOYEES

11.63 By following this checklist, companies can address potential legal and reputational risks related to employees' use of social media.

11.64 Establish guidelines for social media engagement.

11.65 Ensure employee understanding of social media usage expectations by either implementing a separate policy or including it in the employee handbook.

11.66 Remind employees that social media activity at work can be monitored and may lead to disciplinary action, as outlined in the employee policies. Additionally, it should be reminded that engaging in harmful online behaviour towards the company may be considered misconduct or even gross misconduct.

11.67 Provide the necessary restrictions that are applicable.

11.68 Employees' use of company IT resources.

11.69 Employees accessing and using company intellectual property and privileged information.

11.70 Use of third-party intellectual property by employees.

11.71 Safeguarding the privacy and confidentiality of third parties.

11.72 Harassment or bullying of fellow employees is strictly prohibited.

11.73 Discrimination is prohibited.

11.74 The company prohibits negative comments about itself, its employees, business contacts, or competitors.

11.75 Verify that the social media policy is in harmony with the rest of the policies.

11.76 Safeguard valuable business connections and cultivate a positive company image by:

1. Making sure the employment contract explicitly forbids defamation on social media.
2. Updating policies to emphasise the connection between employees' social media posts and their employer's image. One option is to mandate employees to include a disclaimer in their social media posts stating that their opinions are not reflective of the company.
3. Safeguard classified and exclusive data.
4. Educate employees about the risks associated with revealing or misusing the company's confidential information or intellectual property in the context of social media. The disclosure or misuse of confidential information or intellectual property by an employee might cause:

There has been a breach of the terms of employment

11.77 Violate a confidentiality agreement between the company and a third party, resulting in the company also being in breach.

11.78 Threaten the company's ability to maintain ownership of its intellectual property.

11.79 Cause employees or clients to feel embarrassed or confused.

11.80 Put legal privilege between the company and its internal legal counsel at risk.

11.81 Violations of securities laws can happen when material non-public information is disclosed without appropriate cautionary statements or necessary information, or when false or misleading information is used to create a deceptive market impression for a company's securities.

11.82 Formulate company policies and employment contracts that address these risks.

11.83 Take measures to prevent harassment and bullying on social media.

11.84 Ensure that social media is incorporated into the anti-harassment and anti-bullying policies, as well as in all training programs aimed at preventing workplace harassment.

11.85 Ensure that the corporate response to harassment, including both sexual and non-sexual forms, and bullying via social media aligns with the response to harassment and bullying in other situations.

TRAIN EMPLOYEES

11.86 Deliver comprehensive training to human resources management on effectively monitoring and enforcing company policies, restrictions, guidelines, and contract provisions related to social media. It is imperative to adhere to employees' privacy rights when carrying out any actions.

11.87 It is advisable to refrain from imposing any unnecessary limitations.

11.88 Unbalanced constraints can have a detrimental effect on employee morale and open the door to non-compliance, providing no tangible benefits to the company in terms of protecting its property, reputation, or workforce.

IN SUMMARY

11.89 Do:

a. Implement a social media policy to promote responsible utilisation of social media by employees.

b. The policy is intended to prevent employees from engaging in social media activities that may negatively impact the company.

c. Conduct training programs for employees to ensure their understanding of appropriate social media usage, and enforce compliance monitoring measures.

11.90 Do not:

a. Grant employees permission to divulge or misuse confidential or proprietary information.

b. Allow employees to utilise social media as a tool for harassing their coworkers.

c. Implement excessive constraints on the employee's access to social media platforms.

WHAT IS SOCIAL MEDIA AND WHY DOES IT MATTER?

Social media classifications

11.91 There are several fundamental categories that encompass social media sites, applications, and services. Certain websites, web services, and applications can fall into multiple categories, while others may transition into different categories over time. When assessing the legal issues associated with each category, it is essential to comprehend their respective characteristics.

11.92 A blog is a self-published website where authors, also known as bloggers, list information and other content in reverse chronological order. It is commonly hosted on platforms like WordPress, Tumblr, and Blogger. Certain blogs allow for user comments, thus classifying them as a type of social media.

11.93 A social or business networking platform refers to a website or application that enables individuals, corporations, and organisations to establish connections with other users and showcase their networks of friends and contacts, allowing other users to establish connections with them. Notable illustrations consist of Facebook, Google+, and LinkedIn.

11.94 A website designed for the purpose of digital media sharing, enabling users to upload and share videos, photographs, and accompanying text. Snapchat, Instagram, Pinterest, YouTube, and Flickr are illustrative examples within this category.

11.95 A crowdfunding site is an online platform that facilitates users in seeking investments from a broad spectrum of individuals who contribute nominal amounts of financial support. Among the examples are Kickstarter, GoFundMe, and Funding Circle.

11.96 A wiki is a type of database that allows live editing by the general public, as seen in websites like Wikipedia and Wikitravel.

WIDELY USED SOCIAL MEDIA SITES AND SERVICES

11.97 Social media platforms facilitate the connection between users, new content, and communication channels, enabling an immediate and enduring online presence. Numerous websites incorporate conventional communication features into their exclusive technologies, such as email, chat (eg, instant messaging), blogging, and more. The primary purpose of the majority of social media platforms is to facilitate the sharing of links among users, making them publicly accessible.

11.98 Presented below is an inventory, inclusive of descriptions, of renowned social media sites, services, and applications.

11.99 ASKfm and Quora are social networking sites that facilitate the exchange of questions and answers among users.

11.100 Discord is a targeted social networking platform aimed at connecting individuals within the online gaming community. Users can simultaneously overlay voice calls during gaming, establish servers and communities, and engage in real-time text chat.

11.101 Facebook is a social networking site that is under the ownership of Meta. Members have the ability to engage with friends and individuals in their network, sharing links, comments, photos, and videos. They can also participate in public discussions by writing on members' 'walls'. Additionally, it provides the option for members to post private messages that are not accessible to the public.

11.102 Flickr is an internet-based application designed for photo management and sharing. Its members can upload and make their photo and video content accessible for viewing and commenting on the web, both publicly and privately. The usage of Flickr is limited to personal use only, excluding commercial purposes.

11.103 Geni.com, MyHeritage, and Ancestry.com are online platforms that facilitate private communication between family members, allowing them to share photos and messages within their digital family tree. Users construct their family lineage by establishing connections with other relatives who are registered members of the website and uploading personal genealogical information.

11.104 Google+ is a social networking platform that allows users to connect with friends and individuals in their network and view their stream of posts.

11.105 Instagram is a platform owned by Meta that enables users to share photos and videos. Within their community, users are able to share photographs and videos, tag fellow users, and engage in direct messaging.

11.106 Kickstarter is a website that facilitates crowdfunding, where members can invest in projects and receive non-financial compensation.

11.107 LinkedIn is a professional networking website that enables members to maintain connections, establish contacts, and seek assistance in job searches and other career objectives.

11.108 Meetup is a social networking platform that facilitates group organisation and the planning of in-person meetings and events based on shared interests and hobbies.

11.109 Pinterest is a social sharing site that adopts a pin-board style, allowing users to create and manage image collections centred around themes such as events, interests, and hobbies. Users are able to engage in the action of "re-pinning" images from other users onto their personal board, expressing their liking for images and exploring categories of their interest.

11.110 Reddit is a social news platform where users can submit content for voting, which determines the ranking and positioning of posts on the site's pages.

11.111 Snapchat is a multimedia messaging application that enables users to send and receive pictures, videos, and messages that automatically disappear after a short duration.

11.112 Telegram is a multimedia messaging app that is both free and prioritises security, implementing end-to-end encryption for all media transmitted within chats and groups.

11.113 Threads is a microblogging platform under the ownership of Meta, designed as a competitor to X (formerly known as Twitter).

11.114 TikTok is a short-form video sharing platform that provides users with the ability to create and share videos that can range from 15 seconds to 10 minutes.

11.115 Tumblr functions as a blogging website that allows its members to create and share diverse types of content, including text, photos, links, music, and videos, across various platforms such as browsers, phones, desktop computers, and e-mails.

11.116 Twitch is a digital platform that offers live-streaming services primarily for the online gaming community. By means of instant text chat, users have the ability to interact with an audience while streaming their online gaming sessions.

11.117 Microsoft's Viva Engage is a microblogging site specifically created to streamline internal workplace communications. While employee usage is complimentary, companies seeking administrative control and management of their corporate networks are required to pay a fee. The transfer of Yammer to Viva Engage took place in 2023.

11.118 WhatsApp messenger is a free instant messaging app, owned by Meta, that enables users to communicate through voice or video calls and exchange messages in multiple formats including text, audio files, images, and documents.

11.119 WordPress is a software program that is open-source and facilitates website publishing, blog management, mailing list administration, and online store operation.

11.120 X (formerly known as Twitter) is a microblogging platform where users can post concise updates about their thoughts or activities, limited to 140 characters or less. These updates can be shared through instant messages, mobile texts, or the website.

11.121 YouTube serves as an online video community where users can publicly post, share, and view original videos, accompanied by a forum for user comments and a platform for creating individual channels.

Here is an example of a social media policy

About this policy

11.122 This policy is in place to minimise the risks to our business through use of social media.

11.123 This policy deals with the use of all forms of social media, including Facebook, LinkedIn, X (formerly Twitter), Wikipedia[, TikTok][, Instagram][, Snapchat][, Tumblr] and all other social networking sites, internet postings and blogs. It applies to use of social media for business purposes as well as personal use that may affect our business in any way.

11.124 This policy does not form part of any employee's contract of employment and we may amend it at any time.

Personal use of social media

11.125 [Personal use of social media is never permitted during working hours or by means of our computers, networks, and other IT resources and communications systems.

OR

Occasional personal use of social media during working hours is permitted so long as it does not involve unprofessional or inappropriate content, does not interfere with your employment responsibilities or productivity, and complies with this policy.]

Prohibited use

11.126 You must avoid making any social media communications that could damage our business interests or reputation, even indirectly.

11.127 You must not use social media to:

a. defame or disparage us, our staff or any third party;

b. harass, bully or unlawfully discriminate against staff or third parties;

c. make false or misleading statements; or

d. impersonate colleagues or third parties.

11.128 You must not express opinions on our behalf via social media, unless expressly authorised to do so by your manager. You may be required to undergo training in order to obtain that authorisation.

11.129 You must not comment on social media about sensitive business-related topics, such as our performance, or do anything to jeopardise our trade secrets, confidential information and intellectual property. You must not include our logos or other trade marks in any social media posting or in your profile on any social media.

11.130 [You are not permitted to add business contacts made during the course of your employment to personal social networking accounts.

OR

The contact details of business contacts made during the course of your employment are our confidential information. On termination of your employment, you must provide us with a copy of all that information, delete all that information from your personal social networking accounts and destroy any further copies of that information that you may have.]

11.131 Any misuse of social media should be reported to [POSITION].

Guidelines for responsible use of social media

11.132 You should make it clear in social media postings, or on your personal profile, that you are speaking on your own behalf. Write in the first person and use a personal email address.

11.133 Be respectful to others when making any statement on social media and be aware that you are personally responsible for all communications which will be published on the internet for anyone to see.

11.134 If you disclose your affiliation with us on your profile or in any social media postings, you must state that your views do not represent those of your employer (unless you are authorised to speak on our behalf as set out in paragraph 3.3). You should also ensure that your profile and any content you post are consistent with the professional image you present to clients and colleagues.

11.135 If you are uncertain or concerned about the appropriateness of any statement or posting, refrain from posting it until you have discussed it with your manager.

11.136 If you see social media content that disparages or reflects poorly on us, you should contact [your manager OR [DEPARTMENT]].

Breach of this policy

11.137 Breach of this policy may result in disciplinary action up to and including dismissal. [Any member of staff suspected of committing a breach of this policy will be required to co-operate with our investigation.]

11.138 You may be required to remove any social media content that we consider constitutes a breach of this policy. Failure to comply with such a request may in itself result in disciplinary action.

CHAPTER12

INTERNATIONAL LAW AND INTERACTION BETWEEN STATES

Benjamin Ang and Tan E-Reng

12.01 A business or other private organisation could be the victim of a State-sponsored cyber-attack. For example, in recent times, North Korea has been blamed for the attack on Sony, Russia has been blamed for the attack on the US Democratic National Convention, and the US and Israel have been blamed for the attack on the Natanz nuclear power plants in Iran. If a cyber-incident can be attributed to a Nation-State (which is not a trivial task), this escalates it beyond conventional cyber-crime, and the relevant government may want to explore if international law applies.

DETERMINING IF INTERNATIONAL HUMANITARIAN LAW / LAW OF ARMED CONFLICT APPLIES

12.02 In the past, 'military objects' and 'civilian objects' could be more clearly distinguished. Military objects were considered as valid targets during an armed conflict, whereas civilian objects were to be avoided. However, as civilians and civilian objects today are highly interconnected to military personnel and objects, the risk of harm to civilians and civilian objects is very high in cyber-warfare.[1]

12.03 Because of these risks, there has been much debate on the application of international law to cyber-operations in general and cyber-warfare in particular. Cyber-warfare describes cyber-operations conducted in or amounting to an armed conflict.[2] This could include developing malware to target an adversary's computer or systems, infiltrating networks to collect, export, destroy, or change data (such as wiping out surveillance data), or to trigger, alter, or manipulate processes that are controlled by computer (such as shutting down a power station).

12.04 The law applicable during armed conflict is referred to as both International Humanitarian Law (IHL) and the Law of Armed Conflict (LOAC).[3] The core principles of IHL rules governing the conduct of hostilities, such as

1 Diamond, E. (2014, July). *Applying International Humanitarian Law to Cyber Warfare.* Retrieved from Institute for National Security Studies: www.inss.org.il/publication/applying-international-humanitarian-law-to-cyber-warfare/.

2 ibid.

3 Brown, G. D. (2017, November). *INTERNATIONAL LAW APPLIES TO CYBER WARFARE! NOW WHAT?* Retrieved from Southwestern Law Review: www.swlaw.edu/sites/default/files/2017-08/355%20International%20Law%20Applies%20to%20Cyber%20Warfare-Brown.pdf.

distinction, proportionality, and the duty to employ precautionary measures, are broad enough to cover cyber-operations as well.[4]

12.05 To attempt to give the matter some clarity, the United Nations Group of Governmental Experts (UNGGE) on Developments in the Field of Information and Telecommunications in the Context of International Security agreed that 'international law, and in particular the Charter of the United Nations, is applicable' to cyber-warfare.[5]

12.06 One these core principles, the 'distinction' rule, is that military personnel and objects can be targeted during an armed conflict, but civilians and civilian objects should not be. In the case of cyber-operations, this distinction is difficult to apply.

12.07 As the name implies, LOAC applies only during armed conflict. Some of the key challenges in applying LOAC to a cyber-operation include:

(1) What types of cyber-operations amount to 'armed conflict' (if not, LOAC does not apply);

(2) What types of intrusions into a country's computer systems are equivalent to military invasions of territorial sovereignty;

(3) Which computer systems are relevant, because civilians and military share much of the same computer infrastructure and networks; and

(4) How to distinguish between cybercrime, cyber-espionage, and cyber-warfare. (Brown, 2017)

12.08 This can be illustrated by looking at several scenarios.

1. A cyber-operation occurs during peacetime:

    (a) If the cyber-operation has kinetic effects (property destruction, injuries, death), then it can be treated like a kinetic operation (invasion, missile), and would amount to starting an armed conflict.[6] LOAC would apply.

    (b) If the cyber-operation does not have kinetic effects, but causes harrasment, disruption, and interference, then it is not clear when that alone would amount to armed conflict. LOAC might or might not apply.[7]

4 Diamond, E. (2014, July). *Applying International Humanitarian Law to Cyber Warfare.* Retrieved from Institute for National Security Studies: www.inss.org.il/publication/applying-international-humanitarian-law-to-cyber-warfare/.

5 U.N. Secretary. (2013). *Report of the Group of Governmental Experts on Developments in the Field of Information and*. 19, U.N. GAOR, 68th Sess., U.N. Doc. A/68/150.

6 Brown, G. D. (2017, November). *INTERNATIONAL LAW APPLIES TO CYBER WARFARE! NOW WHAT?* Retrieved from Southwestern Law Review: www.swlaw.edu/sites/default/files/2017-08/355%20International%20Law%20Applies%20to%20Cyber%20Warfare-Brown.pdf.

7 ibid.

2. A cyber-operation occurs during an ongoing war or armed conflict, where LOAC applies:

   (a) If the cyber-operation has kinetic effects (property destruction, injuries, death), then it can be treated like a kinetic operation (invasion, missile), then it would be unlawful under LOAC

   (b) If the cyber-operation does not have kinetic effects, but causes harrasment, disruption, and interference, then it might not be unlawful under LOAC

12.09 The LOAC should apply to cyber-attacks inside an armed conflict; a cyber-attack defined as 'a cyber-operation that is reasonably expected to cause injury or death to persons or damage or destruction to objects'.[8] This means that cyber-operations that cause inconvenience, even extreme inconvenience, but no direct injury or death, and no destruction of property, would not amount to 'cyber attacks' and LOAC would not apply. Possible examples could include disruption of major airlines or airport computer systems, causing huge financial losses, or shutting down traffic control systems, or deleting or modifying balances in bank accounts.[9]

12.10 This approach would potentially leave the economy and civilian livelihoods unprotected by LOAC. Some international law experts have thus suggested a 'functionality' approach to deciding whether a cyber-operation amounts to a cyber-attack (thereby making LOAC apply).[10] Loss of functionality would occur when the cyber-operation:

(1) physically damages a component of a computer system;

(2) causes a computer system to cease functioning until the operating system is reinstalled, or

(3) causes a computer system to cease functioning by deleting or interfering with data on the system[11]

12.11 This could mean that LOAC applies to cyber-incidents such as the following:

(1) a malware that causes hard-disks or computer fans to overheat (such as the Stuxnet virus that disabled the Natanz nuclear power plants in Iran);

(2) ransomware that locks up computers and prevents them from functioning (such as the Petya malware), or

8 Tallin Manual 2.0. (2017). *Tallinn Manual 2.0 on the International Law Applicable to Cyber Warfare.*

9 Washington Times. Brown, G. D. (2017, November). *INTERNATIONAL LAW APPLIES TO CYBER WARFARE! NOW WHAT?* Retrieved from Southwestern Law Review: www.swlaw.edu/sites/default/files/2017-08/355%20International%20Law%20Applies%20to%20Cyber%20Warfare-Brown.pdf.

10 Tallin Manual 2.0. (2017). *Tallinn Manual 2.0 on the International Law Applicable to Cyber Warfare.*

11 ibid.

(3) deletion of software, which causes the computer to cease functioning (such as the NotPetya malware).

12.12 The second interpretation of functionality is preferred by Michael Schmitt, General Editor of the Tallinn Manual, writing in his personal capacity.[12] The third (and broadest) interpretation of functionality is consistent with the position of the International Committee of the Red Cross and Red Crescent (ICRC), which states:

> '[T]he fact that a cyber-operation does not lead to the destruction of an attacked object is also irrelevant. Pursuant to article 52(2) of Additional Protocol I, only objects that make an effective contribution to military action and whose total or partial destruction, capture or neutralization offers a definite military advantage, may be attacked. By referring not only to destruction or capture of the object but also to its neutralization the definition implies that it is immaterial whether an object is disabled through destruction or in any other way.'[13]

12.13 The ICRC view would make many non-lethal but disruptive cyber-operations illegal under LOAC. While these interpretations appear attractive, some experts argue that it is not desirable to render non-destructive, non-lethal cyber-operations (eg disruption of air traffic or trade) illegal under LOAC, because such cyber-operations could actually be less harmful for the civilian population than destructive, lethal kinetic attacks (eg bombs, missiles, invasions) – 'If States are permitted to employ a broad range of disruptive cyber options, even against civilian objects, in many cases it could offer a rational alternative to the collateral damage and casualties likely to result from lawful kinetic attacks'.[14]

12.14 At the end of the day, these interpretations are not binding on States. The ICRC is not the United Nations. The Tallinn Manual was developed by an independent international group of experts, at the invitation of the NATO Cooperative Cyber Defence Centre of Excellence, but is not a NATO directive. This means that the international law governing cyber-operations is still not settled.

APPLYING PRINCIPLES OF IHL AND LOAC

12.14 Assuming that IHL and LOAC apply to a cyber-incident, there are three core principles of distinction, proportionality, and military application.

12 Schmitt, M. (2014). Rewired Warfare: Rethinking the Law of Cyber Attack. *INTL REV OF THE RED CROSS*.

13 Droege, C. (2012). Cyber Warfare, International Humanitarian Law, and The Protection of Civilians. *INT'L REV. OF THE RED CROSS*.

14 Brown, G. D. (2017, November). *INTERNATIONAL LAW APPLIES TO CYBER WARFARE! NOW WHAT?* Retrieved from Southwestern Law Review: www.swlaw.edu/sites/default/files/2017-08/355%20International%20Law%20Applies%20to%20Cyber%20Warfare-Brown.pdf.

(1) **Principle of Distinction**: Parties may direct their operations only against military objectives. However, most cyber infrastructure is dual use, serving both civilian and military purposes. That makes them military objectives because of the military purpose they serve, and therefore valid targets under IHL/LOAC. This could mean that cables, routers, nodes, and satellites are valid targets – even though civilians also rely on this infrastructure.[15]

(2) **Principle of Proportionality**: Parties cannot attack if such attacks 'may be expected to cause incidental loss of civilian life, injury to civilians, damage to civilian objects, or a combination thereof, which would be excessive in relation to the concrete and direct military advantage anticipated.' This principle would not apply to a cyber-incident that falls short of these criteria. One challenge would be the definition of 'damage' – whether the 'functionality' approach proposed in the Tallinn Manual above could be applied.

(3) **Principle of Precaution**: Parties are to take care to spare the civilian population and civilian objects from harm. Again, the challenge lies in the definition of harm.

If any of these principles are contravened, the next question is how the government could respond.

NATO RESPONSES

12.15 NATO has 'decided that a cyber-attack can trigger Article 5, meaning that a cyber-attack can trigger collective defence',[16] ie an armed attack on one NATO member is considered an attack on all members, with the caveat that 'it's also important to understand that cyber is not something that always triggers Article 5'. The Secretary General acknowledged that one of the difficulties would be in attributing a cyber-attack to the true attacker. However, NATO has not defined what would amount to a cyber-attack.

12.16 One wonders what NATO would do today, if there was a repeat of the 2007 denial-of-service attacks on Estonian private and government websites, which were largely attributed to Russian government hackers.[17] At the time, the Estonian government declared the incident an act of terrorism instead of an act of war, so IHL and LOAC did not apply.

12.17 Under the current ICRC or Schmitt interpretations of functionality, such denial-of-service attacks could arguably amount to cyber-attacks where IHL and

15 Diamond, E. (2014, July). *Applying International Humanitarian Law to Cyber Warfare.* Retrieved from Institute for National Security Studies: www.inss.org.il/publication/applying-international-humanitarian-law-to-cyber-warfare/.

16 Stoltenberg, J. (2016). *Press Conference following the North Atlantic Council meeting at the Level of NATO Defense Ministers.* Retrieved from North Atlantic Treaty Organization: www.nato.int/cps/en/natohq/opinions_132349.htm?selectedLocale=en.

17 BBC NEWS . (2007, May). *The Cyber Raiders Hitting Estonia.* Retrieved from BBC NEWS: www.bbc.co.uk/2/hi/europe/6665195.stm.

LOAC apply. On the other hand, in hindsight it also appears that the Estonian government may have decided not to declare the denial-of-service attacks as acts of war because of political rather than technical legal reasons, to avoid escalating the situation with Russia.

12.18 At the end of the day, private organisations who are victims of State-sponsored attacks may well find that even if their cases can technically be classified as subject to IHL/LOAC, their government may not want to pursue the issue for political reasons, especially if the alleged attacker is a global superpower or has significant economic influence.

UNITED NATIONS CHARTER RESPONSES

Use of force

12.19 Article 2(4) of the United Nations Charter states, 'All Members shall refrain in their international relations from the threat or *use of force (emphasis added)* against the territorial integrity or political independence of any state, or in any other manner inconsistent with the Purposes of the United Nations.' This means a cyber-incident would violate Article 2(4) if it rises to the level of a 'use of force', for example if it:

(a) violates the territorial integrity (has a physical /kinetic effect within the territory of the State victim); or

(b) violates the political independence of the State victim, or

(c) is inconsistent with the Purposes of the United Nations.

The attacker State would then be in violation of the UN Charter and would be subject to penalties and sanctions.

12.20 It may be surprising to businesses and private organisations that there are certain actions, which though commercially egregious and possibly amounting to cyber-crime, would not be subject to IHL or LOAC. For example, international law does not prohibit propaganda, psychological operations, espionage, or mere economic pressure per se.[18] These types of action are 'presumptively legal' under international law, because acts that are not forbidden (by customary law or treaty) are permitted.

ARMED ATTACK AND RIGHT OF SELF-DEFENCE

12.21 If the cyber-incident was more severe than a 'use of force', and was an 'armed attack', then the victim State could be entitled under Article 51 to use

18 Thelen, J. (2014). *Applying International Law to Cyber Warfare.* Retrieved from RSA Conference: www.rsaconference.com/writable/presentations/file_upload/law-f03a-applying-international-law-to-cyber-warfare.pdf.

its 'inherent right of individual or collective self-defence', which could include sanctions, launching a cyber-attack on the attacker, or even use of force. This would also depend on the victim State's risk appetite and assessment of whether the situation might escalate.

12.22 From past cases of small scale bombings and aerial attacks, an 'armed attack' would be one that involves destruction of property or loss of life.[19] That would mean that a denial-of-service attack per se might amount to a use of force (if it meets the criteria in the previous paragraph) but would not amount to an armed attack. The victim State would have to rely on the operation of Article 2(4) and would not be entitled to self-defence.

NON-STATE ACTORS

12.23 The principle of law is that 'a party to an armed conflict shall be responsible for all acts by persons forming part of its armed forces.' (ICJ in *Democratic Republic of the Congo v Uganda*,[20] Armed Activities on the Territory of the Congo.)

12.24 This principle applies to hackers who are soldiers, or employed by the government, or by private defence companies that are authorised by a government to engage in active offensive or defensive measures. The principle is more difficult to apply where the cyber-attack is carried out by mercenaries instead – it must be shown that 'the person or group of persons is in fact acting on the instructions of, or under the direction or control of, that State in carrying out the conduct.'[21] This is difficult at the best of times, and even more difficult in the case of cyber-operations, where there is the perennial problem of attribution of cyber-attacks, which can be routed through multiple servers in multiple countries.

12.25 The use of mercenaries or 'cyber proxies' is very attractive to attacking States because of they can deny responsibility while achieving their political goals.[22] According to legal expert Tim Maurer, there are three main types of proxy relationships:

(1) Delegation – The State has significant or overall control over the proxy.

(2) Orchestration – The State supports the proxy and they share a common ideology, but the state does not give specific instructions.

(3) Sanctioning – The State provides an enabling environment by deliberately turning a blind eye to the proxy's activities.

19 Gervais, M. (2012). Cyber Attacks and the Laws of War . *BERKELEY J. INT'L L.*
20 *Dem. Rep. Congo v Uganda*, 2005 I.C.J. 168, ¶ 214 (Dec. 19)
21 Gervais, M. (2012). Cyber Attacks and the Laws of War . *BERKELEY J. INT'L L.*
22 Maurer, T. (2018). *Cyber Mercenaries.*

12.26 Maurer suggests that the principles around privateering could apply, but also notes that normative taboos against cyber-privateering are unlikely in the foreseeable future, largely because of the shortage of cyber-expertise within governments and armies around the world, that 'fuels a dependence on non-state actors.'[23]

CYBER NORMS AS THE BASIS FOR INTERNATIONAL LAW

12.27 The evolution of IHL to cover cyber-operations is difficult because international norms cannot be enacted by the legislature of any single State, but emerge only when multiple States express their consent to be bound by it.[24] The basis of this consent would be the development of internationally agreed norms of behaviour in cyberspace, because 'norms reflect the international community's expectations, set standards for responsible State behaviour and allow the international community to assess the activities and intentions of States.'

UNGGE CYBER NORMS

12.28 With the intention of developing said norms, the UN convened the United Nations Group of Governmental Experts on Developments in the Field of Information and Telecommunications in the Context of International Security (UNGGE) in 2004, consisting of initially 15 countries, and finally 25 countries in 2016. In 2013, the third GGE report stated that:

- International law, and in particular the Charter of the United Nations, is applicable ....
- State sovereignty and international norms and principles that flow from sovereignty apply to State conduct of ICT-related activities....
- State efforts to address the security of ICTs must go hand-in-hand with respect for human rights and fundamental freedoms ....
- States must meet their international obligations regarding internationally wrongful acts attributable to them. States must not use proxies to commit internationally wrongful acts. States should seek to ensure that their territories are not used by non-State actors for unlawful use of ICTs.

12.29 The fourth GGE report in 2015 observed that:

- States have jurisdiction over the ICT infrastructure located within their territory.

23 ibid.

24 Diamond, E. (2014, July). *Applying International Humanitarian Law to Cyber Warfare.* Retrieved from Institute for National Security Studies: www.inss.org.il/publication/applying-international-humanitarian-law-to-cyber-warfare/.

- In their use of ICTs, States must observe, among other principles of international law, State sovereignty, sovereign equality, the settlement of disputes by peaceful means and non-intervention in the internal affairs of other States.... States must comply with their obligations under international law to respect and protect human rights and fundamental freedoms.
- [T]he Group noted the inherent right of States to take measures consistent with international law and as recognized in the Charter.
- The Group notes the established international legal principles, including, where applicable, the principles of humanity, necessity, proportionality and distinction;
- States must not use proxies to commit internationally wrongful acts using ICTs, and should seek to ensure that their territory is not used by non-State actors to commit such acts.
- States must meet their international obligations regarding internationally wrongful acts attributable to them under international law.

12.30 Eleven norms were agreed upon at the time, and NATO Cooperative Cyber Defence Centre of Excellence has helpfully divided them into two broad categories:[25]

(1) Limiting norms:

(a) states should not knowingly allow their territory to be used for internationally wrongful acts using ICTs;

(b) states should not conduct or knowingly support ICT activity that intentionally damages critical infrastructure;

(c) states should take steps to ensure supply chain security, and should seek to prevent the proliferation of malicious ICT and the use of harmful hidden functions;

(d) states should not conduct or knowingly support activity to harm the information systems of another state's emergency response teams (CERT/CSIRTS) and should not use their own teams for malicious international activity;

(e) states should respect the UN resolutions that are linked to human rights on the internet and to the right to privacy in the digital age.

(2) Good practices and positive duties:

(a) states should cooperate to increase stability and security in the use of ICTs and to prevent harmful practices;

25 NATO CCDCOE. (2015, August). *2015 UN GGE Report: Major Players Recommending Norms of Behaviour, Highlighting Aspects of International Law.* Retrieved from NATO CCDCOE: https://ccdcoe.org/2015-un-gge-report-major-players-recommending-norms-behaviour-highlighting-aspects-international-l-0.html.

(b) states should consider all relevant information in case of ICT incidents;

(c) states should consider how best to cooperate to exchange information, to assist each other, and to prosecute terrorist and criminal use of ICTs;

(d) states should take appropriate measures to protect their critical infrastructure;

(e) states should respond to appropriate requests for assistance by other states whose critical infrastructure is subject to malicious ICT acts;

(f) states should encourage responsible reporting of ICT vulnerabilities and should share remedies to these.

12.31 When the UNGGE met in 2017, they were unable to produce a consensus report on implementing the said norms. Apparently, this was because of the objections of a small number of States, including Cuba (the only one who made an official statement) and, reportedly, Russia and China, to three legal principles 1) the right to respond to internationally wrongful acts (a veiled reference to countermeasures); 2) the right to self-defence; and 3) international humanitarian law.[26]

The last GGE met between 2019 and 2021 and finally agreed on a consensus report.

12.32 In 2019, under resolution 73/27,[27] the General Assembly established an Open Ended Working Group on Developments in the Field of ICTs in the Context of International Security (OEWG) for all member states to develop a more robust system of rules, norms, and principles to guide responsible state behaviour in their usage of ICTs and in their conduct of activities in cyberspace.[28]

12.33 In December 2020, following a successful initial round of discussions and negotiations, the OEWG was further renewed for the term of 2021-2025, under resolution 75/240.[29] [30] This OEWG uniquely allows participation from non-state stakeholders, subject to the ability of states to veto. Participants of the OEWG, in parallel with related UNGGEs, have continually focused their efforts on addressing and discussing topics such as existing and emerging cybersecurity threats, the application of international law in the context of ICT use, cyberspace

26 (Schmitt & Vihul, International Cyber Law Politicized: The UNGGE's Failure to Advance Cyber Norms, 2017).

27 United Nations General Assembly. (2018, December). *A/RES/73/27*. Retrieved from *United Nations*: https://undocs.org/Home/Mobile?FinalSymbol=A%2FRES%2F73%2F27&Language=E&DeviceType=Desktop&LangRequested=False.

28 Oxford Martin School. *The CMM at the UN OEWG: The UK encourages Member States to undertake national cybersecurity capacity assessment*. Retrieved from *University of Oxford*: https://gcscc.ox.ac.uk/article/cmm-at-the-un-oewg.

29 ibid.

30 United Nations General Assembly. (2021, January). *A/RES/75/240*. Retrieved from *United Nations*: https://undocs.org/Home/Mobile?FinalSymbol=A%2FRES%2F75%2F240&Language=E&DeviceType=Desktop&LangRequested=False.

norms and rules for states and state actors, as well as measures for building confidence and capacity.[31]

12.34 In December 2022, The General Assembly adopted resolution 77/37, titled 'Programme of action to advance responsible State behaviour in the use of information and communications technologies in the context of international security'.[32] [33] This resolution articulated the General Assembly's support for the proposal to formally establish a permanent, dedicated mechanism within the United Nations that facilitates the implementation of norms promoting responsible State behaviour when using ICTs and operating within cyberspace.[34] If the proposed programme of action is successful, it will become a permanent successor to the OEWG 2021-2025 when the latter concludes in 2025.[35]

12.35 The OEWG 2021-2025 has faced many challenges in reaching consensus because states disagree on issues like Russia's proposal for a legally binding convention, supply chain, and human rights. This is exacerbated by geopolitical tensions, arising from Russia's invasion of Ukraine, tensions in the South China Sea, and US – China competition in trade and technology.[36]

12.36 Besides the UNGGE's proposed eleven norms,, there are five other major governmental proposals that are significant the global dialogue on cybersecurity norms.[37]

1. Confidence building measures developed by the Organization for Security and Co-operation in Europe and published in December 2013 (OSCE CBMs).
2. The Code of Conduct submitted to the United Nations General Assembly by Member States of the Shanghai Cooperation Organisation in January 2015 (SCO proposal).
3. Norms outlined in remarks delivered US government officials in May 2015 (USG proposals).

31 United Nations Office for Disarmament Affairs. *Developments in the field of information and telecommunications in the context of international security*. Retrieved from *United Nations Office for Disarmament Affairs*: https://disarmament.unoda.org/ict-security/.

32 ibid.

33 United Nations General Assembly. (2022, December). *A/RES/77/37*. Retrieved from *United Nations*: https://www.undocs.org/Home/Mobile?FinalSymbol=A%2FRES%2F77%2F37&Language=E&DeviceType=Desktop&LangRequested=False.

34 ibid.

35 Digital Watch Observatory. (2022, November). Resolution on the programme of action (PoA) on cybersecurity adopted. Retrieved from Digital Watch Observatory: https://dig.watch/updates/resolution-on-the-programme-of-action-poa-on-cybersecurity-adopted.

36 Avoiding deadlock ahead of future UN Cyber Security Negotiations. Royal United Services Institute. (2023, August 31). https://www.rusi.org/explore-our-research/publications/commentary/avoiding-deadlock-ahead-future-un-cyber-security-negotiations.

37 Microsoft. (2017). *From Articulation to Implementation: Enabling progress on cybersecurity norms*. Microsoft.

4. Agreement between the US and China in September 2015 regarding cyber-enabled theft of intellectual property, law enforcement collaboration, and other cyber-security measures (US-China agreement).
5. G20 Leaders Communique from the G20 regarding cyber-enabled theft of intellectual property, privacy, and international collaboration for cybersecurity (G20 Communiqué).

12.37 In ASEAN, Singapore originally allocated US$7.3 million (S$10 million) to build an ASEAN Cyber Capacity Programme under its Cybersecurity Strategy to 'Forge International and ASEAN Cooperation to Counter Cyber Threats and Cybercrime'. This fund was used to host international and regional exchanges on norms, and to run training programmes with partner countries for building awareness and capacity in cyber norms.

12.38 In 2018, Singapore announced that it would be allocating a further budget of approximately US$22 million (S$30 million) for the establishment of the ASEAN-Singapore Cybersecurity Centre of Excellence (ASCCE), [38] as an institute with the primary function of producing research and providing training in international law, cyber strategy, cyber defence, legislation, norms, and policy, among other related domains.[39]

12.39 One initiative at the ASCCE is the UN-Singapore Cyber Fellowship Programme, which is jointly run twice a year by the National University of Singapore and the Cyber Security Agency of Singapore, through the ASCCE and the United Nations Office for Disarmament (UNODA).[40] Its inaugural programme in August 2022 was attended by high-profile national cybersecurity officials whom, over the course of its six-day programme, underwent training in supervising policy-making, strategisation, and operations within the collective realm of cybersecurity.[41]

12.40 At the ASEAN Ministerial Conference on Cybersecurity in 2018, the ASEAN members states agreed in principle to accept the eleven cyber norms. Subsequently in 2020, ASEAN member states, led by Singapore and the UNODA, started to develop a Norms Implementation Checklist, meant to

38 Kono, K. *ASEAN Cyber Developments: Centre of Excellence for Singapore, Cybercrime Convention or the Philippines, and an Open-Ended Working Group for Everyone*. Retrieved from *The NATO Cooperative Cyber Defence Centre of Excellence*: https://ccdcoe.org/incyder-articles/asean-cyber-developments-centre-of-excellence-for-singapore-cybercrime-convention-for-the-philippines-and-an-open-ended-working-group-for-everyone/.

39 Cyber Security Agency of Singapore. (2021, October). *ASEAN-Singapore Cybersecurity Centre of Excellence*. Retrieved from *Cyber Security Agency of Singapore*: https://www.csa.gov.sg/News-Events/Press-Releases/2021/asean-singapore-cybersecurity-centre-of-excellence.

40 NUS School of Continuing and Lifelong Education. (2022, September). *NUS jointly launches inaugural UN-Singapore Cyber Fellowship Programme*. Retrieved from *NUS News*: https://news.nus.edu.sg/nus-jointly-launches-inaugural-un-singapore-cyber-fellowship-programme/#:~:text=From%201%20to%206%20August,%2C%20strategies%2C%20and%20operations%20effectively.

41 ibid.

establish a framework of steps that should be undertaken by countries in order to implement the norms in an actionable and tangibly effective manner.[42]

12.41 Malaysia and Singapore also agreed to jointly chair the development of a Matrix for ASEAN's Plan of Action on the Implementation of Norms of Responsible States Behaviour in Cyberspace, having initiated and facilitated a workshop to co-develop this Matrix with their fellow ASEAN member states in a manner that would allow them to implement the eleven UNGGE norms at a manageable pace.[43]

12.42 There are also norms proposed by the private sector, such as by multinational technology giant Microsoft.[44]

THE FUTURE FOR CYBER NORMS

12.43 There have been other efforts to develop international norms of behaviour in the cyber domain. They include:

- The 'Hague Process', which facilitated State input into the Tallinn Manual 2.0 project;
- The Global Commission on the Stability of Cyberspace;
- UNIDIR workshops on international cyber-security issues;
- CSCAP Study Groups and ARF ISM on ICT (ASEAN Regional Forum's Inter-Sessional Meeting on Info-Communication Technology).

12.44 Through advocacy and dialogue with governments, the private sector can also continue to play a role in advancing the development of cyber norms. These will help to create an international law framework that will govern cyberspace in a clearer, more comprehensive and coherent way.

Interaction Between States

12.45 This section examines how States cooperate to combat international challenges of cyber-crime, to develop international norms of behaviour in cyber-operations, and examines Singapore as a case study of international cooperation in cyber-issues. Singapore recognises that 'cyber threats are borderless, and

42 Cyber Security Agency of Singapore. (2020, December). *The Geopolitics of Cybersecurity*. Retrieved from *Cyber Security Agency of Singapore*: https://www.csa.gov.sg/News-Events/News-Articles/2020/the-geopolitics-of-cybersecurity.

43 ASEAN. (2022). *ASEAN Cybersecurity Cooperation Strategy (2021-2025)*, 3-vi. Retrieved from *ASEAN*: https://asean.org/wp-content/uploads/2022/02/01-ASEAN-Cybersecurity-Cooperation-Paper-2021-2025_final-23-0122.pdf.

44 Microsoft. (2017). *From Articulation to Implementation: Enabling progress on cybersecurity norms*. Microsoft.

strong international collaboration in cybersecurity is necessary for our collective global security, and strong international partnerships enable countries to deal with cybercrime more effectively'.[45]

INTERNATIONAL CHALLENGES OF CYBER-CRIME

12.46 Cyber-crime is a huge and growing problem in Southeast Asia, with a recent INTERPOL investigation identifying nearly 9,000 servers in this region that are being used for cyber-crime, including command-and- control for malware, launching distributed denial-of-service (DDoS) attacks, spreading ransomware, and sending spam, with victims and suspects in China, Indonesia, Malaysia, Myanmar, Philippines, Singapore, Thailand, and Vietnam.

12.47 This is part of the international problem of cyber-crime, where cyber-criminals based in Romania, Estonia, Lithuania, and Russia, have committed large scale crimes ranging from 'phishing' (sending millions of email luring users to fake banking websites to steal their banking passwords), theft of credit card numbers and ATM PINs, computer intrusion, wire fraud, illegal appropriation of money, and installing malware that intercepts bank account passwords.

12.48 For all of its benefits, global technology can be used for committing criminal acts with a transnational reach, posing a huge challenge for local law enforcement. The aforementioned cyber-criminals committed their crimes without ever physically stepping into the same country as their victims. Fortunately, there are international legal instruments that local law enforcement can use to address this challenge.

CRIMINALISING TRANSNATIONAL CYBER-CRIME

12.49 Some countries have domestic legislation that provides jurisdiction over cyber-crime activity affecting their citizens or property, even if the criminals are located outside the country's borders. However, merely criminalising transnational cyber-crime is not effective. Successfully combatting cross-border cyber-crime, however, requires more than just criminalisation. Success requires effective international cooperation.

12.50 However, there are fundamental challenges to international cooperation in cyber-crime cases. Foreign authorities may be reluctant to recognise legal traditions and systems, particularly if they are requested to assist in a manner which is different from their own national law or principles. States are also naturally reluctant to transfer their citizens to another State for criminal prosecution. Some

45 Cyber Security Agency. (2016, October). *Singapore's Cyber Security Strategy.* Retrieved from Cyber Security Agency: www.csa.gov.sg/news/publications/singapore-cybersecurity-strategy/.

countries rely upon a tradition of non-intervention and may view investigation assistance as burdensome or intrusive absent a treaty for cooperation.

CONVENTIONS, TREATIES AND MUTUAL LEGAL ASSISTANCE

12.51 Where law enforcement agencies in different countries are able to cooperate, this can be either formal or informal. Formal mechanisms include bilateral or multilateral treaties for mutual legal assistance. This is the process by which States request and provide support in criminal cases.

12.52 The Council of Europe's Convention on Cybercrime ('Budapest Convention') has long been the most significant instrument in this field. Article 22(1)(a) of the Budapest Convention requires signatories to recognise computer crimes that are committed in their territory, while Article 23 requires signatories to provide cooperation to the widest extent possible, including collection of evidence.

12.53 Through resolution 74/247,[46] adopted by the United Nations General Assembly on 27 December 2019, the Ad Hoc Committee to Elaborate a Comprehensive International Convention on Countering the Use of Information and Communications Technologies for Criminal Purposes was established as an open-ended committee of cybersecurity experts from across multiple governments across various regions.[47] This Ad Hoc Committee holds the responsibility of drafting and developing a new, internationally standardised convention on cybercrime that, in its current draft as of 29 May 2023, details the proposed sets of conventions and common *modus operandi* to be adopted by member states in dealing with various aspects of cybercrime within the context of the international arena.[48][49] In its current draft, the key aspects of the convention are articulated over nine chapters, the titles of which are listed below:

I. General provisions.

II. Criminalisation.

III. Jurisdiction.

IV. Procedural measures and law enforcement.

46 United Nations General Assembly. (2020, January). *A/RES/74/247*. Retrieved from *United Nations*: https://undocs.org/Home/Mobile?FinalSymbol=A%2FRes%2F74%2F247&Language=E&DeviceType=Desktop&LangRequested=False.

47 United Nations Office on Drugs and Crime. *Ad Hoc Committee to Elaborate a Comprehensive International Convention on Countering the Use of Information and Communications Technologies for Criminal Purposes*. Retrieved from *United Nations Office on Drugs and Crime*: https://www.unodc.org/unodc/en/cybercrime/ad_hoc_committee/home.

48 Digital Watch Observatory. *Ad Hoc Committee on Cybercrime*. Retrieved from *Digital Watch Observatory*: https://dig.watch/processes/cybercrime-ad-hoc-committee.

49 United Nations General Assembly. (2023, May). *A/AC.291/22*. Retrieved from *United Nations*: https://www.undocs.org/Home/Mobile?FinalSymbol=A%2FAC.291%2F22&Language=E&DeviceType=Desktop&LangRequested=False.

V. International cooperation.

VI. Preventive measures.

VII. Technical assistance and information exchange.

VIII. Mechanism of implementation.

IX. Final Provisions.[50]

12.54 Interpol's Cyber Capabilities & Capacity Development Project (C3DP) (formerly known as the ASEAN Cyber Capacity Development Project) is another recent project specifically targeted towards cybercrime in the Southeast Asia region.[51] Financially backed by the United States Department of State with a budget of US$2 million and with a stated timeframe of September 2021 to September 2023, C3DP is a project that seeks to enhance the capacity of ASEAN countries in fighting cybercrime, and also to foster regional cooperation among ASEAN member states.[52] Current, ongoing activities conducted by C3DP include specialised training courses for cybercrime personnel on threat response, table-top simulation exercises, an open knowledge base accessible to regional peers, expert groups in emerging new areas of interest such as cryptocurrency and malware analysis, as well as an e-learning course on obtaining electronic evidence from ICT service providers—whether they be located domestically or across jurisdictional lines.[53]

12.55 Other important instruments are the Economic Community of West African States (ECOWAS) Directive on Fighting Cybercrime within ECOWAS, Commonwealth of Independent States (CIS) Agreement on Cooperation in Combating Offences related to Computer Information, Shanghai Cooperation Organization (SCO) Agreement on Cooperation in the Field in International Information Security, African Union (AU) Draft Convention on the Establishment of a Legal Framework Conducive to Cybersecurity in Africa, and League of Arab States (LAS) Arab Convention on Combating Information Technology Offences.

12.56 Mutual Legal Assistance Treaties (MLAT) treaties, between individual nations, have established streamlined procedures for rapid cooperation between law enforcement authorities. Speed is vital in combating cyber-crime, as computer evidence is highly volatile and easily destroyed. These treaties provide for expedited preservation of evidence and disclosure of stored computer data. They may also provide for mutual assistance in the real-time collection of traffic data, and the interception of content data.

50 Ibid.

51 Interpol. *Cyber Capabilities & Capacity Development Project.* Retrieved from *Interpol*: https://www.interpol.int/en/Crimes/Cybercrime/Cyber-capabilities-development/Cyber-Capabilities-Capacity-Development-Project.

52 ibid.

53 ibid.

12.57 In the interests of speed, States also agree to designate points of contact who can be reached on a permanent basis. Other contact resources include the UNODC Online Directory of Competent National Authorities, Commonwealth Network of Contact Persons, European Judicial Network, and Eurojust.

LIMITATIONS TO MUTUAL LEGAL ASSISTANCE

12.58 Mutual Legal Assistance treaties have some limitations imposed by agreements and domestic legislation. In some cases, assistance will not be provided if the acts are political offences, not criminal offences in the assisting State, or where implementing the request could violate the assisting State's sovereignty, security or order. Despite these limitations, law enforcement agencies in many countries have found success in transnational cooperation to combat transnational cyber-crime.

12.59 Some success stories include instances where US law enforcement officials have cooperated with their counterparts in Lithuania, Estonia, Spain, and Bulgaria, in arresting a number of cyber-criminals, and in many cases extraditing them to the US for trial. These are good indicators of the effectiveness of cooperation and international legal instruments in the battle against transnational cyber-crime.

CASE STUDY: SINGAPORE'S INTERACTIONS WITH OTHER STATES ON CYBER-ISSUES

12.60 One country that has taken concerted steps towards cooperation with other States on cyber-issues is Singapore. One of the four pillars of Singapore's Cyber Security Strategy is 'Step up efforts to forge strong international partnerships, given that cyber threats do not respect sovereign boundaries'.[54]

12.61 In this national document, Singapore has committed itself to strong international collaboration in cyber-security; active cooperation with the international community, particularly ASEAN, to address transnational cyber-security and cyber-crime; champion cyber-capacity building initiatives; and facilitate exchanges on cyber-norms and legislation. Having set aside US$7.3 million (S$10 million) over 10 years for its ASEAN Cyber Capacity Programme (ACCP), the city State has launched or participated in numerous activities since the launch of the Strategy and ACCP in 2016.

54 Cyber Security Agency, 2016.

COOPERATION IN FIGHTING CYBERCRIME

12.62 In ASEAN, Singapore is the Voluntary Lead Shepherd on cyber-crime, leading ASEAN Member States (AMS) in coordinating the regional approach to cyber-crime, and working together on capacity building, training and the sharing of information.

12.63 Singapore has partnered with INTERPOL and other countries in capacity building initiatives, and in bringing global experts and thought leaders together to discuss the latest threats, trends and solutions in the cyber-domain, and share best practices and solutions. For example, Singapore hosts the INTERPOL Global Complex for Innovation (IGCI), a sprawling modern building that is INTERPOL's global hub on cyber-crime. Singapore has led the IGCI Working Group and INTERPOL Operational Expert Group on Cybercrime, working with other INTERPOL member countries to define INTERPOL's cyber-crime programme.

12.64 Together with INTERPOL and Japan, Singapore rolled out several programmes such as the two-year (2016–2018) ASEAN Cyber Capacity Development Project. This project has hosted workshops for Decision Makers and Heads of Cybercrime Units of ASEAN Member States, to raise the level of awareness and knowledge in the region.

12.65 Singapore has also collaborated with the Singapore-United States Third Country Training Programme, the ASEAN Plus Three Cybercrime Workshop (involving the People's Republic of China, Japan and the Republic of Korea) in conducting capacity building programmes.

12.66 The ASEAN Cybercrime Prosecutors' Roundtable Meeting also brings together specialised cyber-crime prosecutors and law enforcement experts from across ASEAN, to take stock of the legal capacities of ASEAN, and to raise the overall capabilities in the region.

12.67 The collaboration extends beyond training, into coordinating international operations on cyber-crime for all INTERPOL member countries. One notable case of international cooperation is the arrest of the 'Messiah' hacker James Raj Ariokasamy in Kuala Lumpur, by Malaysian police acting on information provided by their Singapore counterparts.[55] More recently in April 2018, Singapore Police Force's Technology Crime Investigation Branch (TCIB), in cooperation with US Law Enforcement officials, arrested a Singaporean computer hacker who had infiltrated the US National Football League's official Twitter account in 2016.[56]

55 Lim, Y. L. (2013, November). *Hacker who calls himself 'The Messiah' charged.* Retrieved from *The Straits Times*: www.straitstimes.com/singapore/hacker-who-calls-himself-the-messiah-charged-with-hacking-more-being-investigated.

56 Blake, A. (2018, April). *Singapore sentences Twitter hacker over NFL breach.* Retrieved from *The Washington Times*.

COOPERATION IN JOINT ACTIVITIES BETWEEN ASEAN MEMBER STATES

12.68 The ASEAN Member States participate in various activities to build cooperation in cyber issues:

- The ASEAN Regional Forum (ARF) was established to foster constructive dialogue and consultation on political and security issues of common interest and concern, and to make significant contributions towards confidence building and preventive diplomacy in the Asia-Pacific region.
- The ASEAN Network Security Action Council (ANSAC) was set up as a multi-stakeholder organisation to promote CERT cooperation and sharing of expertise.
- The ASEAN CERT Incident Drill (ACID) is an annual exercise aimed at strengthening cooperation among CERTs in ASEAN and its Dialogue Partners. The exercise tests the coordination amongst the incident response teams and their incident handling procedures. Singapore has convened ACID since 2006.

COOPERATION THROUGH MEMORANDA OF UNDERSTANDING

12.69 In addition to the multilateral cooperation in combating cyber-crime, Singapore has also formalised cooperation through the signing of bilateral memoranda of understanding with eight countries. The common features of these agreements are mutual assistance and information sharing to 'strengthen the cybersecurity landscape of both countries' and 'working together to promote voluntary norms of responsible state behaviour to support the security and stability of cyberspace'.[57] The agreements include:

> France (May 2015): Singapore and France agreed to strengthen national cyber-security capabilities through more regular bilateral exchanges, sharing of best practices and efforts to develop cyber security expertise.
>
> United Kingdom (July 2015): Singapore and the UK agreed to cooperate in four key areas, including cyber-security incident response and cyber-security talent development; and also on joint cyber-research and development collaboration between the UK and Singapore, with funding being doubled over three years, from S$2.5 million to S$5.1 million.
>
> India (November 2015): Singapore and India agreed to establish formal cooperation in cyber-security between the Singapore Computer Emergency Response Team (SingCERT) and the Indian Computer Emergency Response Team (CERT-In). The MOU focused on five key areas of cooperation. They are (i) the establishment of a formal framework for professional dialogue; (ii) CERT-CERT related cooperation for operational readiness and response;

57 Cyber Security Agency. (2016, October). *Singapore's Cyber Security Stragegy.* Retrieved from Cyber Security Agency: www.csa.gov.sg/news/publications/singapore-cybersecurity-strategy.

(iii) collaboration on cyber-security technology and research related to smart technologies; (iv) exchange of best practices; and (v) professional exchanges of human resource development.

The Netherlands (July 2016): Singapore and The Netherlands committed to regular bilateral exchanges, sharing of cyber-security best practices and strategies aimed at protecting critical information infrastructures as well as access to training and workshops.

United States (July 2016): Singapore and the US agreed to cooperate through regular CERT-CERT information exchanges and sharing of best practices, coordination in cyber-incident response and sharing of best practices on Critical Information Infrastructure protection, cyber-security trends and practices. They also committed to conducting joint cyber-security exercises and collaborate on regional cyber-capacity building and cyber-security awareness building activities.

Australia (June 2017): Singapore and Australia agreed to cooperate in key areas similar to the other MOUs, such as sharing of information and best practices, cyber-security training, joint cyber-security exercises with a focus on the protection of Critical Information Infrastructure and a commitment to promote voluntary norms of responsible State behaviour in cyberspace. As a first step, the two countries will organise an ASEAN cyber-risk reduction workshop at the end of 2017.

Germany (July 2017): Singapore and Germany agreed to cooperate in regular information exchanges, joint training and research; and sharing of best practices to promote innovation in cyber-security. Both parties also committed to promote voluntary norms of responsible State behaviour in cyberspace.

Japan (September 2017): Singapore and Japan agreed to cooperate in regular policy dialogues information exchanges, collaborations to enhance cyber-security awareness, joint regional capacity building efforts, and sharing of best practices.

COOPERATION IN DEVELOPING INTERNATIONAL AND REGIONAL NORMS

12.70 As mentioned earlier in this chapter, Singapore has devoted significant resources to promoting the development of norms in ASEAN, especially in hosting international and regional exchanges on norms during the annual Singapore International Cyber Week events.

12.71 With the help of the aforesaid exchanges, ASEAN has expressed support for cyber norms: ASEAN Member States agreed on the value of developing a set of practical cyber-security norms of behaviour in ASEAN (ASEAN Ministerial Conference on Cybersecurity, 2016), and ASEAN Member States support development of basic, operational and voluntary norms, referring to UNGGE 2015 report.

12.72 These are significant developments for the ASEAN Member States. Smaller States have limited options in the use of force or diplomatic sanctions to deter cyber-attacks. The rule of law is therefore very important for smaller States, and the formation of internationally agreed norms of behaviour are the foundation for developing international law in the cyber domain.

CREATING THE NEED FOR COOPERATION THROUGH NATIONAL LEGISLATION

12.73 The Singapore Parliament passed the Cybersecurity (Amendment) Bill (the Bill) on 7 May 2024, making significant amendments to the Cybersecurity Act 2018 (the Act). The 2024 Bill appends new amendments and provisions to the Act to account for the various new technologies – and by extension the various new cybersecurity threat vectors – that have emerged over the course of the past six years since the Act was initially passed.[58]

12.74 One of these technologies is cloud computing, which has been adopted by approximately 60% of all businesses in Singapore in some way as part of their operations and business models.[59] A large number of businesses in Singapore no longer solely rely on physical systems that are wholly owned and controlled by themselves to operate their Critical Information Infrastructure (CII), having moved to employing the use of cloud computing technologies for this purpose.[60]

12.75 As a result, CII-related provisions in the Act have been updated through the 2024 Bill, expanding the definitions of the terms 'computer' and 'computer system' to include 'virtual computers' and 'virtual computer systems'; the provisions no longer solely apply to physical computer systems that are used to operate CII – they now also apply to cloud based systems as well.[61] These changes are of particular relevance to providers of essential services, many of whom now use virtualised, cloud-based, and 'outsourced' third-party systems to operate their CII.[62] The new definitions introduced by the Bill make it clear that it is the owners of the CII, whether physical or virtual, who are the ones that are ultimately responsible for the cybersecurity and cyber-resilience of their CII.[63] Responsibility cannot be 'outsourced' to the third-party vendors who might be the ones supplying the underlying physical infrastructure and systems.[64] State to state cooperation will be needed to enforce this law because many of the virtualised, cloud-based, and outsourced third-party systems may be physically located outside of Singapore.

12.76 The Bill also introduces new regulations for providers of essential services within Singapore, which m*ay operate their CII using either overseas and/or third party vendors, under a new* Part 3A introduced by Clause 14 of

58 Bryan Tan. 'Singapore passes Cybersecurity (Amendment) Bill.' *ReedSmith*, May 17, 2024. https://www.reedsmith.com/en/perspectives/2024/05/singapore-passes-cybersecurity-amendment-bill.

59 Ibid.

60 Ibid.

61 Ibid.

62 Ibid.

63 Ibid.

64 Ibid.

the Bill.[65] Again, responsibility for the continuous operation and function of essential services lies with the providers of these services, who must take all necessary measures to ensure that the systems they employ, including third-party systems, are able to comply with the cybersecurity standards required of a CII, and ensure that they commit to this compliance via legally-binding contracts.[66] Clause 8 of the Bill also introduces a new Section 7(1A) which enables the CSA to designate and regulate CIIs that are entirely located outside Singapore, something which had previously not been possible under the initial principal Act due it only allowing the CSA to designate computer systems as CIIs if they were located partly or wholly within Singapore.[67] State to state cooperation will also be needed to enforce this law.

12.77 The Bill also expands the Act to regulate what is called Systems of Temporary Cybersecurity Concern (STCCs), which have been defined as systems that are, for limited stretches of time, at high risk of being compromised by means of a cyberattack, and whose compromising could potentially lead to serious negative effects for Singapore's national interests. [68] Examples of such STCCs would include systems that are put in place to operate over the duration of certain important events, which could range from key international summits and diplomatic exchanges, public health emergencies, or even international sports and entertainment events. [69] The effective cyber-protection of these systems, even if for a limited period of time, would help to ensure public international confidence in Singapore's ability to manage such events.[70] The Act imposes similar obligations to those placed on CII owners to STCC owners.[71]

12.78 In one incident that took place prior to these amendments, a call between senior German military officers was hacked (allegedly by Russia) and the contents leaked to embarrass the German government, and the breach was attributed to one of the officers joining the call through an unsecure hotel connection while he was attending the Singapore Air Show, an important international event with diplomatic exchanges.[72] In future, this new section could enable CSA to designate hotel systems in similar situations as STCCs.

THE FUTURE OF INTERNATIONAL LAW AND INTERACTION BETWEEN STATES IN CYBERSPACE

12.79 When the first round of the UN Open Ended Working Group concluded in 2021, its final report was hailed for broadly reflecting points of consensus and

65 Ibid.
66 Ibid.
67 Ibid.
68 Ibid.
69 Ibid.
70 Ibid.
71 Ibid.
72 Parker, J. (2024, March 8). Singapore Sting: How spies listened in on German general. BBC News. https://www.bbc.co.uk/news/world-europe-68479836.

moving forward discussions on emerging threats, voluntary behavioural norms, international law, capacity building, confidence-building measures, and potential formats for regular UN dialogue. Most importantly, the report reiterated the UN GGE recommendations on voluntary norms and international law, reaffirming the 2015 GGE conclusions that were endorsed by all UN member states in 2015. The report also endorsed capacity building in international law, supported the responsible reporting of vulnerabilities by states, and encouraged states to protect the integrity of the supply chain for ICT products. However, states did not agree on many issues including the call for a legally binding convention.[73]The UN Open Ended Working Group 2021-2025 process faces even more challenges in reaching consensus because of heightened geopolitical tensions. Not least is the disagreement on whether the process should be renewed in the same form after 2025 (proposed by Russia and China and others) or whether it should be conducted under a Programme of Action (proposed by France and Egypt and others) or whether it will continue on both tracks in parallel, which would be enormously taxing on small states to participate.

12.80 Nonetheless, the current UN OEWG has succeeded in enhancing interaction between states, such as operationalising the Point of Contact Directory in 2024. As of 9 May 2024, 92 states had nominated points of contact, and the first ping took place on 10 June 2024. This is regarded as a 'significant step towards enhancing international cooperation and resilience in addressing cyber threats', [74] and is highly beneficial to interactions between states.

12.81 Another encouraging development is the publication in January 2024 of the Common African Position on the Application of International Law to the Use of Information and Communication Technologies in Cyberspace, by the African Union Peace and Security Council. This document thoroughly and helpfully sets out the positions shared by all member states of the African Union on the applicability of international law, including Sovereignty, Due diligence, Prohibition of intervention, Peaceful settlement of disputes, Use of force, Attribution, International humanitarian law (jus in bello), International armed conflict, Non-international armed conflict, Conduct of hostilities, Attacks against persons, Proportionality, Specially protected persons, objects and activities (international humanitarian law), International human rights law, and state responsibility.[75] It is hoped that more regions do the same, to help build a common understanding of the application of international law in cyberspace.

73 Gold, J. (2021, March 18). Unexpectedly, all UN countries agreed on a cybersecurity report. so what?. Council on Foreign Relations. https://www.cfr.org/blog/unexpectedly-all-un-countries-agreed-cybersecurity-report-so-what.

74 Global Poc Directory established by OEWG on ICT security. Digital Watch Observatory. (2024, May 13). https://dig.watch/updates/global-poc-directory-established-by-oewg-on-ict-security.

75 NATO CCDCOE. (2024, February 21). Common position of the African Union (2024). International cyber law: interactive toolkit. https://cyberlaw.ccdcoe.org/wiki/Common_position_of_the_African_Union_%282024%29.

CHAPTER 13

SECURITY CONCERNS WITH THE INTERNET OF THINGS

Kevin Curran

INTRODUCTION

13.01 The Internet of Things (IoT) also known as Web of Things (WoT) is a concept where everyday devices – home appliances, sensors, monitoring devices – can be accessed through the internet using well known technologies such as URLs and HTTP requests. This chapter highlights some of the aspects of the Internet of Things which are causing global security issues and suggests some steps which can be taken to address these risks.

13.02 The IoT will offer the ability for consumers to interact with nearly every appliance and device they own.[1] For example, your refrigerator will let you know when you are running low on cheese and your dishwasher will inform you when it's ready to be emptied. It is possible that consumers will be receiving more text messages from their devices than human beings soon. We are seeing elements of the IoT in the marketplace already, with home automation having a strong consumer pull, from controlling the lights and temperature to closing the garage door while away from the home. In a more comprehensive way, IoT transforms real world objects into smart objects and connects them through the Internet.[2]

13.03 In contrast with the current Internet, IoT depends on a dynamic architecture where physical objects with embedded sensors will communicate with an e-infrastructure (ie a cloud) to send and analyse data using the Internet Protocol. IoT envisions a future in which digital and physical entities can be linked, through their unique identifier and by means of appropriate information and communication technologies.[3] However, like any new technology or idea, there are kinks that need to be worked out. If IoT is campaigning to run nearly every aspect of our digital lives, considerations need to be made to ensure a seamless and safe introduction. Security, standards and overburdening the

1 McKeever, P., McKelvey, N., Curran, K., Subaginy, N. (2015) The Internet of Things. Encyclopaedia of Information Science and Technology, 3rd Edition, IGI Global Publishing, USA, 2015, pp 5777–5784, ISBN: 9781466658882, DOI: 10.4018/978-1-4666-5888-2.

2 Fathi, A., Curran, K. (2017) Detection of Spine Curvature using Wireless Sensors. Journal of King Saud University – Science, 29(4), October 2017, pp 553–560, Elsevier, ISSN: 1018-3647, DOI: http://dx.doi.org/10/1016/j.jksus.2017.09.014.

3 Curran, K., Curran, N. (2014) Social Networking Analysis. Big Data and Internet of Things: A Roadmap For Smart Environments, pp 366–378, DOI: 10.1007/978-3-319-05029-4, ISBN: 978-3-319-05029-4, Springer International Publishing Switzerland 2014.

network are just some of the requirements that need to be focused on before implementing for mass adoption in the modern business place.[4]

13.04 Being connected to the IoT in the very near future is going to happen seamlessly through modern technologies such as connected home appliances and wearables.[5] For instance, the Mimo baby monitor is a body suit that monitors a baby's body temperature, motion, and breathing patterns. Sensors use Bluetooth wireless communication to relay this data to a base station, which then transmits it to the internet to be analysed by the company's sleep analysis software.[6] Lively is a system composed of activity sensors placed on objects around the home that monitors the daily behaviour of an individual living alone. For example, sensors may be placed on a refrigerator door, a pill box, and car keys to collect data on an individual's eating, medication, and sleep habits. Shockbox[7] is a small, flexible sensor that fits inside of a sports helmet and monitors the history of head impacts athletes sustain. Shockbox sensors communicate using Bluetooth to immediately alert parents, coaches, and trainers in the event of a concussion-level impact.

13.05 The Nuubo Smart Shirt[8] is a sensor-equipped shirt that monitors a patient's vital signs and movement. The sensors in the shirt can take regular measures on items such as heart rate, blood pressure, and body temperature. In addition, it can conduct an electrocardiogram (ECG). The shirt sends data wirelessly to a server for data analysis where, for example, software can detect anomalies in the ECG. The CardioMEMS Heart Sensor[9] is an implantable medical device for monitoring heart failure. The device, which is about the size of a paper clip, is implanted into a patient's pulmonary artery using a minimally-invasive technique and measures pulmonary arterial pressure. Data from the device is collected wirelessly and transmitted to a central database for the patient's health care providers to review. The 'always ready' capability leads to a new form of synergy between human and computer, characterised by long-term adaptation through constancy of user-interface.

13.06 The arrival of wearable devices has been made possible by advancements in miniaturising electronics and in part to advances in battery technologies.

4 IEEE 802.15.4f (2012a) IEEE Standard for Local and metropolitan area networks-- Part 15.4: Low-Rate Wireless Personal Area Networks (LR-WPANs) Amendment 2: Active Radio Frequency Identification (RFID) System Physical Layer (PHY); IEEE 802.15.6 (2012b) IEEE Standard for Information Technology – Telecommunications and Information Exchange Between Systems – Local and Metropolitan Area Networks – Specific Requirements – Part 15.6: Wireless Medium Access Control (MAC) and Physical Layer (PHY) Specifications for Wireless Personal Area Networks (WPANs)used in or around a body.

5 Carlin, S., Curran, K. (2014) An Active Low Cost Mesh Networking Indoor Tracking System. International Journal of Ambient Computing and Intelligence, 6(1) January-March 2014, pp 45–79, DOI: 10.4018/ijaci.2014010104.

6 Rodriguez McRobbie, L. (2014) Selling Fear – Smart monitors cannot protect babies from SIDS, so what are they for? Slate, February 2014, www.slate.com/articles/life/family/2014/02/mimo_and_ other_smart_baby_monitors_don_t_protect_from_sids_so_what_are_they.html.

7 www.theshockbox.com/.

8 www.nuubo.com/.

9 www.sjm.com.

Connecting these devices to the IoT will usher in a new world of truly big data.[10] Consumer electronics are benefitting from the IoT. Samsung Electronics president, Boo-Keun Yoon has said that 90% of the company's household appliances (as well as its TVs, computers, smartphones and smartwatches) will be IoT devices within two years, and that the entire tech industry will fall into line within five.[11] Some estimations are that the worldwide market for IoT solutions will grow to $7.1 trillion in 2020. Like many technologies however, there are negative as well as positive aspects to consider.

13.07 Positive aspects of IoT are demonstrated by environmental industries which are using multifaceted IoT solutions to protect our environment.[12] These include clean water, air pollution, landfill waste, and deforestation. Sensor-enabled devices are already helping monitor the environmental impact of cities, collect details about sewers, air quality, and garbage. In rural areas, sensor-enabled devices can monitor woods, rivers, lakes, and our oceans. Many environmental trends are so complex, that they are difficult to conceptualise, but collecting data is the first step towards understanding, and ultimately reducing, the environmental impact of human activity (Carlin & Curran, 2014).[13] WaterBee[14] is a smart irrigation system that collects data on soil content and other environmental factors from a network of wireless sensors to reduce water waste. The system analyses the data it collects to selectively water different plots of land based on need. Waterbee can be used for a variety of commercial applications, including on farms, vineyards, and golf courses. Smart irrigation systems save energy, water, and money.[15] Using a prototype, 14 sites in Europe were able to reduce their water usage on average by 40%.

13.08 Z-Trap helps prevent crop damage by using pheromones to trap insects and then compile data on the number of different types of insects in the trap. Z-Trap wirelessly transmits the data, including its GPS coordinates, allowing farmers to view a map of the types of insects that have been detected. Construction is also benefitting from the IoT. For instance, wireless bridge sensors can help

10 Smedley, T. (2016) Wearables for babies: saving lives or instilling fear in parents?, Guardian, 30 May 2016: www.theguardian.com/sustainable-business/2016/may/30/wearables-for-babies-saving-lives-or-instilling-fear-in-parents.

11 Tibkem, S. (2015) Samsung, SmartThings and the open door to the smart home (Q&A), CNET, 12 January 2015: www.cnet.com/g00/news/smartthings-ceo-on-samsung-being-open-apples-homekit-and-more-q-a/.

12 Deak, G., Curran, K., Condell, J., Bessis, N., and Asimakopoulou, E. (2013) IoT (Internet of Things) and DfPL (Device-free Passive Localisation) in a disaster management scenario. Simulation Modelling Practice and Theory, 34(3), pp 86–96, DOI: 10.1016/j.simpat.2013.03.005, ISSN: 1569-190X, Elsevier Publishing.

13 Carlin, S., Curran, K. (2014) An Active Low Cost Mesh Networking Indoor Tracking System. International Journal of Ambient Computing and Intelligence, 6(1), January-March 2014, pp 45–79, DOI: 10.4018/ijaci.2014010104.

14 http://waterbee-da.iris.cat/.

15 Schneps-Schneppe, M., Maximenko, A., Namiot, D., Malov, D. (2012) Wired Smart Home: energy metering, security, and emergency issues, Ultra Modern Telecommunications and Control Systems and Workshops (ICUMT), 2012 4th International Congress on, IEEE (2012), pp 405–410.

reduce this risk by monitoring all aspects of a bridge's health, such as vibration, pressure, humidity, and temperature. The US Geological Survey Advanced National Seismic System uses accelerometers and real-time data analysis to monitor the structural health of buildings in earthquake prone regions. Sensors detect the degree of the building's movement, the speed that seismic waves travel through the building, and how the frame of the building changes.[16]

13.09 There are however quite a few risks. Technical challenges include government regulation with regards to spectrum allocation, security, battery issues, costs and privacy. One of the successes of the UK IoT has been the introduction of 'smart meters'. These are network connected meters which 'broadcast' our power usage to the power company. There is, however, a real possibility that unscrupulous individuals can commit a crime by manipulating the data captured by the meter. A hacker for instance could compromise a smart meter to find out about a home owners' peaks of use to learn when they are likely to be out. On a larger scale however, there is a threat whereby smart meters which are connected to smart grids could be attacked leading to complete failure of the system.

13.10 Manufacturers of devices which will contribute to the IoT need to consider the correct forms of cryptographic algorithms and modes needed for IoT devices. There is an international ISO/IEC 29192 standard which was devised to implement lightweight cryptography on constrained devices. There was a need for this as many IoT devices have a limited memory size, limited battery life along with restricted processors. Traditional 'heavy' cryptography is difficult to deploy on a typical sensor hence the deployment of many insecure IoT devices. Regulations for the IoT need to address issues of 'minimum specifications' for IoT devices.

13.11 Ultimately, we can expect to see an explosion in the amount of data collected. There is much value in that data, but one needs to be trained and have a good knowledge of Big Data.[17] Big data is a term for large data sets where the traditional data processing approaches simply do not work due to their complexity. These data sets however possess potential to reveal business trends, identification of diseases, combat crime and much more. There is a great need for people with Business Analytics skills to mine big data. The role of a business analyst is to aggregate data to work out how an organisation can leverage data to operate more efficiently. Predictive analytics is one of the tools which can deal with the sheer complexity of a global IoT. We next look at how implementing security in the IoT differs than traditional methods of rolling out security mechanisms.

16 Gubbi, J., Buyya, R., Marusic, S., Palaniswami, M. (2013) Internet of Things (IoT): a vision, architectural elements, and future directions, Future Gener. Comput. Syst., 29 (2013), pp 1645–1660

17 Zaslavsky, A., Perera, C., Georgakopoulos, D. (2013) Sensing as a Service and Big Data arXiv arXiv:1301.0159.

HOW ORGANISATIONS CAN SECURE IOT

13.12 Hackers attempting to attack an IoT device typically try to either take control of the device, steal information, or disrupt the service it is offering. A rudimentary way to prevent these attacks is to prevent communication with the devices they are trying to hack with a firewall and an Intrusion Detection & Prevention System (IDPS). Here a firewall blocks that which should not be passing through. The IDPS monitors the system and network to detect, block, and report suspicious events.

13.13 The problem however to regular IT security is that firewalls and antivirus programs require a lot of storage space and sufficient processing power to run but many IoT devices are not powerful enough to run these. Therefore, IoT security is different in that we must recognise that IoT devices are primarily embedded dedicated computer systems – and quite limited at that. They are often single purpose devices performing specific functions within a wider more complex system eg Light bulb, TVs, pacemakers, plant watering control systems, kettles. Providing only limited functions allows them to be lean and cheap.

13.14 Here then, the security mechanisms must be equally specialised and aimed at protecting against more targeted attacks which are quite often unique to the functionality of that device. Adopting security support ecosystems such as large databases of malware signatures is unlikely to find adoption or be implementable on these devices. A more practical solution is to enforce rules-based filtering so that for instance white-list rules allows communications only from specific authorised devices. Firewall policies like this allow a much-reduced rule set to be adopted. IoT manufacturers such as Intel, McAfee and Zilog are building these embedded security technology practices into the hardware and software for IoT devices.

13.15 Unfortunately, there are many older IoT devices which are unable to be updated to support these policies in their software so in those cases, an intermediate firewall needs to be added to the network to defend those devices against outside attacks. Firewalls only prevent a subset of attacks however and other problems such as eavesdropping require additional mechanisms in place.

13.16 Organisations need to ensure they deploy IoT devices with sufficient security policies in place such as firewalls and intrusion detection and prevention systems, but they also need to ensure they cater for the confidentiality of their customers' data. This is where encryption plays a core role. All devices need strong passwords. It is also good practice to enforce certificate-based authentication which identifies communicating individuals and authorised devices. This is currently used in point of sale (POS) terminals, petrol pumps, and ATMs. Device management agents can also highlight failed access attempts and attempted denial-of-service attacks. All non-IoT devices must also be patched and kept malware free. These could as likely be the pivot point for infecting IoT devices. Biometric authentication methods are increasingly being offered to add another layer.

13.17 Many of the steps in securing IoT activities are like security steps within the larger enterprise system. Organisation do however need to be aware that privacy issues can arise due to their IoT data collection mechanisms which may lead to user profiling and identification of individuals in unforeseen use case scenarios. The greatest care needs to be taken when deploying data collection devices with regards to their lifecycle, data collection mechanisms and overall security protocols. It is crucial that information security, privacy and data protection be addressed comprehensively at the design phase. We need to start training our graduates in best practice aggregation and anonymity of data. Yes, collect data which benefits society but we need those who do so to know how to scrub if first from individual identifying information which invades our privacy.

13.18 Companies will have to pay more attention to the secure storage of data collected via the IoT as legal repercussions creep in and the increase in data being collected.[18] This data is generally being stored in the cloud.[19] Therefore, all the recommended practices applicable to securing data in the cloud equally applies here. Companies with large data sets due to the multi-tenant nature of a cloud platform should pay extra attention to the data lifecycle phases and ensure that aspects such as data destruction is provided and auditable as part of the service. The fact that any company is allowing confidential datasets to reside outside the company network should lead them to examine how they can robustly protect that data.

13.19 Ultimately, it is critical that they implement a layered security strategy regarding cloud services as their data is more exposed than previously. It is critical to get buy in from upper-management. More so than ever, security breaches can greatly affect their reputation. Cybercrime is on the rise therefore we should think about security in terms of process, people and technology. This will involve creating security policies with internal departments, performing audits, implementing physical security control and classifying risk.

13.20 The rapid rollout of IoT devices and connectivity to external parties has led to increased risks to an organisation's internal assets.[20] Information that is more valuable than ever before is more accessible and easier to divert. Organisations that fail to address the broader security issues that accompany this change will have insufficient controls in place to minimise risks. These risks

18 McBride, B., McKelvey, N., Curran, K. (2015) Security issues with contactless bank cards. Journal of Information, 1(3), pp 53–55 DOI: 10.18488/journal.104/2015.1.3/104.3.53.58.

19 Zhou, J., Leppänen, T., Harjula, E., Ylianttila, M., Ojala, T., Yu, C., Jin, H. (2013) Cloudthings: a common architecture for integrating the internet of things with cloud computing, Computer Supported Cooperative Work in Design (CSCWD), 2013 IEEE 17th International Conference on, IEEE (2013), pp 651–657.

20 Lee, I., Lee, K. (2015) The Internet of Things (IoT): applications, investments, and challenges for enterprises, Bus. Horiz., 58, pp 431–440.

could lead to significant financial, legal difficulties and reputation risk for these organisations.[21]

13.21 Appropriate preventive, detective and corrective controls in the form of policies, standards, procedures, organisational structures or software/technology functions and monitoring mechanisms are therefore required to minimise the risks associated with the confidentiality, integrity and availability of information assets within an organisation. These aspects of security should be the underpinnings of any IoT Regulations policy.

13.22 There is no established formula for balancing risk with security level and the subsequent investment. However, companies who follow industry standards such as ISO 27001 which is a specification for an information security management system will tangentially balance risk with investment. This standard seeks to provide a model for establishing, implementing, operating, monitoring, reviewing, maintaining and improving an information security management system so adhering to the recommended best practices should ensure at least a minimum outlay in security measures. Of course, organisations will differ. No one questions that a military organisation will require an equivalent budget (or percentage) to a corner shop but auditing risk should flag the critical weak points and lead to investment in securing those aspects.

INDUSTRY-WIDE INITIATIVES FOR IOT SECURITY

13.23 There are several industrywide initiatives for IoT security currently (IEEE 2011; IEEE 2012c). It is not an easy task as regulating IoT devices means devising a rule that would be broad enough to cross many sectors and cover all these products. The security expert Bruce Schneier intelligently said that a good starting place would be 'minimum security standards, interoperability standards, the ability to issue a software update or patch after a product has hit the market, and even placing code in escrow so that problems can still be managed in case a company goes out of business'. It is hard to argue with that. The reason for the delay is simply due to many IoT devices being low-margin products hence the lack of urgency from manufacturers.

13.24 It would be fair to say that there is no overarching IoT security initiative but rather several standards which address aspects of security that can be applied to the IoT, including IEEE P1363, a standard for public-key cryptography; IEEE P1619 addresses encryption of data on storage devices; IEEE P2600 addresses the security of printers; and IEEE 802.1AE/IEEE 802.1X address media access control security (IEEE, 2013).

21 Mc Kelvey, N., Clifton, M., Quigley, C., Curran, K. (2014) Internet Copyright Laws and Digital Industries. International Journal of E-Business Development (IJED), 3(4), pp 174–178, ISSN:2225-7411.

13.25 The National Institute of Standards and Technology has created a voluntary cyber-security framework that companies, and organisations can use as a guide to identify and protect against cyber risks. However, it was intended to protect critical infrastructure such as the electricity grid and water treatment plants and does not have specific recommendations for IoT devices. Other security standards for the IoT include the North American Electric Reliability Corp. who have outlined critical infrastructure protection standards to secure the electric grid.

13.26 The US Food and Drug Administration has a set of guidelines to help product makers better protect patient health and information. The Open Interconnect Consortium comprised of companies such as Cisco and Intel have developed interoperability standards for the IoT which also include security aspects. IEC 62443/ISA99, Industrial Automation and Control System Security Committee has defined procedures for implementing secure industrial automation and control systems. Finally, the International Standards Organization (ISO) has a special Working Group on the IoT and this is important as their security standard ISO 27000 is globally popular.[22]

13.27 Whilst not a standard, there are also initiatives to increase IoT security such as where Microchip Technology and Amazon.com have created an add-on chip to make devices more secure. Cloud services are a key part of IoT where connected IoT devices rely on large-scale cloud infrastructure but this chain from device to owner and back is a weak link for spoofing attacks.[23] The AWS-ECC508 provides end-to-end security between the IoT device and the cloud infrastructure by verifying the identity of the AWS cloud service and the IoT device. The identities are based on cryptographic keys which traditionally relied on the original manufacturer to securely generate keys. Now however, the AWS-ECC508 can generate its own keys that Amazon will accept as authentic. It also adopts an 'elliptic curve cryptography' algorithm which is more efficient and uses less computing resources and is designed to protect against hardware attacks, such as removing the casing to probe the circuitry. This is a step in the right direction for securing the IoT.

FUTURE IOT INNOVATIONS

13.28 Edge computing is innovative with regards to IoT devices. An edge device is anything that provides an entry point to a network so by embracing edge computing for IoT devices, they can more efficiently reduce latency

22 Calder, A. (2006) Information Security Based on ISO 27001/ISO 17799: A Management Guide Van Haren Publishing 2006.

23 Ksiazak, P., Farrelly, W., Curran, K. (2015) A Lightweight Authentication Protocol for Secure Communications between Resource-Limited Devices and Wireless Sensor Networks. International Journal of Information Security and Privacy, 8(4), pp 62–102, October-December 2015, DOI: 10.4018/IJISP.2014100104, ISSN: 1930-1650, IGI Global.

for critical applications, remove dependency on the cloud, and ultimately reduce the network loads from data being generated. Examples would be edge IoT computing devices that rapidly react to alarms by taking autonomous decisions.

13.29 The rise of home assistants will continue not just in the form of Amazon echo and Google Home, but voice assistants baked into everyday devices. Many of us are using chatbots already in the form of Apple's Siri, Amazon's Echo and Microsoft's Cortana. For instance, if you ask Siri what the weather will be like for an upcoming event, you are basically chatting to a chatbot more commonly known as a personal assistant. We can expect to see more of these.

13.30 Incorporation of machine learning on wearable IoT devices. Deploying intelligent algorithms on IoT devices in healthcare enables self-monitoring of health. It also allows the mining of the data streams to pre-empt future health problems, incorporating flags in order that individuals become aware of possible health problems long before they manifest themselves in the real world. In addition, predictive modelling, can help researchers understand and mitigate the behavioural, genetic and environmental causes of disease. More innovation in this IoT space will see the market for wearables expand.

13.31 The Blockchain also has an important role to play in IoT in the days ahead. Scaling the IoT will prove difficult using traditional centralised models. There are also inherent security risks in the IoT such as problems when disabling them should they become compromised and become parts of botnets which has become a serious problem already. The Blockchain however with its solid cryptographic foundation offers a decentralised solution which can aid against data tampering thus offering greater assurances for the legitimacy of the data. Blockchain technology could potentially allow billions of connected IoT devices to communicate in a secure yet decentralised ecosystem which also allows consumer data to remain private.

13.32 There are already Blockchain-based IoT frameworks such as ChainAnchor which includes layers of access to keep out unauthorised devices from the network. The IBM Watson IoT Platform enables IoT devices to send data to Blockchain ledgers for inclusion in shared transactions with tamper-resistant records. It also validates the transaction through secure contracts. Another Blockchain solution from Australian researchers uses a block miner to manage all local network transactions to control communication between home-based IoT devices and the outside world. It can authorise new IoT devices and cut off hacked devices. Telestra is using Blockchain to secure smart home IoT ecosystems by storing biometric authentication data to verify identity of people. IBM's Blockchain provide audit trails, accountability, new forms of contracts and speed for IoT devices. They see the benefit of underpinning the IoT with Blockchain as trust, cost reduction and the acceleration of transactions.

FUTURE SHORT-TERM CHALLENGES

13.33 Security of IoT device remains a challenge.[24] Compromised IoT devices have been responsible for many large-scale botnets in recent times. Security standards are a key requirement that need to be focused on before implementing for mass adoption in modern life and more accountability for manufacturers with regards roadmaps for updates for any devices they sell.

13.34 Good throughput is also a challenge for IoT. Although it is still a concept, 5G has some wonderful attributes – not least – conservation of battery life which may transform the IoT in the future. Multiple input multiple output (MiMo) technology is set to be a key part of these efficiency measures. Existing IoT sensors however are not equipped to take advantage of 5G technology. Samsung, Huawei and others are already playing with new 5G technologies and leading the way.

13.35 Companies will have to pay more attention to the secure storage of data collected via the IoT as legal repercussions arrive in the form of the EU GDPR. IoT data is generally stored in the cloud, therefore all the recommended practices applicable to securing data in the cloud equally applies here. Companies with large data sets due to the multi-tenant nature of a cloud platform should pay extra attention to the data lifecycle phases and ensure that aspects such as data destruction is provided as part of the service.

13.36 To date, only a few IoT manufacturers are considering the correct forms of cryptographic algorithms and modes needed for IoT devices.[25] There is an international ISO/IEC 29192 standard which was devised to implement lightweight cryptography on constrained devices. There was a need for this as many IoT devices have a limited memory size, limited battery life along with restricted processors. Traditional 'heavy' cryptography is difficult to deploy on a typical sensor hence the deployment of many insecure IoT devices. Severe pressure needs to be placed on IoT manufacturers to implement best practice in securing these devices before they leave the factory. We know the public will be unaware of the need to update their lightbulbs so we in the security industry must force the manufacturers to not make it so easy for the hackers to exploit them. As we have seen lately, we are now all at risk from IoT devices which were thought to be too dumb to cause harm. The opposite is the truth. Unpatched, poorly deployed dumb devices have the power to bring the Internet to its knees.

24 Ksiazak, P., Farrelly, W., Curran, K. (2018) A Lightweight Authentication Protocol for Secure Communications between Resource-Limited Devices and Wireless Sensor Networks. Security and Privacy Management, Techniques, and Protocols, April 2018, ISSN: 1522555838 IGI Global.

25 Curran, K., Maynes, V., Harkin, D. (2015) Mobile Device Security. International Journal of Information and Computer Security, 6(3), January 2015, pp 55–68, ISSN: 1744-1765.

CONCLUSION

13.37 There is an argument for organisations to keep it simple when it comes to the IoT. A basic rule of thumb in security is that the more devices you have exposed to the internet, then the more exposure you must have to being hacked. It simply means that you are more likely to have neglected devices which are not updated and hence more vulnerable. It is crucial that IT departments monitor their networks 24-7, looking for potential intrusions and unusual activity on the network but not many do this and take appropriate actions.

13.38 The sheer scale of deployment of these limited-function embedded devices in households and public areas can lead to unique attacks. There is also the worry of the domino effect where if one device becomes 'owned' – it can easily spread to the remainder of the cluster. The privacy issues arise due to the data collection mechanisms which may lead to user profiling and identification of individuals in unforeseen use case scenarios. The utmost care needs to be taken when deploying IoT devices with regards to their lifecycle, data collection mechanisms and overall security protocols. We have now seen a major issue with IoT devices due to their implementation of default passwords which are known to hackers in addition to many of these devices have pre-installed unchangeable passwords which is utterly careless on behalf of the manufacturers. The days ahead may see IoT hardware manufacturers being held more accountable for the security of the products they ship and having to ensure any vulnerabilities are patched in a timely acceptable fashion.

CHAPTER 14

MANAGING CYBER-SECURITY IN AN INTERNATIONAL FINANCIAL INSTITUTION

Cosimo Pacciani

THE LIQUID ENEMY: MANAGING CYBER-RISKS IN A FINANCIAL INSTITUTION

> 'Cyber attacks may take the form of persistent malicious action by third parties intent on creating systemic harm or disruption, with concomitant financial losses. It may be extremely hard to determine the extent of an event, how to remedy it and how to recover. The very unpredictability of cyber risk dictates the urgency of having a proper approach in place to manage it' (BIS, 2014[1])

THE LIQUID ENEMY

Foreword

14.01 This chapter provides an overview of the challenges posed by cyber-risks and how to manage them[2].

14.02 This chapter is structured as follows:

- This **first section** reviews how cyber-security and cyber-risks escalated the level of attention of risk practitioners and why they can be defined as 'liquid risk';
- The **second section** provides some ideas on how a Chief Risk Officer (with additional responsibilities as Head of Compliance) believes cyber-risks should be addressed;
- The **third section** discusses, in a forward-looking manner, ideas around emerging risks associated with cyber-security and information security and also around some bigger challenges related to the society changes occurring around us;
- The **fourth section** concludes the chapter by identifying longer-term trends in the financial industry and in society at large and by showing how they

1 Bank for International Settlement, 'Cyber resilience in financial market infrastructures', Basel, November 2014.
2 Looking at the usual cycle of risk identification, monitoring, measurement and management.

are relevant to people tasked with managing current issues with a long-term sustainability target.

14.03 A word of caution: given the speed of change we are currently witnessing in Information Technology (let alone the birth of Artificial Intelligence (AI)), any overview of current trends has the potential to become obsolete very quickly. Timeliness is the main challenge for risk managers in relation to any risk evaluation, but even more so when it comes to cyber-risks. Risk managers must protect the present by keeping an eye on different future scenarios, bearing in mind that whatever we imagine now is unlikely to coincide with what is going to actually happen.

Cyber risk, the liquid enemy

14.04 In the 1990s, communication consisted of a fax machine, a telephone system and frequent mutual visits with headquarters and clients. The first email system and addresses, with a slow internet access, were supplied to employees only in 1998. Shortly thereafter, we had to start dealing with the emerging risks of viruses and we had to get ready for the risks arising from the so-called Millennium Bug of the year 2000, by putting in place readiness plans. This was the first time when cyber-security became a risk to be managed by the financial services industry. The sheer possibility that an IT issue could for the first time harm the entire financial system can therefore be considered as the beginning of the *cyber age* we now live in.

14.05 The increase in the speed of the transmission of data, computation analysis and mobile capacity have radically changed the way in which financial institutions work. The pace of technological change has been exponential, beyond what we could have imagined at the end of the last century. However, the same speed and depth of advancement has created a series of gaps and weaknesses on information platforms that are therefore at risk of being manipulated by external agents (eg hackers).

14.06 That the threat posed by the expansion of, and our reliance on, advanced technology will generate additional risks and potential losses is increasingly obvious and is on the top of the emerging risk lists of governments, financial institutions, think tanks and research institutes. Technology risks are currently assimilated to other operational risks and managed accordingly. This chapter is looking more closely to a sub-category of technology risks, defined as 'cyber risks'[3], as they will require a specific level of attention.

14.07 A different approach from the traditional operational risk one, inspired by Zygmunt Bauman's notion of *liquid modernity*:

3 www.theirm.org/knowledge-and-resources/thought-leadership/cyber-risk/.

> 'What was some time ago dubbed (erroneously) "post-modernity" and what I've chosen to call, more to the point, "**liquid modernity**", is the growing conviction that change is the only permanence, and uncertainty the only certainty. A hundred years ago "to be modern" meant to chase "the final state of perfection" -- **now it means an infinity of improvement**, with no "final state" in sight and none desired.'[4]

14.08 Cyber-risks are the first example of liquid or post-modern risk: they are based on perpetual or continuous change, they are pervasiveness and elude control, as they keep changing depending on infinitely variant situations and contexts.

14.09 Using another Bauman's category, the one of *continuity*, cyber-risks can be understood as building their strength on our expectation that, once they have reached a steady state, those risks will become manageable, following a predictable, if not linear, evolution. Information Technology in fact changes in response to sudden innovation and with unexpected changes. Cyber-risks resemble a mutating virus because they adapt to new living conditions and get ready to attack once the 'host' shows weakness. As such, these risks need to be fought by means of continuous research and remedies. And, as with pandemics, knowledge and information sharing can help us fight cyber infections.

14.10 From a risk management perspective, cyber-risks can therefore best be understood as 'liquid' for the following reasons:

- **The IT services industry is built around permanent change**, through, for example, software and hardware updates. However, what makes cyber-risks even more pervasive is the domination of specific solutions and technological platforms on a global scale. The uniformity of products, coupled with hyper-connectivity between users, otherwise known as *homogeneity* and *consistency*, are positives in IT terms, but they also open up any system to attackers in a serial manner. Interconnectivity allows infections to spread fast, which is itself another element of criticality. Also aggravating is the *risk of failed updates*: when a software or hardware provider (as it was the case in the WannaCry crisis) provides patches and remedies, the speed through which these are applied by an institution is critical.
- **Advanced computing technologies are accessible to everybody:** They provide individuals with the capacity to have access to more and more powerful computers; technological advancements creates a convergence between what companies and institutions can do and what individuals can achieve from their kitchen tables. Furthermore, the introduction of new ledger-based technologies like Blockchains will create even bigger challenges, in terms of controlling information assets and financial transactions.

4 Zygmunt Bauman, 'Liquid Modernity', p 82.

- Cyber-attacks can be provoked by criminal organisations, individuals and, interestingly, government agencies. **The threat can be external and/or internal.** Apart from financial motivations behind recent attacks to payment systems, hackers or perpetrators could have a sort of personal reputation or political motivations. This is what Marxist theories define 2.0 industrial sabotage and it is well exemplified by the Wikileaks and Anonymous cases. Cyber-events could also be triggered by incompetence or human errors, used then by other agents to exploit the open channels.
- **Availability to multiple agents of advanced technologies and pervasiveness of the cyber space on our daily works and lives** will impose a set of controls overarching from the public to the private and from the professional to the personal, with a series of implications. Personal and professional data have a higher and higher degree of correlation or contamination. People disclose any kind of information on the internet and identity theft and industrial espionage, just as much as big data analysis, rely on this proliferation of spots where sensitive information is stored.
- **Financial systems are less and less based on physical platforms and increasingly built on digital ones**: all the work required to defend data, information and avoiding hacking of one's infrastructure will absorb substantial resources and it will require a complete redefinition of the lines of defence, let alone the skills required to monitor this risk. The threat for a financial institution is also in the exposure of potential weaknesses on their own payment and settlement systems – as the reputation of a financial institution is also built on its capacity to execute payments, transfer money and/or financial assets.

14.11 So, the characteristics of liquidity and non-linearity of cyber-risks should make us consider them as a class of their own, with an important caveat: any form of human activity, referencing Bauman again, is moving from being accessible locally (own servers) to becoming located in different servers, in different geographies, creating the idea of data being 'vaporised' in the air (or the Cloud). Although the physical infrastructure is still needed, the fact that there is not a direct ownership or control on information creates a series of technical, legal and operational implications, including some in terms of risk remediation.

The next paragraphs are about how these challenges require an equivalent shift in terms of risk management practice.

CODING A FINANCIAL INSTITUTION APPROACH TO CYBER-RISKS

Three lines of defence and Cyber-risks

14.12 The European Stability Mechanism (ESM)started its operation in 2010 as the European Financial Stability Facility (EFSF). The ESM was set up in 2012 as a permanent institution[5]. The institution is therefore very young and, although

5 For more information on the European Stability Mechanism, see www.esm.europa.eu.

it could benefit from starting with a blank canvas, it had to start its operations in a very short time frame. The way in which it was set up reflects in some of the initial choices made by the ESM management, including the imperative to be lean and able to operate in the markets in the most effective and as short a time possible. It has also been one of the main drivers for the **outsourcing model** adopted by the ESM. The institution operates its IT services via a small, highly skilled internal team and its IT operations (eg storage) are cloud-based. The physical infrastructure operated and directly controlled by the institution is kept to a minimum. Maintenance services are also outsourced to external suppliers.

14.13 When an IT infrastructure is built, the initial optionalities are between *an insourced or outsourced model and a local/owned vs. cloud-based/remote infrastructure*. Each institution faces similar choices, with the obvious advantage the ESM had to being in a position to make a fresh choice, being a new and relatively small institution. For larger and well-established financial services companies, this optionality requires a substantial shift in their operating models, which involves additional costs.

14.14 This chapter will be aimed at the small or new institutions, not only in the public space but also in the growing number of newcomers to the financial industry, in the fund and fin-tech space. In a nutshell, it explores how to build defences in an outsourced 'starting-up' new financial institution.

14.15 Implementation of an outsourcing model should weight benefits and challenges from a risk governance perspective: it should allow for the proper implementation of a *three lines of defence* model, which is a traditional risk governance approach adopted by many institutions and defined in their own Risk policies. In reality, in the industry there is a debate if the three lines may be become at least four, as they should include the role of public agencies, or even five, to include the protection offered by the outsourcing supplier and the software/hardware companies.

14.16 However, for the purposes of this chapter, we shall discuss the traditional three lines model, similar to the one used by the ESM, inside a framework defined by two **shields**, an external and an internal one.

External shields

14.17 Layers of controls and risk/threat management built around the service provider and the regulators/specialised agencies:

14.18 The **outsourcing entity** provides a first important layer of external protection, based on vigilance of security threats and monitoring of events that could affect the network and the institution's access to IT services. The level of control is usually regulated contractually by detailed Key Performance Indicators (KPIs), Key Risk Indicators (KRIs) and Service Level Agreements (SLAs), so that the institution receiving services can monitor any potential risk.

This level of control is defined as the **external shield** in the picture below and it allows for the institution receiving the service to rely on the internal processes and procedures (including the expected risk controls) provided by the outsourcer. It is also standard practice for the outsourcing entity's staff to work alongside the institution's own staff so that issues can be resolved in a shorter time frame.

14.19 A further layer of protection associated with outsourcing entities is the shield of protection offered by software and hardware companies (eg Apple, Microsoft), or systems used by a financial institution (eg Bloomberg, Swift). Usually, these companies continue to supply maintenance and updates to their own clients in order to guarantee the highest possible level of protection from external threats. In the figure below, these are represented as 'alerts' or filters.

14.20 Another institutional external layer of defence is represented by the link between a public financial institution and **relevant national or multilateral security agencies and regulators**. This layer of defence is what could be defined a fourth line of defence, echoing the best practice proposed by the BIS, of I. Andorfer and A. Minto[6]. In Europe, for example, this role is fulfilled by the Computer Emergency Response Team for the EU institutions, agencies and bodies (CERT-EU), whose mission is to monitor and protect EU institutions. The team consists of IT security experts from the main EU institutions. CERT-EU monitors an institution's IP range of addresses and informs linked institutions of any malware/viruses they detect.

Internal shields

14.21 These shields are built around the layering of internal controls ensuring the traditional set of controls and oversight associated with other operational risks, in line with the traditional *three lines of defence*:

First internal line of defence

14.22 A dedicated IT/Information Security team, led by the so-called Chief Information Officer (CIO) with a lean structure, but with different skills set, provides protection to the institution, as first point of contact/engagement with the supplier, filtering and assessing reports from users and looking at diagnostics on the system. Key controls are established for each process used to deliver the IT services or to warrant a safe environment from a security point of view. These controls should be documented on specific maps and guidelines as part of an internal control framework regularly validated and tested.

14.23 The most important task of the first line of defence in relation to the second one and the management of the institution is to act as a filter, meaning that

6 Isabella Arndorfer and Andrea Minto, 'The four lines of defence model for financial institutions', Occasional Paper n.11 – Bank for International Settlement December 2015 .www.bis.org/fsi/fsipapers11.pdf.

any new implementation of software, hardware or new technologies needs to be explained to the institution, while simultaneously guaranteeing the detection, and collection from the users and their own usage patterns, of essential information to identify threats or how to avoid them.

14.24 As part of the process of translating technical aspects into information suitable to be used by the risk and the management board, monitoring dashboards and ad-hoc reports should be developed, showing how the institution (and in the case here its outsourcing entity) complies with defined key controls and key risk indicators. This function does not need to be a bureaucratic task, but it does involve a degree of synergy between the first and second line of defence aimed at determining risk appetite, tolerance and what key controls are to be monitored. This task therefore involves embedding alerts and signals on the network which triggers a response by the controllers.

14.25 **A significant role of the first line of defence is fulfilled by the users** (or the employees), as main customers of the institution's applications and infrastructure. This is why training and awareness sessions, as explained below, are essential.

14.26 Concrete and lean escalation chains will allow a constant flow of information, which is a key element in the early detection of threats. Given the interconnected nature of daily lives, it is also important to provide support to staff members on how to manage their own devices or how to create effective barriers and guidelines in order to avoid the risk of 'cross-contamination'.

Second internal line of defence

14.27 The Risk Management function should be tasked with providing a constant oversight and review of the IT and Information security framework used by the institution.

14.28 The risk function will also have to develop internal risk policies and risk appetite or risk tolerance statements in relation to cyber-risks (see some ideas below).

14.29 In most institutions, the oversight of IT and Information security risks resides with the Operational Risk function. In the future, it may be possible to imagine a separation between the traditional operational risk side, as recipient of information to define the financial impact of operational risk events, and a more focused and properly staffed cyber-risk unit. This development will depend on resources and the technological requirements of the institution.

14.30 One of the conundrums in the industry is where the responsibility for managing Information Security and related processes should be sitting, whether with the CIO or with independent functions devoted to the information side of the IT platform (lead by a 'CISO', Chief Information Security Officer). This choice will also determine whether the Information Security function should be a first or second line of defence.

14.31 However, pragmatism should prevail in order to avoid creating roles that exceed the immediate need for a lean and operational channel of communication between lines of defence. This principle is even truer for small institutions.

14.32 The starting point for assigning roles is defined by the risks that need to be covered and monitored (risk-based approach). For the kind of activities carried out by an international financial institution, data and information security roles should be shared by the CIO and the CRO: an institution's information system should work like a synapse, where the information required to take action sits between two neural cells. This set up will warrant not only the required level of independence (and reduce potential conflicts) but, in line with the concept of 'liquidity', the building up of a core of experience and excellence, whereby a risk is analysed both from a business and a risk management perspective, with additional focus on compliance and legal implications. So, the creation of a CIO and a CISO role may not be as efficient as the integration of both CTO and CRO roles (and their teams) for specific tasks and duties related to the management of the risk appetite for cyber data protection and information security matters.

14.33 The proactive engagement between first and second line of defence rests on maintaining specific expertise on IT and cyber-security matters in the risk function, which is a relatively new element in the context of operational risk matters.

14.34 As part of the first line of defence, operational risk experts will not only have to consider the potential reputational risk and the operational implications of a cyber-attack, but they will also need to define operational costs (expressed in terms of additional intervention, services and man-days used to resolve the event) or, in some cases, losses associated with specific events.

14.35 Cyber-security, precisely because of its pervasive nature, needs a level of alert to both official and declared threats (usually well known in the market and by the suppliers) and another kind of threat, which stems from one-hitters or rogue agents that are not linked to major attacks but are instead instigated by individuals trying to exploit the system's weaknesses to their own advantage or to sell information to other parties. This risk is particularly sensitive for institutions with a high political profiling.

14.36 As of today, financial institutions in the private and public spheres are moving towards more innovative approaches, not only based on a passive approach towards threats, but looking at proactive strategies: pen tests and ethical hackers are, for example, becoming common processes and figures inside any major financial institution and they are associated with real time monitoring of any cyber-activity linked to the institution itself.

14.37 The second line of defence, precisely because of the kind of sensible data it deals with (institutional, price sensitive and also private and personal data) needs to be supported and linked to the Compliance function and a figure known as Data Protection Officer. This function (individual or team) will have to maintain awareness on system accesses, review the handling of data and be sure that any form of usage of such information happens inside the strict and tight boundaries of existing and upcoming legislation. A key element of defence is the inclusion of cyber and information security tests on any form of anti-money laundering or anti-fraud exercise.

14.38 The Compliance function and each operation around IT and Information Security need the vital support of the Legal function of the institution. This principle applies not only to handling of information and data, but also to the maintenance of adequate contractual arrangements with suppliers and the development of consistent policies and rules inside the institution.

14.39 Special attention needs to be paid to forensic activity, where the second and third lines (eg Compliance, Legal and Audit) need to be independently able to review any specific case where investigations are required.

Third internal line of defence

14.40 Audit in the context of cyber-risks retains its traditional role of oversight and regular check through yearly plans. However, the audit function should also be involved in investigations when either major events of clusters or small events occur. This principle also applies to cyber-risk events, mainly to determine whether the accident itself was due to unavoidable conditions or if it was down to detectable gaps.

14.41 The increase of cyber-crimes and incidence of cyber-risk events pose a challenge for the traditional audit function, because it involves incorporating the higher technological advancement of an institution inside the regular audit plans and determining how to develop relevant skills.

14.42 The spectrum of action of an audit function should not be limited to regular reviews but should also extend to specific analysis and examinations, where an independent view is sought.

14.43 Along with Risk and Compliance, Audit also needs to provide advice to the institution on best practice and how to have deep investigations into specific areas. To some extent, the audit function should also administer itself as a 'positive and ethical' hacker, testing how the system supports enquiries and access and to determine whether there are weaknesses that could be exploited by external parties or internally (as it is the case with fraud events).

14.44 The capacity of the above-mentioned lines of defence to protect an institution from cyber-risks relies mainly on three factors:

1. *Early detection* – As in a viral infection, the capacity of the institutional system to survive and resist an attack is based on the capacity to detect

signals or alerts at the ground/operational level, in association with the better known and more diffused threats (hence captured by the external shield's activities).

2.- *Awareness of escalation chains* – staff members should know who to call, how to report an issue and what the immediate actions to take are.

3.- *Transparency and communication across lines of defence* – When a cyber-risk event manifests itself, the first two lines of defence should coordinate, thus providing support to each other, either to define the root cause or to implement short-term patches or longer-term mitigation actions. 'External shields', especially when outsourced, should come with alerting and communication functions as part of the contractual arrangements, including minimum standards and penalties/warranties in case the outsourcing company is not able to inform its clients in a timely fashion.

14.45 The next section provides a series of building blocks for what could constitute best practice foundation for cyber risks' protection, assuming that the above-mentioned lines of defence are working effectively.

Key building blocks for managing cyber risks

14.46 From whatever angle we look at cyber-risks, there are common themes across many organisations. The key question for a Chief Risk Officer is to determine if his/her institution's IT framework and related defences are able not only to monitor potential threats but if the same threats can be managed so that disruption is minimised and costs are kept under control. The aftermath of a cyber-risk event is always characterised by an 'all hands to the pump' approach and, as a result, a significant waste of resources (and often time).

14.47 Cyber-risks are particularly dangerous not only because of their liquidity and the capacity for small agents to interfere and disrupt any kind of institution, but also because a single incident can pervasively influence all functions of an institution, as opposed to being limited to a single division or subset of functions.

14.48 Furthermore, the growing confusion between professional and personal profiles, activities and also accesses to systems (eg hacking via Wifi on airports, use of social media) lends a completely new dimension to these risks.

14.49 The following 'building blocks' are essential to building or reinforcing the management of cyber-risks:

Determine your Information assets

14.50 Relevant literature defines an information asset as a piece of knowledge or data that has some importance for an institution and, as such, it needs to be maintained, protected and stored for identification and usage purposes. The first important task for any institution therefore involves defining what set of knowledge/information constitutes an 'asset' to be protected. This task could be carried out by considering the criticality of the asset itself (eg the preciousness of the information contained), like a specific data set, or by identifying the documentation that needs to be protected, for its confidentiality, from external access or disruption.

14.51 Protection from the risk of information assets being depleted or impacted by an attack requires substantial work on mapping and understanding how the institutional data framework is built. For complex institutions, this task can be challenging, especially when they span across multiple businesses or locations. It is therefore important that each function (eg first line of defence) of an institution should have clarity on the data needed to accomplish its own tasks, how data are managed and what the expected output is (eg regular reports). As argued by Susan Landau in a recent book, simplification and stripping down of systems and data needs could be an optimal strategy.[7]

14.52 In relation to price-sensitive or secret information, it is important that each institution should develop a clear classification for document categorisation. Depending on this initial taxonomy, different protocols and measures can be adopted for storing such information. For example, for public institutions, a mix of electronic and physical storage for key documents may be adopted and contingent arrangements are needed, in order not to not lose these institutions' 'historic memory'.

Keep a robust understanding of your infrastructure

14.53 Any institution relies on a mix of physical and virtual/electronic infrastructures. Although cyber-risks are mostly related to virtual elements, like the cloud, electronic devices and software, there is a connection between virtual and physical assets that needs to be properly understood. The capacity to isolate servers and to remove compromised software and replace it needs to be catered for within business continuity plans, alongside the need to have a separate network, often also with a different logistic/location in case of emergencies (eg data warehoused in the central system should not be accessed directly; users/employees should access to a parallel network instead).

Controlled access to systems

14.54 Having established what information needs protecting and where it should be stored, financial institutions should tend to another task, namely deciding who has access to the information and how such access should be protected. From a risk management and data protection perspective, the capacity of the institution to log accesses to different systems is very important, in order

7 Susan Landau, *Listening – Cybersecurity in an insecure age – 2018*, Yale University Press.

to build not only an audit trail but also to be alerted by unusual occurrences. These are the gateways to the institution and any use of data should be reviewed on a regular basis, including access rights and security arrangements on web pages and portals used by the financial institution. As best practice, the definition of User Access Reviews for key operational systems and for key data bases is recommended, with the capacity to identify a series of key risk indicators in order to capture, for example, unauthorised accesses or stale ones (eg leavers). Another source of risk are the 'dormant' accounts, with potential lack of review of the access profiles that more and more privileges without detailed checks.

Maintain human capital

14.55 Cyber-risks are mainly originated by human agents with the determined objective to profit from an IT system's weakness or to harm an institution or individuals. So, as a good countermeasure, an institution should be in a position to hire profiles with specific IT and Information security knowledge, not only on the support functions but also on Risk, Compliance and Audit, with a mind-set able to predict how attackers will behave. We discuss below the use of ethical hackers, but even more crucial is the need for institutions to have IT experts across the lines of defence with the 'capacity' to read human behaviour and understand how the 'offending mind' may think – a kind of cyber-profiling of expected actions: the robustness of the defence relies mostly on the capacity of individuals to speak the same language and cross-contaminate their relevant experience across the institution, thinking like hackers. Cohesion and coordination are required to reduce potential overlap between lines of defence, since it is normal for institutions to tend to 'overprotect' themselves with redundant controls.

14.56 In relation to human capital, given the rapid development of new technologies, versatility and capacity to understand latest trends are important assets and, in the selection of new hires, Information Security seems to be an area where updated knowledge trumps experience (or, where, potentially, Millennials have a higher level of understanding of protocols and issues to deal with).

Raise awareness among staff

14.57 Another element linked to human capital is the need, for any institution, to keep training staff on new threats and to get their support when they report issues. The kind of training needed in a financial institution can be divided into different components.

Technical knowledge

14.58 How to use internal systems and software, including traditional solutions like Microsoft Office, to file sharing solutions. Training improves efficiency and it allows correct usage of platforms and, even more crucially, it provides users with tips on how to cope with threats from internet and emails, which are still the main source of phishing and malware attacks.

Awareness training

14.59 How to detect anomalies hinting to applications that steal information. As the threat has expanded to smartphones and tablets, it is important that early diagnostics are provided to users, let alone the necessary training on how to report specific events to the function responsible for Information Security, and/or, in case of personal data issues, to the Data Protection Officer of the institution. Timeliness of reporting is a key element to stop the threat and isolate the impacted elements (hardware or software).

Testing of attitude/behaviours

14.60 More and more institutions apply to IT matters the same approach used in relation to the so-called 'clean desk policies': for example, phishing attacks and social engineering attacks could be simulated in order to test the employees' reaction. It may be in the form of a fake email offering free iPads or in the form of fake links to apparently legitimate pages offering discounts or, in some cases, also apparently legitimate emails from colleagues asking for specific actions to be completed. We are at a much more sophisticated level of the initial scam e-mails that populated the earlier days of internet communication (although it seems that scam letters were already very popular in the times after the French revolution – as a testament that some of the most effective phishing techniques appeal to our own human behaviours, from greed to empathy[8]). These tests are very helpful to demonstrate to users the vulnerabilities they are exposed to and provide practical tips on how to discern fake from proper email addresses or internet pages. In a nutshell, this form of testing is aimed to create a positive doubting on what seems legitimate, thus to be verified. From a risk perspective, it may not cover all the cases of phishing but it relies on the fact that perpetrators of such attacks need to have a broader approach. Social Engineering techniques are much more difficult to detect and they herald an era where the capacity for hackers to use personal information or simulate legitimate email addresses may require additional defences (eg detection of suspicious IP protocols).

Passwords/Encryption up to date

14.61 Last but not least, our first line of defence, as much as in our houses, is the quality of the locks we use. Encouraging staff members to change passwords regularly (blocking accounts), or to protect documents with encryption, may not be enough and, in some cases, password protection should become an enforced process. The same principle applies to the capacity to upload and download documents through USB keys or download services on the net.

8 Brian Kaun Wood 'I must first apologise', from *The Internet does not exist, e-flux journal* (Sternberg Press 2018), p 189.

14.62 In terms of delivery of awareness, physical dissemination is important: information provided via leaflets, posters, also in unusual places like lifts and canteens, allows for a more efficient spreading of key news, from password protection protocols, to alert on specific threats.

Run your own penetration tests

14.63 The plural in 'tests' is especially significant here: institutions with outsourcing arrangements usually get contractual arrangements for the running of specific penetration tests by their suppliers. These exercises aim to find weaknesses and gaps in the protection layers of the institution, where the outsourcer acts as a hacker. However, it is becoming more and more common to have Risk or Audit to ask specific companies and consultants in the realm of ethical hacking to run independent penetration tests, to check if the results obtained by these parallel and alternative tests align with the ones carried out by the outsourcing company. In the context of cyber-attacks, the capacity to simulate how different classes of attackers may behave is becoming a vital imperative.

14.64 Given the high probability that a cyber-attack could originate internally or could be perpetrated by former staff or former supplier staff members, some pen tests use a 'white-box' perspective, ie, the hacker knows everything about the company.

Define policies aligned to your desired level of protection

14.65 A good risk management and compliance approach involves defining policies and controls beyond what the company regards as pre-requisites. Given the 'liquid' and ever-developing nature of cyber-risks, it is important that the policies associated with the definition of security standards in an institution are kept as broad as possible. In the context of a financial institution, it is important to have an Information Security Policy that, in plain English and with a lean approach, defines for all the employees:

- the assets to be covered/protected;
- how information assets are classified and what the staff is expected to do;
- the threats to be defined in the policy;
- who is responsible for alerting/escalating and who is responsible for mitigating the risk.

Maintain strong internal controls

14.66 Each institution has its own set of controls and, in relation to IT and cyber-risk measures, the creation of internal controls should follow the same route as normal controls.

KRIs and KPIs as alerting system

14.67 Each institution should define a set of key performance indicators to be applied to their internal services delivering IT and Information security, or, when this service is outsourced, these key performance indicators should be embedded into the contractual terms and tested regularly (at least quarterly – although some of these indicators can be tested in real time, like the downplay time of a supplied service). In addition, it is important to define a set of key risk indicators, or values/deliverables that indicate a heightened state of risk or vulnerability for an institution (for example: the percentage of laptops not updated to last available security software). In this context, the creation of specific General Computing Controls plays a critical role in protecting the network, as they should flag issues not only from a cyber risk perspective, but also in terms of the capacity of the system to deal with stress situations;

Risk register as record of issues

14.68 As example of best practice, some institutions have developed forms of IT risk register: a file-based risk management tool acting as a repository for all identified cyber-risk events and including information about the nature of each risk or event, reference, impact and mitigation measures. This risk register then can become a dashboard subject to regular assessment by the Risk function and used to represent the level of preparedness, updates to the system and also flagging specific events or incidents (eg an idle desktop, the need for a new anti-virus version, malware events), ultimately looking for patterns of higher risk areas that need to be monitored closely. In addition, the register can support the work required to allocate capital requirements of the institution, based on the experience of costs and losses incurred to remedy events.

Have the capacity to execute forensics on risk events

14.69 In case of a certified cyber-attack or even when one is suspected, it is important that the institution has the capacity to run forensics and analysis by drawing on skilled individuals. These activities will need to happen under the strict control of privacy rules, while avoiding further disruption to the service providers and the users. A key element of these activities is the limitation and strong control on who is authorised to have access to the information and how the staff members need to be informed. This is a decision that each institution needs to take on the basis of specific knowledge, tasks and levels of independence needed.

Have a task force ready

14.70 Many institutions, in case of a cyber-attack, set up a 'war room', a task force of individuals with the sole scope of dealing with the event, once the necessary conditions of working for the whole institution have been implemented. Some of the key questions that need to be answered immediately concern the channel of the attack, if it was a single attempt or one of many. It is also important to determine how much the 'infection' has spread and what key actions need to be taken immediately.

RIDING THE WAVES: SOME POINTS FOR A NEW APPROACH TO RISK MANAGEMENT OF CYBER-SECURITY

14.71 Defending an institution from the cyber-liquid risks is a daily challenge: small and apparently minor incidents could be just the symptom of a wider problem. In addition, as risk practitioners, the concern for present issues needs to be continuously projected into the near future: on how technological changes could create conditions for bigger cyber events or crises – even accounting for geopolitical tensions where cyber-threats are de facto becoming weapons in virtual conflicts. This type of risk is well illustrated by real-time cyber-attack maps from information security consultants like Norse.[9] We are already in some kind of global cyber-war.

14.72 A Chief Risk Officer should become, over time, a Chief Information Risk Officer, because, in a few years' time, all activities will take place on electronic platforms and risk management systems and intelligence will need to adapt.

14.73 The following points illustrate how the increasing dangers from the net require an even more disciplined approach from a risk management perspective. Not knowing when the 'liquid enemy' will strike next, the following are ideas on how to be ready.

Definition of 'cyber-risk' as stand-alone category

14.74 Each institution has its own risk language, referencing to risk categories and how these are managed in practice. This is the concept of **risk taxonomy**, an internal description that allows each individual to identify risks. Financial regulators are trying to introduce standardised definitions for each class of risk[10], as this will help the analysis of each risk component of an institution. However, the same risk class may have slightly different meanings in any given institution. For example, an investment fund and a bank will have slightly different nuanced interpretations of what constitutes a credit risk: for a fund manager this will be more related to counterparty risk for transactions, whereas for a bank it is more directly linked to general retail and corporate customers. The taxonomy of risks therefore defines the internal language chosen by each institution. It is then essential to define the institution's defences and requirements in terms of monitoring. Traditionally (as explained in **14.12**), **Cyber Risk** is a component

9 http://map.norsecorp.com/.
10 On this aspect, see this interesting on-line article from Marco Folpmers: www.garp.org/#!/risk-intelligence/all/all/ a1Z40000003Ll7sEAC/call-to-overhaul-traditional-risk-taxonomy.

of the taxonomy definition of Operational Risk: any cyber-risk event could have a wide impact on the infrastructure and regular functioning of the institution, similarly to a system or infrastructure.

14.75 These tasks gained so much relevance for the financial sector that, in 2017, the European Banking Authority published a report titled '*Guidelines on ICT Risk Assessment under the Supervisory Review and Evaluation Process (SREP)*'[11] aimed to define for each financial institution regulated by the authority a clear risk taxonomy related to the whole of the IT and information Security risk spectrum. The report provides a good set of ideas for best practice. Nevertheless, there is scope for identifying a definition of Cyber Risk even more precisely, as follows: *any cyber disruption event within a financial institution resulting either in denial of service, data corruption and loss or on a delayed capacity to intervene, in the context of a very interconnected world (where short-term financial transactions won't be able to happen outside of an electronic platform).*

14.76 In a recent study of the Cambridge Centre for Risk Studies,[12] the financial dimension of cyber-risks is defined as 'cyber-loss processes', or events that could lead to substantial costs or losses for the institution impacted: data exfiltration, contagious malware, financial theft, outage and denial of service attacks are the main ones described. Each one of them has the potential to create substantial damage to either a single institution or the whole system.

14.77 Although the report ends posing the rightful question about the capacity to model financial losses derived by these events and define a potential capital hit (in line with the operational risk framework), it also hints that it may be difficult to define amounts. Given the lack of historic trends, it is difficult to assimilate cyber-risk events to default on mortgages or interest rate volatility.

14.78 However, we live in times of value adjustments (all the XVAR family), where, for any accessory risk, financial institutions adjust their own pricing for their own transactions in the capital market. Therefore, it should not be difficult, at least theoretically, imagining an adjustment of both pricing offered to clients and the internal VAR limits with a defined link to the risk of miscalculation because of 'data exfiltration' or financial theft. This would oblige an institution to focus on mapping its own data sources and computation capacity, alongside its own capacity to protect such information (information assets point as above) and, given the market impact, it will trigger additional transparency and communication on how different institutions deal with cyber-risks (and how they cater for their remediation).

11 European Banking Authority, 'Final Report. Guidelines on ICT Risk Assessment under the Supervisory Review and Evaluation process (SREP) – 11 May 2017, EBA/GL/2017/05, London.

12 Cambridge Centre for Risk Studies, Cyber Risk Outlook, 2018.

Cyber Risk Appetite

14.79 Each risk category of an institution is defined in terms of statutory amount of risk and related losses/costs associated to it or what can be defined as a level of **risk appetite/tolerance.**[13] For example, this is what Value at Risk limits help to define for the evaluation of market risk. Financial speaking, this value is the maximum amount of capital loss that the institution can afford to absorb. When looking at cyber-risks, a similar approach should be followed, whereas up until now the dominant view has been that these kind of events should be regarded as an exception, hence not computed into an institutional running costs.

14.80 Looking at a potential concept of cyber-risk appetite, the first question to ask is what kind of costs need to be covered, as they will help to define a potential loss profile and the severity of each cyber-event. Below are some examples of potential costs and risks associated with information security and risk events to define what could be defined as a 'risk budget', similarly to the concept used in portfolio management to allocate risks and potential losses to different asset classes.

14.81 In relation to Information Security and cyber-risks, the concept of *Risk budget* could be defined in terms of how much money the company is ready to use to maintain the IT framework and how it is going to invest or cater for costs and losses, in case of events. This type of risk is like a level of risk tolerance, as we need to realise that, in relation to cyber-risks, it is not about if, but about when, they are going to happen. Some examples are as follows.

Cost of immediate disruption

14.82 When an event occurs, institutions should be in a position to determine the direct implications and consequences, in terms of failed processes and errors leading to business disruption, for both the institution and its customers or stakeholders. This is the 'first day' cost and it is important that the 'task force' mentioned above is called upon, following a protocol planned in advance, to provide patches to impacted areas and an initial reaction. From a risk appetite perspective, the key questions are:

- what kind of activities are vital and what should the support from the task force focus on? Each institution should have maps of its vital processes and use them in case of a deep attack;
- what kind of data can an institution afford to lose and what part of the infrastructure is not replaceable and by-passable in case of attack.
- do we have alternative processes in place?

13 For some definitions of Risk Appetite, see the book by David Hillson and Ruth Murray Webster *A short guide to Risk Appetite* (Gower 2015).

Cost of Contingencies/remedies

14.83 A 2016 report by the Ponemon Institute[14] states that, in case of a cyber-risk event, information loss or theft represented an average of 39% of the associated costs, followed by business disruption at 36%. Most of these costs related to short-term solutions and intervention, with obvious consequences for contingency planning. Rebuilding the business capacity to perform duties may be costly, but, in these cases, the real loss to remedy is the one of reputation. Although immediately difficult to determine in monetary terms, nowadays the capacity of an institution to react and take action in case of a cyber-event (which may need to be reported and communicated to stakeholders) can be assessed and used to rebuild the reputation.

Cost of low awareness

14.84 In the second paragraph above, it was emphasised how training and awareness of staff are paramount to detect cyber-risk events. In a potential definition of a risk appetite (and risk budget), an institution should also establish the cost of keeping its staff trained. A recent report by Willis Towers Watson, an UK insurance company[15], shows that employee negligence and malicious acts account for a staggering 66% of cyber breaches, where 18% were directly driven by an external threat and only 2% related to cyber extortion. These numbers show clearly what in information security language is described as the *enemy within*. These 'enemies' can be divided into two groups:

- staff not aware of threats or not using precautions in relation to their technological platforms (eg smart phones and emails, mainly), exposing the institution to gaps in its security protocols;
- insiders and staff members with intentionality to damage the institution they work for or to exploit loopholes and gaps in its defence mechanisms for their own reason. In this case, it is important to make staff aware of the consequences of their wrongdoing and the potential impact from a disciplinary point of view.

14.85 So, devoting financial and human resources to ongoing training (and related costs) will be the best risk mitigant for the risks deriving from staff members.

Deep and Dark webs: Alice's mirrors

14.86 With the growing scale of cyber-risks and threats, institutions have started associating their information security functions to additional diagnostic

14 Ponemon Institute, '2016 Cost of Cyber Crime Study and the Risk of Business Innovation', October 2016.

15 Willis Towers Watson ' Decoding Cyber Risk – UK Results' – www.willistowerswatson.com/en/insights/ 2017/06/2017-cyber-risk-survey-report.

and forensics tools. One of the areas where institutions are investing in is the creation of internal capacity or the hiring of experts to monitor the Deep Web and the Dark Web, a kind of '*hidden lands*' behind a kind of Alice in Wonderland's mirror of the surface web. Both webs originated from a legitimate function as '*laboratories*' for the surface web used by developers, have now become the market place for hackers and criminal organisations who sell and exchange data, personal details and methodologies to hack systems. Therefore, more and more institutions are devoting resources to scan both webs in order to find what is called, in anti-terrorism language, murmurs, or information concerning potential new threats, not only general ones, but also related to specific companies and networks or individuals in important positions.

14.87 From a risk management perspective, new threats require new tools, also because the '*liquid enemy*' will continue to morph and adapt to the counter-activities of monitoring, in ways that are difficult to predict. Therefore, it is important for institutions and corporates to continue to invest in detecting software, able to scan deep and dark webs as to highlight potential weak points or if some piece of information assets, including the physical infrastructure, becomes compromised. Development of an in-house capacity for dark web and cyber-crime investigation seems a common orientation of large institutions. For smaller institutions, there will be additional requirements, especially they opt to hire private consultants and companies to perform dark web monitoring, in terms of reliability and maintenance of high ethical standards.

Personal data protection issues

14.88 The management of information security deals with a series of issues related to personal data about all the stakeholders (from clients and suppliers to employees). To this day, the difference between professional and personal usage of software, hardware and networks is blurry. On the other hand, and especially in Europe with the General Data Protection Regulation (GDPR)[16], there is a well-defined principle of defence of individuals' information. These regulations create a series of conundrums for the management of information security, which are widely discussed in this book. Different countries have different approaches, as it is indeed the case when it comes to the protection of customers in other areas. We should similarly focus on the inclusion of transparency measures on how data is handled and on the quality and depth of scrutiny from service providers or employers of their own staff.

14.89 From a risk practice point of view, there are a few points to consider:

16 Reg (EU) 2016/679 of the European Parliament and of the Council of 27 April 2016 on the protection of natural persons with regard to the processing of personal data and on the free movement of such data, and repealing Dir 95/46/EC (General Data Protection Regulation) ([2016] OJ L119, p 1).

1. *Transparency on data processing* – Institutions need to be sure that the process through which personal data is handled and stored is well document and transparent/easily understandable to auditors, regulators and customers.

2. *Proportionality principle* – There should be a process defining the kind of personal information stored for individuals and employees and, as per European regulation, an independent Data Protection function not only created but tasked with enquiry powers in case of forensics.

3. *Human rights to privacy to be preserved* – The role of risk and compliance managers are also as guarantors of the private information of customers and staff alike. The potential intrusion into personal matters needs to be managed correctly and it should be handled either via specific guidelines on how staff members should use social media and personal emails in the work place and, in addition, via a protocol through which this information can be used appropriately. Breach of Data privacy protection measures could outweigh the potential benefit of protecting the institution, via a reputational risk event.

CONCLUSION: CYBER-RISKS IN AN ERA OF AI CONTINUITY

14.90 The management of cyber-risks in a financial institution is quite unique because financial institutions are still a people business (eg finance is the means through which resources are allocated to individuals) but they are fast developing into a highly informatised industry – ergo much less dependent on human labour.

14.91 Consequently, the management of cyber-risks in a financial institution involves handling ever-larger amounts of data and information, a vast ocean of data points that will be become readable only by sophisticated thinking machines. As risk practitioners, we need to look forward into a world where Artificial Intelligence (or AI) will start being used in a more pervasive way – not at the extreme level hinted at by Stephen Hawking in a famous quote from a BBC interview,[17] ('*AI could spell the end of the Human race*') but at a level where some challenges will be unavoidable. Below are some examples of such '*not so tail-risks*'.

14.92 Human hacking activity will become a residual component of cyber threats, and will be replaced by complex machine networks, which are bound to produce a completely different battlefield from the one we are used to today, with frequencies and speeds similar to the ones deployed in high speed trading. This analogy is quite fitting, given that the capital and equity markets are already making pervasive use of primordial forms of artificial intelligence not only to administer market orders (and worth noting, in this respect, is the fact that some recent collapses in some stock exchanges have been attributed to algorithms), but also to provide advice to investors. Hackers are already using

17 www.bbc.com/news/technology-30290540.

bots and sophisticated automated mechanisms to attack their targets, but in the future cyber-attacks will play out as an internecine war between machines able to modify their behaviours depending on the kind of opposition they encounter – with light speed adaptation capacity.

14.93 Institutional knowledge and wisdom will be at risk – Reliance on electronic platforms exposes any institution to the risk of losing stored data and documents and income – and, in extreme case scenarios, to the risk of having all this information not only no longer accessible but also corrupted or wiped out. However, there is much more at stake: as 'thinking machines' will perform tasks and take decisions, the institutional knowledge – defined as an organised and structured set of experience and understanding of one's own business – is at risk of being undermined.

14.94 In the information technology era, knowledge remains one of the key competitive assets, let alone the founding stone of any corporate and institutional identity. In a 'people' business, there is always the inherent risk of losing the identity and exposing the institution to disaffection from its own employees or to a serialised and not engaged workforce. It is not difficult to see potential risks of neo-luddism[18] and sabotage arising, as AI continues to grow.

14.95 Does the net require a new morality? The risk of optimisation – One of the drivers of the recent introduction of a new European regulation on General Data Protection is the building of defence lines to protect individuals from threats deriving from decisions arising from machine learning, algorithms and automated decision-making. In a brilliant recent article, David Weinberger[19] questions the set of principles on which automated learning technologies are built on, and especially when they are built to advise or take decisions. He sums up his concerns as follows:

> 'We think of these systems as making decisions, and we want to make sure they make the right moral decisions by doing what we do with humans: we ask for explanations that present the moral principles that were applied and the facts that led to them being applied that way. "Why did you steal the apple?" can be justified and explained by saying "Because it had been stolen from me," "It was poisoned and I didn't want anyone else to eat it" or "Because I was hungry and I didn't have enough money to pay for it." These explanations work by disputing the primacy of the principle that it's wrong to steal.'

14.96 Given the complexity of the scenario he outlines, Weinberger argues that any Artificial Intelligence or Machine Learning system should derive their internal ethics not from the developer itself but by specially advocated or created public sector bodies. A kind of return to the Laws of Robotics by Isaac

18 www.theguardian.com/technology/2018/mar/04/will-2018-be-the-year-of-the-neo-luddite.
19 David Weinberger on www.medium.com: https://medium.com/berkman-klein-center/optimization-over-explanation-41ecb135763d.

Asimov,[20] where the key expectation is to optimise the outcome: for Asimov and Weinberger, the primary outcome is the protection of human life; for financial institutions, the primary objective is to have artificial intelligence built around a set of critical societal values, like transparency, fairness and respect, that will allow for the best outcome for both the institution (optimisation of efficiency) and its staff, clients and stakeholders.

14.97 From a cyber-risk point of view, 'optimisation' as detailed by Weinberger represents the major challenge for the future and it confronts us with key questions:

- How do we want to manage an institution exposed not only to human-driven but also to machine-driven attacks, where the attack itself (or its success) remains an amoral event?
- What capacity of reaction and proactive and direct action are institutions going to need not only to defend infrastructures, databases, or their reputation, but, in some cases, their role as moral and social leaders who aim to enhance rather than damage human experience?

14.98 So, to sum up, the main defence against the 'liquid enemy' remains our ability to change and adapt, which is best described as 'plasticity', namely the capacity of our brain to change as a result of experience. Plasticity is what we want machines to replicate. We must however also bear in mind the fact that there are other aspects of the human experience, like wisdom and empathy, that we might not want machines to be able to reproduce, because they might be our biggest asset against disruptive behaviour and any type of aggression – whether human or otherwise. It would therefore be prudent to end with an appeal to maintain a 'human line of defence' as the most important strategy to counter cyber-attacks. It seems that we need to develop a cyber-anthropology[21], as a way to understand the existential risks we are running, regulate and mitigate them.

A brave and new tech world.

> 'But God doesn't change. "Men do, though." "What difference does that make?"' All the difference in the world.'
>
> Aldous Huxley[22]

20 https://en.wikipedia.org/wiki/Three_Laws_of_Robotics.

21 Philipp Budka 'From Cyber to Digital Anthropology to an Anthropology of the Contemporary?'- *Working Paper for the EASA Media Anthropology Network's 38th e-Seminar* (22 November – 6 December 2011) www.media-anthropology. nethttp://www.media-anthropology.net/file/budka_contemporary.pdf.

22 Aldous Huxley, Brave New World.

CHAPTER 15

EMPLOYEE LIABILITY AND PROTECTION

Sally Penni

15.01 This chapter will be covering in the most practical of terms, confidential information, Trade secrets, databases, employer liability, employer and business measures and procedures that employers can take against them. It will refer to legal cases where these are a useful reference in order to illustrate this point.

OVERVIEW AND INTRODUCTION OF THE PROBLEM

15.02 Business's confidential information faces a big threat from employees or insiders within the business. The data and research actually illustrates that employees acquire information and remove the information whether to secure future employment to use in direct competition to an employer. So this has meant, according to a report in 2014, that the misappropriation of data by employees was for use with an existing competitor or in at least 30% of cases to set up a competing businesses. The prevalence of this sort of action is of course not uncommon. This chapter seeks to identify the methods by which employers can protect information and immediate practical steps.

Why do employees take the information?

15.03 The vast majority of people, employees and staff taking the information felt that they:

(a) had the right to remove the data because they had been involved in the creation;

(b) some felt there was an expectation to bring the taken or stolen information with them to the new employer;

(c) a survey revealed that they would take confidential data if faced with redundancy and some were already storing the data to enhance their value in the employment market.

15.04 Moreover, the common online nature of most businesses and the contact requirement to have an online presence means that there is an increased danger to employers through their liability of their employees. This makes the employers vicarious liable. In the context of cyber-law this could be through:

(a) the act of an employee visiting an offending website;

(b) emails containing inappropriate content;

(c) defamatory statements;

(d) sharing sexually explicit materials to individuals.

15.05 There have been many cases which have resulted from such computer misuse by employees from discrimination cases to health and safety breaches and harassment. To cover all of these is beyond this chapter. Essentially an employer cannot use statute to seek protection. Companies cannot intercept emails but only monitor as a way of controlling misuse. The only effective course of protection is incorporating this into the contract of employment and having employees accept that whilst at work only the proper use of the internet and emails are acceptable. This means that any breaches would result in disciplinary action and ultimately summary dismissal.

WHAT INFORMATION IS CONFIDENTIAL?

What is confidential information?

15.06 Before we can determine what is confidential information to the employer, it is important to make a distinction. The distinction is between the employer's property and information which has become part of the general knowledge through his increased skills and experienced gained as a result of working for the employer or business.

15.07 We can derive some assistance from case law. In FSS *Travel and Leisure Systems Ltd v Johnson* [1998] IRLR 382, CA the Court of Appeal said it must be possible to identify how the information is used in the relevant business and the use of the information is likely to cause harm to the employer and business.

15.08 Often the employer will seek protection against the information being disclosed by relying on an implied obligation of confidentiality both during the employment and post termination of the employment.

15.09 In *Faccenda Chicken Ltd v Fowler* [1986] IRLR 69, CA the Court of Appeal said at page 137 onwards, that in order to determine whether the information could be protected after termination of employment under the implied duty of confidentiality a court should have regard to the nature of the employment and the nature of the information. They stated:

> 'We are satisfied that the following two matters which attention must be paid
>
> (a) The nature of the employment where confidential material habitually handled may impose a high obligation of confidentiality because the employee can be expected to realise its sensitive nature to a greater extent than if employed in a capacity where such material reaches him only occasionally or incidentally.

(b) The nature of the information itself. In our judgement the information will only be protected if it can properly be classed as a trade secret or material which while not properly to be described as a trade secret, is in all the circumstances of such highly confidential nature as to require the same protection as a trade secret …..The restrictive covenant cases demonstrate that the covenant will not be upheld on the basis of status of the information which might be disclosed by the former employee if he is not even restrained, unless it can be regarded as a trade secret or equivalent.'

15.10 What this case tells us is that the duty of confidentiality arises where the employees' job needs routine handling of confidential information so that actually he ought to be aware of its sensitivity and he or she has been informed about the confidentiality of the information. Moreover the information must be properly characterised as a trade secret or similarly highly confidential to be protected post termination and it must be free or separable from other information which the employee would be free to use or disclose. This means that the employee cannot have any genuine interest in protecting information which is confidential because, for example, it has already been published or where it would not harm the business interests of the employer if it were so.

WHAT INFORMATION WILL THE COURTS PROTECT?

15.11 It is important to look at the cases in this area from 1979 to more recent cases.

Thomas Marshall Exports Ltd v Guinle [1979] CH 227 established the four-part test for confidential information. It states that whether an employer can protect this will be dependent on:

(a) the nature of the information;

(b) the commercial damage which might be done to the employer;

(c) the extent to which the confidential material was explained to the employee, or

(d) the extent it would have been apparent.

15.12 So, so long as an employer/the business can establish that the information was confidential the misuse by of information provided to the competitor is actionable in court.

15.13 What caselaw is there that can assist employers with confidential information? *Crowson Fabrics Ltd v Rider* [2007] EWHC 2942 demonstrates that establishing that information is confidential is not straightforward but that in failing to meet the required threshold tests the employer has protection. This case reflect how businesses are run these days.

15.14 Facts: Crawson Fabrics Ltd was the claimant who was in design production and supply of fabrics for home and commercial furnishings and decorations. The chairman and sole shareholder did not attend to the business full time but had hands on control by proxy, making all the important decisions. The first defendant was Paul Rider, the product and distribution director. He was part of the senior management of the company and inner circle that the Chairman relied upon. The second defendant was Warren Stimson who was the UK and Export Sales Manager. He was not invited into strategic meetings. There were no restrictive covenants within the employment contracts of either of them.

15.15 Held: The claimant company asserted that both defendants had access to confidential information specifically customer contracts and supply information this was because the defendants had decided to set up a competitive company. As one would expect they handed in their notice but did not inform the employer of their intention to set up a rival company. During the notice period the first defendant was asked to prepare a Supplier Bible listing 3,500 of the claimant's customers whilst the second defendant used the claimants email system to contact customers and notify them of the rival company. The claimants' claim was that the first defendant was an employee and owed a duty of good faith and fidelity and so was subject to an implied obligation not to copy, remove or misuse any of the claimant's confidential business information. Moreover by virtue of his seniority it was argued that he owed a fiduciary duty to act in good faith. By way of response the defendants claimed that none of the material that they had created or used or retained at the end of their employment contained any confidential information. They claimed all the information was available in the public domain. They also claimed in the absence of restrictive covenants they were free to use all the material as they had gathered the knowledge and acquired this knowledge over the course of the employment and were free to use it.

15.16 The case was heard in the High Court and the Judge, Smith J, found that the first defendant was a fiduciary and that both defendants had breached their duties not to copy and retain information such as the supplier bible and not to communicate with the claimant's company to solicit them. However he found that the confidential information did not have the confidence necessary and all the information was in fact in the public domain. The only information capable of protection post termination was in the nature of trade secrets. He found as to the manner in which they obtained the information was in an illuminate way. As to the database, the Judge held that the claimants had established a database right and the extraction of the database right.

15.17 Let us take a look at what happens when large amounts of confidential data is transferred not for rival use but to personal computers for use in the future. This is what happened in the next case *Brandeaux Advisers UK Ltd – Chadwick* [2010] EWHC 3241 IRLR 224.

15.18 Facts: The defendant had transferred information to her personal computer and when redundancy arose she threatened to use the data against the company unless she was offered an alternative post. The employer placed her on garden leave and when they discovered the transfer of confidential information she was dismissed for gross misconduct.

Held: the confidential information had to be returned but there was no order for damages as the company had not suffered any loss.

ADVICE

Employer beware

15.19 To prevent and avoid these instances, employers should have regard to employees who have recently left their employment and think of ways to protect themselves such as:

(a) employees can be made aware of the high levels of confidentiality that the employer/business holds the information;

(b) remind employees of their duties as a fiduciary, and

(c) remind employees of their duties under contract of employment as to duties of fidelity.

15.20 It is important for employers to be aware that once employees have left, information and evidence can be lost once accounts and personal emails are deleted or removed.

15.21 Finally in more recent cases, it's important to understand what would happen if the employees does none of the above but uses the confidential information to win business for his new employer. Is the new company liable for the actions of the new employee even if the new employee is acting on their own, an old term called acting on a frolic of their own?

15.22 In *Pintorex Ltd v Keyvanfar* & Ors [2013] EWPCC 36, this is what happened. The company was found to be vicariously liable. The defendant company was found to be jointly liable for the actions of the employee. The third defendant director was not found to be personally liable because he had not known of the employee's intention to misuse the confidential information. However, this case was decided on the facts and does not afford directors of businesses a defence by simply asserting this. Interestingly the detrimental effect of losing confidential information is not limited to the company asserting that they own the information.

Employer beware

15.23 This of course means that there is a risk for any employer when recruiting new employees. The difficulty for businesses is in protecting themselves from the risk of liability they also need to grow their businesses and often the whole point of recruiting new employees is for their acquired knowledge.

15.24 What is the relevant test for protecting confidential information? The test was established in an old case called *Coco v A N Clark (Engineers) Ltd*: ChD *19688* page 415. So in every case we must ask the following questions:

1. Does the information itself have a necessary quality of confidence about it?
2. Has the information been imparted in circumstances imparting an obligation of confidence?
3. Has there been an unauthorised use of information to the detriment of the party that is communicating it?

15.25 The first test means that the legal test actually requires businesses and employers to apply protective measures, systems and procedures in order to protect their information. This means that software businesses, for example, should take measures, for example ensuring their source code is a trade secret and ensuring they have non disclosure agreements. Similarly third parties should do the same, thus ensuring disclosure is only in limited circumstances.

Breach of confidence cases

15.26 If a case is brought for breach of confidence, the courts will expect to see what measures were in place to keep the information in question confidential. They will need specifics of the information being asserted as being confidential. So for example the courts will generally accept as confidential so the issues remaining will be the circumstances of the obligation of confidence and what the authorised use was that caused a detriment.

15.27 But in order for business to assert that they are confidential things like algorithms and programming language should be protected as intellectual property right and must not be released into the public domain deliberately or inadvertently. This remains a difficult area particularly in the open source sector and arena. Comments on source code, preparatory works like design may be confidential but unlikely to be protected by another means and may not be covered by copyright or data protection.

15.28 If you start an action, then a request for pre-action disclosure of specific information the defendant or employee holds can be useful. A proper request not a fishing exercise of what the employee has can be immensely powerful because once such a request has been granted it compels the defendant or employee to admit to possessing and producing the relevant confidential information.

Employer beware

15.29 Vicarious liability for employees' actions is becoming more and more common with courts applying personal liability to company directors so businesses should be aware. This is because a new employer may owe a duty of confidence to the ex-employer if they had knowledge of the employee abusing confidential information but turned a blind eye to it. Especially if the information was generating income and profits. So employers should be aware of this potential secondary liability when recruiting from competitors. As we know from the earlier cases once the information is in the public domain the damage has been done. But it useful to seek injunctive relief that can restrict a competitor from entering into the market by preventing them from using the information for a certain time.

Trade secrets

15.30 Trade secrets are confidential processes normally associated with techniques of manufacturing, special formulae, chemical or recipes, methods of business, as opposed to the structure of business. In fact the term trade secret suggests the highest level of secrecy. The Information Tribunal has explained in the case of *Department of Health v Information Commissioner* [2008] that the ordinary understanding of trade secrets suggests something technical, unique, ordinary and achieved with a degree of difficulty and investment. Coco Cola and Pepsi would agree the recipes were trade secrets. So the cause of action is a breach of confidence and the same test applies.

15.31 The owners of trade secrets should prove that they have taken reasonable steps or made reasonable efforts to keep the information confidential. If they can do this then even if through illegal acts a competitor can obtain their trade secrets then it may remain legally protected. The problem is for businesses and employers who cannot show they have made reasonable efforts to protect their trade secrets. So showing evidence of practical steps such as shredding documents or collection of confidential waste is important.

WHAT PROTECTION DOES THE EU OFFER ON TRADE SECRETS?

The Trade Secret Directive 2013

15.32 The EU proposed a creation of a Directive to try to harmonise the protection of trade secrets. Its aim was to make it easier for national courts to deal with people misappropriating confidential business information. Amongst other things it makes it easier for the claimant or victim to receive compensation for illegal breaches.

The Trade Secrets Directive in short

15.33 On 8 June 2016 following a proposal from the European Commission, the European Parliament and the Council adopted a Directive that aims to standardise the national laws in EU countries against the unlawful acquisition, disclosure and use of trade secrets. The Directive is entitled: Directive (EU) 2016/943 on the protection of undisclosed know-how and business information (trade secrets) against their unlawful acquisition.

15.34 The Directive harmonises the definition of trade secrets in accordance with existing internationally binding standards. It also defines the relevant forms of misappropriation and clarifies that reverse engineering and parallel innovation must be guaranteed, given that trade secrets are not a form of exclusive intellectual property right.

15.35 Without establishing criminal sanctions, the proposal harmonises the civil means through which victims of trade secret misappropriation can seek protection, such as:

- stopping the unlawful use and further disclosure of misappropriated trade secrets;
- the removal from the market of goods that have been manufactured on the basis of a trade secret that has been illegally acquired;
- the right to compensation for the damages caused by the unlawful use or disclosure of the misappropriated trade secret.

15.36 EU countries must bring into force the laws and administrative provisions necessary to comply with the Directive by 9 June 2018.

What will change?

15.37 Companies, inventors, researchers and creators will be put on an equal footing throughout the Internal Market, and the EU will have a common, clear and balanced legal framework which will discourage unfair competition, and facilitate collaborative innovation and the sharing of valuable know-how to make the EU a stronger and more competitive economic region.

Will the Directive have any impact on the freedom of expression and the right to information?

15.38 No. Journalists will remain free to investigate and publish news on companies' practices and business affairs, as they are today. The Directive only deals with unlawful conduct by which someone acquires or discloses, without authorisation and through illicit means, information with commercial value that companies treat as confidential in order to keep a competitive advantage over their competitors. If no unlawful conduct takes place, the relevant disclosure of the trade secret is out of scope of the Directive and therefore not affected by it.

15.39 Even when a trade secret is misappropriated, the Directive foresees a specific safeguard in order to preserve the freedom of expression and right to information (including a free press) as protected by the Charter of Fundamental Rights of the European Union. The safeguard is operative if the divulgation of the trade secret that was acquired by, or passed to the journalist, was through the use of illicit means such as the breach of law or contract.

Will companies be able to hide information on matters of public interest, such as public health, the environment or the safety of consumers?

15.40 No. The draft Directive does not alter the current legal obligations on companies to divulge information for such public policy objectives. The public interest prevails over private interest in such matters. Companies are subject to legal obligations to disclose information of public interest, for example, in the chemical and pharmaceutical sectors. Such regulations, which ensure a high level of transparency, will not be affected. The draft Directive does not provide any grounds for companies to hide information that they are obliged to submit to regulatory authorities or to the public at large.

15.41 Moreover, the draft Directive does not alter and does not have any impact on the regulations that foresee the right of citizens to access documents in the possession of public authorities, including documents submitted by third parties such as companies and business organisations.

15.42 In addition, the draft Directive expressly safeguards those who, acting in the public interest, disclose a trade secret for the purpose of revealing a misconduct, wrongdoing or illegal activity. This safeguard is operative if the trade secret was acquired or passed to the whistle-blower through the use of illicit means such as the breach of law or contract. If no unlawful conduct takes place the disclosure of the trade secret is out of the scope of the proposed directive and therefore no safeguards are necessary.

Our eminent departure from the EU means we will have to await to see what happens to this directive.

WHAT IS COPYRIGHT?

15.43 EU Law – Another useful EU Directive is 2009/24/EC on the Legal protection of Computer Programs commonly referred to by scholars as the Software Directive. It requires all EU Member States to protect computer programs by copyright as literary works.

UK LAW AND THE COPYRIGHT, DESIGNS AND PATENTS ACT 1988

15.44 UK Law – The Copyright, Designs and Patents Act 1988 (CDPA 1988) governs this area in the UK. Essentially it states that copyright arises automatically on the creation of an original literary, dramatic, musical or artistic work. The Act as amended establishes that copyright in protected works lasts until 70 years after death of the creator. In computer generated works the period is 50 years.

WHAT ARE THE CATEGORIES OF PROTECTION IN UK LAW?

15.45 with the categories are:

(a) literary work includes computer programs;

(b) be a dramatic work;

(c) be a musical work;

(d) be an artistic work;

(e) film;

(f) sound recordings;

(g) broadcasts.

15.46 Because of the changing nature of businesses and the ever-increasing requirement for businesses to use computer programs and have an online presence, be more digital etc, it is necessary to spend a little time exploring this. The EU Software Directive also makes allowances. The author of a computer generated work had the first ownership of copyright. The exception is if this is made in the course of employment by an employee. Under CDP 1988, section 11(2), his employer is the first owner of any copyright in the work subject to any agreement to the contrary.

Sections 50A–50C deal with copying computer programs after purchase.

15.47 In order for copyright to subsist under the CDPA 1988 the author must be a qualifying person at the relevant time. Namely the relevant time was either at the time of creation or for an unpublished works at the time of publication. A qualifying person needs to a British person or a person protected within the meaning of the British Nationality Act 1981 (BNA 1981) or be an individual who is domiciled or resident in the UK or a body incorporated under the law as part of the UK or of another country which relevant sections of the Act apply.

Employer beware

15.48 Regardless of the protection afforded by the Act and the EU an employee can easily replicate unprotected functionality without ever needing to copy the protected source code. The leading cases illustrate the limitations of copyright protection.

WHAT DOES THE CASELAW OFFER BY WAY OF PROTECTION ON COPYRIGHT?

15.49 The limitations of protection afforded to computer programs as literary works are clearly defined within *Navitaire* Inc *v Easyjet Airline Co & Another* [2004] EWHC 1725 page 1725. Here there is very little protection from an employee who has assisted in developing the functionality of a computer program then moves to competitor and replicates the software for an employee.

15.50 Whereas the protection to be given to artistic works within computer programs was scaled back in *Nova Productions Ltd v Mazooma Games Ltd & Ors* (CA) [2007] EWCA Civ 219 page 219 and Business La reports page 1032. In this claim there was a breach of a game called Pocket Money and a game called Jackpot Pool and Trick Shot. The Court of Appeal dismissed the appeal and held that although individual works were graphic works for the purpose of section 4(2) of CDPA 1988 and so were capable of protection, it reasoned that a series of such frames providing an illusion of movement was not a single graphic work in itself and was therefore incapable of protection under the Act. Especially as there had been no frame by frame bitmap graphics there was no breach of the claimants copyright in its artistic works. In summary this means that in order for artistic copyright to subsist within a computer program the image created must be identical to a work which exists and was created through sufficient skill and labour in order to attract protection.

15.51 In *SAS Institute Inc v World Programming Limited* [2010] EWHC 1829, the High Court dismissed again a software developers claim that a competitor had infringed copyright and acted in breach of a licence in creating a computer program emulating much of the functionality of its own programmes. However the High Court held that manuals that accompanied the WPS software did infringe the copyright that protected the SAS manuals. They said that WPL had infringed copyright in the SAS manuals by substantially producing them in the WPL Manual. The Court of Appeal upheld the High Court's decision, saying that the manuals constituted the reproduction of the expression of the intellectual creation of the author. So what was important was the expression of the intellectual creation of the author of the manual not the intellectual creation.

15.52 In light of these cases the courts have stated that the functions of computer programs are not a form of expression that can be protected through copyright. Ideas and principles which underline any element of a program including interfaces are explicitly excluded. So this poses a neat set of problems because whilst the source code is protected by copyright an ex-employee is entitled to reproduce the functionality of a valuable assets without using the original source code either in competition or for a competitor.

THE EU AND THE SOFTWARE DIRECTIVE

15.53 Protection is defined in Article 1 of the EU Software Directive 2009/24/EC on the Legal Protection of Computer Programs, commonly referred to by scholars as the Software Directive. It requires all EU Member States to protect computer programs by copyright as literary works. As you can see the protection of copyright covers the code that creates the program. The author of the expression. The form or purpose is irrelevant. Subject to instances of creation under contract, Article 1(2) states that:

> 'Protection in accordance with this Directive shall apply to the expression in any form of computer program. Ideas and principles which underlie any

element of a computer program, including those which underlie its interfaces, are not protected by copyright under the directive'.

15.54 The definition of 'expression in any form of a computer program' actually includes the source codes and objects codes of a program. The function that the code produces is not copyright. This means that an ex-employee going to a competitor would not be prohibited under UK Law or the software directive from reproducing the functionality of a software developed by the past employer provided that he does not copy the base if the code.

WHAT IS THE DEFINITION OF THE FUNCTIONALITY OF COMPUTER PROGRAMS WITHIN THE SOFTWARE DIRECTIVE?

15.55 These are further defined as interfaces. The functional *interconnection and interaction* is generally known as *interoperability*. This is the ability to exchange information and use the mutually exchanged information. The Software Directive makes it explicit that neither can be protected as a literary work. It means therefore that programming which consists of merely algorithms and ideas or principles are not protected. However programs incorporated into hardware and preparatory design work which may result in later computer programs is protected because the protection extends to the source code.

WHAT PROTECTION IS THERE IF THE PROGRAM WAS CREATED BY THE EMPLOYEE ACTING IN THE PERFORMANCE OF HIS DUTIES?

15.56 These are contained under Article 2(3):

> 'where a computer program is created by an employee in the execution of his duties or following the instructions given by his employer, the employer exclusively shall be entitled to exercise all economic rights in the program so created unless it is otherwise provided by contract.'

15.57 The Software Directive grants the author exclusive rights to prevent unauthorised reproduction of his work. So that any translation or transformation of the code will amount to an infringement of these exclusive rights of the author.

WHAT IS PERMITTED UNDER THE SOFTWARE DIRECTIVE?

15.58 Obtaining a licence to use a computer program does not prevent one from performing acts necessary to study the function of the program or observe the program provided it does not infringe the copyright in the program. This means that a competitor could be entitled to reverse engineer a legally purchased computer program as long as the original source code is not reproduced. Under Article 5 subsection (3) of the Software Directive, this could be with or without a former employee who could have worked on the development of the program and then moved to the competitor.

15.59 Whereas under Article 6 of the Software Directive, independently produced computer programs made need to have copyrighted source code to interact with the protected computer program. As long as the goal is interoperability with an independently created computer program rather than the development, production or marketing similar to the protected program.

Advice

15.60 The Software Directive does not limit other forms of copyright protection which may apply to elements of computer programs. The case law shows the courts have found for claimants on the basis of protected artistic works.

15.61 In order to establish an evidential link recruiting and instructing forensic experts is essential to assist in any internal investigation into copying because to prove copyright infringement an ex-employer must prove *causal connection* between the original work and the copy.

WHAT PROTECTION IS OFFERED TO DATABASES?

15.62 The protection of databases is derived from EU law though the Database Directive and the corresponding protection introduced by the Copyright and Rights in databases Regulations 1997. These provide a separate means of potentially enforcement from those provisions contained in the software directive.

What is a database?

15.63 A database is defined as a collection of independent works, data or other materials that are arranged in a methodical way and accessible individually by electronic means or other means. Databases themselves may have a commercial value to be protected. The Software Directive specifically exclude logic, algorithms and programming languages as ideas and principles. But these may find protection if they are compiled into a relevant database.

Issues with a database?

15.64 The Database Directive defines two independent protections. Essentially EU Member States are required to copyright a database that constitutes the authors own intellectual creation by the selection or by the arrangement of their content. Article 3 of the Directive was incorporated into UK law under section 3A of the CDPA 1988.

15.65 Section 3A (1) states that:

> Database means a collection of independent works, data or other materials which
>
> (a) are arranged in systematic or methodical way and
>
> (b) are individually accessible by electronic or other means
>
> (2) a literary work consisting of a database is original if, and only if by reason of the selection or arrangement of the contents of the database constitutes the authors own intellectual creation.

15.66 The author of a database is defined in the same as any other copyright with the CDPA 1988. Any contractual term seeking to negate the permission to use a database appears to be null and void. This is because it is not an infringement of copyright in a database (under licence) to do anything that is exercising that right.

15.67 Furthermore, Article 7 of the Database Directive creates a right where the maker of a database can show that there has been qualitative and quantitatively substantial investment in the obtaining and verification of the presentation of the contents of the database.

WHAT PROTECTION OF DATABASES IS AVAILABLE FROM EU DIRECTIVES?

15.68 In the Copyright and Rights in Databases Regulations 1997, Regulation 13 creates a database right and Regulation 16 defines actions which would contravene the database right.

Regulation 13 states:

> 13 (1) A property right (database right) subsists in accordance with this Part in a database if there has been a substantial investment in obtaining, verifying or presenting the contents of the database
>
> 13 (2) For the purposes of paragraph (1) it is immaterial whether or not the database or any of its content is copyright work, within the meaning of Pat I of the 1988 Act.

15.69 Regulation 16, Acts Infringing database right states:

> (1) subject to the provisions of this Part, a person infringes database right in a database if without the consent of the owner of the right, he extracts or re-utilises all or a substantial part of the contents of the database.
>
> (2) For the purposes of this Part, the repeated and systematic extraction or re-utilisation of insubstantial parts of those contents.

15.70 So this means the owner of the rights in Regulation 13 at the time of compilation must be resident in the ECCA or Isle of Man and that he must be the person taking the initiative in obtaining verifying or presenting the contents of the database and who assumes the risk of investing obtaining verification or presentation. As before, a database made in the course of employment means that the employer will be regarded as the maker. This is subject to any agreement.

15.71 In Regulation 16, extraction means permanent or temporary transfer of those contents to another medium by any means or in any form. Reutilisation within Regulation 16 in relation to contents of a database means making content available to the public by any means. The lawful use of a database following purchase of licence does not breach the right. The database right under the EU expires after 15 years. This is from the end of calendar year in which the database was completed. Substantial changes or additions to the database will create a new 15 year period of protection of investment in practical terms.

IS THERE ANY PROTECTION OF DATABASES TO PROTECT SOFTWARE?

15.72 At first it appears as though there is an additional cause of action in the courts for a company to prevent a former employee from utilising what could be valuable information as we saw in the *Crawson* case. However, in the case of *Cantor Gaming Ltd v GameAccount Global Ltd* [2007] EWHC 1914, the courts appeared reluctant to allow a claim in copyright when underlying material is not protected or where the company can more properly rely on a breach of confidence to bring the claim. In this case the High Court found in favour of the claimant Cantor Gaming.

15.73 This case suggests that the database right may be a useful protection to prevent competition from illegitimate actions with protected material. Notably in this case possession of the database was sufficient to infer use. However, the subsistence copyright in the material was not found in the database. So that copyright did not subsist in the material contained within the database.

THE FACTS

Navitaire v Aasyjet

15.74 In this case an alternative approach to databases was taken by the High Court, because the judge concluded that the structure of the database had not been copied to the extent that there had been infringement of copyright. Interestingly in this case the judge drew a distinction between a database constituting the dataset contained and the structure which defined the limits of the database. Moreover he found that the structure for an electronic database was a computer program which would be protected by the Software Directive where as the Database Directive protected the dataset.

15.75 In the *EasyJet* and *Cantor Gaming* cases, the defendants had not infringed the relevant copyright. This was because simply possessing part of the database not sufficient to constitute extraction or use.

In *Flogas Britain Ltd v Calor Gas Ltd* [2013] EWHC 3060, vicarious liability arose.

Facts

15.76 Flogas maintained a database of information on their customers. They operated in the market of propane gas. A former Flogas employee joined Calor Gas as an area sales manager and in doing so passed the Flogas database to the head of marketing at Calor Gas. Calor Gas used the database to invite and win the Flogas customers to switch to Calor Gas giving them £100 in return. The customers rang Flogas to report this. The offending new employee was dismissed when the MD was notified and the database was deleted. Calor Gas admitted a breach of confidence but Flogas argued that Regulation 13 of the Copyright and Databases Regulation applied, arguing that there had been substantial investment in obtaining, varying and presenting the customer database and a right existed under that regulation which made Calor Gas vicariously liable.

Held

15.77 In this case the judge held:

> 'that the defendant had been vicariously liable for the infringement of Flogas Database right……The infringement of Flogas's database right arose on exactly the same facts as the liability for breach of confidence. As to damages Flogas could not be compensated twice for the loss that they had suffered.'

WHAT DO THESE CASES TEACH ABOUT PROTECTION FROM EMPLOYEES?

15.78 The *Cantor* and *Flogas* cases demonstrates that additional protection is available and can be used to prevent the use of database material from being used by an ex-employees.

Advice

15.79 Businesses should be aware when an ex-employee leaves to go to go to a competitor to create a functionally similar piece of software that was sold by his former employer. It appears that even if there is no evidence of source code copying, it might well be that he has secured a commercial advantage by copying a database that is functionally important to the software. Or where the ex-employee can show a substantial investment which the competitor has avoided through tempting an ex-employee to disclose the database then the right will subsist. But if a software company creates data itself including test data, that test data is unlikely to be protect by the database right which extends to substantial investment in obtaining verifying or presenting not in creating the data.

15.80 The *EasyJet* case appears to impose limitations on reproducing functionality. So that if the database could be reproduced without having to apply a protected structure or via independent work then the protection may not apply. It is important to remember that copyright protection is not in the data itself but rather in the manner and way that the data is selected or arranged. The authorities also seem to demonstrate an unwillingness and reluctance to rely on the database right preferring instead to use alternative protections such breach of confidence or a copy clearly defined copyright.

15.81 It will be interesting to see how this pans out post Brexit. Not least because the legal provisions relating to data management, storage and cyber issues are inextricably linked with European legislation.

EMPLOYERS' LIABILITY

15.82 Potential liability does not stop with a new employee or the use of information, inappropriately or otherwise. More and more commonly employers need to be fully aware of how they may be liable and put in place procedure that will mitigate unwanted behaviour by employees. For example employer's systems – emails and websites or staff internet searches can facilitate discrimination in the workplace harassment and health and safety breaches.

WHAT IS BEING DIRECTLY LIABLE AND CAN THE EMPLOYER BE VICARIOUSLY LIABLE FOR THE CONDUCT OF AN EX EMPLOYEE?

15.83 Compensation in damages from an employee who uses your confidential information or utilises protected material without permission will mean that the new employer or the recruiters or competitor who has recruited will be joined as a party to the case. This will be on the basis of the new employer being directly liable or on the basis of being vicariously liable for those actions. This means we need to explore what these terms mean and what protections and measures and systems employers can put in place in order to protect themselves.

What is direct liability?

15.84 Direct liability applies to a company or organisation when the employer directs or authorises the performance of an act by the employee. In the old case of *Tesco Supermarkets v Nattrass* [1972] AC 153, Lord Reid provided the context in which limited companies could be directly liable. A director or someone in upper management is the person speaking as the company. However a director can delegate their functions so that means direct liability can extend to employees acting with delegated authority.

When does direct liability arise?

15.85 Instances of online harassment or discrimination are unlikely to be classed as direct liability. Company directors speaking for the company will not encourage employees to engage in racial or sexual abuse. But the email traffic by an employee will be relevant and essential in the misuse of information, competitive tendering or Bribery Act 2010. So for instance a company director may aggressively encourage an employee or director to tender for work and if the employee crosses an unacceptable line then it is plausible that direct liability could arise.

15.86 The wonders of an online presence could also facilitate breaches of health and safety or advertising regulations. Moreover a company director will be liable for online advertising instigated by an employee regardless as to whether the specific content was approved by a director if the compliance had been delegated without procedures in place. Making the need for procedures vital.

15.87 In the *Tesco* case, the Law Lords held that a limited company can establish a defence against certain statutory offences if it has set up an efficient system for preventing the commission of offences and offences are committed because of employee default. This is even if the employee is responsible for the supervision of others. Section 7 of the Bribery Act 2010 imposes criminal liability on a company for failing to prevent bribery but it is a defence for the company to prove that adequate procedures were in place designed to prevent employees from undertaking such conduct.

15.88 TIP – companies need well formulated compliance procedures which in so far as can be reasonably expected, these procedures contemplate the cyber-systems in place and prevent instances of information misuse, bullying or improper behaviour within and outside the company or workplace.

What is vicarious liability?

15.89 Vicarious liability, often referred to as VL, is the imposition of liability on one person for the actionable conduct of another, based solely on the relationship between the two persons. Vicarious liability for the actions of the employee is imposed on an employer either at by law or by statute. The test for vicarious liability is that the action of the employee must have been committed in the course or scope of the employment. The Act is within the scope of employment if the employee was retained to perform the act or if its performance is reasonably incidental to the matters which is the employee was retained to do. It is important to note that within the scope of employment is a broad term. Because the misuse of confidential information and infringements of copyrights have long been considered tortious and it follow that the principles of vicarious liability apply to this behaviour.

VL and harassment

15.90 Harassment is a statutory tort to which vicarious liability equally applies. This was illustrated In *S&D Property Investments Ltd v Nisbet* [2009] EWHC 1726 (Ch) where the claimant was entitled to damages for anxiety as a result of harassment by a company director in the course of seeking to recover a debt to the company. The director had sent emails to the claimant suggesting he should sell his property to meet the debt. The company was vicariously liable for the director's actions and it was equitable for those damages to set off against the sum claimed from the claimant in the company's original debt action.

And discrimination under the Equality Act 2010

15.91 Section 109 of the Equality Act 2010 extends vicarious liability for employers through discrimination. So this means that anything done by a person in the course of their employment is also treated as being done by the employer. This is even in the circumstances where the employer had no knowledge or disapproved of the conduct in question (see Equality Act, section 109(3)). What falls into the course of employment was defined and considered by the courts in *Waters v Commissioner of Police* of the *Metropolis* [1997] ICR 1073. In this case an employer was held not liable for an assault occurring to an employee who was off duty but was on the premises controlled by the employer.

15.92 Further two years later in the case of *Chief Constable of the Lincolnshire Police v Stubbs* [1999] IRLR 81, it was held that social gatherings were an extension of employment. In that case it was held that an employer could be liable for discriminatory acts or behaviour if it occurred during a social gathering.

VL and internet usage

15.93 As to the internet usage, an employer is vicariously liable for emails sent by employees to other employees and customers, but may be liable for conduct and or behaviour outside of hours of employment unrelated to work. For example sending emails to personal friends after work if it is facilitated through the company's personal email account. This means that employers need to be very aware and careful of the fact that misbehaviour and conduct towards protected characteristics could result in liability and actionable cause. In certain circumstances however, an employer can escape direct liability if they can establish *all reasonable steps were taken by the employer to prevent the employee from committing the act of discrimination*. This was illustrated in *Croft v Royal Mail* [2003] IRLR 592 EWCA Civ 1045.

DIRECTORS' LIABILITY FOR BREACH OF CONFIDENCE

15.94 The question of the state of mind of a director necessary to render him or her liable for a breach of confidence was considered in the case of *Vestergaard Frandsen A/S & Ors v Bestnet Europe Ltd & Ors* [2013] UKSC 31 by the then President of the Supreme Court Lord Neuberger and others. They were dealing with breach of confidence. Although in principle director liability could be applied to liability in other torts, whether the definition is defined by statute or the common law, it is unlikely that provisions under the contract could deal with tortious actions such as harassment or assault. Contractual terms may however be useful and to the relevant to the use of copyright and confidential information.

IN WHAT WAYS CAN A DIRECTORS LIABILITY BE IMPOSED?

15.95

(1) By Contract.

(2) By Common Design.

(3) By Dishonestly turning a blind eye.

15.96 In the *Vestergaard* case above, the claimants' case was that a senior employee was liable for a breach of confidence on the basis of common design. The argument was that the employee had worked with others to design, manufacture and market products and that those products were designed by one of the group in such a way as to involve the wrongful use and misuse of the claimants' trade secrets. There was no doubt that the former employee was liable to breach of confidence but it was asserted that by working together others were also liable. The SC held that the common design principle could be invoked against a defendant in a claim of misuse of confidential information. But in order for the defendant to be party to a common design, 'she must share with the other party, or parties, to the design, each of the features of design which would make it wrongful If and only if, all those features are shared, the fact that some parties to the common design did only some of the relevant acts, whilst others did only some other relevant acts it will not stop them all from being jointly liable.'

15.97 So in this case the defendant was not in possession of the relevant trade secrets and even more importantly did not have knowledge of their misuse. The defendant therefore did not have the necessary state of knowledge or state of mind. Therefore, although they were party to the activities which may have rendered other parties liable for misuse of confidential information, the defendant was not liable under common design. They said and gave an analogy with a criminal case. Namely that

> 'A driver of the motor car who transports a person to and from a bank to enable him to rob it would be liable in tort for the robbery under the common design or some similar principle but only if she knew that her passenger intended to rob or had robbed, the bank. So in this case, given the ingredients of the

wrong misuse of confidential information. Mrs Sig cannot be held liable in common design for exploiting with others, on behalf of Intection and then Besnet, a product which, unknown to her was being and had been developed through the wrongful use of Vestergaard's trade secrets.'

15.98 This means a director cannot evade liability by avoiding the requisite state of mind if blind eye knowledge can be interred. A director cannot merely turn a blind eye to obvious misuse of information just so that he or she can negate liability. However in order to infer such knowledge according to Lord Neuberger held that the director must also be found to be dishonest.

15.99 This seems to have been the case in the earlier case of *Royal Brunei Airlines Sdn. Bhd. v Tan* [1995] 2 AC 378 where the House of Lords suggested that acting in reckless regard of others' rights or possible rights can be a tell-tale sign of dishonesty. They said.

> 'The only answer to these questions lies in keeping in mind that honesty is an objective standard. The individual is expected to attain the standard which would be observed by an honest person placed in those circumstances. It is is impossible to be specific…Ultimately in most cases an honest person should have little difficulty in knowing whether a proposed transaction or his participation in it would offend the normally accepted standards of honest conduct.'

15.100 This means that a company director may be personally liable for the behaviour of an employee through common design or if he dishonestly turns a blind eye to behaviour he knows to be unacceptable. So in this modern tech savvy and digital age it is not rocket science for company directors to realise that if they know of discriminatory conduct in the work place via being cc'd into an email they are likely to be personally liable.

15.101 TIP: Companies should be protecting themselves very early on, not only against this but also by taking reasonable provisions protecting against secondary vicarious liability as well as direct liability. Let's now look at ways to protect against employer liability.

WHAT MEASURES, SYSTEMS AND PROCEDURES ARE SUFFICIENT TO AVOID EMPLOYER LIABILITY?

15.102 The size of the company will be crucial in determining whether all reasonable steps have be taken by companies and whether all due diligence has been exercised in order to avoid secondary liability. So a failure to take steps to prevent online tortious activity will cause a company to be liable for an employee's actions and would likely render any claim of ignorance or good faith to be irrelevant. This means that contracts of employment of the employee is the first and best place to protect the company from liability in relation to email and internet. It is also useful to prevent loss of confidential information and trade secrets and assert copyright protection. Other areas are which are useful are:

(a) Taking practical steps to maintain confidence or prevent unwanted behaviour.

(b) Have written procedures.

(c) Regularly review and revise your procedures.

(d) Do not ignore improper conduct as you may become personally liable.

CONTRACTS OF EMPLOYMENT AS A MEANS OF PROTECTION

15.103 Employers should ensure that they give a contract of employment to an employee. In an employment tribunal there would be an uplift for lack of a contract. But in truth the contract of employment is the basis of the working relationship and should be the foundation of the protection in the place of the employer. In cyber-security and dealing with information and cyber-related information, the terms of use should be clear even before an employee is recruited. Revision of the employee handbook is useful to include data protection procedures; health and safety, discrimination and sexual harassment policies especially given the '#metoo' climate. More importantly have clear procedures for when there is a breach. For example, the procedure for investigation and sanctions. Most policies are out of date or do not deal with cyber-terms.

15.104 Unprotected assets such as software functionality and ideas and principles within the Software Directive could be protected through appropriate contract drafting and provisions. For example even a very basic contact should contain a term for the protection of confidential information while an employee is employed under that contract. Go beyond the traditional garden leave prohibitions and incorporate the employer's cyber-terms of use to protect clearly defined information such as ideas, or functionality and protect these for a time period or indefinite periods.

15.105 The employee must be aware if the information that they deal with and handle and use the employer considers to be confidential. There cannot be any misunderstanding. So employees could keep an additional log in the employee handbook. If they are specific to certain departments and teams they could be potentially protectable. Furthermore, most modern companies now have Key Performance Indicators and so the contract of employment could ask that all ideas and principles used to meet these key performance indicators are recorded in a log as part of employee handbooks. Any logs would form part of the contract of employment and employees would have to agree not to copy, remove or download any such logs if they depart from the company. Illegitimate retention of the logs would then not be permitted by the courts. The only arguable issue would be if sufficient skill or labour was expanded in making these logs, there may be a claim to copyright to prevent reproduction even from memory like in the *Sas v WPL* case where it might copy a competitor's manual subconsciously. There may even be a database right argument if the format of the log and the information are construed in a certain way. The risk with this sort of restrictive covenant covering logs in this way is that one is risking compiling confidential information into one single source which could be disastrous. Plus these sorts of terms are yet to be tested fully. But in reality the court will have to balance the interest in companies protecting important information following substantial investment and employees trying to utilise their skill and experience legitimately obtained. It is important for employers to be vigilant as the work environment is increasingly becoming virtual and misuse and misconduct is not as easy to detect. For other practical and common-sense measures could include the following:

> PRACTICAL MEASURES Lets go back to basics and make it simple for employees and protect your selves. You can do this by communicating with them so that they are aware.
>
> COMMUNICATION OF THE INFORMATION communicate the terms to the employee and have a record of them signing to say they have received the contract and read the handbook when they start their employment.

Notices

15.106 Have notices to identify confidential waste and then their proper disposal been put up? Like having shredders. Improper disposal of confidential information will not be protected by the courts.

Training employees

15.107 Monitor that employees read the relevant procedures you have in place and that they understand the systems in place. Perhaps generate a survey monkey the free online tool. Invite into the workplace outside trainers or Solicitors or Barristers or even specialist online video webinars. Make the training compulsory. Ask them to do a test afterwards to see they understand. You could set up a newsletter using mail chip which reminds them monthly or quarterly (depending on the size of your organisation) of what confidential information is. Or even call it cyber-security with a check list at the end.

Disciplinaries as a means of protection

15.108 You as the employer should get your managers and middle managers to review disciplinaries and use them when it is necessary. Often there can be three strikes of written warning and action. They can be rigid so that they don't actually address often minor or inappropriate behaviours which then continue and is never really dealt with. Whether it is data misuse or harassment its useful to send employees on active training. A better approach is to be flexible and transparent. Only escalate matters where appropriate and also. Keep records. As all inappropriate behaviour requires action from verbal warning or formal disciplinaries leading to summary dismissal. You simply do not want to become personally liable. You as the employer must protect yourselves from liability.

CONCLUSION

15.109 Given we are in a post Brexit era, only time will tell whether the protections afforded to us by the EU in Directives and regulations remain in force. At the time of writing the Facebook scandal and data protection breaches alleged by Cambridge analytics illustrate the difficulties with protection.

Always seek early legal advice and take pre-emptive protection from liability.

CHAPTER 16

DATA SECURITY – THE NEW OIL

Ryan Mackie

DATA SECURITY IN AN AGE WHEN DATA IS THE NEW OIL

16.01

> 'Secure web servers are the equivalent of heavy armoured cars. The problem is, they are being used to transfer rolls of coins and cheques written in crayon by people on park benches to merchants doing business in cardboard boxes from beneath highway bridges. Further, the roads are subject to random detours, anyone with a screwdriver can control the traffic lights, and there are no police.' www.azquotes.com/quote/743367 – *Gene Spafford (a.k.a 'Spaf') is a Professor of Computer Science at Purdue University and a leading Information Security Expert.*

16.02 Data has become, in the twenty-first century, what oil was to commerce and industry in the eighteenth century – a seemingly infinite and untapped commodity – and as was the case with oil, businesses which can successfully identify the fundamental value that lies in Data (and the benefits that can be gained from mastering how to use, extract and monetise it) will leave their competitors struggling to keep up.

16.03 The analogy of data as the new oil has never been more pertinent, especially in the realm of Artificial Intelligence (AI). As AI continues to redefine the boundaries of possibility, the upcoming legislation in the EU and the UK seeks to navigate the complex interplay between innovation and data security/privacy. This new regulatory terrain will not only safeguard personal information but also ensure that the lifeblood of AI – data – is harnessed responsibly, promoting sustainable advancements while mitigating the risks associated with data misuse. Just as regulations evolved to ensure the sustainable extraction and usage of oil, the upcoming legislation aims to create a framework that governs the responsible harnessing of data, ensuring that AI technologies are utilised ethically and transparently.

16.04 Also, in a time when an organisation's data infrastructure is still seen as a cost centre for the business, if that organisation takes the necessary steps to identify what Data it is processing and knows what value it can assign to that Data, then there's no reason why the organisation's data infrastructure can't become a profit centre for the business by looking at ways to 'monetise' the underlying value in the Data it is processing. Once the organisation understands the value of Data it is processing, it will see that it needs to start treating that Data just like it would any other valuable business asset (eg intellectual property rights, cash in the bank, etc.) and put in place suitable security measures to protect that Data.

16.05 The fact that Data Security Incidents are on the rise in the UK (and globally for that matter) suggests that businesses have been slow to realise the potential value of their own Data – something that cyber-criminals have been faster to grasp and quick to exploit. In this regard, the UK's Data Protection Regulator, the Information Commissioner's Office (ICO), recently published a useful and interactive summary report on the UK's Data Security Incident trends from 2019–2022 – the chart below highlights the key areas where Data Security Incidents (only those that have been reported of course) have occurred during this time frame.

UK ICO DATA SECURITY INCIDENT TRENDS[1]

16.06

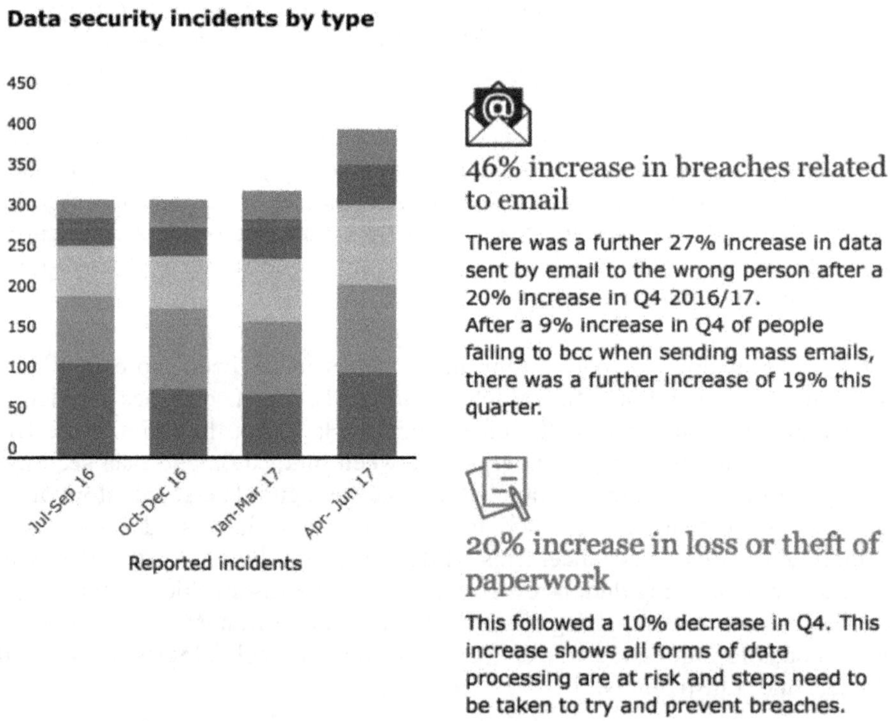

1 https://ico.org.uk/action-weve-taken/data-security-incident-trends.

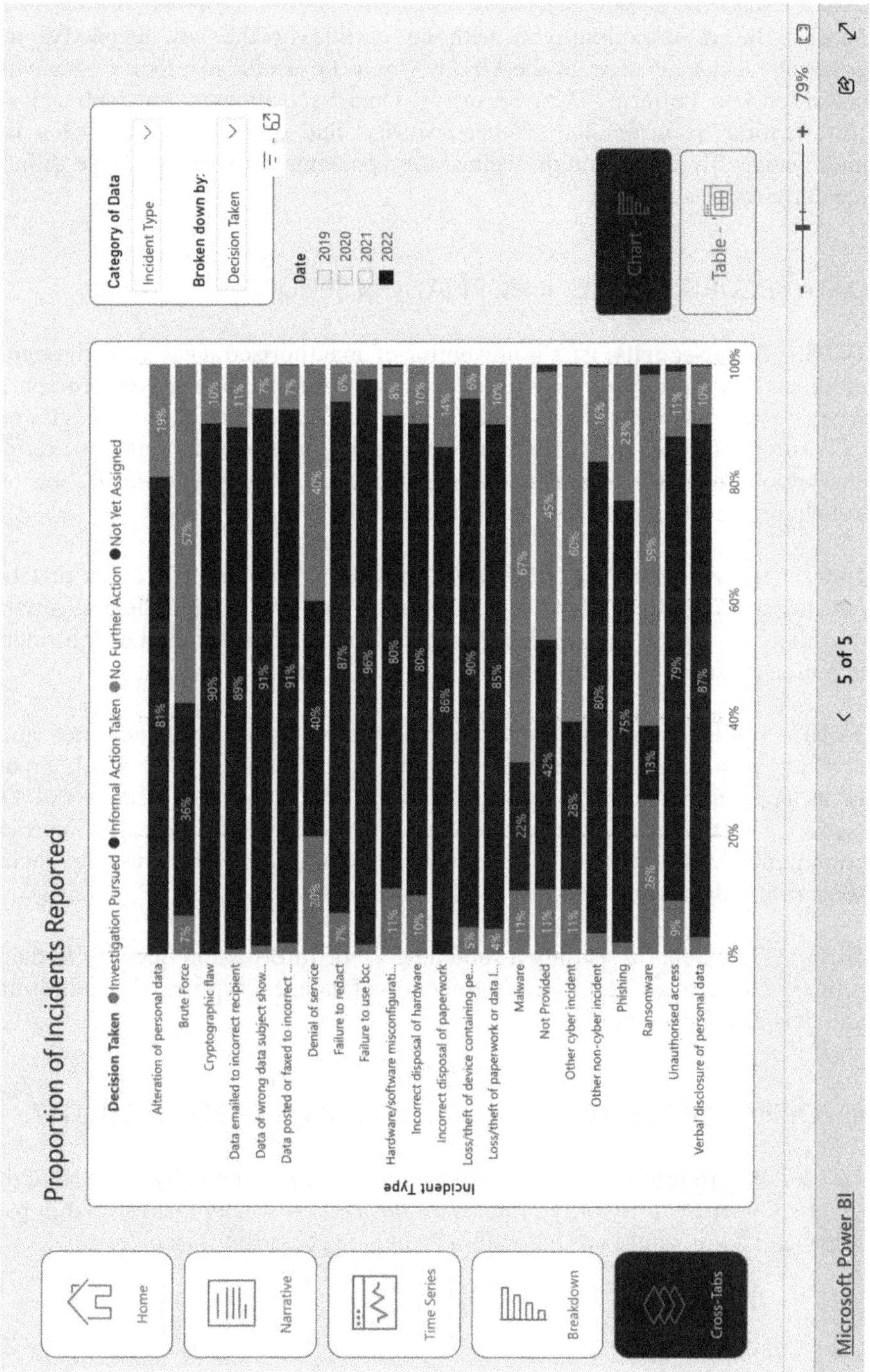
Proportion of Incidents Reported
Decision Taken ● Investigation Pursued ● Informal Action Taken ● No Further Action ● Not Yet Assigned
Incident Type
Alteration of personal data
Brute Force
Cryptographic flaw
Data emailed to incorrect recipient
Data of wrong data subject show...
Data posted or faxed to incorrect ...
Denial of service
Failure to redact
Failure to use bcc
Hardware/software misconfigurati...
Incorrect disposal of hardware
Incorrect disposal of paperwork
Loss/theft of device containing pe...
Loss/theft of paperwork or data l...
Malware
Not Provided
Other cyber incident
Other non-cyber incident
Phishing
Ransomware
Unauthorised access
Verbal disclosure of personal data
0%
20%
40%
60%
80%
100%
Category of Data
Incident Type
Broken down by:
Decision Taken
Date
2019
2020
2021
2022
Chart
Table
Home
Narrative
Time Series
Breakdown
Cross-Tabs
Microsoft Power BI
5 of 5
79%

DATA SECURITY VERSES INFORMATION SECURITY VERSES CYBER-SECURITY

16.07 Before providing you with an outline of the key legislative texts governing Data Security in the UK, it would be useful to provide you with a definition for the term 'Data Security'. Data Security is often confused with 'Information Security' and 'Cyber-Security' and these terms are often used interchangeably even though, technically speaking, they clearly have different meanings in practice.

DATA SECURITY VERSES INFORMATION SECURITY

16.08 Data Security[2] is: 'the prevention of unauthorised access, use, disruption, modification, corruption or destruction of data *in storage* (eg computers, databases and websites) throughout its lifecycle.' Examples of technologies used to ensure Data Security include backups, data masking and data erasure, data encryption, tokenisation and key management practices which are all tools used to help protect data across all applications and platforms.

16.09 Information Security[3] (also known as 'InfoSec') 'ensures that both physical and digital data is protected is the term used to refer to the prevention of unauthorised access, use, disruption, modification or destruction of information in a broader sense' – ie not only in storage or 'at rest'.

16.10 While Data Security relates specifically to security measures aimed at Data in storage, the definition for Information Security is much broader in its application, ie it is focused more on the end-to-end security of Data (securing Data that is incorporated within particular processes, user interfaces, communications, automation, computation, transactions, infrastructure, devices, sensors and data storage).

16.11 Data Security is only a sub-category of Information Security in that its primary concern is with physical protection of data, encryption of data in storage and data remanence issues.

INFORMATION SECURITY ('INFOSEC') VERSES CYBER-SECURITY[4]

16.12 Where InfoSec aims to keep data *in any form* (both physical and digital) secure, Cyber-Security only protects *digital Data* – so any Data stored in paper (physical) form would not fall within Cyber- Security's remit to protect.

2 https://simplicable.com/new/data-security-vs-information-security.

3 ibid.

4 www.secureworks.com/blog/cybersecurity-vs-network-security-vs-information-security.

16.13 Cyber-Security, is the practice of defending an organisation's networks, computers and data from 'unauthorised digital access, attack or damage by implementing suitable controls in the form of processes, technologies and practices'[5].

As is the case with Data Security, Cyber-Security is also a subset of Information Security.

16.14 This chapter is only concerned with the law and practice in the UK as it relates to Data Security – ie to 'the prevention of unauthorised access, use, disruption, modification, corruption or destruction of data (in any form) *in storage*.'

UK DATA SECURITY LAW

16.15 This chapter will attempt to summarise the key UK legislation (both Civil and Criminal) in the realm of Data Security.

CIVIL LAW

16.16 As the use of online services involving financial transactions increased the 1990s, so did the amount of financially motivated digital crime (cyber-crime), but the digital security environment at the time wasn't mature enough to deal with the problem, so further solutions were required.

16.17 In 1995, the Data Protection Directive (Directive) was introduced at EU level and this piece of legislation made it obligatory for organisations processing Personal Data to implement 'an appropriate level of security', in response to which the UK adopted several industry specific digital security standards, eg in relation to public electronic communication networks and for use in the financial services industries.

16.18 The Directive required Data Controllers to implement technical and organisational measures which would 'ensure an appropriate level of security, taking into account the state of the art and the costs of their implementation in relation to the risks inherent in the processing and the nature of the data to be protected', but due to the rapidly changing state of the art at the time, it was difficult to identify what technical measures were suitable as implementation costs would often far outweigh the value of the Personal Data being processed. The Directive served as the precursor to the UK's Data Protection Act which came in to operation in 1995.

16.19 The EU adopted the General Data Protection Regulation (GDPR) in May 2018 and the Network and Information Security Directive (NISD) in July 2016

5 ibid.

– which was recently replaced by Directive (EU) 2022/2555 (known as NIS2) which entered into force on 16 January 2023 – to help bring Data Security laws up to speed with the technological advancements in the area of Data Security and to help in the fight against the advanced methods and technologies being used by cyber-criminals. Due to improvements in computer processing (and in particular the improvements in power and functionality of mobile devices) devices can quite easily run sophisticated encryption software (with features like real time detection, prevention and remediation) at a fraction of the cost of what it took to do the same in the 90s, so businesses no longer have any excuses when it comes to implementing the appropriate technical and organisational controls to design more compliant Data Security systems.

UK GENERAL DATA PROTECTION REGULATION[6] ('UK GDPR') AND DATA PROTECTION ACT 2018 ('DPA 18')[7]

16.20 In the UK, the principal legal frameworks which oversee data protection are the UK General Data Protection Regulation (UK GDPR) and the Data Protection Act of 2018. These laws have been in force since 1 January 2021, following the UK's exit from the EU on 31 January 2020.

16.21 For matters concerning electronic communication, notably marketing practices, the Privacy and Electronic Communications Regulations 2003 (PECR) work in tandem with the UK GDPR and the 2018 Act to provide specialised guidelines.

16.22 The Retained EU Law (Revocation and Reform) Bill, currently under consideration by the UK Parliament, has the potential to significantly reshape UK data protection laws. Unless explicitly incorporated into domestic legislation or granted an extension (possibly up to 2026), most of the retained EU laws, specifically the UK GDPR and PECR, will expire on 31 December 2023.

16.23 Although the 2018 Act will remain in force irrespective of the aforementioned bill, it mostly acts as a supplementary provision to the UK GDPR. Therefore, its inability to serve as a complete framework for the vast majority of data controllers and processors is anticipated to prompt the UK Government to unveil plans for legal reform in data protection later in 2023.

16.24 A prior draft legislation, the Data Protection and Digital Information Bill, intended to modify the UK GDPR and the 2018 Act, was withdrawn in September 2022 due to a change in government. Its future status, whether it will be reintroduced in its original or a revised form, remains uncertain.

6 https://eur-lex.europa.eu/legal-content/EN/TXT/PDF/?uri=CELEX%3A32016R0679&from=EN.
7 https://www.legislation.gov.uk/ukpga/2018/12/contents.

UK GDPR

16.25 The UK GDPR is essentially an adapted version of the General Data Protection Regulation (Regulation (EU) 2016/679), modified and integrated into British law by the European Union (Withdrawal) Act of 2018. This was further revised by the European Union (Withdrawal Agreement) Act 2020, known as 'the Withdrawal Act', and by a series of changes put forth in the Data Protection, Privacy and Electronic Communications (Amendments etc) (EU Exit) Regulations of both 2019 and 2020. This framework has been operational in the UK since 1 January 2021.

16.26 As things currently stand, the GDPR and UK GDPR remain largely analogous, with no major differences between the two frameworks. However, the UK's Department for Digital, Culture, Media & Sport (DCMS) revealed on 10 September 2021, that the government has initiated a public consultation to contemplate alterations to the country's data protection landscape. This opens the door to potential future discrepancies between the UK GDPR and the EU's GDPR.

16.27 The Retained EU Law (Revocation and Reform) Bill could have a marked impact on the UK GDPR. Unless it is formally integrated into domestic legislation or granted an extension, which could be until 2026, the UK GDPR is set to expire on 31 December 2023.

Such developments could eventually result in diverging paths for the two sets of regulations.

The DPA 18

16.28 The DPA 18 serves to augment and specify the guidelines outlined in the UK GDPR, including certain additional limitations and exceptions as permitted under Article 23 of the UK GDPR.

16.29 Originally enacted on 25 May 2018, the DPA 18 underwent revisions after Brexit, and its current iteration has been in force in the UK since 1 January 2021. Any changes to the DPA 18 post 1 January 2021 are catalogued in the Keeling Schedule.[8]

16.30 While the Retained EU Law (Revocation and Reform) Bill won't influence the DPA 18 directly, its scope is supplementary to the UK GDPR and cannot independently govern the processing of personal data, except in the areas of law enforcement and intelligence. Hence, it's anticipated that the Government will introduce a scheme for amending data protection laws later in 2023, which will have notable implications for the DPA 18.

8 https://www.dataguidance.com/sites/default/files/2018-03-05_keeling_schedule.pdf.

This chapter will only discuss the key sections of the DPA from a Data Security perspective.

This summary outlines the existing legal landscape for data protection in the UK up to 31 December 2023.[9]

UK GENERAL DATA PROTECTION REGULATION ('UK GDPR')[10] AND EU GENERAL DATA PROTECTION REGULATION (EU GDPR)[11]

16.31 Instead of repeating much of what has already been said about the GDPR in **Chapter 6**, this chapter will only focus on the key UK / EU GDPR provisions that might apply in practice from a Data Security perspective.

16.32 In this regard, the key Data Security provisions under UK/EU GDPR are:

- Article 5(1)(f) – **Principles relating to processing of personal data**

  > 'Personal data shall be: processed in a manner that ensures appropriate security of the personal data, including protection against unauthorised or unlawful processing and against accidental loss, destruction or damage, using appropriate technical or organisational measures ('integrity and confidentiality')'.

  Although Data Security is already a key consideration under the Directive, Article 5 confirms Data Security as a key Data Protection principle under both the UK and EU GDPR and establishes a baseline for organisations to work towards to that their respective systems, processes and/or applications are compliant from a UK/EU GDPR perspective.

16.33

- Article 28 – **Processors**

  Article 28(1) states that:

  > 'Where processing is to be carried out on behalf of a controller, the controller shall use only processors providing sufficient guarantees to implement appropriate technical and organisational measures in such a manner that processing will meet the requirements of this Regulation and ensure the protection of the rights of the data subject'.

  Under UK/EU GDPR, Data Controllers will need to exercise more care when selecting their personal data processing service providers (Data Processors) which means re-evaluating their procurement processes and ensuring that any requests for tender documents are regularly assessed to ensure these processes ensure that sufficient due diligence had been carried out on potential Data Processors.

9 https://www.dataguidance.com/notes/uk-data-protection-overview.
10 https://eur-lex.europa.eu/legal-content/EN/TXT/PDF/?uri=CELEX%3A32016R0679&from=EN.
11 http://eur-lex.europa.eu/legal-content/EN/TXT/PDF/?uri=CELEX:32016R0679&from=EN.

Data Controllers also need to ensure that they have written contracts with any service providers that are required to process Personal Data on their behalf. These contracts must include a number of Data Security obligations, eg the obligation to provide the Data Controller with assistance where a security breach occurs, to implement appropriate technical and organisational security measures taken and to assist the Data Controller in carrying out any Data Security audits. The same provisions will need to flow down into any contracts that the Data Processor has with its sub-processors.

16.34

- Article 32 – **Security of processing**

The UK/EU GDPR requires that Personal Data be processed in a manner that ensures its security, which includes the protection against unauthorised or unlawful processing and against accidental loss, destruction or damage of that Personal Data.

Article 32 requires that the appropriate technical or organisational measures are used and Article 32(1)(a)-(d)[12] suggests a number of security measures, such as:

- 'the pseudonymisation and encryption of personal data;
- the ability to ensure the ongoing confidentiality, integrity, availability and resilience of processing systems and services;
- the ability to restore the availability and access to personal data in a timely manner in the event of a physical or technical incident;
- a process for regularly testing, assessing and evaluating the effectiveness of technical and organisational measures for ensuring the security of the processing'.

In addition to implementing industry standard security controls to ensure the ongoing confidentiality, integrity, availability and resilience of processing systems (eg access controls, data minimisation, etc.) the UK/EU GDPR specifically call for the use of pseudonymisation (a technique of processing personal data in such a way that it can no longer be attributed to a specific 'data subject' without the use of additional information, which must be kept separately and be subject to technical and organisational measures to ensure non-attribution) and encryption (when data is coded in such a way that only authorised parties can read it) of Personal Data as privacy-friendly techniques and organisations should consider implementing (where feasible of course) these technical controls if they are looking for 'easy wins' when it comes to being audited on Data Security measures under UK/EU GDPR.

12 https://gdpr-info.eu/art-32-gdpr/.

16.35

- Article 33 – **Notification of a personal data breach to the supervisory authority**

  Article 33(1) states:

  > 'In the case of a personal data breach, the controller shall without undue delay and, where feasible, not later than 72 hours after having become aware of it, notify the personal data breach to the supervisory authority competent in accordance with Article 55, unless the personal data breach is unlikely to result in a risk to the rights and freedoms of natural persons. Where the notification to the supervisory authority is not made within 72 hours, it shall be accompanied by reasons for the delay'.

  The UK/EU GDPR introduces a new 'security breach communication framework' for all Data Controllers regardless of which sector they might operate in and Data processors must report personal data breaches to Data Controllers.

  Data Controllers must report any personal data breaches to their supervisory authority and in some cases, affected data subjects and any non-compliance can lead to an administrative fine of up to €10,000,000 or in case of an undertaking, up to 2% of the total worldwide annual turnover of the preceding financial year, whichever is higher.

16.36

- Article 34 – **Communication of a personal data breach to the data subject**

  Article 34(1) states that:

  > 'When the personal data breach is likely to result in a high risk to the rights and freedoms of natural persons, the controller shall communicate the personal data breach to the data subject without undue delay'.

  Basically, this Article provides the Data Subject with a right to know when their personal data has been hacked, so organisations will have to inform individuals promptly of serious data breaches. They will also have to notify the relevant data protection supervisory authority.

  The above breach reporting requirements will not apply if:

  - the breach is unlikely to result in a high risk for the rights and freedoms of data subjects concerned;
  - the appropriate technical and organisational controls were in place at the time of the incident (eg pseudonymisation was used or the data encrypted); or
  - the efforts required to notify data subjects would be unreasonably disproportionate.

THE DATA PROTECTION ACT 2018 ('DPA 18')

16.37 The UK GDPR establishes the fundamental principles, entitlements, and responsibilities for the majority of personal data handling within the UK. However, it excludes law enforcement and intelligence services, which are governed by Part 3 and Part 4 of the Data Protection Act 2018, respectively.

16.38 The key Data Security provisions under Parts 3 and 4 of the DPA 18 can be summarised as follows, but the topic under consideration is too expansive to be included in this chapter and falls outside the scope of this chapter:

Part 3[13] – Law Enforcement Processing:

Section 40[14] – The sixth data protection principle

> 'The sixth data protection principle is that personal data processed for any of the law enforcement purposes must be so processed in a manner that ensures appropriate security of the personal data, using appropriate technical or organisational measures (and, in this principle, 'appropriate security' includes protection against unauthorised or unlawful processing and against accidental loss, destruction or damage)'.

Section 66[15] – Security of processing

> '(1) Each controller and each processor must implement appropriate technical and organisational measures to ensure a level of security appropriate to the risks arising from the processing of personal data.
>
> (2) In the case of automated processing, each controller and each processor must, following an evaluation of the risks, implement measures designed to —
>
> (a) prevent unauthorised processing or unauthorised interference with the systems used in connection with it,
>
> (b) ensure that it is possible to establish the precise details of any processing that takes place,
>
> (c) ensure that any systems used in connection with the processing function properly and may, in the case of interruption, be restored, and
>
> (d) ensure that stored personal data cannot be corrupted if a system used in connection with the processing malfunctions'.

13 https://www.legislation.gov.uk/ukpga/2018/12/part/3.

14 https://www.legislation.gov.uk/ukpga/2018/12/section/40.

15 https://www.legislation.gov.uk/ukpga/2018/12/section/66.

Part 4[16] – Intelligence services processing

Section 91[17] – The sixth data protection principle

'(1) The sixth data protection principle is that personal data must be processed in a manner that includes taking appropriate security measures as regards risks that arise from processing personal data.

(2) The risks referred to in subsection (1) include (but are not limited to) accidental or unauthorised access to, or destruction, loss, use, modification or disclosure of, personal data'.

Section 107[18] – Security of processing

'(1) Each controller and each processor must implement security measures appropriate to the risks arising from the processing of personal data.

(2) In the case of automated processing, each controller and each processor must, following an evaluation of the risks, implement measures designed to —

(a) prevent unauthorised processing or unauthorised interference with the systems used in connection with it,

(b) ensure that it is possible to establish the precise details of any processing that takes place,

(c) ensure that any systems used in connection with the processing function properly and may, in the case of interruption, be restored, and

(d) ensure that stored personal data cannot be corrupted if a system used in connection with the processing malfunctions'.

For more detail on this topic, please refer to the ICO's guidance on its website.[19]

16.39 The UK government is being proactive in its attempts to balance the Data Privacy rights of the individual against the rights of the State to take measures to protect the security of its citizens – eg against terrorism – and it will be interesting to see how these derogations work hand in hand with other key legislation in the realm of UK national security, such as the Regulation of Investigatory Powers Act 2000 (RIPA) and the Investigatory Powers Act 2016 (IPA), both of which are discussed in more detail below.

UK PRIVACY AND ELECTRONIC COMMUNICATIONS REGULATIONS 2003 ('PECR')[20]

16.40 PECR works in conjunction with the UK's data protection framework, namely the UK GDPR and the Data Protection Act 2018. Both PECR and data

16 https://www.legislation.gov.uk/ukpga/2018/12/part/4.
17 https://www.legislation.gov.uk/ukpga/2018/12/section/91.
18 https://www.legislation.gov.uk/ukpga/2018/12/section/107.
19 https://ico.org.uk/for-organisations/law-enforcement/guide-to-le-processing/.
20 www.legislation.gov.uk/uksi/2003/2426/contents/made.

protection aim to safeguard individual privacy. Adherence to PECR can assist in meeting data protection obligations, and the reverse is also true. The PECR specifically regulates the use of electronic communications (email, SMS text, cold calls) as a form of marketing and allow individuals to prevent further contact. The UK Information Commissioner (ICO) has some useful guidance on this piece of legislation on its website[21] which can be referred to when confronted with issues on this topic.

THE PRIVACY AND ELECTRONIC COMMUNICATIONS DIRECTIVE 2002/58/EC (THE 'EPRIVACY DIRECTIVE') AND THE PROPOSED 'EPRIVACY REGULATION'[22]

16.41 Following a study commissioned by the European Commission in 2015 on the effectiveness of the ePrivacy Directive and a subsequent consultation in 2016, on 10 January 2017, the European Commission announced that it aims to implement a new ePrivacy Regulation (ePR) which, amongst other things, is also intended to complement the EU/UK GDPR. As with EU GDPR, the ePR will pass into law in the form of a Regulation (and so will be directly applicable in all EU Member States), with the aim of improving harmonisation across all EU Member States. As is the case with the EU GDPR, the proposed ePR also has extraterritorial effect and any infringements of the new law could attract fines of up to 4% of annual worldwide turnover – similar to those prescribed under EU GDPR.

16.42 The initial deadline for implementation of the ePR was the 25 May 2018 – but the deadline has slipped due to frantic lobbying from various stakeholders that will be effected by the new legislation – eg telecoms and social media providers. Negotiations continue, but it's still unclear when, or if, the Draft ePR will be finalised and enacted into law.

16.43 The ePR will replace the 2002 ePrivacy Directive (which was amended in 2009 and is also known in practice as the 'Cookie Directive'), which gave us the UK's Privacy and Electronic Communications Regulations (PECR).

16.44 The ePR is intended to protect the following forms of communication data (excluding Personal Data which is protected under GDPR):

- processed via business-to-business (B2B) communication; or
- processed via communication between individuals.

21 https://ico.org.uk/for-organisations/direct-marketing-and-privacy-and-electronic-communications/guide-to-pecr/guidance-on-direct-marketing-using-live-calls/what-else-do-we-need-to-consider/#:~:text=PECR%20sits%20alongside%20the%20data,protection%20requirements%20and%20vice%20versa.

22 https://ec.europa.eu/digital-single-market/en/news/proposal-regulation-privacy-and-electronic-communications.

16.45 The new rules that have been proposed under ePR are designed to grant EU citizens and companies specific rights and protections, which are not covered under EU GDPR – eg all providers caught by the ePR must guarantee the confidentiality and integrity of a user's device (ie laptop, smartphone, tablets, etc.) and ensure that any communications data that is held on that device is only accessed by a third party if the user has given their permission.

16.46 The ePR also aims to make the rules surrounding the use of cookies a lot stricter – eg by making it obligatory for device manufacturers, web browsers and software providers to block the use of third party cookies by default.

16.47 From a Data Security perspective, the ePR makes a clear distinction between 'communications content' and 'communications metadata'.

16.48 In this regard, the ePR guarantees privacy (and security) for both:

- communications content – text, voice, videos, images, and sound; and
- communications metadata – a set of data that describes and identifies other data such as source and/or location, time, date and duration data of communications.

16.49 The ePR requires that all communications metadata should be anonymised or deleted unless consent has been obtained from the users to the continued use thereof or if the data is necessary for other lawful purposes, eg detecting or stopping fraudulent telecommunications services.

16.50 When the ePR is finally adopted by the EU, it will need to be implemented into local law by the relevant EU Member States (and organisations will need to comply with these new laws) within six months of its adoption – this is a much tighter deadline for implementation that was the case under GDPR, where Member States had two years to transpose the provisions into local law and business had two years to prepare.

CRIMINAL LAW

Cyber-crime

16.51 The Budapest Convention on Cyber-crime (which forms the basis for all EU cyber-crime law) was only negotiated by the Member States of the Council of Europe together with Canada, Japan, South Africa and the US, and was subsequently opened for signature in Budapest, Hungary, in November 2001, but in the UK the Computer Misuses Act has ensured that hackers and other online 'cyber' criminals can be prosecuted for their crimes since as early as 1990, so the UK has had a head start on other EU States when it comes to fighting cyber-crime. Other international jurisdictions have also since introduced similar legislation to deal with cyber-crime and its related offences.

UK Criminal Law

16.52 The UK Crown Prosecution Service ('CPS') is a useful source of information and guidance when it comes to trying to understand the topic of cyber-crime in the UK. The CPS has published some very useful guidance on this topic on its website, which includes a definition of cyber-crime (from a UK perspective) and an overview of the key cyber-crime offences in the UK[23]:

- The definition of cyber-crime;
- Cyber-dependent crimes and the legislation which should be considered when reviewing and charging a cyber-dependent case;
- Cyber-enabled crimes and the legislation which should be considered when reviewing and charging a cyber-enabled case; and
- Practical and operational points to consider when prosecuting a cybercrime case.

16.53 According to the CPS guidance document[24] referred to above, the term 'Cybercrime' refers to: 'any type of criminal activity conducted through, or using, an Information and Communications Technology (ICT) device' and the purpose of that 'activity' being to commit malicious acts, such as:

- sexual offences (eg grooming or viewing and sharing indecent images);
- taking control of or corrupting computer systems;
- stealing goods, money, information or data; or
- to trade a wide range of commodities online, for example, drugs, firearms, indecent images of children.

16.54 The term 'Cybercrime' describes two criminal activities – these activities were published in the government's National Cyber Security Strategy[25] in November 2016 – and although these terms have different meanings, they often overlap in practice. The two cyber-crimes are defined as follows[26]:

1. '**Cyber-dependent crimes** – crimes that can be committed only through the use of Information and Communications Technology (ICT) devices, where the devices are both the tool for committing the crime, and the target of the crime (e.g. developing and propagating malware for financial gain, hacking to steal, damage, distort or destroy data and/or network or activity).
2. **Cyber-enabled crimes** – traditional crimes which can be increased in scale or reach by the use of computers, computer networks or other forms of ICT (such as cyber-enabled fraud and data theft).'

23 www.cps.gov.uk/legal-guidance/cybercrime-legal-guidance.

24 ibid.

25 www.gov.uk/government/publications/national-cyber-security-strategy-2016-to-2021.

26 www.cps.gov.uk/legal-guidance/cybercrime-legal-guidance.

16.55 From a Data Security perspective, it's evident (from the above definitions) that the unlawful appropriation of Data (personal and non-personal) for commercial gain or some other malicious purpose (eg to manipulate or destroy the integrity of the Data) is a key motive or driver for committing each type of offence and so, arguably, one of the aims of the associated criminal laws is to help prevent the infringement of the Data Security rights of the affected individuals and organisations in the UK.

Cyber-Dependent Crimes

16.56 Cyber-dependent crimes can be split into two categories:

- ***'illicit intrusions into computer networks'*** – from a Data Security perspective, this might include the act of hacking (unauthorised use of, or access into, computers or networks by exploiting identified security vulnerabilities) to unlawfully extract personal data or information which might be of use to criminals; and
- ***'the disruption or downgrading of computer functionality and network space'*** – from a Data Security perspective, this might include the act of introducing malicious software ('Malware') such as 'Spyware' and malicious computer programs, for example, 'Trojans' to steal Personal Data. Other acts that are employed to enable the 'disruption of computer functionality' include Denial of Service ('DOS') and Distributed Denial of Service ('DDOS') attacks, but these methods are more concerned with the actual disruption of service than they are with obtaining Personal Data and other types of valuable information – eg commercially sensitive data.

16.57 Cyber-dependent crimes can be committed by a broad spectrum of perpetrators – ie individuals (eg insiders or employees), groups (eg 'Hacktivists' or organised criminal gangs) or even sovereign States (eg to gather intelligence or compromise UK government defences and government and civilian economic and industrial assets).

CYBER-DEPENDENT CRIMES – OFFENCES AND LEGISLATION

16.58 The CPS guidance on cyber-dependent crimes, suggest that the following offences (and associated legislation) should be considered when reviewing and charging a cyber-dependent case.

COMPUTER MISUSE ACT 1990[27] (CMA)

16.59 The CMA was enacted in response to the failure to convict two individuals (Gold and Schifreen – the 'Defendants') in what amounted to 'hacking' offences under the Forgery and Counterfeiting Act 1981.

27 www.legislation.gov.uk/ukpga/1990/18/contents.

16.60 Steve Gold and his fellow journalist, Robert Schifreen, managed to gain unauthorised access (by using the credentials of a BT Prestel engineer which Schifreen had managed to acquire by looking over the engineer's shoulder while at a trade show) to BT's Prestel Viewdata service, and then famously accessing Prince Philip's inbox.

16.61 Although the Defendants were initially convicted of the charges, the verdict was successfully overturned on appeal and so the CMA was intended to deter criminals from using a computer to assist in the commission of a criminal offence or from impairing or hindering access to data stored in a computer. Basically, the CMA cites three criminal offences for computer misuse:

1. unauthorised access to computer material;
2. unauthorised access with intent to commit or facilitate commission of further offences;
3. unauthorised modification of computer material.

16.62 The CMA is the UK's main piece of legislation when it comes to offences or attacks targeted against computer systems such as hacking or DOS.

16.63 Given the frantic pace at which modern technologies are constantly developing, the CMA deliberately refrains from defining what is meant by a 'computer'. In *DPP v McKeown* and, *DPP v Jones* [1997] 2 Cr App R 155 HL[28], Lord Hoffman defined computer as: 'a device for storing, processing and retrieving information.'

16.64 This means that mobile smartphones or tablet devices could, arguably, also be regarded as 'computers' in the same way that 'desk-top' computers and 'PCs' are.

16.65 The CPS has jurisdiction to prosecute any CMA offences if there is 'at least one significant link with the domestic jurisdiction (England and Wales) in the circumstances of the case'[29] and so includes instances where the accused or the target computer was situated in England and Wales, so the extent of the CPS' jurisdiction is quite broad in this regard.

16.66 The CPS also has the power to charge offenders with the following offences under the CMA – further (and more detailed) guidance can be found in the CPS' legal guidance on the Computer Misuse Act 1990[30]:

- '**Section 1** – unauthorised access to computer material. This offence involves 'access without right' and is often the precursor to more serious offending. There has to be knowledge on the part of the offender that the access is unauthorised; mere recklessness is not sufficient. There

28 https://publications.parliament.uk/pa/ld199697/ldjudgmt/jd970220/mcke01.htm.

29 /www.cps.gov.uk/legal-guidance/cybercrime-legal-guidance.

30 /www.cps.gov.uk/legal-guidance/computer-misuse-act-1990.

also must have been an intention to access a program or data held in a computer.

- **Section 2** – unauthorised access with intent to commit or facilitate commission of further offences.
- **Section 3** – unauthorised acts with intent to impair the operation of a computer. The offence is committed if the person behaves recklessly as to whether the act will impair, prevent access to or hinder the operations of a computer. Section 3 should be considered in cases involving distributed denial of service attacks (DDoS).
- **Section 3ZA** – Unauthorised acts causing, or creating risk of, serious damage, for example, to human welfare, the environment, economy or national security. This section is aimed at those who seek to attack the critical national infrastructure.
- **Section 3A** – making, supplying or obtaining articles for use in offences contrary to sections 1, 3 or 3ZA. Section 3A deals with those who make or supply malware.'

REGULATION OF INVESTIGATORY POWERS ACT (RIPA) 2000[31]

16.67 RIPA regulates the powers of public bodies to carry out surveillance and investigations and also deals with the interception of communications. The Home Office offers guidance and codes of practice relating to RIPA.

16.68 Section 1(1)(b) of RIPA makes it an offence for a person to: 'intentionally and without lawful authority to intercept, at any place in the United Kingdom, any communication in the course of its transmission by means of a *public telecommunication system*'.

16.69 Section 1(2) makes it an offence for a person to: 'intercept any communication in the course of its transmission by means of a *private telecommunication system*'.

16.70 Where content (which can include Personal Data) is unlawfully intercepted through cyber-enabled means, it can be argued that either or both of the offences cited under Sections 1(1) and 1(2) above could apply in a case involving 'hacking' and so the CPS guidance on RIPA suggests that Prosecutors should consider whether to charge offences under RIPA instead of or in addition to CMA. In this regard, the CPS states that it would be advisable to rely on RIPA if material was unlawfully intercepted in the course of its transmission, whereas the CMA probably be more appropriate in circumstances where material is acquired through unauthorised access to a computer.

31 www.legislation.gov.uk/ukpga/2000/23/contents.

16.71 A Draft Investigatory Powers Bill has since passed through Parliament and received Royal Assent as the Investigatory Powers Act 2016 (see below) which Act seeks to reform the requirements of RIPA.

INVESTIGATORY POWERS ACT 2016 (IPA)[32]

16.72 The Investigatory Powers Bill received Royal Assent on Tuesday 29 November 2016, and will now be known as the Investigatory Powers Act 2016 (also known as the 'Snooper's Charter'). The IPA provides a new framework to govern the use and oversight of investigatory powers used by law enforcement and the security and intelligence agencies.

16.73 According to the GOV.UK website, the IPA effectively does three things:[33]

1. 'Brings together all of the powers already available to law enforcement and the security and intelligence agencies to obtain communications and data about communications. It will make these powers and the safeguards that apply to them clear and understandable.
2. Radically overhauls the way these powers are authorised and overseen. It introduces a 'double-lock' for interception warrants, so that, following Secretary of State authorisation, these (and other warrants) cannot come into force until they have been approved by a judge. And it creates a powerful new Investigatory Powers Commissioner to oversee how these powers are used.
3. Ensures powers are fit for the digital age. It makes provision for the retention of internet connection records for law enforcement to identify the communications service to which a device has connected. This will restore capabilities that have been lost as a result of changes in the way people communicate.'

16.74 A public consultation on draft codes of practice under the IPA was published on 23 February 2017[34], but this falls outside the scope of this chapter.

16.75 The GOV.UK website also contains useful fact sheets and guidance relating to the Investigatory Powers Bill[35] which might be worth reading for more background on this important piece of legislation.

16.76 From a Data Security perspective, RIPA and IPA both play an important role in granting UK law enforcement officials the powers to help preserve the Data Security rights of its citizens, but these powers need to be used with caution to ensure that the delicate balance between protecting UK citizens' national

32 www.legislation.gov.uk/ukpga/2016/25/contents/enacted.
33 www.gov.uk/government/collections/investigatory-powers-bill.
34 www.gov.uk/government/consultations/investigatory-powers-act-2016-codes-of-practice.
35 www.gov.uk/government/publications/investigatory-powers-bill-fact-sheets.

security doesn't mean we end up living in a 'Big Brother' type State where national security trumps other individual rights such as Data Security.

DATA PROTECTION ACT 2018 (DPA 18)[36]

16.77 The Data Protection Act of 2018 (DPA 2018) was enacted on 25 May 2018, superseding the Data Protection Act from 1998. This new act incorporates both the General Data Protection Regulation (GDPR) and the Law Enforcement Directive (LED) into British legislation.

Crimes Introduced Under the DPA 2018

Section 119 – The provision criminalises interference with an ICO inspection of EU data systems, necessary for fulfilling the UK's international commitments. Intentional obstruction or failure to assist in these inspections is illegal.

Section 132 – The section updates the previous law, making it a crime for current or former ICO staff to reveal data acquired during their duties. The section clarifies permissible disclosures.

Section 144 – Making a false or recklessly false statement in response to an information request from the ICO is a criminal offence.

Section 148 – The section criminalises the destruction, concealment, or falsification of data and documents. It also encompasses causing or permitting such actions.

Section 170 – Building on earlier laws, the section makes it illegal to knowingly or recklessly obtain, disclose, or keep personal data without the data controller's permission. Exceptions and defences are provided.

Section 171 – This new crime involves the unlawful re-identification of anonymised personal data. Defences are outlined for this and the subsequent processing of re-identified data.

Section 173 – Criminalises the intentional alteration or destruction of data to prevent its disclosure upon request. Defences are detailed.

Section 184 – Makes it illegal to request certain records related to employment or service contracts. Defences are listed.

Schedule 15, Paragraph 15 – Obstructing or providing false statements during a warrant execution under this schedule is illegal.

All offences are subject to fines only, with no custodial sentences or arrest powers being granted to the relevant authority(ies).

Schedule 15 delineates conditions for the ICO to apply for a search warrant.

36 https://www.cps.gov.uk/legal-guidance/data-protection-act-2018-criminal-offences.

The DPA 2018 abolished Section 77 of the Criminal Justice and Immigration Act 2008 concerning penalties for unlawful data handling.

Notification Requirement

Organisations must pay a data protection fee to the ICO unless exempt, replacing the prior notification requirement under DPA 1998. The Information Commissioner holds the authority to implement the DPA 2018 and can levy financial sanctions on those who fail to pay the requisite data protection fee

Data Subject Rights

The GDPR enumerates various rights for individuals, such as the rights to be informed, access data, correct data, erase data, restrict processing, data portability, object, and rights concerning automated decisions and profiling.

16.78 From a Data Security perspective, Individuals and organisations need to take note of these new offences as it might be tempting to take steps to re-identify or alter personal data – eg by re-identifying Personal Data after it has been pseudonymised with a view to repurposing it – as this could constitute a criminal offence.

CYBER-ENABLED CRIMES

16.79 Cyber-enabled crimes include crimes which depend entirely on the use of computer hardware or networks to commit the offence, but instead use the internet and various types of communications technology to allow for the scalability of offences. According to CPS guidance on this topic, these crimes can be categorised as follows[37]:

- 'Economic related cybercrime, including:
  - Fraud
  - Intellectual property crime – piracy, counterfeiting and forgery
- Online marketplaces for illegal items
- Malicious and offensive communications, including:
  - Communications sent via social media
  - Cyber bullying / Trolling
  - Virtual mobbing
- Offences that specifically target individuals, including cyber-enabled violence against women and girls (VAWG):
  - Disclosing private sexual images without consent
  - Cyber stalking and harassment
  - Coercion and control

37 www.cps.gov.uk/legal-guidance/cybercrime-legal-guidance.

- Child sexual offences and indecent images of children, including:
  - Child sexual abuse
  - Online grooming
  - Prohibited and indecent images of children
- Extreme pornography, obscene publications and prohibited images, including
  - Extreme Pornography
  - Obscene publications.'

16.80 The only cyber-enabled crime that is likely to overlap with the topic of this chapter (ie Data Security) is Fraud, so this is the only cyber-enabled crime that will be discussed in this chapter.

16.81 However, it is suggested that you refer to the CPS' guidance on the other cyber-enabled crimes listed above if you'd like to gain a better understanding of how they occur in practice and how the CPS goes about prosecuting these types of offences.

CYBER-DEPENDENT CRIMES – OFFENCES AND LEGISLATION

Fraud

16.82 From a Data Security perspective, the cyber-enabled crime of Fraud (or online fraud) is probably the most common and frequently publicised cyber-crime offence. Cyber-criminals use various methods to obtain both personal (names, bank details, and National Insurance numbers, client databases) and financial data (company accounts and intellectual property – eg new and yet undisclosed innovations, designs and patents) for fraudulent purposes.

16.83 Some of the methods used by cyber-criminals to commit Fraud include:[38]

- '*Electronic financial frauds*' eg online banking frauds and internet enabled card-not-present (CNP) fraud – involving transactions conducted remotely, over the internet, where neither the cardholder nor the card is present.
- '*E-commerce frauds*' which generally includes fraudulent financial transactions (perpetrated against both businesses and customers) related to retail sales and which are carried out online.
- '*Fraudulent sales through online auction or retail sites* or through fake websites' which involves:
  - the offering of goods or services online that, once paid for, are not provided, or

38 www.cps.gov.uk/legal-guidance/cybercrime-legal-guidance.

  - 'online ticketing fraud' – this is where buyers are induced to buy tickets to music, sports and other entertainment events, only to discover that, after payment has been made, the tickets are fake.

- '*Mass-marketing frauds and consumer scams*' which include:
  - '*Phishing* scams' – these scams involve the mass dissemination (to a broad range of targets) of fraudulent emails which are disguised as legitimate emails and which attempt to solicit (or fish) for personal and/or corporate information (eg passwords or bank account details) from users;
  - '*Pharming*' involves the act of directing a user to a fake website (often by including details for that website in a phishing email) in an attempt to get the user to input his/her personal details so they can be used for fraudulent means; and
  - '*Social networking/dating website frauds*' – this is where scammers use social networking or dating sites to persuaded individuals to part with personal information and/or money following a lengthy online relationship.

According to the CPS,[39] the following offences (and associated legislation) should be considered when reviewing and charging a cyber-enabled fraud case:

THE FRAUD ACT 2006 (FRAUD ACT)

16.84 By focusing on the underlying dishonesty and deception exhibited by the perpetrators, the CPS is able to rely on the offences under the Fraud Act. For example, the following acts could constitute offences under the Fraud Act:

- setting up fake social networking accounts or aliases if there was a financial gain to be made from this act;
- the possession or making or supplying of articles for use in frauds – which includes any program or data held in electronic form that can be used in the commission of the fraudulent act – could constitute an offence under Section 8.

The CPS has published further legal guidance on the Fraud Act[40] which you might find useful in this regard.

16.85 The UK has created a national centre called *Action Fraud* where individuals and corporations that have been scammed, defrauded or experienced cyber-crime can report the fraud and cyber-crime. Action Fraud's website[41] is a useful source and provides useful guidance about specific types of cyber-fraud.

39 www.cps.gov.uk/legal-guidance/cybercrime-legal-guidance.

40 www.cps.gov.uk/legal-guidance/fraud-act-2006.

41 www.actionfraud.police.uk/about-us.

THE THEFT ACT 1968[42]

16.86 The CPS guidance on relying upon this piece of legislation to prosecute cyber-dependent crimes states that:

> 'Prosecutors should note that if an offender accesses data, reads it and then uses the information for his/her own purposes, then this is not an offence contrary to the Theft Act. Confidential information per se does not come within the definition of property in section 4 of the Theft Act 1968 and cannot be stolen: Oxford v Moss 68 Cr App R 183 DC. It is likely however that this would constitute an offence under section 1(1) Computer Misuse Act 1990. Also, if it was done with the intent to commit or facilitate the commission of further offences, it would constitute an offence contrary to section 2(1) Computer Misuse Act 1990.
>
> Where there are a number of suspects allegedly involved in an online fraud, a statutory conspiracy under section 1 of the Criminal Law Act 1977, or common law conspiracy to defraud may be appropriate. Prosecutors should consider the *Attorney General's Guidelines on the Use of the common law offence of Conspiracy to Defraud* before making a charging decision. Where several people have the same access to a computer, one way to seek to prove the involvement of suspects will be to follow the payment trail as payments will often be required to be sent to a designated account, and may be attributed to an individual.'

16.87 In this regard, it is important to bear in mind that the nature of the offending act(s) will most likely shape the appropriate charges, and that the authorities are also encouraged to consider offences under other pieces of legislation if necessary – eg the Theft Act 1978, Computer Misuse Act 1990, Forgery and Counterfeiting Act 1981 and Proceeds of Crime Act 2002.

CONCLUSION

16.88 The '*data is the new oil*' analogy does have some truth to it and in the same way that the explosion in the use of internal combustion engines (and mitigating the associated risks and safety issues that arose as a result) changed the way that society looked at oil as a commodity, if individuals and organisations can start to acknowledge that their Data (personal and non-personal) is a valuable asset and take appropriate steps to protect how it is processed, that Data can become a valuable commodity to help drive innovation and add value to the bottom line.

16.89 To compound matters even more, AI amplifies the capacity to scrutinise personal data in manners that could potentially infringe upon privacy rights, thereby creating complex legal challenges. Typically, concerns regarding AI and privacy fall into two categories: 'input issues', which involve the incorporation

42 www.legislation.gov.uk/ukpga/1968/60/contents.

of expansive datasets containing personal data (both sensitive or otherwise), and 'output issues,' a more recent development due to AI advancements, which pertain to the conclusions drawn by AI systems.

16.90 The proposed EU AI Act (EUAIA) promises to be a watershed moment for data security within the European Union and efforts made by the UK Government to provide guardrails for the responsible use of AI will also have an impact on how organisations deal with data security from a UK perspective. By setting stringent standards for AI systems and their operators, the EUAIA aims to elevate the level of data protection and data security, thereby reinforcing user trust and promoting ethical AI use.

16.91 However, as the regulatory landscape evolves, it will be crucial to monitor how these proposed rules align with existing data protection frameworks like the GDPR/UK GDPR, to ensure a harmonised and effective approach to data security in the EU, UK and further afield.

CHAPTER 17

DATA CLASSIFICATION

Dr Reza Alavi

INTRODUCTION

17.01 In today's landscape, information security is deeply integrated into the various functions of an organisation. A robust security posture requires a nuanced understanding of each component within the IT infrastructure, from data acquisition and access to transfer and storage. Effectively classifying data and implementing appropriate levels of security are critical aspects of an organisation's overall information security strategy. The identification, authentication, and authorisation processes, captured within an access control matrix, shape the organisation's security posture and define its risk tolerance.

17.02 This chapter offers a comprehensive overview of several critical areas related to data management: data classification, data processing, data security, and data loss prevention, as well as control mechanisms. We aim to provide a balanced perspective on the critical importance of data classification and the potential ramifications should this process fail. The chapter delves into the complexities organisations encounter in safeguarding data: Confidentiality, Integrity, and Availability. Additionally, this chapter explores the interconnectedness of data classification with Business Impact Analysis (BIA), shedding light on how these two processes mutually influence each other. While offering insights into a successful data classification project, we will also distinguish between data security and data privacy, two closely related yet distinct areas. The chapter then defines various controls and their relevance to data security. In conclusion, we evaluate the significance of asset recovery processes and the role of data loss prevention tools within the broader scope of data classification.

What is Data?

17.03 In the context of technology and computing, data encompasses various elements critical to multiple applications. Raw data is unprocessed information from sources like logs, while structured data is organised into tables or fields for easy analysis, contrasting with unstructured data that lacks this organisation. Specialised technologies like Hadoop and Spark address the challenges of managing and processing Big Data, enormous datasets that exceed the capabilities of traditional databases. Techniques like data mining employ statistical analysis and machine learning to glean insights from data. Data warehousing systems focus on efficiently storing and retrieving large data volumes, optimised more for query and analysis than for transactional processing. Metadata describes other types of data, offering contextual information. Ensuring data integrity, or the accuracy and consistency of data, is crucial, especially in applications like databases. Data security measures protect against unauthorised access or alterations. Depending on its use in computations, data can also be categorised into various types – such as integers or strings. Finally, data encoding and decoding convert data from one form to another for transmission or storage.

Data Classification

17.04 Data classification can be described as the systematic organisation of data into distinct categories to optimise its use and management. It is an indispensable tool for organisations to locate and retrieve the data they need efficiently. An intelligently designed data classification system is essential for effective risk management and compliance, as it establishes the sensitivity levels associated with various data types. Ownership of the data is another crucial consideration in this process. Data classification guidelines set forth the criteria and categories organisations use for this purpose, delineating the roles and responsibilities of different team members.

17.05 Moreover, the data classification process helps meet the requirements of security standards, such as ISO 27001, by outlining best practices for handling, storing, modifying, and transmitting data throughout its lifecycle. The classification level assigned to a particular data set reflects its importance and relevance to an organisation. Therefore, any data classification scheme should prioritise criticality, sensitivity, and ownership, which we will explore later in this discussion.

17.06 The risk of unauthorised disclosure plays a significant role in classifying data and information assets. Examples of such risks include accidental or intentional data loss. Consequently, data with high associated risks typically receives a 'Confidential' classification, demanding more protective measures. On the other hand, data posing a lower risk may be labelled as 'Internal,' requiring less stringent security controls. Ineffectual data classification can have severe consequences, potentially leading to large-scale data breaches resulting from a single unaddressed risk. This amplifies the importance of meticulous data classification. In many organisations, there is an inadequate segregation between highly sensitive and less sensitive data, often due to weak password practices. According to a Verizon report, weak passwords account for 81% of hacking-related breaches. Therefore, the classification of an entire dataset often hinges on the classification assigned to its most sensitive elements.

The Benefit of the Data Classification

17.07 Beyond meeting legal and regulatory requirements, implementing a data classification framework offers numerous advantages to organisations. First and foremost, it demonstrates an organisation's commitment to safeguarding its invaluable data and information assets. The process aids in pinpointing the most critical or valuable assets, thereby guiding the organisation in choosing appropriate protection mechanisms.

17.08 Equally important, data classification helps organisations establish well-defined access levels and permissions for authorised users, enhancing security and operational efficiency. It also lays out procedures for the declassification and eventual destruction of data that has outlived its usefulness or relevance, helping to optimise data storage costs and management. Moreover, attributing value to data enables organisations to make informed decisions in aligning their financial strategies, ensuring that resources are allocated effectively to protect and manage data assets.

17.09 Allocating precise value to information assets parallels how organisations assign value to other types of resources. However, valuing information can be particularly challenging. For instance, some data, like trade secrets, are irreplaceable, while others might be challenging to substitute. In the case of non-replaceable assets such as trade secrets or specialised knowledge, the data becomes invaluable and necessitates robust protective measures. A well-defined data value, aligned with appropriate classification levels, establishes clear accountability for data ownership.

In Summary: Key Benefits of Data Classification

17.10 The merits of a structured data classification approach are manifold and can be outlined as follows:

- Determining the Value of Data: Classification helps attribute value to different data types, guiding protection efforts.
- Managing Sensitive and Valuable Data: Identifies which data requires the most stringent protective measures.
- Assigning Accountability: Clarifies the roles and responsibilities for data stewardship, ensuring data integrity and security.
- Increasing Effectiveness of Data Security: Enhances the efficiency of security protocols by targeting the most critical assets.
- Fulfilling Legal and Regulatory Obligations: Ensures compliance with laws and industry standards, mitigating the risk of penalties.
- Business Continuity and Disaster Recovery Planning: Enables more effective planning by identifying the most critical data to ongoing operations.
- Optimising Security Investment: Allows for a more targeted allocation of resources towards safeguarding valuable data assets.
- Enhancing General Information Security Awareness: Fosters a culture of security consciousness within the organisation.
- Aligning Data Security with Governance and Compliance: Ensures security measures align with organisational policies and regulatory requirements.

- Automated Data Discovery, Tagging, and Classification: Streamlines the data management process through automation.
- Comprehensive Controls: Facilitates the identification of all-encompassing controls such as data loss prevention, monitoring, and reporting.

17.11 Despite its critical importance, the extensive benefits of a comprehensive and robust data classification system are sometimes overlooked by organisations. Such a holistic approach offers robustness and simplicity, serving as the cornerstone for an adequate data protection strategy and broader information security governance. A well-designed data classification framework adds multiple layers of strength to an organisation's security posture by providing a clear mandate and enabling more accurate metrics for assessing information security maturity. In essence, the merits of a thorough data classification strategy go beyond compliance and immediate security needs. They embed a culture of continuous improvement and accountability, ensuring that data protection is not just a checklist item but an integrated, evolving aspect of organisational excellence.

Data Classification Process

17.12 Initiating the Data Classification Process: Organisations need to establish the metrics for data protection before diving into data classification. These metrics should help answer key questions about data nature, location, users, and usage purposes. Answering these questions enables organisations to develop a more robust and efficient data classification strategy. Following identifying the right metrics, organisations should formulate a formal policy outlining their approach to data classification.

17.13 Key Elements of the Data Classification Policy:

- **Purpose**: The policy should articulate why the organisation has adopted this framework and how it aims to ensure the confidentiality, integrity, and availability of its data in line with its overall information security and data protection goals. This section should also specify the organisation's stance on guarding data against unauthorised access, disclosure, and modification.
- **Scope**: The scope should clarify if the policy applies to all data types, regardless of where it's stored or what device it resides on. It should also outline the user base and any third parties who might interact with the data.
- **Assumptions**: This clarifies that all participants and stakeholders have the necessary technical knowledge for policy implementation and are aware of legal and regulatory obligations.
- **Stakeholders**: All user categories and stakeholders are identified here, and their roles and responsibilities are documented.
- **Roles and Responsibilities**: This provides a detailed account of who has access to what data for what duration and clarifies access levels relative to data sensitivity.

- **Data Retention and Disposal**: Organisations should have clear guidelines on data retention periods. Given varying industry and governmental regulations, organisations may retain data records for varying durations. This section also aligns with GDPR requirements around personal data management.
- **Data Transfer**: The core aim of data classification is to secure data based on its sensitivity and significance tags. These protective mechanisms should also be in place during data transfer activities.
- **Data Inventory**: Defines the types of data the organisation holds and where they are located.
- **Ownership and Approval**: Ownership must be clearly established for meaningful data classification. Regular internal audits should confirm data ownership, and these audit reports need senior management approval to lend the policy weight and legitimacy.
- **Change Record**: Managing record changes is crucial for data integrity and confidentiality. This is inextricably linked to an organisation's broader change management strategy, which should be geared to assess the impact of proposed changes on data protection capabilities.

17.14 By rigorously adhering to this structured policy, organisations solidify their data classification schemes and garner senior management support, which is vital for meeting legal obligations and securing financial backing for the project.

Data Classification: A Practical Example

17.15 Data classification in organisations can be a complex but essential process, often guided by a set of standardised criteria tailored to the entity's specific needs and strategic goals. These criteria commonly include considerations like the data's value to the organisation, its lifespan concerning data management cycles, the extent of personal information involved, and guidelines for disclosure and modification. Other dimensions, such as who has legitimate access, how the data is monitored, and storage and backup requirements, are also vital. In some cases, national security considerations may come into play, usually dictated by government regulations. By understanding these various dimensions, organisations can create a robust data classification scheme that enhances data management, optimises security, and ensures compliance with diverse regulations.

17.16 Before looking at the challenges and possible solutions, we should look at an example of the classification:

- **Public Access**
  - Data is open to the general public, with no legal restrictions on access or usage.

  - Examples include news articles, marketing materials, and job advertisements.
- **Internal**
  - Data is restricted within an organisation due to ethical or company policy concerns.
  - There are no legal mandates for restriction, but only employees with a legitimate need can access it.
  - Includes general employment data or business partner details without personally identifiable information.
- **Confidential**
  - Highly sensitive data requiring stringent authorisation for access.
  - Includes personal privacy data, financial data, and other sensitive personal information.
- **Secret**
  - Data with restricted access, often relating to national security.
  - Unauthorised exposure could have significant impacts and cause critical damage.
- **Top Secret**
  - The highest data classification level is generally used for ultra-sensitive national security information.
  - Unauthorised exposure would result in severe impacts and potentially catastrophic damage.
- **Classified Information**
  - The categories of "Confidential," "Secret," and "Top Secret" are collectively termed as classified information.
  - Disclosure of the classification level to unauthorised parties may be considered a violation.

17.17 'Confidential,' 'Secret,' and 'Top Secret' are generally grouped under 'classified information.' Revealing the classification level or labelling to unauthorised parties may be deemed a data security breach. Typically, the label 'classified' is reserved for data that exceeds the 'sensitive but unclassified' security threshold."

17.18 Organisations must adopt a standardised vocabulary and establish clear connections between various data classification tiers, ensuring transparent communication with stakeholders. Such classification not only aids in risk identification but also informs the subsequent actions to be taken when handling incidents or breaches, including response strategies, escalation protocols, and notification procedures.

Challenges of Data Classification

17.19 In today's interconnected world, data flows freely across geographical and digital boundaries through various platforms like websites, social media, cloud services, and more. While this accessibility enhances business operations and decision-making, it also presents significant challenges for data security. Effective data classification is pivotal for implementing robust data protection measures that are both agile and adaptable. However, classifying data is far from straightforward and often lacks intuitive ease.

17.20 Human nature tends to categorise things quickly but not always accurately, a tendency that adds complexity when organisations attempt to standardise data classification. Policies shaped by multiple individuals further complicate the process. Additionally, the need for vast, detailed market data to support predictive analytics and diverse communication channels and devices exacerbates compliance issues. These factors collectively make data classification an overwhelming challenge. Common pitfalls include an over-reliance on human judgment without a strategic vision, a failure to integrate data classification into organisational processes, and the absence of practical, operational tools to support the task.

17.21 Often, organisations classify data at the point of creation, ignoring the changing business context that could influence the classification later. Another complexity is terminological – terms like 'sensitive but unclassified' are often misunderstood outside specialised sectors like the military and government. Given these challenges, organisations must explore various approaches and solutions to make data classification manageable and effective.

The Ramification of Failure of Data Classification Scheme

17.22 Organisations must fully grasp the significance of their data to implement the proper controls that mitigate risk. Failing to classify data correctly can result in deploying insufficient security measures, posing a real threat. Take, for example, a financial firm that loses a backup containing employee financial information. If that data were classified as 'confidential' on the primary system but not the backup, the company's security measures would be flawed and inadequate. To avoid such issues, it is essential for organisations to accurately locate and classify their data based on factors like criticality, sensitivity, and business value. By doing so, organisations can implement cost-effective, consistently applied protective measures, regardless of where the data resides.

17.23 Conversely, correct classification helps organisations identify non-critical or non-sensitive data, allowing them to allocate resources more efficiently. Organisations can focus on what genuinely needs protection instead of guarding data that holds little value. Hence, proper data classification is crucial for risk mitigation and serves as a cornerstone for a cost-effective and robust security program.

Data Classification and Business Impact Analysis (BIA)

17.24 Within an organisation's IT infrastructure, various systems and services need safeguarding. Business Impact Analysis (BIA) is vital for identifying and evaluating these elements. BIA helps organisations gauge the potential fallout should these systems or services fail. Below is a list of some typical services and systems that may require attention:

- Data deemed sensitive or critical, the loss of which could harm the organisation.
- Physical files that contain sensitive information.
- Backup files and media storage.
- Communication tools, both hardware and software.
- Password repositories and databases.
- Libraries of application programs and source codes.
- Essential directories, files, and address tables.
- Proprietary software and packages.
- Storage hardware and other forms of media.
- Security logs, system logs, and audit trails.
- Incident reports.

Role of Business Impact Analysis (BIA) in Risk Management

17.25 After completing a risk assessment, Business Impact Analysis (BIA) is the cornerstone for quantifying an organisation's risk exposure. The risk assessment process yields crucial information about the resources essential for the organisation's operations. BIA then assesses the implications of resource loss, setting the stage for quantifying data loss value. Organisations can leverage this information to formulate strategies that mitigate potential negative impacts. Therefore, BIA plays a pivotal role in determining the criticality and sensitivity of systems, data, and information and in shaping an organisation's approach to data classification. This, in turn, influences plans for business continuity and disaster recovery.

Integrating Business Impact Analysis (BIA) into Data Management

17.26 The BIA process begins with formulating a threat and risk assessment, which lays the groundwork for identifying data-related threats, their associated risks, and the types of data impacted. This threat assessment serves as the foundational input for the BIA and kickstarts the procedure for determining concrete data classifications. Organisations should align their data classification efforts with existing data protection regulations, leveraging these as part of their business case for data classification and in the BIA and subsequent planning phases. In essence, BIA allows organisations to:

- Pinpoint key information components;
- Assess risks linked to the loss of confidentiality, integrity, availability, and compliance;
- Evaluate the impacts and risks tied to data loss and
- Establish clear roles and responsibilities

Implementing Resource Allocation through Data Classification

17.27 This methodology enables organisations to allocate resources to specific classifications, deploying unified controls to counter potential risks. Organisations must weigh factors such as the data's sensitivity, the simplicity of its recovery process, and its overall importance in classifying data.

A Keys to a Robust Data Classification Strategy

17.28 Organisations must first profoundly understand their operational landscape for a successful data classification program. This includes recognising the types of data managed and how it is utilised. A granular understanding of how employees and other data users interact with the system daily is crucial. Secondly, pinpointing critical and valuable data within the organisation is essential. Some organisations have obscure corners filled with "dark data" that remains unexamined. A comprehensive scan across different data repositories is necessary to bring this data to light.

17.29 Knowing what and where this data resides is pivotal for assigning the appropriate level of protection. Organisations should adhere to established standards and frameworks like ISO 17799 and COBIT for optimal results. Both frameworks mandate identifying data owners and classifying each data set. Leveraging these frameworks can help in devising a successful classification strategy. Effective policies should be formulated, and these can then be overseen, evaluated, and enforced by senior management. These policies must also align with IT controls that facilitate rather than obstruct day-to-day work.

17.30 Organisations need to nurture a culture that respects data compliance. Routine training on privacy and security can elevate employee awareness. Integrating privacy and security considerations into daily operations fosters an ongoing culture of awareness. Adopting a 'security and privacy by design' methodology can be a strategic approach. Senior management should be proactive champions in harmonising the relationship between various business units and IT, instilling a robust security culture.

17.31 Before diving into Data Loss Prevention (DLP), it's crucial to define and distinguish between 'Data Security' and 'Data Privacy.' Understanding these terms is vital as they relate to asset recovery.

DATA PRIVACY AND SECURITY

What is Data Security?

17.32 Organisations consider customer data – personal or financial – as well as trade secrets and intellectual property as their most valuable assets. Data Security is the discipline focused on safeguarding these assets from threats and unauthorised access. It involves a suite of tools and methods, such as data classification, permission management, and identity and access management. The primary objective of implementing these measures is to shield critical organisational data from compromise or loss.

What is Privacy?

The Essence of Privacy

17.33 In sociological terms, privacy is an individual's entitlement to freedom from intrusive observation. In a technological context, it pertains to safeguarding a person's information, the 'Data Subject' under data protection laws. These laws empower individuals with the 'Right to be Forgotten,' allowing them to request data deletion from organisations. Privacy, thus, serves as the bedrock of individual rights and freedoms, and it is intrinsically tied to the overarching aims of data security and classification.

Navigating Privacy in Organisations

17.34 Privacy takes centre stage in any organisation's activities, affecting digital and physical realms, including hard copy records. Accountable for data protection, senior management must be cognisant of pressing privacy concerns – regulations such as the EU's GDPR address many of these, necessitating organisational compliance efforts.

Compliance and the Role of the Data Protection Officer

17.35 Individuals possess the right to inquire about the data organisations hold on them and can demand its deletion. Organisations must erase this data from all repositories, internal systems, third-party entities, or cloud services. Organisations must grasp the legal landscape regulating this data, including laws, standards, and contractual obligations. Organisations should designate a 'Data Protection Officer' (DPO), as the GDPR mandates, to ensure continued compliance.

Policy Considerations for Data at Rest

17.36 Addressing privacy also means having policies for data at rest. Questions like where the data is stored, how long it is retained, and how it is lawfully destroyed must be answered. Should data be transferred to a different data centre in another country, specific privacy implications come into play. An apparent retention and destruction policy should be established. Ultimately, true privacy cannot exist without the underpinning of confidentiality. To this end, technologies like Public Key Infrastructure (PKI) play an enhancing role in ensuring privacy.

Why is Data Security Mistaken for Privacy?

17.37 A common misconception among organisations is that robust data security equates to compliance with data privacy regulations. While both are intertwined and aim to protect sensitive information, they serve different purposes and require distinct considerations. Even with stringent data security protocols, a lack of understanding regarding privacy policies among stakeholders with access to sensitive data can result in improper data handling. Therefore, organisations must recognise that data security is just one aspect of a multifaceted privacy compliance framework.

Types of Controls

17.38 Controls serve as the linchpin of a risk assessment strategy, functioning to assess and mitigate the possible threats facing an organisation. However, relying solely on one type of control – preventative or detective – is unlikely to provide a comprehensive defence against cybersecurity threats. Organisations should employ a layered approach for a genuinely resilient framework, incorporating multiple categories of controls to create a "defence-in-depth" strategy. Below, we delve into the various types of controls that can be utilised.

Directive controls

17.39 Directive controls provide a structured framework for reducing cyber threats using policies, guidelines, procedures, standards, and regulations. These controls are geared toward fulfilling legal obligations and achieving compliance. An Acceptable Use Policy (AUP) guides employees on acceptable data handling practices and sets the groundwork for disciplinary actions for violations.

Preventive Controls

17.40 Preventive controls work to pre-emptively stop unwanted incidents. Although they might be expensive, they often prove cost-effective in the long run. Tools like firewalls, anti-virus software, encryption, and practices like risk analysis and job rotation are employed. The concept of Privacy by Design, highlighted by the EU GDPR, underscores the importance of preventive measures in data protection.

Detective Controls

17.41 Detective controls aim to identify errors and violations. They include audit trails, logs, and Intrusion Detection Systems (IDSs) and Intrusion Prevention Systems (IPSs). The latter are essentially detective controls with auto-response capabilities.

Corrective Controls

17.42 Corrective controls work to mitigate the effects of an attack. They include incident handling procedures, Business Continuity Planning (BCP), and recovery procedures. The focus is minimising the impact and risk of a security incident.

Recovery Controls

17.43 Recovery controls aim to restore systems to their pre-incident state. They are tightly interwoven with business continuity and disaster recovery plans, including system restoration, backups, and contingency plans.

Application Controls

17.44 Inserted into software and applications, these controls are designed to manage transactions and operational anomalies. One of their objectives is to limit system utilities that can bypass application controls.

Transaction Controls

17.45 These controls are applied throughout the transaction process to ensure integrity and completeness. They are designed to reasonably assess transaction data quality from the initiation to the output stage.

Input Controls

17.46 Input controls ensure authorised transactions are wholly and correctly entered into the system. Examples include data counting and time stamping.

Processing Controls

17.47 These controls validate transactions during processing, ensuring the correct program is employed. They also identify and reprocess incorrect entries.

Output Controls

17.48 These controls safeguard the confidentiality and integrity of processed data, ensuring they are accessible only to authorised recipients. Policies for privacy and data retention are essential aspects of output controls.

Change Control

17.49 Change control, often managed through configuration management systems, ensures that any modifications to a system are adequately reviewed, documented, and effectively implemented. Backup systems like BCP and DRP must be updated to accommodate these changes.

Test Controls

17.50 Test controls, often a part of the change control mechanisms, aim to maintain data integrity and confidentiality. For instance, data sanitisation processes disguise sensitive information in test databases.

Operational controls

17.51 According to NIST (2013), operational controls are mechanisms implemented by the organisation's staff or outsourced to third parties. They address the daily functioning of security systems and can be crucial in responding to real-time challenges.

17.52 The multifaceted nature of these controls signifies the importance of a layered approach, often called 'defence-in-depth', which can provide a robust security posture for organisations, especially those handling sensitive financial data or operating under stringent regulatory requirements.

Asset Discovery

17.53 With the surge in cloud-based solutions, virtualisation technologies, and the widespread adoption of Bring Your Own Device (BYOD) policies, organisations now operate more complex and diversified IT landscapes than ever before. This complexity has given rise to new layers of information security risk, making asset management a difficult but critical task. Unmapped devices and services increase an organisation's vulnerability, providing potential entry points for cyber-attacks. Asset discovery tools are now essential for gaining comprehensive visibility into network infrastructure.

Asset Visibility Strategies

17.54 Organisations must have a comprehensive understanding of all their assets to enhance cybersecurity resilience. This includes not only hardware and software but also services and data streams that are critical to business processes. An effective asset inventory system should document detailed information on each asset, including its physical location, backup protocols, and ownership. Policies for regular updates, asset disposal, and new hardware and software onboarding should augment this.

Asset Classifications

17.55 Assets in an organisation can be broadly classified into hardware, software, information (both tangible and intangible), human resources, services, and systems. While the focus here is primarily on information assets, it's essential to recognise that these categories are interdependent and collectively contribute to an organisation's overall information security posture. Effective asset management helps streamline stakeholder access and pre-emptively identify unauthorised or insecure configurations. Moreover, it provides a framework for safeguarding intangible assets like reputation, which executive teams should quantify and consider in data risk assessments.

Automated Asset Management

17.56 Among the most effective strategies for asset management is the deployment of automated solutions. Such platforms offer real-time data about devices connected to the network, including their configurations, maintenance status, and the data they can access. Automation also allows for a more detailed view of remote devices. Organisations can leverage dynamic host tracking and other advanced methods to refine asset visibility and data classification processes further. This granular insight aids in tagging and identifying assets across multiple environments – cloud, on-premises, or hybrid – based on technical specifications, ownership, and geographical location.

Data Loss Prevention (DLP)

17.57 Data Loss Prevention (DLP) is a critical mechanism for organisations to combat the challenges associated with data loss. Implementing a robust DLP strategy is essential, backed by the appropriate technology infrastructure. While the practice of data classification can be intricate, it remains a cornerstone for the effectiveness of DLP solutions. Data and assets must be meticulously categorised based on their level of sensitivity, facilitating quick identification and pre-emptive action against potential data loss events. Adding these confidentiality labels within documents simplifies the search for lost or misplaced data and immediately informs users about the permitted activities concerning the document they are handling. The consequences of data loss can have devastating impacts, such as tarnishing an organisation's brand and eroding its reputation. Hence, a comprehensive solution continuously monitoring and enforcing data security across all communication channels is indispensable for upholding an organisation's policy integrity. So, what exactly does DLP entail?

A Definition of Data Loss Prevention (DLP)

17.58 Data Loss Prevention (DLP) refers to policies, procedures, and tools designed to protect sensitive data from unauthorised access, misuse, or unintended dissemination. At its core, DLP aims to maintain the confidentiality of private and sensitive information. DLP solutions commonly leverage data classification schemes to safeguard critical and confidential data. These tools act as gatekeepers, preventing users from inadvertently or maliciously sharing information with unauthorised parties, thereby mitigating organisational risk. Additionally, DLP technologies monitor data traffic within an organisation's network, enabling real-time surveillance and governance over data flow and endpoint activities.

Why adopt Data Loss Prevention Software

17.59 Adopting Data Loss Prevention (DLP) software within organisations is motivated by various factors, but regulatory compliance and legal ramifications are often at the forefront. Stringent data protection laws levy heavy fines for data breaches, making compliance a financial imperative. Equally critical is the internal threat landscape: employees, partners, and contractors continuously interact with sensitive data, creating a minefield of potential vulnerabilities. Moreover, the threat posed by malicious or disgruntled insiders who intentionally seek to undermine security measures is natural and elusive to combat. Email communication remains a significant conduit for data loss and should be a focal point of any DLP strategy.

17.60 DLP solutions provide a multifaceted approach to safeguarding sensitive data, whether in use, transit or at rest. 'In-use' refers to actively processed data, a state in which it is highly vulnerable to insecure endpoints and unauthorised data routes. The absence of robust data classification protocols can result in accidental data leaks. 'In-transit' data, which moves across network points during transactions, poses particular security challenges. Mitigating the risks of transferring data beyond organisational boundaries necessitates a comprehensive understanding of the data journey, from authentication to authorisation. Finally, 'data at rest' is stored in various repositories like servers, backup tapes, and portable devices. Here, encryption serves as a critical defence mechanism. Encryption tools must be rigorously evaluated for relevance, effectiveness, and timeliness. While DLP is a robust set of preventive controls, particularly against insider threats, it is not a stand-alone solution. Additional security controls must complement it for a holistic security posture.

Example (The Importance of Email in Data Loss Prevention)

17.61 Email is a significant conduit for transmitting sensitive and confidential information within organisations. Despite its pivotal role in business communications, email is frequently weak due to employee non-compliance with organisational policies for handling sensitive data. Organisations must implement a robust Data Loss Prevention (DLP) solution to address this vulnerability. An effective DLP tool must secure all classified data and manage associated risks with minimal impact on user productivity.

Conclusion and Future Outlook

17.62 In this chapter, we've delved into the multifaceted domain of data management and security, emphasising the critical role of data classification. We've also examined essential control measures such as Data Loss Prevention (DLP) and asset discovery. Business Continuity Planning (BCP), Business Impact Analysis (BIA), and disaster recovery were scrutinised, showcasing their indispensability in the grand scheme of data security. The growing interconnectivity of today's corporate landscape, spurred by technological advancements, presents opportunities and challenges. On one hand, it unlocks unprecedented avenues for productivity and efficiency. On the other, it introduces complex risks, especially concerning data assets' integrity, confidentiality, and availability. Expanding regulatory frameworks, such as the EU's General Data Protection Regulation (GDPR), have only intensified these challenges, extending their reach beyond regional borders.

17.63 Any organisation interacting with EU citizens' data must now adhere to stringent data protection standards, irrespective of their geographical location. Moreover, the competitive landscape has evolved, amplifying the need for robust data security measures. Information is not just an operational asset but a competitive one. Competitors are increasingly looking to leverage data for market insights, thereby making the security of such data not just a compliance requirement but a strategic imperative. Thus, organisations find themselves at a crossroads. The urgency to protect and adequately classify data assets has never been more crucial. As the stakes continue to rise, with mounting legal obligations and the intensified competitive environment, a holistic approach to data security is not just advisable – it's essential. The road ahead requires ongoing vigilance, investment in cutting-edge technologies, and a proactive cybersecurity posture. Data management and security parameters will continue to evolve, and organisations must be prepared to adapt, reassess, and optimise their strategies accordingly. This is about risk avoidance and securing a competitive advantage in a digitally interconnected world.

CHAPTER 18

LIABILITY FOLLOWING A DATA BREACH

Mark Deem and Adelaide Lopez

LIABILITY ISSUES FOLLOWING A CYBER-ATTACK

18.01 Cyber-attacks are not born equal. Indeed, no two cyber-attacks are the same: whether taken from the point of view of the damage suffered by the threat victim or the motivation of the threat actor,[1] each attack will possess unique qualities. The cyber-attack will impact different stakeholders in different ways and, accordingly, any consideration of legal liability and what action might be taken necessarily requires an appraisal of the ultimate aims of the party suffering loss, as to what represents a genuinely appropriate outcome.

18.02 Resulting claims might be brought by and/or against an enterprise[2] which has been impacted by an attack and experiencing losses. As a putative claimant, the enterprise might seek to bring action against the threat actor, whether an employee, contractor, partner, joint venturer or other third party, with the aim of achieving recompense for the losses it has suffered. As a putative defendant, the enterprise might be vulnerable to claims based upon breach of contract for its failure to meet its agreed commitments in respect of data or information security, or in negligence for its failure to patch, fix or otherwise update and/or secure its network systems to establish and maintain appropriate resilience.

18.03 Claims might be brought by data subjects for any violation of the integrity of their data, whether against the party controlling, processing or targeting their data asset and whether on a group basis, or by way of a representative action.

18.04 Third parties to the actual attack might also seek to assert claims for losses suffered, not necessarily as a direct result of the attack, but as a result of the wider manner in which the targeted individual or enterprise has been impacted by the cyber-attack – this is especially true, for example, where the impact and effects of an attack are experienced at other points of supply chain.

18.05 Further satellite claims might be considered necessary by affected parties in an attempt to secure recovery of data assets; to prevent use of those data

1 The terms 'threat actor', 'threat vector' and 'threat victim' refer to the perpetrator, the particular type of cyber-attack and the party who suffers loss, respectively.

2 The term 'enterprise' is used deliberately to cover all forms and sizes of business or organisation, which might experience a cyber-attack.

assets in a manner inconsistent with the interests of its rightful owner(s); or to seek further information which could ultimately lead to the proper identification of those responsible for the cyber-attack.

18.06 Defences to any liability will focus on the precise contractual obligation which is alleged to have been breached; the basis upon which it is alleged that a duty has been imposed; or the factual basis upon which it is said that the alleged threat actor is responsible.

18.07 For those enterprises against whom regulatory action has been taken in respect of a cyber-attack, claims may be asserted to attack the nature and imposition of any enforcement action or penalty, as well as seeking to challenge the basis upon which the original regulatory decision was taken.

18.08 In framing an appropriate legal response for each individual cyber-attack, questions of civil and criminal law will necessarily arise; and the involvement of independent regulators cannot be ignored. In short, we are compelled to consider proper redress for significant losses, involving myriad stakeholders, all set in a rich, liability landscape.

THE LIABILITY LANDSCAPE

18.09 The liability landscape emerges from the 'perfect storm', which is created by three interdependent factors: specifically, significant, rapid technological advancement; the broad spectrum of threat actors; and the ever-increasing sophistication of the threat vectors themselves. These have all evolved in recent years and, when operating in combination, create significant potential liability.

Technology

18.10 From the technology perspective, the particular trends and behaviours which feed directly into the question of liability are the heightened data sharing by – and greater personalisation of services for – an increasingly peripatetic workforce. Whether by accident or design, the convergence of our personal and professional lives from a technology perspective has resulted in data subjects entrusting and enterprises accepting the custody and control of huge volumes of data assets, which previously would either not have existed or would have been more closely guarded by the data subject. This dramatically increases the exposure and potential liability of the enterprise to data subjects.

Developments in recent years have only compounded this phenomenon, making social engineering even easier. Already changing working patterns were accelerated both during and post the Covid-19 pandemic impacting everything from technology developments to transport patterns. Meanwhile, the introduction of generative AI into the fabric of everyday services has made new and less transparent use of personal data more prevalent: highlighting the increasing appetite for data by technology more generally.

Threat Actors

18.11 The class of threat actors engaging in cyber-attacks has become broader and now encompasses an entire spectrum ranging from the poorly-resourced (but highly motivated) 'script kiddies', through to the incredibly well-resourced (and highly, politically motivated) 'State actors'.[3]

18.12 The full spectrum of threat actors is explored elsewhere in this book, but from a liability perspective the spectrum is best defined by – and can only properly be understood by reference to – the motivation of each particular actor. For the script kiddies, the motivation is invariably the kudos and bragging rights accompanying the successful deployment of any threat vector; for the 'hacktivists', the aim is usually media attention for the attack and the concomitant public recognition of its wider cause; for the criminals, the motivation is ordinarily one of a personal, often financial, gain; for those engaging in commercial espionage, the motivation generally is the attainment of a valuable, competitive advantage; and for State actors, the motivation is frequently one of seeking to gain political advantage. A particularly significant addition to the spectrum in recent years has been the emergence of the insider threat, the internal actor whose motivation may be deeply personal (whether personal gain or revenge) or whose actions might be classified as human error or simple carelessness.[4]

18.13 Whilst motivation will not be determinative of any liability, it is invariably a useful indicator when seeking to attribute threat vectors to potential actors, the pre-cursor to any finding of liability.

Evolution of Threats

18.14 In recent years, we have also experienced an evolution in the nature of the threat vectors themselves: greater sophistication is now evident in all forms of phishing, spear-phishing and whaling attacks through social engineering; the planting of malware on network systems; and the targeted threats to Supervisory Control and Data Acquisition (SCADA) systems and industrial controls. This evolution has been accompanied by the increased potency of such threats, which now have an ability to result in a category 1 attack, capable of devastating the

3 The term 'state actor' as used here encompasses those acting directly or indirectly on behalf of a governmental body, whether with appropriate authorisation or not. Issues concerning the legal implications of cyber-attacks by 'state actors' and liability as a matter of public international law, which could form the basis of a study in and of itself, is identified here for completeness only.

4 The 2017 US State of Cybercrime Survey (conducted by Carnegie Mellon University) found that 20% of cybercrime is suspected or known to be caused by insiders; 30% of respondents thought that damage caused by insider attacks was more severe than damage from outsider attacks. (See 7th edn of Carnegie Mellon's *Common Sense Guide to Mitigating Insider Threats* (2022)).

financial services sector and energy supplies.[5] This goes to the heart of the potential liability and damage suffered as a result of an attack.

How threat vectors manifest themselves as a potential liability

18.15 In considering what legal and/or regulatory liability might arise from this ever-evolving landscape, it is helpful to group threat vectors into four distinct categories.

1. First, those attacks which seek to compromise the network security of an enterprise, with the ultimate aim of a threat actor gaining unauthorised access to infect the network with malware or to otherwise enable the exfiltration or deletion of data assets. The classic example here is one of phishing or hacking, where known or perceived vulnerabilities are exploited, possibly with the assistance of 'innocent' players, who are encouraged to open infected, embedded items or clicking on hyperlinks which route the innocent user into hostile environments.

   As well as the threat actor being liable, the focus of any enquiry into liability for other stakeholders will be on the extent to which the data asset has been compromised; the degree to which contractual commitments to the data subject or supply chain have been achieved; the adequacy of security implemented by the enterprise; whether all reasonable steps have been taken by the enterprise to update, fix and patch the network; and the role of the 'innocent' player in facilitating the success of the threat vector.

2. Secondly, those attacks which seek to cause business disruption, but which do not necessarily compromise the integrity of the data or network. This is exemplified by the distributed denial of service attack (DDoS), where multiple, compromised computer systems are used to target a website, server or other network resource, with a view to slowing down or preventing legitimate connection requests and denying access to users. Ransomware may also fall into this category, in circumstances where access to the network or data assets is prevented unless a payment – usually in a form of cryptocurrency to a hard-coded wallet – is made in a timely manner.

   In this scenario, the existence of liability beyond the threat actor is unlikely to arise from any compromise to the data or adequacy of security, but from the reputational, financial and commercial disruption to an enterprise and its ability to meet its own, wider contractual commitments.

3. Thirdly, where data has been captured in an unsecure state, possibly in transit, outside of the enterprise's network. Examples of this scenario would

5 A C1 attack is classified by the National Cyber Security Centre as a 'national cyber emergency' – an attack which causes essential services or affects UK national security, leading to severe economic or social consequences or to loss of life. The NCSC established a framework in 2018 which has six levels of severity and is to be applied uniformly across all sectors including government, critical national infrastructure, charities, universities, schools, as well as small businesses and individuals.

be the unencrypted laptop or media storage device which has fallen into the hands of a third party; the interception of unencrypted communications made through unsecure channels (for example on open, public Wifi); or data being placed in unsecure locations.

Again, liability beyond that of the threat actor will depend upon the extent to which the data subject or enterprise is responsible for allowing the situation to arise – were they in some way complicit, negligent or otherwise facilitated the attack?

4. Finally, there is the scenario where the enterprise is not the intended target of the threat actor, but has been impacted by a threat vector introduced into the supply chain, possibly even behind the firewall of a given enterprise.

   In addition to the liability considerations set out in the other scenarios (recognising that the threat actor may be seen as less culpable for any loss), the focus of any liability enquiry will necessarily extend to the commercial relationships which exist within the wider supply chain.

Civil Liability

18.16 The liability landscape is complex and has the potential to give rise to competing or alternative civil claims, depending upon the particular threat vector and the nature and terms of relief sought. From a practical point of view, the viability of any litigation strategy will depend to a considerable extent on whether a given cyber-attack can be *attributed* to the actions of an identifiable threat actor, over whom *jurisdiction* can be asserted and against whom a judgment can be *enforced*. None of these factors should be assumed and frequently they will represent the biggest obstacles to achieving a successful outcome.

18.17 The main civil causes of action which may follow a cyber-attack are set out below. Rather than provide comprehensive and exhaustive discussion of all aspects of these particular civil actions, the commentary below identifies certain of the particular features relevant to establishing each form of civil liability, with a particular focus on their potential use in response to a cyber-attack.

UK General Data Protection Regulation

18.18 For those cyber-attacks, which have resulted in the compromise of the integrity of data and/or a violation of network security, the UK General Data Protection Regulation (as retained in UK law from EU GDPR by virtue of section 3 of the European Union (Withdrawal) Act 2018 and as amended by Schedule 1 of the Data Protection, Privacy and Electronic Communications (Amendments Etc) (EU Exit) Regulations 2019 (SI 2019/419)) (UK GDPR) creates a number of areas of potential liability for an enterprise.

18.19 For present purposes, it is noted that liability is most likely to derive from a breach of the integrity and confidentiality principle of the UK GDPR, which mandates that 'personal data must be processed in a manner that ensures appropriate security of the personal data, including protection against unauthorised or unlawful processing and accidental loss, destruction or damage, by using appropriate technical or organisational measures'.

18.20 Breach of this integrity and confidentiality principle of processing could result in either regulatory action involving the data supervisory authority (which, in the UK is the Information Commissioner's Office (ICO)) or civil proceedings.

Regulatory Action

18.21 Regulatory action may result either from an investigation by the ICO (whether acting of its own volition or in response to a complaint from a data subject) or following formal notification of a breach under the UK GDPR by a data controller or processor.

18.22 Implementation of the GDPR brought with it significant fines and penalties which can be imposed by supervisory authorities. Whilst breach of the basic processing principles (of which the integrity and confidentiality principle is the most relevant in relation to a cyber-attack) could lead to fines of the higher of up to £17.5 million or 4% of annual worldwide turnover of the preceding year for the enterprise's group, it should also be noted that the ICO enjoys wide investigative and corrective powers, including the power to undertake audits on-site and issue public warnings, reprimands and orders requiring certain, specific remediation activities.[6]

18.23 These sanctions can be imposed alone, or in combination with fines and, although nothing in the UK GDPR requires the ICO to impose a fine, the authority remains under a duty to ensure that any sanctions imposed are effective, proportionate and dissuasive.[7]

18.24 Any data subject or enterprise dissatisfied with the decision or action of the ICO is permitted to challenge in court the exercise of certain of its powers, including the nature of any penalty fine issued or for failing to make a decision.[8]

18.25 In practice, between December 2021 and January 2024 the ICO issued 55 monetary penalties, 68 reprimands and 44 enforcement notices. In the face of

6 Art 58, UK GDPR.
7 Art 83(1), UK GDPR.
8 Art 78, UK GDPR – although note that this does not extend to measures taken by supervisory authorities, which are not legally binding, such as opinions or advice.

significant cyber-attacks the ICO has responded robustly issuing fines in some cases in the millions and tens of millions of pounds.[9]

Follow-on civil claims

18.26 For the data subject, the UK GDPR provides a number of rights against enterprises, whether performing the role of data controllers or processors.

18.27 In addition to an ability to lodge a complaint with the ICO, where a data subject's asset has been compromised in the course of a cyber-attack and not processed in a compliant manner,[10] any data subject who has suffered damage as a result of such a breach has a statutory right to receive compensation from the data controller/processor. This damage can be of either a material or non-material nature[11] – ensuring the right of data subjects to be able to bring a compensation complaint for distress and hurt feelings, should they be unable to prove financial loss.[12]

18.28 Data subjects can initiate claims on their own; be part of a group action; or can mandate representative bodies to exercise rights on their behalf. This represents a marked change from the previous regime, which existed prior to the GDPR, where group and representative actions were both problematic to set up (predominantly as a result of the costs-shifting mechanism in English litigation) and therefore seldom occurred in practice.[13]

18.29 The introduction of representative actions allows a representative body (defined as a not-for-profit organisation, active in the field of data protection and which has statutory objectives which are in the public interest) to lodge a complaint and seek judicial remedies against a decision of a data supervisory authority or against data controllers/processors. These rights can be exercised either on behalf of a data subject or independent of any such mandate.

9 In 2018 Ticketmaster was fined £1.25 million for failing to protect its customers' data from an attack on a chatbot installed on the company's online payments page which affected 9.4 million customers and was not identified and addressed for nine weeks. In 2020 British Airways was fined £20 million (the highest fine as of the date of writing, although reduced from the original fine of £183 million) for a cyber-attack which accessed the personal data of over 400,000 customers and staff, including credit card and CVV numbers. The same year, Marriott International was fined £18.4 million for failing to secure the details of 339 million guest records from a 2014 attack. Like British Airways, the Marriott fine was reduced from the £99 million fine originally issued.

10 Art 77, UK GDPR.

11 Art 82(1), UK GDPR.

12 This places on a statutory footing the position recognised in *Vidal Hall v Google* [2015] EWCA Civ 311.

13 Indeed, under the Data Protection Act 1998 (**DPA 1998**), one of the only reported examples of an opt in group action in response to a data breach was *Various Claimants v WM Morrisons Supermarket PLC* [2017] EWHC 3113 (QB).

18.30 While, in theory, this option of bringing or funding group data breach claims exists, its efficacy has been tested. Claimants wishing to bring a representative action must clear high hurdles, including showing that damage has been suffered for loss of control of personal data by all members of the class on a lowest common denominator basis;[14] or, their claims must be brought separately.[15] This presents difficult practical considerations in cases where each data subject has suffered varying levels of distress. The class taken as a whole will have to surpass the *de minimis* threshold for mere loss of control damages.[16]

18.31 Given the current practical limitations faced by groups attempting to bring representative actions, some claimant classes have sought Group Litigation Orders (**GLO**) instead, but similarly, this has faced challenges when trying to establish that the claimants have suffered compensable harm.[17] Under this standard, applying for a GLO risks whittling down the size of the claimant group. In *Bennet v Equifax Ltd* the application for the GLO was made on behalf of 100,000 potential claimants; although at the time of writing it remains to be seen how many will meet that standard if the GLO is pursued further.

18.32 Separately, Article 80 of the UK GDPR does allow data subjects to nominate a 'not for profit body, organisation or association' whose objectives 'are in the public interest and is active in the field of the protection of data subjects' rights and freedoms' to exercise data subjects' rights, including by way of representation before the courts. However, should such action be unsuccessful, due to the practical challenges outlined above, data subjects will only be left with the Article 80(2) right to complain to the ICO. Although such an action could lead to a fine of the controller, it would not provide compensation for the data subject(s) for any harm suffered.

18.33 In addition to having primary liability for a breach of a processing principle under the UK GDPR, an enterprise could potentially have vicarious

14 See *Lloyd v Google LLC* [2021] UKSC 50. In that case the Supreme Court did emphasise that the claim was founded 'solely' in section 13 of the DPA 1998, which explicitly stipulates that 'damage' must be suffered, therefore leaving open the possibility of a similar claim being brought under the UK GDPR and DPA 2018.

15 Under CPR 19.8(1) (previously CPR 19.6) claimants must show they have the 'same interest' in the claim. If a representative action were proceeding on an opt out basis, it would be both administratively and practically difficult to ascertain if all claimants had the same losses. The claim in *Lloyd v Google* was brought under this procedure, but the Supreme Court found that the claim would be unable to show: (1) material damage (distinct from the unlawful processing) suffered; and (2) that unlawful processing relating to a given individual actually occurred.

16 The same issue has been tried by the CJEU in the case of *UI v Osterreichische Post AG* Case C-300/21 [2022]. There the Court held that minimum thresholds for damages suffered due to loss of control of data are not unlawful under the GDPR.

17 See *Bennett and Ors v Equifax Ltd* [2022] EWHC 1487. There the claimants were unsuccessful in seeking a GLO, although the Senior Master deferred his reasons for doing so to the CMC, by which point the claimants had changed tact and sought a preliminary issue trial instead.

liability for breaches committed by its own employees, even where there is no finding of primary liability.[18]

Breach notification

18.34 In addition to regulatory activity and civil proceedings under the UK GDPR, there is the mandatory requirement to notify data breaches to the ICO and affected individuals.

18.35 Although this does not amount to a cause of action, the costs of notification are not insignificant. Failure to comply with the mandated regime concerning data breach notification can lead to fines of the higher of up to €10 million or 2% of annual worldwide turnover of the preceding year for the enterprise's group. These fines can be imposed on both the data controller and data processor and, as noted above, could trigger fines for a breach of the processing principles and a fine of €20 million or 4% of annual worldwide turnover.

Breach of confidence

18.36 Cyber-attacks, which involve the compromise of the integrity of data and/or the violation of network security might also give rise to an equitable claim for breach of confidence. Although breach of confidence may be based upon an express or implied contractual or fiduciary obligation – and this may well be the case in the event of a cyber-attack of an enterprise legitimately in possession of confidential and/or personal data – the existence of such an obligation is not strictly required.

18.37 The three constituent elements of a breach of confidence require that the information must have 'the necessary quality of confidence about it'; it must be 'imparted in circumstances which import an obligation of confidence'; and there must be 'unauthorised use of that information to the detriment of the party communicating it'.[19]

18.38 These will need to be considered against the particular facts of a cyber-attack and the means by which a threat vector is deployed by a given threat actor,

18 See *Various Claimants v WM Morrisons Supermarket* PLC [2017] EWHC 3113 (QB), where a supermarket employee stole the personal data of almost 100,000 employees, which he then uploaded to a file sharing resulting in over 5,000 claims against the supermarket chain. The Court of Appeal held that there was a sufficiently close connection between the actions of the employee and his employment for the supermarket to be found vicariously liable. However, the Supreme Court held that there was not a '*close* connection' between the actions leading to the breach and the remit of the employee's role in that case, noting that the employee's motive was relevant. While this is useful for employers, its utility should not be overstated, as the case was determined under DPA 1998 and the court noted in obiter that the DPA 2018 does not exclude vicarious liability.

19 See *Coco v AN Clark (Engineers) Limited* [1968] FSR 415, as reaffirmed by the House of Lords in *Douglas & Others v Hello! Limited & Others* [2007] 2 WLR 920.

prior to commencing any claim. For present purposes, however, the following parties could be considered putative defendants in any breach of confidence claim:

- a party who is directly entrusted with confidential data – for example by virtue of an employment relationship or other commercial contract;
- a party who has come into possession of confidential information, even if this has been obtained improperly – for example, a data breach which arises as a result of a lost unencrypted mass storage device;[20]
- a party who, serendipitously or by accident, has come into possession of information known to be confidential – for example, a data breach which arises from the purchase of second-hand hardware, which has not been successfully wiped;[21] and, by extension
- a party who intentionally obtains information in unauthorised circumstances, where it is known that a reasonable expectation of confidentiality exists – for example, the threat actor.[22]

18.39 Actions for breach of confidence can give rise either to a claim in equity for damages (which are entirely discretionary in nature), or by way of injunctive relief to restrain further use of the data asset.

Misuse of private information

18.40 Closely aligned to breach of confidence, although now considered to be a tort in its own right, is the misuse of private information[23] – which had its origins as a claim for breach of confidence where an expectation of privacy existed. For those claimants seeking a group action, this cause of action could proceed on an opt-in basis, as compared to GLOs which operate on an opt-out basis. In the instance that there are too many data subjects for this to be a practical means to

20 Following *Duchess of Argyll v Duke of Argyll* [1967] Ch 302.

21 See Lord Goff *AG v Guardian Newspapers (No.2)* [1990] Ch 302: '…it is well settled that a duty of confidence may arise in equity independently of such cases; and I have expressed the circumstances in which the duty arises in broad terms, not merely to embrace those cases where a third party receives information from a person who is under a duty of confidence in respect of it, knowing that it has been disclosed by that person to him in breach of his duty of confidence, but also to include certain situations, beloved of law teachers – where an obviously confidential document is wafted by an electric fan out of a window into a crowded street, or when an obviously confidential document, such as a private diary, is dropped in a public place, and is then picked up by a passer-by.'

22 See *Imerman v Tchenguiz & Others* [2011] 2 WLR 592. It is submitted that this case is also good authority, irrespective of whether the party in possession of the data has no intention to use it.

23 See Tugendhat J in *Judith Vidal-Hall & Others v Google Inc* [2014] EWHC 13.

bring a claim, the group of data subjects may choose to bring the most egregious claim first in an attempt to set a precedent for the other claimants to follow suit.[24]

18.41 In order to establish such a claim the court is required to consider two, distinct issues: first, whether the information can properly be said to be 'private', applying the reasonable expectation of privacy test – specifically, what would a reasonable person of ordinary sensibilities feel if placed in the same position as the claimant;[25] and, secondly, whether in all the circumstances, the claimant's privacy interest under Article 8 of the European Convention on Human Rights, should properly yield to the freedom of expression conferred by Article 10.

18.42 Whilst it is by no means certain that a claim for misuse of private information could be sustained in the event of a cyber-attack compromising the integrity of a data subject's assets (much will depend upon the precise fact pattern), there is undoubtedly a prevailing trend for this tort to be pleaded as an alternative head of claim and alongside any action for breach of confidence, as it opens up the potentially more lucrative tortious measure of damages – as opposed to the entirely discretionary damages for breach of confidence. It additionally remains to be seen, whether or not such actions in misuse of private information can sustain a group action by data subjects following a cyber-security incident.[26]

Contractual claims

18.43 A cyber-attack could also give rise to liability for a party who has undertaken a contractual obligation in respect of either a data asset or network infrastructure which has been compromised. The extent of the liability will be defined by the precise nature of the promise, but contractual liability may exist for an enterprise in many circumstances, including where it has suffered a cyber-attack (including a DDoS or business impairment attack) and is unable to deliver on promised safe custody of data; where it is unable to deliver on promised services; and/or where a member of a supply chain has been exposed as a result of a failure to implement agreed security measures.

24 See, for example *Lawrence & Ors v Associated Newspapers Ltd* [2023] EWHC 2789 in which Baroness Lawrence along with six other claimants, including the Duke of Sussex and Elton John, brought a representative action for misuse of private information against the publisher of The Daily Mail, The Mail on Sunday and MailOnline, which they allege used unlawful methods to acquire their personal and confidential information. Associated Newspapers made a preliminary application for strike out of the claims for *inter alia* being out of time. The court held that the claimants had a real prospect of success with respect to limitations and allowed the claim to proceed.

25 See Lord Hope in *Naomi Campbell v MGN Limited* [2004] 2 AC 457.

26 In *Prismall v Google UK Ltd & Ors* [2023] EWHC 1169 the High Court summarily dismissed a representative claim for misuse of private information brought against Google's AI arm, Deepmind Technologies on behalf of 1.6 million patients whose data was transferred to Google by the Royal Free Hospital in 2015. There the judge held that without being able to establish that every member of the class had a reasonable expectation of privacy the claim was bound to fail. At the time of writing the case awaits permission to appeal to the Court of Appeal.

18.44 There might also be contractual liability for an enterprise supplying security measures to a compromised threat victim, where promised service levels or protections have not been achieved.

Further tortious claims

18.45 A cyber-attack has the potential to create further tortious liability in a number of ways:

1. In addition to any breach of the UK GDPR for failure to implement appropriate technical measures, liability could arise in tort for the negligence of an enterprise for a failure to establish and maintain a degree of resilience in the security of a network. Although a sufficiently proximate relationship between the enterprise and the data subject would need to be established, in order that a duty of care be imposed, there is no conceptual reason why such a duty could not arise. In these circumstances, an enterprise may be negligent by, for example, failing to download and install security patches in a timely manner.
2. Equally, tortious liability could arise for an enterprise making representations about the resilience of its systems or security of data, in reliance upon which a data asset is entrusted to the enterprise and subsequently compromised in the course of a cyber-attack.
3. The tort of trespass applies to all unauthorised incursions onto property. This can extend to actual, unauthorised access to computer networks.[27]
4. The tort of unlawful interference with goods has been established in relation to the unauthorised deletion of computer files and removal of back-up files.[28]

NIS ('Cybersecurity') Directive

18.46 For those enterprises identified as either operators of essential services (OES) or digital service providers (by virtue of providing online marketplaces, online search engines or cloud computing) for the purposes of the Network and Information Securities Directive,[29] which was transposed into English law by virtue of Network and Information Systems Regulations 2018 (2018 No 506), there is the potential for further civil liability in respect of the same cyber-attack

27 A tort of cyber trespass is not recognised in the UK, unlike the US.

28 Approved in principle by Chadwick LJ in *Taylor v Rive Droit Music Limited* [2005] EWCA Civ 1300.

29 Dir (EU) 2016/1148 of the European Parliament and of the Council of 6 July 2016 concerning measures for a high common level of security of network and information systems across the Union. The NIS 2 Directive (Dir (EU) 2022/2555) came into force in 2023, expanding the scope of the rules to new sectors and entities. Having been enacted post-Brexit, however, the relevant framework for the UK remains the NIS Regulations 2018.

in circumstances where the attack has occurred as a result of a failure to meet mandated security resilience levels.

18.47 Maximum fines issued by the ICO under the NIS Directive are up to £17.5 million and can be imposed *in addition* to any fines levied by the data supervisory authority under the UK GDPR for the same cyber-attack.

Criminal Liability

18.48 The criminality of any cyber-attack is addressed in **Chapter 21**. For present purposes, however, it is noted that criminal law represents a significant way for redress against the threat actors to be achieved, although it will not result in compensation for losses.

18.49 Broadly, the main criminal offences are found in the Computer Misuse Act 1990 and the Criminal Damage Act 1971. (Notably both acts received Royal Assent a considerable time before the anatomy of a modern cyber-attack had been witnessed, let alone understood. Accordingly, it is often noted that the offences could be triggered for threat vectors which might not ordinarily be instantly recognised as cyber-attacks.)

18.50 Offences have been created and maintained by the DPA 2018 and the Investigatory Powers Act 2016 (which came into force in June 2018) (**IAP 2016**). In particular, it is an offence to knowingly or recklessly obtain, disclose or procure the disclosure of personal data, without the consent of the data controller; and also an offence to sell, or offer to sell, illegally obtained personal data. This offence, which is extended under the UK GDPR to include the retention of personal data, means that a threat actor who is now merely in receipt of data will commit an offence by failing to delete or destroy that data. The IAP 2016 makes it an offence to intentionally intercept a communication without lawful authority, in the course of its transmission by means of a public or private telecommunication system or a public postal service.

Interim Relief & Remedies

18.51 Whilst an appreciation of potential liability in the event of a cyber-attack is undoubtedly important, for impacted data subjects or enterprises securing appropriate relief or remedies for its losses will be of paramount importance.

Interim Relief

18.52 For data subjects or enterprises who have lost custody or exclusive control of confidential or personal data as a result of a cyber-attack, damages at trial over a defendant may not in and of itself provide adequate relief. Indeed, damages are seldom seen as an adequate remedy in circumstances where the confidentiality of data is in issue in an injunction application and the balance of convenience test, which is required under the relevant *American Cyanamid* guidelines[30] will generally favour restraining the further use of the data assets.

18.53 For a data subject and an enterprise victim, a number of different interim orders are potentially available, depending upon the facts of the precise cyber-attack, including:

i) a detention, custody or preservation order in order to secure and maintain the 'integrity' of compromised data, pending trial – Civil Procedure Rule (CPR) rule 25.1(1)(c);

ii) a search order – in circumstances where the threat actor has been identified and the data assets are known to reside or likely to reside on certain premises – CPR rule 25.1(1)(h);

iii) a mandatory injunction requiring information concerning the location of the confidential or personal data assets;

iv) a delivery-up order in respect of the confidential information, requiring return or destruction of information; and

v) an injunction restraining a further breach of confidence.

Persons unknown

18.54 Unfortunately, the reality remains that in many cyber-attacks, a threat victim may not know the threat actor and may not be able to know against whom an application for interim relief should properly be brought. This is particularly true in the case of anonymous hackers; DDoS attacks; and ransomware cases.[31]

18.55 Even if a traditional *Norwich Pharmacal* order[32] might conceptually be possible against banks or internet service providers, many threat actors will have successfully masked their digital footprint and, in the case of ransomware, the use of cryptocurrencies and hard-coded digital wallets will generally mean this is a less than fruitful exercise.

18.56 The English courts, however are rapidly developing jurisprudence to enable interim relief to be sought against 'persons unknown' and therefore obviate the prior need for *Norwich Pharmacal* relief to have been sought, as

30 These are the guidelines set out in the case of *American Cyanamid Co (No 1) v Ethicon Ltd* [1975] UKHL 1, which are used to establish whether an applicant has an adequate case for the granting of an interim injunction.

31 Jurisdictional issues will also frequently arise, where the English court may not feel it has the requisite in personam jurisdiction against a given threat actor.

32 An order requiring a respondent to disclose certain documents or information to the applicant. These orders, whose origins are in the case of *Norwich Pharmacal Company v Commissioners of Customs and Excise* [1974] AC 133, are commonly used to identify the proper defendant to an action or to obtain information in order to plead a claim.

affirmed by the Supreme Court.[33] The origins of this type of order can be traced to a case involving the unauthorised leak by a printing firm of early copies of the *Harry Potter & the Order of the Phoenix*, which were then being offered for sale to the mainstream press. Given that the description of the putative defendants was sufficiently certain, there was found to be no impediment to granting interim relief against unnamed defendants.[34]

18.57 This jurisdiction was confirmed in the context of an application for a worldwide freezing order, following a cyber-attack.[35] During the attack a number of unidentifiable individuals gained unauthorised access to the email account of a senior manager of the claimant company, enabling a number of significant payments to be made. Even though the threat actors were initially unknown at the time of making the order, the approach of the Court emphasised that care is needed in any application to ensure that those who fall within the order and those who do not fall within the order are sufficiently clear.

18.58 The court has even gone so far as to make a final third-party debt order for nearly £3 million against persons unknown in a cryptocurrency fraud claim. In that case, the applicants believed they had been victims of a cryptocurrency ICO fraud in that they were induced by persons unknown to transfer to them cryptocurrancy equivalent to over £500,000 each.[36]

Remedies

18.59 Where traditional remedies at full trial are sought, as noted above, success will very much depend upon the ability of a putative claimant successfully to attribute liability for the threat vector to a threat actor; to establish jurisdiction over the threat actor(s); and then, ultimately to seek enforcement of any judgment.

18.60 From a practical point of view, detailed consideration should be given at an early stage as to these three issues, as this will have a direct impact on which particular head of liability should be pursued.

33 See *Wolverhampton City Council & Ors v London Gypsies and Travellers & Ors* [2023] UKSC 47 where the UKSC confirmed courts' powers to grant final injunctions against persons unknown including, in that case, against unknown and unidentified persons (and 'newcomers') from forming unauthorised encampments on land owned by the local authority. There, the court noted that such injunctions could also be justified in the context of cyber-security breaches.

34 See *Bloomsbury Publishing Plc & Another v Newsgroup Newspapers Limited* [2003] EWHC 1205 (Ch). In this case it was decided that it was sufficiently clear a party would know if it properly was within the class of potential defendants, or not.

35 See HHJ Waksman QC in *CMOC v Person Unknown* [2017] EWHC 3599 (Comm). The case is also notable, in that it was one of the earlier cases to enable service of the order by an online cloud storage solution and via Facebook accounts. In that case, the claimant was ultimately successful in obtaining judgment against the defendants. See also *World Proteins KFT v Persons Unknown* [2019] EWHC 1146 (QB), in which the court agreed to continue an interim injunction against persons unknown arising out of an email fraud.

36 See *Ion Science Ltd v Persons Unknown* (unreported), 28 January 2022, (High Court).

18.61 Generally speaking, a threat victim can seek to recover by way of damages all the costs, losses and fines which have been caused by the threat actor's breach. Quantification and recoverability of losses is, however, very important and may present further difficulties, especially in relation to the loss of the value of data and potential loss of business. Accordingly, an early assessment should be taken as to all potential heads of loss and the extent to which they might properly be recoverable.

Insurance as a means of mitigation of liability

18.62 Given the very considerable costs which might flow directly or indirectly from a cyber-attack for enterprises of all sizes, as well as the oft-repeated refrain that we should treat cyber-attacks as a case of 'when and not if', the insurance industry has an important role to play in the mitigation of this risk.

18.63 Cyber-liability products in the London market have matured considerably over recent years. Cover can be provided on a first-party insurance and third-party basis. The purpose of any cover is to protect and reimburse the enterprise for the costs of dealing with the cyber-attack, rather than reimbursing an enterprise for the losses – for example stolen money – in the course of the attack.

18.64 First-party insurance will cover an enterprise's own data assets and can be obtained in relation to data recovery, business recovery and business interruption losses (the costs incurred to restore data and lost revenues); losses suffered as a result of reputational harm; and costs which might be incurred through cyber-extortion and ransomware.

18.65 Third-party cover will cover an enterprise's liability to meet costs as a result of data assets belonging to others and can be obtained in relation to security and privacy liability (where the enterprise might be sued by the data subject); breach response costs (the costs of notification, forensic investigation and offering credit monitoring services for impacted data subjects); regulatory defence costs (the legal costs of dealing with regulatory action against the enterprise); and multimedia liability (the costs of investigation, defence costs and civil damages from defamation, breach of copyright in electronic or print media).

18.66 Mandated breach notifications and significant fines under the UK GDPR have been a catalyst for many companies seeking to off-load potential risk for a cyber-attack through the use of insurance. Whilst the former head of loss is undoubtedly covered by breach response costs, care needs to be taken as cover may not extend to penalties: the rationale being that public policy generally prevents personal punishments being passed to other parties, where the punishment is for a party's own negligence or where it was at fault.[37]

37 See *Safeway Stores Limited & Ors v Twigger & Ors* [2010] EWHC 11 (Comm).

18.67 As with all forms of insurance, exclusions will apply to deny cover in certain circumstances (for example, war and terrorism). In cyber-liability insurance cover, it is worth noting that exclusions may try to limit the territorial reach of the policy and the policy may not cover physical damage caused to property caused by a cyber-attack.

CHAPTER 19

CRIMINAL LAW

Jill Lorimer and William Christopher[1]

INTRODUCTION

19.01 Cyber-crime is a term used to cover a range of criminal offences including what are termed 'cyber-dependant' as well as 'cyber-enabled' offences. Cyber-dependant offences are those in respect of which a computer is the target of the behaviour, such as hacking, theft of crypto-assets, the deliberate spreading of viruses and distributed denial of services attacks. Cyber-enabled offences, on the other hand, are those in respect of which a computer is merely the conduit by which the substantive offence is committed. These include the sending of malicious communications, online harassment or stalking, the publication or distribution of indecent or obscene material, data protection breaches and cyber-fraud.

19.02 This chapter explains how these types of conduct fit within the often archaic framework of English criminal law. It identifies the primary statutory provisions under which these offences are prosecuted, provides examples of reported cases and sets out the penalties which these offences carry. It goes on to briefly discuss the role of the civil courts in assisting victims of cyber-crime.

MISUSE OF COMPUTERS

19.03 The Computer Misuse Act 1990 ('the 1990 Act') was introduced primarily to criminalise computer hacking and hacking-related conduct which was not covered by earlier legislation and which was, as a result, virtually impossible to prosecute. The original Act created three main offences and has since been amended by the Police and Justice Act 2006 and the Serious Crime Act 2015 to revise the definitions of these offences, increase the available sentences and create two further offences.

19.04 While most offences of dishonesty, committed using computers, are prosecuted under the Fraud Act 2006, the 1990 Act, as amended, remains the principal statute under which hacking and other cyber-dependant offences will be prosecuted. However, the Online Safety Bill, once passed, will make a number of significant changes in this area, consolidating the existing law as well as

1 With special thanks to Phil Taylor for his assistance with the preparation of this chapter.

introducing a number of new offences relating to fraudulent internet advertising and unsolicited sexual communications.

Unauthorised access to computer material – section 1 offence

19.05 Section 1 of the 1990 Act makes it an offence to cause a computer to perform any function with intent to secure or enable access to any program or data held in a computer where such access is unauthorised and where the defendant knows at the time that the access is unauthorised. The offence is one which carries a maximum sentence of two years' imprisonment and/or a fine.

19.06 This section criminalises the basic offence of hacking: it would cover, for example, unauthorised access to a company's systems, or to another person's email or social media accounts. The key to the offence is unauthorised access: it covers any method of effecting such access, including where the password had been provided to the defendant but for a different purpose, or where permission to use it had been withdrawn or revoked.

19.07 Reported case law provides a number of examples of conduct capable of constituting hacking, including the accessing of another person's social media account by using the log-on details of the person controlling the account,[2] unauthorised use of a university's computer systems by a former student,[3] the accessing by a police officer of his force's intelligence system to carry out checks on individuals for personal purposes[4] and the accessing by a former employee of a company's system to terminate its servers by way of revenge.[5]

19.08 We tend to associate the hacking of a company's systems with the actions of a hostile external party. However, case law illustrates that the offence of hacking can equally be committed by those within the organisation: indeed, many of the prosecutions brought under section 1 concern access by employees, particularly public servants, to their employers' computer systems other than in accordance with the access which they have been granted. Their use of the system may have exceeded the use which has been authorised or it may have been for purposes other than those which had been authorised. It has been established that such access is capable of constituting the offence: authority to access a particular piece of data does not equate to authority to access other similar data in the absence of permission to do so.[6]

19.09 The offence does not necessarily require that one computer be used with intent to secure access to another; using a computer to gain unauthorised access to a program or data on the same computer could also constitute the offence.[7]

2 *R. v Crosskey* [2012] EWCA Crim 1645.
3 *Ellis v DPP (No.1)* [2001] EWHC Admin 362.
4 *R. v Nichols* [2012] EWCA Crim 2650.
5 *R v Needham* [2019] EWCA Crim 1541, 2019 WL 04345361.
6 *R. v Bow Street Magistrates Court Ex p. Allison (No.2)* [2000] 2 AC 216.
7 *Attorney General's Reference (No.1 of 1991)* [1993] QB 94.

Unauthorised access with intent to commit or facilitate commission of further offences – section 2 offence

19.10 The second offence under the 1990 Act consists of committing the basic unauthorised access offence but with the additional intent of committing, or facilitating the commission of, further offences, whether by the defendant himself or herself or a third party. The section 2 offence carries a maximum sentence of five years' imprisonment and/or a fine.

19.11 There is no definitive list of 'further offences' capable of founding the second limb of this offence but these are defined as being ones which carry a fixed sentence or a sentence of five years or more which, by definition, excludes minor offences. However, most frauds, however small in value, are prosecuted under the Fraud Act 2006, which carries a maximum sentence of ten years. Therefore unauthorised access with intent to commit even a minor fraud will potentially fall within this section.

19.12 Reported cases of prosecutions under this section are mostly fraud cases, including, for example, that of a bank employee who provided bank customers' details to associates who went on to attempt to commit fraud on those accounts[8]; and an individual who hacked the website of Camelot, the operator of the UK National Lottery, in order to steal customer information which he used to bypass security questions when telephoning the customer services department in an attempt to obtain banking information.[9] While this section is most commonly used where the ultimate aim of the unauthorised access is some form of fraudulent gain, there are instances of this section being used to prosecute those who gain unauthorised access to computer systems with the intent of hacking the voicemails of others or of remotely taking over the webcams of others for voyeuristic purposes.

19.13 The provision makes it clear that the further offence need not be committed at the same time as the first offence, and that the defendant may be guilty of the section 2 offence even where the circumstances are such that the commission of the further offence is factually impossible.

Unauthorised acts with intent to impair, or with recklessness as to impairing, operation of computer, etc – section 3 offence

19.14 The section 3 offence is committed where the defendant does any unauthorised act in relation to a computer, knowing at the time that the act is unauthorised, where he either intends by doing the act to impair the operation of any computer, program or data or preventing or hindering access to any program

8 *R. v Delamare* [2003] EWCA Crim 424.
9 *R. v Akala* [2021] EWCA Crim 199.

or data, or is reckless as to whether his or her act will have any of these effects. This offence carries a maximum penalty of ten years' imprisonment and/or a fine.

19.15 The original wording of the section referred to 'unauthorised modification' but it was amended to 'unauthorised impairment' by the Police and Justice Act 2006 which had the effect of widening the definition of the offence so that neither modification nor deletion of data is now required. The purpose of this amendment was primarily to criminalise the malicious spreading of viruses and distributed denial of service attacks.

19.16 Case law has demonstrated that a wide range of conduct and potentially harmful effects may fall within the scope of this section. Conduct potentially falling foul of the section has included the use of a program to send 500,000 emails to a company to impair the operation of that company's systems,[10] gaining unauthorised access to a company's website in order to make unauthorised modification to its content,[11] creating computer programs designed to carry out distributed denial of service attacks on websites,[12] initiating a cyberattack on an internet service provider,[13] infiltrating the systems of a software company in order to steal commercially sensitive data for ransom,[14] and releasing computer viruses onto the internet.[15]

19.17 It does not have to be proved that the defendant had any specific computer, program or data in mind at the time the act was carried out.

Unauthorised acts causing, or creating risk of, serious damage – section 3ZA offence

19.18 This offence was added to the 1990 Act by the Serious Crime Act 2015 and was intended to target cyber-threats to critical national infrastructure.

19.19 Section 3ZA of the amended 1990 Act makes it an offence for a person to do any unauthorised act in relation to a computer, knowing at the time it to be unauthorised, where the act either causes, or creates a significant risk of, serious damage of a material kind and where the person either intends to cause such damage or is reckless as to whether such damage is caused.

19.20 How is 'serious damage of a material kind' defined? The statute sets out a fairly limited – and exhaustive – list of categories, which comprises damage to human welfare in any place, the environment of any place, the economy of any

10 *DPP v Lennon* (2006) 170 JP 532.
11 *R. v Lindesay* [2001] EWCA Crim 1720.
12 *R. v Mudd* [2017] EWCA Crim 1395.
13 *In the matter of an application by Aaron Sterritt for Judicial Review* [2021] NICA 4.
14 *R. v Kurtaj and another,* unreported, 23 August 2023, Southwark Crown Court.
15 *R. v Vallor* [2003] EWCA Crim 2288.

country and the national security of any country. The act in question need not cause the damage directly or be the main or only cause of the damage.[16]

19.21 The maximum sentence for the offence depends upon the type of damage caused, or at risk of being caused: where the damage or potential damage is to human welfare or national security, the maximum sentence is one of life imprisonment and/or a fine, while the other types of harm give rise to a maximum sentence of 14 years and/or a fine.

Making, supplying or obtaining articles for use in computer misuse offences under section 1, 3 or 3ZA – section 3A offence

19.22 Section 3A, added to the 1990 Act by the Police and Justice Act 2006, creates three variants of a new offence, the aim of which was to criminalise the making, supplying and obtaining of malware and other software tools aimed at hacking into and/or causing damage to computer systems. It is important to note that mere possession of such items is not illegal. In one reported case, an individual was prosecuted under this section for possessing pieces of software used for instigating cyberattacks, in conjunction with multiple other counts under sections 1, 2 and 3 of the 1990 Act.[17]

19.23 The first variant relates to the making, adapting, supplying or offering to supply of any article intending it to be used to commit, or to assist in the commission of, an offence under section 1, 3 or 3ZA of the 1990 Act.

19.24 The second relates to the supplying or offering to supply of any article believing that it is likely to be used to commit, or to assist in the commission of, an offence under the same three sections.

19.25 The third relates to the obtaining of an article either intending to use it to commit, or to assist in the commission of, an offence under these sections or with a view to it being supplied for use to commit, or to assist in the commission of, an offence under these sections.

'Article' in this section is widely defined to include 'any program or data in electronic form'.

19.26 This new offence came under criticism at the time of its introduction as it did not take sufficient – if any – account of the fact that such tools may be legitimately created and supplied by professionals working in the IT security field. The word 'likely' in the section is not defined and has also been criticised for potentially extending the offence to capture those who supply ordinarily legitimate programs but are aware that some customers may misuse them in a certain way. The sensible interpretation of the section has therefore been

16 1990 Act, s 3ZA(4).

17 *R v Martin (Lewys Stephen)* [2013] EWCA Crim 1420.

entrusted to the courts. While there have to date been no reported cases in which an arguably overly-broad interpretation of this section has been applied by the courts, it remains a poorly-drafted section with scope for misapplication.

The maximum sentence for an offence under section 3A is two years' imprisonment and/or a fine.

Jurisdictional issues

19.27 A prosecution under the 1990 Act has always required that there be a 'significant link' to England and Wales – typically, that the defendant or the computer targeted by the offending is located in that jurisdiction.[18]

19.28 However, the Serious Crime Act 2015 extended the reach of the 1990 Act to allow for the prosecution of an offence contrary to sections 1, 3, 3ZA or 3A[19] by a UK national whilst outside the UK where there is no other link to the UK beyond the accused's nationality, providing the act was also unlawful in the jurisdiction in which it occurred.[20]

Review of the 1990 Act

19.29 Since 2021, the UK government has been engaged in reviewing the 1990 Act. This has involved issuing a Call for Information, as a result of which the government concluded that the 1990 Act remained largely effective, reflecting its 'technology-neutral nature'. However, a number of issues were raised in relation to specific areas of the law and related law enforcement powers, and as a result a public consultation was conducted, closing in April 2023. This covered three proposals for legislation: domain name and IP address takedown and seizure, the power to preserve data, and data copying. At the time of publication, the government is considering the results of the consultation on these proposals.[21]

19.30 The government also concluded that there were number of areas raised during the review of the 1990 Act that warranted further consideration by way of a "multi-stakeholder programme". These included: extra-territorial provisions, statutory defences for those in the cybersecurity industry who are "taking action to protect the UK in cyberspace"; and sentencing.

18 1990 Act, s 4.

19 1990 Act, s 4A, which requires a significant link with the domestic jurisdiction in relation to the offence.

20 1990 Act, s 5(1).

21 See https://www.gov.uk/government/consultations/review-of-the-computer-misuse-act-1990.

MALICIOUS COMMUNICATION AND HARASSMENT

19.31 The development of the internet and the continued expansion of social media platforms have created a proliferation of opportunities for the sending of abusive and threatening messages to and about other parties. It has been an on-going challenge for law-makers to fit ever more creative examples of virtual unpleasantness into the existing legislative framework, while respecting the fundamental tenets of free speech.

Malicious and offensive communications

19.32 Such conduct currently tends to be prosecuted under one of two statutory provisions:

First, section 1 of the Malicious Communications Act 1988 Act ('the 1988 Act') makes it an offence for a person, with the intention of causing distress or anxiety, to send a letter, electronic communication or article to another person which conveys an indecent or grossly offensive message or which is itself of an indecent or grossly offensive nature, or which conveys a threat or information which is false and known or believed to be false by the sender. The maximum penalty is two years' imprisonment and/or a fine.

19.33 Second, section 127(1) of the Communications Act 2003 ('the 2003 Act') makes it an offence to send through a 'public electronic communications network' a message or other matter that is 'grossly offensive' or of an 'indecent, obscene or menacing character'. Section 127(2) provides that it is an offence to send a false message 'for the purpose of causing annoyance, inconvenience or needless anxiety to another'. The offence carries a maximum penalty of six months' imprisonment. A recent high-profile prosecution under this section concerned an individual who recorded a video on his mobile telephone of a burning cardboard effigy of the Grenfell Tower fire which he shared in two WhatsApp groups.[22]

19.34 In contrast to the 1988 Act, which covers all types of communication, whether electronic or not, the 2003 Act offence covers only messages sent through a public electronic communications network. However, the 2003 Act offence does not require an intention on the part of the perpetrator to cause distress or anxiety: it only requires that the purpose of sending the false message was to annoy, inconvenience or cause needless anxiety. It also need not be received; only sent. As such, the 2003 Act offence is generally one which is more easily proven. Charges under the 2003 Act offence would therefore typically be preferred in respect of communications where it may be more difficult to establish level of intent required under the 1988 Act.

22 *DPP v Bussetti* [2021] EWHC 2140 (Admin).

19.35 There is, in addition to the two communications offences noted above, a patchwork of other criminal statutes which may be engaged by particular types of online abuse, including harassment, stalking, threats to kill and a number of sexual offences. These typically offer greater sentencing flexibility and may reflect more accurately the true extent of the criminality involved.

19.36 It is worth noting that current Criminal Prosecution Service (CPS) Guidance[23] (last updated in September 2019) specifically distinguishes four different types of communications sent via social media, namely those which:

1. are a credible threat (violence to the person or damage to property);
2. specifically target an individual or individuals and which may constitute harassment or stalking, controlling or coercive behaviour, disclosing private sexual images without consent, an offence under the Sexual Offences Act 2003, blackmail or another offence;
3. are breaches of court orders or a statutory provision; and
4. are grossly offensive, indecent, obscene or false.

19.37 The Guidance recommends that those cases falling within categories 1, 2 and 3 should be prosecuted robustly under the relevant legislation. However, it states that cases falling within category 4 will usually be considered either under section 1 of the 1988 Act or under section 127(1) of the 2003 Act, and notes that such cases will be subject to a high threshold and that in many cases a prosecution is unlikely to be in the public interest.

19.38 This is a deliberate attempt to distinguish communications which constitute a breach of the wider criminal law. For example, threats to kill, threats to cause criminal damage, harassment or controlling or coercive behaviour

from those which do not constitute any criminal offence beyond the sending of an abusive message. The Guidance sends a clear signal that the latter category – communications which may be highly offensive but do not breach any other law – will be less likely to be prosecuted due to the balance which must be struck with the public interest in free speech.

19.39 This approach was a response to a number of widely-criticised decisions by the CPS to institute criminal proceedings against individuals in respect of messages – typically tweets – which, while ill-judged, were perhaps not an appropriate target for the full force of the criminal law.

19.40 At the time of publication, the Online Safety Bill is nearing the end of its lengthy passage through Parliament. If passed, this would, among other things, repeal significant parts of section 1 of the 1988 Act (so far as it extends to England, Wales, and Northern Ireland) and section 127 of the 2003 Act. Those

23 CPS Cybercrime Prosecution Guidance (www.cps.gov.uk/legal-guidance/cybercrime-prosecution-guidance).

provisions would be replaced by new clauses of the Bill, setting out an offence committed where a person sends a message conveying information known to be false with the intention of causing non-trivial psychological or physical harm to a likely audience, and a separate offence committed where a person sends a message conveying a threat of death or serious harm with the intention of causing an individual encountering the message to fear that the threat would be carried out, or being reckless as to this outcome.

19.41 In the rest of this section, we will look at some of the principal ways in which abusive communications are sent online and consider to what extent these may engage a wider range of criminal offences beyond the 1998 and 2003 Acts.

Cyber-stalking and harassment

19.42 The internet and, in particular, social media platforms offer unlimited opportunities for individuals to engage in unwanted and/or threatening contact with or regarding other individuals which has the potential to cause significant distress. This can include sending threatening or obscene emails or messages on social media sites and making personal and abusive posts on public forums and message boards. It can also take the form of a wide range of other malicious online activity, such as spamming, trolling and targeting with malware or viruses. The possible motivations behind such campaigns are many and varied: while the aim may be to initiate or sustain a personal relationship of some description with the target, it may alternatively be to cause distress to him or her or to damage his or her reputation.

19.43 Prosecutors have increasingly sought to pursue the most serious examples of unwanted virtual contact, not only as breaches of section 1 of the Malicious Communications Act 1988 or section 127(1) of the Communications 2003 Act, but also as breaches of legislation proscribing stalking and harassment. Increasingly, cyber-harassment is found not to constitute an isolated act or series of acts but rather to form part of a wider campaign of harassment extending to a whole spectrum of behaviour, including 'real life' acts. The distinction between virtual and non-virtual harassment is becoming increasingly artificial as such campaigns frequently straddle both types of conduct: indeed, it is often the ubiquitous nature of the contact which makes it particularly distressing for the individual concerned.

19.44 The offences of stalking and harassment are found in the Protection from Harassment Act 1997 ('the 1997 Act'). Section 2 of the 1997 Act defines harassment as pursuing a course of conduct – which is defined as conduct on at least two occasions – which the defendant knew or should have known to have amounted to harassment. Harassment is not defined but is stated to include alarming another person or causing him or her distress. For conduct to constitute harassment it must be objectively judged as oppressive and unacceptable, which may depend upon the context in which the conduct occurred. Section 2 harassment, carries a maximum sentence of six months' imprisonment and/or a fine.

19.45 Section 4 of the 1997 Act creates a more serious harassment offence which is predicated upon a course of conduct which causes another person to fear – again, on at least two occasions – that violence will be used against him or her, where the defendant knew or should have known that his or her conduct would have had that effect. The maximum sentence for this more serious variant is ten years' imprisonment and/or a fine.

19.46 In September 2022, a former BBC radio presenter, Alex Belfield, was sentenced to five and a half years' imprisonment for a number of offences under sections 2 and 4 of the 1997 Act in respect of a campaign of on-line stalking and harassment via YouTube and Twitter of a number of BBC personalities and employees.

19.47 The Protection of Freedoms Act 2012 added two parallel stalking offences to the 1997 Act. Stalking is not defined but acts associated with stalking are stated to include a number of activities which may be conducted on a virtual basis, including contacting or attempting to contact a person, publishing material purporting to relate to or originate from that person, and monitoring his or her use of the internet or emails. The section 2A stalking offence carries a maximum sentence of six months' imprisonment and/or a fine, while the maximum sentence for the more serious section 4A stalking offence which involves fear of violence or serious alarm or distress is ten years' imprisonment and/or a fine.

Trolling

19.48 Trolling is the word used to describe the practice of deliberately posting offensive, inflammatory or provocative content online for no reason other than to disrupt normal discourse on the part of other users and/or to provoke an emotional reaction from these other users.

19.49 Trolling in its pure form, while generally recognised as a nuisance, rarely constitutes a criminal offence. Where trolling has given rise to criminal charges, it is invariably where the content of the posts is highly offensive, often racist or misogynistic, or of such a nature as to constitute harassment or a breach of public order legislation.

19.50 Section 1 of the Malicious Communications Act 1988 and section 127(1) of the Communications Act 2003, referred to above, are the primary tools used to target trolls who post content which is deemed so offensive as to warrant criminal sanction. These Acts have been used to prosecute those who deface or post abusive messages on social media tribute sites commemorating deceased persons, for example, and those who send obscene or threating messages to public figures on Twitter who express views with which they disagree. Where the content of these messages reflects racist motivation or other aggravating features, this may be reflected in the sentences ultimately imposed.

19.51 The Protection from Harassment Act 1997, also referred to above, is another tool which may be used to prosecute those whose trolling consists of a course of conduct targeting a specific individual sufficient to constitute stalking or harassment of that individual. Once the Online Safety Bill has become law, this will introduce a number of other relevant offences onto the statute books including a new offence of encouraging a person to cause serious self-harm.

19.52 Where a person posts offensive comments of a particularly inflammatory nature, he or she may also be liable for prosecution under one or more of the various public order offences, including, where appropriate, their racially-aggravated versions. In 2012, a student who sent a tweet mocking the on-pitch collapse of Bolton Wanderers footballer, Fabrice Muamba, was convicted and imprisoned under section 4A of the Public Order Act 1986.[24] This offence is based upon the use of threatening, abusive or insulting words or behaviour, with the intent to cause harassment, alarm or distress. This offence carries a maximum sentence of six months' imprisonment and/or a fine, while the racially aggravated version[25] carries a potential two-year sentence.

19.53 There are those who object to the characterisation of these sort of communications as trolling. Certainly, trolling in its true sense can be a clever, amusing, and thought-provoking exercise of free speech. The issue is, as ever, is where the line is to be drawn.

Revenge porn

19.54 Revenge porn – the disclosure of sexual or intimate photographs, usually of a former partner, with the intention of causing him or her distress or embarrassment – has been a specific criminal offence since April 2015.

19.55 Under the current law, section 33 of the Criminal Justice and Courts Act 2015 creates an offence of disclosing or threatening to disclose a private sexual photograph or film without the consent of an individual who appears in the photograph or film, with the intention of causing that individual distress. It carries a maximum sentence of two years' imprisonment and/or a fine.

19.56 The definition of the offence extends not just to the individual who initially uploads or posts such an image but also anyone who subsequently forwards, reposts or retweets it. However, it must be established that the defendant had the intention to cause the victim distress: the wording of section 33(8) makes it clear that such an intent cannot simply be inferred on the basis that

24 Liam Stacey's appeal against the sentence imposed by the magistrates' court was dismissed by Swansea Crown Court on 20 March 2012; see *R v Liam Stacey*, A20120033.

25 Under s 31 of the Crime and Disorder Act 1998.

causing distress was a natural and probable effect of the disclosure. Where he or she simply thought it would be amusing to do so, for example, this would not be sufficient for the offence to be made out.

19.57 Where posting such material does not fall within the remit of this offence, for whatever reason, it may fall within either section 1 of the Malicious Communications Act 1988 or section 127(1) of the Communications Act 2003.[26] Publication of such material may also constitute a breach of the Obscene Publications Acts.[27] Repeated instances of such conduct may amount to stalking or harassment under the Protection from Harassment Act 1997.[28]

19.58 The Online Safety Bill, as currently drafted and once it has been passed into law, will introduce significant reforms to the law in this area, repealing existing legislation and replacing it with a set of new offences: an offence of sharing an intimate image without consent, two offences based on intent to cause humiliation, alarm, or distress and for obtaining sexual gratification, and a specific offence covering threats to share intimate images. The reforms will remove the requirement for prosecutors to prove defendants intended to cause distress. The new Act will also criminalise the non-consensual sharing of 'deepfake' pornography.

SENDING OF EXPLICIT IMAGES

19.59 As social media and communications apps have become ever more popular, so have incidences of the sending of unsolicited explicit images. The Online Safety Bill seeks to address this. Once passed, it will insert into the Sexual Offences Act 2003 a new section 66A which makes it a specific criminal offence for a person to intentionally send or give (electronically or by any other means) a photograph or film (moving image) of any person's genitals to another person, where they intend to cause alarm, distress or humiliation, or for the purpose of obtaining sexual gratification while reckless as to whether the recipient will be caused alarm, distress or humiliation. The new offence will be punishable by up to two years in prison.

INDECENT AND OBSCENE MATERIAL

19.60 The rapid growth of the internet has facilitated a proliferation in the volume of indecent and obscene material, which can now be produced, shared and accessed with unprecedented ease. Material that would once only have been available upon the expenditure of time, effort and money on the part of those wishing to access it is now freely available in the privacy of their own homes to anyone with an internet connection.

26 See **19.31** et seq above, Malicious and offensive communications.
27 See **19.60** et seq below, Indecent and obscene material.
28 See **19.42** et seq above, Cyber-stalking and harassment.

19.61 The social and psychological issues arising from the vast increase in the accessibility of such material, particularly to minors and vulnerable individuals, are well-documented. The focus of this section, however, is to summarise how the production, dissemination and consumption of such material falls within the criminal law and to consider to what extent legislation pre-dating the internet age is capable of addressing the challenges of technological developments which would have been inconceivable at the time these laws came into force.

Obscene publications and extreme pornography

Obscene publications

19.62 The principal laws governing obscene material are the Obscene Publications Acts 1959 and 1964. The 1964 Act amends and strengthens the terms of the 1959 Act.

19.63 Section 2(1) of the 1959 Act makes it an offence to publish an obscene article, whether for gain or not, or to have an obscene article for publication for gain, whether the gain was to the defendant or another. Both offences carry a maximum sentence of five years' imprisonment and/or a fine.

19.64 What is 'obscene'? Section 1(1) of the 1959 Act provides that an article shall be deemed to be obscene if its effect is 'such as to tend to deprave and corrupt persons who are likely, having regard to all relevant circumstances, to read, see or hear the matter contained or embodied in it'. Courts have tended to adopt a wide interpretation of 'deprave' and 'corrupt'. In the famous Lady Chatterley case, in which Penguin Books Ltd was acquitted of the offence, Byrne J articulated the meaning of the words in the following terms: 'To deprave means to make morally bad, to pervert, to debase or to corrupt morally. To corrupt means to render morally unsound or rotten, to destroy the moral purity or chastity, to pervert or ruin good quality'.[29]

19.65 What if the intended audience for the material in question is likely to be those whose morals are already in a state of depravity and corruption? The courts have consistently taken the view that the 1959 Act is concerned not only with the protection of the innocent from corruption, but also with the protection of the less innocent from further corruption.[30] This is a very significant point in cases in which the publication of pornographic material was aimed primarily or exclusively at experienced purveyors of such material.

19.66 Section 4 of the 1959 Act sets out what is called the 'defence of public good': no offence is committed if it is proved that publication of the article in question is justified as being for the public good on the ground that it is in the interests of science, literature, art or learning, or of other objects of general

29 *R. v Penguin Books Ltd* [1961] Crim. LR 176 at 177.
30 *DPP v Whyte* [1972] AC 849, HL.

concern. It is also a defence under section 2(5) of the 1959 Act for the defendant to prove that he or she had not examined the article and had no reasonable cause to suspect that it was obscene.

19.67 The 1959 Act has been amended and, where necessary, updated to confirm that website content and other material stored electronically falls within its terms. Section 1(3) has been amended to extend the definition of 'publication' to include the transmission of electronic data[31] and case law has established that transmission of data, both uploading and downloading, is sufficient to constitute publication.[32] It has also been held that publication to only one other person – for example, in the context of a private fantasy chat of a paedophilic nature between two consenting adults – was capable of falling within the Act[33] as it was not necessary that publication be to more than one person. Therefore such conduct may be prosecuted under the 1959 Act, with the greater sentencing powers that it offers, in preference to proceeding under section 127(1) of the Communications Act 2003.

19.68 There are of course jurisdictional difficulties in bringing a prosecution under English law in cases where the material is hosted overseas. The CPS has published guidance upon the factors which may determine whether a particular case can be brought before the English courts.[34] However, case law demonstrates that where content is downloaded in England from a website which is hosted abroad, such publication may constitute an offence prosecutable in England on the basis that the mere transmission of data – including the downloading of content by a single individual within the jurisdiction – constitutes publication.[35]

Extreme pornography

19.69 The offence of possession of extreme pornographic images was created by sections 63 to 67 of the Criminal Justice and Immigration Act 2008 ('the 2008 Act') and came into force on 26 January 2009.

19.70 Section 63 of the 2008 Act makes it an offence for a person to be in possession of an extreme pornographic image.

19.71 An image, to be 'an extreme pornographic image', must meet all the following criteria:

31 The Criminal Justice and Public Order Act 1994, s 168(1) and Sch 9, Para 3(a) amended the definition of publication under s 1(3) of the 1959 Act to include the words: '*where the matter is data stored electronically, transmits that data*'
32 *R. v Perrin* [2002] EWCA Crim 747; Waddon, unreported, 6 April 2000.
33 *R. v G.S.* [2012] 2 Cr. App. R. 14.
34 CPS Obscene Publications Legal Guidance, revised January 2019 (www.cps.gov.uk/legal-guidance/obscene-publications).
35 See Perrin, *supra*, (website in France) and Waddon, *supra* (website in the US).

- 'pornographic', which is defined as being 'of such a nature that it must reasonably be assumed to have been produced solely or principally for the purpose of sexual arousal'.[36] This is normally a matter for the judge or jury to determine based on their own judgement and not a matter for expert evidence;
- 'extreme', which is defined as grossly offensive, disgusting or otherwise of an obscene character; and
- one which portrays in an explicit and realistic way any of the acts set out in section 63(7), namely acts which threaten a person's life; acts which result in or are likely to result in serious injury to a person's anus, breasts or genitals; bestiality; or necrophilia.

19.72 The 2008 Act was amended in April 2015[37] to include extreme pornographic images depicting non-consensual penetration and rape.

19.73 It is important to note that the new offence under section 63 only relates to material which is, by virtue of the Obscene Publications Act 1959 ('the 1959 Act'), illegal to publish or distribute in England; in other words, it does not apply to material which would not in any case found a prosecution under the 1959 Act. As the relevant CPS Guidance[38] puts it, all extreme pornography is obscene but not all obscene material is extreme. The difference, as far as material meeting both definitions is concerned, is that mere possession is sufficient to engage the section 63 offence; unlike under the 1959 Act, no act of publication or distribution is required for the offence to be committed.

19.74 Section 65 of the 2008 Act sets out the defences to a charge under section 63, which are essentially: possession for a legitimate reason; possession in circumstances where the defendant had either not seen the image and had no reason to suspect that it was an extreme pornographic image; or had been sent the image without prior request and did not keep it for an unreasonable amount of time. There is a further defence at section 66 which may apply where the defendant had consensually participated in the acts depicted and there was no non-consensual infliction of harm on any person.

19.75 The maximum sentence for possession of extreme pornography depends upon the nature of the acts depicted: images of acts threatening life or which result in or are likely to result in serious injury carries a maximum sentence of three years' imprisonment and/or a fine; while the other two categories of image can lead to a sentence of up to two years' imprisonment and/or a fine.

36 The 2008 Act, s 63(3).

37 Criminal Justice and Courts Act 2015, s 37.

38 CPS Extreme Pornography Legal Guidance (www.cps.gov.uk/legal-guidance/extreme-pornography).

Indecent images of children

19.76 Section 1 of the Protection of Children Act 1978 ('the 1978 Act') prohibits the taking, making, distribution, showing or possession with a view to distributing any indecent image of a child.

19.77 While the statutory provision pre-dates the internet as we would recognise it today, the word 'make' was added in 1995[39] to respond to the proliferation of such material on-line.

19.78 In applying section 1 to the facts in an array of cases in the internet era, it is plain that courts have stretched the logical definition of the word 'making' to find that a basis upon which a broad range of actions – or, sometimes, no action at all – on the part of the defendant can be said to fall within the terms of the offence in order to target the conduct which the 1978 Act was introduced to curtail.

19.79 The word 'make' has since its addition been widely interpreted by the courts to include accessing a webpage incorporating indecent images of children, printing them, copying them, enlarging a thumbnail of such an image while web-browsing, opening an email attachment including such an image, downloading such an image onto a computer screen and storing such an image on a computer.[40] Where indecent images of children appeared by way of a 'pop-up' or automatic redirection on a legal pornography website and were automatically stored on his or her computer without any action on the part of the defendant, the defendant could be held to have 'made' such images where the jury was sure that he knew about the 'pop-up' activity when he visited the legal site and that there was a likelihood that these 'pop-ups' would include illegal material.[41]

19.80 The defences to a charge for the distributing, showing and possession offences are essentially legitimate reason for the conduct in question and the fact that the defendant himself or herself had not seen the images and did not know or have any cause to suspect them to be indecent. There is no defence to the taking or making offence but it is clear from case law on the section that the act of taking or making must be a deliberate and intentional act done in the knowledge that the image taken or made is, or is likely to be, an indecent image of a child.[42]

The maximum sentence for an offence contrary to section 1 of the 1978 Act is ten years' imprisonment and/or a fine.

39 Criminal Justice and Public Order Act 1994, s 84(2)(a)(i).

40 See inter alia *R. v Bowden* [2000] 1 Cr. App.R.438; *DPP v Atkins v DPP* [2000] 1 W.L.R. 1427; *R. v Smith* [2002] EWCA Crim 683; *R. v Jayson* [2003] 1 Cr. App. R. 13, CA.

41 *R. v Harrison* [2008] 1 Cr. App. R. 29, CA.

42 *R. v Smith, R. v Jayson, R. v Harrison, supra.*

19.81 Applicable sentencing guidelines[43] require the court to determine the offence category, based on the nature of the image[44] and the defendant's activity,[45] which then determines the sentencing starting point and range. For example, the starting point for the simple possession of category A images, the most serious category of images, leads to a starting point of one year's custody with a range between 26 weeks' to three years' custody. The consideration of aggravating and mitigating factors will then guide the court as to where the appropriate sentence lies within that range.

19.82 Section 160 of the Criminal Justice Act 1988 ('the 1988 Act') prohibits the simple possession of indecent images of children. There are defences to a charge under section 160, which are essentially: legitimate reason for the possession, not having seen the image and not knowing or having any cause to suspect that it was indecent, and the image having been sent to him or her without prior request and it not having been kept for an unreasonable amount of time. An offence contrary to section 160 of the 1988 Act carries a maximum sentence of five years' imprisonment and/or a fine.

19.83 'Possession' consists of a physical and mental element. A charge for possession can be problematic in the case of electronic images as the physical element can be difficult to establish where images have been deleted or stored on a part of the device from which the defendant may not, himself or herself, be able to retrieve them. The mental component can be equally problematic where images, or footprints of images, are retrieved from a device in circumstances where they may have been automatically cached without the defendant necessarily having had knowledge of the existence or nature of these files. For these reasons, a 'making' charge under section 1 of the 1978 Act is frequently preferred by prosecutors and charges under section 160 in respect of electronic material are comparatively rare.

19.84 For both offences, 'indecent' is a matter of fact for the judge or jury to decide in accordance with recognised standards of propriety.[46] While the term 'image' is commonly used in respect of these offences, these should more correctly be referred to as 'photographs and pseudo-photographs', which are defined to include not just still images but also films, negatives, electronic data which is capable of conversion into a photograph and tracings.[47]

19.85 For the purposes of both Acts, a 'child' is a person who is under the age of 18.[48] A person is assumed to have been a child at any material time 'if it

43 See https://www.sentencingcouncil.org.uk/offences/magistrates-court/item/possession-of-indecent-photograph-of-child/.

44 Category A – images of penetrative sexual activity, bestiality and sadism; Category B – images of non-penetrative sexual activity; and Category C – other indecent images.

45 Possession; distribution; and production.

46 *R. v Stamford* [1972] 56 Cr. App. R. 398.

47 Protection of Children Act 1978, s 7.

48 The 1978 Act, s 7(6).

appears from the evidence as a whole that he was then under the age of 18'.[49] While this is ultimately a finding of fact for the judge or jury to make, and expert evidence on this point is not admissible,[50] the defence may adduce documentary and other evidence in support of the contention that the person in question was not in fact under 18 at the relevant time.

19.86 Finally, section 62 of the Coroners and Justice Act 2009 created a further offence of possession of a prohibited image of a child, which carries a maximum sentence of three years' imprisonment and/or a fine. Photographs and pseudo photographs are expressly excluded from the Act:[51] the offence was created to target computer-generated images, animations and drawings.

DATA BREACHES

19.87 Since the 1990s, there has been an increasing awareness of the value and sensitivity of individuals' personal data and the need to have suitable safeguards in place to ensure that the collection, use and dissemination of such data is appropriate.

19.88 The Data Protection Act 1998 heralded a new regime in the protection of individuals' personal information, a regime which has more recently been built upon and updated. The creation of a number of criminal offences, backed up with potentially very significant fines, forms part of the toolkit available to the Information Commissioner's Office in taking enforcement action against errant firms and individuals.

Data Protection Act 1998

19.89 In October 1995, the European Commission and Parliament issued a Directive to address, amongst other things, the increasing ease with which personal data was being processed and exchanged due to the increasing use of computers. The Directive created protections for individuals 'with regard to the processing of personal data and on the free movement of such data'. In direct response to this Directive, the Data Protection Act 1998 ('the 1998 Act') was implemented, and came into force on 1 March 2000.

Data Protection Act 2018

19.90 After 20 years, the 1998 statute was repealed and replaced by the Data Protection Act 2018 (the '2018 Act'), which represented the UK's implementation of the EU General Data Protection Regulation (GDPR) (and is structured to be

49 The 1978 Act, s 2(3).
50 *R. v Land* [1998] 1 Cr. App. R. 301.
51 The 2009 Act, s 65.

read alongside what is now the retained EU law version of the GDPR), and a significant reform and modernisation of the UK's data protection laws.

The 2018 Act and the UK GDPR regulate the processing of personal data. 'Personal data' is defined very widely as any information relating to an identified or identifiable living individual, ie a living individual who can be identified, directly or indirectly, in particular by reference to an 'identifier' (such as a name or identification number) or one or more factors specific to the physical, physiological, genetic, mental, economic, cultural or social identity of the individual.

The 2018 Act sets out six data protection principles which must be followed by anyone responsible for using personal data. The 2018 Act also strengthened protections for sensitive personal data, namely information about a person's race, ethnic background, political opinions, religious beliefs, trade union membership, genetics, biometrics (where used for identification), health and sex life or orientation.

Enforcement

19.91 The Information Commissioner's Office (ICO) uses the 2018 Act to address the methods by which organisations and individuals are processing data. The ICO has numerous options available for taking action, which include:

- serving information, assessment and enforcement notices;
- powers of entry and inspection;
- issuing monetary penalty notices and fixed penalty charges;
- negotiating undertakings; and
- prosecuting criminal offences under the 2018 Act.

19.92 The options above are only a selection of the powers available to the ICO. The ICO also has the ability to deploy several different strategies at once, as the actions are not mutually exclusive.

Criminal offences

19.93 The 2018 Act contains a number of criminal offences relating to the misuse of data.

Crucially, as with the previous statute, the 2018 Act provides no power to arrest but does allow for the Information Commissioner to apply for a search warrant, pursuant to section 154 and the powers outlined at Schedule 15.

19.94 The principal offences under the 2018 Act include:

- Unlawful obtaining or disclosing of personal data – section 170(1)

Section 170(1) of the 2018 Act echoes section 55(1) of the 1998 Act by making it an offence to knowingly or recklessly obtain or disclose personal data or procure the disclosure to another person of the information contained in personal data without the consent of the data controller. However, under the 2018 Act it is also an offence to knowingly or recklessly retain personal data (even it was lawfully obtained) without the consent of the data controller.

The data controller is the person who determines the purpose for which, and the manner in which, any personal data are to be processed. The data controller can be a company or other legal entity or an individual.

- Re-identification of personal data – section 171

  It is an offence under section 171(1) to re-identify personal data that has been 'de-identified' (i.e., it has undergone a process to remove or conceal personal data). Defences are set out at subsections 3 and 4, and include that the re-identification was necessary for the purposes of preventing or detecting crime or was justified as being in the public interest.

  Under sub-section 5, it is an offence for a person knowingly or recklessly to process personal data that is information that has been re-identified.

  These are offences which were not found in the 1998 Act.

- Selling personal data – section 170(4) and (5)

  If a person sells, or offers to sell, personal data which has been obtained or subsequently obtained in contravention of section 170(1), then the person is guilty of an offence. The section 170(5) offence can be committed by advertising that personal data is (or may be) for sale.

  It is important to note that a person can also be found guilty of data protection breaches under the accessory principles of criminal law, such as conspiracy.

  A breach of these provisions is punishable by an unlimited fine.

  Section 198 of the 2018 Act makes provision, where a criminal offence is committed by a corporate body, for liability to extend to the company's directors and other officers if it can be shown that the offences in questions were committed with the consent or connivance of, or due to any neglect on the part of, the officer concerned.

Defences – section 170(2) and (3)

19.95 The Act sets out a number of statutory defences to the section 170(1) offence. These are, under sub-section (2), that the obtaining, disclosing or procuring was:

- necessary for the purposes of preventing or detecting crime;
- required or authorised by or under any enactment, by any rule of law or by the order of a court; or

- in the particular circumstances, justified as being in the public interest.

19.96 Under sub-section (3), it is a defence where a person acted:

- in the reasonable belief that he had a legal right to obtain, disclose, procure or retain the personal data;
- in the reasonable belief that he would have had the consent of the controller if the controller had known of the obtaining, disclosing or procuring, and the circumstances of it; or
- for special purposes (defined at section 174(1) as journalism, academic, artistic or literary purposes), with a view to publication by a person, and in the reasonable belief that in the particular circumstances the obtaining, disclosing, procuring or retaining was justified as being in the public interest.

Sentencing

19.97 As with the previous statute, offences under the 2018 Act are punishably only by way of a fine:[52] there is no provision for imprisonment, however manifest the breach.

The 2018 Act provides for maximum fines up to £17.5 million or 4% of an undertaking's total annual worldwide turnover.

19.98 In accordance with the ICO's Prosecution Policy Statement,[53] the ICO will seek to apply the Proceeds of Crime Act 2002 ('POCA') in cases which concern the unlawful trade of personal data which involved substantial sums of money. The deployment of POCA provisions would allow the ICO to apply for confiscation of the proceeds of the unlawful activity. The decision to commence POCA proceedings is within the Commissioner's discretion.

FRAUD

19.99 The phenomenal growth in internet usage over the last 30 years has presented a commensurate surge in the opportunities that it offers for the dishonest appropriation of other people's money and property. The web offers speed and – to a certain extent – anonymity, as well as the unprecedented ability to reach millions of potential victims at virtually no cost. It has provided untold opportunities for ingenious and persistent fraudsters, located all over the world, to defraud companies and individuals on a scale which was simply unthinkable in a pre-internet era and in a way which frequently evades the capacity of national and international law enforcement agencies.

52 2018 Act, s 196.

53 https://ico.org.uk/media/about-the-ico/policies-and-procedures/1882/ico-prosecution-policy-statement.pdf.

19.100 The challenges facing law enforcement agencies are immense, with recent statistics revealing that fraud accounts for 40% of all crime committed across the UK,[54] with cybercrime as a whole reaching 2.39 million instances in 2022, and approximately 49,000 instances of fraud as a result of cybercrime.[55]

19.101 This section will consider the main genres of cyber-related fraud and how these fit within the framework of criminal fraud legislation. It will also explore the civil causes of action associated with them and outline measures which victims can utilise to attempt to recover their losses.

Fraud Act 2006

19.102 The vast majority of cyber-fraud cases are ones which, insofar as they can be prosecuted at all, tend to be prosecuted under the Fraud Act 2006 ('the 2006 Act').

19.103 In summary, section 1 of the 2006 Act provides that a defendant is guilty of fraud if he is in breach of any of the following three sections:

- Fraud by false representation (section 2). The defendant must be shown to have dishonestly made a false misrepresentation with the intention to either make a gain for himself or herself or another, or to cause loss to another, or expose another to a risk of loss.
- Fraud by failing to disclose information (section 3). It must be proven that the defendant dishonestly failed to disclose information which he or she is under a legal duty to disclose with the intention to either make a gain for himself or herself or another, or to cause loss to another, or expose another to a risk of loss.
- Fraud by abuse of position (section 4). A person is in breach of this section if he or she occupies a position in which he or she is expected to safeguard or not act against the financial interests of another person with the intention to either make a gain for himself or herself or another, or to cause loss to another, or expose another to a risk of loss. An abuse of position may consist of an omission rather than an act.

19.104 There is thus a single offence of fraud but three different ways in which it may be committed. A conviction for fraud, of any of the three variants, carries a maximum sentence of ten years' imprisonment.

54 https://www.gov.uk/government/publications/national-fraud-initiative-reports/national-fraud-initiative-report-december-2022-html.

55 https://www.gov.uk/government/statistics/cyber-security-breaches-survey-2023/cyber-security-breaches-survey-2023.

19.105 The mental state, or *mens rea*, required for fraud is dishonesty. Prior to 2017, the test for dishonesty had been that set out in the case of *Ghosh*:[56] this was a two-part test requiring the Prosecution to establish that the defendant's dishonesty was both subjectively appreciated by the defendant and also objectively dishonest judged by the standards of ordinary decent people.

19.106 However, since the Supreme Court decision in the 2017 civil case of *Ivey v Genting Casinos (UK) t/a Crockford*,[57] this test has been replaced with a new two-stage test, aligned with the test in civil cases, namely: what was the defendant's actual state of knowledge or belief as to the facts, and, irrespective of the defendant's belief about the facts, was his or her conduct dishonest by the objective standards of ordinary decent people? The Court of Appeal has since confirmed[58] that the new test in Ivey is the one which applies in criminal fraud cases.

19.107 Section 6 of the 2006 Act makes it an offence to possess or have in one's control any article for use in the course of or in connection with a fraud, while section 7 outlaws the making, adapting, supplying or offering to supply an article either knowing that it is designed or adapted for use in the course of or in connection with a fraud or intending it to be used to commit or assist in the commission of fraud. These offences carry a maximum sentence of five and ten years' imprisonment respectively.

19.108 The majority of cyber-fraud within the jurisdiction of English law constitutes fraud by false representation (under section 2). However, possessing, making or supplying articles associated with such frauds – for example, phishing kits, malware and identity theft tools – may incur liability under section 6 or 7 of the 2006 Act.

Variants of cyber-fraud

19.109 Cyber-fraud comes in as many shapes and sizes as traditional non-virtual fraud, and is only limited by the ingenuity of humankind. Some of the principal methods of committing fraud in breach of the 2006 Act include the following:

- Authorised push payment (APP) frauds take place with the victim's knowledge. Criminals will target a victim and put pressure on them to act quickly, with the aim of causing the victim to panic and not think through the transaction properly. Many of the typologies described below fall into this category.
- In contrast, in one type of online banking fraud, a fraudster may represent himself or herself as the victim to the victim's bank in order to persuade it to make a payment to a third-party account without the knowledge or consent of

56 *R v Ghosh* [1982] EWCA Crim 2.

57 *Ivey v Genting Casinos (UK) Ltd t/a Crockford* [2017] UKSC 67.

58 *Booth and another v R* [2020] EWCA Crim 575.

the victim. This fraud typology is distinct from many of the others described below as it is the bank which is deceived rather than the victim.

- Email intercept or mandate fraud is a variant whereby fraudsters intercept emails between a firm (often, solicitors' firms) and its clients. The fraudster sends an email, purporting to be from the firm, to the client, requesting that the transfer of a deposit or a balance of funds due be made to an alternative account and provides the details of this alternative account. The unwitting client follows the instructions, believing these to have emanated from the firm, and only finds out at a later date that he or she has transferred the funds to a fraudster's account. That account will normally have been cleared as soon as the funds landed and the proceeds laundered through numerous other accounts within a matter of hours.

- A further variant of this is CEO fraud. Here, the emails of a senior executive are compromised and emails sent to the finance function of the company purporting to be from the senior executive and instructing payments to be made, usually on an urgent basis on a Friday afternoon, to the fraudsters' bank accounts. Again, it is the victim who has been deceived.

- There are a number of types of impersonation scams. For example, a criminal may contact a victim and pretend to be from the police, the victim's bank, a utility company, a delivery company or a government department (such as HMRC), claiming the victim must settle a fine, pay a delivery charge, pay overdue tax or return a refund. In some cases, the criminal may impersonate a friend or family member and claim they need help urgently by way of a bank transfer.

- The classic Nigerian 419 fraud, or advance fee fraud, has somewhat faded in popularity, although variants of it have been given a new lease of life due to the ease with which large numbers of emails, SMSs or instant messages can be sent. This makes the chances of finding a victim far higher, and for a very significantly smaller outlay. In this fraud the victim is told one of many variations of a story, such as that a distant relative has died leaving a substantial inheritance which cannot be released until certain payments have been made (the advance fees). Initially these can be described as 'lawyers' fees' then 'taxes', and then even the need to pay off other beneficiaries with an amount representing a very large proportion of the 'inheritance' before the money can be released. The amounts demanded escalate rapidly once the fraudster realises they have a victim who is taken in by the fraud and is able to pay. It is often now seen as part of a hybrid fraud, where it is tacked on the end of an investment fraud, before the "proceeds" of trading (invariably fictional) can be withdrawn.

- Fraud in relation to online retail sites continues to be rife, particularly on the part of unscrupulous sellers. For example, buyers may be duped into paying for items which are either never delivered, are fake or have been grossly misrepresented.

- Online trading platform frauds are also prevalent. Here fantastic returns are promised from online platforms offering binary option, crypto asset or foreign exchange trading. Victims are persuaded to put money into their account in order to make trades. The success or otherwise of these is often manipulated or entirely fictional with the intention of persuading the victims to make further deposits. Accounts are then suddenly closed and the fraudsters refuse to return the deposited funds, or insist on payments being made (see advance fee fraud above) for example in respect of tax, to release the funds. Common features of these frauds are that the company purports to have a prestigious address in the City of London, but is unregulated by the FCA, the funds are paid to bank accounts outside the UK, and to the extent that there are genuine corporate structures involved at all, these are often incorporated in off-shore jurisdictions beyond the reach of UK law enforcement.

- Phishing is a particular type of fraud where emails, which are intended to appear genuine, are sent to potential victims in the hope of persuading them to provide sensitive information such as passwords or bank log-on details to the fraudsters, or to download malware. Smishing is now a common variant of phishing, whereby fake SMS messages are used rather than emails. Fraudsters have become more and more adept at presenting these as legitimate communications, including directing potential victims to sophisticated fake versions of the websites of legitimate financial institutions. For those engaging in this conduct, phishing is an easy and potentially lucrative form of fraud which presents a low risk of detection and apprehension.

- Ransomware attacks are used by cybercrime groups to extort victims, often by threatening to sell or publish stolen data. More recent methods of applying further pressure to a victim include threatening to make stolen data searchable online or threatening a distributed denial of service attack to publicly disrupt a corporate victim's business. Attacks are often targeted at sectors perceived as being under pressure. In the case of *Kurtaj and another*, two teenagers were found guilty in relation to multiple charges involving hacking, fraud and ransom demands targeted at a number of well-known companies including Revolut, Uber, BT and Nvidia. The latter instance included a threat to release approximately 1Tb of sensitive commercial information.

- On the dark web, online marketplaces sell compromised data as well as tools that enable cyberfraud. 'Fraud as a service' has increased in prevalence, whereby criminals (often organised into sophisticated and professionally-run organisations) sell their services and expertise, as well as tools, online, offering to carry out fraud on behalf of paying 'clients'.

- Pharming is a form of activity, often deployed in combination with phishing, which involves the deliberate redirection of users to an illegitimate website for dishonest ends. The websites of banks and other financial institutions are frequently targeted by hackers who implement tools which redirect users away from the legitimate site and to a site under the hackers' control. It is more insidious than phishing, which relies upon the victim clicking upon a link in a fraudulent email: pharming requires no such active participation on the part of the victim, which renders it difficult to identify and avoid.

- Online romance fraud is a particularly unpleasant variant of fraud whereby victims are targeted on social networking or dating sites, befriended by the fraudster who generally adopts a false identity, and persuaded to provide his or her bank details and/or to transfer large sums of cash. As with many forms of cyber-fraud, the perpetrators are generally based overseas and the likelihood of their being caught or the monies recovered is slim.
- A variant of this is known as a 'pig-butchering' scam. It has this name as the fraudsters refer to their victims as 'pigs' to be 'fattened up' and then 'butchered', or conned out of their money. Victims are targeted online, often on dating sites, to build a relationship with the fraudster who then persuades them to invest in an online trading platform, often controlled by the fraudster (see above). They may be encouraged to withdraw early gains, to gain trust and encourage larger investments. When they later come to withdraw the proceeds the fraudster and the platform will disappear, sometimes having extracted further funds through an advance fee fraud.

Crypto asset and Initial Coin Offering fraud

19.110 An area which has seen significant growth is crypto asset-related fraud, including fraud related to Initial Coin Offerings, or ICOs. As is often the case with new manifestations of technology, regulators and law enforcement agencies are one step behind the innovators in the sector which has opened a gap for those with dishonest intent to take advantage of the opportunities which they present while the authorities scramble to catch up.

19.111 Crypto assets are virtual representations of value which use some form of distributed ledger technology ('DLT') and which can be transferred, stored or traded electronically. Instead of individual participants maintaining their own ledgers, the system is underpinned by DLT which means that each and every transaction is simultaneously verified and recorded by all network participants. These include cryptocurrencies, such as Bitcoin and Ethereum, which, unlike traditional government-backed (or 'fiat') currencies, have no centralised authority to issue currency and to monitor transactions. These also include stablecoins, such as Tether, which have their value pegged to a specific fiat currency, and non-fungible tokens (NFTs) which are digital, non-interchangeable representations of artwork or other assets which supposedly derive value from being able to prove their ownership and authenticity on a blockchain (a form of DLT).

19.112 Regulators in most jurisdictions have warned consumers of the risks associated with crypto assets. The main risks arise from the following features:

- Anonymity. In reality, most crypto assets do not offer complete anonymity but a form of disconnection between users' real-life and crypto identities which, depending on the asset, offers varying layers of protection to users with dishonest intent. As more and more jurisdictions crack down on digital currency exchanges – one of the principal means by which funds are transferred from fiat to crypto and back to fiat – by forcing them to implement similar anti-money laundering procedures to traditional banks and money exchanges, it will become more and more difficult to transfer funds in and out of cryptocurrencies without leaving a real world trace.

- Speed of transfer. Funds can be transmitted out of the jurisdiction virtually instantaneously. By the time the user has realised that he or she has been defrauded, it is difficult to trace or recover those funds.
- Lack of centralised controlling authority. This means that, in the event that funds are transferred pursuant to a fraud, there is no agency with capacity to intervene, block transfers or freeze accounts.

19.113 In the UK, crypto assets remain largely unregulated. At the time of writing, the principal forms of regulation are, first, the requirement that firms offering crypto exchange or custodian services be registered with the FCA under the UK Money Laundering Regulations and, second, that activities relating to the relatively small proportion of crypto assets which fall within the FCA's current regulatory perimeter (essentially security tokens) are subject to the same degree of regulation as those relating to mainstream financial products.

19.114 The Financial Services and Markets Act 2023 gives the Treasury to extend the current FCA authorisation regime to what is referred to 'digital settlement assets' (DSAs). As currently defined, that term is intended to capture crypto assets where they are used for the settlement of payment obligations, a description which is likely to apply primarily to fiat-backed stablecoins initially. However, the definition of a DSA can be extended to cover other forms of crypto assets over time.

19.115 On 1 February 2023 HM Treasury published a further consultation into the regulation of crypto assets which envisages the possible extension of the regulatory perimeter to include all crypto assets. It remains to be seen to what extent the UK regime will align with the EU Markets in Crypto-Assets Regulation ('MiCA'), the new EU regulatory framework which is in the course of implementation in EU member states. Both in the UK and in the EU, the trend is towards increasing regulation, driven by the economic imperative to embrace the positive technological opportunities presented by crypto while maintaining or enhancing protections for consumers and market integrity.

19.116 ICOs present regulators and law enforcement agencies with a particular headache. These are essentially capital fund-raising schemes which allow companies and individuals to raise funds from members of the public, typically to finance a new cryptocurrency-related business venture. ICOs are something of a combination between a traditional Initial Public Offering (IPO) and a crowd-funding scheme. They work by inviting investors to contribute sums of an established cryptocurrency, such as Bitcoin or Ethereum, to the company in return, not for shares as would be the case in an IPO, but rather a digital coin or token of some description, in the anticipation that these will increase in value once the funding goal has been reached and the product launches.

19.117 The challenge for regulators is that ICOs are generally, depending upon how they are structured and the jurisdiction in which they are established, unregulated. This means that a company launching an ICO can elicit financial contributions from members of the public, often on the provision of minimal information, for extremely risky, if not downright fraudulent, schemes. If the project fails or the company goes into administration, there is little if any comeback for the investors who are unlikely to see their investment again. ICOs are by nature hugely high-risk and speculative investments even where they have been set up and run in good faith; many are out-and-out frauds: some 80% of ICOs were considered to have been scams according to a recent study.[59]

19.118 Crypto assets and in particular ICOs are likely to occupy an increasingly significant ranking in the league of fraud risks and present challenges which legislators are struggling to address. The direction of travel is very much towards increased regulation, primarily by finding ways of bringing ICOs within existing frameworks of regulated financial products and by increasing the legal requirements which apply to digital currency exchanges.

19.119 The question now is the extent to which crypto assets and ICOs will survive the likely degree of regulation to which they are to be subjected. After all, the lack of regulation is one of the main unique selling points of these products: there may come a point where regulation effectively extinguishes their very raison d'être. It seems likely that we will reach a fork in the road whereby 'legitimate' uses of the considerable opportunities presented by the new underlying technology will be harnessed by compliant companies and individuals while those operating in what will be the diminishing fringes of the unregulated sector will become the focus of regulatory and enforcement scrutiny.

The Civil Perspective

19.120 As with all fraud, the focus of the civil fraud lawyer in cyber-frauds is to recover losses caused to the victim. The civil causes of action available in cyber-fraud claims can equally be used in any civil fraud claims, and are largely common law claims.

19.121 This means that the law is able to develop to keep pace with the changing fraud landscape, and the courts of England and Wales are not afraid to develop the law in response to different challenges. If a victim can show a compelling case and some basis for the court to intervene, there is a willingness from the courts to provide victims with effective remedies. This has been seen to great effect in relation to cyber-fraud and the innovations of the English Courts in frauds involving the theft of crypto assets.[60] These innovations have included recognising crypto assets as property, establishing a way to establish jurisdiction

59 https://research.bloomberg.com/pub/res/d28giW28tf6G7T_Wr77aU0gDgFQ.

60 See **19.149** to **19.159** below.

for disputes, a change in procedure in the Civil Procedure Rules to make service out of the jurisdiction easier and allowing service by NFT. Enforcement has also seen innovation with liquidation of crypto assets being compelled and the proceeds paid into Court. This has prompted some commentators to suggest that The English Court should have its own crypto wallet.

19.122 As with all frauds, a victim should consider not only the claims they have against the fraudsters themselves, but also claims against third parties who might be easier to identify and serve, and who might have deeper pockets than the fraudster who will have taken steps to conceal their assets or the assets misappropriated in the fraud.

19.123 A common feature in cyber-fraud is the relative ease with which it is possible to follow the money through the banking system (unless and until it is converted to cash, or possibly cryptocurrencies), contrasted with the relative difficulty of identifying and serving the fraudsters. This is often because the fraudsters' involvement is to pretend to be someone they are not, for example in the CEO fraud mentioned above.[61] They are also very often in jurisdictions which are different either from the place where the loss was suffered, where the victim is, or even where the money is sent, either initially or in subsequent transactions made to launder the money and make it more difficult and expensive to follow the money. However, fraudsters have reacted to the fact that money can be followed through the banking system and as well as using banks in different jurisdictions have also habitually transferred money from the recipient bank account in many different tranches to several different bank accounts, and then transferred on again in the same fashion, making it less and less cost effective to try and follow the money. This has led to an increase in attempted claims against parties other than the fraudster, primarily banks, as to which see further below.

Potential Civil Causes of Action and Targets[62]

19.124 In order to take advantage of the draconian remedies available in the Courts of England and Wales such as freezing orders and search orders, the victim (the claimant in civil proceedings) must show a good arguable case against the defendants. It is necessary, therefore, to assess both who the claimant might want to sue, and what causes of action there might be against them. Below are brief descriptions of the main causes of action which can be deployed against potential targets in a civil fraud claim. It is not the intention to provide an exhaustive list together with a detailed exposition of the law, rather to provide a starting point for considering the claims which might be able to be brought.

61 See **19.109** et seq Variants of cyber fraud.

62 See further Paul McGrath QC, *Commercial Fraud in Civil Practice* (2nd edn, Oxford University Press 2014).

The Fraudster

19.125 Set out below are the main causes of action which can be deployed against the fraudster themselves.

- **Deceit.** The main cause of action against the fraudster will be the tort of deceit or fraudulent misrepresentation. The elements of this are similar to the fraud offences in the Fraud Act set out above.[63] In a deceit claim the victim must show:

  - the fraudster made a representation of fact to the victim;
  - which they intended the victim to rely on;
  - and which they knew to be false or were reckless as to whether it was true or false;
  - which the victim did rely on and this caused the victim loss.

  If all of the above elements are made out the claimant can claim all loss flowing from the fraudulent misrepresentation. There is no requirement that the loss needs to be reasonably foreseeable, just that it is caused by the misrepresentation. This can include a loss of opportunity.

  In *4Eng v Harper and another*[64] the claimants brought proceedings in deceit in respect of the purchase of a company's shares from fraudsters who had been using the company to commit wholesale fraud on Mars in relation to the maintenance of their factory. The claimants argued that but for being persuaded by fraudulent misrepresentations to buy the shares they would have invested in a different company. They were able to prove that this was more than a possibility and that there would have been finance available. The Court found that there was an 80% chance they would have invested, and an 80% chance that having done so the company would have continued to be as successful as it actually was. This meant that subject to those two 20% reductions the claimant's damages were both the loss of profits for the length of time they said they would have held the company, together with the profit realised on the sale of the business.

- **Unjust enrichment.** Here the claimant must show that the defendant has been enriched, that this is unjust and it is at the expense of the claimant. It is not difficult to see how these elements might be made out in a claim against a fraudster.

- **Conspiracy.** Often in fraud cases there are multiple defendants, all of whom are said to have been involved in some way in the fraud. One very useful cause of action to bring in all the actors in a fraud is a conspiracy claim. This is examined in more detail below.[65]

63 See **19.102** Fraud Act 2006.
64 *4Eng v Harper and another* [2008] EWHC 915 (Ch).
65 See **19.128** Accomplices.

- **Inducing a breach of contract.** Here the fraudster can be held liable as the accessory if they have persuaded another to breach a contract with the victim. This could be the case if the fraudster has persuaded an insider to assist them in the fraud. The elements of this tort are as follows:
  - the fraudster must have knowledge of the contract between A and B (the victim);
  - they must intentionally induce A to breach the contract or procure the breach;
  - this in fact causes A to breach the contract;
  - this causes loss to B; and
  - A has no justification for their actions.
- **Breach of Trust or Fiduciary Duties.** If the fraudster has been in a position of trust there may be claims for breach of trust or fiduciary duty. These provide powerful remedies for a claimant to require the fraudster to account or to assert proprietary interests against assets in order to assist in tracing them. This can be particularly useful where there are competing creditors, or there is an insolvency situation, as a proprietary interest can be asserted over assets which will prevent them being available for other creditors. This can be equally useful where a fraudster has invested wisely as the profits from an investment can also be claimed.
- **Constructive Trusts.** It may also be possible to assert that the fraudster holds stolen assets as trustee for the victim. Not only does this allow proprietary claims to be asserted over the assets and tracing claims to be pursued, it also brings into play the possibility of making claims for dishonest assistance in a breach of trust, even where there was no formal trust which the fraudster has breached. This will be examined further below when looking at accessory liability and other potential targets.[66]

19.126 Other less fraud specific causes of action should be considered where appropriate, such as breach of contract or negligence. It is not the purpose of this chapter to explore these in detail. A victim should be seeking to find the cause of action which is easiest to prove, but which still provides a remedy which is effective.

19.127 Causes of action such as deceit which require elements of dishonesty are more difficult to prove than When assessing causes of action which do not. The House of Lords explained this as follows[67]:

> 'the probabilities the court will have in mind as a factor, to whatever extent is appropriate in the particular case, that the more serious the allegation the

66 See **19.128** Accomplices and **19.129** Other accessories or facilitators.

67 (*Re H (Minors) (Sexual Abuse: Standard of Proof)* [1996] AC 563, at 586D-H, as clarified in *Re B (Children)* [2008] UKHL 35).

less likely it is that the event occurred and, hence, the stronger should be the evidence before the court concludes that the allegation is established on the balance of probability. Fraud is usually less likely than negligence.'

Accomplices

19.128 These could include co-conspirators either in the fraud itself, or knowingly in the receipt or laundering of the proceeds.

- **Conspiracy.** The main cause of action to bring in accomplices is a conspiracy claim. This can either be a conspiracy to cause loss by lawful or by unlawful means. Both torts require a combination or understanding between two or more people, and must result in loss being caused to the target of the conspiracy. Whilst an unlawful act is not required for a lawful means conspiracy, the sole or predominant intention or purpose must be to cause loss to the victim. For an unlawful means conspiracy, intention to cause loss still has to be proven, but it does not need to be the sole or predominant intention. An unlawful act has to be involved in the concerted action.
- **Dishonest Assistance.** Dishonest assistance in a breach of trust can be claimed against an accomplice if the following factors are present.
  - there must be a trust or fiduciary relationship;
  - it must have been breached;
  - the third party must have induced or assisted in the breach; and
  - the third party must have acted dishonestly in providing the inducement or assistance. There is no requirement that the trustee has acted dishonestly.
- **Knowing or unconscionable receipt.** The elements required for liability are:
  - the assets must be held under a trust or fiduciary relationship;
  - there must be a transfer in breach of trust;
  - the transfer must be to a third party beneficially (so not as an agent for others eg in a banking relationship);
  - in circumstances where the knowledge of the recipient of the transaction is such that it would be unconscionable to allow them to retain the assets.

Other accessories or facilitators

19.129 These could include parties who, whilst they were not complicit in the fraud, have been drawn into it sufficiently that they can be held to have liability. Banks are an obvious target, although a very difficult one to hit, as detailed further below. Other targets are any party which has received the proceeds of the fraud, including in certain circumstances solicitors or accountants.

19.130 To the extent a contractual relationship can be established there may be breach of contract claims, or even claims in negligence, if a duty of care can be established. For example, in relation to the email intercept fraud described above,[68] where the party to whom funds were to be sent was the claimant's own solicitor they may have a duty of care towards the claimant. In this example it might be to ensure that their email system has not been hacked so as to allow a fraudster to intercept it and send on altered emails to deceive the claimant into making a payment to the fraudster's account. In these circumstances a claim against the solicitors in negligence should be considered.

Banks

19.131 Banks have increasingly been targeted in claims brought by the victims of APP fraud. They are obvious targets, as their involvement in the fraud is immediately apparent, as the bank accounts of both the victim and the fraudster can be quickly and accurately identified, including the identity of the banks in question. Claims have been brought against the victim's bank and the recipient bank into which the funds were transferred.

19.132 A contractual claim was argued in the case of *Tidal Energy Ltd v Bank of Scotland Plc.*[69] Here the claimant was induced in a mandate fraud to send a payment intended for Designcraft Ltd to an account in the name of Childfreedom Ltd by CHAPS. The CHAPS form required the recipient name, sort code, account number and receiving bank. All of these except the recipient name were details of the fraudster's account in the name of Childfreedom. Neither the sending bank nor the receiving bank checked the account holder's name, which enabled this fraud to take place. The claimant in this case argued that for its bank not to check these details was a breach of contract in that the payment instruction had not been performed and as such their account should not be debited. This argument failed both at first instance and in the Court of Appeal on the basis that this is common banking practice.

19.133 In his dissenting judgment Floyd LJ considered that as the payment instruction included four identifiers including the account holder's name, the instruction was not complied with if this identifier was not checked. Permission was given to appeal to the Supreme Court but this appeal was not pursued.

19.134 The prevalence of APP fraud did, however, lead to Which? making a 'super complaint' to the Payment Systems Regulator (PSR) in 2016. In response the PSR worked with the banking industry to report on whether and what steps

68 See **19.109** Variants of cyber fraud.

69 *Tidal Energy v Bank of Scotland* [2014] EWCA Civ 1107.

could be taken to reduce APP fraud. This in turn led to the development of the Contingent Reimbursement Model, which sought to define the circumstances in which banks would be liable to victims of fraud and the levels of care the banks owed to their customers, as well as the levels of care that customers have to protect themselves against APP fraud. The Contingent Reimbursement Model for Authorised Push Payment Scams (the Code) was implemented on 29 May 2019 and has since been amended. It is at present a voluntary code, but most major UK banks are signatories. It requires banks to:

- Take reasonable steps to prevent accounts being opened for criminal purposes;
- Implement Confirmation of Payee (CoP) in a way that the customer can understand and respond to;
- Take reasonable steps to detect accounts which may be being used to receive APP scam funds;
- Where there are concerns that funds may be the proceeds of APP scams take reasonable steps to freeze the funds and repatriate them to the paying bank; and
- Reimburse customers who are the victims of APP frauds unless they can establish that the customer ignored effective warnings, failed to act on a clear negative CoP result or made the payment without a reasonable basis for believing that the payee was the person the customer was expecting to pay.

19.135 CoP specifically addresses the issue highlighted by the *Tidal Energy* case, and requires, in certain circumstances, the recipient bank to check the details of the beneficiary identified on the payment instruction and confirm to the paying bank that the details match. This is generally also confirmed to the customer before a transfer is made. However, there are limitations to this provision:

- It necessarily only applies to payments made between banks which are signatories to the Code;
- It only applies to customer undertaking payment journeys between GPB-denominated UK domiciled accounts; and
- The definition of Customer does not include businesses (other than a micro-enterprise).

Whilst the Code provides a mechanism for reimbursement and assists with APP fraud prevention, it is voluntary and so does not provide a cause of action against either the victim's bank or the recipient bank. It has also prompted a change in approach by fraudsters which is to target international transfers and transfers from non-GPB denominated accounts.

19.136 Claims against the customer's bank in relation to which there are reported judgments have focussed on situations involving APP fraud, in contrast to where the bank has been deceived and breached its duty to its customer in this way. It is supposed that in such cases liability would more easily be established and the bank readier as a result to reimburse. The Supreme Court recently considered a claim against the customer's bank in an APP fraud on the basis that the bank had breached its Quincecare duty, after an implied duty first established in *Barclays Bank plc v Quincecare Ltd*[70] to the effect that a bank should refrain from carrying out a payment instruction if it had reasonable grounds to suspect that the instruction was an attempt to misappropriate the customer's funds. The Court of Appeal in *Philipp v Barclays Bank UK plc*[71] had decided that this duty was directly applicable to APP fraud. In an eagerly awaited judgment the Supreme Court disagreed, and held that provided the payment instruction was clear, and made by the customer or the customer's agent with apparent authority it did not need to make further enquiries and would be in breach of its duty to make the payment if it did not do so. The circumstances in which this duty might provide a remedy for victims of APP fraud are therefore severely limited.

19.137 Claims have also been made against the recipient bank, both seeking to establish a duty owed to the payer by the recipient bank and making claims for unjust enrichment or knowing receipt.[72] None of these have been successful. It seems clear that the recipient bank does not owe duties to third parties, but only to its customer. In *Tecnimont Arabia Ltd v National Westminster Bank Plc*[73] a claim for unjust enrichment was brought on the basis that the mistake in paying over the money caused by the deceit of the fraudster meant that the bank had been enriched unjustly. However, on the facts it was held that this was not at the expense of the claimant (due to the interbank payment mechanism). The court went on to consider whether, if unjust enrichment had been made out the bank would have been able to rely on a defence of change of position, as it had paid the money away at the instruction of the fraudster and as such would be out of pocket. The court found that it would be able to rely on this defence as its conduct was not unjust – its procedures had been followed and they were in line with industry standards. Such delay as there was between the notice of the fraud and the freezing of the account was reasonable.

19.138 The alternative claim in *Tecnimont* for knowing receipt also failed as there was no breach of trust or fiduciary duty – a requirement of the cause of action. The same would be true in relation to a claim for dishonest assistance: there would be no breach of trust, even if the requisite dishonesty by the bank could be established.

19.139 However, a claim could be made if the bank had received the money beneficially (i.e. other than as a deposit taking institution) perhaps in payment of a loan, and a proprietary claim could be established. Here there might be a claim either for knowing or unconscionable receipt or simply a tracing claim that the

70 *Barclays Bank plc v Quincecare Ltd* [1992] 4 All ER 363.

71 *Philipp v Barclays Bank UK plc* [2023] UKSC 25.

72 *Abou-Rahmah v Abacha* [2005] EWHC 2662 (QB); *JP SPC 4 v Royal Bank of Scotland International Ltd* [2023] AC 461.

73 *Tecnimont Arabia Ltd v National Westminster Bank Plc* [2022] EWHC 1172 (Comm).

bank could not defend on the basis they were a bona fide purchaser for value without notice of the proprietary claim.

19.140 This was exactly the situation in a Privy Council case referred from the Gibraltar courts *Credit Agricole Corporation and Investment Bank (Appellant) v Papadimitriou.*[74] Here the claims made against the bank which had received the laundered proceeds of a fraud, were in dishonest assistance, knowing receipt and a tracing claim on the basis that the bank was holding assets over which the claimant had a proprietary claim. The Court at first instance dismissed all the claims. Only one was appealed, being the tracing claim. The bank's defence was that it had received the funds as a bona fide purchaser for value without notice of the fact they were the proceeds of fraud. It is not clear why the knowing receipt claims were not also appealed, as the test in relation to the bank's notice would seem to be very similar for the test for the defence the bank was running. The case might provide the possibility of knowing or unconscionable receipt claims to be advanced by other claimants in the future. The Court of Appeal allowed the appeal on the point argued, which the bank then appealed to the Privy Council.

19.141 The Privy Council found that the bank had failed in its KYC obligations in that it had not asked the appropriate questions about the underlying transactions. If it had, the Court held, it would have ascertained that there were either questions, which if they remained unanswered lead to the conclusion that the transactions were for the purpose of money laundering, or if answered would have inevitably led to this conclusion. The bank therefore was sufficiently on notice of the fact that the funds it had received were the proceeds of fraud that it could not avail itself of the bona fide purchaser without notice defence. There appear to be no other reported cases of banks being held to be liable in similar circumstances, so this is an unusual set of facts which allowed liability to be established in this case.

19.142 Solicitors acting for fraudsters often find themselves having to take great care about the source of the funds they are receiving in payment of their fees. If they are on notice that the funds could be the subject of a constructive trust, then they are potentially liable to pay back the trust money to the claimant. It is a common tactic to attempt to set up this sort of claim, and make life difficult for the solicitors acting for the fraudster.

Civil Fraud Remedies in Cyber Fraud

19.143 Again, these are not in substance different from any other fraud claim. However, one of the defining features of cyber-fraud and cases involving the theft of crypto assets, is that it can be very difficult indeed to identify the fraudsters themselves. Tools which the civil-fraud lawyer can turn to in a fraud claim are set

74 *Credit Agricole Corporation and Investment Bank (Appellant) v Papadimitriou (Respondent)* [2015] UKPC 13 Privy Council Appeal No 0023 of 2014.

out below.[75] What these remedies have in common is that they are almost always obtained without notice to the fraudster, and in the case of disclosure orders against third parties, can be coupled with gagging orders preventing the third party from informing the fraudster that they have been ordered to give disclosure.

- **Freezing injunctions**. These are court orders freezing either the assets of the fraudster, or where there is a proprietary claim the assets which are said to be held on trust for the claimant. They can be made on a worldwide basis. As well as showing a cause of action and identifying some assets the claimant must show a good arguable case and risk of dissipation. As they are obtained without notice there is an onerous duty of full and frank disclosure, and a cross undertaking to pay damages to the defendant if the order is later found to have been wrongly granted is almost always required.
- **Search orders.** These are orders which require the occupant of specified premises to permit entry and allow a search within strictly defined parameters. The requirements are similar as for a freezing injunction, and in addition the claimant must show some evidence that the respondent will not comply with an order to provide disclosure or deliver up evidence. The main thrust of the search in a cyber-crime case (if a premises can be identified) will be for electronic devices which may have been used in the fraud.
- **Third party disclosure orders.** These are either under the *Norwich Pharmacal*[76] jurisdiction, or pursuant to Part 25 of the Civil Procedure Rules.[77] They are often coupled with gagging orders preventing notification to the fraudster. These gagging orders are normally for a short period of time to allow analysis of the material disclosed and further applications either for disclosure or freezing injunctions to be made.

19.144 The first of the recent developments in these remedies was in relation to a CEO fraud.[78] The case is called *CMOC v Persons Unknown*.[79] In *CMOC* the claim arose from an alleged fraud which had been committed by persons unknown by infiltrating the email account of one of the senior management of the claimant. Those persons were then able to send payment instructions purporting to come from that senior manager to the finance function of the claimant, but which were not actually from him. As a result payments totalling around £6.3 million were sent in a number of large payments from the claimant's bank account to various other bank accounts around the world. The English Commercial Court granted a without notice freezing injunction against 'persons unknown'.

19.145 Injunctions against persons unknown have been possible since 2003 when Harry Potter's publishers obtained an injunction against the individuals

75 See also CPR, Pt 25, s I – Interim Remedies.

76 *Norwich Pharmacal Co v Customs and Excise Commissioners* [1974] AC 133.

77 CPR, Pt 25 (1)(g).

78 *See* **19.109** Variants of cyber fraud.

79 *CMOC v Persons Unknown* (2017) EWHC 3599 Comm.

who had stolen copies of the book before its publication and were trying to sell it to newspapers.[80] The key point identified by the Court was to identify the defendants sufficiently that it was clear who was caught by the injunction and who was not. In *CMOC* the Court allowed the defendants to be identified as those who had perpetrated the fraud by reference to the transactions and/or those who were the legal or beneficial owners of the bank accounts into which the money was paid. Orders against Persons Unknown have since been widely deployed in relation to crypto asset cases, as detailed below.

19.146 Another very important point to come out of this case is that the Court granted a blanket order for service of the worldwide freezing order out of the jurisdiction, and made orders for alternative service, by electronic means. The latter point is not new, but the combination of orders was at the time quite exciting in the context of cyber-crime, and has since been the subject of much judicial innovation in the context of claims involving crypto assets.

19.147 Another important development from *CMOC* was in relation to the disclosure order which was obtained against the foreign banks to which the stolen money was paid. Prior to *CMOC* it wasn't completely clear how extra-territorial disclosure orders could be obtained, as at this time it was clear that *Norwich Pharmacal* orders could not be served out of the jurisdiction.[81] There has also been to a change in the Civil Procedure Rules in relation to service of disclosure orders out of the jurisdiction.[82] In *CMOC* the applicant sought orders under the *Bankers Trust*[83] jurisdiction and under CPR, Part 25(1)(g). This was previously a little used jurisdiction and provides that the court can grant:

> 'an order directing a party to provide information about the location of relevant property or assets or to provide information about relevant property or assets which are or may be the subject of an application for a freezing injunction.'

19.148 An important point to note here is that the Court can grant orders in relation to assets which are *or may be* the subject of an application for a freezing injunction. This clearly means that whilst you probably need to have the grounds for a freezing injunction, you do not need to have obtained one before you seek information under this Part. The information obtained may make your application for a freezing injunction stronger or more targeted. It also covers assets which are in other jurisdictions.

80 *Bloomsbury Publishing Group Ltd v News Group Newspapers Ltd (Continuation of Injunction)* [2003] 1 WLR 1633.
81 *AB Bank Ltd v Abu Dhabi Commercial Bank PJSC* [2016] EWHC 2082 (Comm).
82 See **19.152**.
83 *Bankers Trust Co v Shapira* [1980] 1 WLR 1274.

Crypto Assets

19.149 This case generated a lot of interest in relation to its application to fraud claims involving crypto assets, which have been on the increase in the English Courts. One of the key features of crypto assets is the fact that they are simultaneously anonymous, in that the individual behind the public key cannot easily be identified, and completely transparent, in that all of the transactions are recorded and can be seen in the Blockchain. The English courts have been compelled to develop the law in certain key areas to meet these challenges.

19.150 The use of injunctions against persons unknown has become commonplace. The defendants can be identified as those who received the proceeds of a fraud as cryptocurrencies and are the holders of a certain public key. However, there are some unique features of cases involving crypto assets where again the court has had to innovate. The first legal concept the Court was asked to grapple with was whether a crypto asset is property under English law. This was first decided in *Robertson v Person Unknown* 16 July 2019 (unreported) and followed by *AA v Person Unknown.*[84] The latter case was in the context of a ransom paid in bitcoin for the decryption of a company's computer systems hacked and encrypted for this purpose. The insurer who paid the ransom sought a proprietary injunction to freeze the bitcoin it had paid. Previously crypto assets fell outside of the traditional definition on property under English law, meaning a proprietary injunction would not be available. On an interim basis the court decided that English law could recognise a crypto asset as a new form of property. They were definable, identifiable by third parties and capable of assumption by third parties, and they had some degree of permanence.[85] On this basis a proprietary injunction was granted. This has since been followed in *Ion Science Ltd v Persons Unknown* (unreported) and *Fetch.ai Ltd v Persons Unknown.*[86]

19.151 The next issue which arose in crypto cases was the question of jurisdiction and choice of law for claims. This is a novel feature of crypto, because unlike a bank account which must be located in a certain jurisdiction, this is not the case with a crypto asset. This issue was first decided in *Ion Science* which held that the *lex situs* of the crypto asset was the place where the owner was domiciled. This has since been the subject of challenge in *Tulip Trading Ltd v van der Laan*[87] where the Claimant was a Seychelles company, so domiciled in the Seychelles, but held to be resident in England and Wales. The residence point was found to be sufficient to found jurisdiction in England. This was not appealed, and the Court of Appeal did not suggest the conclusion was incorrect. This then is the current state of the law.

84 *AA v Person Unknown* [2019] EWHC 3556 (Comm).
85 *National Provincial Bank Ltd v Ainsworth* [1965] AC 1175, [1965] 5 WLUK 32 followed.
86 *Fetch.ai Ltd v Persons Unknown* [2021] EWHC 2254 (Comm).
87 *Tulip Trading Ltd v van der Laan* [2023] EWCA Civ 83.

19.152 Service of proceedings and injunctions and service of disclosure orders has been the next development. Dealing first with disclosure orders, this has been addressed by a change to the Civil Procedure Rules and the introduction of a new jurisdictional gateway for the service of 'information orders'. These include those granted under the *Norwich Pharmacal* jurisdiction, the *Bankers Trust* jurisdiction and CPR Part 25. The relevant provision in the CPR is Practice Direction 6B 3.1(25) and it became effective from 1 October 2022. This provides that with the permission of the Court a claim form or application may be served out of the jurisdiction where an order is sought for disclosure of:

- The true identity of a defendant or potential defendant; and/or
- What has become of the property of a claimant or applicant.

The claim or application must be made for the purpose of proceedings already started or which are intended to be started in the English Courts. This is expected to provide clarity and make it easier to litigate issues arising in crypto claims. The new procedure has been deployed in the case of *LMN v Bitflyer Holdings Inc and others*[88] where Bankers Trust orders were obtained against several exchanges located overseas. The Court granted the disclosure order and also permitted service out of the jurisdiction against those exchanges under the new provision.

19.153 The courts have also innovated further in relation to service of proceedings and injunctions in these sorts of cases. The author speculated in the previous edition that service may in the future be effected on the blockchain, and this has indeed come to pass. The court has permitted service by NFT in at least 2 cases, being *D'Aloia v Persons Unknown and others* and *Osbourne v Persons Unknown.*[89] The process is that an NFT is minted by the claimant and then airdropped into the wallets identified as holding the stolen NFTs. The service NFT contained a URL which linked to a website holding copies of all of the documents for service, and which could be accessed by the custodians of each wallet. Service was thereby embedded in the blockchain.

19.154 Finally, there is one more recent development, which comes at the end of a victim's journey to seek redress, and this is in the area of enforcement of a judgment. The case is *Law v Persons Unknown and Huobi Global Ltd* (unreported) 26 January 2023. Here a judgment was obtained against the persons unknown who had stolen crypto assets. Huobi operated a crypto exchange which held the wallets into which the stolen crypto assets were transferred. Whilst it was outside the jurisdiction and therefore could not be compelled to comply with an English order, it had indicated to the claimant its willingness to comply and whilst it did not consent to the order had not opposed it. This is also a lesson in good communication as the solicitors for the claimant had been in contact with Huobi and obtained its cooperation. Exchanges will often wish to be seen to be cooperating with the victims of fraud and complying with foreign court orders.

88 *LMN v Bitflyer Holdings Inc and others* [2022] EWHC 2954 (Comm).

89 *D'Aloia v Persons Unknown and others* [2022] EWHC 1723 (Ch) and *Osborne v Persons Unknown* [2023] EWHC 340 (KB) (22 February 2023).

19.155 The order sought was for delivery up of the crypto assets in order that the claimant could enforce against it. The way the court gave effect to this was to order that first the crypto asset was converted to fiat currency, and then that this fiat currency was paid into court in England, allowing the claimant to then seek an order to enforce against it. It is the slightly cumbersome procedure which has led some commentators to suggest that it might be time for the English court to have its own crypto wallet.

Other Civil Remedies in Cyber-Crime

19.156 This chapter would not be complete without mentioning a trend in the High Court's Media and Communications List and the development of the jurisdiction to grant injunctions against 'persons unknown' in order to respond to it. The trend is in relation to hacking and blackmail claims.

19.157 The hacker will hack into a company's systems and steal confidential information, and then threaten to publish it unless large sums of money are paid. A reasonably early example of a case involving these circumstances is *PML v Person(s) Unknown (responsible for demanding money from the Claimant on 27 February 2018)*.[90]

19.158 As is apparent from the case title, the injunction was granted against persons unknown, but with sufficient detail about their identity that it is clear who is caught by the injunction and who is not. As in *CMOC* a blanket order for service out of the jurisdiction was granted and that service was permitted by email to the email address from which the blackmail demand had been sent. The judgment is worth reading as it sets out the steps which the claimant went to in order to close down the threat to publish its confidential information, and how successful those steps appeared to have been.

19.159 Since this case several more injunctions and judgments have been obtained in similar cases and there is now a fairly well-established procedure for bringing them.[91] The cases will generally satisfy requirements for the interim injunction to be granted without notice and for the hearing to be held in private. Often the Claimant will be anonymised. Service out of the jurisdiction will generally be permitted given the difficulties with identifying the Defendant, and where they might be located. Alternative service by electronic means will also generally be permitted. Default judgment will often be granted, continuing interim injunctions and with the application being decided on paper and without the need for a hearing in circumstances where the defendants, despite having been served in accordance with the court's requirements, unsurprisingly have not participated in the proceedings.

90 *PML v Person(s) Unknown (responsible for demanding money from the Claimant on 27 February 2018)* [2018] EWHC 838 (QB).

91 *Ince Group plc v Persons Unknown* [2022] EWHC 808 (QB); *Armstrong Watson LLP v Persons Unknown* [2023] EWHC 1791 (KB).

19.160 The development of the remedies available to the victims of cyber fraud and theft of crypto assets highlight and confirm the willingness of the English courts to innovate rapidly and be extremely flexible in meeting the fast-moving challenges of fraud in this area. They also show how effective these remedies can be when coupled with a well thought out strategy, even to the point of being able to enforce against crypto assets held in exchanges located out of the jurisdiction.

CHAPTER 20

THE DIGITAL NEXT WAY

Mark Blackhurst

CYBER ATTACKS

20.01 If there's anything that's guaranteed about the future of the internet, it's that cyber-attacks will continue to be a part of its day-to-day functioning life and that too few online businesses will properly protect themselves. In recent years, the news on a daily basis is littered with stories of companies being hacked, infiltrated or subject to online cyber intrusion and theft. If only these companies would think about this or try to prevent issues at source. In most cases cyber, security issues are preventable and can, with the right planning and strategic partner, be safeguarded against.

20.02 If you run a web-based company, cyber-security arguably is possibly the most important aspect of your business model. Quite simply, if you don't properly protect your business, you're leaving it exposed to being exploited, controlled and irreparably damaged in the future economy. Vast amounts of money are spent on Digital business in today's modern era, especially in the marketing world and at DigitalNext we seek to protect our clients right from the outset. We made this decision a number of years ago, it's a fundamental part of our day-to-day operational thinking and structure.

20.03 Just a few years ago, in 2016, businesses in the UK lost over £11 billion to cyber-crime. That's an average of £210 per person in the country. Up to date recent figures suggest that cyber crime poses a substantial and increasing economic threat to the UK, with an estimated annual cost of £27 billion, which is a substantial increase. Cyber criminals, ranging from individuals to organised groups find cyber crime to be a highly lucrative business, To compound this, the ease of access and anonymity offered by ICT make it an extremely attractive endeavour. Developing a deeper understanding of cyber crime and its economic implications is crucial to combatting this evolving threat effectively and as a company working extremely closely with our clients, we are extremely aware of our important responsibilities and have invested in continually enhancing our security procedures and protocols.

20.04 The first hints that the World Wide Web was potentially flawed came from the fears of the Y2K bug, and while that fizzled out, what it did do was begin or enable conversations about who was responsible for protecting all the information stored online. In our view the Y2K bug was the dawn of the new digital era in the new Millenium and a signal post for the change in the world that was to come.

20.05 From there data poured into all the emerging platforms, governments were caught flat-footed. They hadn't prepared for the internet's success, and they're still scrambling to keep up with the rate of change to this day.

20.06 The debate is still raging about who has to take responsibility for protecting the online population. Facebook, or as we now know it, META, Twitter and even Google are being targeted for not doing enough to protect individuals, as is huge news at the moment, but they're constantly battling to protect themselves. Very few countries are even close to helping protect their citizens, and so it's a real Wild West, where only those who strive to protect themselves will remain secure.

20.07 As the web has developed to a place where an exponentially growing number of people live, work and play there has been a huge growth in the number of unscrupulous characters around the world who spend their time searching for any potential weaknesses. And so, from its inception to its global reach today, companies and individuals could not and will not be able to rely on governmental protection online.

20.08 Computer security on a huge scale is now a constant arms race. As developers work to alleviate one threat, virus writers are already planning ten new ways to infiltrate your business. These aren't your stereotypical people sitting in their parents' basement, they are advanced criminal organisations. Many now run as professional outfits, combing the web to constantly search for points of access that they can exploit for financial gain.

20.09 An example we have observed in particular where a company was held for ransom by one of these unscrupulous criminal outfits, where the effect was worsened by their incumbent agency's previous supplier's bad advice. Access to the site wasn't returned to them until they had handed over a substantial amount of money this would have been easily preventable. The victim didn't have anything physically stolen, but their entire business was tied up in a single website and without it, they were out of business. These kinds of attacks are on the rise, but you can protect your valuable data and online assets from these modern-day thieves with smart security choices. This and similar kinds of situations are ones we have assisted scores of companies with in the past few years, in the post Brexit and lockdown era to a successful conclusion.

PROTECTING YOUR BUSINESS

20.10 In cutting corners with cyber-security, businesses not investing time and resources in their cyber security are not only exposing themselves to a possible security breach further down the line, they're also leaving their customers at risk too.

20.11 When a business doesn't value the security of its customers, it cannot expect to continue gaining their custom. It's at this point, especially when speaking with new potential customers, we are front foot educating about the investment and strategy that needs to be deployed to protect their business' future.

20.12 As you are developing and growing your business, you should be constantly learning from those with more experience. It's a great way of ensuring your security protocols are up to date and helps you to create a safe, secure business network. You should be seeking out people who have years of experience online in order to learn about what your needs are and how to meet them.

20.13 The world right now is in a time of huge transition and disruption. In a disrupted world, it's those who react best to it that will prosper in the future. From an individual's perspective, if you want to be taken seriously in the online world, you should be keeping up to date with all the new ways online security is being threatened. The same can also be said for businesses. Being an outwardly cyber security conscious company is beneficial for your reputation and the public perception of your business, being seen to be secure and aware is certainly something that any company can use to promote themselves as it breeds confidence in them outwardly.

20.14 As a business owner looking for advice, you should look for companies with good accreditation and track record, for example. By looking for a Digital Partner that is an affiliated Google Premier Partner or also looking for further accreditations to their name could be something you do. At DigitalNext the Google Premier partner certificate is something we have now held for a long time. Google is possibly the most trusted name online and companies must work hard to obtain that level of trust from them. Do business with companies like Google and you'll learn a lot about the realities of being successful and safe online.

20.15 The online economy is utterly unique in that it gives your product an almost unlimited amount of potential clients, in the post Brexit world you may want to grow your business more Internationally but you also have to be aware that those working in other countries may not be as safety conscious as we are becoming in the UK.

20.16 You may want to trade with them, but you cannot take their security for granted, just as you can't take yours for granted either.

GDPR

20.17 Increasingly companies are now harvesting vast sums of data from those using their services. And if you're UK-based; you have a legal responsibility under the Data Protection Act (DPA) to ensure you don't put that data at risk, additionally there's an even bigger piece of legislation. The EU's General Data Protection Regulations (GDPR) came into effect on the 25 May 2018, and while it reaffirms much of what the DPA already stipulates, there are new elements and significant enhancements, so you will have to do some things for the first time and some things differently than ever before.

20.18 The GDPR stipulates that in some instances if data is taken maliciously from your company, you don't just have to report this to a central body; you will also have to report it directly to the individuals whose data was stolen.

20.19 So this isn't just yours and your customers' data that's at risk, it's your entire reputation as a business. It's why it can't be said often enough that security really should be top of your agenda.

20.20 Imagine, for a moment, you run a small independent clothing shop. It's your pride and joy, and every night as you leave the shop, you lock the money in the safe, set the alarm, close the shutters and double lock the front door. But you haven't bothered to check the windows, and one is left wide open all night. The contents of that shop get stolen, and your safe is taken too – all because you left the shop unprotected.

20.21 This is exactly what happens online when cyber-security isn't taken seriously, and professional hackers will take seconds to expose that weakness in your defences.

20.22 There are many hundreds of thousands of online businesses that don't use a full 360-degree website, multichannel marketing and security conscious service. They want minimal setup costs and pay next to nothing for a cheap website build. The coding of your site is a big part of its security, and if that's not done well it leaves them exposed. What's more, online businesses can flourish at any moment, and as they grow, they need to update their security. Again though, this is often left until the last minute by many when it should be a priority.

STEPS TO UPDATE YOUR ONLINE SECURITY

20.23 There are some simple steps to help ensure you and your customers remain protected.

20.24 When you visit certain websites, you may not have noticed that some begin with the acronym HTTPS. It stands for Hypertext Transfer Protocol Secure, and it's a huge step in ensuring intruders can't tamper with the communications between your website and your users when they access it from a browser. Those intruders can simply be looking for a way to try and inject bespoke ads into their pages, but they can also be looking for ways to use that data maliciously.

20.25 Once they have that information, it becomes easier for them to trick users in to handing over sensitive information or installing viruses such as malware. There are various types of malware, including spyware, keyloggers, true viruses, worms, or any type of malicious code that infiltrates a computer.

20.26 Again, they can be used by big companies to feed-back data or prevent copyright breaches, but they can also be used by unwanted intruders to gather up your data. They will exploit every unprotected resource that travels between your websites and your users. Images, cookies, scripts, HTML … they're all exploitable.

20.27 Intrusions can occur at any point in the network, including a user's machine, WIFI, or a compromised Internet Service Provider (ISP), just to name a few.

20.28 If you're doing business online, it's essential you use HTTPS. It's where the little green lock appears on your web browser and lets potential customers know your site is safe.

20.29 One of the simplest ways to keep your company well protected is to automate your operating system's updates. Companies like Apple and Microsoft do a lot of the work for you, and constantly offer updates to try and stay one step ahead of the criminals.

20.30 A great example of why this is important is the Wanna Cry ransom ware outbreak that hit back in 2017. It targeted a known issue in Windows operating systems, however users who had run an update were protected. But millions of users worldwide had outdated systems and felt its effects. And once inside, this outbreak, like others before it, attacked entire networks and brought entire businesses, websites, governmental and educational systems to their knees.

20.31 A great way to work against this is also to ensure you keep a constantly updated backup of your entire website. This will hopefully only ever be used as a last resort, but can even come in handy when there's been a catastrophic administrative error, which does happen!

20.32 We often hear of the importance of using 'strong passwords' to protect our accounts from attacks and a good password system is a great first step. Most operating systems and web platforms now require customers and administrator accounts to adopt strong passwords and it's vital this is used. But many now also offer a requirement for users to change their password every few months or so; while that may be annoying for those of us who've used our dog's name as every single password since we first had a Myspace account, it's a brilliant way to increase security, particularly for employee logins.

20.33 For those employees who have access to the backend of your website, it's now recommended that they use Google's 2-factor authentication. It means they don't just enter their user ID and password, but also a Google authentication number, meaning it's much more difficult for hackers to gain access where you least want them. The Google authenticator number is a 1-time code that users access via a mobile app each time they log in. Again, it's one more login step for your employees but is vastly more secure than a simple username and password combination.

20.34 We've all heard of anti-virus software and firewalls, but just like operating systems, these need to be regularly updated. Similarly, these should be set up to update automatically. If you're paying for the software to protect you, it only makes sense that you remain protected against the latest threats.

20.35 Your online business is likely to require payments to be made through your website. The last thing you need is fraudulent activity and payments. Most payment processors enable fraud alerts, but fraud protection shouldn't be taken for granted. Like all security issues, it's beneficial that you understand how they work.

20.36 They stop things like mismatching credit card information being used, or orders being shipped to blacklisted countries, and while some will inevitably slip through, fraud alerts can prevent most fraudsters from using your site.

20.37 If you're a small business, chances are you aren't storing company and customer details on private servers. You'll be paying for the services of hosts to do that heavy lifting for you. But this proves once again why it's essential that you're aware of every possible weakness that can lead to a successful attack on your business. It falls on you as a business owner to ensure your providers work with secure systems and protect all the data being sent between you and your customers. Go to the top providers and ask them questions.

20.38 Only when you're satisfied with the service they're offering should you be willing to give them your money.

20.39 When it comes to taking payments, it may be tempting for some businesses to delve into the world of cryptocurrency. The recent hype around Bitcoin and others has led to a rapid surge in cryptocurrency use across the world. Again, governments around the world are struggling to adapt their regulations to this rapidly evolving marketplace. You need to be extremely well prepared if you want to adopt cryptocurrency into your business model. Stories are already emerging of people losing thousands of pounds through fraud, viruses, hacking and the physical loss or damage of computer hardware. Companies need to be aware and make the right moves in this area to ensure their preparedness for the ever growing Crypto currency and Block chain space.

EMPLOYEE SAFETY

20.40 It is not just the structure of your online presence that can create problems. Each and every member of your workforce with access to your information is not only a potential security threat; they're also a security risk. Employees are the gateway to your business and often that makes them the biggest danger. It's easy enough for them to plug in a memory stick and walk off with years' worth of sensitive information, but it's more likely that they'll grant access to a malicious person unwittingly. It's essential that all your staff remain aware of all best practice when using online resources in the online world.

20.41 Potential hackers aren't only using traditional phishing scams, whereby they seek to gain entry to your servers via email trickery. They will try to encourage employees to open attachments or click on links in emails or on the web that will take them to sites that will attempt to steal their private passwords or information. Those scams are evolving, and now include 'vishing', using voice software and 'smishing', using text messages. Each of these scams is an attempt to access the passwords that can give hackers access to whatever they want to see within your business. It's therefore imperative that each and every employee within your business is aware of these potential threats. Have you considered cybersecurity training sessions for each and every employee? It should really be a part of their orientation into the business.

PROTECTING YOUR REMOTE WORKFORCE

20.42 There's also an increasing trend for remote working and with that comes new dangers. Home Wifi systems are often poorly protected, with some not even demanding a password to be connected. Workers also use shared spaces, cafes and cloud Wifi while they're going about their day. These unsecured networks are a security nightmare and should be avoided at all costs by anyone on your staff using a company machine.

20.43 Businesses where employees sign in remotely should consider setting up a virtual private network (VPN). It allows them to access certain applications via a secure web browser and encrypts the network traffic to make it secure. Users can only access these browsers with a login and password, and some VPNs offer a security token that generates new passwords every few minutes.

20.44 Employees are also fallible, as are we all, so from time to time-sensitive information can be put at risk when a laptop is stolen or misplaced. Biometric fingerprint recognition, which is now available on certain models of laptop, can add another layer of security while full disk encryption is also an option. This will secure any and all information on a computer's hard drive and render the machine useless to any criminal who tries to steal it.

20.45 There is also the more obvious threat of an attack from contractors who are in your building. Staff should remain vigilant, and you need to monitor access to the network via memory sticks or other plug-in devices. It can take just minutes for somebody to steal everything they'd need from you.

20.46 Many businesses now use the services of penetration testers. Otherwise known as ethical hackers, these experts in the field will either come into your place of work or act remotely, to see where the weaknesses in your systems are. While it may seem counter-intuitive to allow someone into your businesses with the sole aim of hacking you, these teams can provide priceless information about where your weaknesses lie. Do your research on them, and find ones who have a strong track record and a long list of testimonials about the work they do.

20.47 It can't be overstated how important cyber-security is. Just by getting the basics right you put yourself in a great position to be well protected.

20.48 The online economy is a fantastic place to work. It offers limitless potential for those ready to explore it. It's become a part of our everyday lives, and there are billions of people ready and willing to give you their money and their data. But with that comes responsibility, and whether personal or professional we all now need to view cybersecurity an essential part of our lives.

CHAPTER 21A

PRODUCT SECURITY AND TELECOMMUNICATIONS INFRASTRUCTURE ACT 2022 (THE ACT)

Helen Wong MBE

OVERVIEW

21.01 The Product Security and Telecommunications Infrastructure Act 2022 is a landmark legislative measure introduced to address the pervasive cybersecurity and privacy vulnerabilities associated with consumer-connected devices, often referred to as the Internet of Things (IoTs). This Act establishes a comprehensive framework to enhance the security of these devices and is a critical component of the UK's strategy to protect consumers in the digital age.

BACKGROUND

21.02 The UK and EU have long been aware of the cybersecurity risks posed by IoT devices, which have become integral to everyday life. These devices include smart speakers, televisions, wearable technology, and various other internet-enabled products. Recognizing the need for robust security standards, the Act was introduced in December 2021. After extensive consultations and amendments, it received Royal Assent on 6 December 2022. The Act is complemented by the Product Security and Telecommunications Infrastructure (Security Requirements for Relevant Connectable Products) Regulations 2023, which were signed into law on 14 September 2023 and is effective from 29 April 2024. Together, these regulations establish mandatory security requirements for IoT device manufacturers.

PURPOSE AND STRUCTURE OF THE ACT

21.03 The Act is divided into two primary sections:

1. **Part 1: Product Security**
   - **Objective**: This section creates a regulatory framework designed to enhance the security of consumer connectable products against cyber threats by setting minimum security standards.

- **Scope**: It encompasses any consumer product capable of connecting to the internet or a network, either directly or indirectly.

2. **Part 2: Telecommunications Infrastructure**

   - **Objective**: This section aims to expedite the deployment and expansion of mobile, full-fibre, and gigabit-capable networks across the UK. It includes amendments to the Electronic Communications Code, which governs the rights of operators to install, maintain, and use communication apparatus.
   - **Impact**: Enhanced connectivity is expected to drive demand for internet-enabled consumer products, necessitating stronger cybersecurity measures to protect consumers.

APPLICABILITY AND SCOPE

21.04 The Act applies to a wide range of businesses involved in the supply chain of consumer-connected devices available in the UK. Specifically, it targets:

- **Internet-connectable products**: Devices capable of connecting to the internet.
- **Network-connectable products**: Devices that can transmit data using electronic or electromagnetic energy, even if they are not directly connected to the internet.

21.05 Certain products are exempt from these regulations due to existing adequate security measures, including:

- Products supplied in Northern Ireland.
- Electric vehicle charge points.
- Medical devices.
- Smart meter products.
- Computers designed exclusively for children under 14.

KEY OBLIGATIONS

21.06 The Act imposes specific duties on three main categories of businesses:

1. **Manufacturers**: Entities that produce or market products under their own name or trademark.
2. **Importers**: Entities that bring products into the UK.
3. **Distributors**: Entities that make products available in the UK.

COMPLIANCE WITH SECURITY STANDARDS

21.07 All relevant products must meet several key security requirements, which include:

- **Minimum Password Standards**: Ensuring devices use strong, unique passwords.
- **Security Issue Reporting**: Providing information on how to report security vulnerabilities to a designated contact point.
- **Security Update Periods**: Specifying the minimum period during which security updates will be provided.
- **Adherence to Standards**: Complying with standards such as ETSI EN 303 645 and ISO/IEC 29147 to achieve deemed compliance.

STATEMENT OF COMPLIANCE

21.08 Each product must be accompanied by a compliance statement that includes:

- Product types.
- Name and address of the manufacturer.
- Declaration of compliance with security standards.
- Defined support period for security updates.
- Signature, name, and function of the signatory.

ADDRESSING NON-COMPLIANCE

21.09 Manufacturers, importers, and distributors must:

- Investigate potential compliance failures.
- Maintain records of investigations and confirmed compliance failures.
- Notify relevant parties and take steps to prevent non-compliant products from being available in the UK market.

ENFORCEMENT MECHANISMS

21.10 The enforcement of the Act's provisions is the responsibility of the Secretary of State, or a delegated authority such as the Office for Product Safety and Standards (OPSS). The enforcement powers include:

- **Compliance Notices**: Requiring businesses to take specific actions to comply with the Act.

- **Stop Notices**: Prohibiting non-compliant activities or restricting non-compliant products from being made available on the market.
- **Recall Notices**: Mandating the return of non-compliant products from consumers and other end users.
- **Monetary Penalties**: Imposing financial penalties up to £10 million or 4% of worldwide revenue.
- **Forfeiture Orders**: Court orders requiring non-compliant products to be delivered up to OPSS or another person, possibly leading to their destruction or disposal.

21.11 The OPSS can also publish details of compliance failures and enforcement actions, serving as a deterrent and informing the public about potential risks.

EU/UK CONTEXT

21.12 The development of the UK's IoT product security regime began collaboratively with the EU, building on the EU standard ETSI EN 303 645. Following Brexit, the UK and EU have developed separate but aligned legislative frameworks. The EU's Cyber Resilience Act (CRA) proposes similar cybersecurity requirements. Companies operating in both jurisdictions must comply with both sets of regulations, reflecting the nuanced differences in each regime.

PRACTICAL IMPLICATIONS FOR BUSINESSES

21.13 Businesses must ensure full compliance with the new regulations by 29 April 2024 to avoid significant sanctions. The Act codifies previously voluntary cybersecurity measures, thereby enhancing consumer protections against cyber threats. Given the rigorous enforcement regime and the substantial penalties for non-compliance, it is crucial for businesses to align their operations with the new requirements to maintain consumer trust and legal compliance.

CONCLUSION

21.14 The **Product Security and Telecommunications Infrastructure Act 2022** represents a comprehensive effort to secure consumer-connected devices and facilitate the expansion of telecommunications infrastructure in the UK. It ensures that enhanced connectivity is accompanied by robust cybersecurity measures, protecting consumers and maintaining trust in the digital marketplace.

21.15 The Act's emphasis on mandatory security standards, detailed compliance obligations, and stringent enforcement mechanisms highlights the UK government's commitment to addressing the evolving challenges of cybersecurity in the IoT era.

CHAPTER 21B

INTELLIGENCE AND THE MONITORING OF EVERYDAY LIFE*

Dr Victoria Wang and Professor John V. Tucker

INTRODUCTION

21.16

> 'The most profound technologies are those that disappear. They weave themselves into the fabric of everyday life until they are indistinguishable from it.'[1]

Our digital world is made from software and data is generated wherever there is software. It is natural to collect data, indeed, it is difficult not to collect it and also difficult to erase it. Digital technologies encourage monitoring of physical and social phenomena. The accelerating growth of data is transforming how we live our lives, and hence on surveillance and intelligence practices broadly conceived. Such a transformation presents many challenges.

21.17 In this chapter, we reflect on the technologies of monitoring in our digital society and offer a conceptual framework for thinking about digital intelligence in general terms. We address the issue of privacy that is increasingly significant as the monitoring of everyday life becomes all-pervasive. At first sight, privacy issues suggest that we should either: (i) not collect certain data, or (ii) limit and regulate access to data collected. Given that data is difficult to manage, and especially to protect and erase, we focus on a third option that is (iii) to hide or mask the identity of the people to whom the data refers. So, we propose that the key to privacy in an increasingly digital world is identity. We outline a theory of identity[2] whose primary purpose is to provide a framework to view the complex path from data to intelligence, and to mark obstacles to personal digital privacy. We use ideas from computer science, surveillance studies, and intelligence studies to guide our arguments.

* This chapter is as published in the 1st edition (September 2018).

1 Mark Weiser, 'The Computer for the 21st Century', *Scientific American* 265/3 (1991), pp 66–75. Mark Weiser (1952-1999) was a pioneer of ubiquitous computing at the Computer Science Laboratory at Xerox PARC.

2 These ideas were first announced in our papers presented at the *6th* Biannual Surveillance and Society Conference, Barcelona, 24-26 April 2014. They have been published in Surveillance and identity: conceptual framework and formal models, *Journal of Cybersecurity*, 3(3), 2017, pp 145–158.

21.18 In the next section, we provide some key background observations of many significant impacts that digital technologies have on surveillance and intelligence practices in our contemporary digital world. From para **21.29**, we briefly describe the concept of surveillance as the monitoring of everyday life and summarise software technologies that are the sources of data. From para **21.48**, we explore how definitions and practices of intelligence may be affected by evolving software technologies and the abundance of data that they generate. From **21.58**, we discuss the concepts of privacy and identity, and their interdependency. From **21.71**, we explain our concept of *identifiers* to make our discussion more precise. We conclude by commenting on some implications of our approach and its possible further development.

BACKGROUND

21.19 In our contemporary digital world, the collection and analysis of data is a phenomenon that is prevalent and a marvel. Why is it so omnipresent? Let us start with the technology and a thesis:

> **Observation.** All aspects of our professional, social and personal lives are, more or less, mediated by software technologies. These technologies collect, store and process our data. Furthermore, they generate data about their own operations, and consequently, about their individual users' actions. As a result, data is generated wherever there is software and it is completely natural to collect and store this data; indeed, difficult *not* to collect it. It is also natural to want to make use of the data. The more software, the more data, the greater the appetite for monitoring, the greater the opportunities for intelligence gathering.

21.20 We explore these propositions and their theoretical implications. By monitoring and intelligence, we have in mind a broad range of contexts and purposes. In the case of intelligence, we will focus somewhat on security and policing, but our discussion is relevant to monitoring and intelligence practices in political, commercial, social and personal spheres.

21.21 Today, complete digital records of employees' performance in both sound and video are quite common.[3] The technical requirements to record a complete life digitally are within reach of consumers. This extraordinary fact has stimulated proposals for computational sociology over a decade ago.[4] The

3 For an early example, body worn video (BWV) is used to record police officers' shifts. *Body-Worn Video* (College of Policing, 2014). library.college.police.uk/docs/college-of-policing/Body-worn-video-guidance-2014.pdf.

4 A more recent example of comprehensive employee monitoring, is a new paradigm of performance management offered by Humanyze, which involves analytics applied to data gathered from a wide range of sensors monitoring individuals. www.humanyze.com. See also in Ben Waber, *People Analytics: How Social Sensing Technology Will Transform Business and What it Tell US About the Future of Work* (Financial Ties/Prentice Hall 2013).
David Lazer, Alex Pentland, Lada Adamic, Sinan Aral, Albert Laszlo Barabasi, Devon Brewer, Nicholas Christakis, Noshir Contractor, James Fowler, Myron Gutmann, Tony Jebara, Gary King, Michael Macy, Deb Roy, and Marshall Van Alstyne, 'Life in the network: the coming age of computational social science', *Science* 323/5915 (2009) pp 721–723.

dramatic improvements in memory capacity and cost suggest that these digital recordings could be of very high quality. Therefore, we may propose that:

> **Thesis.** In principle, an individual's life can be approximated in terms of digital data, and that each approximation can be improved upon by further searches and the deployment of technology.

21.22 The perception of ease in collecting data about everyday life creates a much greater demand for monitoring and subsequently for data analysis and analysts. This in turn affirms the belief that statistical calculation could play a greater role in helping mankind to achieve a better understanding of the world. Rightly or wrongly, this belief in calculation, or in sociological terms 'calculative attitude',[5] has become 'a major motif of social control in the later modern society'.[6] Calculation has led to new developments in surveillance for intelligence purposes. The naturalness can be understood as 'the automation of surveillance', which must be seen as 'an aspect of the way that surveillance occurs as a routine management procedure'.[7]

21.23 Software technologies that capture behaviour and yield data are tools to build a surveillance society, which in turn can be seen as the means to achieve a secure society.[8] For Lyon, we have, for almost 20 years, been living in a surveillance society wherein *the monitoring of everyday life*[9] is a natural phenomenon. In theory, at least, pervasive software technologies could transform our society into a digital panopticon wherein people from all walks of life are monitored at scale.[10] This suggests the concept of perfect surveillance in which every single action can be observed, recorded, archived, replayed, pored over and analysed.[11]

21.24 Since software technologies can be found in every area of everyday life, perfect surveillance is becoming a realistic benchmark for theorising. Undoubtedly, an increasing reliance on software technologies in everyday life might have created two contradictory phenomena: (i) an even larger amount of

5 Anthony Giddens, *Modernity and Self-identity: Self and Society in the Late Modern Age* (Polity Press, 1991) p 28.

6 Jock Young, *The Exclusive Society: Social Exclusion, Crime and Difference in Late Modernity* (Sage 1999) p 66.

7 David Lyon, 'Surveillance, Snowden, and Big Data: Capacities, Consequences, Critique', *Big Data & Society* July-December (2014) pp 1–13.

8 David Lyon, *Surveillance Studies: An Overview* (Polity Press 2007).

9 David Lyon, *Surveillance Society: Monitoring Everyday Life* (Open University Press 2001).

10 Kevin D. Haggerty and Richard V. Ericson, 'The new politics of surveillance and visibility' in K. Haggerty and R. Ericson (eds.) *The New Politics of Surveillance and Visibility* (University of Toronto Press 2006) pp 3–34.

11 Victoria Wang, Kevin R. Haines and John V. Tucker, 'Deviance and Control in Communities with Perfect Surveillance – the Case of Second Life', *Surveillance and Society* 9(1/2) (2011) pp 31–46.

digital data for corporate, police, national and international intelligence, and (ii) a public demand for greater privacy.[12]

21.25 Privacy issues certainly go hand-in-hand with intelligence practices, and the balance between security and privacy has always been difficult to achieve.[13] The data explosion that could be used to inform intelligence has raised questions about user privacy that appear to have no answers. The current increasing attention to various forms of intelligence collection raises worrisome privacy questions.[14] Privacy is personal and highly sensitive to context. Today, attitudes towards what is private are changing – individuals are more willing to place personal information, such as their daily experiences and opinions, into public domains, particularly social media sites.[15] These kinds of behaviours are blurring the boundaries between social and work identities, eg, a candidate for a job could (or should?) be deemed unsuitable if a potential employer finds inappropriate information online.

21.26 We propose that in the digital world, *the protection of privacy is fundamentally the protection of an individual's digital identity.* By digital identity, roughly speaking, we mean data from which an individual can be identified. Identity and identification are complex subjects – questions of personal identity have been topics of philosophical debates for centuries.[16] Concretely, an individual's identity is defined through biometric, biographical and social characteristics (including DNA, irises, fingerprints; nationality, profession, address, bank account; Facebook, Twitter, Instagram account, etc).

21.27 Identity is central to intelligence practices and police investigations, especially, when one of the main purposes of surveillance is social sorting, originally defined as the 'focus on the social and economic categories and the computer codes by which personal data is organized with a view to influencing and managing people and populations'.[17] Currently, personal data is receiving tremendous attention as evidenced by the emergence of identity intelligence – 'a relatively new intelligence construct that refers to the analysis and use of personal information, including biometric and forensic data among others, to identify intelligence targets of interest and to deny them anonymity'.[18]

12 *A Democratic Licence to Operate – Report of the Independent Surveillance Review* (Royal United Services Institute 2015). www.rusi.org/downloads/assets/ISR-Report-press.pdf.

13 Ben Goold and Liora Lazarus, *Security and Human Rights* (Hart Publishing Ltd 2007).

14 Loch K. Johnson and Allison M. Shelton, Thoughts on the State of Intelligence Studies: A Survey Report. *Intelligence and National Security* 28 (1) (2013) pp 109–120.

15 Foresight, *Future Identities – Changing identities in the UK: the next 10 years* (The Government Office for Science 2013). www.gov.uk/government/uploads/system/uploads/attachment_data/file/273966/13-523-future-identities-changing-identities-report.pdf.

16 Ronald L. Jackson (ed.) *Encyclopedia of Identity* (Sage 2010).

17 David Lyon (ed.), *Surveillance as Social Sorting: Privacy, Risk and Digital Discrimination* (Routledge 2003) p 2.

18 David Goldfein, *Joint Publication 3-05* (Special Operations 2014). http://fas.org/irp/doddir/dod/jp3_05.pdf.

21.28 Similarly, in the UK, to strengthen the country's abilities in security, surveillance, intelligence and counter-terrorism, the Investigatory Powers Act 2016 (once nicknamed the Snoopers' Charter) was passed in November 2016. In particular, this Act allowed police, the intelligence officers, etc to (i) view the internet connection records, as part of a targeted and filtered investigation, without a warrant; and (ii) hack into computers or devices to access their data, and bulk equipment interference for national security matters related to foreign investigation. Needless to say that the Snooper's Charter is seen by privacy campaigners as discredited, intrusive and treating all UK residents as potential suspects. Indeed, with numerous counter-terrorism practices in an era of rising national and international security threats, the inevitable conflict between security and privacy has been made even more prominent.

SURVEILLANCE AS THE MONITORING OF EVERYDAY LIFE

21.29 Today, the monitoring of everyday life, enabled by software technologies, provides a unique resource for intelligence practices. Access to how an individual lives his or her life is key to understanding or predicting actions and events – past, present and future.

Established Surveillance Technologies

21.30 Increasingly, in intelligence gathering, surveillance is as much about objects as people.[19] There are general technological devices specifically designed for surveillance purposes, including:

> *General Technologies.* CCTV,[20] automatic number plate recognition (ANPR),[21] voice recognition,[22] global positioning systems (GPS),[23] drones,[24] and satellite imaging.[25]

19 Kevin D. Haggerty, 'Tear down the walls: on demolishing the panopticon' in D. Lyon (ed.) *Theorizing Surveillance: the Panopticon and Beyond* (Willan 2006) pp 23–45.

20 Kirstie Ball and David M. Wood, *A Report on the Surveillance Society: Summary Report* (The Information Commissioner 2006). https://ico.org.uk/media/about-the-ico/documents/1042391/surveillance-society-summary-06.pdf.

21 Alan Travis, ''Big brother' traffic cameras must be regulated, orders home secretary', *The Guardian* (2010) 4 July.

22 Jon Stokes, 'The new technology at the root of the NSA wiretap scandal', *ars technica* (2005) 20 December.

23 Mike Nelli, 'Mobility, locatability and the satellite tracking of offenders' in K. Aas, H. Gundhus and H. Lomell (eds.) *Technologies of Insecurity: The Surveillance of Everyday Life* (Routledge 2008) pp 105–124.

24 Roger Clarke, 'The Regulation of the Impact of Civilian Drones on Behavioural Privacy', *Computer Law & Society Review* 30/3 (2014) pp 286–305.

25 Chad Harris, 'The Omniscient Eye: Satellite Imagery, "Battlespace Awareness," and the Structures of the Imperial Gaze', *Surveillance & Society* 4(1/2) (2006) pp 101–122.

Identity Managements. Many forms of surveillance systems are supported by identity management systems that provide information[26] on identity. There are international systems of fingerprinting,[27] iris scans,[28] facial recognition[29] and DNA comparisons.[30] There are national systems of registration of citizens by passport,[31] and driving and vehicle licensing, which in the UK are used for personal identification in the absence of a National Identity Register (NIR).[32] New domain-specific identity management services are emerging in particular areas, for example, ORCID for researchers.[33] More generally, services that manage internet user names and passwords are available, eg, logging into sites via a Facebook account. There is excitement about applications to identity management of the Blockchain technology that makes the cryptocurrency Bitcoin possible.[34]

21.31 Currently, besides traditional general-purpose surveillance technologies, the availability and capabilities of data technologies – sensors, actuators, card readers, cameras, communications, software and hardware – require a re-examination of the scope and magnitude of intelligence practices. The internet is increasingly becoming an important collection of information sources, especially 'open source' information. It is said that strategic analysis relies on open sources for 90% of its evidence and research material.[35] It is now widely recognised that commercial and social activities are responsible for the staggering growth of large datasets of personal information.

21.32 In fact, our world is made from technologies that depend on software, which is designed to process data. An excellent example is the smartphone whose software can monitor the life of its owner. These technologies have surveillance capabilities, which may be unintended rather than intended. Indeed, all software technologies that we use in everyday life naturally collect, store and process data *about their own operation* and, therefore, can be used in surveillance.

26 In the context of criminal intelligence, the terms information and intelligence are often use interchangeably. United Nations, *Police Information and Intelligence Systems – Criminal Justice Assessment Toolkit* (United Nations Office on Drugs and Crime: Vienna 2006). www.unodc.org/documents/justice-and-prison-reform/cjat_eng/4_Police_Information_Intelligence_Systems.pdf.

27 Simon A. Cole, *Suspect Identities: A History of Fingerprinting and Criminal Identification* (Harvard University Press 2001).

28 Ball and Wood, *A Report on the Surveillance Society: Summary Report.*

29 Lucas D. Introna and David M. Wood, 'Picturing Algorithmic Surveillance: The Politics of Facial Recognition Systems', *Surveillance & Society* 2(2/3) (2004) pp 177–198.

30 Helen Wallace, 'The UK National DNA Database – Balancing crime detection, human rights and privacy', *Science & Society, EMBO reports 7* (2006) pp S26-S30.

31 John Torpey, *The Invention of the Passport: Surveillance, Citizenship and State* (Cambridge University Press 2000).

32 UK government, *The Identity Card Act 2006: Elizabeth II. Chapter 11* (London: The Stationary Office 2006).

33 http://orcid.org/.

34 Phil Champagne, *The Book of Satoshi: The Collected Writings of Bitcoin Creator Satoshi Nakamoto* (e53 Publishing LLC 2014).

35 United Nations, *Police Information and Intelligence Systems – Criminal Justice Assessment Toolkit.*

21.33 Biometric identifiers have long been prominent in investigations. Matching DNA involves advanced bio-science and computer science, and can raise subtle issues of identity. For example, cases involving differentiating between twins can be difficult.[36] Further, there are extra-ordinary cases, where thousands of DNA samples are collected in the belief that suspects will be revealed. Some investigations indeed are heroic for their scale, depth and cost, an example of this being the *Guerinoni* case of 2015.[37]

21.34 At first sight, the Driver and Vehicle Licensing Agency (DVLA) can be seen as a factory for identity. Since the 1970s, it has maintained two giant databases, one for drivers, and one for vehicles. Its licences fix identities and grant permissions, and gather billions of pounds in tax. The curation of these data is excellent and in practice – without any official approval – drivers' licences are regularly used as personal identifiers in daily life. The DVLA has provided information for the UK Police National Computer (PNC) since its inception, and indeed, this service was one among several explicit motivations for the creation of the DVLA.[38]

21.35 Wherever permission to access databases is an issue, then so is identity. If permission is the main business of the DVLA, then the rise of software in motor vehicles – including GPS technologies, dashboard cameras and other monitoring systems – together with the evolution of autonomous vehicles and smart roads promise dramatically more data and additional means for surveillance.

Technologies of Daily Life

21.36 Besides established surveillance technologies, more and more aspects of our daily lives are mediated by software technologies. These generate and store large amounts of data that can be easily accessed. Some examples would include:

> *Web Services*. These have surveillance capabilities although they might not be used for surveillance purposes. Online banking, retailing, gaming, gambling and social networking sites are great repositories of data about people's activities that are often time-stamped. Many established databases have long been computerised, such as health, social security, tax and vehicle records, and are connected to the web.
>
> *Embedded Systems*. Many objects contain central processing units (CPUs) and software that allow them to be branded smart. Often users can communicate with them by using an app on a smart phone or tablet. Everyday examples of

36 www.eurekalert.org/pub_releases/2013-12/emo-esd120913.php.

37 Tobias Jones, 'The murder that has obsessed Italy', *The Guardian* (2015) 8 January. www.theguardian.com/world/2015/jan/08/-sp-the-murder-that-has-obsessed-italy.

38 Jon Agar *The Government Machine: a Revolutionary History of the Computer* (MIT 2003) Chapter 9. *Guidance – Police National Computer (PNC) – version 5.0* (Home Office 2014). www.gov.uk/government/uploads/system/uploads/attachment_data/file/488515/PNC_v5.0_EXT_clean.pdf.

remote access include web cameras, heating systems and smart white goods, such as ovens and fridges.

Mobile Technologies. Mobile technologies, such as smart phones, tablets and watches, make computers easily accessible to individuals and more useful for their personal lives. They encourage significantly more software to be involved in individuals' private interests and daily routines, and must lead to more data that document their lives. Moreover, technologies that are spatially aware can increase significantly both their utility and their surveillance potential. As satellite position systems multiply with higher spatial resolutions, radically new applications will emerge for monitoring smart objects.

Environments. Technologies with embedded software can create environments. These technologies, which may be stationary or mobile, can be connected directly or indirectly together or to web services. Examples of environments are emerging as the components identified above are used to build smart (districts of) cities and digital homes.

21.37 Let us now consider the most personal aspects of an individual's life – his or her home.[39] Our homes have long been wired to the outside via telephone lines. Current state of the art technologies are capable of creating a comprehensive domestic digital environment – the digital house. Domestic life is supported by smart personal digital assistants like Amazon's Alexa, which through voice interaction, plays music, makes lists, offers reminders, provides news, weather, traffic reports, and all sorts of real-time information. Personal assistants can also control domestic products. A digital house will have *many* such personal assistants.

21.38 Currently, advanced and increasingly fanciful examples of domestic products include cameras at entrances that have facial recognition software; clothes made with smart fabrics that can regulate our body temperature and monitor our health; kitchen surfaces that can identify what is on them and have the ability to react according to personal needs by, for example, keeping coffee cups warm; refrigerators that can advise on recipes based on what is in stock when shopping and can also suggest personal diets. Our doctors can give us virtual medical checks by using toilets that analyse waste.

21.39 These advanced domestic conveniences and services involve technologies that are internet enabled and linked to the house's router using the IP address provided. The scenario illustrates domestically the idea of the Internet of Things.[40] The networking of the objects extends outside the home for a variety of reasons. The software in the technologies may need maintenance but more likely what makes the device smart is the connection between the software and the systems of a service provider, which could be either the manufacturer or an

39 Martyn Campbell, 'Smart Internet will help Manage your Home and Life by 2027', *Plusnet* (2012) 23 February. http://community.plus.net/blog/2012/02/23/smart-internet-will-help-manage-your-home-and-life-by-2027/.

40 Dave Evans, *The Internet of Things: How the Next Evolution of the Internet Is Changing Everything* (Cisco 2011).

independent company. These connections enable data about usage to be collected and stored in databases online.

21.40 Consider the smart TV in the living room. Quite recently, a range of smart TVs manufactured by Samsung caused a stir in the news, when it became publicly known that the voice recognition facility enabled a service provider, Nuance, to eavesdrop on conversations in the living room.[41] In contrast, just a year or so later, there is no similar reaction to the reality of personal digital assistants permanently monitoring sounds in several rooms awaiting their wake up call. Yet, users' confidence in the controlling of their digital devices is not always high, as the frequency of seeing covers over the camera lenses built into computers suggests.

21.41 With such monitoring capacity available we can expect, roughly speaking, that personal data collection will be a natural and inevitable feature. Just as the computer, phone and car generate information about us, we can expect all of our products belonging to our personal Internet of Things to do likewise.

Perfect Surveillance

21.42 In the execution of software, the creation and storage of digital data is continual. Software technologies normally maintain detailed logs of their operations and so when individuals engage with these technologies these engagements will be logged in time and space. Thus, the digital approximation of our lives becomes possible since our lives are mediated by software. The faithfulness of the digital approximation increases as we engage with more software in more aspects of our daily lives. We provide a working definition of digital trace as follows:

> A *digital trace* of an entity is a sequence of data representing observations of the entity's behaviour in a context; it is equipped with an identifier that distinguishes the entity from other entities in that context, and records time/place of the observations.

21.43 So, in a context where every action requires engaging with software, a faithful digital approximation is achievable.

21.44 Cyber-communities, like Second Life, are such contexts. Second Life is a cyber-community launched in 2003. The environment is created totally by software technologies, which have in-built surveillance capacity to collect and store a vast amount of information. There is no absolute privacy for anyone once he/she enters Second Life. The creator of the software, Linden Lab, can watch, record, store and replay all the time. By December 2007, Linden Lab had stored

41 'Not in front of the telly: Warning over 'listening' TV', *BBC* (2015) 9 February. www.bbc.co.uk/news/technology-31296188. 'Samsung hit by latest smart TV issue', BBC (2015) 26 February. www.bbc.co.uk/news/technology-31642195.

around 100 terabytes of digital data, which is equivalent to the total internet traffic in 1993.[42] All these data are stored in the database of Isilon Systems, Inc. – a global company based in Seattle, USA.

21.45 Let us now return to the real world. Given the ubiquity of software, to what extent is the digital trace an approximation of an individual's activities over a fixed period or location? That the traces are approximations typically may mean that the information they contain has gaps, inconsistencies and errors. Any incompleteness of the record in time and space will be expected to introduce ambiguities and inconsistencies. Such problems are characteristic of intelligence. However, expectations of the continuity and 'completeness' of surveillance, together with the wide spectrum of information sources and sheer volume of the data available, means intelligence practices will be transformed in scope and boundaries. Let us note first where exactly the data is derived:

> The data available from which a digital trace may be made originates in physical objects with software interfaces. Thus, the data collected represent observations of the behaviour of physical objects.

21.46 The digital trace is a composite record of the behaviour of a variety of software systems accessed by a variety of digital technologies. This most obviously includes computers, phones, tablets, but also less obviously, by a manifold of embedded systems in the street, office, home and motor cars. Thus, we have the following:

> Surveillance directly observes devices and only indirectly observes people.

21.47 In principle, digital traces are approximations to the behaviour of individuals, since these observe and record *what individuals do with technologies*. The question arises – how do we know who is employing the device? While we may be certain as to the identity of the device, our confidence as to the identity of the user engaging with the device may be variable, since most of the technologies we have in mind are networked and are accessible remotely. The identity of the user may be hidden and protected. Indeed, in some cases an autonomous piece of software may be the user, or the device could be hacked.

DIGITAL INTELLIGENCE

21.48 We have reflected on the nature and extent of data that may already *exist* about an individual's activities; the scale, intimacy and comprehensiveness of data available is astonishing. However, *access* to the data may be difficult since its sources are diverse, eg, owned by organisations and companies, located in many countries, that process, store and secure the data using many different data

42 Stephen J. Dubner, 'Philip Rosedale Answers Your Second Life Questions Rosedale', *The New York Times* (2007) 13 December. freakonomics.com/2007/12/13/philip-rosedale-answers-your-second-life-questions.

representations and software technologies, and subject to the laws and regulations of different jurisdictions.

21.49 Intelligence is a broad concept. It encompasses State intelligence, police intelligence, corporate intelligence, open source intelligence, etc. Focusing on State intelligence, Warner suggested that intelligence is a secret State activity to understand or influence foreign entities.[43] In the corporate world, intelligence has been associated with automated data gathering and processing, and more recently, has become increasingly dependent on new techniques of data analytics.[44] Actually, corporate intelligence has become a central sociological topic in the surveillance studies community.[45] In 2013, Alan Breakspear examined various key components of intelligence and proposed a new universal definition. This is: 'Intelligence is a corporate capability to forecast change in time to do something about it. The capability involves foresight and insight, and is intended to identify impeding change, which may be positive, representing opportunities, or negative, representing threat'.[46] Breakspear's definition may serve the needs of the majority of intelligence scholarship. However, its exclusive focus on forecasting is a limitation.

21.50 In policing, the term *criminal intelligence* is often used, and understood, as any information with additional value that can be used by law enforcement to deal with crime. Criminal intelligence is not confined to predicting or pre-empting crime. It is the basis of an effective policing model and regularly plays a role in the investigation of crimes committed. This includes the search for case evidence, and the planning and allocation of manpower.[47]

21.51 According to UN guidelines, criminal intelligence is a process involving the following stages: (i) collection of data, (ii) evaluation, (iii) collation, (iv) analysis, (v) dissemination and (vi) direction.[48] Once information has been *collected*, it will be *evaluated* according to the reliability of its source and *collated* – cross referenced and ordered ready for use. The actual *analysis* will then consider the information in context and draw conclusions as to its meaning. Finally, that meaning will be *disseminated* to those who *need to know* it. The need to know principle is fundamental to working with sensitive information and intelligence. Unless there is a clear professional reason for sharing information with another person that information should not be shared.

43 Michael Warner, 'Wanted: A Definition of "Intelligence"', *Studies in Intelligence* 46 (2002) pp 15–22.

44 McConnell, *Vision 2015 – A Globally Networked and Integrated Intelligence Enterprise.*

45 Lyon, *Surveillance, Snowden, and Big Data: Capacities, Consequences, Critique.*

46 Alan Breakspear, 'A New Definition of Intelligence', *Intelligence and National Security* 28/5 (2013) p 678.

47 Marilyn Peterson, *Intelligence-Led Policing: The New Intelligence Architecture* (US Department of Justice Office of Justice Programs 2005).

48 ACPO, *Practice advice – Introduction to intelligence-led policing* (National Centre for Policing Excellence 2007). www.fairplayforchildren.org/pdf/1291430265.pdf.

21.52 Of the six stages in the process of criminal intelligence, collection, is particularly interesting. First, the methods of collection are many and varied.[49] Secondly, for each form of data collection, there is a process of *curation*. Not all information that is collected is worthy of preservation. Information needs to be classified in different ways to determine appropriate means of selection, preservation and retrieval for future use. Curation is adapted to methods for collecting information, according to the ACPO:

- '*Routine Collection* – the collection of information as part of routine operational policing activity, such as crime recording, case files, operational databases (e.g., HOLMES 2), fixed penalty and other traffic enforcement databases …;
- *Volunteered information* – information office by the general public, community contacts and partners, such as crimestoppers, neighbourhood watch…; and
- *Tasked information* – the prioritised collection of information, such as CCTV system, Automatic Number Plate Recognition (ANPR) system, surveillance techniques, human sources'.[50]

21.53 These categories seem adequate to organise the new sources of data described in the previous section. Routine collection refers to the police's own data; volunteered information might be extended through the immense traffic of social media much of which, although personal, is publicly available or can be accessed easily. Task information meanwhile captures the bulk of the data generated by the software technologies embedded in everyday life.

21.54 For a host of reasons, the role of the internet with its global reach has long been a source of concern for intelligence and policing agencies.[51] Indeed, open source intelligence is a huge area of interest of security and policing agencies, companies and individuals. For example, this last point is well made in national

49 According to the UK National Intelligence Model, the main sources of information available to the Police Service include: 'victims and witness, communities and members of the public, crimestoppers, prisoners, covert Human Intelligence Sources (CHIS), covert operations, e.g., surveillance, CCTV and Automatic Number Plate Recognition (ANPR), crime and disorder reduction partnerships, commercial agencies, e.g., banks and credit card agencies, fixed penalty tickets database, Forensic Science Service (FSS), Internet – Open Source (e.g., http://www.homeoffice.gov.uk), media, NCPE Opsline, Neighbourhood Watch Scheme, Police IT systems, eg, Police National Computer (PNC), other law enforcement agencies, eg, Serious Organised Crime Agency (SOCA), Primary Care Trusts (PCTs), Local Education Authorities (LEAs), National Firearms License Management System (NFLMS)'. ACPO, *Practice advice – Introduction to intelligence-led policing* p 18.

50 ibid p 19.

51 eg, in 2008 the US Director of National Intelligence's paper focused on cyberspace: John M. McConnell, *Vision 2015 – A Globally Networked and Integrated Intelligence Enterprise* (US National Intelligence 2008).

and international guidelines for intelligence in policing, and extends to the UK's ACPO[52] and the UN's criminal justice assessment toolkit.[53]

21.55 This interest is propelled by the availability of various kinds of technological tools to collect and analyse large datasets. Currently, Cambridge Analytica has become famous as a producer and user of these tools. As clearly stated in its strapline – 'data drives all we do' – and it combines techniques including data mining, data brokerage, and data analysis with strategic communication to change people's behaviour.[54] In March 2018, the company was reported to have gathered vast amounts of personal information from Facebook – without permission of users or the company – to profile people psychologically in order to influence the outcome of the 2016 US presidential election.[55] Actually, the current state of intelligence studies is becoming dominated by various software tools that can be used to analyse large datasets.[56] To advocates of this approach, *more* quantitative work is needed to allow repetitive patterns across time and space to emerge, enabling the identification of both strengths and weaknesses in theoretical speculations. To critics of quantitative analysis, an over-reliance on data is the biggest problem in the intelligence profession, since what informs intelligence should not be data, but knowledge and insight. The focus on data is a key phenomenon of the so-called 'digital revolution' in intelligence. For Michael Warner, we have little understanding of the current wave of technological change that is washing over intelligence profession.[57]

21.56 This wave of technological change has also perplexed the battleground for privacy. Currently, in the realm of organisational security, a new form of intelligence practice – 'Identity and Access Intelligence'[58] – is becoming lucrative in IT security, particularly, for cloud computing. Its related practices, such as Privacy as a Service (PaaS)[59] and Identity Management (IdM),[60] provide consistency in defining roles and delegating access privileges. This state of affairs

52 ACPO, *Practice advice – Introduction to intelligence-led policing* (National Centre for Policing Excellence 2007). www.fairplayforchildren.org/pdf/1291430265.pdf.

53 United Nations, *Police Information and Intelligence Systems – Criminal Justice Assessment Toolkit*. See also Christopher Eldridge, Christopher Hobbs and Matthew Moran, Fusing algorithms and analysts: open-source intelligence in the age of Big Data, *Intelligence and National Security*, 33/3 (2018) pp 391–406.

54 Cambridge Analytica. https://cambridgeanalytica.org.

55 BBC 'Cambridge Analytica: Facebook boss summoned over data claims', *The BBC* (2018) 20 March. www.bbc.co.uk/news/uk-43474760.

56 Loch K. Johnson and Alison M. Shelton, 'Thoughts on the State of Intelligence Studies: A Survey Report', *Intelligence and National Security* 28/1 (2013) pp 109–120.

57 Michael Warner, 'Reflections on Technology and Intelligence Systems', *Intelligence and National Security* 27/1 (2012) pp 133–153.

58 *Identity and Access Intelligence: Transforming the Nature of Enterprise Security – An Enterprise Management Associates (EMA™)* (IBM 2012). www-01.ibm.com/common/ssi/cgi-bin/ssialias?infotype=SA&subtype=WH&htmlfid=WGL03028USEN#loaded.

59 Wassim Itani, Ayman Kayssi and Ali Chehab, 'Privacy as a Service: Privacy-Aware Data Storage and Processing in Cloud Computing Architectures', *Eighth IEEE International Conference on Dependable, Autonomic and Secure Computing, IEEE Computer Society* (2009) pp 711–716.

60 Kenji Takahashi and Elisa Bertino, *Identity Management: Concepts, Technologies, and Systems* (Artech House Publishers 2011).

and its future development add significantly to the challenges facing intelligence. For example, in terms of open source intelligence, individual providers of social media data might not be aware of its availability to both the general public and governments. In the US, the PRISM program appears to provide the National Security Agency (NSA) with direct access to the servers of some of the largest tech companies, including Apple, Facebook, Google, Microsoft, Skype, Yahoo and YouTube.[61] In the UK, the Tempora program appears to give similar access for the General Communications Headquarters (GCHQ).[62] The PRISM and Tempora programs have the capabilities to tap cables and networks, known as 'Upstream', to intercept any internet traffic.[63] The Communications Security Establishment of Canada (CSEC) collects data from airport Wifi systems to build and analyse a dataset to warn when a 'suspect' appears; such a dataset could also be used for surveillance purposes.[64]

21.57 In the UK, the police can count on one general information source: CCTV. The UK processes a large, heterogeneous and dispersed collection of videos of the everyday comings and goings of people – a general purpose surveillance library. However, gaining access and piecing them together to form video traces and continuous narratives, is neither easy nor quick, even though tools to mine relevant information from thousands of hours of video exist. To this complex library of video of streets and shops is being added many more individuals' collections of video data, posted on social media sites. For the police, the magnitude of data in existence brings new challenges and opportunities, ethical and technological, which require new technologies, procedures and laws.[65] It does little to reduce their workload however. Ethical and social reflections lead to questions about rights, responsibilities and best practices. To citizens, technology reduces their privacy; to the courts, it increases the quality of their evidence. The importance of digital traces that approximate the activities of people are evident since:

> In any investigation, access to how an individual lives his or her life is a key to understanding or predicting past, present or future actions and events.

61 Glenn Greenwald and Ewen MacAskill, 'NSA Prism program taps in to user data of Apple, Google and others', *The Guardian* (2013) 7 June. www.theguardian.com/world/2013/jun/06/us-tech-giants-nsa-data.

62 Ewen MacAskill, Julian Borger, Nick Hopkins, Nick Davies and James Ball, 'GCHQ taps fibre-optic cables for secret access to world's communications', *The Guardian* (2013) 21 June. www.theguardian.com/uk/2013/jun/21/gchq-cables-secret-world-communications-nsa.

63 Lyon, *Surveillance, Snowden, and Big Data: Capacities, Consequences, critique*.

64 Greg Weston, Glenn Greenwald, Ryan Gallagher, 'CSEC used airport Wi-Fi to track Canadian travellers: Edward Snowden documents', *CBCnews* (2014) 30 January. www.cbc.ca/news/politics/csec-used-airport-wi-fi-to-track-canadian-travellers-edward-snowden-documents-1.2517881.

65 David Anderson, *A question of trust – report of the investigatory powers review* (Her Majesty's Stationary Office 2015).

PRIVACY AND IDENTITY IN DIGITAL INTELLIGENCE

21.58 Let us consider the impact of what we have discussed on privacy from a practical and technical perspective rather than an ethical or a legal position.

On Privacy and Identity

21.59 Given the monitoring of everyday life, we leave traces of ourselves everywhere we go, in person and online. Often, we are unaware how much we disclose, or are observed, or how our privacy is affected. Face-to-face interactions could be perceived as more private than online interactions since we could have more control over face-to-face interactions. In a seminal book[66] Irwin Altman wrote:

> 'Privacy mechanisms define the limits and boundaries of the self. When the permeability of these boundaries is under the control of a person, a sense of individuality develops. But it is not the inclusion or exclusion of others that is vital to self definition; it is the ability to regulate contact when desired. If I can control what is me and what is not me, if I can define what is me and not me, and if I can observe the limits and scope of my control, then I have taken major steps toward understanding and defining what I am. Thus, privacy mechanisms serve to help me define me'.

21.60 In short, to Altman, the word *boundary* is a key feature of what privacy really entails. *Self-boundary* is a boundary that is modified by self-disclosure, whereas a *dyadic boundary* involves the comfort that the discloser feels if, or when, his or her information is leaked to a third party.[67] Both types of boundaries touch on the main issues related to defining privacy, which are disclosure and violation.

21.61 Privacy means different things in different contexts.[68] Some examples are identified below:

- A classic understanding of privacy is 'the right to be let alone'.[69]
- A legal theory of privacy can be 'a value so complex, so entangled in competing and contradictory dimensions, so engorged with various and distinct meanings…'.[70]

66 Irwin Altman, *The Environment and Social Behavior: Privacy, Personal Space, Territoriality and Crowding* (Brooks/ Cole 1975) p 50.

67 Irwin Altman, 'Privacy Regulation: Culturally Universal or Culturally Specific?' *Journal of Social Issues* 33/3 (1977) pp 66–84.

68 Anderson, *A question of trust – report of the investigatory powers review* pp 25–38.

69 Samuel D. Warren and Louis D. Brandeis, 'The Right to Privacy', *Harvard Law Review* 4/5 (1890) p 205.

70 Robert C. Post, 'Three Concepts of Privacy', (*Yale Law School Legal Scholarship Repository* 2001) p 2087.

- In legal practices, privacy can be a positive right to conceal or hide information about ourselves.[71]
- Of course, 'privacy can also be understood in terms of control' – since knowledge is power, and thus 'the transfer of private information to the state can be seen as a transfer of autonomy and of control'.[72]

21.62 In digital intelligence, information is reduced to digital data, which is processed by software. Privacy can be reduced to an operational problem that requires an operational approach from information security professionals. Here are some examples of how they conceive of privacy:[73]

- Privacy can be individuals exercising control over information about themselves to which others have access.
- Privacy can be only doing things that have been expressly permitted with personal information.
- Privacy may include preventing others from knowing any type of information which one knows, but do not wish others to know.
- Privacy not only concerns information about a person but also information about his/her activities, which may include all data that the person is working with, such as emails, malware collections, program sources etc.
- Privacy may extend to a right to prevent being contacted or approached by others without consent.[74]

21.63 For information security professionals, it would appear that the notion of privacy is closely associated with personal data. However, like privacy, personal data can also have different meanings. The UK's Information Commissioner has a strong definition: 'data which relate to a living individual who can be identified – (a) from those data, or (b) from those data and other information which is in the possession of, or is likely to come into the possession of, the data controller, and includes any expression of opinion about the individual and any indication of the intentions of the data controller or any other person in respect of the individual'.[75] In particular, the intention seems to be that personal data can identify a unique individual.

21.64 The protection of privacy is fundamentally the protection of data representing characteristics from which an individual can be identified, which constitutes an individual's identity. An individual's 'identity' is often based on

71 *R v Spencer*, (2014) SCC 43 (CanLII), para 35 et seq. https://scc-csc.lexum.com/scc-csc/scc-csc/en/item/14233/index.do.

72 Anderson, *A question of trust – report of the investigatory powers review* p 26.

73 Sarah Gordon, *Privacy: A Study of Attitudes and Behaviors in US, UK and EU Information Security Professionals* (Symantec Security Response 2006).

74 Some individuals' perspective on unsolicited commercial email, or spam, illustrates this view of privacy.

75 *The Guide to Data Protection* (Information Commissioner's Office 2014) p 7.

a selection of characteristics from biometric through biographical to social and could be understood as 'those characteristics which determine who a person is: this includes an individual's perception of him as similar to, or different from, other people, but identities can also be imposed by others'.[76] Examples of characteristics include DNA, irises, fingerprints; nationality, profession, financial status; family, place attachment, community, etc. This notion of identity includes both characteristics from embodied individuals (which are often turned into digital data and stored in various databases), and increasingly, characteristics about these individuals to be found, in terms of digital data in multiple databases, circulating on the Internet.[77]

On Digital Privacy

21.65 Over the past decade, methods for analysing large quantities of data have been developed into a new data science largely through commercial and bureaucratic applications. The popular term *big data* describes data sets with the characteristics of *volume*, *velocity* and *variety*.[78] The description is a technical one and comes from computer science. The magnitude of the data has brought new challenges. For example, how do we distinguish useful information, given the vastness of the data sets? New concepts of *value* and *veracity* are introduced to deal with this social and economic need.[79]

21.66 Big data is a product of the monitoring of everyday life. New communications technologies are radically advancing our freedoms and are enabling unparalleled invasions of privacy. Our mobile phones help us keep in touch with friends and family. However, at the same time, it makes it much easier for security agencies to track our whereabouts. Our web searches might appear to be private between us and our search engines, but search companies are creating a treasure trove of personal information by logging our online activities, and can make it available to any party wielding enough cash. Our social media posts on sites such as Facebook and Twitter are stored, owned and ready to be mined for information by private companies, such as Echosec and Cloudera.[80]

21.67 Surveillance is inevitable: the creation, collection and storage of digital data representing the behaviour of people is a necessary consequence of our digital world. Thus, the data exists to manufacture digital traces of individuals. The completeness of an individual's digital approximation depends on the

76 Foresight, *Future Identities Changing identities in the UK: the next 10 years*.

77 David Lyon (ed.), *Surveillance as Social Sorting: Privacy, Risk and Digital Discrimination* (Routledge 2003).

78 Volume refers to the size of the data set; velocity refers to the speed of change of the data set; and variety refers to the types of data in the data set. The characterisation is called V^3 definition and is due to Doug Laney. Doug Laney, '3D Data Management: Controlling Data Volume, Velocity and Variety', *Application Delivery Strategies* (2001) 6 February.

79 Value refers to the usefulness of the data set in some context while veracity refers to the accuracy.

80 www.echosec.net/ and www.cloudera.com/content/cloudera/en/home.html.

ability to find these custodians of data and then to get access to the multitude of databases in which data is stored. Each individual has many identities provided by many organisations, public and private. Thus, there are many independent *custodians* of identities. So, gaining access to these databases becomes a key and also complex issue in digital intelligence gathering. It involves ethical, legal, political, financial and technical considerations, which depend on events.

21.68 It would appear that, in practice, national security is often achieved at the cost of individual privacy, especially when it is enabled by a considerable number of technological systems for surveillance purposes. However, respect for individuals' autonomy, anonymity, and the right to free association must be balanced against legitimate concerns, such as public safety and law enforcement. National governments, however, must put legal checks in place to prevent abuse of State powers, and international bodies need to also consider how a changing technological environment shapes security agencies' best practices.

21.69 The notion of identity is indispensable in terms of achieving privacy. Since data about people's behaviour is created automatically, privacy becomes a matter of controlling the identity of the object of the behavioural data, which is the identity of people. Personal data ought to have at least two components: (i) the information that the data records which we might call the *content* and (ii) the means to identify the person which we call the *referent*. In processing personal data, as with surveillance, there are four possible scenarios as illustrated in the table below:

Content	Referent	Surveillance Example
✓	✓	Monitoring email: both links and content
✓	✗	Monitoring search behaviour for marketing
✗	✓	Monitoring email: links but not content
✗	✗	No monitoring

21.70 Privacy depends on (i) the potential difficulty of finding and accessing these referents, and (ii) the difficulty of cross-referencing referents. In particular contexts, identity aggregation can be commercialised, eg, ORCID[81] is used to connect research and researchers by confirming identity.

THEORISING IDENTITY

21.71 The many identities collected by a person may however have some common properties. First, an identity arises from the person belonging to some group or community – which may be formal or informal; voluntary or compulsory; innate, accidental or imposed. Abstractly, we say that identity arises from, or belongs to, some *context*. What is a context? Since our interest is on

81 http://orcid.org/.

monitoring, surveillance and intelligence, the context will have something worth observing.

On Identifiers

21.72 Problems arising in accessing and cross-referencing identities in different databases have led us to attempt an analysis of the general concept of digital identity of people and objects. People and objects can be intimately connected, as in the cases of people and phones, cars, homes etc. Often, objects define the context for the discussion of a person's identity. We use the term *entity* to mean both people and objects. Our analysis of the identity of entities rests on one central concept:

> An *identifier* for an entity is specific data that is associated with the entity for the purposes of recognising, separating or identifying it among other entities within a particular context.

21.73 Thus, we see emerging the abstract idea of a context as having entities that have identifiers. To develop the idea of context we add the idea of the *characteristics* of an entity that are the data associated with the entity for the purpose of *defining* why it belongs to a context. In thinking about context, we accept that entities are 'known' *only* through the data that act as their (i) identifiers and (ii) characteristics.

21.74 Monitoring observes the behaviour of entities in a context and collects the observations. Observing can mean many things, but what is common is the acquisition of data about the behaviour of entities. Thus, if we factor out the mechanisms by which data is obtained we see that the essence of monitoring is that it directly obtains and observes data about the behaviour of entities and only indirectly observes entities themselves. This view builds an abstract concept of context and monitoring that is made from data. To complete the picture, we define a context to consist of the following components:[82]

> ***Entity.*** People or objects belonging to a context that possess behaviour in space and time.
>
> ***Identifiers.*** Data that distinguishes between individuals or objects in a context.
>
> ***Characteristics.*** Data that registers and records properties of the entity that characterises context.
>
> ***Behaviour.*** Data that is the result of observations of the behaviour.
>
> ***Attribute.*** Properties of behaviour to be observed based on rules, norms, practices, expectations, and other observable properties.

82 See: Surveillance and identity: conceptual framework and formal models, *Journal of Cybersecurity*, 3(3), 2017, pp 145–158.

21.75 Consider identifiers that are supposed to identify people. Historically, the identity of a person is reduced to forms of evidence, including personal testimony, biometrics and, especially, records of other confirmations of identity, all of which we gather together under the term data. We also need to consider the *problem of entity authentication*. For a particular context, given any entity and identifier, can we decide whether or not the identifier is associated with the entity? Data is only processed by software. While an identifier is data, what does it mean to input an entity to a software system? In theory and practice, the entity is actually defined by means of identifiers, ie, specific data that is used to identify an entity in a particular context. The data may appear to be varied, in text and biometrics, but it is inevitably in digital form.

21.76 The abstract notion of an identifier proves to be a subtle but useful tool for thought. A list of characteristics needs to be examined in order to understand identity. These include:

- ways identifiers are created;
- how the generation of identifiers depends upon other identifiers and can structure themselves into hierarchies;
- provenance of identifiers and the essential role of context;
- how identifiers are to be compared and when they might be deemed equivalent;
- how identifiers are inter-related and can be conflated or transformed between contexts.

21.77 Software technologies monitor individuals and objects, and capture their attributes in data. Following Altman,[83] to specify a particular context, only those attributes relevant to the context and its purpose need to be specified. Consequently, an entity's behaviour in another context is protected, making it hard to build a more complete picture of the entity.

21.78 The idea of *need to know* can be found in all organisations. It can be simply expressed as needing to have clear professional reasons before sharing information. The idea is likely to be implicit in practices that are features of the profession, organisation and context. In matters of intelligence the idea needs to be explicit and practice regulated. When the information is digital, the demands of software require it to be made very precise. Thus, notions of *information boundaries* need to be formulated. Boundaries are needed in order to be regulated and possibly enforced by the software, preventing information leakage.

21.79 In the context of investigations, by the idea of *need to know*, we might introduce a restriction that limits searching by having to specify questions or topics. Thus:

83 Irwin Altman, *The Environment and Social Behavior: Privacy, Personal Space, Territoriality and Crowding*.

Only information that is directly relevant to a query or question arising in the context of an investigation should be requested and accessed.

Some Observations on Identifiers

21.80 The relationship between entities and identifiers has proved to be very complicated, even within a single context. There are contexts where the association can have these following forms:[84]

1. *Many – One Associations*. Different identifiers can be assigned to the same entity.
2. *One – One Associations*. Different identifiers are assigned to different entities.
3. *One – Many Associations*. An identifier can be assigned to more than one entity but an entity has only one identifier.
4. *Many – Many Associations*. An identifier is assigned to more than one entity and, vice versa, an entity can be assigned more than one identifier.

21.81 For example, in the UK, the association of vehicle registration marks to keepers is many-one at any one time. The association of registration marks to cars is one-one at any time. The association of postcodes to homes is one-many. If more than one computer is accessing the internet at the same time in a period, from the same service, then the association between IP addresses and computers is many-many.

21.82 Many contexts come with monitoring and surveillance which observe the behaviour of entities. These systems actually deal with identifiers for entities, which may narrow the search for entities but need not pin down the particular entity of interest. Thus, one-to-one associations are important because of a *uniqueness principle*: If an association is one-one then given an identifier, there is one, and only one entity with that identifier. There is 'enough data' to distinguish the entity from others in the context. Note, too, the profoundly important practical *enumeration principle*: The addition of a unique number to the data in an identifier of an entity can turn any many-one association into a one-one association.

21.83 Creating identifiers is an everyday occurrence. We open accounts, register for services, apply for permissions, buy products, etc. For many of these actions, we rely on a handful of pre-existing identifiers. To buy a product, an address and a credit card account number are usually sufficient for the vendor. In the UK, to open a bank account and obtain a credit card, we give proof of our identity and our current address, eg, using a passport and a recent utility bill. In turn, the quality of a bank identifier is guaranteed by the databases of the State (passport, driver's licence) and, say, an energy provider (utility bill). The passport

84 See: Surveillance and identity: conceptual framework and formal models, *Journal of Cybersecurity*, 3(3), 2017, pp 145–158.

provides a high-quality identifier based on a birth certificate, a photograph and possibly other biometric data. Many examples illustrate the general *construction principle*: New identifiers are created from pre-existing identifiers.

21.84 The quality of an identifier is essentially a matter of its reliability in use, which in turn depends on its provenance, ie, the process involved in establishing the identifier. In the case of people, a passport is a standard example of a *high integrity identifier* with a rigorous provenance. The driving licence is another example of a high integrity identifier. In the case of a bank, the process of establishing an identifier is weaker because identity and location is devolved.

21.85 Since identifiers are often built from other identifiers, one matter of practical importance is the process of comparing identifiers and reducing one type of identifier to another. In some cases, such as banking, it may be expected or required that the transformations are supposed to be trustworthy and end in high integrity identifiers.

21.86 *Basic personal identifiers* are those upon which we rely to distinguish a unique human being and guarantee their identity, albeit in some context with its own level of rigor. Essential to establishing identity is the collection, storage and processing of data. Indeed, identity is almost purely a matter of data. People and objects are named, labelled or otherwise denoted by data relevant to some context. The data in question captures some relevant aspects of a person or an object. Different identities are managed by different kinds of *identity management systems*.

21.87 Identifiers have several roles in privacy. An identifier implies the existence of information about the entity and its behaviour in a context. First and perhaps most obviously, the information is private if the following applies:

(i) one can know the identifier and *not* have access to the information;

(ii) one can know the information but *not* know the identifier; or

(iii) one knows neither the identifier nor the information, but one knows one or both exist.

21.88 The second case is becoming increasingly common through the open data movement. To take one example, large amounts of data from different sources are being collected and combined for research, policy development and practical management of health services. Patient records are routinely uploaded to databases in an anonymised form. A surgery splits a patient record into two parts containing personal identifiers and treatment record and the parts are both given a new linking identifier. The treatment record is sent to the database, where it is anonymous to users and maintainers of the database whilst the personal identifiers are sent to an independent unit, who create an anonymous identifier, which is attached to the record by the linking identifier. The independent unit does identity management. The term 'metadata' is often used in these situations. Metadata – summarising basic information about data and thus expediting working with data – is generally understood as the 'data about data, such as the IP address, the identity of the contact, the location of calls or messages, and the duration of the contact'.[85] For some scholars, metadata equals surveillance,[86] and by extension, intelligence.

21.89 Although the general ideas of the proposed theory of identity can be motivated by rather simple informally described examples, the concepts are sufficiently abstract to apply to many situations and enable us to formalise them mathematically using elementary algebra and logic. In their mathematical form, the theoretical notions become precise and reveal most clearly the possible structure of ideas.

CONCLUSION

21.90 In conclusion, we have examined the digital approximation of everyday life and discussed some of its consequences for intelligence and privacy, focussing on the relationship between monitoring, privacy and identity. To map the nature of identity in a digital world, we have proposed a concept of identity based on data, called identifiers. The emerging theory is intended to provide a conceptual framework to reveal and analyse the fundamental role of identity in privacy and the path from data to knowledge.

21.91 The development of software technologies will continue to surprise and challenge all of us. The daily life of citizens is being monitored through their use of these technologies. Most of the monitoring data is unused but its existence, however temporary or obscure, is an important fact. Moreover, its use in intelligence and surveillance seems inevitable. Technological innovations enable the tasks, routines and other trivialities of everyday life to be recorded and managed, the data belonging to third parties, such as phone companies, app manufacturers, or security or regulatory bodies.

21.92 The Internet of Things is central to research and development manifestos, such as Web 3.0[87] and Industry 4.0.[88] New technological discoveries will improve the resolution and connectivity of this world of data. The instances of a person's identity, and the number and form of their identifiers, are destined to grow as they avail themselves of more smart products and web services. Moreover, with the growth of sensor-based technologies that can be embedded into the human body, the Internet of Things is by no means restricted to personal possessions as people become nodes of the Internet of Things.

85 Lyon, *Surveillance, Snowden, and Big Data: Capacities, consequences, critique*.

86 Bruce Schneier, 'Metadata Equals Surveillance', *Schneier on Security* (2013) 23 September. www.schneier.com/blog/archives/2013/09/metadata_equals.html.

87 Péter Szeredi and Gergely Lukácsy, *The Semantic Web Explained: The Technology and Mathematics behind Web 3.0* (Cambridge University Press 2014).

88 Mario Hermann, Tobias Pentek and Boris Otto, *Design Principles for Industrie 4.0 Scenarios: A Literature Review* (Technische Universität Dortmund 2015).

CHAPTER 22

CYBER SECURITY LAW AND LEGISLATION: PROTECTING DATA IN THE UK, EU, AND USA: BREACHLESS LIABILITY

David Clarke

INTRODUCTION

Importance of Cyber Security Law

22.01 Cyber security law is an important player in protecting data across the UK, EU and USA. It puts forth a legal framework that organisations must be in compliance with in order to safeguard confidential information. These laws address the high level of risks associated with a more digitised environment which can lead to data breaches putting lives and businesses at risk. When organisations adhere to cyber security and data protection law, they are able to create a policy framework to manage the risks connected to unauthorised sharing of data, ensure openness in managing data, and put in place sufficient cyber-security measures. These laws establish a basis for efficient data protection and serve to retain the trust of the customer and stakeholders. In the ever-changing landscape of cyber threats, the rise of cyber security law cannot be overemphasised. The adherence to these laws is necessary for a positive security posture of organisations; in addition, they serve to make the online space safer for all users.

BREACHLESS LIABILITY

22.02 Breachless liability means this legal obligation for data breaches and preventative compliance, along with the fines and damage to image and reputation that can be realised. Within the framework of Cyber Security and Data Protection Law, breachless liability includes unauthorised data disclosure, privacy blackouts, insufficient cybersecurity, and nonadherence to regulatory orders; such breaches result in rigorous legal repercussions alongside hefty fines for institutions. In order to curtail the threat of breaches, appropriate cyberspace and data protection controls should be employed for example, strong password policies, timely updates of systems, multi-factor authentication and encryption of sensitive information. However, organisations are bound by essential law that controls data frauds, for example, the following sample (a larger list is below), Data Protection Act 2018 (UK), General Data Protection Regulation (EU),

California Consumer Privacy Act (USA), Computer Misuse Act 1990 (UK), and Health Insurance Portability and Accountability Act (USA). Data protection and data privacy need to be embraced fully and, of great importance, comply with the cyber security and data protection laws to ensure that cyber threats or breaches are mitigated with resources and available using best practices.

SCOPE OF THIS CHAPTER

22.03 The overview of this chapter is to investigate the subject of the law and legislation on cyber security in favour of data security in the UK, EU, and USA. It looks at the core preventative measures that should be present to ensure effective cyber security such as strong password policies, constant system updates, multi-factor authentication, encryption of confidential data and employee education and engagement. The aspect of adhering to legislation and possible legal consequences of data breaches had also been highlighted in the chapter. It gives a general overview of the 21 plus existing laws which are being added to daily. Examples of these breaches are British Airways Data Breach, and Facebook-Cambridge Analytica Scandal The book seeks to demonstrate the real-life consequences of data breaches, alongside, their legal implication. Finally, the chapter highlights complying with cyber security law and roadmaps future issues in this sphere.

TOP 21 CYBER SECURITY AND DATA SECURITY MEASURES TO ASSIST IN BREACHLESS LIABILITY

22.04 Asset Management Register: Maintaining a comprehensive record of all assets within the organisation, including equipment, software, and data, to ensure efficient management and tracking.

22.05 Systematic IAR Setup: Establishing a structured process for setting up and configuring the Incident Response System to effectively handle any security incidents that may arise.

22.06 Records Management Security: Implementing measures to secure and protect sensitive and confidential records from unauthorised access, loss, or theft.

22.07 Asset Classification Process: Developing a standardised procedure for categorising assets based on their criticality and sensitivity, enabling prioritisation of security measures accordingly.

22.08 IAR Design and Upkeep: Designing and maintaining the Incident Response System to ensure its effectiveness and efficiency in addressing security incidents.

22.09 Cybersecurity Strategies: Developing comprehensive strategies to safeguard against cyber threats, including proactive measures to prevent attacks and reactive measures to mitigate potential damages.

22.10 XDR Strategy Implementation: Implementing the Extended Detection and Response (XDR) strategy to detect and respond to security incidents across different endpoints, networks, and cloud environments.

22.11 ZTNA for Secure Access: Incorporating Zero Trust Network Access (ZTNA) to ensure secure and controlled access to resources, regardless of the user's location or device.

22.12 Robust MFA Utilisation: Leveraging Multi-Factor Authentication (MFA) to add an extra layer of security by requiring multiple factors, such as a password and biometric verification, for user authentication.

22.13 Standardise Endpoint Security: Establishing standardised security measures for all endpoint devices, including desktops, laptops, and mobile devices, to protect against malware, unauthorised access, and data breaches.

22.14 Offline Insurance Contact List: Maintaining an offline list of important contacts, such as insurance providers, to ensure immediate access in case of a security incident or emergency.

22.15 Control Organisational Communications: Implementing measures to control and secure organisational communications, including email encryption, secure messaging platforms, and employee training on safe communication practices.

22.16 Manage Unused Account Risks: Regularly reviewing and managing unused user accounts to minimise the risk of unauthorised access and potential security breaches.

22.17 Apply Least Privilege Principle: Granting users the minimum privileges necessary to perform their tasks, reducing the risk of accidental or intentional misuse of elevated privileges.

22.18 Scalable Backup Systems: Implementing backup systems that can accommodate the organisation's growing data needs and ensure efficient data recovery in the event of a security incident or data loss.

22.19 Web Usage Filtering: Implementing filters to control and monitor employees' internet usage, minimising the risk of accessing malicious websites or downloading potentially harmful content.

22.20 Monitor for Data Loss: Deploying tools and systems to monitor and detect any unauthorised or accidental data loss, ensuring the organisation can take prompt action to prevent further damage.

22.21 Executive Cybersecurity Updates: Providing regular updates to executive management on the organisation's cybersecurity posture, highlighting potential risks, and recommending necessary measures for improvement.

22.22 Urgent Security Patching: Promptly applying critical security patches and updates to software, operating systems, and network infrastructure to address vulnerabilities and reduce the risk of exploitation.

22.23 Legal Breach Consultation: Seeking legal consultation in the event of a cybersecurity breach to ensure compliance with data protection laws, mitigate legal risks, and take necessary actions to protect the organisation.

22.24 Organisational Cyber Commitment: Demonstrating a strong commitment to cybersecurity practices and policies across the organisation, fostering a culture of awareness and accountability.

22.25 Continuous Security Improvement: Implementing ongoing assessments, audits, and updates to enhance the organisation's security posture and adapt to emerging threats and technology changes.

22.26 Ensure Executive Alignment: Ensuring that executive leadership understands the importance of cybersecurity and aligns their decisions and actions with the organisation's security objectives.

22.27 Additional Security Actions: Implementing additional security measures specific to the organisation's needs and risk profile to further enhance protection against cyber threats.

22.28 Comprehensive MFA Approach: Adopting a holistic approach to Multi-Factor Authentication (MFA), covering various systems, applications, and user accounts, to ensure comprehensive security across the organisation.

22.29 Proactive XDR Use: Leveraging Extended Detection and Response (XDR) solutions proactively to detect, investigate, and respond to security incidents, enhancing the organisation's threat detection capabilities.

22.30 Inactive Account Removal: Regularly reviewing and removing inactive user accounts to minimise the risk of account takeover and unauthorised access to sensitive information.

Ensure Executive Alignment

22.31 It is important for breachless liability to be achieved in organisations that rely on executive alignment. The leadership team spearheads the instillation of security and data protection consciousness that is known to have many benefits to a company. By making cybersecurity and data protection a priority, executives effectively create a culture where employees know they must protect sensitive information.

22.32 The concept of executive alignment refers explicitly to the inclusion of top-level management into the cybersecurity decision-making processes. Executives should be aware of the latest threats/happenings, ongoing technologies, and law upon data protection. Through the provision of these periodic cybersecurity updates to executives, they thus remain aware of upcoming dangers and the patterns of dealing with them.

22.33 In addition, executive alignment goes with making clear channels for reporting cybersecurity incidents. The following should be provided; the executives should be reachable to facilitate the delivery and timely reporting of any breaches or vulnerabilities detected in the organisation. This allows making quick decisions, and what is most important is the choice of effective countermeasures aimed at the avoidance of data loss or, at the same time, unauthorised access.

22.34 In conclusion, executive alignment is an essential aspect of managing breachless liability. Through direct legal participation of the top-level management in the implementation of cybersecurity practices in and decision-making of the organisations, its data is preserved from potential attacks and the knock on effects of non compliance.

Continuous Security Improvement

22.35 Continuous security improvement is a critical aspect of effective cybersecurity management. By implementing a range of measures, organisations can enhance their cyber resilience and reduce the risk of data breaches. These measures include:

1. Organisational Cyber Commitment: Establishing a culture of cybersecurity within the organisation is crucial. This involves promoting awareness and accountability among employees, as well as providing the necessary resources to implement robust security measures.
2. Legal Breach Consultation: Seeking legal advice regarding breach management and ensuring compliance with relevant laws can help organisations mitigate the legal consequences of data breaches.
3. Urgent Security Patching: Timely installation of security patches and updates is essential for addressing vulnerabilities and preventing unauthorised access to sensitive data.
4. Executive Cybersecurity Updates: Regular updates and briefings to organisational executives on cybersecurity risks and trends enable informed decision-making and allocation of resources.
5. Monitor for Data Loss: Implementing robust data loss prevention measures, such as real-time monitoring and encrypted communications, can help detect and prevent unauthorised data transfers.
6. Web Usage Filtering: Utilizing web filtering systems can restrict access to potentially risky websites, reducing the likelihood of falling victim to phishing attacks or malware downloads.

7. Scalable Backup Systems: Regularly backing up data and ensuring the availability of scalable backup systems can mitigate the impact of data breaches and enable swift recovery.
8. Apply Least Privilege Principle: Limiting user access rights to only what is necessary reduces the risk of unauthorised access to sensitive information.
9. Manage Unused Account Risks: Regularly reviewing and deactivating unused accounts helps minimise the risk of compromised credentials and unauthorised access.
10. Control Organizational Communications: Establishing secure communication channels and implementing email encryption protocols can protect sensitive information from interception or unauthorised disclosure.

22.36 Incorporating these continuous security improvement measures into an organisation's cybersecurity strategy strengthens its overall security posture and contributes to breachless liability.

Organisational Cyber Commitment

22.37 Organisations have a significant responsibility to ensure that data safety is maintained, and when there is a breach of this, they are quick to fix it. For breachless liability, some cyber security necessities need implementation. The measures that are in part regular, urgent cybersecurity updates, policies and processes, and tracking to identify weaknesses in process and policy. There are also important web usage filters and the least privilege principle. Risk management of un-used accounts and taking control of all organisational communications maintain the right environment. Moreover, keeping an offline the insurance contacts' list, standardising endpoint security, and ensuring a powerful MFA also bolster protection. Two critical strategies – the necessity for zero trust network access (ZTNA) and an XDR plan – should intensify right now's intensely convoluted assault terrain. Protection of records management, security, and keeping control over an asset management register are critical elements of organisational cybersecurity. Additionally, clearly articulating the cybersecurity strategies, asset classification process, and IAR setup systems are vital to breachless liability. Organisations can help ensure the integrity and protection of data with these measures if they focus especially upon them.

Legal Breach Consultation

22.38 Legal Breach Consultation is a crucial aspect of ensuring breachless liability in the realm of cyber security law. It involves seeking expert legal advice and guidance to assess the potential breaches that an organisation may face and devise strategies to mitigate them.

Urgent Security Patching

22.39 Urgent security patching contributes significantly to being a breachless liability. It is basically about immediately correcting flaws in software and systems to thwart possible cyber-attacks. Through the application of security patches punctually, organisations can improve their cybersecurity sentinel and safeguard confidential data. The aforementioned vulnerabilities should be dealt with on time; if not, systems are left open for attacks, which directly will be inclusive of chances of hacking. Organisations should take pressing security patching as their organisational priority in order to safeguard the continuity of networks and information assets' protection.

Executive Cybersecurity Updates

22.40 To achieve breachless liability and data protection one needs to update themselves from time to time. Regular reporting to executive management on the organisation's cybersecurity state, outlining potential threats and advising on appropriate measures to develop positive change.

Monitor for Data Loss

22.41 Monitor for Data Loss: The aspect of monitoring for data loss is highly significant in as far as making the liability of the breaches zero is concerned in the world of cyber security. Through establishing effective data loss monitoring systems, organisations can transform potential attacks into small incidents that remain unnoticed to the rest of the world. Such systems function by tracking network traffic, user activity, and data transfers, all in an effort to signal off suspicious or unauthorised behaviour to security teams. Such leaks of the data are reduced with the use of the data loss prevention tools which apply policies that make it impossible for the sensitive data to be leaked or promiscuously shared. Data loss by setting up this priority, company security systems are being reinforced to control the situation in the event of data breaches or the associated legal implications, which can become more manageable.

Web Usage Filtering

22.42 Web Usage Filtering concerns limiting and monitoring the usage of the internet by employees or individuals within an institution to discourage unauthorised usage, malware attacks, and data leakage. It entails the choice of technologies and rules that rather limit or filter Internet access to the sites or categories of sites that might cause potential security loss. As one of the measures that help boost cybersecurity, web usage filtering is essential to reducing the negative effects of unscrupulous online activities in the UK, EU, and USA and, consequently, the protection of data. Organisations can reduce the potential of data breaches and almost an entire class of cybersecurity incidents by blocking access to malicious or inappropriate websites.

Scalable Backup Systems

22.43 Breachless liability is important in the field of cyber security, since Scalable Backup Systems are essential for such a goal. These systems provide firms with opportunities of daily or even more frequently performing full data backup, so that in case of a breach or loss they can easily restore the information and, thus, prevent negative consequences. The appropriate backup systems are supposed to be scalable in order to support the increasing data volume and redundancy measures to avoid data loss. Furthermore, companies have to set up a safe and disconnected backup storage to lock their protected backups from computer attacks. With the right planning and implementation of scalable backup systems, companies can increase data security measures, reduce hacking exploitations, and enable better cyber defence measures overall.

Apply Least Privilege Principle

22.44 The idea of the least privilege principle is one of the core elements of cybersecurity and it limits accordingly individuals or systems access privileges to only comprising of what is necessary for them to do to operate within their role requirements. With such an applied principle, organisations can avoid exposure to unauthorised access of confidential information and decrease the possibility of sustained damage following a data breach.

22.45 Applying the least privilege principle means that the user should be afforded the lowest possible level of access privileges, whereby such levels of access privileges remain sufficient for the smooth performance of their duties. This secures a user's account, as in case of compromise, the attacker would still have limited access to sensitive data or critical systems.

22.46 In order to ensure efficient accountability through the least privilege principle, organisations can be periodically set to undertake reviews of access undertaken to eliminate privileges that are redundant. With the use of RBAC (Role Based Access Control) systems management by access privileges based on job roles can be simplified and the risks of data leaks can be considerably reduced.

Manage Unused Account Risks

22.47 Manage Unused Account Risks: Managing risks of UA, this area is of paramount importance in the field of cyber security. The accounts that are obsolete ought to be monitored actively in an attempt to limit vulnerabilities. With a systematic review and inactivation of such accounts, companies minimise threats of illegitimate access and possible cases of information spillage. Compliance with relevant cybersecurity legislation and protection of sensitive information requires businesses to focus on the optimisation of unused accounts.

Control Organisational Communications

22.48 Control Organisational Communications: Communication and information management in organisations is quite an essential extension of the process of cyber protection and sensitive data protection. No incident operation can function properly without effective communication protocols and the fact is that these protocols are very critical when it comes to risk mitigation and breachless liability. This can be realised through designing escalation and structured processes for communication in organisations and this consequently improves overall security posture.

Offline Insurance Contact List

22.49 An integral component of a full-scale cyber security plan is offline risk coverage. A data breach is an instance that offline details insurance may assist in rapidly assisting in an incident solution in offering technical and incident support and support to organisations that may have been affected by the breach. These providers can provide customised policies that protect from illegal data sharing, opacity, insufficient security protection, and non-conformity as to regulations, they can also help the recovery process.

Standardise Endpoint Security

22.50 The best practice of endpoint security practices in is important in securing information and breach prevention. If all endpoints are consistently secured, vulnerabilities are reduced, and potential gateways for a cyberattack are minimised. This entails implementing reliable security measures that include implementing strong anti-malware programs regularly patched with patch management plus the use of encryption protocols.

22.51 Adapting a preventive approach toward threat discovery and management is another vital facet of endpoint security. Through continuous monitoring and threat intelligence, the detection and control of risk is efficient. Endpoint security as well as control of access and user authentication measures – including, multi-factor authentication (MFA) – help to strengthen the endpoint security and avoid unauthorised use.

22.52 In addition, organisations can utilise ZTNA (Zero Trust Network Access) to limit technology and applications, improving secure admittance to the organisation and applications. ZTNA applies the identity verification as well as granular controls over the access, verifying only the authenticated and authorised people are granted the access to the resources.

22.53 Adoption of XDR (Extended detection and response) strategies further makes endpoint security more stringent. XDR solutions have the capability of integrating and correlating data from many security products enabling more efficient close monitoring in the detection of threats and incident response. Aggregating and analysing data from across endpoints, networks and cloud environments enables organisations to make a holistic assessment of the risks involved.

22.54 In the end, end point practices standardisation can be crucial for data protection and incident management Through the implementation of ZTNA security vulnerabilities can be lowered, threats can be identified in an early warning manner, and threats can be responded to effectively, solidifying breachless liability.

Robust MFA Utilisation

22.55 Some critical steps towards breachless responsibility are the significant adoption of MFA. By MFA, the users need to submit more evidence to prove their identity, therefore increasing the level of information security. It can be both some acknowledged to the user setting (eg, a password) or devices, information possessed by the user (eg, his mobile phone) or even the same user himself or herself, MFA deployment by organisations can lower the possibility of unauthorised access to sensitive data, as well as limit the consequences of incidents. Governments and experts advise the adoption of MFA as standard cybersecurity practice. Organisations can use MFA to boost their overall cybersecurity and also to authenticate how critical data is secure from malicious actors.

ZTNA for Secure Access

22.56 ZTNA, or Zero Trust Network Access, is a critical component of secure access in the realm of cyber security. With the increasing sophistication of cyber threats, traditional perimeter-based security measures are no longer sufficient. ZTNA offers a new approach by verifying and authorising every access attempt between devices and systems, regardless of the user's location or device. By adopting the ZTNA framework, organisations can minimise the risk of unauthorised data sharing, enhance transparency, and form robust cybersecurity measures. It serves as a proactive strategy to prevent breaches and maintain compliance with regulatory orders.

XDR Strategy Implementation

22.57 Secure access in cyber security includes the important element of ZTNA or Zero Trust Network Access. As the sophistication of cyber threats advances, the more traditional perimeter-based security measures are proving inadequate. ZTNA assists by authenticating each user at the entrance to a system or an application to allow or deny access to the converter depending on the user's location and type of device. Through the adoption of the ZTNA framework organisations can reduce the risk factor of data loss caused by unauthorised sharing of data and implement strong cyber security measures.

Records Management Security

22.58 Records Management Security refers to having and keeping records protected and well managed in an organisation. It includes activities including the keeping of accurate inventories, implementing control of access, and planning appropriate right disposal – plans. Organisations need to make sure that they focus on the security of records management so as to prevent unauthorised sharing of data and in ensuring transparency and adhering to regulatory demands. A records management security depends upon effective asset management, now in terms of asset registers and a systematic information asset register IAR establishment. These steps help to find, classify, monitor usage, and employ security controls for special category data.

Cybersecurity Strategies

22.59 In this section, we discuss some of the main measures for breachless liability in the UK, EU, and USA. These actions include Records Management Security, Asset Management Register, as well as the Systematic IAR Setup. It concludes that a successful Asset Classification Process and appropriate Cybersecurity Strategies are necessary to sustain data integrity. If organisations can follow these tactics, they reduce the potential risk of data leakage and the legal implications that arise from data leakage, lack of transparency, poor cyber security measures and noncompliance with regulatory orders.

Asset Classification Process

22.60 The asset classification process plays an integral role within the cybersecurity and data protection entities. It includes classification and naming of goods as per value, sensitive nature, or organisation-specific nature. Throughout this procedure, there is the possibility of pinpointing which security measures are applicable to various resources, increasing defence level of the most important and secretive data.

22.61 Classification of assets helps organisations define the necessary security controls, access restrictions, and data handling practices. Assets can be grouped under various categories which include public, internal, confidential or highly confidential based on the sensitivity and damage the effect of such an asset could cause if it were compromised. It is a starting point for formulating mechanisms of protecting data and allocating resources meaningfully.

22.62 When classifying assets, the significance of assets are reviewed, the potential risks facing the assets and threats to the assets are identified and appropriate security controls employed to protect the assets. It also entails periodic revision and rectification of asset lists as circumstances change and new risks keep surfacing.

Systematic IAR Setup

22.63 A vital part of no breach liability in the field of cyber security is Systematic IAR Setup. Towards the accomplishment of this process, an engineered Incident and Response (IAR) system is incorporated that plays a critical role in the efficient management and mitigation of possible data breaches. With the establishment of structured IAR Setup, organisations can anticipate, best prevent attempts at attacks from hackers, thus helping to respond timely and with minimum impact of impending threats. The associated activities usually involve the development of incident response plans, the creation of incident response teams, regular testing and evaluation of the system, as well as constant refinement guided by the lessons learned. In the grand scheme of things, it is meant to develop a solid system that sufficiently offers quick and decisive responses to emerging cyber onslaughts. The importance of a well-established, continuous, systematic IAR Setup to entities is to improve their cybersecurity posture, protect sensitive data, and meet compliance according to the applicable legislation and regulations.

KEY LEGISLATION FOR DATA BREACHES AND BREACHLESS LIABILITY

UK Data Protection Act 2018 Fines

22.64 Penalties for data breaches as prescribed in the UK Data Protection Act 2018 include the imposition of fines and regulatory actions. This act is also very essential whereby it is protection of data in the UK, and can incur breachless liability. It ensures entities are responsible for the unauthorised transaction of data. With compliance with the Data Protection Act 2018, possibilities of breaches in the systems are reduced and the integrity of digital systems is maintained.

UK Network and Information Systems (NIS) Regulations 2018

22.65 In accordance with NIS Regulations 2018 of the UK, fines and regulatory action follow the breach of data for the cyber attack. Such rules are intended to develop the reliability of network and information systems grounded on the responsibility of organisations for the breaches. Fines promote cybersecurity measures to be observed. Through the introduction of these regulations, the UK is taking a preventive stance aimed at boosting cyber security and safeguarding confidential data. These regulations must be observed by organisations in the UK to prevent possible legalities. Not only are their own data protected, but also those of their customers especially those who are part of or supply critical national infrastructure.

Telecommunications (Security) Act 2021

22.66 Telecommunications (Security) Act 2021 covers the necessity of effective security measures to safeguard data in the UK. The law entails charges against unauthorised sharing of data, lack of transparency, inadequate cybersecurity measures and non-compliance with regulatory orders. As a way to have data integrity and confidentiality the following act enforces breachless liability. These steps reveal the development of cyber security law compliance and the necessity to secure personal data with the formulation of the new premises of the modern digital world.

USA (Virginia) Consumer Data Protection Act (CDPA)

22.67 The Consumer Data Protection Act (CDPA) in the USA (Virginia) is an important piece of legislation that aims to protect consumer data. It establishes fines and regulatory actions for unauthorised data sharing, lack of transparency, inadequate cybersecurity measures, and non-compliance with regulatory orders. The CDPA plays a crucial role in breachless liability by holding organisations accountable for safeguarding sensitive information. By implementing robust cybersecurity measures and following the provisions of the CDPA, companies can mitigate the risk of data breaches and protect the privacy and security of individuals' data. This legislation reflects the growing importance of cyber security law in the digital age, where data breaches have significant legal consequences and require comprehensive measures to prevent and address them.

USA (Colorado) Colorado Privacy Act

22.68 In the USA (Virginia), there is an Act known as the Consumer Data Protection Act (CDPA) which seeks to protect the rights that consumers are entitled to with regard to their data. It provides fines for unauthorised sharing of data and regains actions for lack of transparency; for inadequate cybersecurity measures; and for non-compliance with regulatory regulations. The CDPA leaves a huge role that the CDPA takes up the liability of breachless as it requires organisations to effectively secure personally identifiable information. Through adopting cybersecurity programs and adherence to the tenets of CDPA, companies can reduce risks associated with data breaches and secure the privacy and security of individuals' information.

USA (Nevada) SB 220

22.69 Thus, USA (Nevada SB 220) is an important piece of legislation where State of Nevada information pertaining to data security. It has the potential for penalties and other measures for unregulated information sharing, transparency, poor cyber security measures, and non-compliance. This law may act as a major deterrent for entities dealing with confidential data making them focus on strong cybersecurity protocols. SB 220 intends to cultivate breachless liability by putting the corporate accountability compared to the indication that the corporate should be liable for data loss under the SB 220 if the company is found responsible for a data breach, the company could be fined; for this reason, the companies should be aware of regulation around the UK, EU, and USA regulation in the USA, securing data for the modern society.

USA (Maine) LD 946

22.70 US ME LD 946 is a statute that lays down penalties for data breaches in the State of Maine. including the civil penalty amongst others, and regulatory action. It discusses the, inappropriate cybersecurity measures. Protecting data within the United States is a broader initiative that this law accommodates. LD 946 has penalties for data breaches in order to make companies adhere to robust cybersecurity measures and relevant compliance regimes.

USA (New York) SHIELD Act

22.71 The SHIELD Act in the US states encompasses the New York chapter and is an important legislation catering for data protection and breachless liability. It puts fines and policy enforcement actions on illegal data sharing, lack of disclosures, and insufficient security measures. It remains one of the principal data breach prevention efforts made in the US, besides gatekeeping organisations to take responsibility for sensitive information security.

USA (California) California Consumer Privacy Act (CCPA)

22.72 In the USA (California), CCPA is a significant factor that should be considered while gathering information about data Under this act, unauthorised sharing of data attracts penalties alongside regulatory action against data sharing lacking in transparency, insufficient cybersecurity measures and noncompliance with orders issued by regulatory officials. The CCPA focusses on ensuring that consumers have control over their personal information and hence certain rights pertaining to their data. By means of this act, individuals ask businesses about their collection and utilisation of data. In addition, the option is there, where they can opt-out of the sale of the personal information and can ask for the deletion of the data. The CCPA places an emphasis on the need to protect data supported by privacy and security, setting a precedent for other states in the USA.

China Data Security Law of the People's Republic of China

22.73 Penalties for data security law violation in the People's Republic of China are fines and suspension of business, according to China Data Security Law. This act greatly contributes to the breachless liability within the country.

EU Digital Operational Resilience Act (DORA)

22.74 EU Digital Operational Resilience Act (DORA): Specifically, DORA defines fines punishable under EU legislation for different cybersecurity violations. The purpose of this legal act is to improve the resistance of digital operating activities of financial institutions including banks, etc. The digital infrastructure stability and security addressed by Dora in the EU. It works alongside other major EU cybersecurity legislation. DORA in the EU is aimed at securing data and continuity of digital services particularly in the financial sphere.

EU Cybersecurity Act

22.75 EU Cybersecurity Act: The EU Cybersecurity Act plays a major role in securing data in western Europe. The Act provides a certification process for cybersecurity products, services and processes enabling digital security. It seeks to increase trust and confidence in digital services and enhance the cybersecurity capacities of the EU. Setting up the certification framework, the Act guarantees the level of measured cybersecurity since consumers and businesses can be protected from cyber attacks. This act will form a major step towards a safer digital environment in the EU.

EU Network and Information Systems Directive (NIS Directive)

22.76 Organisations that come under NIS Directive in the UK, EU and the USA are liable to fines and regulatory enforcement for breach of data. This imperative is intended to strengthen essential service providers and digital service providers to make them secure and adaptable.

EU General Data Protection Regulation (GDPR)

22.77 The EU General Data Protection Regulation (GDPR) it also has an important function of ensuring the security of data in the UK, EU, and USA. Violating the GDPR results in fines and regulatory actions for unauthorised data sharing, lack of transparent mechanisms. This piece of legislation makes an organisation accountable for any violations that occur that were not expected.

USA Health Insurance Portability and Accountability Act (HIPAA)

22.78 The USA Health Insurance Portability and Accountability Act (HIPAA) is key legislation for data breaches in the United States. HIPAA imposes fines and regulatory action for unauthorised data sharing, lack of transparency, inadequate cybersecurity measures, and non-compliance with regulatory orders. This act specifically focusses on safeguarding the privacy and security of protected health information. It requires covered entities and their business associates to implement comprehensive security measures to protect patient data from unauthorised access or disclosure. HIPAA violations can result in substantial penalties, including fines and potential criminal charges.

USA Gramm-Leach-Bliley Act (GLBA) Fines

22.79 USA Gramm-Leach-Bliley Act (GLBA): Fines have been established under the Gramm-Leach-Bliley Act (GLBA) to address data security breaches. This legislation targets financial institutions and requires them to implement appropriate measures to safeguard customer information. Failure to comply with GLBA regulations can result in significant fines.

USA Cybersecurity Information Sharing Act (CISA)

22.80 The Cybersecurity Information Sharing Act (CISA) in the USA is important legislation aimed at enhancing the sharing of cybersecurity threat information between private companies and government agencies. It encourages the voluntary sharing of cyber threat indicators and defensive measures to improve the overall cybersecurity posture. The act provides liability protection to entities that share information, ensuring that they are protected from legal actions arising from the sharing of such data. By promoting collaboration and information sharing, CISA aims to strengthen the nation's ability to prevent and respond to cyber threats. This legislation plays a crucial role in fostering a culture of shared responsibility and cooperation in the fight against cybercrime.

India Personal Data Protection Bill 2022

22.81 The Personal Data Protection Bill 2022 in India focusses on safeguarding personal data and regulating its usage. It aims to provide transparency, accountability, and consent in the processing of personal data. The bill introduces strict data protection standards and grants individuals the right to access, correct, and erase their personal data. It also establishes a Data Protection Authority to oversee enforcement and impose fines for non-compliance. The bill addresses various aspects of data protection, including cross-border transfers, data breach notifications, and the processing of sensitive personal data. By implementing robust regulations, the Personal Data Protection Bill 2022 aims to strengthen data security and protect individuals' privacy in India.

India Information Technology Amendment Act 2018

22.82 The India Information Technology Amendment Act 2018 introduces fines for non-compliance with cybersecurity measures, unauthorised data sharing, and lack of transparency. The Act also includes provisions for imprisonment in certain cases. It aims to strengthen data protection and privacy in India, confirming that organisations implement adequate cybersecurity measures to prevent data breaches. By imposing fines and penalties, the Act serves as a deterrent against non-compliance with regulatory orders and promotes a culture of cybersecurity compliance in the country. The introduction of this legislation highlights the growing global concern for data protection and the need for robust cybersecurity laws to safeguard sensitive information.

UK Online Safety Bill 2023 Fines, regulatory action

22.83 The UK Online Safety Bill 2023 introduces fines and regulatory action for data breaches, aiming to enhance cyber security and protect valuable data. This legislation addresses key issues such as unauthorised data sharing, lack of transparency, inadequate cybersecurity measures, and non-compliance with regulatory orders. The fines and regulatory actions act as a strong deterrent to companies to prioritise the protection of data and prevent breaches from occurring. This legislation is a crucial step towards achieving breachless liability and the security of data in the UK.

UK Network and Information Systems (NIS2) Directive

22.84 EU Network and Information Systems (NIS2) Directive imposes fines and regulatory action for data breaches. It focuses on the importance of potential breachless liability for critical national infrastructure and addresses unauthorised data sharing, lack of transparency, and inadequate cybersecurity measures.

DATA BREACHES AND LEGAL CONSEQUENCES

Summary of Unauthorised data sharing, breach and transparency issues

22.85

1. Non-compliance with cybersecurity regulations.
2. Inadequate incident reporting and remediation.
3. Risks of harmful online content.
4. Unauthorised access and data tampering.
5. Retention and misuse of shared information.
6. Lack of data protection and privacy standard adherence.
7. Failure to report data breaches.
8. Security incident notification deficiencies.
9. Non-compliance with encryption standards.
10. Unauthorised data handling and access.
11. Cross-border data transfer non-compliance.
12. Consumer rights and data selling issues.
13. Data retention, disposal, and consent problems.

NON-COMPLIANCE WITH CYBERSECURITY REGULATIONS

22.86 Failure to abide by cybersecurity laws has far-reaching legal implications for the organisation. Compliance with these laws is supported by penalties such as fines, regulatory action and other forms of legal sanctions upon failure to follow them. Cybersecurity measures can be implemented to mitigate the risk of non-compliance. These actions are executive alignment, continuous security improvement, organisational cyber commitment, legal breach consultation, urgent security patching, executive cybersecurity updates, data loss monitoring, web usage filtering, scalable backup systems, applying the least privilege principle, managing unused account risks, organisational control of communications, maintaining an offline insurance contact list, standardising endpoint security, strong multi-factor authentication.

INADEQUATE INCIDENT REPORTING AND REMEDIATION

22.87 Ineffectiveness in the reporting and rectification of data breaches is poor incident reporting and remediation. It states the delayed detection and remediation of cybersecurity events may result in additional vulnerabilities with impact 2. As such, poor incident reporting leads to delays in breaches, which may be identified late, thus causing further damages. Likewise, successful remediation ensures corrective actions to minimise the impact of a breach which includes vulnerability patching as well as improved security measures. The insufficiency of incident reporting and remediation leads to long exposure to threats and liabilities as it makes it impossible to observe cybersecurity regulations and to protect valuable information. Incident reporting and remediation should be considered key elements of a successful organisation's cybersecurity strategy, focussing on transparency, early actions and timely response to attacks to provide data security and avoid regulatory noncompliance.

RISKS OF HARMFUL ONLINE CONTENT

22.88 However, in the context of cyber security, the risks of exposure to potential harmful online content may have serious legal implications. Illegal data sharing and opacity represent statistics that pose serious threats even possible frauds related to mismanagement of cybersafety rules. Risk factors also include non-compliance with regulatory orders, poor incident reporting and remediation. Thus, web usage filtering continuous security improvement, and advanced multi-factor authentication plan must be a priority for such organisations.

UNAUTHORISED ACCESS AND DATA TAMPERING

22.89 Cases of unauthorised access and data tempering form a very critical part of the cyber security law and legislation. Unauthorised access is defined as unauthorised entry into any computer systems or networks often for malicious purposes. This might lead to unauthorised data modification, stealing, or destruction which can cause significant harm to not only individuals but organisations. In contrast, data corruption includes making changes to data because approval is done for mischievous purposes that may result in serious damages or disruptions.

22.90 To deal with the mentioned threats in the UK, EU, and USA, some measures and legislation have been enacted. Organisations should adopt stringent measures to ensure that unauthorised access to their premises does not take place and also that no data of the records has been tempered with; continuous security improvement, web usage filtering, and scalable backup systems are some of the major resolutions. The risk of unauthorised access can be limited by the use of appropriate controls.

FAILURE TO REPORT DATA BREACHES

22.91 The consequences of failure to report data breaches in the UK, EU, and USA within various time scales can initiate legal ramifications. The law requires organisations to immediately notify the law enforcers of any data breach, especially if it involves organisation information. The data breach reporting failure poses sensitive data into a risk as it hinders essential mitigation, and hence, increases the likelihood of a data breach leading to unauthorised access and tampering. It also reveals the lack of capability of data protection and privacy policies.

NON-COMPLIANCE WITH ENCRYPTION STANDARDS

22.92 It is one of the most serious threats in terms of data security in the UK, EU, and USA, because the encryption standards are not aligned with them. Compliance with encryption, especially considering the facts that this is a fundamental security aspect, can have severe repercussions when it is poorly implemented. Therefore, much emphasis needs to be put on the compliance of data encryption standards to ensure data protection and reduce the risk of legal and reputational consequences that might arise.

CROSS-BORDER DATA TRANSFER NON-COMPLIANCE

22.93 One of the most important problems in the area of cyber security law and regulation is the non-compliance with cross-border data transfer. The violation of regulations related to cross-border data transfer by organisations can give rise to legal and security implications

CONSUMER RIGHTS AND DATA SELLING ISSUES

22.94 Two important issues of cyber security law and legislature that should be taken into account are consumer rights and data selling. The greatest concern is data sharing being conducted without authorisation and due to the lack of transparency; consumers' privacy may be violated. Poor cybersecurity practices and failure to adhere to regulatory mandates make the situation worse. It is indeed breaches of the consumer rights that arise from the improper retention and misuse of the shared public information.

FUTURE TRENDS AND CHALLENGES IN CYBER SECURITY

22.95 Making mention of the future of cyber security, some emerging trends and trends and challenges can be noticed as technology continues to upgrade with cyber threats becoming advanced. One of the significant trends is the development of emerging technologies represented by the advent of artificial intelligence, machine learning, while limitless and independent aspects of quantum computing are capable of both reinforcing and thwarting current security mechanisms.

22.96 The growth of remote working and the usage of cloud services has increased the dependency on third parties, a new breed of vulnerabilities and attacks that potentially follow it. In addition, with the growth in mobile devices and proliferation of 5G networks yet another significant risk emerges, that of massive data breaches.

22.97 Cyber threats are constantly changing and thus imply continuous adaptation and improvement of security policies. Advanced persistent threats, ransomware attacks, and social engineering techniques necessitate organisations to deploy integrated and dynamic security solutions.

22.98 The cyber security regulatory landscape is never static. Changes are being made for the onset of new dangers and for the protection of personal data. Organisations need to keep track of such legal developments to be in full compliance, or a costly penalty may be imposed.

22.99 Finally, the cyber security of the future shall demand organisations to adopt new technologies, enhance their team to counter ongoing sensitive alterations, and remain concerned with the changing legislation related to digital generation. Companies can prevent the threats and protect important data by being active, and always improving their security approaches, and following government guidelines and best practices.

NUMBERED CHECKLIST SUMMARISING THE CYBER SECURITY/DATA PROTECTION RECOMMENDATIONS

22.100

1. **Asset Management**: Maintain a comprehensive asset register for efficient management and tracking.

2. **Incident Response System (IAR) Setup**: Establish a structured process for configuring the Incident Response System.
3. **Records Management Security**: Implement security measures to protect sensitive records from unauthorised access.
4. **Asset Classification**: Develop a standardised process for categorizing assets based on sensitivity.
5. **Cybersecurity Strategies**: Formulate comprehensive strategies to guard against cyber threats.
6. **Zero Trust Network Access (ZTNA)**: Incorporate ZTNA for secure and controlled access to resources.
7. **Multi-Factor Authentication (MFA)**: Utilise MFA to add an extra security layer for user authentication.
8. **Endpoint Security**: Standardise security measures across all endpoint devices.
9. **Security Patching**: Apply critical security patches and updates promptly.
10. **Legal Breach Consultation**: Seek legal advice in the event of a cybersecurity breach.
11. **Cyber Commitment**: Foster a culture of cybersecurity awareness and accountability.
12. **Continuous Security Improvement**: Regularly assess and update security measures to enhance protection.
13. **Executive Alignment**: Ensure executive leadership understands and prioritises cybersecurity.
14. **Compliance with Legislation**: Adhere to relevant cyber security laws and regulations.

22.101 This checklist is designed to assist organisations in establishing robust cyber security practices and achieving breachless liability by adhering to legislative requirements and implementing best practices in data protection.

CONCLUSION

Importance of Compliance with Cyber Security Law

22.102 The issue of cyber security in the UK, EU and USA is of significant importance in protecting data according to cyber security laws. It's intention companies implement the appropriate actions to avoid illegal data sharing, insufficient transparency and how to enhance cybersecurity and data protection approaches.

CHAPTER 23

DATA ARCHITECTURE: CYBERSECURITY'S SILENT PARTNER[1]

Kevin Murphy

ABSTRACT

23.01 Central tenets of this chapter include:

- Optimising insights from data analytics is vital to securing the enterprise and achieving broader business objectives.
- Understanding data points relating to 'identity' is central to mitigating cyber attacks.
- As data is now the locus of decision-making, technology and security strategies should be re-aligned to serve an over-arching data strategy.

23.02 It has been estimated an additional $13 trillion could be added to global GDP by 2030 as a result of digitisation, automation, and AI.[2] The value is a direct result of new business opportunities and productivity gains created by technology.[3] Public cloud providers have enabled this growth by providing businesses access to the latest technology and scope to aggressively iterate. Within this context, and whether through incumbents or digital natives, customer or regulatory expectations, the modern enterprise is continually challenged to provide new services at an unprecedented level of pace and scale.

23.03 The velocity and range of competitive pressures have established agile methodology as the primary ethos supporting change delivery. Bringing business and technology teams together and simplifying processes to optimise output has similarly influenced the provision of cybersecurity. Exemplified through

1 This chapter was written for general information purposes only. It is intended to apply to a variety of factual circumstances and industry stakeholders. The information is advisory only. Once published, the information may not contain the most up to date information. As such, this document is not intended to constitute compliance or legal advice. Readers should consult a subject matter expert if they wish to take action on any of the information contained herein. Reference to any commercial product does not imply any endorsement, merely to illustrate a point of argument.

2 McKinsey Global Institute (MGI), '*Twenty-five years of digitisation: Ten insights into how to play it right*', May 2019.

3 Ibid.

'DevSecOps', security is now a core element of the developer lifecycle.[4] But digitisation has also had a profound influence on data; increasing both volume and the need for integrated insights. Most large enterprises now have data strategies with the objective of leveraging this range of information to improve consumer experience.[5] This has resulted in significant investment in data science and analytics.[6]

23.04 Using data to improve business decisions and deliver intuitive products also presents significant value in securing the enterprise. It is the purpose of this chapter to outline the fundamental importance of data in delivering cybersecurity. Specifically, highlighting the primacy of a 'cybersecurity data architecture' as the cornerstone of protecting the enterprise. An architecture predicated on data integration, profiling, and automated decision-making has the dual benefit of reducing the enterprise risk profile, and operational expenditure related to compute.

23.05 To understand the core components of this cybersecurity data architecture, an analysis of the threat environment shall help prioritise the data points most important to mitigate cyber-attacks; those relating to 'identity'. The historic challenges of securing identity shall then be used to inform the creation of a data architecture to support cybersecurity operations; based on the concepts of profiling and intelligent 'data fabric'. To realise this data-led cybersecurity operating model, a new approach shall be proposed in relation to people capability and risk management. Finally, this new architecture shall be envisioned in strategy. A paradigm shift where cybersecurity and technology strategies are for the first-time servant to the locus of decision-making; the data strategy.

DATA AND ATTACK VECTORS: RE-INTERPRETING THE THREAT LANDSCAPE

23.06 The most realistic threat scenarios remain ransomware, supply chain compromise, and insider risk, with data loss and business interruption being the most likely impacts. Assessing each threat scenario in turn can help identify the common data points required to mitigate these attacks.

Ransomware

23.07 Ransomware costs the world economy $20 billion in 2021. This figure is expected to rise to $265 billion by 2031.[7] With the example of Trikbot, a

4 DevSecOps: Short for development, security, and operations—automates the integration of security at every phase of the software development lifecycle, from initial design through integration, testing, deployment, and software delivery. Definition found in 'What is DevSecOps', IBM website, September 2023.

5 *Weaving data fabric into hybrid multicloud'*, IBM Institute for Business Value, p 3.

6 *From Data Science to Diplomacy'*, IBM 2019.

7 *'Ransomware Statistics, Trends and Facts for 2023 and Beyond'*, Cloudwards, April 2023.

successful exploit is typically a trojan distributed through spear-phishing emails containing a malicious link or word attachments that, through selection, activate malware. Once inside the enterprise, the malicious actor will then use a range of tools to map the network and expand access; with the ultimate goal being administrator privilege and access to the crown jewels of sensitive information.[8] Weak identity controls remain the persistent cause of ransomware attacks. For example, 88% of impacted enterprises do not employ best practice such as multi-factor authentication, just in time access, and privilege access workstations; core functionality which would significantly reduce a malicious actor's ability to gain access and persistence in the network.[9]

Supply Chain

23.08 The dominant role of identity is further reflected by compromised credentials featuring in over half of cybersecurity incidents in 2023.[10] As a root cause, this trend continues with supply chain compromise. In the context of data breaches, supply chain attacks surpass malware (including phishing) by 40% as a threat vector.[11] Unlike ransomware, where attack vectors are primarily limited to phishing and remote desktop vulnerabilities, the scope of supply chain compromise is often more ubiquitous and difficult to detect.

23.09 Exemplified by the SolarWinds attack in 2020, it was inevitable malicious actors would target the increasingly complex supply chain. A complicated patchwork of dependencies which has largely originated from a more diverse developer environment and increased business dependency on third-party solutions.[12] SolarWinds was notable as the perpetrator used legitimate software and trusted channels to initiate the attack, denuding the ability of many traditional point detection tools to identify what appeared as legitimate actions.

23.10 Similarly, the Lazarus Group has continued to focus on exploiting the supply chain through the open-source ecosystem. Using social engineering to engage developers, the group lures victims to collaborate on open-source platforms such as GitHub, where they inadvertently install malicious packages to compromise the estate.[13] It is important to note that in both incidents, attackers sought to compromise the identity infrastructure of the enterprise. Namely stealing password hashes to elevate privileges (known as 'Kerboroasting'); SAML certificates to enable identity authentication by cloud services; and

8 For an overview see '*Conti ransomware explained: What you need to know about this aggressive criminal group*', CSO Online, 31 May 2022.

9 '*Digital Defence Report*', Microsoft, 2022, p16.

10 '*Threat Horizons Report*', Google, p 4.

11 '*Supply chain attacks cause more data compromises than malware*', HelpNetSecurity, January 2023.

12 For a full explanation of the incident see '*Solarwinds hack explained: Everything you need to know*', TechTarget, June 2023.

13 '*Lazarus Group Launches First Open Source Supply Chain Attacks Targeting Crypto Sector*', Medium.com, August 2023.

creation of new accounts on the Active Directory server to evade detection. In sum, identities form the connective tissue through which malicious actors move through the attack lifecycle.[14]

Insider Risk

23.11 Defined as a security threat where the attack originates from within an organisation being attacked or targeted. The significance of insider risk to the enterprise should not be understated. Popularised by Wikileaks, high-profile insider breaches are regularly reported as affecting major organisations and service providers.[15] To provide context and scale, an 'insider' is 20% more likely to perpetrate a security incident than an external attacker. Nearly half of all corporate data breaches can be attributed to employees through account misuse, unintentional data loss, and fraudulent activities.[16] It is estimated that up to 50% of technology spend is on information technology, which is created, modified, and maintained outside routine governance routes. Termed 'shadow IT', these assets are generally not onboarded nor visible to security tooling and so operate from an inherently insecure posture.[17]

23.12 Insider threat can extend beyond the present employee or stakeholder to include former employees, board members, or anyone who at one time had legitimate access to proprietary information from within an organisation.[18] Illustrated by the Ubiquiti incident, a former employee stole confidential data only then to pose as a whistleblower and attempt to extort $2 million through a ransom demand. Using their experience as developers, the perpetrator used their cloud administrator credentials to clone hundreds of GitHub repositories, steal data, and then hide this activity through the alteration of log files.[19]

23.13 Similar to SolarWinds, malicious actors operating with legitimate credentials are difficult to detect. To mitigate insider risk, the concept of 'identity' has had to evolve beyond the authentication of access, to authenticating user profiles. Technical and behaviour indicators are key in providing this 'profile view' of normalised, abnormal, and malicious user behaviour. Data points of value can include unusual data access, device, configuration, irregular network traffic, and the sudden movement of large volumes of data. Behavioural patterns such as atypical log-on times, connections from different geo-locations, and higher absence rates can further be correlated to indicate insider risk. Due to

14 '*Top lesson from Solarwinds attack: Rethink identity security*', Kyle Alspach, Venture Beat, 18 November 2021.

15 '*Uber engineer Levandowski, accused of massive theft from Google, has been fired*', Joe Mullan, Arstechnica, 30 May 2017.

16 Professor Bill Buchanan, School of Computing Napier University, SC Roundtable June 2017.

17 '*45+ Shadow IT Statistics for 2023*', Kevin Shuler, Quandary Consulting Group, 14 February 2023.

18 '*Unmasking Insider Threat*', Securonix eBook, pp 3–5.

19 '*Former Ubiquiti dev charged for trying to extort his employer*', Sergiu Gatlan, 1 December 2021

the volume and pace of data points relative to the individual user, the ability to reduce false positives in identifying high-risk patterns of user behaviour has remained an industry challenge.

PRIMACY OF 'IDENTITY' DATA POINTS

23.14 Identity compromise is the common denominator in ransomware, supply chain, and insider attacks. Within this context, malicious attackers are increasingly using legitimate and authenticated credentials to perform exploits; a vector, that by definition, is difficult to detect. In articulating a desired architecture to mitigate identity and access management (IAM) risk, it is important first to understand the traditional challenges and enterprise context in which IAM controls are applied.

Historical Challenge of Managing Identity: Complexity

23.15 At the enterprise level, identity operates in a flux of complexity. In the consumption-based model of technology, the business tends to own an application and supporting business processes, but technical teams are responsible for the management of the supporting compute environment. Allocating responsibility to maintain and modernise the identity estate is often frustrated due to split and often competing interests of ownership.

23.16 In terms of scope, identity can extend from the management of modern Kubernetes workflows, range of third-party SaaS cloud applications, to the maintenance of legacy mainframes. Populations can comprise permanent, contingent, and third-party colleagues across varied geographic locations. In summary, ownership, visibility, and managing change across the IAM estate remain thematic challenges. With 80% of organisations reporting an identity related breach through June 2022, it is clear this enduring statistic is a function of a fertile attack surface that is often legacy-based, inadequately governed, and inherently insecure.[20]

To Protect, First Modernise

23.17 As demonstrated, threat actors log-in and break into systems when perpetrating ransomware, supply chain, and insider-based attacks.[21] With a complex mix of legacy and cloud, it can be a challenge to convince business owners to modernise the application estate when operations are ostensibly running as intended. IAM is viewed as an application function, not a high priority attack vector; and so unlikely to be prioritised until there is a significant breach.

20 '*80% of Firms Suffered Identity-Related Breaches in Last 12 Months*', Robert Lemos, Dark Reading, 22 June 2022.

21 Bret Arsenault, Microsoft Entra presentation, 11 July 2023.

Support for IAM modernisation therefore becomes dependent on the articulation of risk to a non-technical audience.

Identity: Risk Beyond IT – Ensuring Business Engagement

23.18 To obtain business engagement, the risk profile of identity management must be presented as a technical and financial risk. To illustrate the scale of the challenge, 50% of identities have access to all permissions and resources; 75% of critical containers have the same 'run' permissions as root. 80% of workload identities are inactive, and 60% of human identities are inactive.[22] Credential compromise is commonly a by-product of systemic operational misconfiguration.[23]

23.19 In the context of the consumer-based cloud model, where on average 65% of resource groups are underutilised, the optimisation of identity management will clearly result in significant cost savings related to licensing, monitoring, and storage of logs.[24] As a function of the split-ownership model, IAM remediation therefore presents significant opportunity in reducing a range of non-IT enterprise risks. For example, well-configured resources will reduce the operational risk of outages, and the financial risk of underutilised resources. In turn, sustainability risk shall be addressed as the energy consumption of the technical estate is optimised.[25] The articulation of IAM as a holistic enterprise risk will ensure the business case for modernisation shall have the broadest support.

Modernising the IAM Estate: An Emerging Architecture

23.20 Once business support has been achieved, it is then possible to engineer an identity architecture optimised to mitigate the cyber threat environment. As shown in the SolarWinds attack, the centralised storage of identity has created a prime target for attackers.[26] To address this, the concept of decentralised identity (DCI) has emerged. With the example of 'confidential ledgers', distributed ledger technology is being used to share identity across a range of nodes while using cryptographic techniques to authenticate.[27] Similarly, FIDO2 functionality uses asymmetric cryptography to allow local, overcentralised authentication to

22 Ibid.

23 '*Security Misconfiguration: Impact, Examples, and Prevention*', Admir Dizdar, Brightsec.com, 29 May 2022.

24 A statistic shared during author's Microsoft delivered Azure cloud architect training, January 2022.

25 The link between compute overhead and sustainability is a feature benefit of increased telemetry and should form a data indicator for related metrics. Point made by Derek A Whigham, Chief Product Owner, Lloyds Banking Group, 22 September 2023.

26 For a full explanation of the incident see '*Solarwinds hack explained: Everything you need to know*', TechTarget, June 2023.

27 For an excellent overview confidential ledgers see Microsoft's learning and development series: https://learn.microsoft.com/en-us/azure/confidential-ledger/overview.

reduce reliance on passwords.[28] Whilst mathematically secure, the medium-term application of DCI is limited due to the significant compute resources involved.

23.21 The architectural picture is further complicated through the advent of 'Open IAM'. Providing a platform to manage all enterprise identities, whether on premise or in the cloud, these solutions are influenced by an emerging theme within technology procurement: convergence.[29] Aiming to consolidate solutions, rather than add to the traditional point focused estate, OpenIAM seeks to provide an agnostic data layer for identity, which can then serve single-sign-on, social media authentication, self-service, and ultimately a unified view of use identity across the enterprise.

Zero Trust Architecture

23.22 Placed within the broader eco-system of technology, it is arguable the concept of zero trust architecture (ZTA) provides the most achievable architecture to protect identity. A default closed architecture in contrast to OpenIAM. Based on the concept of segmentation, zero trust can best be understood as a security framework requiring all users to be authenticated, authorised, and continually validated against policies before being granted access to applications and data.[30] Operating from policy decision and enforcement points, the zero-trust engine integrates both resource and user telemetry; analysing identities, credentials, operations, endpoints, hosting environments, workloads, and interconnecting infrastructure. For implementation, the consumption-based model of cloud computing is ideally suited for ZTA, as all assets that are chargeable are in some way visible and subject to policy.

23.23 Through the deployment of network and application security groups, it is possible to group compute requirements and define access based on policies.[31] Linked to resource groups, compute can then be mapped to specific business areas within the enterprise, providing both visibility and ownership.[32] Building on the principle of convergence, public cloud providers are offering holistic identity management suites which incorporate both legacy on-premise and multi-

28 Instead of a user's machine transmitting a one-time-password to a server for authentication, FIDO uses asymmetric public key cryptography. For more detail see 'FIDO2 is touted as a security panacea: Why isn't it everywhere?', Eliot Beer, The Stack, 18 October 2022.

29 For an overview of OpenIAM see 'openiam.com', September 2023.

30 For a full explanation see '*Zero Trust Architecture*', NIST Special Publication 800-207.

31 Compute: Terms to describe networks, virtual machines, storage and applications.

32 'A resource group is a container that holds related resources for an Azure solution. The resource group can include all the resources for the solution, or only those resources that you want to manage as a group. You decide how you want to allocate resources to resource groups based on what makes the most sense for your organization. Generally, add resources that share the same lifecycle to the same resource group so you can easily deploy, update, and delete them as a group'. Found in Azure documentation September 2023.

cloud environments.[33] Incorporating human, machine, and workload identities, developer, and production environments; converged identity architectures offer the functionality of simplified workflows and centralised management, which addresses both technical and financial risk in the consumption of compute.

ZTA Foundations

23.24 Successful ZTA deployment is primarily dependent on simplifying existing identity management and then providing a governance platform that can be easily integrated with the wider technology ecosystem.[34] From a foundational level, ZTA must be mapped against the most accurate baseline of the asset estate to ensure adequate coverage. As a result of change, an enterprise baseline remains dynamic and must be supported by continuous device discovery activity that flows through to asset management repositories. Similarly, all traffic should be observable to ensure network access is appropriately scoped, allowing assets to reach policy enforcement points.[35]

23.25 To date, the introduction of zero trust architecture (ZTA) at the enterprise level has proved challenging. This has been the function of existing unreliable and complex identity infrastructures, as detailed above, which are largely legacy based, complex, and ultimately neglected, which has resulted in widespread misconfiguration.[36] Beyond the realm of cybersecurity, implementation of ZTA is often dependent on an overarching enterprise-wide infrastructure modernisation strategy.

ZTA Performance: Secure the Data Plane

23.26 Notwithstanding the challenges noted above, ZTA is an enterprise goal to be nurtured. Following the engineering of a zero-trust architecture, focus can then turn to operation. To optimise ZTA performance, the enterprise should determine between agent- or gateway-based deployment. Agent-based requires a software component to be installed on assets to direct traffic to a policy enforcement point. Gateways act as a proxy for the resource and communicate directly with the policy administrator. Both architectures require integration with the enterprise asset registry. Due to no installation being required, less bandwidth, increased scalability, and lower costs, the industry is moving towards

33 As an example of a vendor solution, 'Microsoft Entra' is the product family name for all identity and network access solutions from Microsoft. This includes multi-cloud and on-premise, identity and privacy governance; all in one over-arching solution. Found in Microsoft Documentation, September 2023.

34 As detailed in the 'Microsoft Entra' solution.

35 For an excellent overview of the core components required by a zero trust architecture, see '*Zero trust blog series – blog 2: Architecting for zero trust*', Ismael Valenzula, SANS blog, 10 August 2023.

36 '*Security Misconfiguration: Impact, Examples, and Prevention*', Admir Dizdar, Brightsec.com, 29 May 2022.

agentless based deployment models.[37] This trend is being aided by abstraction. With the example of eBPF, it is now possible to run a limited set of instructions on a virtual machine running telemetry directly from a kernel without loading a module, significantly improving visibility.[38]

23.27 The primacy of identity in the security hierarchy is reflected by the growing number of identity threat detection and response tools.[39] For an attacker, a breach of an identity repository will result in open access to a technology enterprise as credentials are used to legitimately pivot across the estate. From a ZTA perspective, securing identity starts with ensuring the data and control planes supporting a ZTA policy enforcement engine are separated; good practice from both a security and business continuity perspective and an argument against OpenIAM.[40]

How ZTA Informs Cybersecurity Data Architecture

23.28 Historical analysis of IAM challenges helps build a picture of the core components of a cybersecurity data architecture. A modernised application estate is required, which can only be achieved through business sponsorship. This support is achieved through business reporting relating to the financial and operational risk of IAM misconfiguration. As a solution architecture, ZTA highlights the breadth of the required telemetry and dependency on accurate baselines to inform policy-based decision making.

23.29 Comprising functionality relating to detection, protection, and governance, IAM platforms are fundamental components in ZTA. To optimise the detection of identity-based risks, these platforms must reflect the increasingly federated compute environment. Primarily, be able to manage the increasing business dependency on third parties, internal and external access administration, and the burgeoning SaaS estate.[41] IAM platforms must therefore offer customisable reporting to reflect compute resource groups mapped to business units to ensure accountability, continuous authentication through user lifecycles to limit lateral access, and increased API functionality with existing security products to ensure the correlation of data across the enterprise.

37 '*What's the difference between agent based and agentless architecture?*', Perimeter 81 blog, found September 2023.

38 eBPF: 'A revolutionary technology with origins in the Linux kernel that can run sandboxed programs in a privileged context such as the operating system kernel. It is used to safely and efficiently extend the capabilities of the kernel without requiring to change kernel source code or load kernel modules'. Found at 'https://ebpf.io/what-is-ebpf/', September 2023.

39 '*How identity threat detection and response are the latest tools in cybersecurity arsenals*', Taryn Plumb, Venture Beat, 6 October 2022.

40 '*Zero trust blog series – blog 2: Architecting for zero trust*', Ismael Valenzula, SANS blog, 10 August 2023.

41 The SaaS market is growing 18% year on year. '*The State of SaaS in 2022: Growth Trends & Statistics*', Laura Schiff & Chrissy Kidd, BMC Blog, 17 September 2021.

From Data Points to 'Profiles': Emerging IAM Data Architecture

23.30 To optimise mitigation, identity platforms increasingly rely upon enhanced data analytics to meet the challenge of profiling user behaviour. Platforms are addressing this challenge through the introduction of code-level traces that span customer and user lifecycles. Through the provision of unique IDs at the transaction level, an ID persists through the user journey, capturing relevant data that is used for anomaly protection.[42] Augmented by graphs, relationships between identities can then be mapped and profiled, with any exceptions being alerted and automatically terminated through policy.[43] Such functionality should be viewed as standard in IAM platform selection criteria.

23.31 Within a data-led environment, platforms must provide low-code interfaces to allow developers to build dynamic and fine-grained authorisation flows based on allocated risk scores derived from historic pattern analysis. For example, privileged actions such as payment initiations should be subject to both 'just enough' and 'just in time' access to limit both the time and scope of functions. The provision of journey time orchestration can equally help understand the friction in customer journeys as it can identify malicious bots, aiding dynamic configuration and the identification of cyber-enabled fraud.[44]

Beyond Identity: IAM Data Architecture to Ubiquitous Visibility Across the Cyber Risk Profile

23.32 ZTA is predicated on protecting identity. But a cyber risk profile comprises many risks, including, but not limited to, data loss prevention, vulnerability management, physical security, and monitoring. Whilst these risks may orbit around identity, they still require bespoke treatment in the protection of the enterprise. Again, the concept of ZTA provides the foundations for holistically mitigating aggregate cyber risk.

23.33 Using persistent IDs, not only shall it be possible to link devices, workloads, and processes to an identity, but by extension also link data, applications, and infrastructure. This functionality offers significant insight when risk scores are linked to a persistent ID, which not only includes access but can factor vulnerabilities, secrets management, and API hygiene into an emerging risk profile. Depending on the breadth of the architecture, further data points could

42 For a commercial application see Dynatrace's 'Pure Path' technology: 'Dynatrace's patented distributed tracing and code-level analysis technology. It automatically integrates high-fidelity distributed tracing with user experience data, data from open-source technologies, and code-level, including OpenTelemetry, and code-level analytics'. As found on Dynatrace's web page September 2023.

43 A graph is an abstract data type that can be used to represent complex, non-linear relationships between objects. For more information see the website 'ISAAC Computer Science'.

44 The Darwinium platform is a good example of how profiling user journeys has been leveraged to identify fraud and automated bot attacks. Found at 'darwinium.com', September 2023.

include threat intelligence, user behavioural analytics, device configuration, and network traffic.

23.34 Protecting identity therefore requires profiling an ever-increasing range of data points encompassing the entire portfolio of cyber risk. The ability to provide a platform to make sense of this data is the fundamental mission of a data-led cybersecurity architecture. The ability to provide insight from data creates significant overhead, which requires management. In differentiating signals from noise, it is clear an effective cybersecurity operating model requires a new relationship with data.

SECURITY OPERATIONS: IDENTITY PROFILES AND THE FOUNDATIONS OF A NEW DATA ARCHITECTURE

Scale of IAM Threats: Detecting Compromise

23.35 Recent high-profile incidents demonstrate the breadth of identity based cyber-attacks. This has raised the question of whether IAM platforms alone can best mitigate this threat vector. For example, in 2020, a former CISCO employee was sentenced to prison for accessing the company's AWS cloud infrastructure and deploying code from his personal Google Project account which resulted in the deletion of 450 virtual machines. In 2022, Slack reported attackers were using stolen employee tokens to access and download private code repositories from GitHub. The same year, the Lapsus$ Group utilised stolen code signing certificates to sign malware, tools, and malicious drivers as they stole data from NVIDIA.[45] The emerging picture is of an evolving array of identity-based attack vectors across an increasing range of technology. The challenge then becomes how best to augment existing identity data points in the detection of cyber-attacks.

Re-imagining Security Operations – Historic Challenge

23.36 A security operations centre (SOC) is generally defined as a strategic command facility that protects the enterprise through intelligence gathering, threat analysis, and ongoing monitoring.[46] As a function, the SOC has evolved with the environment it protects. Emerging from network monitoring in the 1980s, the SOC now reflects an enterprise where the perimeter is far from defined and extends well beyond traditional on-premise data centres.

23.37 The sheer breadth of available data points – from desktop events to third party data connections and Kubernetes – has significantly challenged the ability of the SOC to effectively manage events. Lack of context, visibility across the

45 '*Threat Horizons Report*', Google, August 2023, pp 20–22.
46 Definition from Technopedia, 25 March 2020.

enterprise, orchestration, and a high-number of manual operations through a lack of automation continue to be the most common operational problems reported by SOC practitioners.[47] Root cause of these challenges can be seen as a function of technology scope and data volume.

Danger of a Myopic Architecture

23.38 Many established SOCs are predicated on a 'point and click' architecture with specific tools engaged to monitor different infrastructure and platform environments. This approach made sense for the monolithic enterprise, which operated from a limited number of on-premise data centres with data confined to platforms based on business use (ie, Human Resources). As technology has evolved to include cloud computing and a broader range of operating systems, tooling has proliferated as a means to accommodate the increased range of telemetry to be ingested. The result is a patchwork of alerting that lacks a holistic view and requires significant manual intervention to obtain value.

23.39 Technology has responded to these challenges through the availability of security orchestration, automation, and response (SOAR) tools. SOAR works in conjunction with the security incident and event management (SIEM) tool. SIEM collects and analyses log data from various sources, where SOAR automates and orchestrates the response to those threats. It is important to note that the effectiveness of both SIEM and SOAR tools requires continual tuning by skilled analysts to achieve value.[48]

23.40 To adequately defend the enterprise, there must be an acknowledgement we now operate in a period of ubiquitous computing that is not limited to a specific device, location, or operating system and can be accessed anytime and anywhere. Within this context, computing is increasingly abstracted, as demonstrated through the now routine use of virtualisation and decentralised technology such as distributed ledgers. It is within this maelstrom of competing technology that the SOC is challenged to detect malicious behaviour. This will only be achieved by exploiting the one common denominator of technology: data.

THE SILENT PARTNER: DATA DRIVEN SECURITY ARCHITECTURE

23.41 It is forecast that an enterprise will create more data in the next three years than it did in the previous 30 years.[49] To solve the challenge of detecting cyber events, the central focus of the SOC should not be tooling, but the creation of a bespoke and intuitive data platform that brings together data, governance,

47 '*SANS 2023 SOC Survey*', SANS, June 2023, p 7.
48 '*SANS 2023 SOC Survey*', SANS, June 2023, p 2.
49 Microsoft CEO and Chairman, Satya Nadella's 'Microsoft Inspire' 2022 Keynote Speech. As found on YouTube, September 2023.

and analytical services across the organisation.[50] In sum, creating an intelligent 'data fabric' that can seamlessly transform 'data points' to an integrated 'point of view'.[51] Having limited visibility and silos of data are no longer defensible.[52]

23.42 Best understood as a 'unified data architecture' that promotes standardised storage locations, formats, and data minimisation; this data fabric moves beyond the concept of integrating fixed data stores into a series of platforms, but more enables the flow of data into an agnostic data layer.[53] Utilising core feeds from security monitoring, including firewalls, databases, applications, network connections, and identity and access management tooling; security data can be streamed to the consolidated data layer, providing end-to-end visibility and near real-time data analytics across the enterprise.[54]

Taming Volume

23.43 The consolidation of data provides accessibility to an increased volume of curated data sets. With the application of feature engineering, raw security data can more easily be transformed into optimised formats which can then be ingested by machine learning models. Through structuring security data into a graph, interactions between entities such as IP addresses, user names, applications, and events can be identified. This graph structure is then converted into vectors to summarise relationships. These vectors are known as 'features' and can be clustered into a model, which can be termed as either a known pattern, emerging pattern, novelty, or noise.[55] Applied to event-driven architecture, the SOC can institute policies which automatically initiate based on actions related to identified features; the 'intelligent' component of the unified data fabric. For example, a data loss prevention policy may restrict a data transfer to a vector that indicates a previously unknown destination. To manage volume, automated actions are a critical output of the data architecture.

50 Derek A Whigham, Chief Product Owner, Lloyds Banking Group, is a leading pioneer of this new SOC architecture. As propounded in his '*Security Operations of the Future*' seminar at PriceWaterouseCoopers, Edinburgh, 23 February 2023.

51 An intelligent data fabric extends beyond an architecture and provides a set of data services which enables consistent data capabilities across a range of computer environments. Aiding the unified data architecture, a fabric standardises data management practices across cloud, on premise, and edge devices. '*What is data fabric?*', NetApp.com, 21 September 2023.

52 '*Weaving data fabric into hybrid multicloud*', IBM Institute for Business Value, p 4.

53 Ibid, p 3.

54 Derek A Whigham, Chief Product Owner, Lloyds Banking Group, is a leading pioneer of this new SOC architecture. As propounded in his 'Security Operations of the Future' seminar at PriceWaterhouseCoopers, Edinburgh, 23 February 2023.

55 '*What is Feature Engineering – Importance, Tools, and Techniques for Machine Learning*', Harshil Patel, Towarddatascience.com, 30 August 2021.

The 'Silent Partnership': Foundations of Data Good Practice

23.44 The phrase 'silent partner' is applied to the relationship between cybersecurity and data as the underlying functionality of the cybersecurity data architecture, which marries data analytics to automated actions, should largely be transparent to the end-user. As a feed to security tooling, it is evident the output of information shall only be a reflection of the quality of data ingested. To understand the dependency cybersecurity has on this underlying data fabric, it is important first to outline the core foundations of a well-constructed data architecture.

23.45 The first challenge is to map the array of data source systems required to be ingested by the data platform. The objective being authoritative data sources of certified data that support the cybersecurity operating model.[56] This can be a function of identifying the required feeds from existing security tooling (ie, vulnerability scanners). Evaluating source systems should address the characteristics of the data source (ie, an application or IoT device), how long the data is persisted, rate the data is generated, level of consistency, and schema.[57] For established enterprises, this can involve legacy data types, which may require data integration engineers to modernise. Where possible, parquet, over other file format types such as CSV should be preferred due to high performance, retrieval, and accessibility to all major coding languages.

23.46 Once the data sources have been assessed, it is important to evaluate storage. Key questions include compatibility with the architecture's read and write speeds, ability to handle future scale, data sovereignty, and the support of complex query patterns (ie, SQL or MongoDB). Similarly, considerations for data ingestion should include reliability, data destination after ingestion, and the logging of metadata.[58] As the data fabric can employ application programmable interfaces (APIs) to deliver insights through integration with applications and business flows, telemetry relating to these APIs should feed into security monitoring tools.[59]

23.47 Understanding the data lifecycle from on premises to cloud and open-source systems is critical both in terms of security and cost. As shown in the Capital One breach, misconfigurations can lead to high profile security incidents. Again, it should be emphasised that reducing the attack surface of the cloud is also good practice from a cost optimisation perspective. For example, underutilised resources, idle instances, and redundant backups should be configured for automatic removal based on the comparison of usage against historic cost

56 'What Constitutes an Authoritative Data Source?', Roger Westman, Mitre Corporation, 2 September 2009.

57 '*Fundamentals of Data Engineering*', Joe Reis and Matt Housley, O'Reilly, 2022, p 38.

58 Ibid, p 40.

59 For an overview of API security, see Salt security '*Understanding API Attacks*' ebook. Found on the Salt website: www.content.salt.security.

profiles.[60] Data retrieval is costly and should be modelled on business use. Similarly, file structure should be scrutinised to optimise performance.[61] For highly regulated industries such as banking and utilities, log data can be required to be held for extended periods.

23.48 In the consumption-based model of cloud computing, controls such as asset tagging and auto-scaling can leverage data profiles to identify waste and provide right-sizing recommendations for compute such virtual machines and containers. Through data analytics, return on security investment will then evolve to integrated cost management across the technological estate.[62]

From Data Engineering to Data Science

23.49 Once the data sources have been mapped and storage and ingestion lifecycles optimised, the cybersecurity data architecture is then ready to be operationalised. Where a data engineer creates the architecture, a data scientist creates value from the data. The first steps in enabling a data scientist are the creation of a data catalogue, which helps summarise key attributes such as location, format, structure, and lineage of data assets. A data scientist can thereafter use modelling to structure and present the data in a manner most useful to the business.[63]

23.50 In the SOC example above, this involved feature engineering and predictive analytics. It is important to note data featurisation is a transformation process. Data considerations for machine learning therefore include quality, discoverability, and ingestion; preferably through batch processing, which is easier to consume.[64] In terms of tooling, low-code platforms utilising python are preferable due to accessibility and extensive libraries that support data analysis, machine learning, and visualisation.

Enhancing SOC Performance

23.51 Working from a unified security data architecture, over point reporting from tools, has the potential to significantly improve the security risk profile of an organisation. Beyond device telemetry, the data platform can consume feeds from asset management databases, which can in turn be mapped to critical business processes and security test data, identifying distinct devices that may be specifically vulnerable and require an enhanced level of security control.

60 For an overview of cost monitoring alerting in public cloud, see Microsoft Azure documentation '*Use cost alerts to monitor usage and spending*', 4 June 2023.

61 '*Fundamentals of Data Engineering*', Joe Reis and Matt Housley, O'Reilly, 2022, p 42.

62 'What is Feature Engineering – Importance, Tools, and Techniques for Machine Learning', Harshil Patel, Towarddatascience.com, 30 August 2021.

63 '*Fundamentals of Data Engineering*, Joe Reis and Matt Housley, O'Reilly, 2022, pp 292–298.

64 Ibid, p 353.

Allied to the concept of 'event chaining', such vectors can be applied to industry frameworks such as the MITRE ATT&CK framework; identifying the most likely attack paths.[65]

23.52 As we enter the era of augmented artificial intelligence (AI), an optimised cybersecurity data architecture shall provide the perfect scaffold for the application of security 'co-pilots'.[66] Extending beyond the ZTA policy-based decision-making model detailed above, security co-pilots shall use enhanced feature engineering to provide security practitioners with recommendations to improve the control environment. These recommendations could be supervised – requiring human intervention, or automated – changing detection rules in real-time. Such capability will improve the detection of events and release resources for more sophisticated tasks.[67] This approach has been proven to significantly reduce false positives and handling costs on a per incident basis.[68]

23.53 Through the use of workbenches, security data is now multi-modal with the ability to categorise risk profiles based on an individual, asset (such as an application or database), data type, underlying code, and flow. This granular level of visibility can be critical in limiting containment actions and minimising business interruption. Further, thematic trends resulting from incident and vulnerability analysis can be fed back into developer loops, ensuring the promotion of secure code and images.

Assuring Cybersecurity Data Sources

23.54 As a cornerstone of security tooling, which in turn drives decision-making, it is imperative that cybersecurity practitioners periodically assure authoritative data sources most critical to the cybersecurity operating model. Leveraging the data catalogue, there should be a modular view of critical data sources that are mapped to key security risks such as IAM, SOC, vulnerability management, and data loss prevention. Based on risk assessments, cybersecurity data assurance activities will include metrics of the components detailed above relating to availability, security, reliability, performance, and cost. As a function, the cybersecurity operating model must formalise roles and accountabilities as a data owner, and consumer, with the rest of the enterprise.

65 Derek A Whigham, Chief Product Owner, Lloyds Banking Group, is a global pioneer of this new SOC architecture. As propounded in his '*Security Operations of the Future*' seminar at PricewaterhouseCoopers, Edinburgh, 23 February 2023.

66 'Announcing Microsoft Co-Pilot, your everyday AI companion', Satya Nadella, Microsoft Events, 21 September 2023.

67 Derek A Whigham, Chief Product Owner, Lloyds Banking Group, is a leading pioneer of this new SOC architecture. As propounded in his '*Security Operations of the Future*' seminar at PricewaterhouseCoopers, Edinburgh, 23 February 2023.

68 Ibid.

Beyond Security: Predictive Analytics and Automated Interventions

23.55 From a strategic perspective, an intelligent data fabric that transparently marries data analytics to automated actions clearly has use cases beyond security. Focussing on the concept of identity, feature engineering extends to a trust fabric where profiles can allow or deny actions based on predicted behaviour. For example, validating cloud workloads through the correlation of logging, configuration parameters, and actions. Authenticating third party code signing through the comparison of hash values linked to other vectors, such as session windows and utility tokens. Transaction monitoring could equally be authenticated on the same vectors to identify and prevent fraud.

23.56 With the availability of federated learning, unified data architectures have the ability to extend beyond an individual organisation and collate datasets from multiple organisations, aiding collaboration and industry response to common threat vectors.[69] Through the tagging of assets to cost profiles, the availability of quantum simulators provides increased probabilistic analysis, which can aide scenario modelling and investment for the range of use cases detailed above.[70] Finally, through the emergence of industry clouds, the integration of telemetry relating to customers, suppliers, partners, and regulators has the potential to identify and contain malicious actors in near real time.

PROFILING: FROM DATA TO PEOPLE

Talent Shortfall

23.57 Improving the detection of cyber-attacks inevitably focusses on technology, specifically enhancing the view of behaviour profiles. But to realise the data architecture that underpins the emerging cybersecurity operating model, we must also focus on the 'profile' of our people capability and seek to understand the requirements a data-led architecture places upon desired skill sets. This is first achieved by understanding the context in which cybersecurity practitioners operate.

Business Agility: Devolved Cyber Decision-Making

23.58 Through the agile delivery model, the procurement, installation, and deployment of technology is rapidly being devolved from centralised IT functions to the business as a means to improve delivery time. 50% of all advertised roles

69 For further information on federated learning see the excellent range of white papers provided by the 'Confidential Computing Consortium' found at 'confidentialcomputing.io', September 2023.

70 For availability see '*Azure Quantum Computing Service*' found at 'azure.microsoft.com', September 2023.

now require technology skills, with this expected to increase to 75% in 2030.[71] As a result, 88% of boards now recognise cyber risk as a business risk, with remediation decisions increasingly dependent on business input.[72]

23.59 Such trends are particularly challenging for cybersecurity. With 60% of the world's corporate data stored in the cloud and a 20% year-on-year increase in public cloud spending, there is a corresponding demand for experienced cloud practitioners.[73] With 70% of enterprises struggling to drive customer value through the cloud, it is evident talent shortages are translating into execution risk, negatively effecting business objectives.[74] The operational risk resulting in a lack of cybersecurity expertise is not lost on financial regulators, with Hong Kong, Singapore, and the US Securities and Exchange Commission each increasingly focussing on enterprise capability.[75]

23.60 Not surprisingly, therefore, cloud and emerging technology cybersecurity practitioners remain at the top of the pyramid as the most in-demand resource.[76] Incredibly, one leading technology training vendor alone has seen a 2,367% increase in the consumption of cloud-related training.[77] Focussing on the SOC specifically, lack of skilled staff is consistently reported as a primary factor in preventing full utilisation of the capabilities.[78] Add in data science, AI, and blockchain, and the ability of an enterprise to fulfil the required skill resource within IT is a significant challenge, regardless of derogating technical decision-making to a previously unencumbered business.[79]

Cyber Skill Development: A Strategic View

23.61 To develop the required skill profile, an enterprise must support the professionalisation of cybersecurity. Primarily, any 'people' strategy must reflect the two distinct pathways of cybersecurity: that of 'administrator' (ie, governance,

71 *'Technology in the Workplace Statistics for 2023: Is Tech Helping of Hurting Us?'*, blog found at 'teamsgate.io', September 2023.

72 *'Why accountability for cybersecurity risk can't only fall to the CISO'*, Barnaby Clarke, Panaseer Blog, 19 April 2023.

73 *'34 Amazing Cloud Statistics (2023)'*, Josh Howarth, found at 'explodingtopics.com', 24 November 2022.

74 *'State of Cloud: How orgs are maturing in the cloud'*, Pluralsight, June 2023, p 2.

75 *'Publicly traded companies aren't moving to add cyber experts to their boards'*, Derek B. Johnson, SC Media, 20 March 2023. Whilst boards may not be increasing cyber representation meantime, this will change with increased regulatory scrutiny. The New York State Financial Services Directive (2017), Hong Kong and Singapore Monetary authorities, each have mandates to assess cybersecurity expertise. The US Securities and Exchange Commission are developing new rules in this regard.

76 *'State of Upskilling Report'*, 2021, Pluralsight, p 3.

77 *'State of Cloud: How orgs are maturing in the cloud'*, Pluralsight, June 2023, p 10.

78 *'SANS 2023 SOC Survey'*, SANS, June 2023, p 7.

79 Interesting to note high profile cyber incidents labelled as artificial intelligence have still been a result of mis-configuration. *'Microsoft worker accidentally exposes 38TB of sensitive data in Github blunder'*, Jessica Hardcastle, The Register, 18th September 2023.

risk management), and 'practitioner' (ie, those who run the technology; cloud architects and SIEM engineers).

23.62 Once a colleague has selected a career path, individual roles and team-based learning objectives should be mapped against broader strategic cybersecurity objectives and measurements. As detailed above, objectives should include the wider operational landscape. For example, there is real value in security professionals obtaining broader technology qualifications relating to cloud architecture, distributed ledger technology and, of course, data science, as a means of understanding how this compute operates to enable the implementation of security controls that factor in user experience.

23.63 Career progression and training remain a primary method to attract and retain staff.[80] Relevant industry accreditations must therefore be mapped to role profiles and form part of a visible career path. The format of the accreditations should also be acknowledged. For governance professionals, traditional exam-based qualifications may provide the necessary learning for a role. For operational teams such as the SOC, time-bound performance-based qualifications available both for the individual and teams may provide more value.[81]

Retaining Cyber Talent

23.64 Financial inducements should be awarded for in-grade progressions based on skills attainment, which is tracked through personal development plans, a key feature in both attracting and retaining talent. To ensure knowledge transfer, successful colleagues should be included in a mentor network where they can support aspiring candidates to achieve the same accreditations. For example, 35% of enterprises struggle to align cloud skills to business outcomes.[82] To realise return on investment to the business, candidate skill sets should be mapped to enterprise projects and workstreams to enable application of theory to meaningful business outcomes.

23.65 It is important to note that whilst there may be two career paths (administrator and practitioner), colleagues from across the business should be able to experience both as enterprise needs dictate, through shadowing opportunities or the acquisition of accreditations. Operating as composable skills paths, this will prevent colleagues becoming too weighted towards one area of expertise and enable accessibility. It shall also allow for the development of behavioural abilities such as adaptability, relationship building, and empathy as colleagues are tasked in a range of different teams.[83] In this context, it is notable SOC practitioners list risk management and business acumen as being

80 '*SANS 2023 SOC Survey*', SANS, June 2023, p 16.
81 Both ISACA and SANS provide lab based technical training. For further details see 'isaca.org' and 'sans.org'.
82 '*State of Cloud: How orgs are maturing in the cloud*', Pluralsight, June 2023, p 17.
83 'Preparing for What's Around the Corner', Chartered Banker, Summer 2023, p 18.

the primary non-technical skills they seek to recruit; traditional staples of the administrator career profile.[84]

Cyber Skill & User Experience: Return on Investment

23.66 Upskilling cybersecurity across the enterprise can be a significant outlay in terms of colleague abstraction and training costs. It is therefore important to articulate the value of this investment. 90% of employees have admitted intentionally behaving in an insecure manner, a form of 'insider risk' as detailed above.[85] The primary motive for evading security controls remains the achievement of a business objective.[86] The root cause of such actions remains security controls being externally implemented on a business process by an IT department rather than being created by the business themselves.

23.67 Having a cyber-skilled workforce at every level of the enterprise – even at a rudimentary level – will intuitively help the business create processes with security in mind. With users building controls, resource experience is less likely to cause friction and result in evasion. For example, using an invisible challenge and response to authenticate identity, or improving the time to verify a transaction through a secondary control. Broad cyber skill attainment should therefore be positioned as a means to improve user experience, security control compliance, and reduce operational and data loss risk as a result.

RISK MANAGEMENT

Data Fabric Enabling Continuous Risk Assessment

23.68 Distributed technology across the enterprise has federated the volume and pace of security risk decision-making. Traditional stage gates and manual risk assessments will no longer meet the range and depth of enterprise change. Compounded by the lack of skilled security resources, the ability to make consistent decisions within appetite would appear limited. Intelligent data fabric and the provision of recommended actions from data again offer a solution.

23.69 Continuous adaptive risk and trust assessment (CARTA) methodology uses data analytics to provide risk scores based on historic behaviour.[87] Originally intended for access controls, CARTA delivers continuous context aware security assessments that, through data engineering and machine learning, can now be applied across the entire security suite. For example, based on high-risk scores, breach attack simulators can now consume vulnerability data, which can

84 '*SANS 2023 SOC Survey*', SANS, June 2023, p 17.
85 '*90% of Employees Admit to Violating IT Policies*', Kayla Elliott, PC Matic, 7 November 2016.
86 '*Negligence Drives 90% of Data Breaches*', Cybelangel.com, 28 October 2020.
87 For a comparative discussion of CARTA compared to 'zero trust', see '*Zero trust vs.CARTA. Is one actually part of the other?*', Christopher Hines, Zscaler blog, 26 April 2019.

automatically amend SOC detection rules and developer guardrails in real-time; continually testing the attacker lifecycle to protect assets at source. Similarly, the CARTA model has been applied 'as-a-service' in red teaming solutions to automatically resolve identified vulnerabilities.[88] The emergence of security co-pilots as detailed above will inevitably increase the scale of automated decision making across the cybersecurity risk profile.

23.70 Collecting data from multiple sources (sensors, devices, networks, people) and applying a risk score based on historic normalised behaviour is now a common reporting functionality across all major security tooling platforms.[89] However, to provide all important operational context and facilitate independent cyber judgement at scale, the output of data architecture requires a feedback loop that includes cyber practitioners, data scientists, risk architects, and most importantly, the end consumers; the business stakeholders themselves.[90]

23.71 With the increasing prominence of AI to inform risk-based decision making, the cybersecurity data architecture must be able to validate the output from data modelling. The scope of this validation must include the design, development, use, and evaluation of AI products, systems, and services.[91] Key outcomes being ongoing assurance relating to the accuracy, security, and explainability of the data model.

23.72 Due to the ubiquitous nature of computing, security risks must be reported for business decision making at a legal entity, division, and business unit level. The security risk must further be bespoke to localised business and rooted in the prioritised threats at the enterprise level, namely malware, third parties, and insiders. Examples of reported metrics being easily consumable data relating to endpoint protection coverage, completion of user entitlement reviews, and remediation of outstanding critical supplier reviews.

An Agile Data Architecture: Supporting Risk Decision Making

23.73 As a result of digitisation, hybrid work, and increased technical autonomy from the business, Chief Information Security Officers (CISOs) are increasingly viewing themselves as risk decision facilitators.[92] The agile delivery model has

88 '*Tech Mahindra Partners With FireCompass To Launch CARTA*', Market Watch, 15 July 2022.

89 For cybersecurity vendors such as 'Crowdstrike' are leaders in this field. For extensibility, the same detection methodology is also being used to detect financial crime. For example 'Napier.ai' uses a risk based scorecard to assess a customer risk level as means to comply with 'know your customer' financial legislation.

90 As shown from studies relating to the 2008 financial crisis, the vast majority of statistical modelling were wrong. Prediction of events remains volatile and requires significant caveats. As detailed in 'Anti-Fragile: Things that gain from disorder', Nassim Nicholas Taleb, Penguin, 2013, p 149.

91 See NIST's artificial intelligence framework.

92 '*From control owners to risk decision facilitators: Mathan Babu Kasilingam, Vodafone Idea*', Muqbil Ahmar, CISO Economic Times, 22 August 2023.

displaced the role of the CISO from 'control owner' to 'strategic partner' with the business in the treatment of security risk.[93] Similarly, in the consumption-based model of computing, the businesses are assuming increased accountability for cyber risk, and security practitioners are now operating as consultants.

23.74 A risk framework should reflect this balance of accountability and specialism by mapping ownership for decision making against risk scoring. The highest rated risks therefore require the authority of the CISO and security experts to approve. The technical capability of the business should further be supported by specialist tools and training; and then measured by scorecards linked to operational objectives.[94]

Composable Security Requires Composable Data

23.75 To effectively manage risk, the underlying data architecture of the cybersecurity operating model requires being agile. Reflecting the concept of 'composable security', where security products become modular so they can be easily built into non-security components such as serverless functions; data artefacts must also be consumable to reflect the changing demands of the business.[95] In the scope of the cybersecurity data architecture, this necessitates a data fabric that is inextricably linked to risk management. For example, data pertaining to IAM solutions automatically feeds into the risk management system through API integration, changing control effectiveness and risk ratings in real-time. Threat intelligence, cybersecurity incidents, audit findings, and regulatory important assets should also be linked to the risk management system, triggering out-of-cycle re-assessments and related remediating action plans as required.[96]

23.76 Streamed risk data has broader operational value to the business. A common challenge of risk management systems is that risks and controls are equally reported. By factoring routine control assessments into threat intelligence, incident and business change data, it becomes possible to continually assess the control environment and provide weighting and scaling to risk and control clusters based on potential attack vectors. This functionality is critical in understanding the cost of controls (ie, cost profiles) in mitigating specific security risk profiles, demonstrating return on investment to accountable business owners, and supporting investment cases moving forward.

93 Ibid.

94 *'Preparing your teams for digital transformation: An interactive strategy workbook'*, Pluralsight.com, pp 16–23.

95 A design principle based on modulatory where security components (such as privilege access management) can be independent and interchangeable based on need and function. *'Introduction to Cybersecurity First Principles'*, Matt Hale, GitHub, 2022.

96 The risk management framework should factor the regulatory responsibilities of the enterprise. For example, in financial services assets related to reporting and subject to Sarbanes-Oxley compliance should by definition be treated as a priority.

BRINGING IT ALL TOGETHER: CYBERSECURITY STRATEGY – PATHWAY TO SUPPORTING THE DATA-LED ERA

Core Components

23.77 Every enterprise is a technology enterprise. The most successful enterprises shall be those that best integrate technology and business models. As shown, this has resulted in an operating environment responding to a surge of innovation related to technological advancements. Through solutions such as GitHub Co-Pilot, it has never been easier for developers to publish new code. Confidential computing has created a platform where operations can be performed over encrypted data, greatly expanding use cases related to the lifecycle of sensitive data.[97] AI and security co-pilots have the potential to significantly re-shape security role profiles across the enterprise as many tasks move from manual to automated. Importantly, each of these ground-breaking technologies is accessible to functions outside the realm of IT and is creating data at a rate faster than can be understood. In sum, the security landscape has never been more complex or challenging.

23.78 It is the role of strategy to turn a developing situation into a desirable outcome.[98] The overarching aim of a cybersecurity strategy is to protect the enterprise while enabling the business to grow and change. As shown, the enterprise must prioritise activity to support outcomes related to addressing the threat environment, enabling the value of data, ensuring ubiquitous visibility, developing people skills, and mitigating risk through change. In this context, it is evident the strategy that has led enterprises to the point of rapid digitisation shall not deliver the required value or security moving forward.

Common Strategic Limitations

23.79 Historic challenges related to cybersecurity strategy ('security strategy') have focussed on currency; it has been routine for a strategy to be developed and published, then not revisited or reported upon until the next iteration, sometimes years later. Similarly, an overarching security strategy can lead to a proliferation of sub-strategies such as IAM, vulnerability management, and third-party suppliers. Cybersecurity strategies also tend to be insular, regularly failing to acknowledge dependencies on other areas of the business. Ultimately, what is created is a poorly understood complex monolith.

97 As an emerging technology, confidential computing has not received the same level of attention as artificial intelligence or quantum computing. With a total addressable market of $1.9bn in 2021, and expected growth rate of 45% through to 2026, the availability and extensive use cases of this technology will see far greater use in the near term. For further information see the excellent range of white papers provided by the 'Confidential Computing Consortium' found at 'confidentialcomputing.io', September 2023.

98 Lawrence Freedman, *Strategy: A History* (Oxford University Press) p xiii.

New Approach: First Principles

23.80 With security decision making increasingly residing in the business, a new approach to cybersecurity strategy is required. The components of the strategy remain standard: The first step in articulating strategy is identifying the primary threats an enterprise faces. As detailed above, this remains mitigating malware, third party security, and insider risk. To help prioritise activity, threats should then be quantified into the risk posed to the enterprise; this is achieved through scenario analysis and forecasting. Once a risk profile has been created, desired security outcomes can be agreed. Finally, based on security outcomes, people, processes, and technology can be allocated to a roadmap of activity supported by performance measures.

Agile Strategy

23.81 If the format of the security strategy remains consistent, delivery requires a fundamentally new approach. Reflecting the operating environment, the security strategy should be constructed with extensive business engagement throughout the lifecycle and the ability to change in result of material events such as breaches. Progress should be measured at the business unit level through metrics that are directly rooted in prioritised enterprise-level security risks. For example, to mitigate IAM risk, a business unit should report on the number of outstanding privilege entitlement reviews.

23.82 To ensure currency and reflect change, each business unit should have strategic security objectives and related metrics that are reported monthly to inform the localised risk picture. Owned by the CISO, but with accountabilities across the enterprise, the security strategy must support a consequence model that reflects actions and impacts beyond the traditional realm of IT and has meaningful accountabilities for the wider business.[99] As such, the strategy must be open to constant real-time feedback from the business to ensure engagement and investment. Through this approach, delivery of the security strategy is driven from the business unit, instead of a central security forum.

23.83 Accessibility of the strategy beyond the security function should be enabled through self-serve business apps such as PowerBI. It should be possible for any colleague to access a pillar of the security strategy and cut the data relative to their business unit. Localised metrics should reference both the overarching strategic objective and be used as real-time data indicators for relevant risk and control profiles within the enterprise risk management system.

99 Derek A Whigham, Chief Product Owner, Lloyds Banking Group. As propounded in his '*Security Operations of the Future*' seminar at PricewaterhouseCoopers, Edinburgh, 23 February 2023.

Strategic Inter-dependencies: Technology, User Experience, & Data

23.84 As an enabler, the security strategy is ultimately driven by business objectives. Whether a merger and acquisition, increased third party integration, or use of a new hosting functionality, the north star of the security strategy must be measured by the ability of the business to operate at scale and pace without incident. Further measures should reflect time to implement security controls, security cost profiles per risk and control, and time to remediate incidents.

23.85 It is important to note the security strategy operates in a broader ecosystem of strategic objectives that include – but are not limited to – technology, data, and resiliency. As an extension of protecting information technology, the security strategy has revolved around and supported the overriding technology strategy. As argued, the increasing prominence of data not only within the cybersecurity operating model, but the broader enterprise, challenges this paradigm. As a fundamental component to decision making, now is the time technology and security strategies serve the data model and strategy, rather than vice versa.

Modernisation & Simplification: Factoring the Legacy Estate

23.86 Technology allows the business to engage with customers and maintain operations. Themes such as modernisation and simplification shall be relevant to most organisations. The security strategy should both support and advance the broader technology strategy. It is a common weakness that most strategies only look to the future and focus on leveraging the latest technology. Modernisation requires both a forward and retrospective view of the enterprise.

23.87 Recent studies have shown two-thirds of the Fortune 500 companies, and 45/50 of the world's top banks are still heavily reliant on legacy architecture such as mainframes. With customer information control systems (CICS) dating back to the 1960s, mainframes pose a significant currency risk to the enterprise. Maintaining a strong security posture requires a constant assessment of system configuration changes and software upgrades. With 89% of mainframe practitioners being aged over 50, the ability to service this estate is becoming increasingly limited.[100] The security strategy should reflect and address this capability risk by ensuring knowledge transfer through a blend of formal training and on-the-job shadowing opportunities.

23.88 To support simplification of the enterprise technology estate, the security strategy should advance the principle of 'convergence' as detailed previously; where security tools are consolidated to reduce licensing costs and management

100 '*The Role of IBM Mainframes in Cybersecurity*', Robert S Hanschel presentation, MIT Cybersecurity Research Council, February 2023.

overhead.[101] Bespoke security tooling, for example cloud container monitoring, should only be used where the use case identifies no modular equivalent with existing vendors. To ensure operational resilience, convergence should be factored against concentration risk to ensure operational resiliency.

User Experience is a Cybersecurity Strategic Imperative

23.89 The security strategy operates in a broader kaleidoscope of competing enterprise objectives. To enhance customer and colleague experience, the strategy should have objectives relating to the improvement of consumer journeys. This could result in the implementation of transparent security controls in place of manual prompts such as traditional 'captcha' authentication methods. Metrics could then determine friction levels through consumer abandonment.[102] Core objectives of an operational resilience strategy such as 'resiliency by design' should both inform and support zero trust architecture.

Data: Protecting & Leveraging

23.90 Returning to the fundamental premise of this chapter, the common denominator of all relevant enterprise strategic objectives is the effective use of data. Most enterprise data strategies shall seek to provide a unified data architecture, consistent formatting to provide availability, and a single view of data priorities. Protecting the data lifecycle through the use of encryption, applying enhanced analytics to maintain change within appetite, and providing real-time data to automate risk decisions, the security strategy must function as a pioneering blueprint of what can be achieved from a data-led culture for the rest of the enterprise. In this vein, whether supporting the data lifecycle, or modernising the estate, security and technology strategies must serve the overarching data strategy in protecting and assuring data as it is used in ubiquitous decision-making.

MOVING FORWARD

23.91 It is an exciting time to be involved in cybersecurity. Through rapid digitisation, cybersecurity practitioners are immersed in the latest technology

101 A good example being the convergence of cloud monitoring tools: Cloud infrastructure entitlement management (CIEM), Cloud Workload Protection Platform (CWPP), Cloud Security Posture Management (CSPM), Cloud Native Application Protection Platform (CNAPP), and Cloud Access Security Brokers (CASB); all previously point solutions are now being provided as modular services in centralised 'cloud security' product. As an example vendor see Lacework; found at 'go.lacework.com', September 2023.

102 A function of application performance management, both application observability and fraud detection tools are measuring customer journeys to profile the user experience. See Dynatrace – 'www.dynatrace.com', and Unit21 – 'unit21.ai' to see how vendors are correlating indicators to profile customer journeys for different use cases.

developments as the business seeks to leverage commercial opportunities presented by AI, quantum computing, and data science. But through this world of rapid flux, complexity, and change, there remains a common denominator in protecting the enterprise: data.

Forging a path forward, security leaders must acknowledge the critical value of a well-architected cybersecurity data architecture; both in protecting the enterprise and in identifying cost opportunities in the consumption-based model of cloud computing. This includes the creation of an intelligent data fabric that brings together data analytics, automation, and risk management to help the enterprise manage change securely. Transforming 'data points' to an integrated 'point of view' is in direct correlation to the visibility of security risk across the enterprise. Conversely, failure to appreciate the relationship between data and security will accentuate the risk of shadow IT and extend an attack surface already primed for exploit through systemic misconfiguration.

23.92 Creation of a cybersecurity data architecture is predicated on profiling. To operationalise the architecture, this involves a new profile in terms of an enterprise's people capability. Against a backdrop of a significant talent shortfall, the cybersecurity strategy must develop capability from within. This includes traditional cybersecurity roles but must also address skills relating to technology (such as cloud architects), data science (ie, feature engineers), and emerging compute (quantum). Failure to embrace these skill sets is tantamount to sleepwalking into redundancy.

23.93 With use cases extending to fraud, transaction monitoring, and portfolio optimisation, the silent data architecture that underpins cybersecurity will clearly find a significant voice beyond realising traditional IT objectives. To effectively enable decision making at pace and scale, the hierarchy of enterprise strategic objectives must prioritise data with the strategic objectives of technology and security servant components. More than addressing a primary operational risk, cybersecurity data architecture has now become the vanguard for business decision-making and enterprise change.

CHAPTER 24

MERGERS AND ACQUISITIONS CORPORATE DUE DILIGENCE AND CYBER SECURITY ISSUES

Vijay Rathour

THE SINS OF OUR FATHERS

24.01

> 'I don't throw darts at a board. I bet on sure things. Read Sun-tzu, The Art of War. Every battle is won before it is ever fought.'

In the 1987 film 'Wall Street', Gordon Gekko reminds us that due diligence is an essential element of all major decisions, wars, and his rabid appetite for company acquisitions.

24.02 Cyber-crime is not a new phenomenon, but the incidence and impact of computer and data-related crime is growing at an accelerating rate. It is on track to cost businesses nearly $15 trillion annually in 2024[1]. Trust and confidence in our economies will be damaged and every enterprise will suffer from the increased cost of doing business, while every consumer will be impacted by the rising cost of resisting increasingly sophisticated cyber-criminals. These highly focused, highly organised and persistent attackers continue to raise the bar and find means to gain access to our businesses, our commercial secrets, our personal and private data, our money and our intellectual property. And in the vast majority of attacks, they get away with their crimes, often leaving little evidence for law enforcement to identify, if the attack is spotted at all. According to Europol, cyber-crimes committed on businesses are on track to become more profitable than the global trade of all major illegal drugs combined. Perhaps you have already acquired a business that's become a victim, or you may be the next.

24.03 In August 2017 a US court handed down a ruling that confirmed US company Verizon Communications Inc's worst fears. A judge decided that its subsidiary Yahoo! would face litigation from more than a billion account holders. The claimants said their personal information was compromised in successive cyber-attacks on Yahoo! – which went completely undetected at the time. Verizon became liable for these breaches after completing its acquisition of Yahoo! in June.

1 https://www.weforum.org/agenda/2024/01/cybersecurity-cybercrime-system-safety/.

24.04 Marriott International's acquisition of Starwood Hotels in 2016 culminated in enormous regulatory fines and reputational hard as a result of a sophisticated cyber incident on their collective systems. The Starwood systems had not completed incorporation into the parent Marriott IT infrastructure during this time. A subsequent attack on the reservation system resulted in hundreds of millions of customer records, including personally sensitive information such as credit card numbers and passports, were stolen by the attackers.

24.05 The UK's Information Commissioner's Office (ICO) fined Marriot £99 million for breach of the GDPR. A major factor in the size of the fine was the failure to mitigate security flaws that should have been identified by effective due diligence prior and post-acquisition.

24.06 The General Data Protection Regulation (GDPR) came into force across the EU on 25 May 2018. This regime radically shakes up European data protection laws and policies. Regulators such as the UK's Information Commissioner's Office, are granted dramatically greater powers to regulate, sanction and interrogate the controls and breaches of data governance of businesses across Europe. The impact of this regulation persists well beyond Brexit, and it creates stringent new requirements on businesses, and creates additional rights for individuals as data subjects. The maximum fines enforceable by the Information Commissioner's Office in respect of data breaches jumps from the current £0.5 million to £20 million or 4% of annual global turnover, with a now mandatory requirement to report most serious data breaches, typically within 72 hours.

24.07 When you acquire a business, you pay careful heed of its obligations, its weaknesses, its staff and its assets, and you value, warrant or dispose of each carefully following appropriate diligence. But what about the cyber-risks? If you acquire a business that has suffered a data breach, you also acquire its obligations and the fall-out that will flow from them. After May 2018 those multi-million euro fines will land at your door.

24.08 The scale and nature of the corporate cyber-crime threat has grown increasingly alarming over the past few years. Alleged State-sponsored attacks, organised hacktivism, leaked and pirated entertainment content and global ransomware attacks are becoming all too commonplace.

24.09 Surveys[2] of global businesses, insurers, risk consultants, underwriters, senior managers and claims experts in corporate insurance have placed cyber-incidents (defined to include cyber-crime, IT failure, data breaches and related incidents) as the top business risk they face.

24.10 As corporate IT systems grow and evolve, the 'attack surface' grows alongside them, presenting new vulnerabilities to be exploited. Cyber-criminals have often weaponised exploits within days or weeks of discovering a vulnerability

2 Allianz Risk Barometer 2023.

in the system architecture. Yet despite advancements in counter-cyber-crime technologies in recent years, breaches take some 204[3] days on average to detect, and a further 73 days to contain once discovered. Given the scale of the damage cyber-attacks can do, it can take weeks or months for a listed company's market valuation to recover from the impact.

24.11 With a breach costing the targeted organisation some £3.5 million on average, containing and mitigating a breach quickly after the event is critical, but having the ability to identify that it occurred is even more so.

THE 'NEW OIL'

24.12 Increasingly, data is the lifeblood of a modern and connected organisation. For many businesses it can be where the majority of its value lies, moving away from tangible physical properties to ephemeral concepts such as subscriber information, targeted advertising profiles, electronic transactions in games, your unique trading algorithm and logistics solution. Businesses are increasingly deriving value from otherwise intangible bits and bytes. Theft, loss and contamination of such data could critically impact the valuation of that business.

24.13 A breach of the organisational safeguards, resulting in the digital property leaving the confines of the business, can present a major operational risk. Cyber-attacks and data breaches can impact a company's value in a number of ways, some more obvious than others:

- they can result in IP theft;
- they can cause significant business interruption if systems cease to function due to attacks from hackers;
- your brand will be damaged as your customers question your operational integrity, particularly if you do business via online ecommerce platforms;
- revenues will be lost;
- investigating a cyber-attack to an appropriate level of objectivity to allow lessons to be learned requires investment in diligent and effective internal and external computer forensic experts;
- addressing operational weaknesses and undertaking other remedial action requires analysis and budget;
- regulatory investigations will attract not only significant fines, but cause reputational harm, impact insurance premiums, and potentially increase scrutiny over general data governance, including increasing numbers of Data Subject Access Requests;

3 Cost of Data Breach Study, IBM, 2023.

- customer relationships and notifications require a structured approach and delicate handling in line with the company's value and character;
- legal costs will inevitably follow if and when regulatory and customer notifications are required, and these can often precede civil and criminal litigation against the business; and
- longer-term impacts may include the increased cost of raising finance and securing specialist cyber-insurance.

24.14 Despite these risks, mergers and acquisitions (M&A) practitioners have been routinely overlooking cyber-security when valuing and buying companies. Reports have shown that almost four in five dealmakers were not including tests of cyber-security as part of their due diligence process.[4]

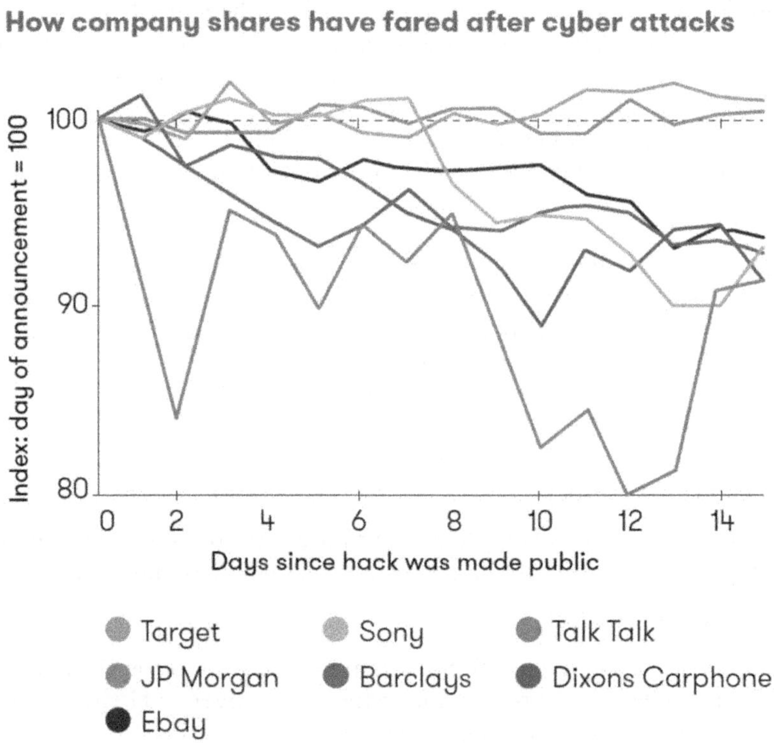

24.15 On 29 November 2017 the world's largest shipbroker, Clarkson PLC, issued a public statement[5] declaring that it had been 'subject to a cybersecurity incident which involved unauthorised access to the Company's computer systems'. The press release continued with a comment by the CEO of the business stating:

4 Cybersecurity in M&A, Freshfields Bruckhaus Deringer, 2014.
5 www.clarksons.com/media/1129201/notice_of_cyber_security_incident.pdf.

'Issues of cybersecurity are at the forefront of many business agendas in today's digital and commercial landscape and, despite our extensive efforts we have suffered this criminal attack. As you would rightly expect, we're working closely with specialist police teams and data security experts to do all we can to best understand the incident and what we can do to protect our clients now and in the future. We hope that, in time, we can share the lessons learned with our clients to help stop them from becoming victims themselves. In the meantime, I hope our clients understand that we would not be held to ransom by criminals, and I would like to sincerely apologise for any concern this incident may have understandably raised.'

24.16 Shares in Clarkson PLC fell by over 2% after the public announcement detailing the incident, despite the business stating that it had worked to invest 'heavily' to minimise the risk of further data breaches. It had insisted that the breach would not affect its ability to do business.

24.17 The variables impacting how quickly a business begins to recover from a share price fall following a breach include multiple factors such as the appointment of a dedicated incident response team, board-level involvement, appointing a CISO and CPO, the use of a mobile platform and many others[6]. Effective public-relations and pro-active crisis management can dramatically impact the 'bounce back' post a cyber-incident, but many businesses suffer a permanent negative share price impact following a significant breach. It is not unusual for the business to lose as much as 10–20% of its valuation in these circumstances.

UN-DUE DILIGENCE?

24.18 Following on from financial recessions and the loss of trust in the integrity of financial markets, the corporate world has begun to recover and indeed grow with renewed vigour for corporate consolidation through mergers and acquisitions.

24.19 Recent studies[7] have surveyed hundreds of directors and officers of public companies to assess their views on the impact of cyber-security threats on their approach to mergers and acquisitions. Although many respondents expressed only limited familiarity with the value of cyber-security diligence, 76% of them agreed that a high-profile data breach would have serious implications on the pending transaction.

24.20 The M&A community is becoming alert to the risks of inheriting potentially tainted cyber-properties – 80% of practitioners consider cyber-due diligence to be 'highly important'.[8] Cyber-due diligence is becoming the

6 Cost of Data Breach Study, IBM, 2023.
7 https://kpmg.com/us/en/media/news/2024-cybersecurity-survey.html.
8 Testing the Defenses: Cybersecurity Due Diligence in M&A, West Monroe, 2016.

M&A practitioner's first line of defence against hackers decimating the value of a target business.

24.21 A typical cyber due diligence assessment begins with a comprehensive audit of the governance, procedures and controls that an organisation uses to keep its information assets safe. An effective cyber-due diligence exercise should therefore involve at least the following four measures:

1. A review of the target business' current cyber posture, including:
   a. data protection measures, seeking to identify any vulnerabilities that need addressing before the transaction goes through;
   b. breach management, disaster recovery and business continuity plans;
   c. compliance with industry-specific data regulation – for example, FCA risk management standards in financial services; PCI DSS standards for credit card handing in retail; OfCom regulations for telecom providers etc.
2. Penetration testing of the target business' cyber-defences, and potentially those of its suppliers.
3. An OSINT (open source intelligence) and dark web search for signs of a breach – for instance, elements of the target business' intellectual property, customer and client personal data or brand sensitive material being offered for sale.
4. A valuation of the target firm's information assets.

24.22 Increasingly, regulatory and commercial considerations require these assessments to broaden to assess the quality and effectiveness (or potential bias) of algorithms used by the business, and increasingly the AI used to help deliver services and judgements over individual data subjects. The European Union's regulation on Artificial Intelligence will require increasing scrutiny over businesses operating in the region. Sister regulation, Digital Operational Resilience Act (DORA), will also require a careful review of the effectiveness of cyber resilience preparations. The US Securities and Exchange Commission (SEC) has emphasised the importance of disclosing cybersecurity risks and incidents, especially following M&A activity.

24.23 Legal clawbacks and warranties may give you some capacity to recover or withdraw from mergers and acquisitions where parties have failed to be entirely honest about their disclosures. In the UK 'Material Adverse Change' provisions may allow parties to allocate risk in such transactions, providing a formal structure and exclusions when the exception is triggered. However, establishing the exclusions can be difficult, particularly where these relate to the state of knowledge of a potentially latent and undiscovered data breach. If a business sincerely does not know that it has suffered a breach or cyber-incident, its knowledge may be flawed but honest.

Warranty and Indemnity Insurance

24.24 In recent years the use of buy-side warranty and indemnity insurance has grown to help address some of these potential pitfalls. Although these products had once been considered to be expensive, proportionate to the risks, the market for innovative products has grown to address practical requirements. Such products have greatly increased certainty for buyers by providing coverage for losses arising from a breach of a warranty given in a sale and purchase agreement (SPA).

24.25 When these mechanisms are effectively drafted and executed, they can, like cyber-due diligence, provide visibility over issues that may remain otherwise undisclosed. Failure to provide fulsome responses and disclosure against the warranties can result in the purchaser being able to recover compensation for the diminished value of the acquired business.

24.26 Warranty and indemnity insurance coverage typically requires that the buyer has undertaken a thorough due diligence exercise. A less than robust due diligence process (including, potentially, cyber-due diligence) could have cost implications or indeed result in a complete denial of the policy.

24.27 Insurers are unlikely to provide coverage against issues and failures that were within the buyer's knowledge before it acquired the target business. The buyer will be unable to claim on the policy if the issues at fault had been disclosed to the buyer, or which it had discovered during the due diligence process. Given the long latency period of many cyber-attacks, it is critical to note that the buyer cannot enter into a transaction with knowledge that there was an issue or failing with respect to which it intended to claim under the policy – warranty and indemnity insurance is not a guarantee of performance or compensation under any circumstances.

THE OBSERVER EFFECT

24.28 In quantum physics, it is well understood that the mere act of observing a situation can change that phenomenon. We must likewise be wary that the act of conducting an overt cyber-diligence exercise may cause consequences counter to those desired or expected by our observations.

24.29 As part of the high-level measures considered within the cyber-due diligence audit described above, a review should seek as much detail as possible to facilitate an objective assessment of the business, its data estate and its commercial risks. These assessments should include:

1. A review of the cyber-security history of the acquisition target, including security logs, alerts and infrastructure.
2. A review of current incident response plans and postures, and the security around applications and platforms.

3. Active testing and reviews of recent audits, including penetration tests, security reviews and objective assessments of the strengths and weaknesses of the business IT environment.

24.30 The majority of M&A practitioners surveyed[9] would be 'somewhat likely' to allow the discovery of a major security incident in a target business to affect the acquisition. However, although the tangible benefits of obtaining greater insights into the business you are acquiring are undeniable, the mechanism is not without risks.

24.31 A potential commercial acquisition typically requires a strong wall of confidentiality and secrecy around acquisition strategy, strengths and weaknesses, longer term plans post integration (including layoffs and divestment of business units) etc. Maintaining secrecy for the entire period leading up to an acquisition can be very difficult, and it is likely that anyone that discovers the plans will have views to express about it. It is not assured that all of those privy to the information will keep it secret, so a new threat of a leak of commercially sensitive information may arise.

24.32 Corporate psychologists can express views on managing corporate culture pre- and post-integration, but through the lens of cyber-security, it is helpful to pre-empt the impact on corporate culture and the morale of those within the businesses. An open and inclusionary approach can lead to greater loyalty and perhaps manifest as a closer-knit team. However, only a single leak of potentially sensitive information, on to social media, through a financial trading forum, or perhaps at a price on the dark web, can be enough to dramatically increase the number of cyber-predators eyeing your business. Such an incident may also require regulatory notification, for example to stock exchanges.

24.33 An acquisition can significantly impact your own cyber-security, for example by broadening the attack surface from one business to two. The physical and logistical exercises required to send out new corporate information, update all customers by email, provide new credit/payment cards or equipment, for example, can all invite opportunities for spammers and hackers to steal customer information, or expose recipients to payment diversion frauds and man-in-the-middle attacks. These threats can also be turned back on to your own security, where for example, an unexpected alert from the new business' firewall may go overlooked by the acquiring business due to lack of familiarity by the new teams, staff and infrastructure.

24.34 The mere act of conducting an overt cyber-due-diligence review may give the acquired business the opportunity to present a rose-tinted view of its security. The evolving ingenuity of organised cyber-criminals leads to an arms race between attackers and defenders, and so the quality and probity of the assessment is critical. A 'light touch' review may be unable to identify latent threats, Remote Access Trojans (RATs) that open back doors in to the business, and legacy command and control centres (C2) that are monitoring and impacting

9 Cybersecurity and the M&A Due Diligence Process – Veracode 2016.

the business in real time. It is essential that the appetite for risk is measured against the budget and time invested in the review. An incomplete appraisal of the business may fail to spot historical or ongoing attacks and vulnerabilities, communicating perhaps an undue confidence in the business.

OILING THE SUPPLY CHAIN

24.35 The GDPR will continue to place pressure on businesses to manage the risks of their suppliers with almost as much scrutiny as themselves. Within the complicated data processor and data controller environments, a breach of your data by a third party may place significant burdens on your business. Certainly as far as your customers and the general public are concerned, blaming a third party is unlikely to assuage those who have had their data jeopardised as a result of doing business with you.

24.36 Internal IT teams, and those of suppliers, may be disinclined to elaborate on historical and current flaws in their cyber-resilience. The dispassionate scrutiny and cyber-due-diligence by an objective third party can go a long way to uncovering those latent weaknesses, if any, and help the respective businesses and their legal counsel to construct appropriate safeguards, warranties and exceptions, where necessary, to manage the risks.

MORRISONS AND THE DISGRUNTLED INSIDER

24.37 On 1 December 2017, the High Court of England and Wales ruled that Morrisons Supermarkets was liable for the acts of a rogue employee who was responsible for a deliberate data breach. His actions resulted in a leak of personal data regarding almost a hundred thousands of his colleagues. The factual history of this incident date back to 2013, and yet over four years later the business has found itself liable for his actions and will be responsible for the damages that may become payable to that class of individuals damaged by the rogue employee's deliberate data breach.

24.38 Even though the employee here intentionally sought to cause harm to his employer by leaking the confidential and private data on to the internet, his employer was found to be legally responsible for his actions. The data included personal data such as bank details, National Insurance information, addresses, phone numbers and other Personally Identifiable Information. The English courts ruled that the employer was vicariously liable for these activities (ie that it effectively inherited the actions of its employee) because the malicious act was still sufficiently closely connected to the employee's authorised duties that he was considered to still be acting as an employee when committing the data breach.

24.39 The employee had originally received the data that he subsequently leaked when he was acting as an employee and undertaking his conventional and contracted activities: as part of a statutory audit he had been provided with payroll data on an encrypted USB stick. He subsequently took a copy of the data and stored it on his personal computer, and at a later data published the material on a public file sharing website. The courts found that there was a continuous sequence of events linking his employment to the publication.

24.40 This is a very new concept within this jurisdiction and creates a disturbing precedent for employers in monitoring and safeguarding against the activities of its business and its employees. The judges had acknowledged that there was no reason for the business to distrust the employee with the data, and it had taken some precautions to control the data by limiting access to it. Unfortunately, a relatively minor oversight of failing to put in place an organised or proactive deletion policy for this and similar data types meant that the employer had failed to satisfy its legal requirements and became liable for the actions.

24.41 There is likely to be a very significant financial cost flowing from the employee's activities; legal costs and individual claims from the thousands of employees could stretch into the millions of pounds. With businesses in the retail sector increasingly approaching administration or proactively seeking financial strength through mergers and acquisitions, the apparently minor and nuisance cyber-breaches and transgressions of a rogue employee may create significant and costly legal burdens. However, the slow rot of these behaviours may mean that the financial harm does not come to light for many years after the acquisition completes and a future business owner will become responsible for the historical sins that have been committed.

24.42 Businesses should, of course, work to ensure that their organisational controls are fit for purpose and allow it to minimise the risks of a data breach. Cyber-due diligence exercises are designed to identify exactly these types of incidents, potentially saving millions of pounds of costs, years of legal proceedings, and damaging brand and reputational harm.

CONCLUSIONS

24.43 Cyber-due diligence presents many opportunities to identify, mitigate and remediate breaches and systemic weaknesses in the acquired business. When properly executed by computer forensics experts, the analysis will help businesses to identify cyber-security risks and vulnerabilities in the target entity.

24.44 The exercise should also bring to light any previous breaches that the target firm may have unknowingly suffered, or indeed those that they had discovered but omitted to disclose. The exercise will thereby also help evaluate the likely costs of a past or potential breach while simultaneously helping to reduce the risk of future breaches and liabilities, avoid fines, litigation, brand damage and loss of customers.

Ultimately, it will enable the correct valuation of the target's information assets – leading to a more accurate assessment of the value of the business as a whole. And most of all, it will help you to preserve that value in the future.

CHAPTER 25

PROTECTING ORGANISATIONS

Gary Hibberd

INTRODUCTION

25.01 The purpose of this chapter is to make the case for organisations to consider and to implement security standards, such as Cyber Essentials, ISO27001, ISO27701, ISO27018, CSA STAR and PCI DSS. Each will be discussed, an overview of the standard provided and the merits of each considered, however it is not the intention to state that one is better than the other, but each will be considered on their effectiveness and validity.

25.02 There has never been a more pressing time to consider implementing a security standard within your organisation, as protecting the information you hold is of paramount importance. Not just because of the negative effect a breach could have on your reputation and your financial stability, but because all that information you hold relates to real people. In the last five years we have lived through a pandemic which has increased our reliance on data and digital technology, and the 'rise' and proliferation of Artificial Intelligence (AI) tools, like ChatGPT.

25.03 In an increasingly complex digital environment, this chapter will outline ways to approach the protection of your organisation, by using frameworks and standards that make the process easier to follow. Ultimately aiming to provide an outline of the standards which will make you more secure.

THE UK'S NATIONAL CYBER SECURITY STRATEGY

25.04 On 15 December 2021, the UK government released its latest strategy to combat the growing threat of cyber-attacks, both home and abroad. The 'National Cyber Security Strategy 2022' sets out the UK government approach to protecting and promoting the UK's interests in cyberspace. In previous years there have been three pillars (Defend, Deter, and Develop), and these have been replaced with five new pillars which broaden the discipline and focus of the strategy. These five pillars are:

Pillar 1: Strengthening the UK cyber ecosystem, investing in our people and skills and deepening the partnership between government, academia and industry

Pillar 2: Building a resilient and prosperous digital UK, reducing cyber risks so businesses can maximise the economic benefits of digital technology and citizens are more secure online and confident that their data is protected

Pillar 3: Taking the lead in the technologies vital to cyber power, building our industrial capability and developing frameworks to secure future technologies

Pillar 4: Advancing UK global leadership and influence for a more secure, prosperous and open international order, working with government and industry partners and sharing the expertise that underpins UK cyber power

Pillar 5: Detecting, disrupting and deterring our adversaries to enhance UK security in and through cyberspace, making more integrated, creative and routine use of the UK's full spectrum of levers

25.05 The National Cyber Security Strategy states that the vision is to create 'cyber power' in support of national goals. Making the point that cyber power is becoming an ever more vital lever of national power and a source of strategic advantage. The report goes on to state that cyber power is the ability to protect and promote national interests in and through cyberspace.

25.06 The strategy recognises that in this digital age, the UK's ability to be a cyber power will hinge on the ability to deliver security (and confidence in security) at a national level. It also recognises that we require an integrated approach to cyber security, building on organisational resilience which is fundamental about removing 'gaps' within governance, risk and compliance (GRC). Finally, and importantly, the strategy clearly recognises the importance of involving the whole of society. This became increasingly important during the Pandemic, when a whole new range of digital technologies and new digital users were relied upon to support families, organisations, and the economy.

25.07 For example, grandparents and parents who were previously unaccustomed to technology were suddenly 'hosting' virtual family gatherings, to ensure that connections with loved ones remained. In economic and business terms, organisations were quickly forced to adopt 'Work from home' practices, which pushed IT strategies and functions to the limit, as technology was pushed to the fringe of the networks. The challenges faced by the nation were clear, and it is interesting that the strategy was in full development, and published during this period, and it is clear on reading the strategy that this played a big role in shaping the five pillars mentioned above.

25.08 Being able to successfully defend against cyber-crime or defend against human error can only be achieved when we engage at every level of society or within an organisation. We need clear objectives, strategies, tactics and operational steps to follow. In a word, we need 'structure'. In business this is relatively simple to implement as there are a number of frameworks or standards which set out clear rules for us to follow in order to protect our organisation. But what standards exist? Which is best? And which is the right standard to achieve?

Standard Practice

25.09 Throughout the remainder of this chapter we will explore some of the most popular and recognisable security standards available. Whilst the perspective is

UK based, the standards selected are internationally recognised, and where they are not, they are seen as being desirable to achieve, internationally. Each standard will be explored in some detail, with the 'pros' and 'cons' of each discussed and reconciled. However it is important to state at the outset that adopting 'standard practices' of any kind can only be a positive thing, as it clearly demonstrates a desire by the organisation to improve its security posture.

25.10 The remaining pages of this chapter will discuss the following standards:

- PCI DSS – Payment Card Industry Data Security Standard.
- Cyber Essentials and Cyber Essentials Plus.
- ISO27001:2022 – Information Security, Cybersecurity, and Privacy Protection
- ISO27018:2014 – Code of practice for protection of personally identifiable information (PII) in public clouds acting as PII processors.

25.11 As we approach the topic of protecting organisations the chapter would not be complete if we did not discuss security frameworks, which are different from the standards above as organisations do not 'certify' against frameworks. Frameworks are often adopted as a way to help build a security posture, upon which the standards above can be achieved. The most common security framework we come across is the National Institute of Standards and Technology (NIST) Of course any organisation can adopt the above standards, and simply use them as a framework too, and simply not go for full certification. The reasons for that decision may be financial or there may be no (perceived) business benefit from achieving the certification. These areas will also be discussed throughout the remainder of this chapter.

PCI DSS

25.12 If your organisation processes card payments, then you are most likely already aware of the 'Payment Card Industry Data Security Standard' (PCI DSS), which is controlled by the PCI Security Standards Council. This includes financial institutions, merchants (of all sizes), point-of-sale vendors and hardware and software developers who are involved in developing processing payment technologies. PCI DSS was released in December 2004 and the PCI Security Standards Council (PCI SSC) was launched on 7 September 2006 to oversee the Payment Card Industry (PCI) security standards. A key focus for the PCI SSC is on improving payment account security throughout the entire transaction process.

25.13 Maintaining payment security is required for organisations that process, store or transmit cardholder data, with guidance on how this data should be maintained and controlled described within a set of technical and operational requirements.

25.14 According to its own website, PCI Data Security Standards help protect the safety of financial (card) data. They set the operational and technical requirements for organisations accepting or processing payment transactions, and for software developers and manufacturers of applications and devices used in those transactions. Whilst we often refer to PCI DSS, it is worth nothing that there are in fact three separate PCI security standards;

- PCI PTS – Manufacturers; PIN Entry Devices;
- PCI PA DSS – Software Developers Payment Applications; and
- PCI DSS – Merchants and Service Providers. Secure Environments.

25.15 PCI DSS, focuses on developing a secure environment, which will help establish a protective framework around our entire organisation and focus on both operational and technical controls involved in the card payment process.

25.16 Although we talk about protecting an 'organisation', the PCI standard uses the term 'Merchant' or 'Service Provider' to describe any organisation who processes or is involved in the processing of card data. And helpfully, the card brands provides us with four levels of Merchant and two levels of Service Provider so that we can better understand (and describe) the level of risk associated to card processing, although this does vary from card brand to card brand, below are examples:

Merchant Level	Processing transactions
1	Over 6M transactions per year.
2	1M to 6M transactions per year.
3	20,000 to 1M transactions per year.
4	Fewer than 20,000

Service Provider Level	Processing transactions
1	Over 300,000 transactions of a single card brand
2	Under 300,000 transactions of a single card brand

25.17 In order for a Merchant or Service Provider to demonstrate it is able to comply with the requirements of the standard, they must complete a 'Self-Assessment Questionnaire' (SAQ) or complete a qualified assessment of their PCI DSS implementation, this is dependent on the level the Merchant or Service Provider operate at. Due to the various approaches to card data processing, the PCI Security Council developed different SAQ assessments based on specific card processing methods. These are:

SAQ ID	Description
A	Card-not-present Merchants, All Cardholder Data Functions Fully Outsourced
A-EP	Partially Outsourced E-commerce Merchants Using a Third-Party Website for Payment Processing

SAQ ID	Description
B	Merchants with Only Imprint Machines or Only Standalone, Dial-out Terminals – No Electronic Cardholder Data Storage
B-IP	Merchants with Standalone, IP-Connected PTS Point-of-Interaction (POI) Terminals – No Electronic Cardholder Data Storage
C	Merchants with Payment Application Systems Connected to the Internet – No Electronic Cardholder Data Storage
C-VT	Merchants with Web-Based Virtual Payment Terminals – No Electronic Cardholder Data Storage
P2PE	Merchants using Hardware Payment Terminals in a PCI SSC-Listed P2PE Solution Only – No Electronic Cardholder Data Storage
D-M	All other SAQ-Eligible Merchants
D-SP	SAQ-Eligible Service Providers

25.18 In order to help protect Merchants, the PCI Security Standards Council states that its goals and objectives surrounding the PCI standard are to:

Build and Maintain a Secure Network

1. Install and maintain a firewall configuration to protect cardholder data
2. Prevent the use of vendor-supplied defaults for system passwords and other security parameters

Protect Cardholder Data

1. Protect stored cardholder data
2. Encrypt transmission of cardholder data across open, public networks

Maintain a Vulnerability Management Program

1. Use and regularly update anti-virus software or programs
2. Develop and maintain secure systems and applications

Implement Strong Access Control Measures

1. Restrict access to cardholder data by business need-to-know
2. Assign a unique ID to each person with computer access
3. Restrict physical access to cardholder data

Regularly Monitor and Test Networks

1. Track and monitor all access to network resources and cardholder data
2. Regularly test security systems and processes

Maintain an Information Security Policy

1. Maintain a policy that addresses information security for employees and contractors

25.19 As we can see from the requirements above, this is a broad range of requirements, and within each requirement (in the standard) we are provided with detailed instructions on what is necessary and how it should be tested/validated. PCI DSS is not truly 'risk based', in that it does not ask an organisation to consider if any of the controls are necessary, it assumes that it knows best and simply requires an organisation to demonstrate it has implemented the control unless justification for non-inclusion can be evidences due to non-applicability ie no card holder data storage. Therefore, the PCI DSS can be relatively restrictive, because of this prescriptive approach.

25.20 It is also worth pointing out that the PCI Security Standards Council does not require, monitor or enforce compliance with the PCI DSS. PCI DSS compliance of merchants is managed and monitored by the merchant banks who are responsible for ensuring compliance and reporting compliance to the card brands. The merchant banks oversee the compliance of their merchants but in some cases the use of other Payment Service Providers (PSPs) can mean that PCI DSS is not enforced as rigorously as it should be, resulting in some merchants not maintaining compliance. Merchants of course risk financial penalties for noncompliance and may even lose card network privileges if they cannot evidence of compliance.

25.21 PCI DSS is primarily a technical set of controls that help an organisation to protect its processors surrounding card data processing but is defined as a 'Business as Usual' method for operating good security practices. If your organisation does this, then you should look at PCI DSS as a good set of controls which you should adopt. More information can be found on the PCI Security Standards Councils website, which includes the SAQ's and the complete standard.

CYBER ESSENTIALS AND CYBER ESSENTIALS PLUS

25.22 In the UK, the government has recognised that implementing security standards can be seen as a costly and complex programme of work. In order to tackle this issue, they set about creating a new standard which would address some of the key issues surrounding cyber-security. Working with groups like the 'Information Assurance for Small and Medium Enterprises' (IASME) and the Information Security Forum (ISF), they created a set of controls for organisations to use, which would help protect them against some of the most common forms of attack.

25.23 The scheme was launched in June 2014 and offers two levels of certification; Cyber Essentials, and Cyber Essentials plus. Both provide the technical controls considered as necessary to protect an organisation, however it is Cyber Essentials Plus which requires a little more evidence than the former, Cyber Essentials (more on this later).

25.24 Importantly, from October 2014 the UK government requires all suppliers of services to government departments (who process sensitive and personal information) to be certified against the Cyber Essentials scheme. This is certainly one of the reasons the scheme has become so popular within the UK, and could be seen as a model for other countries who are struggling to get businesses in their jurisdiction to take cyber-security seriously. The Cyber Essentials schemes were all updated in 2021, and reflect the need for more evidence of compliance and conformity. This means an enhanced audit process which requires a larger sample within the target organisation.

How Cyber Essentials protects your organisation

25.25 The Cyber Essentials Scheme sets out technical controls which it states will help to identify and remediate the most common vulnerabilities within an organisation. It does this by focusing on five key areas of technical security:

- Boundary firewalls and internet gateways
  - Ensuring devices designed to prevent unauthorised access to or from private networks are configured and controlled appropriately.
- Secure configuration
  - Systems must be configured in the most secure way for the needs of the organisation.
- User access control
  - Controls of user access to ensure those who should have access to systems have appropriate controls around them.
- Malware protection
  - Ensuring that virus and malware protection is in place and regularly updated.
- Patch management
  - Ensuring that appropriate patch management processes are in place and are carried out on key systems and services.

25.26 The details of each of the above is covered elsewhere in this book, so to do so here is unnecessary, but it's important to again point out that the only focus of Cyber Essentials (and Cyber Essentials plus) is on technical controls within an organisation.

25.27 When setting out on achieving the standard, the organisation must select an appropriate 'scope' which defines what it is trying to protect. This is of course a technical scope so requires a level of understanding (and ability) to determine and document what the scope is.

25.28 In an attempt to protect your organisation, it makes sense to implement a standard which can address some of the more technical areas of our business; the digital devices. Cyber essentials aims to address what the creators believed were the main areas of concern to an organisation, as they recognise that organisations often have competing priorities for resources. Therefore, by focusing on a small number of technical controls a tangible difference to an organisation's cyber-security could be made, which would minimise the damage caused when someone opened a malicious attachment or clicked on a link. Therefore whilst the focus is very much on the technical areas of the business, implementing these controls will certainly go some-way to protecting the broader organisation.

The Certification Process

25.29 As a Cyber Essentials scheme Applicant, you must ensure that your organisation meets all the requirements set out by the standard. You may also be required to supply various forms of evidence before your chosen Certification Body can award certification at the level you seek.

25.30 As stated above there were several bodies involved in bringing Cyber Essentials into being, one of which is the IASME Consortium (www.iasme.co.uk/cyberessentials/). On their site you can gain access to the questions that must be completed in order to achieve certification (currently 80 questions).

After submitting the questionnaire it will be assessed remotely and based upon your evidences, you will either achieve certification, or not.

Cyber Essentials Plus

25.31 Once an organisation has achieved the perceived 'minimum' of control around cyber-security, then they have the option to go to the next level of Cyber Essentials plus. The steps taken for this certification are almost the same, with the same set of controls as outlined above, however this time the verification of your cyber security is carried out independently by a Certification Body. This means that rather than simply submitting the 'Self-Assessment Questionnaire', the certification body will visit you and independently audit your approach to the controls required by the standard.

25.32 Following the internal audit, an internal and external 'Vulnerability Scan' must be carried out on the technical infrastructure. For example, part of the process will be to use an (approved) vulnerability scanner to scan the external IP range for all IP addresses within the specified ranges (provided by the organisation). Note this is not a full 'Penetration Test' which explores the ability for a vulnerability to be exploited, but merely sets out to determine if a vulnerability exists.

25.33 As you can see, the key difference between Cyber Essentials and Cyber Essentials plus is the more 'hands-on' approach, which is a more rigorous and beneficial certification to hold, because it is independently assessed, but is based on 'actual' evidence witnessed onsite. Therefore there are a number of problems with the Cyber Essentials scheme.

The problem(s) with Cyber Essentials

25.34 Like PCI DSS, Cyber Essentials is based on a 'Self-Assessment-Questionnaire' (SAQ). This means that theoretically anyone with a degree of knowledge in networks and cyber-security could complete the SAQ and submit it to a remote auditor who has nothing to base their understanding of the organisation on, other than what they see in the SAQ. Of course the evidence provided will (and should) include screen shots, so this isn't quite as easy to carry out as suggested, but still there are clear issues with a certificate that is based purely on a remote audit. For this reason the Cyber Essentials Plus scheme is more favourable, giving confidence that an external body has been involved in attesting the credibility of the technical controls in place.

25.35 Cyber Essentials is also 'rule' based, which means that it sets out a set of 'rules' for an organisation to follow, based on the five areas discussed. For example, Cyber Essentials makes the following statement when talking about Malware Protection; 'The Applicant must implement a malware protection mechanism on all devices that are in scope.' It then proceeds to list possible mechanisms that can be used. Although it would seem sensible to have malware protection on devices, it may not always be necessary and/or desirable. A 'Risk based' approach to security allows an organisation to decide upon the most appropriate controls to implement, based on their particular requirements. Indeed where some larger organisation have Cyber Essentials in place, it is questionable how they achieved this standard because of either their ability to apply every rule to their business, or the scope of the certificate itself (eg in a business of 10,000 people/mobile devices what malware protection is in place? And how is this being maintained and managed?). The majority of (if not all) international standards are moving to a 'risk based' approach to their controls, requiring organisations to consider the risks to their business, and/or the data subjects they deal with and implement appropriate risk mitigation controls accordingly. Cyber Essentials does not provide this flexibility or level of business assessment.

25.36 Whilst Cyber Essentials is a good thing, indeed any attempt to improve security is a good thing, it is concerning that it only aims to improve the security of the IT systems used by an organisation. The standard is aimed at an enterprise's IT, and based around a simple risk scenario. This scenario is one that assumes the attacker had some technical knowledge, they are sitting somewhere on the internet, and are using attack tools which are freely available on the internet (aka 'Commodity attack tools'). Tools such as NMAP, Nessus, and Metasploit. It is understandable that we must start somewhere, and it seems logical to start with the devices, and how they are protected. But this leaves many to believe that protecting an organisation starts and ends with the IT department. This is a little like looking at car accidents and believing the ONLY way to improve road safety is to make safer cars. Yes, the vehicle needs to be well maintained, but the driver just might need some training too.

Benefits of Cyber Essentials

25.37 Although there are short-comings of the Cyber Essentials scheme, any demonstration of commitment to cyber-security is a positive thing. Holding the Cyber Essentials scheme does offer a level of protection for your organisation, and when it is done well it is an outward demonstration to your clients, customers, partners, suppliers and regulators that you take the protection of information seriously. In addition, it is currently mandated (in some situations) by UK government bodies, and therefore could assist you in helping to grow your business by winning government contracts.

25.38 Cyber Essentials is seen as the 'entry level' when demonstrating that an organisation is thinking about cyber-security, so what does it say about organisations who have *not* implemented these controls? Clearly this scheme can be used for commercial and competitive advantage, and is often used in marketing and commercial discussions.

25.39 Ultimately, Cyber Essentials (and Cyber Essentials plus) helps you to protect your organisation's reputation and potentially its profitability (by avoiding data breaches or cyber-attack). So although Cyber Essentials has its faults, it is certainly better than nothing at all.

25.40 However, if we want to truly protect our organisation then we need a standard that considers not just the 'Cyber' Essentials, but the what is essential to our organisation; People, Premises, Processes and Providers. And the only standard which does this is the international standard for Information Security Management; ISO27001:2013

ISO27001:2022

25.41 ISO27001, is just one of the standards which comes from the International Standards Organisation (ISO), an independent body which has members from 162 national standards bodies from around the world. In the UK, the British Standards Institute (BSI) is the organisation that helps determine what standards are developed. There are literally hundreds of standards which outline the way that jet engines should be developed through to medical devices. But no matter what the standard is, they're all essentially about developing 'quality' and ensuring there is a consistent approach to the creation of whatever they are focusing on.

25.42 ISO27001 is part of what many call the '27000 family', which includes ISO27005 (Information security risk management), ISO27008 (guidelines for auditors on information security controls) and ISO27010 (information security management for inter-sector and inter-organisational communications). It's important to note that there is more than 27001 to be aware of, because whilst our focus is going to be on two main ISO standards, it is helpfully to remember there are actually 12 ISO standards within the 27000 family.

ISO27001 & ISO27002

25.43 Like Cyber Essentials, ISO27001 offers you a framework that you can apply to your organisation in order to build a more secure business. However unlike Cyber Essentials, ISO27001 isn't only focused on technology. ISO27001 is a standard that has been around for many years, having started out as a British Standard in 1995. Developed by the BSI, BS7799 was made up of two parts and was aimed at protecting against the broadest range of security risks and vulnerabilities. Originally it was developed around the 'Plan-Do-Check-Act' methodology, but has today moved away from this approach (although it still has elements of this within it).

25.44 ISO27001 provides organisations with a truly holistic approach to Information Security because it allows organisations to focus on risks to the '5 P's' of Information Security:

- People;
- Premises;
- Processes;
- PC's; and
- Providers.

25.45 Whilst this standard isn't overtly structured around the above (ie you won't see chapter headings of the above), the standard does ensure that none of the above is neglected.

25.46 The standard has maintained this approach since it became an international standard in 2005 and then again later when it was replaced by ISO27001 in 2013. The latest version of the standard was released on 21 October 2022, and is a much needed change.

25.47 When organisations implement ISO27001, they are said to be building an 'Information Security Management System' (ISMS), which a systematic approach to managing information that is risk based. This is an important point, because building a security framework which is focused on risk ensures the standard is as applicable to small organisations as it is to large organisations.

25.48 Once you have purchased the standard (and yes, you have to buy it from the certification body), you will see that following an explanation of standard terms and definitions that the ISMS is structured around six key areas.

Each will be discussed in detail to demonstrate that the ISO27001, and ISO2702 are about more than the technical aspects of a business, and that we need to think broader in terms of Information Security.

Context of the organisation

25.49 When implanting the ISMS, the standard firstly requires you to explain and articulate 'what' your organisation is, and describe its place in the world. The standard states that 'the organisation shall determine external and internal issues that are relevant to its purpose and that affect its ability to achieve the intended outcome(s) of its information security management system.'[1]

25.50 This section of the standard requires the organisation to identify and describe key aspects of the business (in context to Information Security), including who interested parties are (internally and externally), and the scope of the ISMS itself.

25.51 By clearly articulating which functions, people, and locations are in scope you can begin to build a picture of the size of your implementation. Also, by describing who the interested parties are (eg employees, customers, suppliers, regulators) you begin to build a picture of what needs to be done to ensure their needs are being met.

25.52 By doing this, you can clearly set the 'scope' of your ISMS, which essentially means describing what the ISMS will cover. It is important that the scope be broad enough to be useful but not too broad that it will be difficult to control. Selecting the right scope is important, as some organisations try and build the scope around one department, meaning everything outside the department is (by definition) out of scope and therefore of no interest to ISO27001. This creates complexity because people within the organisation aren't sure when they are and when they are not, expected to behave in a certain way. So it's important to develop a scope that is meaningful to your organisation (and meets the needs of the interested parties).

Leadership

25.53 The next section of the standard is extremely important, because without clear leadership there is little point in progressing in your development of the ISMS. In earlier versions of the ISO standard, Leadership was implicit, but it was felt that this topic was so integral to the success (or failure) of the ISMS that the sensible decision was made to give it its own section. The section opens with the following: 'Top management shall demonstrate leadership and commitment with respect to the information security management system'[2]

25.54 The standard requires your organisation to demonstrable leadership and commitment from the head(s) of the organisation with clearly defined roles,

1 ISO27001:2013 – 4.1 Context of Organisation.
2 ISO27001:2013 5.1 Leadership.

responsibilities and authorities. In this section we see that the standard seeks to understand how policies have been defined, signed-off and communicated.

25.55 If leadership isn't in place or cannot be demonstrated then there is little point in pursuing the remaining parts of the standard. This again is why the setting of the scope is so important, and of course is easier in smaller organisations than in larger ones. Firm commitment from the top must be in place if there is any chance of this standard being achieved.

Planning

25.56 Once you have your commitment from the leaders in your organisation, then the standard requires you to start planning your implementation. This starts by identifying the actions required to address risks (and opportunities) that the interested parties (internal and external) might be interested in.

25.57 Performing a risk assessment is important here, and focusing on the '5 Ps' mentioned earlier will help you to identify the risk areas. It is here that we make our first reference to the 'Annex A Controls' (herein referred to as 'Annex-A', which are part of the ISO27001 standard). Annex-A will be discussed later, but it is important to note that any risks identified should be tied to the controls associated to the various sections in Annex-A, and as you'll discover later the 14 areas of this section cover broadly the '5 Ps' we need to consider.

25.58 In this section of the standard we also identify our security objectives, because without clearly defined objectives we won't know what we're trying to achieve. As always, good objectives should be specific, measurable, attainable, realistic and timed (SMART), and whilst the standard doesn't make reference to SMART objectives, you do need to specify what your objectives are, what resources you need, and if possible how you'll measure them.

Support

25.59 Now you have your commitment and your plans in place it's time to identify the resources you need to ensure the ISMS is successful. In this section of the standard you're required to determine the resources you need to establish, implement and maintain the ISMS (and of course continually improve it). Resources can range from securing a budget for Information Security, through to the people you will need to help you with the ISMS.

25.60 In terms of people, the standard asks you to determine the 'competence' of the people involved in the building and implementation of the ISMS, and it is down to you to determine what evidence you need to provide. This is an important point to make, as the role of implementing an ISMS is sometimes handed to someone who is a programme manager, and doesn't have the necessary technical skills required by the standard. The person(s) involved in the ISMS need to have the skills, but also the TIME to implement the standard (time is a resource), so care should be taken when implementing the standard.

25.61 It is in this section that we are also expected to demonstrate that we have raised awareness of the ISMS, and that the interested parties (internal and external) are, where necessary, informed of what their roles and responsibilities are. Again, this is a good indication that we're taking security away from being an IT problem, and placing expectations on people and their behaviour.

Operation

25.62 Now the plans are in place and we have our resources, we need to put the ISMS into operation. Ensuring you have operational plans in place will be evidence that the ISMS is being controlled effectively.

25.63 This means having a clear plan around auditing of your ISMS, and development and auditing of your policies and procedures. This is about demonstrating that your ISMS isn't merely something which 'sits on a shelf', but is actually being maintained within the organisation. Updating your risk register, for example, and maintaining it on an ongoing basis is a good example of the ISMS 'in operation'.

Performance evaluation

25.64 At the start you set out clear objectives which were SMART, so now you will need to demonstrate that the ISMS is being monitored, measured, analysed and evaluated. Of course it is down to you to determine what is measured, how and how often. But having clear evidence that this is taking place is required by the standard.

25.65 Importantly it is here that we again see an expectation placed on management that they periodically review the ISMS and ensure it is operating effectively. The standard outlines the kinds of things that it expects management to assess and review, and also states that it requires 'documented information as evidence of the results of management reviews.'[3] (it's almost like they don't believe they would happen!)

Improvement

25.66 Finally, the ISMS requires us to demonstrate that we are continually trying to improve the security capabilities in our organisation, by assessing and understanding any issues, non-conformities, or incidents that occur. These

3 ISO27001:2013 9.3 Management Review.

can be discovered through audit, management reviews or incidents, but having an approach to improving the ISMS is important. Indeed, before we move into the final section of the ISMS, the 'Annex A Controls', the final words of the ISO27001 standard are: 'The organisation shall continually improve the suitability, adequacy and effectiveness of the information security management system.'[4]

Annex A Controls

25.67 The final section of the ISO27001 standard is where the greatest strength of the standard rests. The 'control objectives' listed in the table are meant to be used in context of the risks that were identified during the risk assessment carried out previously (under section 6 of the ISMS).

25.68 Each control area covers a different aspect of Information security, and focuses the users attention on key aspects of the business. These are now:

- Organisational controls.
- People Controls.
- Premises Controls.
- IT Controls.

Where there were once 114 controls across 14 areas, there are now 93, across the four areas named above. There have been some significant changes in the new standard, with the introduction of 11 new controls, the merger of 24 and updating of 58 others.

CONCLUSION

25.69 In order to protect ourselves and our organisations, we must stop concentrating on only the technical aspects of information security. Good information security requires us to consider the physical, logical and technical aspects of information, indeed it requires us to think of security in all its forms; information on paper, in our heads and on devices.

25.70 To put in place a security framework that only focuses on the technology is like believing the way to safer roads is ONLY through more robust cars. Safer roads requires investment in the physical environment, training AND the vehicles themselves. If we continue to focus on technology we are going to continue to be vulnerable. We need to see beyond the vehicle and look at our environment, and ask ourselves how we can engage on every level. Only then will we be able to truly protect our organisations.

4 ISO27001:2013 10.2 Continual Improvement.

CHAPTER 26

PUBLIC PRIVATE PARTNERSHIPS

E Rudina

INTRODUCTION

26.01 This chapter looks the public-private partnerships and the role of independent Computer Emergency Response Teams (CERTs) in the protection of critical infrastructure against cyber-attacks.

26.02 Cyber-security issues are no longer the preserve of computer security experts and specialised IT companies; they are now considered matters of national and economic security affecting privacy, civil liberties and have even become part of the political debate.

26.03 This is doubly true when it comes to security for critical infrastructure.

26.04 Different countries have different assessments of how vulnerable their critical infrastructure sectors are to cyber-attacks, and the possible impact of those attacks. Cyber-security strategies, which are formulated by most countries, describe the different approaches to countering such attacks. In some countries the responsible agencies adopt a more secondary role, only providing regulatory oversight, while others play a more proactive role, getting involved in the development of technical cyber-security measures to protect critical infrastructure. There is no doubt that on the strategic level success depends on the relations between government agencies and the critical infrastructure sectors represented by the relevant government departments, the largest enterprises in a sector, and the authorities regulating issues of security and safety.

26.05 There are several reasons for this. In different sectors the processes, technologies and requirements may vary drastically. Cyber-security measures must be elaborated that take into account all the specific needs of a particular sector. At the same time, cyber-security measures must not raise additional issues (eg, they must not affect safety). This requires the participation of domain area experts in the development of security measures. Last but not the least, facilities may be privately owned and operated, making it necessary to establish a public-private partnership in order to provide security.

26.06 Not surprisingly, many cyber-security strategies place an emphasis on some kind of public-private partnership. At the same time, the goals, scenarios and extent of the relationships between the parties are not the subject of this strategy. These parameters are established in the corresponding government programs. An example of a public program is the UP Kritis program, the initiative for cooperation between the economy and the state in order to protect critical infrastructure in Germany. This public-private cooperation between critical infrastructure operators, their associations and the responsible government agencies covers eight of the nine of the ten Critical Infrastructure sectors (energy, health, ICT, transport and traffic, media and culture, water, finance and insurance, food). Only the state sector and administration are based on other security activities Federal, state and local level covered.

26.07 The members of UP KRITIS work in committees, both sector-specific and cross-sectoral, in technical, organisational and political issues. The works serve to prepare for and prevent security incidents and supply failures. In order to counter current threats, the members exchange information on technical issues such as the current threat landscape, the consequences of current incidents and procedures for incidents management and incident reporting.

26.08 The Cyber-security Information Sharing Partnership (CiSP) is another example of a joint industry-government initiative implemented in the UK. Its aims are to share information about threats and vulnerabilities in order to increase overall situational awareness of such threats and therefore reduce their impact on UK business. CiSP allows members from across sectors and organisations (strictly from UK, public or private sector) to exchange cyber-threat information in real time, in a secure and dynamic environment, whilst operating within a framework that protects the confidentiality of shared information based on TLP mark.[1]

26.09 The US is classic case because it is here that collaboration between the private and public sectors has historically been one of the pillars of national security. The issue of ensuring security and resilience of critical infrastructure, and protecting this infrastructure against cyber-attacks, is addressed in the framework for a partnership between the government and the private sector and comprises two documents – Presidential Policy Directive 21 (PPD-21): Critical Infrastructure Security and Resilience, and the National Infrastructure Protection Plan (NIPP) 2013: Partnering for Critical Infrastructure Security and Resilience. Cybersecurity and Infrastructure Security Agency's (CISA) Strategic Plan for 2023/25 lays out four strategic goals, and strengthening whole-of-nation operational collaboration and information sharing are among them. The Plan refers the partnership and collaboration as a part of CISA's mission and declares the shared responsibility for securing the nation's cyber and physical infrastructure.

26.10 Hence, within a public-private partnership the State can usually support two types of activities: regulating measures to strengthen the resilience of critical infrastructure against cyber-attacks and observing the current situation in order to take urgent steps when necessary. While regulatory authorities

1 TLP (Traffic Light Protocol) is a set of designations used to ensure that sensitive information is shared with the appropriate audience.

work with potential threats and countermeasures, computer incident response teams deal with the need to exchange information about attacks, exposures, or vulnerabilities that have just been discovered and may therefore require an immediate response.

26.11 Implementing government programs that reflect the overall objective of contributing to the security of critical infrastructure and countering terrorism looks like a reasonable idea. Collaboration between public authorities and private organisations may be limited to a single area, such as sharing information about security incidents, or cover a range of aspects involving specialised governmental committees with high-profile representatives from ICT and different critical infrastructure sectors.

26.12 There is also the subtle issue of relations between government structures and internet service providers, large hardware and software vendors, multinational information corporations (like Google or Facebook) being developed not only in the context of protecting critical infrastructure objects (including government systems) from cyber-attacks but also in the context of more broadly defined national interests. National security concerns can play a decisive role when it comes to the application of methods that may run counter to generally accepted security principles. This issue had assumed special significance in light of recent attacks on digital supply chain.

26.13 CERTs and authorities under government control, inter alia, may be constrained by government policy, while independent research centres, organisations and CERTs usually have no specific restrictions other than those imposed by their professional reputation. The private CSIRTs of commercial vendors primarily the concerns of the particular vendor (both related to financial and reputational risks) and therefore not considered here as independent.

26.14 At the same time, a procedure for cooperation between independent agents and government bodies is an area of cyber-security that has not been formalised by any public strategies or programs that we know of. An enforced partnership between public agencies and a private sector organisation usually imposes a varying degree of obligations on the latter (with regards to those aspects that may affect national security or the security of critical infrastructure) but very rarely imposes any form of responsibility on the public agency.

26.15 Some States provide a 'feedback interface' to gather from independent researchers and private companies any data, analysis or distribution information that may be of interest to a government CERT. However, while the participation of a government CERT as an authoritative body may be helpful, it still plays an indirect role in this case. If such essential data (critical vulnerabilities in popular software or devices, critical infrastructure facilities exposed to threats, information about potential or ongoing attacks against these facilities) are available, distribution or reporting according to the responsible disclosure principle is usually not a problem.

26.16 This is exactly why independent researchers, cyber-security companies and CERTs are the free variables in the public-private partnership equation. The fact that they are not influenced by any factors except their reputation gives us reason to believe that they aim to share information about incidents, threats and vulnerabilities within a holistic security-driven approach.

26.17 The impact of private companies and independent research on critical infrastructure protection cannot be overemphasised. A single researcher is capable of finding a *show-stopping* vulnerability such as heartbleed. A group of computer security experts can discover an incident that is part of a targeted attack such as Stuxnet. A community of such experts can accumulate knowledge about existing vulnerabilities and possible attacks, and distribute the information about vulnerabilities and incidents in line with a responsible disclosure principle. As many years of practice show, this principle facilitates a decrease in the risks related to possible malicious exploitation of vulnerabilities or misuse of information following an incident.

26.18 An independent CERT should be built like a community and managed by principles that do not allow any of the members to harm the security interests of a globally defined critical infrastructure.

26.19 The first of these principles is keeping the appropriate confidentiality. Before sharing the information, which may harm the third parties, the source should take the responsibility. In a group of community of experts who share the goals, practices and informal trust, the purposed notation known to all members may specify the possible regime for data sharing. The source uses this notation to indicate the regime, and the recipients are willing to follow the appropriate rules of sharing. As an example, the Traffic Light Protocol (TLP) was created to facilitate greater sharing of potentially sensitive information and more effective collaboration. TLP is a set of four labels used to indicate the sharing boundaries to be applied by the recipients: TLP:RED, TLP:AMBER, TLP:GREEN, and TLP:CLEAR. TLP is distinct from the Chatham House Rule, but may be used in conjunction when appropriate.

26.20 Confidentiality of the information related to vulnerabilities plays an ambiguous role in supporting security and safety of systems which may be affected by these vulnerabilities. On the one hand, this information should not be widely shared before patching the vulnerability or applying other measures by the system vendor to compensate the risk. On the other hand, not all vendors handle this information in an appropriate way. Sometimes the vendor ignores the information, interpret or manage the risk improperly. In such a case it is important to inform about the vulnerability those who may be affected by the risk (users, customers, other stakeholders or third parties). This managed approach is called *responsible disclosure*. The appropriate processes are to be established and followed by security researchers, groups and companies, including CERTs. The standard ISO/IEC 29147:2018 Information technology – Security techniques – Vulnerability disclosure provides requirements and recommendations to vendors on the disclosure of vulnerabilities in products and services.

26.21 One of the major aspects of the efficient threat prevention and incident handling is prompt data exchange. Emergency response teams deal with attacks which are constantly growing in frequency, complexity and obfuscation. Gathered experience results particularly in data feeds containing information on suspicious and dangerous IPs, URLs and file hashes. These data feeds may be contributed to enhance the process of attack recognition by automated monitoring solutions (like SIEM, SOAR, threat intelligence platforms) and used by other response groups. Having the standard format for the data exchange would help with sharing threat feeds and enhance emergency response. Current proposed standards (OpenIoC, STIX, TAXII) are not used widely.

26.22 The last but not least, CERT functioning must be based on a deep understanding of the current state of cyber-security on a global level, a willingness to improve this state and not do harm.

This relates not only to the financial aspects but also to fundamentals like human life, health or environmental safety – all areas that could be endangered. It is well known that the difference between national and international security is that national security is a policy, while international security is a state of affairs. International cyber-security is necessary to maintain the core values in this state of affairs.

CHAPTER 27

CYBERSECURITY DISPUTES

Ffion Flockhart, Charlie Weston-Simons and Steven Hadwin,
Allen Overy Shearman Sterling LLP

INTRODUCTION

27.01 As other chapters of this book illustrate, cybersecurity incidents may have acute consequences for victim organisations. In addition to immediate operational disruption, the legacy of an incident can be years of litigation as affected parties contest who bears ultimate legal responsibility for financial losses. Commercial disputes of this nature may draw in customers, Managed Security Service Providers or 'MSSPs' or entire supply chains. This type of dispute is only part of the story. As the English Courts have witnessed in recent years, the contentious implications of an incident also extend to personal data breach claims, appeals of ICO decisions to the First-Tier Tribunal (Information Rights) and beyond, and injunctions aimed at preventing the use or disclosure of stolen data. These proceedings are perhaps most associated with ransomware and data extortion. However, other types of incidents present different legal challenges. Just by way of example, disputes commonly arise in business email compromise or 'BEC' scams over which party bears responsibility for losses arising from the original compromise, and in other scenarios efforts can be made (with the assistance of the courts, and at a cost) to recover stolen currency. Overlaying all of this is the possibility of a cyber insurance claim, although, as this chapter will explain, the absence of any reported cases would imply that this is not yet a particularly contentious area.

27.02 This chapter will give an overview of the categories of dispute that are most commonly associated with cybersecurity incidents. The main points are:

(a) At the time of writing, this area of the law is 'on the march'. There have been significant developments in the law as it relates to data breach claims since the implementation of the GDPR and the high-water mark of the Court of Appeal's judgment in *Lloyd v Google LLC*.[1] Outside of that sphere, *Lonestar Communications Corporation LLC v Kaye & Ors*[2] is a very good example of how cybersecurity incidents (in this case, a campaign of Distributed Denial of Service or 'DDOSAttacks') have the potential to give rise to very substantial commercial disputes. By the time that the next edition of this book is published, it is highly likely that cybersecurity case law will have developed significantly.

1 [2019] EWCA Civ 1599.
2 [2023] EWHC 421 (Comm).

(b) The Supreme Court's judgment in *Lloyd v Google LLC*[3] had a chilling effect on data breach claims. Prior to that judgment, there appeared to be scope for representative (ie, opt-out) actions in data breaches. In combination with the practical challenges presented by the High Court's judgment in *Warren v DSG Retail Ltd*,[4] many collective actions that were underway prior to that judgment have now been discontinued; a strong indication that such actions have become less appealing to prospective claimants, claimant law firms and litigation funders than was previously the case. At the time of writing, the English Courts are more or less in step with the Court of Justice of the European Union (**CJEU**) when it comes to interpreting the UK GDPR and what gives rise to a right to compensation.

(c) The disruption caused by cybersecurity incidents provides fertile ground for commercial disputes. This is particularly the case where the victim has customers and other counterparties that are dependent on their services. Where an incident has financial consequences for third parties, claims for compensation may follow based on breach of contractual terms (eg, specifically negotiated Key Performance Indicators and remedies for non-performance) and negligence. For those faced with such claims, liability and quantum will turn on issues such as the extent to which an organisation's security complied with industry standards, the circumstances of the security compromise and speed of recovery, the availability of a force majeure defence, and the effect of any contractual exclusions and limitations on liability.

(d) In any BEC incident, it will be critical for the affected parties to establish where the compromise occurred that enabled the malicious actor to insert themself into the email exchange and (very often) provide false bank account details for the transfer of funds. This is not only important for the affected parties to take swift remedial action, but it will also be a key factor in determining which party bears responsibility for the loss of funds. The prospects of recovering diverted funds are low, but not impossible; see *CMOC Sales and Marketing Limited v Persons Unknown & Ors*[5] for an example of what can be achieved.

(e) In certain cases, cyber-attack victims may wish to apply to the courts for an injunction to prevent the use and disclosure of stolen data. While this is not common practice in the UK, considerations such as the sensitivity of the data, the perceived public relations benefit and the support that an injunction lends to Internet Service Provider (**ISP**) takedown requests should be brought into consideration.

(f) As for insurance, the first litigated cyber insurance dispute is still awaited. Such cases as there have been in other jurisdictions have focussed on the availability of cover for losses caused by cybersecurity incidents under other (ie, non-cyber) insurance policies. To date, the rapid growth and

3 [2021] UKSC 50.
4 [2021] EWHC 2168.
5 [2018] EWHC 2230 (Comm).

commercially competitive nature of the cyber insurance market has seen many claims that might have resulted in litigation being settled commercially (or in a limited number of instances, resolved via confidential arbitration). However, this may change as underwriting becomes more sophisticated and if insurers take a firmer line on policy terms and pre-contractual disclosure.

(g) *DSG Retail Limited v Information Commissioner*[6] illustrates that there is scope for organisations issued with a fine by the ICO following an incident to appeal such decisions to the First Tier Tribunal under Section 162 of the Data Protection Act 2018 (the **DPA 2018**).

PERSONAL DATA BREACH CLAIMS

27.03 In the cybersecurity context, a personal data breach claim is a claim for compensation by an individual who is seeking compensation for alleged losses caused by the compromise of their personal data in a cyber incident. Typical heads of claim include damages for financial loss and distress.

27.04 Such claims typically follow cyber-attacks against organisations, where the sole objective of the attacker is to steal data and extort the victim by threatening to leak it, or double extortion ransomware attacks (where the attacker exfiltrates the victim's data in addition to encrypting it),[7] and where the impacted data includes personal data, prompting the organisation to notify the affected data subjects of a personal data breach because it meets the applicable threshold under Article 34 of the UK GDPR.[8] Article 82 of the UK GDPR and section 168 of the DPA 2018 now provide the statutory basis for a right to compensation for these types of damage arising from a contravention of a data controller or processor's obligations under the legislation. Such contravention often takes the form of a breach of Article 5(f) or Article 32 of the UK GDPR, each of which requires appropriate technical and organisational measures to be in place in order to safeguard the security of personal data.

27.05 Prior to 2021, it had been thought that there may be an automatic right to so-called 'loss of control' damages to compensate the data subject for the loss of control of their data alone (in other words, there was no need for the data subject to establish that they had suffered compensable distress or financial loss to recover damages; the loss of control was a sufficient basis for damages to be awarded). However, the Supreme Court's judgment in *Lloyd v Google LLC* in

6 [2022] UKFTT 2020_0048 (GRC).

7 Such claims also follow triple ransomware attack, where in addition to encrypting and exfiltrating data, an attacker may make other threats such as threatening the victim's customers or performing a distributed denial-of service attack.

8 Article 34(1) UK GDPR: 'When the personal breach is likely to result in a high risk the rights and freedoms of natural persons, the controller shall communicate the personal data breach to the data subject without undue delay.'

2021 and subsequent EU case law relating to Article 82 GDPR,[9] has largely put paid to that notion, and to the corresponding possibility that a highly lucrative (and, for controllers, damaging) representative action could successfully be brought by one affected data subject on behalf of all those whose data had been stolen. That said, it remains possible to bring data breach claims collectively as well as individually, albeit by a less straightforward process.

27.06 It would take several chapters to do justice to all of the jurisprudence that underpins and explains data breach claims in their current form, including the development of the tort of misuse of private information (**MPI**) and cases under the **DPA 1998**. The more limited ambition of this chapter is, instead, to trace the evolution of data breach claims from the point at which the Court of Appeal ruled in *Vidal-Hall v Google Inc*[10] that MPI is a tort, and that data subjects could recover compensation from controllers for distress at common law and under section 13 of the DPA 1998 without proving financial loss. While a number of the cases that are summarised in more or less[11] chronological order below did not involve cybersecurity breaches, they are nevertheless integral to the law in this area and are often cited in argument by personal data breach claimants.

(a) Shortly after *Vidal-Hall*, the measure of damages for MPI was considered in the phone-hacking cases of *Representative Claimants v MGN Ltd*[12] and *Gulati v MGN Ltd.*[13] Those cases held that, in such circumstances, damages could be awarded for distress and loss of control over the use of the claimants' private information.

(b) In *TLT v Secretary of State for the Home Department*,[14] the High Court considered the measure of damages for distress in a case involving the accidental publication of asylum seekers' personal information by the Home Office. Taking into account the claimants' loss of control over their information and the impact of the data breach on each of them, the claimants were awarded damages ranging from £2,500 to £12,500. This award represents a high-water mark in terms of compensation awarded for non-material damage by the English Courts and was often cited by claimants as an initial attempt at quantifying damages for data breach claims arising from cyber incidents. This approach was taken, notwithstanding that the nature of any distress caused to an individual following a large-scale cyber-attack against a company is likely to be significantly less severe than that caused by the unfortunate facts of *TLT*.

9 Article 82(1) GDPR: 'Any person who has suffered material or non-material damage as a result of an infringement of this Regulation shall have the right to receive compensation from the controller or processor for the damage suffered.'
10 [2015] EWCA Civ 311.
11 For efficiency, in one or two cases it has made sense to consider them out of chronological order.
12 [2015] EWCA Civ 1291.
13 [2015] EWHC 1482 (Ch).
14 [2016] EWHC 2217 (QB).

(c) These cases provided the backdrop to *Lloyd v Google LLC*,[15] the Court of Appeal judgment that for the time being represents the high-water mark for personal data breach group actions in the UK. This case arose from the same facts as *Vidal-Hall v Google Inc*; Google's use of the 'Safari Workaround' by which Google was able to circumvent privacy settings on Apple iPhones to place tracking cookies on the devices of millions of users in the UK. A consumer activist sought to bring an 'opt-out' representative action against Google under CPR 19.6 on behalf of all affected users, asserting that a uniform per capita award of damages in the sum of £750 could be made without the need to investigate each claimant's injury or loss because all users had the 'same interest'. This assertion was founded on section 13 of the DPA 1998 and an argument that it included a right to damages for loss of control over personal data in the same way as MPI cases.[16] The Court of Appeal agreed with Mr Lloyd, permitting the representative action to proceed on the basis that damages could be awarded for loss of control alone.

(d) At around this time the British Airways Data Event Group Litigation was also commenced. This litigation involved claims for damages by customers of British Airways following a cyber attack that was identified in September 2018. It was alleged that British Airways had failed to put in place appropriate technical and organisational measures to protect the data of the approximately 430,000 data subjects who were affected, in breach of its obligations under the GDPR, also amounting to a breach of contract and breach of confidence (**BoC**). The losses claimed by customers included financial loss, distress and loss of control of data. Before the litigation was settled in around July 2021, it was the subject of two procedural judgments[17] which considered certain aspects of how the group litigation was to be managed. In contrast to *Lloyd*, this litigation was conducted under a Group Litigation Order (**GLO**).

(e) Next in time, the High Court considered a strike out application in *Warren v DSG Retail Ltd*, a data breach claim that arose from a cyber-attack on the sales terminals of two well-known retail chain stores, in the course of which the personal data of many customers had been accessed. At the time of the hearing, the ICO had investigated the incident and issued on a Monetary Penalty Notice (**MPN**) for £500,000 on the basis that the seventh data protection principle under the DPA 1998[18] (equivalent to the UK

15 [2019] EWCA Civ 1599.

16 The claimants did not claim that Google's use of the Safari workaround was also a misuse of private information. This is probably because it would have been necessary to demonstrate, for each user, that there was a reasonable expectation of privacy, which would be incompatible with the representative action procedure.

17 [2021] EWHC 217 (QB) and [2021] EWHC 520 (QB).

18 'Appropriate technical and organisational measures shall be taken against unauthorised or unlawful processing of personal data and against accidental loss or destruction of or damage to, personal data.'

GDPR security principle[19]) had been breached.[20] The judge found for DSG, striking out the claimant's claims for BoC, MPI and negligence. In relation to the BoC and MPI claims, the judge reasoned that those claims required a positive act on the part of DSG, whereas in this case it was the criminal third party hackers that had disclosed and misused the claimant's data (and therefore, any cause of action would likely sound against the hackers rather than against the victim organisation). Rejecting the negligence claim based on a prior finding[21] that there was no scope to impose a duty of care where the statutory duties under the DPA 1998 operated, it followed that the only viable claim was the statutory claim for the alleged breach of the security principle. This was a highly significant decision. Firstly, and while it is still common for data breach claims arising from cybersecurity incidents to be based on multiple common law and statutory causes of action, the practical effect of *Warren* was that the only relevant basis for such claims is a breach of the security principle. Second and consequently, it made data breach claims materially less attractive to litigation funders because the removal of BoC and MPI as viable causes of action made it impossible for a successful claimant to recover their after-the-event insurance premium from the defendant.[22]

(f) In *Rolfe & Ors v Veale Wasborough Vizards LLP*,[23] the claimants (two parents and their child) sought damages from the child's school for alleged distress arising from the school's error in sending an email accompanied by a statement of account for outstanding school fees to someone else. The judge dismissed the claim, stating that 'In the modern world it is not appropriate for a party to claim … for breaches of this sort which are, frankly, trivial.'

(g) Two months later, the Supreme Court handed down its judgment in *Lloyd v Google LLC*,[24] overturning the Court of Appeal's decision and holding, crucially, that (1) it was not possible to recover damages under section 13 of the DPA 1998 for loss of control of data alone and (2) it was necessary to prove material damage and/or distress, requiring an individualised assessment that was incompatible with the representative action regime. While the Supreme Court indicated that a 'bifurcated process' might work, involving an initial representative action to decide common issues of fact or law, followed by further proceedings (possibly under a GLO) to determine issues that required individual consideration, in the same breath it questioned

19 Article 5(1)(f) UK GDPR: 'Personal data shall be…processed in a manner that ensures appropriate security of the personal data, including protection against unauthorised or unlawful processing and against accidental loss, destruction or damage, using appropriate technical or organisational measures.' See also Article 32 (Security of processing).

20 Subsequently, the MPN was reduced to £250,000 on appeal: see *DSG Retail Limited v Information Commissioner* [2022] UKFTT 2020_0048 (GRC).

21 *Smeaton v Equifax Ltd* [2013] 2 All ER 959.

22 This is because claims for breach of data protection legislation do not fall within the 'publication and privacy' exemption in the Legal Aid, Sentencing and Punishment of Offenders Act 2012.

23 [2021] EWHC 2809 (QB).

24 Above n 3.

how such a process could be funded. From the cybersecurity perspective, the effect of the Supreme Court's decision was that the only way to bring a group personal data breach claim was to actively recruit a sufficient class of individuals who considered that they had incurred actionable distress or pecuniary loss as a result of an incident. However, that type of opt-in exercise would require effort (and therefore up-front investment) which, in combination with *Warren*, represented a significant financial challenge. Importantly, there would also be the uncertain prospects of litigating issues of liability (such as whether the victim / controller had or had not breached UK GDPR by not having appropriate technical and organisational measures, notwithstanding the incident) and loss (such as whether each individual claimant could provide persuasive evidence that they had suffered more than de minimis distress resulting from the loss of their data). Reflecting these points, in the months following *Lloyd* a number of high-profile data-related representative actions that had been commenced or contemplated (some of which arose from cybersecurity incidents) were abandoned. It should also be noted that the Supreme Court's judgment did not resolve two questions: whether 'loss of control' damages could be recovered under the UK GDPR because, in contrast to the DPA 1998, Article 82 confers a right to compensation for 'non-material damage', and whether data breach claims under the UK GDPR are subject to a 'threshold of seriousness' in the same way as claims for MPI (as may have been implied in the judgment in *Rolfe*). These questions have, however, been considered in subsequent European and domestic cases, as outlined below.

(h) *Johnson v Eastlight Community Homes Ltd*[25]was another case of a misdirected email being sent in error to a single individual, this time attaching a compilation of various customers' rent statements (including the claimant's). Three hours after receiving the email, the recipient confirmed they had deleted it. Amongst other points, the Master saw no basis for the claim to have been issued in the High Court, refused to strike it out entirely but described it as a *'very modest claim'* and criticised the claimant's proposed costs of £50,000.

(i) In *Stadler v Currys Group Ltd*,[26] the claimant sought £5,000 in damages for alleged distress arising from Currys' failure to perform a factory reset on a smart television that was considered too costly to repair, whereupon it was sold to a third party who purchased a film from the claimant's Amazon account through the television. Applying *Warren*,[27] the judge struck out the claimant's claims in MPI and BoC, finding that Currys did not make use of the data or information on the television. As in *Johnson*, the judge found that the claim (though not trivial and therefore liable to be struck out) was 'unquestionably of low value' and therefore should be transferred to the County Court and the small claims track meaning that (if successful) the

25 [2021] EWHC 3069 (QB).

26 [2022] EWHC 160 (QB).

27 See also *Underwood & Anor v Bounty UK Ltd & Anor* [2022] EWHC 888 (QB) for a further example of a misuse of private information claim being struck out in accordance with *Warren*.

claimant would only be able to recover fixed costs in a very limited amount. This judgment served to highlight the important part that track allocation played, and still plays, in the context of low-value data breach claims. That is because, in many cases, the claimant may be represented by solicitors acting on a 'no win, no fee' basis; but if the value of the claim is low and the successful claimant cannot recover their full legal costs, there is no financial advantage (or worse) to be gained by the solicitor in assisting the claimant to bring their claim.

(j) *Smith & Ors v Talktalk Telecom Group Plc*[28] concerned a 'mass data breach claim', as they are sometimes described, by various customers of Talktalk whose private information including names, addresses and banking details was alleged to have been taken by dishonest employees of a third party service provider in 2014 and whose personal data was also said to have been accessed in an 'SQL Injection' cyber-attack. Before the same judge who decided *Warren*, it was submitted in response to Talktalk's application to strike out the MPI claim that *Warren* was either distinguishable or wrongly decided. Confirming *Warren*, the judge reiterated his earlier view that it was the third-party attacker who had misused the claimants' information, not Talktalk, and struck out the MPI claim.[29] However, the judge did also observe that, in other circumstances, it might be possible for a controller to become liable, in contract or another tort, if they were responsible for creating a vulnerability. Notably, the judge also permitted the claimants' claim to proceed based on an inference that, where their data had been used by a scammer, the data had been obtained from a vulnerability in Talktalk's systems. It is submitted that the judge's acceptance of this approach may have been a function of the fact that the information that the claimants required to plead a more specific case was in Talktalk's hands; as would generally be the case in claims arising from cybersecurity incidents.

(k) In *Bennet & Ors v Equifax Ltd*,[30] a hearing of an application for a GLO, the Court and parties grappled with the question of how a large number of low value data breach claims can be dealt with most efficiently, in a post-*Lloyd* world. Whereas the claimants contended for a GLO model, the defendant proposed that preliminary issues on causation and loss should be heard first, ahead of liability. The thinking behind this approach was that, if the claims had no or negligible value, there would be no need for a GLO or liability hearing. In the event the Senior Master opted not to decide the issue, remitting it to a managing judge in the High Court. This claim arose from a cyber-attack on Equifax's US parent company that took place in 2017, impacting individuals resident in England and Wales whose personal data was being processed by the US parent on behalf of the defendant. By the time of the hearing, the ICO had issued an MPN for £500,000. In October

28 [2022] EWHC 1311 (QB).
29 Viz. 'Creating a situation of vulnerability (and thus enabling a fraud) is simply not a misuse of information within the tort.'
30 [2022] EWHC 1487 (QB).

2023, it was reported that the claim had been settled out of court – leaving the overall question about how best to handle low-value claims open.

(l) In *Driver v Crown Prosecution Service*,[31] the High Court awarded damages of £250 for distress in a personal data breach claim described by the judge as 'at the lowest end of the spectrum'. This was not a cybersecurity case (it arose from an email sent by the Crown Prosecution Service to a third party about a charging file from which the claimant could be identified) but, usefully, it gives some guidance on quantification of damages for distress in data breach claims. On the same theme, in *Ali v The Chief Constable of Bedfordshire Police*[32] which followed shortly after *Driver*, a claimant was awarded £3,000 for distress 'in the bottom half of the range of awards for "less severe psychiatric harm"' according to the relevant Judicial College Guidelines. The claim arose from breaches of Articles 5(1)(a) and (b) of the UK GDPR; but not Article 5(1)(f) as this was also not a cybersecurity case.

(m) *Beck & Ors v Police Federation of England and Wales (Re Costs)*[33] was concerned with the costs implications of the claimants' late decision to abandon their application for a GLO and agree to the Police Federation's 'lead claimant' model, which presumably envisaged one or more lead claims being determined, and the principles from that exercise being applied to the wider class. This was, therefore, another instance (after *Bennett*) of procedural argument over the most efficient way to manage multiple low value data breach claims through to trial, in this case arising from two ransomware attacks in 2019. The judgment is most noteworthy for the Senior Master's recognition that a GLO may not be the most proportionate procedure for managing such claims due to the significant costs associated with establishing a group register, advertising and compiling schedules of information. In a different way to *Johnson* and *Stadler*, this highlights the importance of case management in the bringing and defence of data breach claims where the only loss claimed is distress. Without an effective approach, there is invariably a risk of disproportionate costs being incurred, making such claims more difficult to resolve.

(n) In *Prismall v Google UK Ltd & Anor*,[34] the claimant brought a representative against Google and DeepMind Technologies on behalf of approximately 1.6 million patients, in connection with the transfer of patient records to DeepMind Technologies for the development of a medical app. In contrast to *Lloyd*, the claimant based its claim on MPI (so not the DPA 1998 or UK GDPR). As described above, in MPI claims damages are recoverable for loss of control of private information, as long as there is a reasonable expectation of privacy in the relevant data and the impact exceeds a *de minimis* threshold. Due to the need for all members of the represented class to have the 'same interest' in order for a representative action to proceed, the

31 [2022] EWHC 2500 (KB).
32 [2023] EWHC 938 (KB).
33 [2023] EWHC 685 (KB).
34 [2023] EWHC 1169 (KB).

judge focused on the characteristics of the 'lowest common denominator' claimant, to identify the harm that all members of the class would have suffered. Having done this, the judge declined to find a reasonable expectation of privacy because the lowest common denominator claimant would have put their information in the public domain, also finding that such claims would not meet the *de minimis* threshold. At the time of writing, the claimant had been granted permission to appeal this judgment to the Court of Appeal. This case is material to cybersecurity-related data breach claims because it represents a further obstacle to opt-out class actions. In order for such actions to be a realistic possibility again, it would seem to require a combination of *Prismall* being successfully appealed, and *Warren* being overturned or distinguished so that cybersecurity claims could be brought in MPI and meet the 'same interest' test for representative actions. Unless that happens, this avenue for opt-out collective redress would appear to be firmly closed.

(o) Finally, in *Farley & Ors v Paymaster (1836) Ltd (Trading as Equiniti)*[35] the High Court considered the claims of over 400 current or former police officers, seeking damages under the GDPR and for alleged distress arising from their annual pension benefit statements being sent to the wrong recipients, also alleging MPI. Ultimately, the judge struck out all but 14 of the claims because, in the majority of cases, it could not be shown that the statements had been opened by the unintended recipient. The judge also observed that the remaining 14 cases may only be eligible for *'very modest damages'* but that they should nevertheless be allowed to go forward. Notably, the judge declined to express a view on whether English law imposes a 'threshold of seriousness' on data protection claims, as it does in MPI and as the Supreme Court in *Lloyd* had suggested may be the case. That is an important question because, if there is such a threshold, it would enable the English Courts to dismiss claims of a trivial nature. For the time being, at least, it remains a live issue, both in this jurisdiction and continental Europe.

27.07 As to the EU, although post-Brexit CJEU decisions are not binding on the English courts following the European Union (Withdrawal) Act 2018, they are still decisions to which the English courts may have regard. This is particularly relevant in the context UK GDPR given its EU origins. In parallel with the judgments described in this section, there have been a number of significant European cases that are, on any view, highly relevant to the development of the law in this area. One such case is the CJEU's decision in *UI v Osterreichische Poste AG*,[36] widely referred to as 'The Austrian Post Case', which considered various issues relating to Article 82 GDPR.[37]

35 [2024] EWHC 383 (KB).

36 C-300/21.

37 Article 82 GDPR, provides that 'any person who has suffered material or non-material damage as a result of a breach of [the GDPR] shall be entitled to receive compensation from the controller or the processor.' Article 82 UK GDPR is in substantively identical terms.

(a) One of those issues was whether every breach of the GDPR, without more, gave rise to a right to compensation; essentially the same issue that the UK Supreme Court had considered in *Lloyd* in the context of the DPA 1998 and 'loss of control' damages. The CJEU concluded that some damage or harm is required.

(b) Another issue was whether 'non-material damage' must meet a minimum threshold of seriousness to warrant compensation under Article 82 of the GDPR. The CJEU decided that there is no such minimum threshold and subsequent case law has affirmed that Article 82 precludes any national law from imposing a minimum threshold in order for non-material damage to be compensable.[38]

27.08 The Austrian Post Case therefore appears to have resolved one of the issues that was left open by *Lloyd* – that is, whether 'loss of control' damages could be recovered under Article 82 of the UK GDPR on the grounds that loss of data is a form of 'non-material damage'.[39] There is no reason to believe that an English court would take a different view of this issue. As to the threshold of seriousness, as set out above, this is a live issue that was considered (but not determined) recently in *Farley*, where there was some debate over the implications of the CJEU's decision. That issue may be considered soon in this jurisdiction, whether in *Farley* or another suitable English case. While there have been other relevant CJEU decisions that have a bearing on the GDPR and cybersecurity disputes, as matters currently stand the English courts and CJEU are taking a broadly consistent approach.

27.09 Other CJEU authorities provide the English courts with useful guidelines as to whether and how technical and organisational measures implemented by a defendant controller should be considered 'appropriate' for the purposes of Article 5(f) and 32 of the GDPR (and therefore, whether the requisite breach of the regulation has taken place). *VB v Natsionalna agentsia za prihodite*[40] in particular makes clear that (i) a personal data breach will not, in and of itself, equate to an absence of appropriate measures; (ii) each case will need to be assessed on its own facts, with reference to the risks associated with the data processing; and (iii) given the principle of accountability in Article 5(2) of the GDPR, the burden of proof in determining whether technical and organisational measures are appropriate will rest with the defendant controller, rather than the claimant. The current English authorities do not suggest that the English Courts would arrive at different conclusions on these points.

27.10 Drawing the threads together, the current status of cybersecurity data breach claims in this jurisdiction may be summarised as follows:

38 For example, *C-456/22 – VX and AT v Gemeinde Ummendorf.*

39 This reasoning has been applied in subsequent cases covering similar subject matter, including *VB v Natsionalna agentsia za prihotide* which re-affirmed that loss of control of personal data is not, per se, compensable.

40 C-340/21.

(a) For the foreseeable future, it is very hard to see how an opt-out group action could be brought.

(b) While alternative group action models are possible – GLO and lead claimant being the obvious ones – they are opt-in and therefore less economically attractive to third party funders.

(c) Unless *Warren* is overturned or, as the judge in *Smith* suggested, on the facts of a case it can be argued that the controller or processor is responsible for creating the vulnerability, the only relevant basis for these claims is likely to be the UK GDPR, specifically Article 82 claims alleging breaches of Articles 5(1)(f) and/or 32. However, MPI remains relevant to data breach claims that do not have as their root cause an alleged cybersecurity failure.

(d) In the light of *Lloyd* and the Austrian Post Case, to recover compensation claimants must prove that they have suffered loss on account of an incident, whether in the form of financial loss or distress. Loss of control is not enough.

(e) It is currently uncertain whether there is a threshold of seriousness below which damages for distress may be recovered. However, cases such as *Rolfe*, *Johnson* and *Farley* indicate that the Courts are alert to the possibility of opportunistic claims, where there is no real prospect of proving compensable distress.

(f) While every claim for distress must be considered independently, the lower end of the compensation scale is currently around £250.

(g) For defendants faced with data breach claims commenced in the High Court, consideration should be given to whether it is appropriate for them to be handled in the County Court on the small claims track. The associated costs implications may assist their prompt resolution.

COMMERCIAL DISPUTES

Background

27.11 The disruptive potential of cybersecurity incidents is clearly illustrated by the scale of the insurance claims brought by Mondelez and Merck in the aftermath of the NotPetya outbreak of 2017. Those claims are considered in more detail later in this chapter, but their quantum ($100 million and $1.4 billion respectively, of which a significant proportion related to business interruption) demonstrate the impact that an incident can have on an organisation's ability to carry on its business activities, particularly where there is a prolonged recovery period.

27.12 However, it may not only be the victim organisation's[41] business that is disrupted. Any provider of goods or services may find itself unable to meet its

41 Referred to as **Victims** for shorthand purposes in this Section.

obligations to customers and clients[42] in the event of a third party incident that inhibits its ability to do business. If those Customers are reliant on the timely delivery of the Victim's goods or services, they may in turn incur significant financial losses. The result is that an incident may not only cause the Victim to incur business interruption losses; the Victim may also face the prospect of contractual claims for damages by Customers for their own losses, comprised of lost profit and their own costs of dealing with the incident. This latter category may include legal and other incident response costs, particularly if the Customer is the controller of data affected by the incident. In that scenario, the Customer will have its own obligations to notify regulators and data subjects in the UK and elsewhere, may retain technical specialists to advise on potential contagion risk and the assurances needed to re-engage, and may itself face compensation claims from data subjects and other parties.

Elements of a typical Customer / Victim contractual dispute

27.13 While practitioners in this area will be familiar with this type of contractual claim, perhaps surprisingly, at the time of writing there have not been any reported decisions in England and Wales. It is submitted that this is likely to be because Customers either determine that the costs of pursuing a claim outweigh the likely benefit due to the applicable contractual framework and defences, or because a way is found to resolve contested claims without the need for formal dispute resolution (ie, litigation or arbitration) or otherwise prior to judgment.

27.14 Notwithstanding the lack of reported decisions, it is nevertheless possible to explain the typical legal basis of such claims and explore the issues that commonly arise. Before doing so, however, it is important to stress the primacy of the terms of the written contract between the Victim and Customer as determinative of the respective rights, obligations and remedies of the parties in such situations. As the relevant terms invariably vary from contract to contract and transaction to transaction, it follows that the starting point for assessing any such claim is a detailed review of those provisions. This may be the case even between the specific Victim and the Customer, who may have contracted on the Victim's standard terms for one transaction disrupted by an incident but on different terms more favourable to the Customer for another such transaction.

27.15 Against that background, the following should be viewed as a non-exhaustive overview of the contractual terms and issues that may be material:

- **Duties**: In each case, the contract may set out a number of duties that are relevant to the Customer's claim, in the sense that the Customer considers that the Victim's failure to perform them was a relevant cause of the disruption and, consequently, the Customer's losses. Duties that are regularly relied on include, *firstly*, the Victim's basic obligation to supply

42 Referred to as **Customers** on the same basis, supra note 36.

the goods or services within an agreed timeframe, *secondly*, a duty to maintain appropriate standards of IT security (sometimes by reference to 'good industry practice', possibly accompanied with specific requirements for regular penetration testing, audits and security-related measures), and *thirdly*, with respect to data protection, an obligation to maintain appropriate technical and organisational measures in connection with the Victim's processing of personal data. In addition to these duties, Customers may also invoke duties implied under statute such as the obligation on suppliers of a service to carry out the service with reasonable skill and care, which arises under section 12 of the Supply of Goods and Services Act 1982. However, where the contract contains express duties such as those already outlined and examined further below in the context of breach, it is submitted that implied duties of this nature are unlikely to make a practical difference to the viability or merits of a Customer's claim.

- **Breach (non-performance)**: Taking the principal duties in turn, there will rarely be any question that the Victim has failed to supply the relevant goods or services within an agreed timeframe, that being the fundamental premise of the Customer's case. However, this may not be enough for the Customer to establish the Victim's liability or achieve its financial objectives. This may be because the contract contains specific remedies for delayed performance, such as agreed compensation for breach of agreed service levels, or because the contract contains a Victim-friendly force majeure clause, or other limitations or exclusions of liability that would bite on non-performance but not or to a lesser extent on other types of breach.
- **Breach (security)**: As IT security requirements are generally framed in relative (ie, by reference to 'good industry practice') rather than absolute (ie, strict liability) terms, where a breach of this duty is alleged, it will be for the Customer to prove that the Victim's IT security fell short of the prescribed standard. To resolve questions of this nature, a court or tribunal will normally require evidence from a suitably qualified expert or experts. In cases where the Victim contests liability, its position will essentially be that the attacker was able to compromise their IT environment successfully, and possibly exfiltrate data and/or deploy malware, in spite of the appropriate IT security measures that the Victim had in place. There is accordingly an overlap between this type of defence and force majeure, considered further below.
- **Breach (data protection)**: Since the GDPR (and subsequently, the UK GDPR) came into force, there has been a requirement for data processing to be governed by a written contract between the controller and the processor covering various matters, including specific provision for the processor to implement appropriate technical and organisational measures.[43] In practice, the relevant provisions tend to be incorporated into wider contracts in a section relating to data protection, or as a separate data processing agreement addendum. It may appear that there is considerable overlap

43 Article 28(3) of the UK GDPR.

between an obligation to include this type of clause alongside an obligation to maintain appropriate standards of IT security in accordance with 'good industry practice'. While contracts do not always seek to rationalise the operation of overlapping security provisions, it is submitted that the answer should be – in a clearly drafted contract – that the obligation to implement appropriate technical and organisational measures in the data protection section of an agreement should only be relevant to the problem that it seeks to address (ie, the secure processing of personal data) whereas a 'good industry practice' type of obligation should have wider operational relevance. The practical effect of this should be that the former type of obligation only becomes material where an incident results in personal data being compromised, causing the controller / Customer to incur losses and/ or liabilities that it looks to recover from the processor / Victim, whereas the Customer may base a claim for business interruption losses on the latter type of obligation. This may seem like a distinction without a difference, but it takes on additional significance where the data protection obligations are subject to a lower liability cap, or none at all.

- **Defences (force majeure / adequacy of security)**: The general purpose of a force majeure clause is to excuse one or both parties from performance of the contract following the occurrence of an event that was beyond the parties' control. Force majeure clauses typically define qualifying force events non-exhaustively, and sometimes include 'cyber-attack' or something similar as a qualifying event. While there is currently no authority on when a cyber-attack will be treated as a force majeure event, in light of wider authorities on force majeure arguments[44] it is submitted that relevant considerations may include the extent to which the Victim may be held responsible for failing to guard against the incident. Consequently, a Victim seeking to rely on a force majeure clause in their contract may find themselves making the same or a very similar argument in this respect as they are making in response to an allegation that they breached an obligation to maintain appropriate IT security (ie, that the cyber-attack occurred despite the appropriate measures that the Victim had in place). It should also be noted that force majeure clauses often require the relying party to give written notice of a force majeure event in order for the clause to be engaged.

- **Defences (exclusions of liability)**: As with any contractual claim, it is important to scrutinise any term that seeks to exclude liability for a particular type of event or loss with great care. Subject to the types of loss claimed by the Customer and the exact wording of the relevant provision, it may be (for example) that certain of the losses claimed may be characterised as indirect or consequential loss, which is a commonly excluded category of loss. Alternatively, the relevant provision may go further by excluding all liability on the Victim's part for loss of revenue or types of costs that commonly form part of a cyber incident disruption claim. While in a

44 See for example *2 Entertain Video Ltd v Sony DADC Europe Limited* [2020] EWHC 972 (TCC).

business-to-business context an extensive exclusion clause may give rise to considerations of reasonableness under the Unfair Contract Terms Act 1977 (**UCTA 1977**), the critical point is that the terms of any potentially relevant exclusion clause must be carefully considered.

- **Remedies (service levels / liquidated damages)**: It is possible that the contract will specify the financial consequences of any delayed performance by the Victim. These provisions may take the form of service level provisions with staged discounts or service credits corresponding to the period of delay, or liquidated damages clauses. If provisions of this nature are present, the Customer's entitlement should still (always depending on the specific terms of the contract) be subject to the availability of any force majeure defence. In light of the relevant terms, it may also need to be determined whether these contractually prescribed remedies are the Customer's sole remedy, taking account of any relevant exclusions and financial limitations on the Victim's liability.
- **Remedies (proving loss)**: Where there is not an agreed contractual remedy, it will be for the Customer to prove that it incurred the losses it is claiming, and that the losses in question were caused by the incident. This may be a significant exercise, not only because the required documentation may not exist (for example, many disruption claims include an element of damages for additional staff working or overtime for which there may not be evidence other than the payments made) but also because the claim may include items such as loss of profits for which technical accounting assistance may be needed. There may also be issues of causation and mitigation. The result is that it may be necessary for the Customer to invest time and money in the process of establishing its claim (and this process might rely on whatever evidence of lost revenue or additional costs could be contemporaneously gathered), or accept some level of discount as part of a commercial settlement which avoids the need for a detailed assessment exercise.
- **Remedies (liability caps)**: Finally, the presence of contractual liability caps may have a crucial bearing. If there are such caps, they may apply to certain breaches but not others. For example, breaches of data protection related obligations are sometimes subject to higher caps than other types of breach, or they may be uncapped. If the Customer has contracted on the Victim's standard terms, they may find that the maximum recoverable amount is significantly lower than the actual value of their losses. While the Customer may wish to argue that the relevant clause should be disregarded under UCTA 1977, such arguments are not straightforward, particularly in the context of a negotiated agreement between sophisticated parties, and the Customer's best prospect of recovering a sum in excess of the liability cap may be to exert whatever commercial leverage that it has.

27.16 We emphasise, again, that this is not intended to be an exhaustive list of the issues that may arise in the context of such claims, and that other issues may arise from the particular wording of each contract. For example, a contract may include a clause that allocates the costs of investigating and resolving an incident involving malware to the party whose environment was initially compromised, or an incident may result in a Customer seeking to terminate their contract early (either exercising a contractual terminate right or alleging repudiatory breach by the Victim). However, this overview should at least provide a framework or foundation for assessing claims of this nature.

Other commercial disputes

27.17 While contractual disputes between Customers and Victims for disruption losses may be the most common type of post-incident commercial dispute, many other types of dispute are possible. This point is illustrated by the subject matter of *Lonestar Communications Corporation v Kaye & Ors*.[45] In that case Lonestar, a Liberian telecommunications provider, was the victim of a campaign of multi-vectored 'DDOS Attacks'[46] for a period of around 18 months which disrupted its network and services. After criminal courts in Germany and the UK had found the campaign was carried out by a Mr Kaye, a 'hacker for hire', it was Lonestar's case that the campaign had been funded and encouraged by two other defendants, the CEO of Lonestar's main competitor in Liberia, Cellcom Liberia, and another employee. The Court agreed with Lonestar, also finding that their actions fell within the scope of their employment by the relevant corporate entities. From that basis, the Court went on to determine the extent of the losses suffered by Lonestar, awarding Lonestar significant damages of approximately $4 million for loss of profit and incident response costs, as well as exemplary damages.

27.18 Notably, the judgment also indicated that the facts of the case would prompt a claim from the buyer of Cellcom Liberia for breach of warranties given under a stock purchase agreement under which the buyer had acquired the company during the period in which the DDOS Attacks had occurred. This points to another category of commercial dispute that a cyber incident may give rise to, quite apart from the array of contentious possibilities presented by scenarios involving the theft and misuse of data, and recovery actions such as *AA v Persons Unknown & Ors*[47] where the Victim's insurer was able to obtain a proprietary injunction over a wallet containing bitcoin with a value of $1.2 million that had been extorted by a cyber-attacker in return for decryption software.

45 [2023] EWHC 421 (Comm).

46 Described in the judgment as 'a form of cyber-attack in which the perpetrator seeks to make a machine or network resource unavailable to its intended users by flooding the target machine or resource from multiple different sources, in an effort to overwhelm it and prevent legitimate requests for connection being fulfilled.'

47 [2019] EWHC 3556 (Comm).

BEC DISPUTES

27.19 The substance of a BEC[48] dispute is helpfully illustrated by the facts of *CMOC Sales & Marketing Ltd v Persons Unknown & Ors*.[49] That case involved CMOC, a business that bought and sold Niobium, a soft metal. In October 2017, CMOC discovered that it had been the victim of a BEC whereby the perpetrators of the fraud had hacked into CMOC's email systems and caused CMOC's bank to pay out approximately $8.2 million via a series of transfers. The perpetrators were able to send emails purporting to come from a director of CMOC to his bank, enclosing fake payment instructions.

27.20 Pausing there, the judgment does not provide details of the steps that CMOC, and possibly its bank, took to establish where the compromise occurred (ie, on CMOC's system or that of its bank). However, that is generally a threshold question in any BEC dispute that is integral to establishing where legal responsibility for the loss lies. In incidents involving banks in particular, there may also be a question whether the bank should have rejected or queried the payment request because there were specific and identifiable grounds for believing that the request was an attempt to defraud the customer (known as the 'Quincecare duty' under English law).[50]

27.21 Plainly, in CMOC's case, it was clear that it was CMOC's email systems that had been compromised, not the bank's. This in turn led to CMOC making urgent applications aimed at locating and freezing the stolen funds, identifying the primary perpetrators and conspirators, and bringing the case against them to trial with a view to recovering the company's losses. The resulting orders enabled CMOC to trace the stolen funds into accounts held with 50 banks in 19 jurisdictions, and to identify 30 individual defendants. Having frozen the funds that could be identified, CMOC then successfully made out (1) a proprietary claim against all defendants who it could be shown received the stolen funds, entitling CMOC to recover approximately $1.5 million from the relevant bank accounts; (2) damages claims for dishonest assistance and unlawful means conspiracy against the defendants responsible for the hack and those who knowingly assisted the fraud; and (3) a claim for knowing receipt against all of

48 The NCSC describes BEC as 'a form of phishing attack where a criminal attempts to trick a senior executive (or budgetholder) into transferring funds, or revealing sensitive information': https://www.ncsc.gov.uk/files/Business-email-compromise-infographic.pdf. It is submitted that the sub-category of BEC that is most likely to give rise to a commercial dispute, considered here, arises where a criminal successfully inserts itself into an email exchange between two commercial organisations, in order to obtain funds by fraudulent means. In addition to the CMOC example, a common type of BEC fraud involves the provision of fraudulent invoices from an authentic (or authentic-seeming) email address.

49 [2018] EWHC 2230 (Comm).

50 See *Federal Republic of Nigeria v JP Morgan Chase Bank NA* [2022] EWHC 1447 (Comm) for a detailed explanation of this duty and *Philipp v Barclays Bank UK Plc* [2023] UKSC 25 in which the Supreme Court declined to extend the Quincecare Duty to circumstances where instructions came directly from a customer (who was being defrauded), rather than from an agent posing as the customer.

the defendants who received the company's funds, whether directly or following a series of transfers.

27.22 As well as illustrating the type of dispute that may arise from a BEC incident, the CMOC case also demonstrates the steps that can be taken to recover stolen funds via the courts, and the importance of taking speedy action in such situations. However, it is striking that, notwithstanding CMOC's extensive efforts, it was only possible to recover around 20% of the stolen funds. While it is not known if CMOC experienced any success enforcing its judgment against the identified defendants, the unfortunate reality is that in most cases the perpetrators of a BEC incident will act quickly to put stolen funds beyond the victim's reach (often by transferring them to accounts in jurisdictions where tracing them would be difficult to the point of impossibility) and that many victims and their insurers will take the view that the material costs associated with taking such action are not justified.

INJUNCTIONS

27.23 In this jurisdiction, the victim of a cyber-attack involving data theft may occasionally apply for an interim or permanent injunction prohibiting the attacker from using or disclosing the stolen data. When such injunctions are obtained, they are made against 'persons unknown'.[51] As the attacker's identity is not generally known, the probability is that they are in a jurisdiction where enforcement is far from straightforward, and their conduct would tend to imply that they are unlikely to pay much regard to an English Court order. Therefore, it might be thought that an injunction would have limited practical value.

27.24 Nevertheless, injunctions are sometimes sought and granted. While each case may raise individual factors, as in *XXX v Persons Unknown*[52] considered below, there is a perception in certain quarters that having an injunction may assist with takedown requests to Internet Service Providers (**ISPs**) following an incident, where an ISP is asked to remove stolen data that was deliberately posted by a cyber-attacker (typically following the victim's refusal to pay a ransom). Another justification that is sometimes given for obtaining an injunction is that it demonstrates to the victim's commercial counterparties and affected data subjects that the victim is 'going the extra mile' to safeguard their interests or has taken 'all possible steps' to bring the stolen data back under its control.

27.25 The *XXX* case is a good case study of a situation where the victim considered it necessary to take this step. Based on the judgment relating to the victim's application for summary judgment in relation to its claim for a permanent injunction, it would appear that principal drivers for the victim's

51 See for example *PML v Persons Unknown* [2018] EWHC 838 (QB), *The Ince Group Plc v Persons Unknown* [2022] EWHC 808 (QB), *XXX v Persons Unknown* [2022] EWHC 2776 (KB) and *Armstrong Watson LLP v Persons Unknown* [2023] EWHC 1761 (KB).

52 [2022] EWHC 2776 (KB).

approach in this case were the highly sensitive nature of the stolen data, some of which was classified and protected by the Official Secrets Act 1989, and the fact that social media users were referring to the stolen data after it was published on the dark web following a ransomware attack in which a ransom of $6.8 million was demanded.[53]

27.26 After an interim injunction was obtained, the Court granted the victim's application for summary judgment, also confirming that the victim should continue to be anonymised. On the latter point, the Court indicated that the fact that a business would be likely to suffer negative commercial and reputational consequences if a cyber-attack on their systems becomes public knowledge is not automatically a sufficient reason to depart from the principle of open justice, also observing that in cases involving significant data breaches the victim will typically have no alternative but to make the breach public. In this case, the Court considered that the particular feature justifying anonymity was the security-sensitive nature of the victim's work and the fact that disclosing its identity could prompt third parties, including hostile nation states, to make contact with the attackers and locate the stolen data on the dark web. This highlights a further consideration to be balanced for any victim thinking of obtaining an injunction, that taking this step may in fact serve to draw attention to the incident.

27.27 While there may be the occasional case such as *XXX* where the expense of obtaining an injunction is justified due to specific factors, and the odd case where a victim is persuaded by the more impressionistic factors referred to above, the current position is that most victims do not go to the trouble and expense of obtaining injunctive relief. Unless and until something happens to make this a more logical step (eg, it becomes a regulatory expectation), it is submitted that this should remain the case. It should also be noted that, in other jurisdictions, it is becoming more commonplace for victims to pursue this option.

INSURANCE CLAIMS

27.28 For many organisations, cyber insurance is a critical component of their framework for managing cyber risk. From its origins in the 1990s where it was bolted on to some liability insurance policies, the product has developed to become a valuable standalone category of insurance covering a range of first third party (eg, incident response costs, extortion payments, business interruption and restoration costs) and third party (eg, privacy and other civil liabilities including defence costs) losses.

27.29 Perhaps surprisingly, given its popularity and the relatively high frequency (and size) of claims, there have not been any reported cases involving cyber insurance coverage disputes. However, there have been high profile claims

53 The judgment also referred to the victim's preference for obtaining summary judgment on the merits 'as this may assist the claimant in having the judgment recognised and enforced in foreign jurisdictions'.

for cyber-related losses under other types of insurance policies (principally property insurance providing 'all risks' cover) arising from the NotPetya cyber-attack in 2017. The claims in question were brought by Mondelez and Merck in the US, seeking indemnification for the significant losses that they had incurred in connection with the incident (as mentioned above, the aggregate value of these claims was in the order of $1.5 billion). In Mondelez's case, the policy was said to respond because it covered losses caused by 'the malicious introduction of a machine code or instruction', and in both cases the central issue was whether the NotPetya attack equated to a hostile or warlike action that was caught by the war exclusion in both policies, in light of the widespread attribution of the NotPetya malware to Russia. Both cases settled after a state appellate court found in Merck's favour.

27.30 In part due to these claims, the insurance industry has made significant efforts in recent years to confirm the extent to which a non-cyber insurance policy (eg, property damage, professional indemnity or marine) will provide cover for cyber-related losses. There has also been a widespread re-modelling of war exclusions in cyber insurance policies, with a view to clarifying when a policyholder can expect to be covered for losses arising from incidents carried out by nation state sponsored actors.

APPEALS OF ICO NOTICES

27.31 Finally, section 162 of the DPA 2018 entitles any person who receives an information, assessment, enforcement or penalty notice to appeal to the First-Tier Tribunal (the **FTT**) for its variation or cancellation. As well as a number of fines by the ICO having been reduced following dialogue with the affected data controllers,[54] there have been a number of such appeals under this section.[55] In the cybersecurity context, these include Ticketmaster's appeal of the ICO's MPN for the sum of £1.25 million which was stayed in 2021 pending the outcome of a concurrent personal data breach claim in the High Court[56] and, most notably, *DSG Retail Limited v Information Commissioner*[57] although it should be noted that the DSG MPN and appeal were made under the DPA 1998 due to the timing of the incident.

27.32 In *DSG*, the subject matter of DSG's appeal was an MPN in the sum of £500,000 which proceeded on the basis that approximately 10 million records of non-financial personal data had been unlawfully processed and exfiltrated from DSG's servers, and that 5,646,417 payment cards were affected as to which

54 The most notable examples being the fines imposed by the ICO against British Airways and Marriott.

55 See for example *Experian v Information Commissioner* [2023] UKFTT 00132 (GRC) where the appeal's subject matter was an enforcement notice relating to Experian's use of credit reference data for direct marketing purposes.

56 *Ticketmaster UK Limited v Information Commissioner* [2021] UKFTT 2020_0359 (GRC).

57 Above n 6.

the PAN[58] of each card constituted personal data. The basis for the MPN was that various aspects of DSG's technical and organisational IT measures had been assessed as inadequate for data security. DSG's challenges to the MPN included that its technical and organisational IT measures were adequate, that the PAN of each card did not constitute personal data in its own right, and that any contravention of the applicable data protection principles was not serious.

27.33 The FTT determined that the fine imposed by the ICO should be reduced by 50%. On the substantive issues, the FTT found that the ICO had placed excessive emphasis on a penetration testing report from around the time of the incident, that not all of the alleged deficiencies were made out, that DSG's Payment Card Industry Data Security Standard (PCI-DSS) compliance was a 'relevant consideration' but not to the extent relied on by the ICO, and that PANs could be regarded as personal data in combination with other information.

27.34 Clearly, the extent to which more appeals of this nature are forthcoming will depend on the ICO's approach to enforcement and regulatory priorities at any given time, and the resulting incidence of MPNs following cybersecurity incidents. Relevant to that, it also remains to be seen whether the ICO's recently published Data Protection Fining Guidance[59] will result in fewer notices being susceptible to appeal.

58 Primary Account Number.

59 https://ico.org.uk/about-the-ico/our-information/policies-and-procedures/data-protection-fining-guidance/.

CHAPTER 28

THE JELLO PROBLEM: KEY FEATURES OF GENERATIVE AI THAT CREATE LEGAL RISK

David Wakeling & Marcus Turner[1]

INTRODUCTION

28.01 In describing a generative AI model as a 'giant ocean of jello—a vast mathematical mixing' whereby the model 'mash[es] up work done by human minds',[2] Jaron Lanier, a computer scientist at Microsoft, provides a metaphor which neatly captures the features of generative AI which drive legal risk for organisations that deploy generative AI systems. Specifically, the application of wildly complex algorithms to a vast mountain of human data, produces something unexplainable, where it is impossible to reliably predict the form of or inspiration for the output. This can broadly be divided into two core features.

28.02 The first feature is the *jello* – caused by complexity at scale. We refer to this as the 'black box' problem.[3] The vastness of the training data and the complexity of the algorithms supporting the model mean that it is difficult to understand the inner workings of a generative AI model and, crucially, when it will make errors. In particular, a generative AI model is: (i) opaque – why a given prompt generates a particular output is unclear and unpredictable; (ii) inconsistent, whereby a different output is generated by the same input; and (iii) prone to 'hallucinations', which is where a model confidently asserts something which is incorrect. This feature of

1 With special thanks to: Alex Shandro, Karishma Brahmbhatt, Jane Finlayson-Brown, Daren Orzechowski, Catherine Di Lorenzo, Peter Van Dyck, Andrew Denny, Lisa Nguyen, Helen Christakos, Neville Cordell, Edward Taelman, Robert Dickens, Beverley Potts, Emma Keeling, Jason Rix, Justin Ormand, William Wray and Mohamed Sacranie.

2 Lanier, J., '*There is no A.I*', New Yorker (2023). URL:https://www.newyorker.com/science/annals-of-artificial-intelligence/there-is-no-ai

3 In '*Explaining decisions made with AI*', the UK Information Commissioner's Office (ICO) defines a 'black box' model as any AI system whose inner workings and rationale are opaque or inaccessible to human understanding. These systems may include: (1) neural networks (including recurrent and convolutional neural nets); (2) ensemble methods (an algorithmic technique such as the random forest method that strengthens an overall prediction by combining and aggregating the results of several or many different base models); and (3) support vector machines (a classifier that uses a special type of mapping function to build a divider between two sets of features in a high dimensional space). For further information, see: ICO and The Alan Turing Institute, '*Explaining decisions made with AI*' (2022). URL: https://ico.org.uk/for-organisations/uk-gdpr-guidance-and-resources/artificial-intelligence/explaining-decisions-made-with-artificial-intelligence/.

generative AI creates and amplifies legal risks in several ways. First, litigation risk arises if the AI model produces inaccurate, inconsistent, or harmful results, which gives rise to potential disputes with customers, third parties, and model providers regarding claims for, among other things, breach of contract, negligence, product liability, or misrepresentation. Secondly, in the context of data protection principles, the two most important issues for a deployer of a generative AI system are: (i) transparency of information to individuals who use the AI or may be affected by the AI; and (ii) assessing fairness and bias in the AI, both of which are particularly difficult in the context of jello feature.

28.03 Turning to the second feature, the reference to *human* data is crucial. The mathematical mixing not only of work done by human minds but also of information about individuals creates significant legal risk in the context of intellectual property and data protection laws. As regards intellectual property, the key risks for a deployer of a generative AI model are: (i) the risk of infringing third party intellectual property rights ('infringement risk'); (ii) the risk to the deployer's own intellectual property, including data leakage ('internal risk'); and (iii) the risk that the deployer may not own its AI-generated output ('ownership risk'). There are also significant questions about privacy and data protection, to the extent that the AI model has been trained using personal data or a user inputs personal data as a prompt.

28.04 These legal risks lie on a spectrum that depend on the organisation's role(s) in the AI value chain.[4] Model development or customisation provides increased control over an AI model, but alters and, in most cases, amplifies the nature of the legal risks. If, for example, an organisation licenses a large language model (LLM) and customises it by fine-tuning for a particular use case, who is liable for any inherent bias in the model that results in a bad outcome for that organisation's customers? Is it the provider of the LLM or the organisation, or both? In practice, there may be multiple relevant actors across the AI value chain that have a causal nexus to a particular AI system, each of which could be liable depending on the use case, jurisdiction, and fact pattern.

28.05 Of course, developers of generative AI models have a different relationship with that vast mountain of human data. Particularly for large, general purpose AI models, more training data increases the probability of better outputs (although quality of output will also be affected by data quality and composition). As such, there is an incentive for AI developers to use as much good quality data as possible to train their models. This leads to additional

4 By the AI value chain, we mean the complex sequence of activities and actors involved in the development, distribution and deployment of AI models. The AI value chain can vary depending on the type, purpose and complexity of the AI model, among other things. The complex nexus of relationships and dependencies between upstream and downstream companies, and the differing levels of control different actors have in respect of an AI model, presents challenges for AI governance and regulation. For further reading see: Küspert, Moës, Dunlop, *The value chain of general-purpose AI*, (Ada Lovelace Institute 2023). URL: https://www.adalovelaceinstitute.org/blog/value-chain-general-purpose-ai/.

legal risk for developers in relation to the data used to train an AI model. These include intellectual property infringement and breach of contract risks (where data is obtained without permission), privacy and data protection risks (where the training data includes personal data) and breach of regulatory responsibilities. Similarly, developers face enhanced obligations to explain the AI model and to manage the risks of the potential bad outcomes for deployers of the AI model. Generally, an increase in the capabilities of an AI model and the quantity of the data used leads to an increase in the AI model's complexity, which in turn makes the model harder to explain. This is the tension – often there is a choice between the competency and transparency of an AI model, but it is very challenging to achieve both.

28.06 The consequence of failing to manage these legal risks is potential litigation or regulatory sanction. Both the litigation and regulatory landscape are changing rapidly, as courts and legislatures try to adapt to the novel and complex issues raised by generative AI. Across jurisdictions, intellectual property laws and guidance in the context of generative AI are nascent. It is likely that substantial changes in legislation and case law will materialise over the coming years, which may affect the nature and extent of these risks. Conversely, data protection regulators have for years been very active in considering the data processing activities inherent in AI, and in many cases will be tasked with applying those regulatory principles to AI systems more broadly. Finally, the arrival of AI-specific regulation, such as the EU AI Act,[5] heralds a new era of complex compliance obligations with different jurisdictions taking different approaches to regulation of AI systems.

SCOPE

28.07 This chapter examines the key features of generative AI that create legal risks for organisations that deploy generative AI systems at an enterprise level. As lawyers, we are naturally focused on LLMs, which are a type of generative AI model trained on large amounts of text data.[6] This chapter will do the same.

5 The text of the AI Act used to prepare this note is the version of 2 February 2024. This version was approved by the European Parliament on 13 March 2024 (European Parliament legislative resolution of 13 March 2024 on the proposal for a regulation of the European Parliament and of the Council establishing a common framework for media services in the internal market (European Media Freedom Act) and amending Directive 2010/13/EU (COM(2022)0457 – C9-0309/2022 – 2022/0277(COD))). It should be noted, however, that small revisions and modifications to the text remain possible.

6 The Alan Turing Institute defines an 'LLM' as a 'deep neural network that has been trained on very large corpora of text, sourced primarily from text-rich sites on the Internet such as Reddit and Wikipedia. An LLM learns patterns in language, such as the likelihood of certain words following others in a sentence, using techniques like next token prediction or masked language modelling to generate or complete text. An LLM does not understand the semantic meaning of a sentence in a linguistic sense, but rather calculates mathematically what the most likely next word should be based on the input to the model.' Adam, C and Richard Carter, 'Large Language Models and Intelligence Analysis,' CETaS Expert Analysis (2023). URL: https://cetas.turing.ac.uk/publications/large-language-models-and-intelligence-analysis.

28.08 Whilst most of the other chapters of this book focus on cyber security, we will not cover the general cyber security and data protection issues that apply to *any* technology deployment (eg, data breaches or hostile attacks) but instead will focus on other risks that arise specifically from the features of generative AI and its deployment by organisations[7].

28.09 We recognise that organisations are increasingly developing or customising their own AI models, rather than relying solely on deploying an AI model 'off the shelf' from an AI Software-as-a-service provider. This chapter will also consider legal risk in the context of the growing trend of businesses training or customising their own AI models for more specialised use cases.[8]

28.10 We will consider the legal issues and risks that have general application across industry sectors, and not delve into the specific application to any particular industry sector or use case. The widespread adoption of AI has become a global phenomenon. We have attempted to give a flavour of the position not just under the laws of England & Wales, but also in the EU and in the US.[9] This better reflects the reality of deployment of AI by organisations that are having to grapple with a cross-jurisdictional nexus of AI systems and actors in the AI value chain.

28.11 AI is quickly becoming ubiquitous, which means that it is impacting almost every aspect of law, from employment, to antitrust, to the detailed nuances of financial services regulation and securities law. In order to provide substantive analysis in one chapter, we have chosen to focus on areas that are most impacted; specifically: intellectual property, privacy and data protection, and litigation. Given the rapid rate of change, our analysis is intentionally thematic, with a view to identifying core principles of legal risk.[10]

7 For the purposes of identifying those legal risks, we assume that the organisation has ensured data security from an operational perspective as part of the information security requirements and enterprise onboarding process.

8 A note on terminology. The EU AI Act defines: a 'deployer' as any natural or legal person, public authority, agency or other body using an AI system under its authority except where the AI system is used in the course of a personal non-professional activity; and 'provider' as a natural or legal person, public authority, agency or other body that develops an AI system or a general purpose AI model or that has an AI system or a general purpose AI model developed and places them on the market or puts the system into service under its own name or trademark, whether for payment or free of charge. We have chosen not to refer throughout to AI 'deployer' and AI 'provider' are not universally applicable to principles outside of the scope of the EU AI Act. Where relevant, however, we do refer to the appropriate regulatory definitions. Where we refer to an AI 'user', we mean any person that uses an AI system. The term AI 'developer' refers generally to any person or entity that creates, designs, or trains an AI system. These terms are not mutually exclusive.

9 When we refer to the 'EU' and the 'US' in this chapter, we recognise that these are not specific legal jurisdictions. Where it is possible to identify common principles across individual jurisdictions, we have attempted to do so. Therefore, additional considerations or nuances may apply to specific jurisdictions within these regions.

10 For example, we have deliberately limited our reference to the dynamic landscape of ongoing litigation with a view to preserving the relevance of this chapter.

28.12 Finally, we are very grateful to our global team of experts at A&O Shearman for their invaluable contributions to the writing of this chapter.

AI-SPECIFIC REGULATION: A RISK-BASED APPROACH?

28.13 In response to the rapid increase in development and deployment of AI systems across the globe, regulators are considering initiatives to regulate the use of AI to protect the rights and interests of individuals and society. While these initiatives differ in their scope, priorities, and stage of development, they share some common themes. These include: (i) the protection of human rights and individuals from the harmful or discriminatory effects of AI, especially in high-risk or sensitive domains such as law enforcement, health, or democracy; (ii) the application of data ethics principles such as fairness and transparency in the design, development, and deployment of AI systems, and the potential trade-offs between these principles and the technical performance or competitiveness of AI; (iii) focus on the distribution of power and responsibility among the actors involved in the AI value chain, and the potential for market concentration or extraterritorial impact of AI; and (iv) requirements and oversight based on the use case for AI and associated risk level. Most jurisdictions support innovation (with the accompanying expectations around economic benefits), and so recognise the need for proportionality and flexibility in their approach to AI regulation. Given the different stages of development of AI-specific regulation in the EU, UK, and US, this section will focus on the high-level themes that provide context to the legal risks identified through this chapter. AI-specific regulation supplements existing regulatory frameworks, which we will consider in later sections.

EU AI Act

28.14 The EU AI Act sets out a comprehensive horizontal legal framework that aims to regulate the design, development, and deployment of AI systems in the EU. The EU AI Act has a very wide territorial and extraterritorial scope and addresses each component in the AI value chain: from developers, importers, exporters to deployers of AI systems. It covers a wide range of AI systems,[11] and introduces different levels of obligations or restrictions depending on the risk and impact of the AI system.

28.15 At a high-level, the EU AI Act identifies three core categories of risk: prohibited AI practices, high-risk systems, and limited risk systems. Prohibited AI practices are those that violate fundamental rights or pose unacceptable risks,

11 The EU AI Act defines an 'AI system' as 'a machine-based system designed to operate with varying levels of autonomy and that may exhibit adaptiveness after deployment and that, for explicit or implicit objectives, infers, from the input it receives, how to generate outputs such as predictions, content, recommendations, or decisions that can influence physical or virtual environments', following the OECD definition set out in the OECD AI Principles (2019). URL https://oecd.ai/en/ai-principles.

including, but not limited to, biometric categorisation systems, classification of individuals based on their social behaviour or characteristics (or 'social scoring'), real-time remote biometric identification systems in publicly accessible spaces, and AI systems that exploit any vulnerabilities of a person or specific group of persons due to their age, disability or specific social or economic situation.[12] High-risk AI systems are classified according to two criteria: (i) AI systems which are products or safety components of products that need a third-party check for EU compliance (such as toys, medical devices, or machinery); and (ii) AI systems which are used for purposes that are assumed to be high-risk, unless proven otherwise, including in relation to biometrics; safety components in critical infrastructure; education; employment; access to essential private or public services; law enforcement; migration, asylum and border control management; and justice and democratic processes.[13] 'Providers' of high-risk AI systems must comply with strict requirements regarding risk management, the quality and relevance of data sets used, technical documentation and record-keeping, transparency and the provision of information to deployers, human oversight, and robustness, accuracy and cybersecurity.[14] 'Deployers' of high risk AI systems must also comply with certain obligations, which can broadly be divided into four broad categories, as follows: (i) governance, (ii) monitoring, (iii) transparency; and (iv) the requirement to perform a data protection impact assessment and a fundamental rights impact assessment.[15] Limited risk systems are AI systems that have a specific purpose and some, albeit not high, risk. For example, for deployers, the most important limited risk AI systems are (a) emotion recognition systems or biometric categorisation systems,[16] and (b) AI systems that can generate or manipulate content such as videos, images, or text.[17]

28.16 The EU AI Act also introduces specific rules for AI systems based on models that can perform many different tasks, called general purpose AI models.[18] Note that large generative AI models, such as GPT-4, are a typical example of a general purpose AI model, given that they allow for flexible generation of content that can readily accommodate a wide range of distinctive tasks.[19] These specific rules include requirements for 'providers' to publish clear summaries of the data used to train the general purpose AI model, provide technical documentation,

12 For a full list of prohibited practices, see Article 5 of the EU AI Act.
13 For a full list of high-risk systems, see Article 6 of the EU AI Act.
14 See Title III, Chapter 2 of the EU AI Act.
15 See Article 29–29a of the EU AI Act.
16 See Article 52(2), EU AI Act.
17 See Article 52(3), EU AI Act.
18 The EU AI Act defines a 'general purpose AI model' as 'an AI model, including when trained with a large amount of data using self-supervision at scale, that displays significant generality and is capable to competently perform a wide range of distinct tasks regardless of the way the model is placed on the market and that can be integrated into a variety of downstream systems or applications. This does not cover AI models that are used before release on the market for research, development and prototyping activities.'
19 See Recital 60(c) of the EU AI Act.

respect the EU law on copyright and related rights,[20] add watermarking for content produced by the model so that it is clear to recipients that it is AI generated, and allow evaluation of the model by the European Commission.[21]

UK White Paper

28.17 The UK White Paper on AI regulation, published in March 2023,[22] proposed a 'pro-innovation' approach to AI regulation based on five cross-sectoral principles: (i) safety, security, robustness; (ii) transparency, explainability; (iii) fairness; (iv) accountability and governance; and (v) contestability and redress. The UK Government published its response to the White Paper in February 2024,[23] after a public consultation and the UK AI Safety Summit.[24] The response outlined the UK's aim to be a global leader in safe AI development and deployment, and announced various initiatives to support AI innovation, regulation, and collaboration. The UK Government decided not to introduce new general AI legislation, but to adopt a context- and sector-based approach, using existing regulators and regulatory frameworks and providing guidance for those regulators. The response document also acknowledged the unique challenges of highly capable general purpose AI models, and indicated that targeted regulatory requirements for developers of these systems were under consideration.

US Presidential Executive Order

28.18 The US Presidential Executive Order on AI, issued by President Biden in October 2023,[25] aims to govern the development and use of AI safely and responsibly. Its scope is inherently limited to government agencies, contracts,

20 See Article 52(c) of the EU AI Act. Providers of general purpose AI models should put in place a policy to respect Union law on copyright and related rights, in particular to identify and respect the reservations of rights expressed by rightholders pursuant to Article 4(3) of Directive (EU) 2019/790.

21 See Title VIIIA, Chapter 2 of the EU AI Act.

22 UK Department for Science, Innovation, & Technology, UK White Paper, '*A pro-innovation approach to AI regulation*' (2023). URL: https://www.gov.uk/government/publications/ai-regulation-a-pro-innovation-approach.

23 UK Department for Science, Innovation, & Technology, Consultation outcome, '*A pro-innovation approach to AI regulation: government response*' (2024). URL: https://www.gov.uk/government/consultations/ai-regulation-a-pro-innovation-approach-policy-proposals/outcome/a-pro-innovation-approach-to-ai-regulation-government-response#:~:text=The%20white%20paper%20proposed%20five,and%20leading%20AI%20safety%20experts.

24 The AI Safety Summit 2023 was a major global event that took place on the 1 and 2 November 2023 at Bletchley Park, Buckinghamshire. URL: https://www.gov.uk/government/topical-events/ai-safety-summit-2023.

25 Executive Order on the Safe, Secure, and Trustworthy Development and Use of Artificial Intelligence (2023). URL: https://www.whitehouse.gov/briefing-room/presidential-actions/2023/10/30/executive-order-on-the-safe-secure-and-trustworthy-development-and-use-of-artificial-intelligence/.

projects, and benefit programs over which the President has authority.[26] It establishes a coordinated federal government-wide approach based on eight guiding principles, such as AI safety and security, innovation and competition, civil rights and privacy, and global leadership. The Executive Order directs various government agencies to develop guidelines, standards, regulations, and best practices for AI in different sectors and domains, such as critical infrastructure, cybersecurity, healthcare, education, and criminal justice. It also creates a White House Artificial Intelligence Council to oversee and coordinate federal AI policies and initiatives. The order recognises the potential benefits and risks of AI and calls for collaboration with Congress, the technology industry, and international partners to advance and govern AI in accordance with democratic values and human rights.

GENERAL LITIGATION RISK

28.19 Generative AI leads to litigation risk in different contexts.[27] This section will focus on some examples of the general litigation risks, in large part arising from the black box problem. We will consider these risks from the perspective of an organisation using AI at an enterprise level in the context of potential disputes with customers, third parties and developers.

Disputes with customers

28.20 A deployer of generative AI may face legal risks in the context of disputes with customers, especially if the AI output is flawed, inaccurate, or discriminatory. Moreover, the difference in output from the same input presents difficulty in the litigation context. For example, this may evidentially be relevant if an AI chatbot gives two customers different financial advice to the same question, and one of the customers has a bad outcome in comparison to the other.

26 The Executive Order sets the stage for substantial federal oversight over the development and use of AI. Because it is an Executive Order – rather than legislation passed by Congress – the Executive Order's immediate effect is largely limited to the government agencies, contracts, projects, and benefit programs over which the President has authority as head of the Executive Branch. But the Executive Order lays the groundwork for a broader policy framework that the White House aims to implement through legislation. Further, the Executive Order does in some instances direct federal agencies to apply their existing legal powers to regulate AI. By way of example, the Executive Order directs the Secretary of Commerce, in accordance with the Defense Production Act, to require developers of large, sophisticated AI models to provide information concerning the ownership, training, development, and production of the models to the government on an ongoing basis.

27 We will address the types of risks that arise in the context of intellectual property and data protection disputes later in this chapter.

28.21 In the context of an organisation using generative AI as an internal resource to support the services it offers to its customers, disputes may arise in the following circumstances:[28]

- *Contractual restrictions.* The organisation may be subject to contractual restrictions on how it uses generative AI to provide services to customers. For example, it may be prohibited from using it, obliged to disclose its use, or restricted from using customer data with it. Not adhering to these terms would be a breach of contract and may give rise to the right to terminate. In addition, customers may have contracted based on the organisation's assurance of not using generative AI, which could give rise to a claim for misrepresentation or negligent misstatement.
- *Flawed services.* If the services delivered are flawed due to reliance on generative AI,[29] the ways in which an organisation could be held liable are the same as they would have been without the use of generative AI, if you were, say, using an out-of-date textbook (ie, primarily contractual and tortious). There are not additional legal risks, though there may be practical ones. If the organisation provides a service that is substandard it cannot point to the generative AI as a way of escaping liability.
- *Discrimination.* A dispute for discrimination may arise if an AI system treats different customers differently. For example, a bank using AI to make credit decisions would, quite properly, discriminate between certain customers. However, the black box problem presents a particularly thorny issue if that bank is required to explain the rationale for a decision. For individuals, there will be equality and data protection laws to consider,[30] regulated sectors typically have rules expressly prohibiting discrimination, and consumer legislation often requires that consumers are treated fairly.[31] Additionally, if the company is in a dominant position there may be anti-trust restrictions to comply with.[32]

28 Other scenarios may be relevant, including for misleading advertisement where systems might be described or marketed as artificially intelligent even though they are not that different from traditional systems. This is a particular focus of the Federal Trade Commission in the US.

29 For example, consider a bank supplying information to a customer about an investment opportunity in circumstances where the information has been generated by AI is inaccurate and has not been checked.

30 For example, in the UK, the Equality Act 2010 legally protects people from discrimination in the workplace and in wider society.

31 For example, in the UK, Financial Conduct Authority's Handbook of rules and guidance includes a requirement for regulated firms to make sure customers are treated fairly. Principle 6 says: 'A firm must pay due regard to the interests of its customers and treat them fairly'.

32 The considerations under US laws will be very similar. this is an area of law which is not harmonised in the EU, so the analysis must be done on a country-by-country basis. Under EU law more broadly, there is no general legal requirement to treat customers equally, provided that you do not discriminate in a manner that is legally prohibited, such as: (i) on the basis of protected characteristics (eg, sex, gender, ethnical origin, etc); or (ii) harms the internal market (eg, by discriminating depending on the country of the customer). However, discrimination is a significant focus of the EU AI Act.

28.22 In the context of an organisation deploying a generative AI system as a service directly to customers, disputes may arise if the service that the AI system provides is flawed. For example, if an organisation deploys a customer-facing chatbot, who is liable if that chatbot makes a mistake?[33] If the customer is a business, an organisation might include disclaimers or try to limit or exclude liability, or include non-reliance provisions. Some jurisdictions (eg, England & Wales) still impose restrictions on what liability can be excluded. For example, the Unfair Contract Terms Act 1977 requires the exclusion of liability for negligence to be reasonable. However, a distinction is drawn between clauses which exclude liability and clauses which define the terms or basis upon which the parties are conducting their business. If the customer is a consumer, then there are typically significant restrictions preventing contractual protections from being effective. For example, in England & Wales provisions which exclude or limit liability for breach of statutorily implied terms that what is being provided is of satisfactory quality, fit for its purpose, as described, and/or provided with reasonable skill and care, will be unenforceable.[34]

Disputes with third parties

28.23 One type of dispute that may arise with third parties is for defamation. This may arise when an organisation deploys an AI system directly to customers, and that AI system generates an output that is defamatory about a third party. For example, a chatbot that summarises legal cases may falsely accuse a named third party of embezzlement. There are a number of arguments the organisation may want to make under English law. However, the position has not been tested before the English courts, and this is a novel and uncertain area of the law.

33 A recent decision from Canada's Civil Resolution Tribunal (*Moffatt v Air Canada*, 2024 BCCRT 149) illustrates this scenario neatly, and likely reflects the approach that an English, US and EU court would take. The facts were that a customer asked Air Canada's chatbot if there was a reduced rate for flights booked for reasons of bereavement. The chatbot indicated that there was, and that it could be applied after a flight had been booked. This was not correct. Customers needed to apply beforehand. When Air Canada refused to apply the reduced rate the customer (who represented himself) issued an online claim with the tribunal. Air Canada argued, in effect, that it should not be held liable for what the chatbot said and that the chatbot should (somehow) be responsible for its own actions as a separate legal entity. The Tribunal said this was a 'remarkable submission' and that Air Canada was responsible for all the information on its website (whether the information came from a static page or a chatbot). It had not taken reasonable care to ensure its chatbot was accurate. It was liable for negligent misrepresentation and ordered to pay damages for the difference between the price paid for the flights and the price that would have been paid had a bereavement discount been applied.

34 In the US (New York and Delaware) the position is similar save that there are no statutory limitations or reasonableness test and with careful drafting sophisticated parties have generally free to limit or even eliminate a great deal of their liability. In the EU, in relation to businesses, the rules on restricting liability vary from country to country but most national tests provide that the liability limitations cannot go so far as to hollow out the essential contractual obligations, meaning that if the liability exclusions (whatever their form) are so extensive that a party could not perform its essential contractual obligations and not be liable for it, such liability exemptions are considered null. In relation to consumers, the EU rules are nearly identical to the UK position and significantly restrict the possibility to limit liability.

28.24 First, pointing to a combination of the terms of use (eg, that prohibits users from enquiring about living individuals), a warning that the chatbot cannot be guaranteed to tell the truth, and the fact the public knows that generative AI hallucinates, the organisation may seek to argue that statement is not defamatory on the basis that the statement does not lower the reputation of the victim in the eyes of so-called 'right-thinking members of the public', the victim has not suffered serious harm, or the true meaning of the statement (when coupled with the disclaimer) is not defamatory.

28.25 Secondly, the organisation may try to argue that it is entitled to rely on certain defences that are available to intermediaries (although this is untested and may well be difficult given the AI has generated the content and so is not entirely passive in the process).

28.26 If the customer has deliberately sought to manipulate the chatbot to provoke a defamatory output, a court or tribunal is likely to be unsympathetic to any claim. The risks are greater if the customer has complied with the terms of use.

28.27 If the customer, in turn, posts the defamatory output on, say, social media, the customer will be liable for that publication. Whether the company might be liable for the original publication comes down to a question of reasonable foreseeability (if the claim is based only on the original publication) or whether the company intended or authorised the republication (if the claim is for re-publication). The company can fortify its position by making expressly clear to chatbot users that it does not authorise the repetition or publication of the chatbot's output.[35]

Disputes with foundation model providers

28.28 Finally, disputes with foundation model providers may arise, for example, if licensing terms are not given careful consideration. For example, usage rights over inputs and outputs are likely to be a key area for negotiation between foundation model providers licensing an AI system and their licensees. Model providers are likely to want to use inputs and outputs to further train and improve the AI model. Licensees will be concerned about confidentiality, intellectual

35 In the US, for a tort claim of this nature, as under English law, contractual exclusions are unlikely to be effective against third parties. These claims are also untested in US courts and will give rise to interesting questions. A similar analysis would apply under New York law. For an original claim, in short, the analysis would come down to foreseeability and, if it came to it, damages are likely to be low. New York generally does not recognise liability for republication (although the courts have suggested there may be exceptions). Similarly, under EU law, contractual exclusions and disclaimers are unlikely to be effective against third parties. The EU is currently consulting on Liability Rules for Artificial Intelligence, which would shed more light on these questions. For further reading see: https://commission.europa.eu/business-economy-euro/doing-business-eu/contract-rules/digital-contracts/liability-rules-artificial-intelligence_en.

property rights and personal data. There is the risk that, notwithstanding contractual commitments and any agreement as to operational protections, the model provider either deliberately or inadvertently does make use of licensee inputs and outputs in breach of contract. In that scenario, then the most helpful form of relief to the user is likely to be an injunction, but other forms of relief (such as damages or an account of profits) may also be possible options (albeit they may be quite limited).

OVERVIEW OF DATA RISKS

28.29 Data protection risk arises where personal data is processed to develop or deploy an AI model. Data protection laws, such as the EU GDPR[36] and UK GDPR[37] and the CCPA,[38] impose various obligations on the parties involved in the processing of personal data, which includes the AI deployer as well as the AI provider.

28.30 Data protection regulators investigate and monitor how personal data is used in connection with AI systems. If found to be in breach of data protection laws, this can result in fines (potentially substantial ones) and liability to pay damages to affected data subjects. This risk is exacerbated in jurisdictions where class actions are available. In addition to legal and financial risk, ethical and reputational risks can also arise. For instance, overly extensive use of AI for monitoring or profiling purposes could be perceived as invasive and may damage the trust and loyalty of customers or employees.

28.31 The data protection risk lies largely with the AI provider in relation to the developing and training of the AI model. However, data protection risk will also arise for the AI deployer, for example, where the deployer provides personal data to train or fine-tune the AI model, or submits personal data to the AI system as part of a prompt.

36 EU GDPR means the General Data Protection Regulation (Regulation (EU) 2016/679) of the European Parliament and of the Council of 27 April 2016 on the protection of natural persons with regard to the processing of personal data and on the free movement of such data, and repealing Directive 95/46/EC (General Data Protection Regulation), [2016] OJ L119/1.

37 UK GDPR means the General Data Protection Regulation (Regulation (EU) 2016/679), as amended and incorporated into domestic law by the European Union (Withdrawal) Act 2018, as further amended by the European Union (Withdrawal Agreement) Act 2020 and the Data Protection, Privacy and Electronic Communications (Amendments etc.) (EU Exit) Regulations 2019, as amended by the Data Protection, Privacy and Electronic Communications (Amendments etc.)(EU Exit) Regulations 2020.

38 CCPA means the California Consumer Privacy Act, 2018 Cal. Legis. Serv. Ch. 55 (A.B. 375) (WEST). All citations to the CCPA are to Section 3, Title 1.81.5 of the CCPA, added to Part 4 of Division 3 of the California Civil Code.

Factors affecting data risk

28.32 It is important to recognise that data risk lies on a spectrum, and there are a number of variables that can amplify or minimise the risk. These variables include: (i) the nature and volume of data processed, (ii) whether any sensitive data is involved, (iii) the jurisdiction(s) in which the data is processed, (iv) the purpose(s) for processing, (v) the impact on the individual or society, (vi) whether the model has been fine-tuned for the specific use case, (vii) the types of security measures in place, and (viii) whether processing involves automated decision making with a legal or other significant effect and the level of human involvement in the decision-making process.

28.33 From a data protection perspective, the use of AI systems will exacerbate existing data risks, rather than introduce new ones. The level of data risk will depend on the specific use case and the guidance or rules that are implemented alongside the AI system.[39] There are several data protection requirements that are nuanced in the context of AI systems, and on which data protection authorities have focused, including individual rights requests, data minimisation, accuracy and security. However, the two core areas that are persistently of concern for regulators, AI providers and deployers are transparency, and fairness and bias.

TRANSPARENCY

28.34 There are a number of transparency obligations under the UK and EU GDPR as well as under the EU AI Act. One of the key GDPR principles is that individuals must be informed about the way in which their data is processed, including information about the consequences for them as individuals (the 'transparency' principle).

28.35 The concept of 'transparency' goes much further than simply updating a privacy notice; in addition to the underlying individuals whose personal data is processed ('data subjects') there are various internal and external stakeholders who will need to be provided with information in relation to the AI system. For example, explanations will need to be documented for internal compliance management purposes (eg, to record a privacy-by-design approach), explanations may need to be given by AI deployers to justify design decisions to experts (eg, regulators or courts) who may challenge the use of the AI system, or detailed information about system choices may need to be given to data scientists to test fairness and outcomes.[40] The type of transparency needed in a given

39 For example, in the context of data protection risks, a potentially *low* risk scenario would be the use of an LLM by an in in-house legal team as a tool for drafting contracts and legal memorandums. This will involve very little personal data such as log-in credentials of the employee using the system. Conversely, an example of a *high* risk scenario would be the use of an LLM to filter CVs for recruitment purposes.

40 References to 'transparency' in this note refer to both internal and external transparency.

circumstance will therefore be context-specific, and will be influenced by the type of stakeholder involved.

Transparency and the GDPR

28.36 The GDPR does not explicitly refer to AI, as it is technology neutral. However, the GDPR will apply to AI systems that involve the processing of personal data and, in particular, where that processing involves automated decision making which has legal or other significant effects on individuals. In the context of the transparency principle, the role of the parties under the GDPR (as a data controller or processor) will affect how transparency obligations are discharged to data subjects and which party is responsible for those obligations.

28.37 To the extent the AI system operates as a black box that makes it difficult to identify the rationale for any given output, it can be difficult for the AI deployer to give individuals meaningful information about the AI model's operations and the envisaged consequences for the individual. Where the use case concerns making an automated decision that has a legal or other significant effect on the individual, under the GDPR, AI deployers need to provide 'meaningful information about the logic involved and the significance and envisaged consequence for the individual', both in privacy notices and in response to a data subject access request.[41]

28.38 An example of what may constitute a 'legal or other significant effect' is where an AI model is used to generate automated decisions about credit applications based on the applicants' personal and financial data (eg, income, debt, credit history, and employment status) and the decisions: (i) are solely based on the output of the AI model; and (ii) do not involve any human intervention or oversight.[42]

28.39 To discharge this transparency obligation, AI deployers would need to obtain sufficient information from the AI provider to provide meaningful information to individuals. The UK Information Commissioner's Office (**ICO**) has published some helpful guidance[43] on the dimensions of effective explainability, setting out a number of different types of explanation that could to be given to individuals, including explanations of the reasons that led to a decision and what steps have been taken to consider and monitor the impact

41 For example, relevant provisions under the UK GDPR: Article 22(1) and (4), Articles 13–15, Article 35, and Article 40.

42 For example, see UK GDPR, Recital 71: 'the data subject should have the right not to be subject to a decision, which may include a measure, evaluating personal aspects relating to him or her which is based solely on automated processing and which produces legal effects concerning him or her or similarly significantly affects him or her, such as automatic refusal of an online credit application or e-recruiting practices without any human intervention.'

43 ICO and The Alan Turing Institute, '*Explaining decisions made with AI*' (2022). URL: https://ico.org.uk/for-organisations/uk-gdpr-guidance-and-resources/artificial-intelligence/explaining-decisions-made-with-artificial-intelligence/. In particular, see p 21.

of a decision made by an AI system on an individual, who was responsible for making the decision, what data has been used, what steps to ensure fairness have been taken, and so on.

Transparency and the EU AI Act

28.40 The EU AI Act makes clear that transparency is a key requirement in respect of certain AI systems. According to the EU AI Act, at a high-level, 'transparency means that AI systems are developed and used in a way that allows appropriate traceability and explainability, while making humans aware that they communicate or interact with an AI system, as well as duly informing deployers of the capabilities and limitations of that AI system and affected persons about their rights'.[44] In particular, there are a couple of key elements to consider in the context of transparency:

- *Restrictions on high-risk AI systems.* The EU AI Act contains specific transparency requirements for high-risk AI systems to avoid such systems becoming incomprehensible or too complex for natural persons;[45] and
- *Transparency obligations for general purpose AI models.* The EU AI Act also contains further requirements for AI systems which are classified as 'general purpose AI'.[46]

28.41 Under the EU AI Act, transparency obligations are similar to those in the GDPR but not identical. There are two main points to note. First, the EU AI Act imposes some limited transparency obligations on AI deployers in the context of high-risk systems. For example, deployers who are employers must inform workers representatives and the affected workers that they will be subject to the system prior to putting it into service or using a high-risk AI system at the workplace.[47]

28.42 Second, the EU AI Act is not fully aligned with other EU rules. For example, the EU AI Act states that if certain high-risk AI systems are used by organisations as a basis for making a decision that significantly affects an

44 See Recital 14(a), EU AI Act.

45 See Article 13(1)-(2) of the EU AI Act: 'High-risk AI systems shall be designed and developed in such a way to ensure that their operation is sufficiently transparent to enable deployers to interpret the system's output and use it appropriately... High-risk AI systems shall be accompanied by instructions for use in an appropriate digital format or otherwise that include concise, complete, correct and clear information that is relevant, accessible and comprehensible to users.'

46 See Article 52(c) of the EU AI Act for specific transparency obligations applicable to general purpose AI models. Note that certain exceptions apply where that general purpose AI model is accessible to the public via an open source license (provided that such open source general purpose AI model does not pose systemic risks).

47 See Article 29(5)(a). Additional obligations apply where deployers of a high-risk system are bodies governed by public law or private operators providing public services and operators deploying high-risk systems.

individual (whether or not those decisions are fully automated), that individual has the right to obtain a clear and meaningful explanation of the role of the AI system in the decision making, the main parameters of the decision taken, and the related input data.[48] The existing GDPR rules for automated decision making only apply to *fully automated* decisions that are taken without any human intervention.

Transparency and US law

28.43 The US does not have a federal-level data protection law.[49] In the absence of comprehensive federal legislation, there is a patchwork of state laws that relate to data protection and AI. The concept of transparency is a key element of the US state laws that have been passed. This transparency obligation, however, only applies to a limited sub-set of companies that fall within the scope of the general privacy laws in California, Connecticut, Colorado and Virginia.[50]

Transparency obligations in practice

28.44 Whilst there is overlap in transparency requirements in the GDPR and EU AI Act, the obligations in the EU AI Act are in many ways broader than those under the GDPR. For example, the automated individual decision making provision of the GDPR only applies in cases of fully automated decisions that are taken without any human intervention. In contrast, the obligations in the EU AI Act apply to decisions taken on the basis of an AI system, whether or not such decision is fully automated.[51] The challenge is therefore to understand how to discharge these obligations in practice, given that neither regulation specifies how deployers can actually ensure transparency, explainability or interpretability.

48 See Article 68(c) of the EU AI Act.

49 The American Data Protection and Privacy Act (H.R.8152 – American Data Privacy and Protection Act, 117th Congress (2021-2022). URL: https://www.congress.gov/bill/117th-congress/house-bill/8152) was introduced in the House of Representatives in June 2022. In December 2022, it was placed on the Union Calendar, and it is unclear whether it will advance in the 118th Congress.

50 Specific legislation includes: (i) the California Bolstering Online Transparency Act requires operators of sites, apps or social networks with 10 million or more monthly visitors to disclose to consumers any communications via bots in certain circumstances; (ii) the Illinois Video Interview Act requires employers to notify the applicant of AI use, explain how the AI works, and obtain their consent; (iii) a recent FTC decision also held that biometric data cannot be used to train AI without the user's prior consent; and (iv) enacted and soon to be enacted general state privacy laws in Colorado, Virginia, Connecticut and California require companies to give notice of use of AI for processing data, and permit consumers to opt-out of such practices in certain circumstances. Those circumstances typically include using data processed by AI to make a decision that results in the provision or denial of financial and lending services, housing, insurance, education enrolment or opportunity, employment opportunities, health care services or access to essential goods or services.

51 See Article 68(c) of the EU AI Act.

28.45 Data protection authorities (such as the ICO) have focused on, among other things, the need for the AI deployer to give individuals meaningful information about the logic involved and the significance and envisaged consequence for the individual.

28.46 Literature on trustworthy AI (for example guidance from the ICO,[52] the Alan Turing Institute,[53] the EU High-Level Expert Group on AI,[54] and the National Institute of Standards and Technology[55]) broadly identifies two components of 'transparency': (i) system transparency, and (ii) process transparency.

System transparency

28.47 This comprises information about the AI system's inner workings (ie, the types of information that the AI system uses in operation, the relationship between input and output data, and the conditions under which the AI system would produce a certain output). It can be difficult to provide system transparency where there are low levels of system interpretability, because the less interpretable the AI system is, the harder it can be to identify the rationale for its output, therefore making the AI system a 'black box'. AI systems can generally be difficult to interpret for two key reasons: (i) the AI system requires a specific skillset to interpret it; or (ii) the AI system is so complex that it cannot be fully interpreted notwithstanding the skillset.

Process transparency

28.48 This comprises information about the AI system's design, development, and deployment (but not its logic, which would be addressed as part of system transparency) to demonstrate that good governance processes have been implemented and best practice has been followed throughout the AI lifecycle. Process transparency encompasses a range of information relating to phases throughout the AI lifecycle:

- *Substantive information* to answer questions about substantive aspects of activities within a given lifecycle phase for an AI system, for example regarding how training data was collected at the testing stage and the sources of that data.

52 ICO and The Alan Turing Institute, '*Explaining decisions made with AI*' (2022). URL: https://ico.org.uk/for-organisations/uk-gdpr-guidance-and-resources/artificial-intelligence/explaining-decisions-made-with-artificial-intelligence/.

53 Ostmann, and Dorobantu, *AI in financial services* (The Alan Turing Institute2021). URL: https://doi.org/10.5281/zenodo.4916041.

54 Ethics Guidelines for Trustworthy AI, European Commission's High-Level Expert Group on AI. For further information, see: https://digital-strategy.ec.europa.eu/en/library/ethics-guidelines-trustworthy-ai.

55 Artificial Intelligence Risk Management Framework, NIST https://nvlpubs.nist.gov/nistpubs/ai/NIST.AI.100-1.pdf.

- *Procedural information* to answer questions about the procedures that were followed in performing the activities within a given lifecycle phase, for example how pre-processing of personal data was carried out at the design stage.
- *Governance information* to answer questions about governance arrangements for activities conducted within a lifecycle phase, for example what internal policies and procedures are in place at the deployment stage.
- *Information on adherence to norms and standards* refers to compliance with norms or standards in the design, development, and deployment of an AI system.

Types of explainability

28.49 One of the key measures for addressing system and process transparency, and therefore helping AI deployers to discharge their transparency obligations, is through explainability methods. A good understanding of the relevant stakeholders and audiences, and effective user engagement and consultation, will be crucial factors in successful implementation of explainability models.

28.50 There are six main types of explanation that can be process-based and provide process transparency, and/or that can provide system transparency and be outcome-based.[56] As mentioned above, the type of transparency needed in a given circumstance will be context-specific, and will be influenced by the type of stakeholder involved. Therefore, AI deployers will not need to use all of these explainability methods in respect of all internal and external stakeholders at all times.

1. *Rationale explanation.* A rationale explanation sets out the 'why?' of an AI decision with a view to helping an individual understand the reasons that led to a decision. It allows an individual to assess whether they believe the reasoning of an AI system of a decision is flawed.
2. *Responsibility explanation.* A responsibility explanation sets out who is involved in the development, management and implementation of an AI system, and who to contact for human review of a decision. This promotes accountability in the AI lifecycle.
3. *Data explanation.* A data explanation sets out what types of data have been used in a particular decision, including the sources of that data and reasons why that data has been used. This helps individuals understand how the AI system was trained and tested, and what data was used as part of a specific AI decision.

56 ICO and The Alan Turing Institute, '*Explaining decisions made with AI*' (2022). URL: https://ico.org.uk/for-organisations/uk-gdpr-guidance-and-resources/artificial-intelligence/explaining-decisions-made-with-artificial-intelligence/. In particular, see p 23.

4. *Fairness explanation.* A fairness explanation sets out the steps taken across the design and implementation of an AI system to ensure that the decisions it supports are generally unbiased and fair, and whether or not an individual has been treated equitably.
5. *Safety and performance explanation.* A safety and performance explanation sets out the steps taken across the design and implementation of an AI system to maximise the accuracy, reliability, security and robustness of its decisions and behaviours. This will help to provide reassurance to individuals that the AI system is secure and reliable and enable them to understand and challenge an AI decision if they think it is unreliable (for instance to allege it is unfair).
6. *Impact explanation.* An impact explanation sets out the steps taken across the design and implementation of an AI system to consider and monitor the impacts that the use of an AI system and its decisions has or may have on an individual and on the wider society. This will help individuals understand the consequences of a decision and why that decision was taken and enable them to decide whether they are prepared to be involved in the particular process.

FAIRNESS AND BIAS

28.51 Fairness is a key component of data protection laws, but also of many sets of AI ethics principles as well as in the EU AI Act, and various laws that have vertical application. It relates to both how one handles the processing, and the way the outcome affects individuals. In simple terms, the principle involves ensuring an AI model is fair on individuals. It typically includes non-discrimination, the avoidance of unfair bias, and other questions of differential treatment. Fairness is included as a principle in several legislative texts and initiatives, both in the US and in the EU.

28.52 In the context of GDPR, the principle of fairness is that personal data should not be used in a way that could have unjustified adverse effects on individuals or in ways that data subjects would not reasonably expect. Applied to AI models, this would also require that the AI system is sufficiently statistically accurate and avoids discrimination.

28.53 Fairness under data protection principles is different to 'algorithmic fairness', which data protection authorities, such as the ICO, see as a statistical approach to fairness that is concerned with the 'distribution of classifications or predictions leading to the real-world allocation of resources, opportunities or capabilities'.[57]

57 ICO, '*Guidance on AI and Data Protection*', (2023). See in particular p 56. URL: https://ico.org.uk/media/for-organisations/guide-to-data-protection/key-dp-themes/guidance-on-ai-and-data-protection-2-0.pdf.

28.54 Fairness and bias risks will vary depending on the variables listed in **28.32** above. As a user of AI systems it may be difficult to control the fairness or bias in the outputs when AI models are intrinsically shaped by the training data. However, guidance from data protection authorities in the UK and EU is that the person deciding the use case of the AI model would be ultimately responsible for the way that the AI model outcome affects individuals.

28.55 In the UK, for instance, the data protection regulator has recommended taking into account factors such as: (i) the underlying structures and dynamics of the environment in which the AI will be deployed; (ii) the implications of creating self-reinforcing feedback loops; (iii) the nature and scale of any potential harms to individuals resulting from the processing of their data; and (iv) how the AI user will make well-informed decisions based on rationality and causality rather than mere correlation.[58][59]

Fairness, bias and the EU AI Act

28.56 Fairness and bias are also key principles in the EU AI Act for certain AI systems considered to be high risk. While most of the fairness and bias obligations would apply to the AI provider,[60] certain limited obligations apply to an AI deployer where a deployer has control over the AI system – especially high-risk AI systems. If that's the case, then deployers have their own set of obligations to ensure fairness and avoid bias. Such obligations for deployers include: (i) to ensure that the data is relevant and sufficiently representative in light of the particular use case if an AI deployer has control over input data (such as prompts and, potentially, data used to fine-tune the system);[61] and (ii) deployers must put in place human oversight measures.[62]

58 ICO, '*What about fairness, bias and discrimination?*' (2023). See in particular p 57. URL: https://ico.org.uk/for-organisations/uk-gdpr-guidance-and-resources/artificial-intelligence/guidance-on-ai-and-data-protection/how-do-we-ensure-fairness-in-ai/what-about-fairness-bias-and-discrimination/.

59 Regarding fairness and bias in the US, there are currently only two enacted state laws that specifically address bias in the use of AI, although there are ten or so other bills that are pending: (i) Colorado SB 21-169 protects consumers from unfair discrimination in insurance practices via automated rate-setting mechanisms; and (ii) New York Local Law 144 states that employers must conduct bias audits of AI-enabled tools that are used for employment decisions.

60 See, for example, Article 10(f)-(fa) of the EU AI Act. As part of their data governance and management practices, providers are required to examine for possible biases that are likely to affect the health and safety of persons, negatively impact fundamental rights or lead to discrimination prohibited under Union law, especially where data outputs influence inputs for future operations. Where biases are identified, providers must take appropriate measures to detect, prevent, and mitigate those biases.

61 See Article 29(3) of the EU AI Act.

62 See Article 13(d) of the EU AI Act.

Fairness and bias during the process

28.57 Several institutions such as The Alan Turing Institute,[63] as well as data protection authorities, have identified four types of fairness in practice:

- *Data fairness*. The AI system is trained and tested on representative, relevant, sufficient, accurate, recent, appropriate, and generalisable datasets.[64]
- *Design fairness*. The model architectures do not include target variables, features, processes, parameters or analytical structures (correlations, interactions, and inferences) which are unreasonable, morally objectionable, or unjustifiable.
- *Outcome fairness*. The system should not have discriminatory or inequitable impacts on the lives of the people they affect. For example, the chatbot should not always direct website visitors of a certain ethnic origin, age, to the most expensive products or services.
- *Implementation fairness*. The system should be deployed by users who are sufficiently trained to implement them responsibly and without bias.

28.58 A key question is to what extent the deployer of the generative AI model could have any control over how fair or biased the system outputs actually are, given that fairness and bias in a system are intrinsically shaped by the quality of the training data? As explained above, the practical risk here will depend on the use case and the types of variables taken into account (eg, nature and volume of data processed).

28.59 Guidance from data protection authorities (such as the ICO) is that the provider, as the person deciding the use case of the model, would be ultimately responsible for the way that the model's outcome affects individuals, and algorithmic fairness is only one aspect of achieving a fair outcome. The ICO has therefore recommended taking into account factors such as:[65] (i) the underlying structures and dynamics of the environment the AI will be deployed in, (ii) the implications of creating self-reinforcing feedback loops, (iii) the nature and scale of any potential harms to individuals resulting from the processing of their data, and (iv) how well-informed decisions will be made based on rationality and causality rather than mere correlation. Having enough of an understanding of the characteristics in the model that could lead to unfair or biased outcomes can help to put in place measures to rebalance the risk when deploying the AI system.

63 Leslie, *Understanding artificial intelligence ethics and safety: A guide for the responsible design and implementation of AI systems in the public sector* (The Alan Turing Institute 2019). URL: https://doi.org/10.5281/zenodo.3240529.

64 For example, the HR LLM (see n 39) will ideally have been trained on data representative of the types of candidates that you want applying for a job.

65 ICO, '*Guidance on AI*', (2023). See in particular p 57. URL: https://ico.org.uk/media/for-organisations/uk-gdpr-guidance-and-resources/artificial-intelligence/guidance-on-ai-and-data-protection-2-0.pdf.

Selecting training data: ethical considerations

28.60 Selecting pre-training data for an AI model is not only a technical and legal question but also an ethical decision. In the context of selecting training data to train a generative AI model, a fundamental question from an ethical perspective is whether the data is relevant, accurate, and sufficient for the purposes for which the AI model is to be used. This includes consideration of the ethical elements of the principles of fairness and bias beyond the strict data protection concepts. In particular, what historical biases are embedded in the environment from which your data has been collected?

28.61 In addition, responsible use of training data concerns not only *what* the data is, but also *where* the data came from. The OECD's AI principle of 'Human-centred values and fairness' requires that 'AI actors' should respect the rule of law, human rights and democratic values, throughout the AI system lifecycle, including in relation to internationally recognised labour rights.[66] For example, some pre-training datasets may have been created or processed using manual human labour in poor working conditions. This raises ethical concerns about the exploitation and dignity of the workers, as well as the potential legal risks of violating labour laws, human rights standards. Where datasets are being acquired from third party sources, it is important to carefully assess the provenance of the pre-training datasets to ensure that they comply with the relevant ethical principles as well as wider consideration of the social and environmental impacts of the data selection. [67]

INTELLECTUAL PROPERTY INFRINGEMENT RISK

28.62 At their simplest, intellectual property rights relate to 'who should get credit for what'. The application of intellectual property rights to generative AI, poses significant legal and policy challenges. The question of who should be credited and rewarded for the outputs of generative AI has not been resolved by courts or legislatures in most jurisdictions. There is no clear consensus on how to balance these interests and values, and different approaches may have different implications for the development and use of generative AI.

28.63 In general terms, therefore, intellectual property infringement refers to certain (infringing) acts being performed without the consent of the owner of the relevant intellectual property right. In the context of generative AI, intellectual property infringement risk exists at the point of *training* and at the point of *use*. A mere deployer or user of AI, who is not involved in the training, is unlikely to be exposed directly to infringement claims at the point of *training*. However,

66 See human-centred values and fairness (Principle 1.2), OECD AI Principles, (2019). URL: https://oecd.ai/en/dashboards/ai-principles/P6.

67 See, for example, Partnership on AI's, '*Data Enrichment Sourcing Guidelines*', (2021). URL: https://partnershiponai.org/wp-content/uploads/2022/11/data-enrichment-guidelines.pdf.

infringement at the point of training exposes AI users indirectly to greater infringement risk at the point of *use*.

28.64 It is also helpful to draw a distinction between *legal risk* and *practical risk*. Legal risk is the risk of an infringement actually occurring. Practical risk is the risk of that infringing output being spotted by the rightsholder and the rightsholder subsequently taking action against the user. Infringement risk is highly fact-specific and the risk profile will be driven by the particular use case.

28.65 Further, intellectual property rights are national rights. As such, the laws for determining whether materials are protected, and whether any intellectual property rights in those materials have been infringed, will vary by jurisdiction.[68] On this basis, the risk profile for particular use cases will also vary by jurisdiction. Some examples are highlighted below in the context of US, English, and EU laws. The question of which jurisdiction would apply for web-based intellectual property infringement claims is complex, and would need to be considered on the particular facts.

Relevant intellectual property rights in training data

28.66 Intellectual property rights will likely be present in the data used by the AI developer to train and test the AI model, including copyright works, trade marks, design rights, moral rights, database rights and personality rights. Copyright protects forms of creative expression, including literary works (including code), artistic works and musical works. Generative AI models are likely to have been trained on data that consists primarily of copyright works.[69] Therefore, copyright is likely to result in the greatest infringement risk, and will be the focus here.[70]

68 In the context of copyright, the Berne Convention provides for a minimum level of protection for literary and artistic works in those countries that are signatories to it. Ultimately, whether a given work is protected in a certain jurisdiction (and the full extent of that protection) is a question for the law of that jurisdiction.

69 For example, on 17 January 2023, Getty Images announced that it had commenced High Court proceedings against Stability AI, the creator of the generative AI model Stable Diffusion. Getty asserted that 'Stability AI unlawfully copied and processed millions of images protected by copyright and the associated metadata owned or represented by Getty Images'. The particulars of claim later released to the public showed that Getty was asserting claims for copyright infringement, as well as database right infringement, trade mark infringement and passing off. On 6 February 2023, Getty filed a complaint against Stability AI in the US District Court for the District of Delaware, setting out a case for copyright infringement as well as trade mark infringement and unfair competition. In both the UK and US copyright infringement allegations, Getty points to three main potentially infringing acts: (i) Stability AI's alleged copying of its images to prior to training the model; (ii) Stability AI's alleged copying of its images during the training of the model; and (iii) Stability AI's alleged copying of its images after the training of the model (i.e. reproduction at the point of use). On 1 December 2023, the English judge refused to throw out Getty's claims, finding that they had a real prospect of success. The case will therefore go to full trial.

70 Other intellectual property rights will be of varying importance in certain use cases. For example, designs and trade marks may come into play more often where generative AI is being used to generate images but, even here, copyright remains the main risk.

Factors affecting the copyright infringement risk

28.67 The factors that may affect the legal and practical risk of copyright infringement at the point of use are varied and will depend on the use case and the facts. They will likely include:

- *Output type*. Whether the user is generating code, text, images, video or music.
- *Task type*. Whether the user is requiring the model to perform a task that leans more heavily on the training data as compared to the prompt.
- *Learning type*. Whether the developer used supervised, unsupervised or reinforcement learning.
- *Origin of training data*. Whether this came from the user, the developer or a third party.
- *Use of the output*. Whether output is used internally or externally, verbatim or for inspiration.
- *Publicising use of AI*. Whether people know you use AI within your business.
- *Jurisdiction*. Where the allegedly infringing act is taking place.

Copyright infringement at point of training (and possible exceptions for the developer)

28.68 Intellectual property infringement is a significant risk in relation to the use of data to train or customise an AI model. More training data can generally increase the probability of better outputs. As a result, AI developers can feel the need to use as much data as possible to train their models. The risk is higher at the point of training than at the point of use, as the training process involves more extensive and intensive acts of copying and processing data.

28.69 The risk will vary depending on the type and source of data, the jurisdiction of training, as well as the availability of statutory exceptions or defences. Broadly speaking, it is possible for AI developers to train models using: (i) their own proprietary data that they control, (ii) data in the public domain,[71] or (iii) data licensed from third parties on terms that allow for machine learning.[72] Each category of data raises specific legal risks. Where the training data is not adequately licensed, the copying, reproduction, modification and communication of those copyright works as part of the training process will infringe that copyright

71 For example, data collected through 'web scraping', of websites that are in front of a paywall or not otherwise access restricted.

72 For example, this may include data licensed from research institutions, data licensed on an open source basis, data licensed from data vendors, and data licensed from commercial counterparties (eg, in a collaboration).

unless you can rely on a legal exception. The legal landscape of copyright law in the context of training AI models appears likely to develop in future.

28.70 Exceptions to copyright infringement are prescribed by statute and help to balance the conflicting interests of rightsholders and third parties by allowing certain types of copying of copyright works for certain purposes (such as copying for text and data mining or copying for uses that are considered 'fair'). Where a user or a developer is able to fall within these exceptions then, even if a copying of a whole or substantial part a work is shown, they will not be liable for copyright infringement.

- *Text and data mining exceptions.* In a number of jurisdictions, including the UK and the EU, a statutory exception to copyright infringement exists where copies are made for purpose of computational analysis. This is also known as a 'text and data mining' exception. The scope of these exceptions vary.[73][74]
- *Fair use / fair dealing.* Within England & Wales and the EU, there are 'fair dealing' exceptions but these only cover use for the specific purposes (such as for criticism, review and reporting current events; or for parody, caricature and pastiche). These purposes are unlikely to apply in the context of a developer of a commercial AI system. In the US, there is a general exception for 'fair use', which is generally considered to be broader than the England & Wales and EU exceptions for fair dealing.[75]
- *Temporary copying exceptions.* Within England & Wales and the EU, there is also a temporary copying exception that might be argued to apply to the

73 In February 2023, the UK Government announced that it was abandoning its plans for a broad TDM exception. Instead, the UK Government was hoping to publish a voluntary code of conduct agreed between the various stakeholders (representing both AI developers and creative industries). However, at the end of November 2023, Viscount Camrose, Parliamentary Under Secretary of State (Minister for AI and Intellectual Property), indicated that no consensus had been reached on this, adding that there will not be any development on this until 2024 and legislation may be required to resolve the current standoff. That said, the UK Government's preferred approach is still to seek a consensual agreement of a 'code of practice' between the various stakeholders because of the risk that strict UK legislation might send AI developers overseas. For further reading see: https://www.worldipreview.com/copyright/uk-govt-confirms-backtrack-on-broad-exceptions-for-ai-24623.

74 On 12 September 2023, eight members of the French Parliament introduced a proposal (the Proposed Legislation No. 1630), to amend the first book of the French Intellectual Property Code with respect to copyright. This legislative change has been proposed to address issues such as the use of copyright works in the development and operation of AI systems and the approach to authorship and copyright ownership of works generated by AI systems.

75 This is likely to be assessed on a case-by-case basis for generative AI models, and not dealt with by way of a blanket ruling as was the case in the Google Books case (*Authors Guild v Google* 721 F.3d 132). In that case, various authors accused Google of copyright infringement by copying, scanning, and making available snippets of copyrighted books. It was possible for the court to reach that blanket determination in relation to Google's use for Google Books because Google explained how snippets were shown and therefore the court knew how much of the copyrighted works were being taken each time. That is not the case with the output of generative AI. The court also determined that Google augmented public knowledge by making available information about books without actually substituting for the books. A court would have difficulty reaching the same decision in a generative AI context.

training process, but this only covers copying for a lawful use of the work, which has no independent economic significance.

Copyright infringement at point of use (and possible exceptions for the user)

28.71 Copyright infringement at the point of use is possible in at least three ways. First, an unlicensed copyright work in the training data may be 'memorised' by the model and later reproduced substantially as output. It is this form of infringement that arises from the infringement at the point of training, and will be the primary focus of this chapter. Secondly, a user may insert another's copyright work as a prompt without the consent of that person (and this becomes more problematic where the model learns from prompts). Finally, a third party may insert their own copyright work into a model that learns from prompts, and the relevant copyright work is later reproduced as output to another user.

28.72 At the point of use, AI models do not contain 'copies' of training data as such. Rather, the weights within the model contain an abstracted representation of all the training data the model has seen. This prompts the question: if a user causes a model to substantially reproduce a copyright work from its training data, has that use of the model generated an infringing copy for which the user could be liable, even when the model itself contained no copy of the original work? In England & Wales, at least, this is likely to be the case and, if so, any further reproduction, storage and distribution of that infringing copy by the user would also be infringing acts.

28.73 At a high level, in England & Wales and the EU, to demonstrate copyright infringement, a rightsholder must prove (i) a 'causal connection' between the original work and the infringing copy, and (ii) that at least a 'substantial part' of that original work has been reproduced. Taking each element in turn:

- *Copying.* Copyright is not a monopoly right. It is possible (if unlikely in many cases) for two people to create the same original work and, if they do so independently, there will be no copyright infringement and each will hold copyright in the relevant work. Therefore, to show copyright infringement, 'copying' must be established. The legal test for copying in England & Wales, the US and the EU is met by establishing a 'causal connection' between the work protected by copyright and the output work, ie, showing that the output has not been independently created.
- *Substantiality.*[76] The legal test of substantiality has different names in different jurisdictions.[77] However, practically, these tend to arrive at the same result.

76 See: Copyright, Designs and Patents Act 1988 of the UK, in particular section 16(3) and Copyright and Information Society Directive 2001 (Directive 2001/29/EC of the European Parliament and of the Council).

77 Specifically, 'substantial similarity' (US), 'substantial part' (UK) and 'expression of the author's own intellectual creation' (EU).

Substantiality is a question of the quality of the extracted part (in the sense of its originality) rather than the quantity taken from the original work, and will always be determined on the facts. The owner of the copyright work alleging copying must be able to point to a single copyright work that has been copied substantially. This may be challenging in the generative AI context. It is not sufficient to point to a mosaic of different works that each have insubstantial elements of similarity with the infringing work.

28.74 Specific considerations will apply to different types of output. For example, reproducing as little as eight seconds of a video of a cricket match[78] or eleven words of a newspaper article[79] have previously been found to infringe copyright in the original work.

28.75 In England & Wales, the US and the EU, in cases where the defendant denies copying, copying will be presumed where: (i) the defendant had access to the copyright work, and (ii) there are objective similarities between the copyright work and the alleged infringing work. Where the presumption of copying arises, the evidential burden (but not the legal burden of proof) shifts on to the defendant to put forward evidence of how the derivative work was created independently in order to disprove copying.

28.76 In the US, one potential distinction is that the copyright owner would have to show that the *alleged infringer* copied the original work. So, for the initial output, where the user did not have access to the training data, it may be difficult for the copyright owner to show that the end user actually copied the underlying work.

28.77 At present, AI developers are secretive about the sources of their training data. However, the EU AI Act includes a requirement for providers of general purpose AI models to put in place a policy to respect Union copyright law, as well as make publicly available a sufficiently detailed summary about the content used for training of the general-purpose AI model, based on a template provided by the AI Office. The summary should not be technically detailed but comprehensive at a general level, while taking into due account the need to protect trade secrets and confidential business information.[80] In Recital 60(i), the EU AI Act states that any use of copyright protected content requires the

78 *England and Wales Cricket Board Ltd & Anor v Tixdaq Ltd & Anor* [2016] EWHC 575 (Ch).

79 *Infopaq v Danske Dagblades Forening* C-5/08, [2009] EUECJ C-5/08 (16 July 2009).

80 See Recital 60(k) of the EU AI Act: 'In order to increase transparency on the data that is used in the pre-training and training of general purpose AI models, including text and data protected by copyright law, it is adequate that providers of such models draw up and make publicly available a sufficiently detailed summary of the content used for training the general purpose model. While taking into due account the need to protect trade secrets and confidential business information, this summary should be generally comprehensive in its scope instead of technically detailed to facilitate parties with legitimate interests, including copyright holders, to exercise and enforce their rights under Union law, for example by listing the main data collections or sets that went into training the model, such as large private or public databases or data archives, and by providing a narrative explanation about other data sources used.'

authorization of the rightsholder concerned unless relevant copyright exceptions and limitations apply. While it remains to be seen how this will work in practice, it is likely to increase the *practical risk* of infringement, as rightsholders will be able to more easily establish whether their works have been used to train certain models.

28.78 Among the most likely defences to be argued by the user of an AI system is 'fair use' in the US or 'fair dealing' in England & Wales or EU, but we consider that these arguments are unlikely to be successful. Critically, the fact that a provider of a commercial AI system will likely lack a defence of fair dealing in England & Wales or EU has a knock-on effect on the ability of the user to rely on such a defence. Even if the user is using the AI system for one of the purposes for which fair dealing in available, if the AI provider's dealing is not fair, then the user's dealing cannot subsequently make the dealing fair.

The results of a finding of infringement

28.79 In England & Wales and the EU, the copyright owner is likely to seek damages based on the reasonable licence fee they would have received for the infringing acts or an account of profits generated through the infringing acts. In addition, they would likely seek an injunction to prevent further infringements. This may include preventing publication of any infringing output and also an injunction against further deployment of the infringing AI system.[81] The foregoing is, of course, aside from other consequences of litigation such as reputational harm and loss of management/employee time.

INTERNAL RISK

28.80 Internal risk is the risk that a deployer's use of generative AI causes damage to the deployer's proprietary intellectual property rights. Internal risk arises in two ways: (i) where a deployer inputs its intellectual property or confidential information as a prompt; and (ii) in relation to generation of software, where the output generated by the model contains open source code that has been reproduced from its training data and which is subject to a restrictive or 'copyleft' licence. This is aside from the reputational risks that these events trigger.

Deployer's intellectual property inserted as a prompt

28.81 Where a deployer inputs its intellectual property or confidential information into a generative AI model as a prompt, there is scope for: (i) loss of

81 In the US a copyright owner can recover actual damages and profits, or it can elect for statutory damages of between \$750–\$30,000 per instance of infringement, with adjustments for innocent and wilful infringement (in the case of the latter, which includes recklessness and wilful blindness, the rightsholder can recover up to \$150,000 per instance of infringement).

confidentiality or trade secrets; (ii) public disclosure of an otherwise patentable invention which prevents patentability; and (iii) the dissemination of copyright works to third parties via the model.

28.82 In a trade secret context, at a high level, the trade secret regimes in the US, England & Wales and EU generally apply to information that has a necessary quality of confidence, or where reasonable steps have been made to prevent the information from being exposed or misused by third parties. As such, any disclosure of confidential information as a prompt could, absent steps to maintain the confidentiality of it, result in that information no longer being considered a trade secret.

28.83 The internal risk is exacerbated where the user's prompts (and corresponding outputs) are fed automatically back into the model for training purposes.[82] However, the risks arise on any deployment of generative AI, as it is likely that an AI developer would seek (via the terms of the contract) to obtain broad usage rights over the inputs (and corresponding outputs) for the purposes of improving, maintaining and operating its model.

Copyleft code in output

28.84 Using generative AI to generate code raises an additional internal risk, where the AI model has been trained on open source code which is reproduced in the output.

28.85 Some open source code is made available subject to licences that are more restrictive than others, and in particular subject to 'copyleft' terms. At a high level, copyleft terms require the licensee to distribute to the public any works that are 'derivative works' of the relevant open source code. As such, if an organisation incorporates open source code into its own proprietary code (for software that is then distributed externally, eg, to customers), these terms could require the public disclosure of that proprietary code on an open source basis (ie, free of charge).

28.86 Whether this risk arises depends on the particular open source licence terms. Not all copying of copyleft code will result in a requirement to license the derivative work on an open source basis, and what constitutes a derivative work under the relevant licence will also vary. This would need to be considered for a particular use case and a particular output.

82 Which, at the time of publication, is the current default setting for ChatGPT.

OWNERSHIP RISK

Subsistence of copyright in AI-generated works

28.87 As at the date of publication, there are no legal regimes that specifically address subsistence of copyright in AI-generated works. In the US, the current guidance from the US Copyright Office is that the output of most current generative AI models is not copyrightable, except to the extent human authors substantially modify the work. This might be by editing or arranging it.[83] The US Copyright Office based this guidance on a view that the elements of 'authorship' for US copyright purposes are determined and executed by the AI, not the human user.[84]

28.88 A very small number of jurisdictions do allow copyright to subsist in *computer*-generated works. For example, in England & Wales, protection is given to original literary, dramatic, musical and artistic works generated by a computer, where there is no human creator, for a period of 50 years from the date the work is made. It is a matter of local law as to whether copyright works, including computer-generated works, are protected in that jurisdiction. Computer-generated works created in England & Wales are not afforded protection in other countries that do not protect such works merely because copyright originally subsisted in England & Wales. Similarly, copyright protection is available in England & Wales for those computer-generated works created in the US, despite those works being without copyright protection in the US.

Ownership of copyright in AI-generated works

28.89 Where copyright does subsist in AI-generated works, there is then some uncertainty as to who would be the author of that copyright. For example, in England & Wales, the author of a computer-generated work is taken to be the person who made the arrangements necessary for the relevant work to be created.[85] In the context of a commercialised AI product, there are likely to be multiple competing claims for authorship, including the AI developer (as the designer and trainer of the model) and the user (as the person who conceived of

83 See US Copyright Office, '*Copyright Registration Guidance: Works Containing Material Generated by Artificial Intelligence*', Library of Congress, (2023). URL: https://www.federalregister.gov/documents/2023/03/16/2023-05321/copyright-registration-guidance-works-containing-material-generated-by-artificial-intelligence#p-52.

84 A recent case in the US involved use of generative AI image generator Midjourney to create images for a graphic novel titled *Zarya of the Dawn*. Although the user allegedly used hundreds of prompts to iterate and refine the output, copyright was refused on basis that, among other factors, Midjourney was a tool that generated images in an 'unpredictable way', so the user inputting the prompts could not be the 'author' of the images. See the US Copyright Office's registration decision here: https://www.copyright.gov/docs/zarya-of-the-dawn.pdf.

85 See Copyright Designs and Patents Act 1988, which includes express provision for copyright protection of computer-generated works that do not have a human creator. Specifically, where a work is 'generated by computer in circumstances where there is no human author' (see section 178), the author of such a work is 'the person by whom the arrangements necessary for the creation of the work are undertaken' (see section 9(3)).

the prompts) – both of whom arguably made the arrangements necessary for the work to be created.

28.90 In the EU, assuming that the output is copyrightable, the question of authorship will be answered under each EU country's national laws. The EU Commission has stated that, generally, authorship will follow the person who made the creative choices that led to the output.[86] Similarly, in the US, assuming again that the output is found to be copyrightable (which currently appears unlikely), there would likely be competing claims for authorship between the AI developer and the user.

28.91 It is likely that (in England & Wales, EU and US) the user's right to authorship of any AI-generated work protected by copyright will differ depending on the level of input by the user of the AI system. Where the user has inserted a simple prompt to create a summary of, for example, recent EU law based on publicly available information, it will be difficult to argue that the user owns any copyright in that summary. On the other hand, if the user inputs a highly detailed prompt asking specifically to focus on certain topics in a given style and format, the user is more likely to have made creative choices that entitle it to authorship of any copyright in the output.

AI-generated inventions and patents

28.92 Changes to laws on the patentability of AI-generated inventions are being deliberated by legislatures around the world.[87] Currently, in England & Wales, EU and US, there is no law or guidance prohibiting an invention devised using AI from being patentable merely because it was created by an AI system. There are, however, question marks around whether AI-generated outputs would be capable of meeting the usual requirements for patentability, which would need to be considered on the facts of each specific case.

28.93 This is distinct from the question of whether an AI system can be named as the inventor of a patent.[88] Currently, in every jurisdiction where the question

86 See Case C-145/10, *Eva-Maria Painer v Standard Verlags GmbH* [2011] E.C.D.R. 297, para 89. In particular: 'author has to express his creative abilities in the production of the work by making free and creative choices'. See: https://curia.europa.eu/juris/document/document.jsf?docid=115785&doclang=EN.

87 For example, in the UK, a recent consultation on patent law considered introducing a new quasi-patent right for AI-generated inventions with limited exclusive rights and a shorter duration. However, the outcome of the consultation resulted in no proposed change to the law on the basis that 'there is no evidence that UK patent law is currently inappropriate to protect inventions made using AI'. See the UK Intellectual Property Office's June 2022 response here: https://www.gov.uk/government/consultations/artificial-intelligence-and-ip-copyright-and-patents.

88 An AI developer called Dr Thaler has been making headlines by pursuing patent applications in the name of his AI system called 'DABUS' in multiple jurisdictions worldwide. See *Thaler v Comptroller-General of Patents, Designs and Trade Marks* [2023] UKSC 49. URL: https://caselaw.nationalarchives.gov.uk/uksc/2023/49.

of AI inventorship has been considered by a court, the courts have held that an AI system cannot be named as the inventor. As set out above, that in itself would not preclude the patenting of an AI-generated invention.[89]

RISK MANAGEMENT FRAMEWORK: THE THREE RISK MANAGEMENT PILLARS

28.94 In A&O Shearman's own deployment of generative AI, we grounded management of legal risk within the framework of the three pillars set out below. These three pillars can be applied to each specific legal risk identified above to help mitigate legal risk.

Use Case +

28.95 This pillar is conceptually divided into two distinct elements:

- *'Use case'*. The first element involves clearly defining a use case for generative AI within an organisation. The flexibility of generative AI models requires careful consideration of how users can safely use them. It is important to create a safe and clear plan that meets strict legal standards and reflects the deployer's business strategy, values, and risk appetite.
- '+'. The second element refers to strict governance controls, which, in simple terms, involves communicating the use case effectively and ensuring that it is followed. It requires enhancement of and integration with existing governance to accommodate generative AI. Such governance should involve ongoing monitoring (by way of a feedback loop) to ensure control of risk and ensure long-term benefits are sustainable. It also requires aligning your goals in respect of generative AI with the organisation's culture and strategy.

89 There was an English High Court decision in November this year (*Emotional Perception AI v Comptroller* [2023] EWHC 2948 (Ch) regarding the patentability of a recommender model for media files, which comprised artificial neural networks. This decision appeared to mark a notable shift in the UK's approach to evaluating the patentability of AI models. In summary, the court found that a trained neural network can be a 'technical effect' and therefore patentable. Following the judgment, pending development of more detailed guidance, UK patent examiners have been instructed to not object to inventions involving artificial neural networks under the 'program for a computer' exclusion. Similarly, the US law on patent eligibility will pose challenges to AI-related inventions because individuals cannot obtain patents on abstract ideas. Following US Supreme Court guidance from 2010 to 2014, US courts have since invalidated many software patents on the grounds that they are fundamentally directed to an abstract idea and simply use generic computer components to effectuate the idea. To obtain a patent in the US, the AI-related invention must provide an 'inventive concept' that goes beyond using computer technology as a tool, such as a solution to a technological problem. The US Patent Office has provided some guidance in an informative decision reversing an Examiner's rejection of claims in a patent application related to 'systems and methods for improving the transcription of speech into text.' *Ex Parte Hannun*, Appeal 2018-003323 (PTAB April 1, 2019).

28.96 These are ingredients of a conventional definition of change management, but this is specifically focused on the vertical slice of change management that applies to legal risk management.

Operational

28.97 This pillar involves practical, operational steps which must be taken to align and integrate the generative AI system within an organisation. Legal departments must work in lock-step with information security teams and those aligning the AI systems with the organisation's technology infrastructure. This includes, among other things, security measures, configuration of the model, and privacy enhancing technologies. The interdependencies between legal, operational and security stakeholders is greater than in non-AI based technology deployment.

Contractual

28.98 Contract terms help to mitigate legal risk, both in the contract between the deployer and the foundation model provider, as well as in contracts between an organisation and its customers, if relevant. There should also be pre-contract due diligence, as well as ongoing contract management such as with respect to audit rights. In negotiations with foundation model providers, there are likely to be red lines for each organisation, such as regarding customer data or trade secrets not being exposed or used to train the models for others.

CONCLUSION

28.99 The deployment of generative AI can make an enormous impact on a business, but it requires a multi-disciplinary collaboration across functions to identify appropriate measures to manage and continuously monitor risk.

28.100 A&O Shearman is the leading law firm in the world for AI. Our lawyers are well-practised in using generative AI tools themselves, and we recently launched ContractMatrix,[90] our proprietary AI contract negotiation platform, which we developed in partnership with Microsoft and Harvey.[91] Because we have built and use AI tools across our multinational network, our AI advice is grounded in a detailed understanding of the latest AI technologies and how businesses can harness those technologies to generate value. We have pioneered risk management frameworks for the expansive legal risks that arise from AI,

90 For further details, see: https://www.allenovery.com/en-gb/global/expertise/advanced_delivery/contractmatrix.

91 For further details, see: https://www.ft.com/content/f1aff4d0-b2c5-4266-aa0a-604ef14894bb and https://www.allenovery.com/en-gb/global/news-and-insights/news/ao-launches-saas-partnership-with-microsoft-and-harvey.

and we are currently advising more than 70 of the largest global businesses on the safe deployment of generative AI, across the Middle East, APAC, US, UK and EU.

28.101 If you are interested in learning more about how we can help you navigate the complex and evolving legal landscape of generative AI, please do not hesitate to contact us.

CHAPTER 29

CYBER SECRET, LIFE SECRETS – ON THE VERGE OF HUMAN SCIENCE

Arthur Keleti

INTRODUCTION

29.01 A turtle's shell is made up of 60 bones, including the backbone, breastbone, and ribs offering an almost perfect protection for the vital body parts of the animal. These bones have evolved over time, shaped and changed into this masterpiece of protection against all types of threats. But nature had over 200 million years to perfect this shield in a relatively slowly changing environment. On the contrary today the digital environment we have created for ourselves generates huge amounts of data every year, and the numbers are only going to keep growing from here on out, reaching zettabytes of information in a few years from now. Today it is not just us who produce data, our systems are making more information by themselves as well. On the top of that with its exponential development AI (artificial intelligence) gives birth to datasets that look like originated from humans. Unfortunately for us all, a Gartner Report from 2013[1] predicted that by 2020, companies and governments won't be able to protect 75% of important data using the available technology. And that was not very far off. It seems that the cyber-ecosystem with its speed and complexity will not let us have enough time or resources to develop such a well-functioning protection for our vital parts of information.

29.02 Hidden among the tons of data that we collaboratively with AI each generate are our secrets – our personal things we don't necessarily want others to know about; after all, that's why we call them secrets. As Will Smith, the actor suggests: 'I've trained myself to illuminate the things in my personality that are likable and to hide and protect the things that are less likable.' Yet we came to know the part of Mr Smith's personality he wanted to hide when he slapped Chris Rock at the 2022 Oscars Gala. Context of this incident had a lot to do with how human secrets could emerge to the surface. There is a lot about context and its relationship to our secrets we will learn more in this chapter.

1 Gartner Reveals Top Predictions for IT Organizations and Users for 2014 and Beyond www.gartner.com/newsroom/id/2603215.

29.03 A form of secrets, cyber-secrets are made of data we hold on our devices, be them computers, smartphones, Internet of Things (IoT) devices or in the cloud on some server somewhere belonging to Google, Facebook or Amazon. Not all data needs to be secret, of course, but a good deal of it does, even if you may not realise so at first glance. A secret is never an independent phenomenon, however, but it's always one of connection and network. The context surrounding certain data is what transforms it into a secret; it's the norms that each individual abides by depending on the societal standards he lives in, the family values he grew up with, the religious constraints he may or may not feel, the needs he feels that require fulfilment. Even the person we are not willing to share information with, or the moment when we do not feel like doing it matters. They all contribute building blocks to the secrets that we keep. In our new digital ecosystem, it is the context that gives the real value to our information and not the content.

SHADES OF SECRETS

29.04 How many secrets do you think you have? That many? Well, you may have a few more than you'd believe. A study of the Columbia University[2] suggests that out of almost 40 different secret categories (such as hidden relationship or social discontent) the average person has 13 (five of which they have never told anyone about). But even more importantly, not all secrets are created equal. Almost twice as many people would hide a secret crush or attraction from their loved one than would hide something shameful, they did as a child.[3] Just like any other information, secrets are subject to personal evaluation, which means that something that one individual may feel needs to be kept secret, another could feel is trivial and can be shouted at the top of their lungs in a crowded market.

29.05 To better understand how we categorise our secrets, a coordinate system of personal or organisational attitudes can be used. This divides our secrets into three large groups – white, grey, and black – judged by the repercussions of revealing a certain secret.

29.06 For instance, white secrets, if exposed, would not cause a major problem for the bearer, they are more unpleasant than problematic. Let's say you are wearing the same pair of socks for a month. Convenient to implement, less convenient to reveal. Black secrets could cause some pretty big issues and embarrassment as well. Grey secrets are somewhere in between, and they can turn white or grey, depending on the norm environments.

2 The Experience of Secrecy – Michael L. Slepian, Jinseok S. Chun, and Malia F. MasonColumbia University www.columbia.edu/~ms4992/Pubs/in-press_Slepian-Chun-Mason_JPSP.pdf.
3 Davis, C.G., & Tabri, N. 'The secrets that you keep: Secrets and relationship quality' (2023) 30(2) *Personal Relationships* 620–635. https://doi.org/ 10.1111/pere.12472.

29.07 In one of BuzzFeed's videos,[4] young couples are telling each other secrets of the embarrassing kind. One of them confessed to her boyfriend on camera that she has been recording him talking in his sleep and uploading the recordings online. While this is considered a white secret at first look, it is uncertain what privacy concerns or inconvenience it may cause for the victim as the recording could be played in a different context where various norm measures may apply. This secret can easily shift into the grey zone.

29.08 Let's apply the model further. Say you have a partner, going steady for a few years. And then, one day, you wonder what your ex from five years ago is doing, so you go online, look them up, and start going through their social media. You may not want anyone to know about your trip down memory lane, but it wouldn't be a tragedy if others found out about it, including your understanding partner. Everyone has a past, right?

29.09 How about if, while going through their Meta posts and Instagram photos, you tap that 'like' button for a picture from their summer vacation two years ago? They may even notice and spark a conversation; innocent chit-chat among people who used to know each other well. Now, that's a grey secret. You probably don't want your partner to find out because, no matter how understanding they may be, they might still get annoyed with you. At the same time, you probably don't have any issues with your friends knowing about your reconnection, and they may even want some details themselves. In this example, the shade of the secret is affected by both the context (who you are telling it to) and the norm surrounding you (relationship rules, personal values, nature of upbringing, common sense).

29.10 Time goes on, and the chatting continues, you may even remember how it felt to be together, how easy it was in the good old days, you may even remember you had feelings for each other. One thing leads to another, and you start exchanging heated messages, maybe even set up a meeting in person. This is serious because no matter how you turn it, you're still cheating on your partner. You definitely don't want them to find out because it could mean the end of your relationship. Even your friends will think you crossed the line, your family will be disappointed because they thought you might be getting married soon, and your life will alter dramatically. That's a black secret because it will have a deep impact on your life, it could cause plenty of embarrassment, and affect more than your relationship with your partner. If this happened after you got married, it would even have legal consequences; a definitely problematic situation.

29.11 Of course, this is just an example. White secrets can be about the things you like to watch on the internet when no one's looking, or that you actually forgot to hand in that report at work that you suggested your boss probably deleted by mistake. Black secrets can also be that you blackmailed an ex with nudes, or that you haven't been paying taxes, not forgetting that in certain norm

4 Couples Tell Each Other An Embarrassing Secret – via BuzzFeedVideo www.youtube.com/watch?v=al4kEWMjUzo.

environments you would receive a pat on the back from your friends for cheating on 'everybody's favourite' tax authority. The famous early philosopher Plato put it best: 'When there is an income tax, the just man will pay more and the unjust less on the same amount of income.'

29.12 The interesting part about secrets is that everyone has their own. What is a secret for someone, may not be a secret for another, because each of us comes from a certain background, we accept some societal norms and disregard others, we abide by religious dogmas or dismiss them completely. Furthermore, something that was a secret for you five years ago, like your sexual preferences, for example, may no longer be so. What is important is that regardless of what information you may want to keep hidden, there's someone who wants to find it. Curiosity is in the human nature. Philosopher and psychologist William James who lived in the late 1800s used to say that curiosity is the impulse towards better cognition,[5] and that may very well be the truth when we're talking in general. A psychologist living in this day and age may also recognise that for good and bad hackers, curiosity is what drives them in their work, in their effort to make money, because secrets, especially when used in the right context, can be used as currency. The core of today's ransomware/extortion issue resonates oddly well with this. As the ransomware gang LockBit 3.0's message to one of their victim reads:[6] 'You can pay 15m (15 million US dollars) and nobody will know about what data we have.' 'You have 2 days until it will be published. All or nothing.'

PRIVACY

29.13 We all care about our privacy. The only problem is that it is really hard to define what we mean by it. Privacy is like a bubble made of fragile soap water. It is a notion that shifts with time; what was private in the past, is no longer private today. Think that a few hundred years ago, most homes didn't have separated rooms. The only walls that offered some sort of shield were the outside ones that would keep the weather at bay. Under these circumstances, families did everything under the same roof, where everyone else could see. In fact, privacy as most of us understand it today, depending on our social environment and norms surrounding us, has only been around for 150 years or so. 'The right to privacy' is a phrase that was coined in 1890, when portable cameras that used photographic film, the Kodaks, first appeared.

29.14 A few decades ago, back when postcards were extremely popular, mail carriers would regularly have fun reading what people were communicating in this manner. In this day and age, correspondence privacy is protected by law.

5 The Psychology and Neuroscience of Curiosity – ScienceDirect www.sciencedirect.com/science/article/pii/S0896627315007679.

6 lockbit3.0, Chat: ************B8DC6D – Ransomchats Viewer ransomch.at/lockbit3.0-sirva_com.

29.15 Privacy today needs way more granularity in law. There are technologies on the horizon like brain to machine interfaces or AI models capable of reading fRMI brain scans. Humans need initiatives including neurorights like mental privacy in law or the French framework of the revision of the bioethics law in 2021 that protects against the abusive use of neural data. As UNESCO addresses this type of risk of neurotechnologies in their recent publication[7]: 'we need to assess how far current human rights frameworks are equipped to protect neural rights, or whether there is a need for a new set of neuro-specific human rights, such as the right to cognitive liberty, mental privacy, mental integrity and psychological continuity.'

29.16 Another interesting aspect of privacy is that the notion is different for everyone. While one individual may feel comfortable with public displays of affection, another may not feel quite so at ease with kissing their partner where everyone can see. While one person may be ok with letting everyone in the office know how their night of drinking went, others may be more restrained in mixing personal and office lives. The problem is well demonstrated in the struggle of smartphone vendors who have been trying to separate work and private instances of the same environment with not too much success. Blackberry's effort back in 2015 with the BES12 platform came close to achieve a decent level of separation, but it has not gained massive popularity. Major smart phone vendors are trying to solve the problem by letting the user adding separate instances to internet browsing like the browsing profiles in Safari in Apple's iOS17 operating system in 2023.

29.17 And yet, privacy has become something of a desideratum for most of the world. Even with the shifting definition of this notion, privacy is something we all hope for. Still, most of us use Meta. Three billion of us, more specifically, as the company announced in Q2 2023. The man behind the company (formerly known as Facebook), Mark Zuckerberg, said in 2010 that privacy is no longer a norm expected by society. 'People have really gotten comfortable not only with sharing more information and different kinds, but more openly and with more people… That social norm is just something that has evolved over time.[8]' He later backpedalled on this statement, but it's still something he said, something he believes.

29.18 He's not necessarily wrong, either. We all share more information than we even know. Sure, you may not make public Meta posts every day, check in every time you eat out or go for a drink, or post pictures to Instagram sharing your location, but you browse the internet still logged into Meta, browse the social network from your mobile device with GPS enabled, use Google for search or query public AI models through Bard, Bing or ChatGPT and so on.

7 *The risks and challenges of neurotechnologies for human rights* – UNESCO, University of Milan-Bicocca (Italy), State University of New York. Downstate Health Sciences University, ISBN 978-92-3-100567-1, https://doi.org/10.54678/POGS7778.

8 'Privacy no longer a social norm, says Facebook founder' – *The Guardian* www.theguardian.com/technology/2010/jan/11/facebook-privacy.

This isn't data you share consciously, but it's still data that can reveal a lot about you – where you go, what you buy, who you spend time with, what interests you have, and much, much more. We have come to the point where you could read from Andy Greenberg of Wired about how to spend $1,000 to easily track someone's location by simply using mobile adverts.[9] No wonder why some part of the intelligence community has already started using features of the ads technology industry through ADINT (advertising-based intelligence).[10]

29.19 Despite all this, we immediately become scandalised when we hear about any threats to our privacy. One of the major dangers to our cyber-secrets, and, implicitly to our privacy, is malware. The internet is full of hundreds of malware strains, dozens of families, wreaking havoc on devices all over the world. A worrying sudden increase in the number of variants of new malware detected by Symantec in February 2017 topped around a hundred million. By 2023, this number had multiplied fivefold. Whether we're talking about PCs running Windows, or phones running Android, there are billions of potential victims. Most of our data nowadays is held on such a device, and yet we still don't know how to properly and consistently protect ourselves. Sometimes, even if we check everything on the list – run security updates, install security software, use unique passwords, or multifactor authentication etc – we're still going to fall victims to hackers.

29.20 Cyber-security professionals are accustomed to this fact already, but the majority of people would hardly believe that they will become a target of hacking or cyber-crime or if they do they don't know how to deal with it. A Canadian study[11] in 2017 showed that less than 44% know how to protect themselves and 38% are aware of how to report a cyber-crime. Despite many countries making it mandatory for organizations to report cyber-crime, according to general observation the number of such reports has decreased by about 5% year on year, while the financial losses due to cybercrime are predicted to increase by 15% annually. Before you know it, your computer, your phone, or literally anything electronic you have, is infected. If you're lucky, you'll stumble upon a malware thread that can be easily removed. But maybe you'll encounter a piece of malware that quickly encrypts all your vacation photos and your work documents and demands that you pay an amount of money to get it all back. You can either pay the hackers, wait to see if there's a decryption tool available online, or just go ahead and format the entire computer, saying goodbye to every piece of data on your device. Or you can turn to your 'probably non-existent/non-reliable' backup from before you got infected.

9 It Takes Just $1,000 to Track Someone's Location with Mobile Ads – Wired www.wired.com/story/track-location-with-mobile-ads-1000-dollars-study/.

10 Defense Ministry sets sights on ADINT companies – Globes, Israel business news, July 16, 2023, https://en.globes.co.il/en/article-defense-ministry-sets-sights-on-adint-companies-1001452394.

11 Canada Cybercrime Survey 2017 – Accenture www.accenture.com/ca-en/company-news-release-canada-cybercrime-survey-2017.

29.21 Ransomware is the malware-of-choice for hackers nowadays, with the dark web being filled with easy-to-buy kits for anyone who doesn't want to go to the trouble of coding their own. These are manufactured by competing ransomware provider crime groups. Security experts don't see an end to ransomware's popularity because it has so many advantages for the attackers – it's easy to deploy, works fast, results in money. Plus, attackers are rarely ever caught, and crypto-wallets make it difficult to track the money.

29.22 Later in 2017, ransomware showed its true potential with two names – WannaCry and NotPetya. WannaCry spread like wildfire across the globe, affecting some 300,000 computers in 150 countries, before one security researcher accidentally pulled the plug. Although it's hard to tell exactly, experts estimate that WannaCry's damage went over $1 billion. $1 billion out of the total $5 billion estimated for all ransomware damage done across the world in 2017.

29.23 A month later, in June 2017, came NotPetya. The name was handed out by Kaspersky Lab because it resembles the Petya ransomware in some aspects, but it's not exactly like it. First of all, NotPetya isn't ransomware, despite displaying a note following file encryption, because its purpose isn't to gain money, but rather to just make everything unreadable. So, the main purpose of this attack was to damage beyond repair all the data on an infected computer.

29.24 A few years later, in December 2022, Medibank, a leading Australian health insurer, experienced a severe data breach. This incident jeopardized the personal data of nearly 9.7 million clients. The notorious REvil ransomware group, based in Russia, is believed to be behind the attack. Evidence surfaced when REvil displayed 6GB of data on a dark web forum. This act hinted at their access to even more confidential information. Their demand was apparent: $10 million in ransom. The compromised data included names, birth dates, passport details, medical bills, and patient histories. There were reports of hackers trying to extort ransom directly from users, suggesting that cybercriminals already use data from the database. Despite the gravity of the breach, Medibank remained steadfast, refusing to pay. The Australian government unprecedently backed up the notion. As a result, Medibank has significantly ramped up its cybersecurity efforts.

29.25 It is the mechanism of ransomware and the logic behind its creation that threatens privacy. The target is something the user has, or something the user values. The ransom works on different levels from threatening with deleting our data to extorting ransom for NOT selling it online. It all depends on the attacker's weapon of choice and his war tactics. This puts the individual in a vulnerable position. As 'Gasland' director Josh Fox said: 'When you're cornered, there are two things you can do: move or fight.'[12] Well, Josh had his camera to protect his family, but what does the average user have against a ransomware armed hacker?

12 Josh Fox IMDB biography – www.imdb.com/name/nm1068198/bio.

29.26 To bring it one level further up perhaps the most damaging to one's privacy is spyware. If your device becomes infected with such a tool, you won't even know it's there, but it will know everything that you type, including on those messaging apps that offer end-to-end encryption. It will even hear your conversations and turn your device into a remote recording tool. All your secrets, be them white, grey, or black, could suddenly be exposed. They could be used as blackmail material by those seeking to gain some money from this. Depending on the individual, such a tool could result in more or less important information gathered. What if the infected device belongs to a bank manager? Or a politician? Or a doctor privy to sensitive information? Plus, in this situation, our secrets and privacy aren't the only ones at risk. In fact, we risk becoming victims of financial schemes, of identity theft, and more.

29.27 Looking through all the options we are left with, we need to come to the sad realisation: there are too many dimensions endangering our privacy. From our own inability to properly define the abstraction of privacy, through various malware targeting it, to the unavailable all-cure potion of a proper anti-something for our devices. Not to mention, smart home and other Internet of Things devices exposed to outside attacks. Device numbers rapidly multiply and have reached 15 billion by 2020, and is expected to double by 2030.

DATA BREACHES

29.28 If we somehow manage to properly protect our computers, smartphones, and tablets, we're still not safe. Data breaches also post a very large risk to our safety. 2017 and 2018, for instance, was a year when barely a week went by when we didn't hear about some company somewhere losing control over their servers, resulting in a data breach. Although the number of individuals impacted by breaches seems to have decreased over the years to 2023, the number of breaches is steadily growing. Whether it was some server left unprotected, or a group of very determined hackers, it was still our data that was exposed. It is tricky to unravel the facts behind the mystical trends. Incident reporting is still something that has not yet become an 'Olympic sport' in every country. So it is hard to say what is really going on behind the closed doors of the boardrooms of companies and organisations. Many of the incidents that have made it to the surface are data losses where the leaked information is already available on the internet. Even in 2023 out of almost a million of incidents know to Version, only a quarter was reported.[13]

29.29 The Equifax data breach, for instance, exposed social security numbers, addresses, and financial history for 143 million people. Uber announced the personal data of some 57 million users had been affected by a data breach. And then there was Yahoo. Even though the company had previously announced two

13 DBIR 2023, Data Breach Investigations Report – Verison, https://www.verizon.com/business/resources/reports/dbir/.

massive data breaches in late 2016 – one that occurred in 2014 affecting 500 million users, and one from 2013 that affected 1 billion users – the company came out and made one correction. There weren't just 1 billion people affected, but 3 billion.

29.30 All of this data can be used against us, it can be used to hack other accounts, or steal our money, or for various other purposes with almost endless combinations. This is why someone is always after our data, after our secrets – money can be made from it. In Bob Dylan's words: 'money doesn't talk, it swears' especially in the hands of cyber-crime organisations.

29.31 As for data, from the privacy perspective, it doesn't always matter if we are giving them out willingly or they are stolen from us. We are under the misguided belief that the services we use online are free. Sure, we may not pay in cash, but we pay with our data. In the event of someone managing to crack open both Meta's and Google's vaults, and to track back to us that anonymous ID they use for advertising, where all the little bits of information about our online activity are stored, we'd all be in deep trouble.

THE RISK PARALYSIS

29.32 When it comes to protection, companies have a particular fetish of risk proportionate protection. Some companies will do pretty much anything to protect their users' data, while others… well, not so much. Unfortunately, anything from non-existing security to 100% protection fits under the idea of proportionate protection. You could not find a cyber-security vendor today that is not selling 'state of the art protection', and there is no company that is not taking cyber-security risks 'seriously'. So, it all boils down to how seriously you can take that risk and how feasible the proposed solution is. Two very subjective perspectives, quite apparent factors when a boardroom or mid-management decides to ignore the threat and 'accepts the risk'. For a light-hearted explanation and for some quality amusement time, search for 'Host Unknown presents: Accepted the Risk' on Youtube.[14]

29.33 Each company has a risk level of its own. Due to their size, some may not even have a good grasp of their real risk level and how complex the protection they need is. For instance, does a bank require more complex protection than a sewage treatment plan? Or does a nuclear plant require more complex protection than a hospital? It's difficult to assess, as most security experts, as well as country leaders, find it near impossible to agree on what counts as critical or vital infrastructure and what doesn't.

14 'Host Unknown presents: Accepted the Risk' – Host Unknown, https://youtu.be/9IG3zqvUqJY.

29.34 That's because circumstances change. A sewage company may have a minor importance at first glance, but everything could change if a flood hits. Similarly, a military coup could suddenly increase the importance of a bakery.

29.35 Information security tries to focus on what risks a company or organisation carries, and suggest protection to match said risks.

29.36 One of the aspects that could be factored in for risk analysis is the sensitivity and importance of the stored data. For its part, data can also be classified on the basis of sensitivity, which, in turn, affect its protection. For instance, in a nuclear plant, it's not as important to protect the information about the temperature inside the reactor, as it is to make sure that no one can tamper with the safety limits set for those temperatures, because that could lead to a disaster.

29.37 Then, the system and the data itself and the procedures defining them are changing all the time, making things that much more difficult, and requiring the reassessment of the risk analysis at each step. The protection needs rethinking in its entirety, not just in segments, because new processes are created all the time, while old processes change. Risk analysis is (or should be) a living entity that changes and adapts.

29.38 But does it? The reality of the situation is that most companies and organisations, and even private individuals, don't reassess the risks and adjust their protections accordingly. Most companies choose a more static protection and therefore sustainable approach. That is why by 2023, more and more organisations prefer ongoingly managing their attack surface and the risks linked to them.

29.39 We also need to consider that this is the type of field where companies are reluctant to invest because they don't see hard evidence that it's working. When an attack is mitigated, most C-level executives can't see the financial impact the attack could have had had it gone through. It's hard to estimate how much money the protections set in place actually save a company. Budgetary managers only see how costly an attack is for a company once it is successful. Legal fees, production setbacks, the cost of cleaning up the systems, potential lawsuits, potential fines from authorities, and so on. These are all contributing to the over 6 trillion US dollars annual cost of cybercrime in the World.

29.40 Then there's the problem of who can access certain data within a company. Rights management is something every company deals with and it's just as difficult to figure out as the risk proportionate assessment. To make the matter even more complicated the popular and efficient idea of microservices, on-demand application and environments technology require instant and temporary rights distribution. To the challenge this poses the security industry responded with zero trust, a nice sounding but rather costly and hard to achieve goal.

29.41 The most common solution is the rights matrices, which are large databases and software that determine who can access which system, process, or data, as well as when and for what purpose. Each user needs to get a level of access and each type of data needs to be assigned a minimum level of access required to open it. As history has proven, it's also extremely important to keep up with the day-to-day situation within a company and to withdraw the access rights when someone is demoted or fired, or to upgrade them once someone gets promoted to a position that requires more access.

29.42 Ideally, the rights matrix looks more like 'who can access what and when'. I'm afraid, however, that in most cases it is rather black and white right now, with no shades of grey. The bad news is that we can't solve access problems real-time properly because there are too many conditions to be met, and too many changes to follow.

29.43 Besides requiring too many human resources, part of the problem is that there are ultimately no working standards to guide us, there is no really right way to do things apart from following the recommendations of certain software solutions. While several companies are trying to fill the gap between what is promised in bigger software distributions and reality, perhaps the rapidly developing generative AI models will figure out the way to deal with this dilemma. But for now, it looks like us humans aren't capable of doing it properly.

29.44 In May 2018, GDPR has taken effect, a new set of rules that are meant to protect internet users. All companies operating within the EU need to comply with these new rules, make sure all user data is obtained with the user's consent, completely protected, and, in the event of a data breach, immediately inform users and the authorities about the situation or face steep fines. Experts agree that the GDPR has proven to offer some really good protection for users. It will, however, continue to cause a lot of problems for many companies involved and users often feeling harassed by necessary GDPR permissions. While GDPR decently helped people understand that they do have data that needs protecting, it remains to be seen if it will solve the confusion about data owners and with cyber-secrets on the long run. The EU remains confident in protecting the privacy and data rights of its users that shows evidently in both the Digital Service Act and the developing AI Act.

AND THEN THERE WERE BUGS

29.45 We like to believe that our data is relatively safe if we keep our operating systems on computers and mobile phones updated and anti-malware software installed, if we avoid downloading things online, installing apps we aren't certain about, or tapping on every link we get. It is coming from our basic human instinct of thinking that what we use more often, becomes less risky to use. We also like to believe we are safe by trusting that the likes of Google, Meta, Microsoft, and Amazon are properly protecting whatever we hold in those clouds. But what if the vulnerability that gets you hacked isn't you? For the most part, each user is at fault for getting hacked to some extent, but if the bug is ingrained in the hardware or the software, what do you do then?

29.46 Numerous vulnerabilities has been discovered in processors that carry critical flaws, which affect every platform they are built-in from computers to tablets and smartphones. Intel's two issues from 2018, dubbed Meltdown and Spectre, existed in the CPU hardware itself, and have pushed the need for a redesign of the kernel software all major operating systems are based on. Windows, Linux, MacOS, Chrome OS, Android, iOS – you name it, it's affected.

29.47 Google described Meltdown as an exploit that breaks the fundamental isolation between user applications and the operating system. Experts believe there's no one solution to actually fixing Spectre because the vulnerability tricks other applications into accessing arbitrary locations in their memory. If you think you're safe because your computer is brand new, think again. Meltdown affects every Intel processor released since 1995.

29.48 A vulnerability recently discovered in AMD's CPU, called 'Zenbleed', allowed for fast and direct reading of private data. This flaw was especially risky in business settings. Imagine someone renting a virtual server being able to access data from other servers on the same CPU cores. Another example, 'Downfall' also from 2022 is equally dangerous to complicated eco-systems. As Daniel Moghimi, the security researcher who found it describes: 'This vulnerability, … enables a user to access and steal data from other users who share the same computer. For instance, a malicious app obtained from an app store could use the Downfall attack to steal sensitive information like passwords, encryption keys, and private data such as banking details, personal emails, and messages. Similarly, in cloud computing environments, a malicious customer could exploit the Downfall vulnerability to steal data and credentials from other customers who share the same cloud computer.'[15]

29.49 Updating your operating system, web browser, and CPU firmware, might help, but they aren't fail-safe. While experts rarely observed any attacks exploiting these vulnerabilities in the wild, they predict it won't be long before that happens. Vulnerabilities like Zenbleed combined with zero-click attacks that require no interaction from the user to be successful pose a greater threat. During the last decade both cybercriminals and intelligence organisations have discovered this potential and keep exploiting them 'in the wild'.

MASS SURVEILLANCE

29.50 When it comes to the value of privacy and secrets, another big issue that we're all facing is mass surveillance. Some years ago, it came like a bomb that the US National Security Agency (NSA) was, in fact, monitoring online

15 Downfal Page – Daniel Moghimi – https://downfall.page.

communications without discrimination. Whether you were at fault for something or not, a suspect in an investigation or not, it didn't really matter. Edward Snowden blew the whistle on the entire operation, shared thousands of documents with the media, showing the widespread operations the NSA was conducting without any kind of oversight. The intelligence agency tried to defend itself to some degree, saying they weren't actually spying on Americans, but only foreigners, but that didn't really stick. And it didn't make things better. As John Oliver put it in an interview with General Keith Alexander, the head of NSA: 'Do you think that the NSA is suffering from a perception problem with the American people at the moment… bear in mind that the answer to that is yes.' [16]

29.51 As far as reactions go, people were either downright scandalised and hailed Snowden as a hero, or indifferent and said Snowden was a traitor, especially since he had run off and settled down in Russia, one of the few nations offering him protection. That is, until John Oliver again put a different perspective on things. He stopped people on the streets and asked their opinion on the NSA surveillance, only to encounter some bland responses. Then he asked if they were bothered the NSA could see their private photographs. Apparently, that's all it took because that did get a response from the people he was interviewing. This shows, once more, that we all care about our privacy, that there are lines we wish no one crossed – like being unable to keep those private photos secret. While many of us will take a naked photo here and there, maybe for ourselves, or maybe to share with our partners, we don't want others to see that. We granted permission to only a handful of people to see those pictures, and when our trust is broken, and others are privy to the same information, we feel betrayed. Inspired by Oliver's unique style, someone even set up a website where the main issues of the NSA surveillance system were listed, complete with the laws that had made this possible in the first place.

29.52 Mass surveillance is probably what all governments wish to do. It is quite likely that they're actually doing it, but the information is not out yet. They're doing it because information is powerful; data is powerful; our secrets are powerful, you can win an election using it wisely. In general, they don't care if you're cheating on your spouse, or are gossiping about your co-workers; they care about information that has the potential of being of national importance. At least that is what the 'national protection narrative' dictates. Maybe there's terrorist chatter, maybe there's an attack of some sort being planned, maybe there's an uprising that needs to be stifled. Reasons are aplenty, and governments like to be in control, so they like to have their hands on any potential information. Since many governments are still lacking all the resources they want, it is uncertain how far this is going to get in the future.

29.53 But if there are governments that can afford to have enough data collected why are there still such terrorist attacks happening? Why are mass shootings

16 General Keith Alexander Extended Interview: Last Week Tonight With John Oliver (HBO) – LastWeekTonight on YouTube www.youtube.com/watch?v=k8lJ85pfb_E.

happening across America every other day, and well-prepared terrorist attacks can happen in such developed countries as Israel? Well, partly because the amount of data that is being transmitted online is massive. Even with a performant system set in place to flag conversations revolving a certain topic, there's nothing to say attackers aren't speaking in code.

29.54 There's also another aspect we need to consider – mass surveillance is seen differently across the globe. While something like this may be frowned upon in the Western world, Easterners have a slightly different view on it. Eastern Europe, for instance, lived in a constant state of surveillance for decades, with people being punished for the things they said in their own homes. This has considerably altered the way people view privacy there, but it has also made them hunger for it more once communism was a thing of the past. The newer generations, at least, have a completely different view on this topic than the previous one did; they're more ready to stand up for what they see as injustice and wrongdoings of their governments based on their personal norms.

29.55 Another vector is at play here: the significant difference in perceiving privacy between generations. Only 12% of Gen Z say they would not share their data, as opposed to 33% of the Non-Gen Z population.[17] This phenomenon adds a new dimension to assessing privacy, which is particularly troubling for legislation as it suggests that not all generations would weigh the value of secrets equally.

29.56 Once we travel further east, however, we again encounter China. Here, the government doesn't even hide the fact that it is constantly surveys its citizens. With the internet making it big in China in about 1994, it wasn't long before the government realised that there was too much freedom, too much information coming through, so they instituted some steps to control everything. By 1998, the Great Firewall was enforced, censoring content from the rest of the internet.

29.57 Nowadays, the Chinese don't have access to tools like Meta, X (formerly known as Twitter), or WhatsApp, these being replaced with local alternatives. YouTube is also blocked, and for a few years, even Wikipedia was off limits.

29.58 A new approach to mass surveillance has surfaced: China's Social Credit System. Originating as a concept in 2007, it evolved into a structured program by 2014 and now profoundly impacts the daily lives of Chinese citizens.

29.59 Actions like jaywalking or playing music loudly in public spaces can incur penalties within this system. This framework assesses citizens' behaviours and reliability in every sphere of life, which might result in the suspension of certain privileges, such as the capability to reserve transportation tickets. The widespread use of facial recognition, network traffic analysis, and the data processing of major China-based tech companies gathering vast amounts of

17 Global Consumer Sentiment Survey – Oliver Wyman Forum – October 2022, N: 9,674, www.oliverwymanforum.com/gen-z/2023/aug/how-gen-z-uses-social-media-is-causing-a-data-privacy-paradox.html.html.

personal data challenge the notion of privacy and the preservation of personal and professional confidence.

29.60 To complicate the scenario further from 2021, China has a comprehensive Personal Information Protection Law, which, while safeguarding individual privacy, also provides governmental agencies the authority to access sensitive personal information.

29.61 Other countries have credit score systems in place, such as the US, but there it only takes into account whether you pay your loans on time, if you max out your credit cards all the time, or how many times you've applied for credit. That's nothing compared to how much information the Chinese authorities are getting.

29.62 But is mass surveillance good or bad? It certainly has some theoretical advantages – like the fight against terrorism and against crime. Governments could also reach a better understanding of their people. The question that comes next is whether or not anything would change once this understanding occurred. Chances are mixed.

29.63 Personally speaking, how much of your privacy are you willing to sacrifice for this protection that may or may not work? The truth is that governments have been, are, and probably will always be slow to react to cyber-threats. Bureaucracy always makes sure too much time passes between someone noticing something is wrong, and someone taking action against that something; whether we're talking about someone with criminal intent or a cyber-threat. In fact, cyber-threats in particular are hard to combat. When someone is sick we call the ambulance, when a house is on fire we call the firefighters, when someone is robbed we call the police, but who would you call when a cyber-thief is taking your data? What is the cyber-crime emergency number in your country? Michael Hayden, former director of the NSA, painted the bleak reality quite well. 'Our government will be constantly, continually, late to need in the cyber domain. Our government will be less capable of keeping us safe up here than it has been keeping us safe down here, forever.' [18]

THE POST-SNOWDEN WORLD

29.64 Regardless of whether you consider Edward Snowden to be a whistleblower or a traitor of his country, no one can deny that he did one thing right – he opened everyone's eyes about the undergoing of one government. The American Intelligence agencies may have been the target of his revelations, but there's nothing to say others don't have similar programs in place.

18 Cyber Security: Why Is This (Still) So Hard? – YouTube – www.youtube.com/watch?v=47zJPU0VHSQ&feature=youtu.be&t=25m53s.

29.65 And yet, Snowden has put the spotlight back on privacy, on the secrets we want to protect. Along with this came something that has become somewhat of an industry standard – encryption. Following the NSA scandal, there's been a full-blown revolution among tech companies. End-to-end encryption was introduced in messaging apps, and it has now reached a point where if this feature isn't provided by such a tool, it's not going to get much of a following.

29.66 Tech companies promised that the data going through their servers was completely encrypted. There was an expectation that emails would be encrypted too, and that also happened, although at a much lower level. In messaging apps, end-to-end encryption works because everyone you communicate with also uses the same tool. With emails, there are so many providers. Google, for instance, encrypts emails when they're being sent, and when they're stored, but that works best if the recipient is also a Gmail user. When the Transport Layer Security (TLS) won't work, Google will notify you of this. If you have to cross platforms, that protection lessens. That's why there are so many own-server-run email services promising end-to-end encryption, but little adoption – if you send a message outside the original platform, that protection disappears completely.

29.67 Then there's SSL, HTTP/2 and all those certificates. Sites today are required to use modern protocols in HTTPS due to the added protection and efficiency this provides. In essence, once someone visits a properly set up HTTPS site, even if they're being monitored, those watching will only be able to tell they visited a certain site, not what they did while there. Browsers have chosen to support HTTP/2 through a TLS connection, taking advantage of a TLS feature named ALPN (application-layer protocol negotiation) which helps decreasing network latency. All in all, it is quite difficult for any user to prefer unencrypted connection in any situation.

29.68 The problem is that we've reached a point where our solution for all-things-privacy is encryption. We encrypt everything, try to protect everything, and then nothing really is special anymore. If we get a tiny string of spyware on our devices, maybe even without clicking a link or opening a file, nothing is protected anymore.

29.69 So if we combine all the above, from zero-click to advanced malware into an application, we get sophisticated software like Pegasus that stepped out of mythology into the reality of tens of thousands of activists and political rivals in at least 50 countries worldwide. The Israeli NSO Groups' advanced spyware can discreetly and remotely retrieve all data from a target's mobile phone, eliminating the need for the user to activate Pegasus by clicking a malicious link. Additionally, they can transform the mobile phone into a tracking and covert recording instrument, enabling the device to monitor its owner. The 2021 release of Citizen Lab's investigation into the matter has moved the spotlight to the privacy aspect of the intelligence industry. The scandal's aftermath has continued to uncover serious privacy violations by governments and intelligence agencies, and it also calls our attention to the lack of local protection of our devices as opposed to the network protection where most of the focus had gone before.

29.70 Plus, for every organisation and authority without access to users' data, the tech giants' habit of encrypting everything is annoying like little else before. Why? Because encryption renders any collected data useless. That might satisfy GDPR enthusiasts, but it practically makes it complicated, if not impossible, for law enforcement to process evidence or efficiently trace the flow of money. Following the terrorist attacks from London in mid-2017 the country's Home Secretary came out and accused WhatsApp of giving terrorists a way to communicate in secret. Forget the 1 billion other people using this app, it was that attacker's messages the authorities wanted and couldn't get.

29.71 After all, let's assume WhatsApp gives backdoor access to authorities, even if that were possible. Who gets a way in? Pretty much any law enforcement agency in the world. How long before someone hacks those agencies and steals the code? How long before one police officer, or federal agent, misuses the code for personal gain? How long before someone mistakenly shares the code with others? Not long. The thing is, encryption doesn't just protect people from the government's mass surveillance habits, it also protects people's communications from hackers. While the government may not want to do you harm, those hackers certainly would like nothing more than to leverage your secrets against you. Furthermore, WhatsApp doesn't actually have access to people's messages in plain text – that's what end-to-end encryption is really about anyway.

29.72 On another note, there have been cases in the past when terrorists did not use WhatsApp, or any other app people can download from the Play Store, or iTunes – they used apps they made themselves, offering the same protections.

29.73 Another entity that has made a habit out of demanding backdoor access to encryption is the FBI. In late 2017 the agency was complaining it had some 7,000 devices that were locked, which made the data on them unusable in investigations. One famous case went down between the FBI and Apple after the December 2015 mass shooting in San Bernardino. The FBI demanded Apple crack open the iPhone of the shooter, something Apple couldn't do even if it wanted to. The case went to court and there was a lot of media hype surrounding it. Until one day, the FBI dropped the lawsuit and said it managed to crack the device on its own. How? Well, they won't say, and the court agreed they don't have to share this information after a group of media outlets sued the Bureau. There are many rumours surrounding the method the FBI used, or, more specifically, the Israeli company they paid to gain access. The irony is that after spending nearly $1 million to get access to the data on the phone, they admitted the device held very little useful information.

29.74 The story and its implications continued to unfold as Apple has made the privacy of its users its key selling point while it keeps troubling agencies. When in 2022, Apple introduced a series of end-to-end encryption protection improvements of its iCloud service, the FBI told the Washington Post that it was 'deeply concerned with the threat end-to-end and user-only-access encryption pose'.[19]

19 Apple says it will allow iCloud backups to be fully encrypted – Washington Post, 12.07.2022 – https://www.washingtonpost.com/technology/2022/12/07/icloud-apple-encryption/.

29.75 Glancing on the other side of the coin raises questions as in the summer of 2023, the Kremlin's Federal Security Service (FSB) accused Apple of informing the NSA about software vulnerabilities within its iPhone series, enabling US intelligence agents to infiltrate and surveil devices owned by diplomats and embassies from countries such as Russia, NATO members, former Soviet states, Israel, China, and more. These accusations were accompanied by discoveries of similarly functioning malware by Kaspersky, Russia's number one cybersecurity firm, on their own devices of top and middle management.One thing is for sure: the cyber-security profession needs to work out a proper solution to the en-decryption paradigm.

THE WORLD OF UNTRUST

29.76 Anton Chekhov, a famous Russian playwright and short-story writer, used to say that you must trust and believe in people, or life becomes impossible. And we do. We all trust someone or something until they prove we misplaced that trust. For instance, we trusted Yahoo with our emails, and then we found out that they had been hacked, knew about it, and said nothing. Trust is gone.

29.77 The same applies with people. You may trust a small group of friends with your secrets, but you must admit that if one of them slips and tells someone else about your adventures one night, your trust in them will lessen and it will take a long time before it's back up again. How can you tell who you can trust and what type of information, what kind of secret, you can trust them with? How about companies? Studies show that once a company suffers a data breach, our trust in that company drops significantly. The data breach at Australia's Medibank impacted the prominent private health insurer significantly. Following the incident in October 2022, the company has grappled with sustained levels of mistrust and after nine months it is ranked as the 6th most distrusted brand[20] in the local market.

29.78 What about the things we see on our Meta feed? There's been a lot of talk in the past few years about fake news – how can one determine if a certain article is fake or not? Well, on one hand that's pretty easy, really because it only requires checking for a few facts, part of the problem is that most people don't do that. On the other hand, hunting for facts becomes more and more of a task in the era of generative artificial intelligence that can produce any text in seconds and automatically distribute information that spreads multiple versions of reality in hours.

29.79 Meta (then Facebook) has been accused of enabling fake news outlets to grow and, in this process, to influence the result of the 2016 US elections when Donald Trump was elected president. Thousands of fake accounts were

20 Distrust after data breaches lingers for months – Roy Morgan Single Source (Australia). Risk Monitor, 12 month average to June 2023 – https://www.roymorgan.com/findings/9306-risk-monitor-quartely-update-june-2023.

discovered, pushing fake news made in some basement somewhere, and countless accounts that had bought ads pushing this type of false content to Trump voters. It has reached a point where many individuals live in an alternative reality where facts don't matter, and when facts are brought to the table, they're dismissed. One of the reasons why this is happening is the fact that Trump keeps pushing this 'fake news' phrase around, especially when it concerns reliable news outlets simply because they criticise his actions. Another is the way the Meta News feed worked. More specifically, when you surround yourself with people that have the same beliefs as you do, you're only going to see articles from certain sources.

29.80 Meta started surveying people to figure out which news sources they trusted, but given its history, not much is going to change – the people that get delivered erroneous articles are still going to get those – because that's what they trust in. As part of the effort to reestablish social media and comply with EU regulations, Meta, among other social media giants, has started publishing Transparency Reports that are available in detail through their Transparency Center. According to Meta on Face Accounts: 'Accounts actioned increased from 426 million in Q1 2023 to 676 million in Q2 2023 due to updates in our calculations to align with the Digital Services Act.' [21]

29.81 A 2017 study from the Pew Research Center[22] shows people are hopeful about the future. Nearly half of those who responded to the questionnaire believed that people's trust in their online interactions would grow over the next decade, while 28% believed the situation would remain the same, while 24% believe trust will be diminished. When asked what they think will help change things, many individuals brought up various advances in security, encryption technologies, as well as Blockchain. According to Pew Research Center's study[23] only five years later shows a majority (61%) of the people are sceptical that anything they do to protect their personal information will make much difference.

29.82 Although the Blockchain technology has been around for more than a decade, ever since Bitcoin was invented by Satoshi Nakamoto, it's still not gaining enough traction as a solution to many issues, including trade chains, financial transactions, and more. The encryption-protected digital ledger is controlled by no one man in particular, and it cannot be altered. A public ledger anyone can inspect can help establish trust between individuals, companies, and governments. Yet it seems that the technology, probably too abstract and without proper backing up or legitimacy of trusted governance, cannot give trust the expected boost.

21 Transparency Center, Face Accounts – Meta, https://transparency.fb.com/reports/community-standards-enforcement/fake-accounts/facebook/.

22 The Fate of Online Trust in the Next Decade – Pew Research Center, www.pewinternet.org/2017/08/10/the-fate-of-online-trust-in-the-next-decade/.

23 Key findings about Americans and data privacy – Pew Research Center, https://www.pewresearch.org/short-reads/2023/10/18/key-findings-about-americans-and-data-privacy/.

29.83 When asked about trust in the 2017 study, answers covered six major themes, ranging from very positive outlook on the situation to some pretty pessimistic views. The first theme claimed that trust would strengthen because systems will improve and people will adapt to them, while a second focused on the fact that the nature of trust will become more fluid as technology becomes a more integral part to human and organisational relationships. Others believed that trust would not grow, but technology usage will continue to rise, as we settle into a 'new normal.' A fourth theme mentioned by respondents put Blockchain at the centre of it all, saying that the technology could help improve things, although others believe its value might be limited when it comes to establishing trust. A fifth theme gathered all the people who believe that the current situation will not change much in the next decade, while a sixth believed trust will diminish because the Internet is not secure.

29.84 Five years later, in 2023, with the emergence of AI, responsible use of the technology concerns many Americans and people worldwide. 70% of the respondents have little to no trust in companies 'to make responsible decisions about how they use AI in their products'.

AI IS THE NEW AUTHENTIC?

29.85 Trust is the brother of authenticity. We cannot build trust without provenance and credibility. And authenticity is closely related to how we perceive our reality, what we think of truth.

We believe there are many sides to the truth. Perspectives, situations, social norms, and time influence what we consider true. When telling the truth, we are often guided by our empathy, our ability to empathise with someone, to put ourselves in their shoes. We don't necessarily agree with the person we are proving right, but we can imagine that from their point of view, according to their set of norms, they are right.

29.86 Since our perceived truth in cyberspace is rooted in facts that we believe are facts, we turn to our technology layer, the IT systems, for storing and retrieving them. That is why it is so essential to build trust in technology. IT systems were created to keep facts: data that we can work with and produce more data from. But it also works the other way around, and we may feel that what is in IT systems are facts.

29.87 The definition of trust between humans may differ when machines are involved, either on the sending or receiving side, and even when we discuss trust between two machines.

As technology advances, machines can communicate in an increasingly 'persuasive' human way, and as a consequence, people's attitudes towards them change.

29.88 The whole picture, of course, also involves the question of human biological perception since we believe in what we see or think we know. Sensory perceptions are increasingly likely to deceive us. This is one of the fundamental problems of the Deepfake phenomenon.

29.89 If the truth, as perceived by the receiving person, is backed up by technology with facts and data in a medium, situation and perception that the receiver currently has confidence in, it will be considered credible and authentic.

29.90 Artificial Intelligence is the kind of technology we more and more trust. AI plays a significant role in operating the mediums we store and retrieve information from. Meta, Twitter, or LinkedIn newsfeeds rely on AI to pick the relevant content for us. AI can produce text that looks human-made and can create artificial sounds, images, and videos of humans that have never existed in real.

So, in that sense, AI, either as a significant contributor, enhancer, or creator itself, is at the centre of our perceived reality. As such, it is also the new foundation of authenticity of people, business and governments. That is why we need to consider AI not just as part of the solution but also as part of the problem.

WHAT'S THE SOLUTION?

29.91 The reality is that there's no solve-all solution here, but here are some suggestions that might oil things up a bit. Artificial Intelligence is a field that is constantly growing and evolving, with applications widening day by day. One of the things AI is great at is sifting through massive amounts of data.

29.92 New LLM (Large Language Models) and LMM (Large Multimodal Models) are available in the hundreds for writing text, generating images, and recognising human context in them. With billions of dollars poured into developing AI the race is on between technology giants. AI is also democratised by thousands of different sizes of open-source models and developers coming up with new ideas daily.

29.93 Comprehensive studies suggest that the AI models we work with today might even be 'partly conscious'.[24] OpenAI's (the company behind ChatGPT) top researcher, Ilya Sutskever, in late 2023, claimed in a Tweet that 'large neural networks are slightly conscious'. The GPT-4 model has reached between IQ140-150, and LMMs are proving to be empathic, understand human context, can reason, and if given memory, can even plan and work with other copies of themselves like humans would. These technological improvements pave the way for a new generation of digital assistants working closely with humans, so much so that they would even deeply understand them.

24 *Consciousness in Artificial Intelligence: Insights from the Science of Consciousness* – Butlin, Pet al. (2023), doi.org/10.48550/arXiv.2308.0870.

29.94 But what if the new digital assistants finally will be able to analyse our daily behaviour? One of more AI, customised for each of us, in our phones and wearable techs, learning about our behaviour, learning what our social norms are, where we live, how we think, and so on. We are just a few announcements away from an AI assistant that would learn what we are likely to consider a secret, what is important for our privacy. Then, it would protect only the data that was essential and, in case of need, surface only the required data.

29.95 Picture this. You have all your secrets on your phone and the police suspect you of selling drugs, for instance. The truth is that you are only smoking pot from time to time, but you're still uncomfortable giving the police access to your phone to exonerate yourself. This AI could, at the specific request of the police, pull out all the data needed to show that you're not involved in distributing drugs, such as the location where you were when a transaction took place, or a lack of conversations regarding actually setting up meetings to sell drugs (maybe come up with a different example). The police got the information it needed, your secrets were protected, the investigation moves on to a different suspect.

29.96 Or, knowing the AI has your secrets encrypted, you wouldn't be too concerned about the police going through your data. Only in case, a special request was made would the AI reveal one of your secrets that is relevant to the case.

29.97 Not only would this type of personal technology protect you from unwanted attention from authorities, but it would also protect you against nosy friends, cybercriminals, hackers, secret agencies of rouge governments, or common thieves.

29.98 Today LLM's can author complete books and graphical neural networks can create 3D models of an object using only a couple of images or turn a picture in bad resolution into a sharper image combining the insufficient information with machine learning and neural network capabilities. It is safe to say that we are on the verge of using machines to resolve problems we haven't been able to sort out amongst ourselves. One of these should be the solution to the cyber-secret paradigm: how to protect our personal and organisational secrets the most human-focused, human-aligned and context-aware way while providing access to only the relevant part of any sensitive information and do so for the necessary duration and scope. That is the challenge today in the shadow of billions of unprotected IoT devices, zettabytes of cyber-space traffic, colourful motivations of cyber-criminals or governments and people who are having a hard time defining what privacy means to them. New AI assistants will be like computers stepping out of a fantastic movie. Our near future of privacy is like the sci-fi encounters of Star Trek's spaceship the Enterprise. Loaded with technology, equipped with thinking and talking artificial intelligence, and facing hard to resolve moral or logical dilemmas all the time. Shields up, secrets ready.

CHAPTER 30

A PLAN FOR THE SME

William McBorrough

BUILDING A SMALL BUSINESS SECURITY RISK MANAGEMENT PLAN

30.01 Many people constantly juggle between the dual roles of a small business owner and information security professional. This requires a balancing act that many small business owners should, but fail to, attempt. The calculus is the same for most businesses: Lower cost, increase revenues. However managing costs, for small businesses, is always a challenge.

30.02 Increasing cyber-security 'awareness' has always been seen as the obvious answer. The reality is that awareness is passive. The implication that greater awareness is sufficient to prompt better behaviour is belied by the fact that many organisations that have reported breaches have some attempts at a 'security awareness training' for their employees.

30.03 Security is a means to an end. This is especially true for for-profit business entities. As a business leader, you are responsible for ensuring the protection of your organisation's assets; this includes its mission critical data, the systems used to store, process and transport them and the employees that utilise and depend on them. To do this in a cost-effective, efficient, and effective manner, you need an enterprise information security management program.

Where do you start?

30.04 Although improving an organisation's security and risk management may seem a daunting task, it doesn't have to be. Adopting simple risk management steps helps small and medium-sized businesses proactively implement simple best practices to protect their businesses. Security should be built into your business processes, information technology (IT), and most importantly your employees and contractors. Each business is unique and faces challenges particular to their operations. There is no magic pill that guarantees 100% security. There are security experts available to help you understand your unique risks and implement solutions that work your particular business environment.

30.05 Many small business leaders are in denial when it comes to cyber-risks. Common excuses are:

1. 'We are too small.'
2. 'We can't afford it.'

3. 'Our IT guy is taking care of it.'

4. 'It's too complicated.'

30.06 But that's not all, is it?

There are always 'more pressing' priorities competing for time, resources, and energy. But let's consider the common misconceptions.

You are not a big, well known business. Why would anyone attack you?

30.07 Most small businesses get their cyber-security information from the news media reports. The stories usually feature large brand names, millions of affected users and millions of dollars lost. What's not reported is that small businesses are experiencing more cyber-attacks than their larger counterparts. After analysing millions of emails from thousands of companies from January 2021 to December 2021, researchers at Barracuda Networks, a leading cloud security company, discovered that employees working in small businesses, with less than 100 staff members, encountered a staggering 350% more social engineering attacks compared to their counterparts in larger enterprises. This finding underscores the pressing need for robust security measures in order to safeguard organisations from such threats.

30.08 As big companies become more and more security conscious, attackers are increasingly turning their sights on small businesses. While it might be the case that well trained, well-funded hackers may not be very interested in the average small company, most online attacks aren't carried out by expert hackers. Attacks are perpetrated by low-skilled, common criminals with access to pre-packaged hacking tools, thereby casting a wide net in the hope of finding an unprotected computer system or network. These tools are easy to use and readily available on the internet, often free of charge. The anonymity of a cyber-attack makes it even more attractive to criminals. Many attackers use safe havens in foreign countries which do not have strong cyber-crime laws or extradition treaties.

30.09 Malicious software like viruses, worms, trojan horses, spam and bots are all vectors of cyber-attacks that are indiscriminately spreading across the internet. These attacks don't only target small business computer systems but also seek to use unprotected systems to launch attack on others.

It's too costly

30.10 According to the 2021 SMB Data Breach Statistics from Verizon, 95% of cybersecurity incidents at SMEs cost between $826 to $653,587. These damages can spiral due to cost of system downtime and recovery, legal fees and compliance fines, damages to reputation, etc. Although the cost of inaction far outweighs the cost of addressing the risks.

30.11 The second primary source of cyber-security information is security vendors. There is an entire eco-system of security products, services, gadgets, widgets, and on and on. Small business owners are constantly bombarded with sales pitches for point solutions to specific security challenges. Each vendor is focused on the specific problem which the tool or service supposedly solves. In order words, if I'm selling hammers, I'm only concerned with your nails. Not your screws, bolts, nuts, etc. Although you might need those more urgently, and can get them at much lower costs.

30.12 The sum of these point solutions quickly add up leaving small business owners with the impression that if they do anything about security, it will likely cost them more than they can afford.

30.13 The reality is that many aspects of a security risk management program don't require an organisation to spend any money at all. Some organisations might need to hire a security advisor to guide them but that expertise will inevitably save them from making unwise financial decisions about procuring security services and/or products. Creating security policies, procedures, and guidelines are the foundation of a security program. Businesses needs a security strategy before spending any money.

Hasn't the IT guy(s) already dealt with this issue?

30.14 Years before 'cybersecurity' became the buzzword it is today, 'information security' or 'information assurance' were the terms more commonly used. The objective was much more obvious then. Provide needed safeguards for protected information in every medium ie verbal, written, digitised. A common example used when illustrating this point is that if one writes down a sensitive account information about a client on a sheet of paper and leave that at a coffee shop, that is considered a security breach or incident, and one that has nothing at all to do with technology. Hence, your IT guy can't save you. Although cyber-security includes traditional 'IT' related issues, it primarily focuses on protecting valuable information from all threats including physical attacks, data corruption, equipment failure, social engineering, and bad security choices due to insufficient security awareness education, etc. Effective security risk management requires specific training related to threats, vulnerabilities, and risks affecting computer systems, business operational processes, and most importantly you and your employees. One's security problems cannot be addressed solely by off the shelf products or IT service management.

Too Complicated?

30.15 Security can certainly be complicated. Consider the fast-moving technology landscape, ever-changing regulatory requirements, business needs, client needs, etc. That's enough to make a small business owner's head spin. That said, the fundamentals of security are and have been constant for quite some time. Protect the confidentiality, integrity and availability of information and information systems by identifying, evaluating and managing risks to them. So how does one do that?

Why you need a formal security program?

30.16 A security program provides the framework for establishing, implementing and maintaining an acceptable level of security risk to your organisation's assets and operations as determined by executive leadership. The scope, scale and complexity of such a program must be driven by your organisation's business and security needs. A security program also allows you to examine your organisation holistically and:

- identify, classify and categorise your assets that need protecting;
- identify and evaluate threats to those assets;
- identify and assess where those assets are vulnerable to evaluated threats;
- manage the resulting risks to those assets through mitigation, transference, avoidance and acceptance.

Current state of security management

30.17 The reality is that all organisations are doing ***something*** with respect to security. Without a formal security program, however, most businesses respond to the ever-expanding landscape of network intrusions, data breaches, system failures and other security incidents in an ad-hoc and reactive manner. They react to the individual crisis du jour without a well thought out approach. This leads to spending unnecessary time, money and other resources to address the symptoms rather than the root cause. A simple root cause analysis will most likely lead to the lack of an organised, enterprise-wide approach to managing your security risks that allows the business to prioritise your security investments and efforts.

30.18 Reports of data breaches are an almost daily occurrence. These breaches often lead to the loss of sensitive, personal and/or valuable information. A commonly reported cause attributed to an unpatched web server or application. Businesses usually respond to this attribution by ordering the IT department or service provider to launch an aggressive patching effort. While applying security patches and fixes to vulnerable servers and applications is definitely needed, having unpatched servers and applications on your network is merely a symptom of a systemic problem. This problem could include lack of proper security oversight, policies, procedures, risk management, security architecture, employee training etc. all of which could have contributed to preventing the breach and resulting loss of reputation, system downtime, recovery cost, legal fees, etc. Unless the multiple causes are addressed, the organisation will continue to *ricochet* from one security incident to the next. Security vendors and service providers are more than willing to sell you point solutions to deal with any subset of technical security challenges but as business managers across industries and sectors face increasing threats and decreasing budgets, you can ill-afford to continue down that path.

Security Program Standards and Best Practices

30.19 There exists a number for frameworks for building, managing and maturing a security program. The International Organization for Standardization (ISO) and the International Electrotechnical Commission (IEC) provides recommendations for information security program management (ISO/ IEC 27002). Other common security frameworks include the National Institute of Science and Technology (NIST),[1] Control Objectives for Information and related Technology (COBIT), Committee of Sponsoring Organizations of the Treadway Commission (COSO) and the HiTRUST Common Security Framework (CSF). Regardless of which framework you employ, it must be tailored to fit your organisation's business model, operations and technology environment.

Security Program Components

30.20 Regardless of industry sector or organisation size, there are five components that are the foundation of any security program:

1. **Designated security leader**

   Security within an organisation is everyone's responsibility. However, your organisation must designate a security officer or manager to lead, implement and manage the security program. This is a requirement for most security regulations and standards, with some requiring that this role be at the executive management level. Your security leader should have the authority and support to champion the cause of security as a business driver and enabler from the boardroom to the operations floor.

2. **Security Policy Framework**

   Your security policy documents the organisation's leadership's goals for managing security risk and protecting the organisation's assets. Your policy framework also includes standards, procedures and guidelines that govern the implementation of the security program across all of the organisation's business units and functions. Your policy framework should be reviewed and updated periodically ensure it keeps pace with the ever-changing regulatory compliance requirements, business operations and technology landscape.

3. **Risk Management Framework**

   Your security program must continuously assess threats and vulnerabilities in order to identify, measure and prioritise risks to the organisation's

1 www.nist.gov/cyberframework.

assets that must be managed. Periodic enterprise risk assessments must be performed to include security penetration testing of security procedures and controls and employee security awareness and practices.

4. **Security Architecture and Operations**

   An enterprise security architecture enables your organisation to implement necessary technology infrastructure that maximises ROI and minimises risk. A layered approach to applying security controls allows you to protect your data, applications, systems and networks. Security event monitoring and response allows your organisation to efficiently detect and mitigate security incidents that lead to data breaches, system downtime and network intrusions.

5. **Security Awareness and Training Program**

   A security awareness program and role-based security training are essential to educating your employees about their roles and responsibilities in helping to maintain a strong security posture. Users are often considered the 'weakest link' in an organisation's security controls, however users that are trained and equipped with the tools needed to perform their duties securely are your first line of defense against security threats.

It's really all about risks

30.21 It is often useful to try to move the focus away from 'cybersecurity' and technology-related threats to business risks. That's why security matters. Not because security is the 'right thing to do' but because it's a means of managing risks to the mission, the business. This approach is independent of the size of the business. The steps are as follows and can be applied to assets, processes, people, etc:

30.22 A risk management approach focusing on assets would be as follows:

- identify what are the assets that the business depends on is critical;
- what are the threats to these assets;
- where are those assets vulnerable to those threats.

30.23 Once those three elements have been established, the business can focus on the high-risk areas that are critical to business' daily activities. This is an exercise that needs to be done prior to a small business (or any business) spending money or a time on security. Basically, 'what is that risk and how do I mitigate that risk'.

Case Study

30.24 To illustrate the point that businesses of any size can adopt this approach let's consider a single person entity – 'Sally, Inc.'

30.25 Sally is a consultant. She is always on the go, has no permanent office and no real IT or business infrastructure. She has no employees and a number of clients whom she services directly. Sally, Inc. has no security program. Sally depends primarily on her handy mobile phone with which she communicates with her clients and business partners, stores clients related data, manage her time and activities.

30.26 As an aside, I would point out that quite a number of our clients are single person entities and because of the industries, are required to maintain a formal information security and risk management program.

Security Risk Management Process

Step 1. Identify Critical Assets

30.27 Sally relies heavily on her mobile phone to conduct much of her business. This makes the device a 'mission critical asset' ie an asset that is critical to achieving the mission on the business. Sally depends on this asset for three critical business functions.

1. Communication

   Sally uses the mobile phone to make calls, send emails and texts, share business updates and marketing via social media, and communicate with current and prospective clients, business associates and others.

2. Data Storage

   Sally uses her mobile phone to store and access contact information, previous communications, saved files and other information necessary to the day-to-day operations of Sally, Inc.

3. Business Operations

   The mobile phone provides Sally with a full suite of applications for productivity, marketing, sales, financial management and other business functions that she depends on to achieve the mission of Sally, Inc.

30.28 Sally has identified the mobile device as mission critical because if it were inaccessible or unavailable to her, that would have a negative impact on her ability to perform the activities critical to achieving her business' mission.

Step 2. Identify Threats

30.29 Threats to this mission critical asset includes anything that could potentially affect the confidentiality (allow unauthorised access to the data or device), integrity (allow unauthorised modification to the data or device) or availability (prevent authorised access to the data or device). There are many potential threats however Sally is concerned with those that could affect her mobile device. Identifying one's mission critical assets allows the business to focus on threats relevant to that asset, not ALL threats. In this case, Sally identifies the following as potential relevant threats:

1. Gravity, clumsy fingers – These could cause the phone to fall or be dropped.
2. Thieves, faulty memory – These could cause the phone to be lost or stolen.
3. Shoulder surfers, nosy people – These could allow others to see sensitive information about Sally's business and clients.
4. Software bugs – These could cause the phone to become unusable.

Step 3. Identify Vulnerabilities

30.30 Vulnerabilities are any weakness or lack of protection that could allow identified threats to cause harm or adversely impact the mission critical asset. Sally is not concerned with all possible vulnerabilities. She identifies corresponding weaknesses relevant to the identified threats as follows:

1. Glass screen – The mobile phone has a glass screen that is used to view data on the phone and also control phone functions (touchscreen). This glass is susceptible to scratches, cracks, breaks if the phone was dropped on a hard surface. Sally recalls how many times she has already dropped the phone.
2. Small, portable – The mobile phone is designed to be small, portable and lightweight. This makes it easy to conceal by a thief or lose tract of by the owner. Sally is very busy and with a wireless headset, recalls how many times she has almost lost her phone on the train, in the gym, left it at home, etc.
3. Screen visibility by third parties – The mobile phone has a clear, bright, glass screen which makes it easy to see what Sally has on the screen, especially in a crowded train, in a coffee shop and all the numerous other places Sally finds herself working during her business day visiting clients, attending events, making sales calls, etc.
4. Poor software development, testing-vendor – Sally knows that she is prompted to update her phone's operating system very often. She is also prompted to perform numerous updates on the many apps she depends on the phone. Sally has no way of verifying these updates and has to trust the vendors and developers. Some of these updates have led to glitches on the past the affected some function that Sally depends on.

Step 4. Assess Risks

30.31 With the asset, threats and vulnerabilities identified, Sally can now consider the resulting risk. Many of the point solutions referenced earlier in this chapter are meant to address specific threats and vulnerabilities. However, Sally is primarily concerned with the associated risk those pose to the mission of the business. Sally knows that she has neither the time, money, nor inclination to combat all threats or address all vulnerabilities. Sally is mission-focused. Risk is assessed by calculating or measuring the likelihood or probability that those identified threats can exploit related vulnerabilities to negatively impact the critical asset thereby affecting the mission of Sally, Inc. The likelihood ranges from Unlikely to Possible to Likely. The impact or consequence can range from Minor to Moderate to Major. The risk can then be assessed as the likelihood that consequence occurring for the business. Risk is measured as Low to Medium to High. This helps Sally prioritize where to focus her security efforts, time and money.

Risk = Likelihood * Consequences

	Consequences		
Likelihood	Minor	Moderate	Major
Likely	MEDIUM	HIGH	HIGH
Possible	LOW	MEDIUM	HIGH
Unlikely	LOW	LOW	MEDIUM

Sally, Inc. Critical Asset Risk Assessment

30.32

1. Clumsy fingers and dropping the phone: Sally is also on the go. It's quite likely she could drop the phone and with a glass screen, it could crack or break. This could disable the phone thus preventing its use for business needs. The likelihood is Likely. The consequence is Major. The assessed risk would be **High**.
2. Losing the phone: Sally is always on the go and the phone is small. Because Sally tries to be careful, the likelihood of losing the phone or having it stolen is assessed at Possible. This would still have a Major impact of her business as she would lose access to data and communications. The assessed risk in this case is still **High**.
3. Screen visibility: Sally stores all her clients' contact information on her phone, including billing information. She has invoicing, project management, marketing and communication applications which she uses daily. Although, she is always conscious of her surroundings. She sometimes has to work in very close proximity to other people in public. The likelihood of someone else seeing sensitive data on her phone is possible. The impact of that could be assessed as moderate depending on the kind of information. That would lead to an assed risk level of **Medium**.
4. Software update: Sally has always updated her phone and applications when prompted. She knows that many of the updates includes security fixes and updated features that would benefit her business. Although she has experienced glitches in the past due to updates, none of them have severely

impacted the phone communication functions nor denied her access to her information. She does realise however that this is a possibility. However, frequently, performing the updates, especially for applications, are required for continued usage. She believes that the likelihood of an update severely affecting the phone is low based on past experiences. The impact would be moderate as most of her applications store their data in the cloud so she would still be able to access it should be need to. This would lead to a risk assessment of **Low**.

30.33 All of the risks have been identified and assessed. Now Sally has the information she needs to make an informed decision as to how to manage the assessed risks to her business.

Step 5. Manage Risk (Avoid, Mitigate, Transfer, Accept)

30.34 There are four basic risk management options:

Mitigation: Employ controls to reduce either the likelihood or impact ie Reduce the Risk.

Avoidance: Change behaviour to avoid the Risk.

Transference: Transfer the Risk to a Third Party.

Acceptance: Accept the risk and carry on.

1. Sally can purchase a protective case and screen cover for her phone thus protecting it from damage of the phone falls on a hard surface – **Risk Mitigation**.
2. Sally can add a password to protect her information in case someone else gains physical access to the phone. She can also back up all her data in case the phone gets lost or stolen. She can also unable or install location tracker functionality to always be able to locate the phone. These are all examples of **Risk Mitigation**. Sally can also purchase insurance on her phone to get it replaced at a lower cost if needed. This transfers the full cost of replacing the phone to an insurance carrier. This is **Risk Transference**.
3. Sally can modify her behaviour to ensure that she only uses the phone to access sensitive information. She can also purchase a privacy screen cover which reduces the visibility of information on the screen to only persons directly facing the screen. These actions are considered **Risk Mitigation**.
4. Sally knows she cannot delay phone and application updates indefinitely. As the risk to her was considered low she decides to continue to install the updates. **This is Risk Acceptance.** Sally also has the option of totally changing the way she runs her business so as not to depend on her mobile phone. This would be **Risk Avoidance.** In this case, this would be reasonable if Sally has other more secure options readily available and easily adoptable.

30.35 With this process documented and repeated periodically for all mission critical assets or processes, Sally, Inc. now has a security risk management program she can maintain with her size of company. Naturally, more mature organisations would have a more mature risk management program. However, if Sally can build a security risk management program, all businesses can as well.

Now that you know

30.36 Consider these important steps.

1. Have you identified your mission critical assets and processes? ***Consider the impact to your business.***

2. Have you thought about the threats that may affect them and adversely impact your business? ***Consider the threat to your assets and processes.***

3. Have you looked for where your assets might be susceptible to those threats? Consider ***Vulnerabilities relevant to identified threats.***

4. Have you assessed the risk by considering the potential likelihood and impact to your business? ***Measure and prioritise the risk.***

5. Have you made an informed, conscious decision in line with your business mission and needs about your risk? ***Make informed business decisions on how to invest time and resources.***

CHAPTER 31

CONCLUSION

Helen Wong MBE

31.01 As of the time of writing, we are now being governed by a Labour Government that recognises the importance of cyber security and AI as both an opportunity and a threat. The sector has effectively created an extra 2,700 job openings and generated a revenue of £11.9 billion. However, the continued threats persist and carry significant risks.

31.02 Key Technology Policies announced in the Labour Manifesto Include:

'Delivering growth and raising productivity depend on fresh thinking and new ideas. Britain has many cutting-edge businesses, but innovation needs to be converted into commercial success in every corner of our country' (Labour Party Manifesto, June 2024)

'DSIT will become the digital centre for government' – Peter Kyle, Shadow Science, Innovation and Technology Secretary and expected to keep this role under within Starmer's first cabinet has stated that he wants the digital centre for government to be responsible for 'delivering common platforms and reforming roadblocks to data exchange across the public sector'.

31.03 The objective is to increase the size of the co-operative and mutuals sector in the UK by double. Our intention is to work alongside the sector to overcome the challenges they encounter, specifically the obstacle of securing financial resources.

31.04 To efficiently combat tax avoidance, it is crucial to prioritise investments in innovative technology and fortify the capabilities of HMRC by implementing modernisation initiatives.

31.05 The most recent update entails the classification of data centres in the UK as critical national infrastructure, alongside emergency services, finance, and healthcare systems, as well as energy and water supplies. Data centres are expansive facilities housing extensive arrays of computers that remotely support various services, including artificial intelligence (AI) applications, data processing, and streaming.

ARTIFICIAL INTELLIGENCE (AI)

31.06 The advent of Artificial Intelligence marks the next progressive phase that the world must navigate, with its prevalence in both Cyber Security threats and solutions. The current focus of the discussion centres around ensuring the ethical advancement and implementation of AI models, as well as implementing regulatory measures on a select group of companies that are spearheading the development of highly advanced AI models.

31.07 The implementation of a strategic plan with the objective of facilitating the growth of the Artificial Intelligence (AI) industry and removing regulatory impediments to the establishment of new datacentres.

INDUSTRIAL STRATEGY AND R&D

31.08 It has been proposed that a statutory Industrial Strategy Council be created to provide expert guidance.

31.09 Furthermore, we aim to improve the national planning policy in order to better accommodate the demands of a contemporary economy, thus streamlining the construction process for laboratories, digital infrastructure, and gigafactories.

31.10 The creation of a National Data Library aims to bring together ongoing research programs, foster data-driven public services, and uphold stringent measures to protect public welfare.

31.11 By replacing short funding cycles with ten-year budgets, we aim to facilitate impactful collaborations between key R&D institutions and industry, thus ensuring the UK's continued leadership in global innovation.

31.12 The objective is to enhance the procurement process and stimulate innovation by minimising micromanagement through a mission-oriented approach.

31.13 The development of a comprehensive ten-year infrastructure strategy, aligned with an industrial strategy and regional development priorities, focused on improving rail connectivity in the northern region of England. The strategy will provide guidance for investment plans and offer the private sector a sense of certainty regarding the project pipeline.

DATA AND ONLINE SAFETY

31.14 In order to ensure the safety of individuals online, particularly on social media platforms, and to effectively combat online threats, it is essential to explore additional measures and enhance fraud strategies.

31.15 The introduction of a National Data Library would foster the amalgamation of existing research endeavours and elevate the provision of data-driven public services, all the while upholding robust security measures.

31.16 It is crucial to prioritise the reinforcement of online security measures for all users, particularly on social media platforms. This can be accomplished by further developing the current Online Safety Act.

CYBER SECURITY

31.17 Given the recent cyber-attacks and the ongoing concerns surrounding safety and security, the Labour Party has decided to conduct a Strategic Defence Review within the first year of assuming government. This review intends to outline a comprehensive plan for achieving a 2.5% growth in defence expenditure.

31.18 The Labour Party intends to develop a comprehensive plan for cyber defence to ensure the protection of critical infrastructure.

31.19 It is crucial to prioritise the thorough preparedness of the United Kingdom in countering hybrid warfare, including cyber-attacks.

CLEAN ENERGY

31.20 Our goal is to transform Britain into a dominant force in clean energy, resulting in reduced costs, job creation, and enhanced security through affordable, zero-carbon electricity by 2030, with an accelerated path to achieving net zero emissions.

31.21 Allocate an annual budget of up to £500 million beginning in 2026 to reward clean energy developers through the implementation of a British Jobs Bonus.

31.22 The introduction of the National Wealth Fund aims to provide assistance in decarbonising the sectors with the highest energy consumption.

BROADBAND AND 5G

31.23 We need to redouble our efforts in order to achieve the objective of complete gigabit and nationwide 5G coverage by 2030.

How does the Labour Manifesto impact the Cyber Security Space?

31.24 The manifesto clearly demonstrates Labour's strong emphasis on technology across its various commitments, providing a reason for optimism among those engaged in the tech sector. The government's manifesto clearly states its intention to harness the transformative power of technology in order to effectively carry out a substantial portion of its key manifesto commitments. Let's consider the NHS as an illustrative example, where technology serves as the foundation for Labour's notable pledge to reduce waiting times. There is a clear acknowledgement that successful implementation requires a substantial investment in new technologies.

31.25 The Labour manifesto consistently embodies a specific viewpoint on technology and its influence on the tech industry, covering diverse domains such as renewable energy, public service restructuring, and the application of Artificial Intelligence. Noteworthy financial commitments within it include a £1.5 billion investment in new gigafactories, a £1 billion investment in carbon capture technology, and £500 million allocated for green hydrogen manufacturers.

31.26 Although not explicitly highlighted, technology is integral to all of Labour's pledges. The Manifesto suggests that technology should be utilised not just for economic growth and enhanced productivity but also as a means to tackle the societal issues faced by the UK.

31.27 Nonetheless, there are individuals within the sector who maintain a measured sense of optimism while addressing the challenges that the tech industry encounters. Although the technology investment plans seem commendable, their feasibility in light of public spending decisions during uncertain economic conditions remains uncertain. The Labour Party's greatest challenge lies in the domain of public sector IT projects. The implementation of efficiency projects can be hindered, especially when the leadership has already presumed the expected savings.

31.28 The book's expert contributions demonstrate that cyber-security is a complex and multifaceted matter. Its impact extends beyond hardware to encompass software, as well as individuals' perceptions and attitudes. It encompasses both criminal and civil laws, prompting governments around the world to develop defensive measures. As the world increasingly emphasises connectivity, digital transformation initiatives, wearables, the Internet of Things, and ubiquitous Wifi, ensuring cyber-security will become an imperative concern for businesses of all sizes and sectors.

31.29 The Cloudstrike incident in 2024 highlights the remarkable proficiency and determination of cyber-criminals. Moreover, the incident known as the 'Clop' cyber-attack, wherein a Russian cyber-criminal group managed to effectively hold sensitive data from well-established institutions such as the BBC, BA, and Boots as ransom, serves as a striking reminder of the necessity to maintain a state of constant vigilance and exercise caution towards potential vulnerabilities. Unfortunately, we cannot escape the reality that these attacks will persist and grow in severity. It is important to note that this issue is not limited to IT. It is of utmost importance that we, as a collective, address this issue, remain vigilant, and take decisive action to eradicate the vulnerabilities within the system. In the pages of this book, we have thoroughly examined the multitude of threats and the corresponding strategies for their conquest. It has been noted that threats can emerge not just from software vulnerabilities, but also from physical breaches, such as neglecting to password-protect your laptop, which can be likened to leaving your front door unlocked. Security should be the foremost concern in both our personal and professional domains.

31.30 Provided below are my cyber-security predictions that I expect to have a lasting impact on us in 2025 and the years to come.

PREVENTION IS BETTER THAN CURE

31.31 In line with human nature, it is customary for both businesses and individuals to postpone the resolution of problems until they have reached a state of dysfunction. The problem with such a mentality lies in the fact that, in the majority of the cyber-attacks we have discussed, no tangible harm was inflicted. It is expected that there will be an increase in cyber-attacks, leading individuals to adopt a proactive approach. The future will see businesses increasingly prioritise the safeguarding of hardware, software, and physical premises. Furthermore, this strategy will yield greater financial advantages in the long run, encompassing both profitability and reputation. In order to attain the most favourable result, it is recommended to give priority to detection, followed by a comprehensive response and subsequent remediation process after any attack. The ongoing battle shows no signs of stopping. The primary concern at present is to determine the parties that will be affected. The pivotal question concerns the point at which an individual will encounter the repercussions. It is strongly recommended to make preparations for future events rather than trying to handle an attack without any support.

INTERNET OF THINGS WILL CAUSE MORE CYBER-ATTACKS AND FINANCIAL LOSS.

31.32 The pursuit of connectivity yields beneficial consequences as it facilitates the transformation of cities into the twenty-first century. Nonetheless, these networks offer a compelling chance for malicious actors to gain access to any interconnected residence or organisation within the realm of Internet of Things (IoT). The attack surface is anticipated to expand, particularly for households lacking comprehensive knowledge of IoT security, rendering them vulnerable to cyber-attacks. Tackling the security challenges associated with the Internet of Things (IoT) requires an extensive educational campaign and a centralised security initiative, spearheaded by the government, aimed at safeguarding numerous devices against infection and cyber-attacks.

THE RISE IN RANSOMWARE

31.33 The concept of ransomware involves cyber-criminals extorting money from businesses and households by restricting access to their computer systems until a monetary ransom is paid. The individual who was once involved in bank robbery has now transitioned to using computer systems to drain bank accounts electronically. The financial burden is ultimately borne by the victims due to their failure to back up their systems and their potential involvement in the attack, such as accepting downloads, disclosing passwords, or unknowingly transferring funds to fraudulent accounts. Please give thought to this idea: the formulation of a contingency plan that would facilitate the continuation of operations in the event of a cyber-attack that cripples the system. It is advised not to make any payments to them. Daily backups of all files are imperative to ensure uninterrupted functioning. It is crucial to remember that when you provide payment to criminals, you inadvertently support the establishment of a sustainable business model.

TO CLOUD OR NOT?

31.34 Regardless of the device being utilised, the prevalence of cloud computing continues to expand. Storing data in the cloud not only increases storage capacity on your devices, but also offers the possibility of cost savings by eliminating the need for larger hardware purchases. Similar to the concept of the Internet of Things (IoT), cybercriminals are unequivocally focussing on cloud infrastructure as a prime target for potential hacking endeavours. Security, trust, and testing are among the key factors.

CAN ARTIFICIAL INTELLIGENCE FIGHT BACK?

31.35 Encryption is being utilised as a measure to ensure the protection of passwords. Furthermore, the emergence of artificial intelligence presents the potential for a redeeming element. Machines have the ability to acquire algorithms, identify pre-emptive issues, and self-instruct in response to cyber threats. For instance, they are able to facilitate the shutdown of a machine prior to the downloading of malware, hinder hackers by detecting flagged anomalies, and comprehend the patterns of potential cybercriminal behaviour. The implementation of artificial intelligence on IoT devices or in the cloud has the potential to identify vulnerabilities and breach points, playing a pivotal role in shaping the future of the cyber-security landscape.

31.36 As the power and capability of AI continue to progress, it is imperative that we acknowledge the escalating conflicts between institutions and malicious groups, which are now unfolding at an accelerated pace.

31.37 There is a growing need for an increased number of proficient professionals, along with advanced tools that improve the effectiveness of cyber-security measures, resulting in advantages for both businesses and their customers. The individuals showcased in this book possess a perfect blend of legal, technical, and business acumen, whom I strongly recommend you consider as your main point of contact.

Best wishes and thank you for reading.

Helen Wong MBE

Appendix 1

Theresa May Speech, Munich Security Conference, February 2018

For more than half a century, this conference has brought nations together from Europe and across the Atlantic to forge our common security. The fundamental values we share – respect for human dignity, human rights, freedom, democracy and equality – have created common cause to act together in our shared interest. The rules-based system we helped to develop has enabled global cooperation to protect those shared values. Today as globalisation brings nations closer together than ever before, we face a host of new and growing threats that seek to undermine those rules and values.

As internal and external security become more and more entwined – with hostile networks no longer only rooted in state-based aggression and weapons designed not just to be deployed on the battlefield but through cyberspace – so our ability to keep our people safe depends ever more on working together. That is reflected here today in the world's largest gathering of its kind, with representatives of more than seventy countries.

For our part, the United Kingdom has always understood that our security and prosperity is bound to global security and prosperity. We are a global nation – enriching global prosperity through centuries of trade, through the talents of our people and by exchanging learning and culture with partners across the world. And we invest in global security knowing this is how we best protect our people at home and abroad.

That is why we are the second largest defence spender in NATO, and the only EU member to spend 2 per cent of our GDP on defence as well as 0.7 per cent of our Gross National Income on international development. And it is why we will continue to meet these commitments. It is why we have created a highly developed set of security and defence relationships: with the US and Five Eyes partners, with the Gulf and increasingly with Asian partners too.

We have invested in critical capabilities – including our nuclear deterrent, our two new aircraft carriers, our world class special forces and intelligence agencies. We are a leading contributor to international missions from fighting Daesh in Iraq and Syria to peacekeeping in South Sudan and Cyprus, and NATO missions in Eastern Europe. And within Europe we are working ever more closely with our European partners, bringing the influence and impact that comes from our full range of global relationships.

And we want to continue this co-operation as we leave the European Union.

The British people took a legitimate democratic decision to bring decision making and accountability closer to home. But it has always been the case that our security at home is best advanced through global cooperation, working with institutions that support that, including the EU. Changing the structures by which we work together should not mean we lose sight of our common aim – the protection of our people and the advance of our common interests across the world. So as we leave the EU and forge a new path for ourselves in the world, the UK is just as committed to Europe's security in the future as we have been in the past.

Europe's security is our security. And that is why I have said – and I say again today – that the United Kingdom is unconditionally committed to maintaining it. The challenge for all of us today is finding the way to work together, through a deep and special partnership between the UK and the EU, to retain the co-operation that we have built and go further in meeting the evolving threats we face together. This cannot be a time when any of us allow competition between partners, rigid institutional restrictions or deep-seated ideology to inhibit our co-operation and jeopardise the security of our citizens.

We must do whatever is most practical and pragmatic in ensuring our collective security. Today I want to set out how I believe we can achieve this – taking this opportunity to establish a new security partnership that can keep our people safe, now and in the years ahead. Safeguarding our internal security

Let me start with how we ensure security within Europe. The threats we face do not recognise the borders of individual nations or discriminate between them. We all in this room have shared the pain and heartbreak of terrorist atrocities at home. It is almost a year since the despicable attack on Westminster, followed by further attacks in Manchester and London. These people don't care if they kill and maim Parisians, Berliners, Londoners or Mancunians because it is the common values that we all share which they seek to attack and defeat. But I say: we will not let them. When these atrocities occur, people look to us as leaders to provide the response.

We must all ensure that nothing prevents us from fulfilling our first duty as leaders: to protect our citizens. And we must find the practical ways to ensure the co-operation to do so. We have done so before. When Justice and Home Affairs ceased to be intergovernmental and became a shared EU competence, of course there were some in the UK who would have had us adopt the EU's approach wholesale, just as there were some who would have had us reject it outright. As Home Secretary, I was determined to find a practical and pragmatic way in which the UK and EU could continue to co-operate on our common security.

That is why I reviewed each provision in turn and successfully made the case for the UK to opt back in to those that were clearly in our national interest. Through the relationship we have developed, the UK has been at the forefront of shaping the practical and legal arrangements that underpin our internal security co-operation. And our contribution to those arrangements is vital in protecting European citizens in cities right across our continent.

First our practical co-operation, including our expedited extradition and mutual legal assistance relationship, means wanted or convicted serious criminals – and the evidence to support their convictions – move seamlessly between the UK and EU Member States. So when a serious terrorist like Zakaria Chadili was found living in the UK – a young man who was believed to have been radicalised in Syria and was wanted for terrorist offences in France – there was no delay in ensuring he was extradited back to France and brought to justice. He is one of 10,000 people the UK has extradited through the European Arrest Warrant. In fact, for every person arrested on a European Arrest Warrant issued by the UK, the UK arrests eight on European Arrest Warrants issued by other Member States. The European Arrest Warrant has also played a crucial role in supporting police co-operation between Northern Ireland and Ireland – which has been a fundamental part of the political settlement there.

Second, co-operation between our law enforcement agencies means the UK is one of the biggest contributors of data, information and expertise to Europol. Take for example, Operation Triage where police in the UK worked extensively with Europol and the Czech Republic to crack a trafficking gang involved in labour exploitation.

Third, through the Schengen Information System II, the UK is contributing to the sharing of real-time data on wanted criminals, missing persons and suspected terrorists. About a fifth of all alerts are circulated by the UK, with over 13,000 hits on people and objects of interest to law enforcement across Europe in the last year alone. The UK has also driven a pan-EU approach to processing passenger data, enabling the identification and tracking of criminals, victims of trafficking and those individuals vulnerable to radicalisation.

In all these areas, people across Europe are safer because of this co-operation and the unique arrangements we have developed between the UK and EU institutions in recent years. So it is in all our interests to find ways to protect the capabilities which underpin this co-operation when the UK becomes a European country outside the EU but in a new partnership with it.

To make this happen will require real political will on both sides. I recognise there is no existing security agreement between the EU and a third country that captures the full depth and breadth of our existing relationship. But there is precedent for comprehensive, strategic relationships between the EU and third countries in other fields, such as trade. And there is no legal or operational reason why such an agreement could not be reached in the area of internal security.

However, if the priority in the negotiations becomes avoiding any kind of new co-operation with a country outside the EU, then this political doctrine and ideology will have damaging real world consequences for the security of all our people, in the UK and the EU.

Let's be clear about what would happen if the means of this co-operation were abolished. Extradition under the European Arrest Warrant would cease. Extradition outside the European Arrest Warrant can cost four times as much and take three times as long. It would mean an end to the significant exchange of data and engagement through Europol. And it would mean the UK would no longer be able to secure evidence from European partners quickly through the European Investigation Order, with strict deadlines for gathering evidence requested, instead relying on slower, more cumbersome systems. This would damage us both and would put all our citizens at greater risk.

As leaders, we cannot let that happen. So we need, together, to demonstrate some real creativity and ambition to enable us to meet the challenges of the future as well as today. That is why I have proposed a new Treaty to underpin our future internal security relationship. The Treaty must preserve our operational capabilities. But it must also fulfil three further requirements. It must be respectful of the sovereignty of both the UK and the EU's legal orders. So, for example, when participating in EU agencies the UK will respect the remit of the European Court of Justice. And a principled but pragmatic solution to close legal co-operation will be needed to respect our unique status as a third country with our own sovereign legal order.

As I have said before, we will need to agree a strong and appropriate form of independent dispute resolution across all the areas of our future partnership in which both sides can have the necessary confidence. We must also recognise the importance of comprehensive and robust data protection arrangements.

The UK's Data Protection Bill will ensure that we are aligned with the EU framework. But we want to go further and seek a bespoke arrangement to reflect the UK's exceptionally high standards of data protection. And we envisage an ongoing role for the UK's Information Commissioner's Office, which would be beneficial in providing stability and confidence for EU and UK individuals and businesses alike. And we're ready to start working through this with colleagues in the European Commission now.

Finally, just as we have been able to develop the agreement on passenger name records in the face of terrorist atrocities in recent years, so the Treaty must have an ability to ensure that as the threats we face change and adapt – as they surely will – our relationship has the capacity to move with them.

Nothing must get in the way of our helping each other in every hour of every day to keep our people safe. If we put this at the heart of our mission – we can and will find the means. And we cannot delay discussions on this. EU Member States have been clear how critical it is that we maintain existing operational capabilities. We must now move with urgency to put in place the Treaty that will protect all European citizens wherever they are in the continent.

EXTERNAL SECURITY

But clearly our security interests don't stop at edge of our continent. Not only do the threats to our internal security emanate from beyond our borders, as we look at the world today we are also facing profound challenges to the global order: to peace, prosperity, to the rules-based system that underpins our very way of life. And in the face of these challenges, I believe it is our defining responsibility to come together and reinvigorate the transatlantic partnership – and the full breadth of all our global alliances – so that we can protect our shared security and project our shared values.

The United Kingdom is not only unwavering in its commitment to this partnership, we see reinvigorating it as a fundamental part of our global role as we leave the European Union. As a Permanent Member of the United Nations Security

Council, as a leading contributor to NATO and as America's closest partner, we have never defined our global outlook primarily through our membership of the European Union or by a collective European foreign policy. So upon leaving the EU, it is right that the UK will pursue an independent foreign policy. But around the world, the interests that we will seek to project and defend will continue to be rooted in our shared values.

That is true whether fighting the ideologies of Daesh, developing a new global approach to migration, ensuring the Iranian nuclear deal is properly policed or standing up to Russia's hostile actions, whether in Ukraine, the Western Balkans or in cyberspace. And in all these cases, our success depends on a breadth of partnership that extends far beyond the institutional mechanisms for cooperation with the EU.

That means doing more to develop bi-lateral co-operation between European nations, as I was pleased to do with President Macron at last month's UK-France Summit. It means building the ad hoc groupings which allow us to counter terrorism and hostile state threats, as we do through the 30 strong intergovernmental European Counter Terrorism Group – the largest of its kind in the world. It means ensuring that a reformed NATO alliance remains the cornerstone of our shared security. And, critically, it means both Europe and the United States reaffirming our resolve to the collective security of this continent, and to advancing the democratic values on which our interests are founded.

Taken together, it is only by strengthening and deepening this full range of partnerships within Europe and beyond that we will be able to respond together to the evolving threats we face.

So what does this mean for the future security partnership between the UK and the EU?

We need a partnership that respects both the decision-making autonomy of the European Union and the sovereignty of the United Kingdom.

This is fully achievable. The EU's common foreign policy is distinct within the EU Treaties and our foreign policies will keep evolving. So, there is no reason why we should not agree distinct arrangements for our foreign and defence policy cooperation in the time-limited implementation period, as the Commission has proposed. This would mean that key aspects of our future partnership in this area would already be effective from 2019.

We shouldn't wait where we don't need to. In turn, if the EU and its remaining Member States believe that the best means to increase the contribution Europe makes to our collective security is through deeper integration, then the UK will look to work with you. And help you to do so in a way which strengthens NATO and our wider alliances too, as EU leaders have repeatedly made clear.

The partnership that we need to create is therefore one which offers the UK and the EU the means and choice to combine our efforts to the greatest effect – where this is in our shared interest. To put this into practice so that we meet the threats we all face today and build the capabilities we all need for tomorrow, there are three areas on which we should focus.

First, at a diplomatic level, we should have the means to consult each other regularly on the global challenges we face, and coordinate how we use the levers we hold where our interests align. In particular, we will want to continue to work closely together on sanctions. We will look to carry over all EU sanctions at the time of our departure. And we will all be stronger if the UK and EU have the means to co-operate on sanctions now and potentially to develop them together in the future.

Second, it is clearly in our shared interests to be able to continue to coordinate and deliver operationally on the ground. Of course, we will continue to work with and alongside each other. But where we can both be most effective by the UK deploying its significant capabilities and resources with and indeed through EU mechanisms – we should both be open to that. On defence, if the UK and EU's interests can best be furthered by the UK continuing to contributing to an EU operation or mission as we do now, then we should both be open to that. And similarly, while the UK will decide how we spend the entirety of our foreign aid in the future, if a UK contribution to EU development programmes and instruments can best deliver our mutual interests, we should both be open to that. But if we are to choose to work together in these ways, the UK must be able to play an appropriate role in shaping our collective actions in these areas.

Third, it will also be in our interests to continue working together on developing the capabilities – in defence, cyber and space – to meet future threats. The UK spends around 40 per cent of Europe's total on defence R&D. This investment provides a sizeable stimulus to improve Europe's competitiveness and capability. And this is to the benefit of us all. So an open and inclusive approach to European capability development – that fully enables British defence industry to participate – is in our strategic security interests, helping keep European citizens safe and Europe's defence industries strong. And Eurofighter Typhoon is a great example of this – a partnership between the UK, Germany, Italy and Spain which has supported over 10,000 highly skilled jobs across Europe.

This is also why the UK wants to agree a future relationship with the European Defence Fund and the European Defence Agency, so that jointly we can research and develop the best future capability that Europe can muster. Last year's 'Not Petya' cyber-attack showed why we also need to work closely to defend our interests in cyber space. This reckless attack – which the UK and partners have attributed to Russia – disrupted organisations across Europe costing hundreds of millions of pounds.

To contend with a truly global threat such as this we need a truly global response – with not only the UK and EU, but industry, government, likeminded states and NATO all working together to strengthen our cyber security capabilities. And as our lives move increasingly online, so we will also become increasingly reliant on space technologies. Space is a domain like any other where hostile actors will seek to threaten us. So we very much welcome the EU's efforts to develop Europe's capabilities in this field. We need to keep open all the options which will enable the UK and the EU to collaborate in the most effective way possible. The UK hosts much of Europe's cutting edge capabilities on space and we have played a leading role, for example, in the development of the Galileo programme. We are keen for this to continue as part of our new partnership, but, as is the case more widely, we need to get the right agreements concluded which will allow the UK and its businesses to take part on a fair and open basis.

CONCLUSION

It was the tragic massacre at the 1972 Olympics here in Munich which subsequently inspired a British Foreign Secretary, Jim Callaghan, to propose an intergovernmental group aimed at co-ordinating European counter terrorism and policing. At the time this was outside the formal mechanisms of the European Community. But in time, it became the foundations for the co-operation that we have on Justice and Home Affairs today. Now, as then, we can – and must – think pragmatically and practically to create the arrangements that put the safety of our citizens first. For ours is a dynamic relationship, not a set of transactions. A relationship built on an unshakeable commitment to our shared values.

A relationship in which we must all invest if we are to be responsive and adaptive to threats which will emerge perhaps more rapidly than any of us can imagine. A relationship in which we must all play our full part in keeping our continent safe and free, and reinvigorate the transatlantic alliance and rules based system on which our shared security depends. Those who threaten our security would like nothing more than to see us fractured. They would like nothing more than to see us put debates about mechanisms and means ahead of doing what is most practical and effective in keeping our people safe.

So let the message ring out loud and clear today: we will not let that happen. We will together protect and project our values in the world – and we will keep our people safe – now and in the years to come.

Dated: 17 February 2018.

REFERENCE

www.gov.uk/government/speeches/pm-speech-at-munich-security-conference-17-february-2018.

Appendix 2

Cybersecurity lexicon for converged systems

CIA Information security policy objectives: Confidentiality, Integrity and Availability.

Computer virus: A program that is run (unwittingly) by the user that executes on the victim system and spreads to other executable programs.

Crypto ransomware: Criminals use malware to encrypt information and then demand payment via digital currency to recover information.

Cyber physical systems (CPS): CPS interface the physical world with the logical, enabling the (Industrial) Internet of Things, data and services. See Operational Technology.

Backdoor: Provides access to a compromised system normally via the internet bypassing legitimate authentication (logon).

Botnet: A large number of compromised systems attack a single target. The Mirai botnet attack used IoT devices, mainly home routers and cameras to create a DDoS.

Denial of Service (DoS): An incident where there is an interruption in services or access to a resource, normally with malicious intent. In a distributed denial of service (DDoS) attack, large numbers of compromised systems (called a botnet) attack a single target.

ePHI: Electronic protected health information (ePHI) refers to protected health information (PHI) from the US Health Insurance Portability and Accountability Act 1996.

Exploit kit: An exploit kit automates the exploitation of browsers and software 'plug-ins' used with them. They are often user-friendly and can be used by non-technical people to run a crime campaign, which might include using compromised machines as a remote platform to launch further attacks.

Functional safety: The freedom from unacceptable risk of physical injury or of damage to the health of people, either directly, or indirectly. Functional safety is the part of the overall safety that depends on a system or piece of equipment that depends on the system or equipment operating correctly in response to its inputs, including the safe management of likely operator errors, hardware failures and environmental changes.

Hacktivist: Short form of *hack*er ac*tivist* – an individual or group that uses computer networks to further their political agenda.

Internet of Things (IOT or IoT): The movement toward connecting physical devices – including the car, fridge, home heating system, lighting, fitness, wellbeing and medical devices etc. – to the internet so that they can be controlled, monitored or supported remotely.

Industrial Internet of Things (IIOT or IIoT): The use of the Internet of Things (IoT) in an industrial capacity. Industrial IoT systems are bound by specific design functionality, and can therefore be distinguished from (non-Industrial) IoT ad hoc groupings of existing devices sharing data to fill an emergent requirement.

Industrial control systems (ICS): Also known as Operational Technology or OT. The systems that control industrial and critical infrastructure. A generic term that encompasses several types of control systems used in industrial sectors and critical infrastructure.

Keyboard/Mouse Jack: The compromise of a wireless keyboard or mouse, where an attacker can circumvent poor or lack of encryption to inject or read key strokes.

Keylogger: Software or hardware that records keystrokes made by a computer user, which can be used to obtain passwords and other confidential information.

Malware: Short for *mal*icious soft*ware* – refers to any intrusive or hostile software.

Man in The Middle attack (MiTM): An attacker intercepts and relays messages between two parties who believe they are communicating directly with each other.

Medjack: The compromise of vulnerable medical devices for use as back doors; providing malicious access to hospital networks.

Operational Technology (OT): IT derived term to distinguish embedded control systems from information processing systems. Comprises the hardware and software that controls or monitors the state of a physical system. See industrial control systems.

Penetration testing: The testing of computer devices, systems, networks or web pages to assess potential vulnerabilities that could be exploited to provide access.

Phishing: Spam email either containing malicious software or links to websites with malicious software.

Remote access trojan (RAT): A trojan can provide access to a target computer, in order to download additional malicious software, which may (amongst other things) encrypt files (ransomware), monitor computer use and control the computer remotely, potentially for attacks on other computers.

Rootkit: A software package that conceals the presence of malicious software on a computer.

Social engineering: The attempt to obtain information by subterfuge from personnel that can then be used to attack computers, devices or networks.

Spear-phishing: Carefully crafted email sent to selected individuals either containing malicious software or links to websites with malicious software.

Spoofing or impersonation: A network term for fooling hardware or software, making communication appear to originate from elsewhere.

SRA: Traditional engineering objectives: Safety, Reliability and Availability.

Trojan: A trojan horse or trojan is any malicious program that is concealed and run by the user.

Update hijack: Legitimate software updates compromised with malicious software.

Waterhole attack: An attack targeted at a particular group of individuals, who visit common websites. A chosen website is compromised in anticipation that it will be visited by a member of the target organisation.

Worm: A malware program that spreads itself (without user intervention).

Agency guidance and security advisories.

European Union Agency for Network and Information Security (ENISA) www.enisa.europa.eu.

UK CareCERT http://content.digital.nhs.uk/carecert.

UK Cyber-security Information Sharing Partnership https://www.ncsc.gov.uk/cisp.

UK Medicines and Healthcare products Regulatory Agency. www.gov.uk/government/organisations/medicines-and-healthcare-products-regulatory-agency.

UK National Cyber Security Centre www.ncsc.gov.uk/guidance.

UK NHS Digital http://digital.nhs.uk/.

US DHS ICS-CERT https://ics-cert.us-cert.gov/.

US FDA Cybersecurity guidance www.fda.gov/MedicalDevices/DigitalHealth/ucm373213.htm.

US National Health Information Sharing Analysis Centre .https://nhisac.org/.

Appendix 3

The Government's National Response

Helen Wong MBE

The government released a statement in February 2018 stating that organisations risked fines of up to £17 million if they did not have effective cyber-security measures.

Bosses of Britain's most critical industries are being warned to boost cyber-security or face hefty fines for leaving themselves vulnerable to attack following our consultation.

Energy, transport, water and health firms could be fined up to £17 million if they fail to have the most robust safeguards in place against a cyber-attack.

New regulators will be able to assess critical industries to make sure plans are as robust as possible.

A simple, straightforward reporting system will be set up to make it easy to report cyber breaches and IT failures so they can be quickly identified and acted upon.

This will ensure UK operators in electricity, transport, water, energy, health and digital infrastructure are prepared to deal with the increasing numbers of cyber threats.

It will also cover other threats affecting IT such as power outages, hardware failures and environmental hazards. Under the new measures recent cyber breaches such as WannaCry and high profile systems failures would be covered by the Network and Information Systems (NIS) Directive.

These incidents would have to be reported to the regulator who would assess whether appropriate security measures were in place. The regulator will have the power to issue legally-binding instructions to improve security, and – if appropriate – impose financial penalties.

Margot James, Minister for Digital and the Creative Industries, said:

> 'Today we are setting out new and robust cyber security measures to help ensure the UK is the safest place in the world to live and be online.
>
> We want our essential services and infrastructure to be primed and ready to tackle cyber attacks and be resilient against major disruption to services.
>
> I encourage all public and private operators in these essential sectors to take action now and consult NCSC's advice on how they can improve their cyber security.
>
> The National Cyber Security Centre (NCSC), the UK's centre of cyber excellence established in 2017, has today published detailed guidance on the security measures to help organisations comply. These are based around 14

> key principles set out in our consultation and government response, and are aligned with existing cyber security standards'.

National Cyber Security Centre CEO Ciaran Martin said:

> 'Our new guidance will give clear advice on what organisations need to do to implement essential cyber security measures.
>
> Network and information systems give critical support to everyday activities, so it is absolutely vital that they are as secure as possible.'

The new measures follow the consultation held last year by the Department for Digital, Culture, Media and Sport seeking views from industry on how to implement the NIS Directive from 10 May 2018.

Fines would be a last resort and will not apply to operators which have assessed the risks adequately, taken appropriate security measures and engaged with regulators but still suffered an attack.

Following the consultation, incident reporting arrangements have been simplified, with operators reporting to their Competent Authority. Penalties will be fixed at a maximum of £17 million and the new legislation will be made clearer for companies to know whether they have to comply with the NIS Directive.

The NIS Directive is an important part of the government's five-year £1.9 billion National Cyber Security Strategy to protect the nation from cyber threats and make the UK the safest place to live and work online. It will ensure essential service operators are taking the necessary action to protect their IT systems.

For the UK government's National Response go to www.gov.uk/government/publications/national-cyber-security-strategy-2016-to-2021.

Appendix 4

Sample Legal Documents

Helen Wong MBE

The below provides some sample letters and policy frameworks that you can use in your organisation.

APP 4.1 BREACH OF DISCLOSURE LETTER

Breach of Disclosure Letter From:[Your Name, & Address here] To:

[Recipient Name & address here]

[Date here]

Dear [name],You are hereby notified that as of [date of violation], you are in violation of our contract signed on [agreement date].

You – [state the nature of the said breach here] — [Here, describe the violation in brief]-We would like to say that we are open for discussion regarding this mater.

As you are responsible for all the damages occurring out of this breach, we need to talk for the suitable compensation for the violation in contract by you.

You have [duration] to offer a compensation for the breach in our contract, after which we will – [State what action you will take].Thanks for your understanding into this matter.

Regards,

[Your name]

Encl: [Enclosures List here]

APP 4.2 SAMPLE OF ACCEPTABLE USE POLICY

App 4.2.1 Unauthorised Information Access

*<Insert organisation name> and third party employees **shall** only be authorised access to information relevant to their work.*

*Accessing or attempting to gain access to unauthorised information **shall** be deemed a disciplinary offence.*

*When access to information is authorised, the individual user **shall** ensure the confidentiality and integrity of the information is upheld, and to observe adequate protection of the information according to the Company's policies as well as legal and statutory requirements. This includes the protection of information against access by unauthorised persons.*

[All staff must be made aware that they have a duty of care to prevent and report any unauthorised access to systems, information and data.]

App 4.2.2 Misuse of Information Systems

Use of the Company's information systems for malicious purposes ***shall*** *be deemed a disciplinary offence. This includes but is not limited to:*

Penetration attempts ("hacking" or "cracking") of external or internal systems.

Unauthorised electronic eavesdropping on or surveillance of internal or external network traffic.

Discriminatory (on the grounds of sex, political, religious or sexual preferences or orientation), or derogatory remarks or material on computer or communications media; this includes but is not limited to sending offending material as embedded or attached information in e-mails or other electronic communication systems.

Acquisition or proliferation of pornographic or material identified as offensive or criminal.

Deliberate copyright or intellectual property rights violations, including use of obviously copyright-violated software.

Storage or transmission of large data volumes for personal use, e.g. personal digital images, music or video files or large bulk downloads or uploads.

Users accessing or attempting to access medical or confidential information concerning themselves, family, friends or any other person without a legitimate purpose and prior authorisation from senior management is strictly forbidden and ***shall*** *be deemed a disciplinary offence.*

Use of the Company's information systems or data contained therein for personal gain, to obtain personal advantage or for profit is not permitted and ***shall*** *be deemed a disciplinary offence.*

If identified misuse is considered a criminal offence, criminal charges ***shall*** *be filed with local police and all information regarding the criminal actions handed over to the relevant authorities.*

[All staff must be made aware of what constitutes misuse and the potential consequences of any misuse of systems, information and data.]

App 4.2.3 Guidelines for IT Equipment Use

App 4.2.3.1 Physical Protection

Users ***shall*** *not eat or drink in the vicinity of any IT equipment.*

Users ***shall*** *not expose any IT equipment to magnetic fields which may compromise or prevent normal operation.*

Users ***shall*** *not expose any IT equipment to external stress, sudden impacts, excessive force or humidity.*

*Only authorised IT support personnel **shall** be allowed to open IT equipment and equipment cabinets.*

*If left unattended in semi-controlled areas such as conference centres or customer offices, laptops **shall** be locked to a fixed point using a physical lock available from IT support.*

*Portable equipment **shall** never be left unattended in airport lounges, hotel lobbies and similar areas as these areas are insecure.*

*Portable equipment **shall** be physically locked down or locked away when left in the office overnight.*

*Portable equipment **shall** never be left in parked cars, unless completely invisible from outside the vehicle and protected from extreme temperatures.*

Portable equipment **shall** not be checked in as hold luggage when travelling, but treated as hand or cabin luggage at all times.

App 4.2.3.2 General Use

*Users **shall** lock their terminal/workstation/laptop/mobile device (using the Ctrl-Alt-Delete function or other applicable method) when not left unattended, even for a short period.*

*Users **shall** not install unapproved or privately owned software on IT equipment.*

*Only authorised <insert organisation name> IT personnel **shall** be allowed to reconfigure or change system settings on the IT equipment.*

*Laptops and mobile devices **shall**:*

Only be used by the Company or third party employee that has signed and taken personal responsibility for the laptop.

Have the corporate standard encryption software installed, rendering the information on the laptop inaccessible if the laptop is stolen or lost.

Have the corporate standard anti-virus, anti-spyware and personal firewall software installed.

Have the corporate standard remote access installed.

If configured according to the specifications above the laptop/mobile device may be connected to wired or wireless access points.

NHS laptops shall never be (via cable or wireless) directly connected to other non-NHS IT equipment or systems.

*Users **shall** not use privately owned storage devices or storage devices owned by third parties for transfers of NHS data.*

*Any device lost or stolen **shall** be reported immediately to the <insert organisation name>Security Team <or equivalent organisation>.*

App 4.2.4 Internet Acceptable Use

*Information found on the Internet is subject to minimal regulation and as such must be treated as being of questionable quality. You **should** not base any business-critical decisions on information from the Internet that has not been independently verified.*

*Internet access via the NHS infrastructure is mainly provided for business purposes. For the purpose of simplifying everyday tasks, limited private use **may** be accepted. Such use includes access to web banking, public web services and phone web directories.*

*Excessive personal use of the Internet during working hours **shall** not be tolerated and **may** lead to disciplinary action.*

*Users **shall** not use Internet-based file sharing applications, unless explicitly approved and provided as a service.*

*Users **shall** not upload and download private data (e.g. private pictures) to and from the Internet.*

*Users **shall** not download copyrighted material such as software, text, images, music and video from the Internet.*

*Users **shall** not use NHS systems or Internet access for personal advantages such as business financial transactions or private business activities.*

*Users **shall** not use their <insert organisation name> identity (i.e. using your <insert organisation name> e-mail address) for private purposes such as on social media, discussion forums.*

App 4.2.5 Email Acceptable Use

*Email services within the Company are provided for business purposes. Limited private use for the purpose of simplifying everyday tasks **may** be accepted but private emails **should** be distributed via web based email services.*

*Users **shall** not use external, web-based e-mail services (e.g. hotmail.com) for business communications and purposes.*

*Private emails **should** be stored in a separate folder named 'Private e-mail box'. If retrieval of business emails is required (due to sick leave etc.) this folder will not be subject to inspection).*

*Private emails **should** be deleted as soon as possible in order to limit storage requirements for non-business information.*

*Users **shall** not broadcast personal messages, advertisements or other non-business related information via the Company e-mail systems.*

*Users **shall** not distribute content that might be considered discriminatory, offensive, derogatory, abusive, indecent, pornographic or obscene.*

*Users **shall** not distribute statements of a political or religious nature, or other information of a personal nature.*

Engaging in any illegal activities via e-mail is prohibited. Discovery of such material **shall**, if deemed as being of a criminal nature, be handed over to the police.

APP 4.3 ACCESS CONTROL POLICY

App 4.3.1 General

*Access **shall** be granted using the principle of '**Least Privilege**'. This means that every program and every user of the system **should** operate using the least set of privileges necessary to complete the job.*

*Each user **shall** be identified by a unique user identity so that users can be linked to and made responsible for their actions.*

*The use of group identities **shall** only be permitted where they are suitable for the work carried out (e.g. training accounts or service accounts).*

*During their induction to the system each user **should** be given a copy of guidelines for staff on use of the system and their user login details, and **should** be required to sign to indicate that they understand the conditions of access.*

*Records of user access **may** be used to provide evidence for security incident investigations.*

App 4.3.2 Physical Access

*Physical Access **shall** only be granted on the authority of the Data/System Owner and **shall** be applied on a strict 'Need to Know' basis.*

*All Company Data/Systems **shall** be physically protected in accordance with their value, Security Classification and Privacy Marking.*

*Data/System Owners **shall** implement physical security measures in order to control Physical Access to their data/systems, in addition to any physical access controls for the buildings in which they are located.*

*The Data/System Owner **should** retain a log 'date/time/name/reason' for access to their data/system.*

*Any unauthorised access **shall** be reported as a Security Incident.*

App 4.3.3 Network Access

*All staff and contractors **shall** be given network access in accordance with business access control procedures and requirements for access defined by their roles.*

*All staff and contractors who access <insert organisation name> networks remotely **shall** only be authenticated using the approved remote access authentication mechanism.*

*Diagnostic and configuration ports **shall** only be enabled for specified business reasons. All other ports **shall** be disabled or removed.*

*Risk assessment **shall** be conducted by <insert organisation name> to determine the requirements for the segregation of networks.*

*Segregation of networks **shall** be implemented as determined by the results of the risk assessment.*

*Network administrators **shall** group together information services, users and information systems as appropriate to achieve the required segregation on networks.*

*Network routing controls **shall** be implemented to support the access control policy.*

APP 4.4 OPERATING SYSTEM ACCESS

App 4.4.1 User Responsibilities

*All <insert organisation name> users **shall** be expected to confirm they are an authorised user at log-on.*

*All <insert organisation name> users **shall** have a unique identifier which **shall** not be shared with other users.*

*All <insert organisation name> users **shall** be required to change their passwords at frequent intervals and in accordance with the password management policy.*

App 4.4.2 System Configuration

*Only authorised personnel **shall** have access to system utilities and access **should** be revoked when there is no longer a business reason for access.*

*Where there is a business requirement for the use of identifiers that are not associated with a single individual (for example, service accounts), these **shall** only be created following consultation with the <insert organisation name> security team and following a formal risk assessment.*

*All user workstations **shall** be configured to lock automatically after a period of inactivity in order to reduce the risk of unauthorised access.*

*Restrictions on connection times to sensitive systems **should** be considered to reduce the window of opportunity for unauthorised access.*

APP 4.5 INFORMATION SYSTEM ACCESS

App 4.5.1 User Responsibilities

*All users **shall** ensure that they lock their screens whenever they leave their desks to reduce the risk of unauthorised access.*

*All users **shall** ensure that their desks are kept clear of any information or removable storage media in order to reduce the risk of unauthorised access.*

*All users **shall** keep their passwords confidential and unique user identities **shall** not be shared.*

*Passwords **shall** be changed at regular intervals and this **shall** be enforced by the system.*

*Passwords **shall** be changed whenever there is an indication of possible system compromise.*

App 4.5.2 Administration

Access to information systems shall be granted using a formal user registration processes.

*Managers **shall** review user access rights on a regular basis and after any changes to user roles and responsibilities.*

*Each user of a system **shall** have a unique user identity, so that the user can be held accountable for any actions carried out by their allocated user identity.*

*A formal record of all users connected to a Company system **shall** be maintained, including the necessary approvals.*

*Privilege access management **shall** be controlled through a formal process and only the minimum privileges **shall** be granted to carry out the role or task.*

*A formal record of all privileges allocated **shall** be maintained.*

*When a user account is no longer required, e.g. through staff resignation or a change in duties the account **shall** be disabled immediately.*

*Unused accounts **shall** be monitored and appropriate action taken in line with NHS procedures for disabling and deleting accounts.*

*Removal of accounts **shall** also include the removal of any associated access rights.*

App 4.5.3 System Configuration

For audit purposes, systems shall be configured to capture the unique user identity being used.

*Where technically possible, all standard accounts that are delivered with operating systems **shall** be disabled, deleted or have their 'default' passwords changed on system installation.*

App 4.5.4 Application and Information Access

*All <insert organisation name> staff and contractors **shall** only be granted access to those application functions required to carry out their roles.*

*All <insert organisation name> staff and contractors **shall** only be granted access to information in applications in accordance with business access requirements and policy.*

*All <insert organisation name> staff and contractors **shall** only have access to sensitive systems if there is a business need to do so and they have successfully completed any additional necessary vetting processes.*

*Sensitive systems **should** be physically or logically isolated in order to meet the requirements of restricted access to authorised personnel.*

APP 4.6 ANTI-VIRUS MALWARE POLICY

App 4.6.1 General

*<Insert name of organisation> systems **shall** run effective anti-virus and anti-malware software.*

*<Insert name of organisation> IT anti-virus and anti-malware software **shall** be configured to detect and remove known viruses and malware.*

*All <insert name of organisation> IT systems (servers, desktops, laptops) **shall** run one of the NHS approved and supported anti-virus and anti-malware software packages.*

*All servers, desktops and laptops **shall** be configured to run only one of the approved products at any time.*

*Anti-virus and anti-malware software **shall** be kept up to date.*

*Anti-virus and anti-malware definition files **shall** be kept up to date.*

*Anti-virus and anti-malware software updates **shall** be deployed across the network automatically following their receipt from the vendor.*

*Virus and malware signature updates **shall** be deployed across the network automatically following their receipt from the vendor.*

*Anti-virus and anti-malware software **shall** be configured for real time scanning and regular scheduled scans.*

*Tamper protection **shall** be enabled to prevent end users or malware altering the anti-virus and anti-malware software's configuration or disabling the protection.*

*All IT equipment and removable media **shall** be scanned for viruses and malware before being introduced to the <insert name of organisation> network, system or device.*

*IT systems infected with a virus and malware that the anti-virus or anti-malware software has not been able to deal with **shall** be quarantined from the NHS network until virus free.*

*Any instance of virus or malware infection or detection **shall** be documented and raised as a security incident.*

App 4.6.2 Administrative

*Changes that are required to the settings of any of anti-virus or anti-malware products **shall** follow the formal <insert name of organisation> change control process.*

*<Insert name of organisation> **shall** ensure that all anti-virus and anti-malware products are regularly and correctly updated from the vendor service.*

*<Insert name of organisation> **may** periodically test anti-virus and anti-malware defences by deploying a safe and non-malicious test file.*

*A log **shall** be kept of all scans undertaken, these logs **should** record as a minimum: Date. Time.*

Addresses of areas scanned.

Malware found.

Any action taken by the anti-virus and anti-malware software (e.g. quarantine or delete).

*To prevent misuse and tampering by unauthorised staff, all administrative settings in the deployed anti-virus and anti-malware products **shall** be secured by means of a password.*

APP 4.7 APPLICATION SECURITY POLICY

*<Insert name of organisation> **shall** ensure that applications utilised by <insert name of organisation> are securely configured and managed.*

*IT Managers **shall** ensure that all applications are captured and maintain an inventory of all authorised applications. The application configuration/patches/ updates undertaken and **shall** cover:*

Software vendor and item identifier.

Version number and licence details of the software.

Serial number.

Date first installed and date of changes with details of person responsible for change/update. (Note: For smartphones where the user controls the update this process will not be possible. The annual review of the applications on the smartphone should record the latest the build and record this.)

*Only applications that are supported by an approved vendor **shall** be procured and used.*

*Full support contracts **shall** be arranged with the application vendor for through life support.*

*No modifications **should** be made to the application without confirmation that the vendor can continue to provide support.*

Updates, patches and configuration changes issued by the vendor ***shall*** *be implemented as soon as practicable.*

Workstations, laptops and tablets ***shall*** *be configured so that unauthorised applications cannot be downloaded.*

Access to application configurations ***shall*** *be restricted to authorised personnel only; i.e. least privilege.*

A full review of applications and licences ***shall*** *be completed at least annually, as part of the regular software reviews. Any anomalies* ***shall*** *be reported to <insert name of organisation> senior management.*

APP 4.8 ASSET MANAGEMENT POLICY

The Asset Management Policy ***shall*** *be used to ensure that all <insert name of organisation> information assets (IT and physical hard copy) are identified, categorised, classified and recorded.*

App 4.8.1 Asset Categorisations

<Insert name of organisation> information assets are defined as the hardware and software that forms constituent parts of the IT system storing and processing the information and physical hard copies. An Asset Register ***shall*** *be used and the processes outlined in this policy* ***shall*** *be adhered to for the asset management.*

The first stage of the process is the categorisation of the assets. The assets ***shall*** *be categorised using the below list as the framework:*

App 4.8.1.1 Hardware

Desktops

Monitors

Laptops

Printers

Media – CDs, DVDs, optical Disks, External Hard Drives, USB memory Sticks (also known as pen drives and flash drives), Media Card Readers, Embedded Microchips (including Smart Cards and Mobile Phone SIM Cards), MP3 Players, Digital Cameras, Backup Cassettes, Audio Tapes (including Dictaphones and Answering Machines), etc.

Photocopiers

Fax Machines

Servers

Firewalls

Routers

Switches

Tokens

Keys

App 4.8.1.2 Software

Databases

Applications

Software Licenses

Support/Warranty Contracts

Development software

Utilities software

Data files

App 4.8.1.3 Physical

Hardcopy documents – files, letters, patient records, etc.

X-rays, CT Scans, MRI reports, etc.

Microfiche

App 4.8.2 Asset Classification

*Each asset **shall** be classified.*

*The assets containing confidential information **shall** be classified as private.*

App 4.8.3 Asset Identification and Register

*All <insert name of organisation> information assets **shall** be recorded in a register. Each register **shall** include, as a minimum, the below information:*

Product Number

Asset Number/Purchase Order No

A unique serial number

Location/User

Support/Warranty Information

Category of asset

Classification of asset

Asset Owner (normally the Information Asset Owner (IAO))

Final disposal details.

App 4.8.4 Asset Management

*Ownership of each Information Asset **shall** be linked to the relevant IAO and recorded on the Asset Register.*

*Each IAO **shall** know:*

What information is held and the nature of the information.

Who has access and the purpose of access?

*IAOs **shall** provide reports to the <insert name of organisation> Senior Information Risk Owner (SIRO), suggested as at least annually on assurance and usage of their assets.*

App 4.8.5 Asset Disposal

*All <insert name of organisation> assets that involve data/information **shall** be disposed of in accordance with the requirements of Government Guidance for the type of asset and its classification.*

The specialists handling the asset shall include the following processes:

*date, time, method and personnel responsible for the disposal of the asset **shall** be recorded in the Information Asset Register.*

APP 4.9 AUDIT POLICY

App 4.9.1 Technical Requirements

*<Insert name of organisation> **shall** implement auditing for all business-critical transactions that create, update or delete data on the System in audit tables which will be available for analysis. Where available this **shall** include:*

User name. Date.

Transaction Start Time.

Transaction End Time.

Satisfactory completion of transactions which have a financial implication to include:

Batch run identifier.

Workstation ID.

Access to and alteration of critical or security data.

Instances when processes are halted because of security or privilege breaches.

*<Insert name of organisation> business-critical system audit logs **shall** be sized appropriately and their contents reviewed regularly by trained staff, with discrepancies being reported to <insert name of organisation> Management and the relevant Information Asset Owner (IAO).*

[The information collected by technical means for system audits should be tailored to meet the requirements and capabilities of the organisation. Too little information may mean that actual or potential breaches and vulnerabilities are missed, too much information may mean that they are lost in a sea of background noise.]

<Insert name of organisation> system audit logs and any associated customer data that is collected, ***shall*** *be safeguarded using a combination of technical access controls and robust procedures, with all changes supported by logging and internal audit controls.*

[It is essential that audit logs and any collected data are protected in accordance with the information to which they refer. Audit logs should also be protected in order to ensure that they cannot be deleted, altered or tampered with.]

The activities of <insert name of organisation> system administrators and the use of powerful system utility tools ***should*** *be audited by independent internal auditors on a regular basis.*

[A process should be established to independently audit and verify the audit processes. This will add a further level of security control against the alteration or deletion of audit records or the misuse of the audit process.]

All critical <insert name of organisation> system clocks ***shall*** *be synchronised daily from a single time source, in particular between the various processing platforms within the IT infrastructure.*

'System time' in any system ***shall*** *not be manipulated, since it could invalidate log contents, which might compromise the investigation of security incidents.*

APP 4.10 DISASTER RECOVERY PLAN

A Disaster Recovery Plan ***shall*** *be produced to enable data and IT systems/functionality to be recovered in a structured and managed manner post an incident.*

The Disaster Recovery Plan ***shall*** *support the requirements of Business Continuity.*

The Plan ***shall*** *be regularly tested, this* ***should*** *be at least annually.*

The Plan ***should*** *cover:*

Ownership – which post owns and controls the plan

Responsibilities – identification of roles and their responsibilities

Identification of critical assets with priority order for recovery/business functionality

Capabilities – identified internal and external capabilities

Resources – allocation of tasks to resources, internal and external

Task flow – including:

Points of contact

Relationship to incident management team

Recovery processes and actions – in a structured order

Recording of recovery actions taken and time when assets recovered/restored.

Post Action Review – lessons learnt.

Test Schedule.

App 4.10.1 Responsibilities

The following roles ***shall*** *undertake the responsibilities listed:*

Senior Information Risk Owner (SIRO) – coordinate the development and maintenance of the Disaster Recovery Plan – ensuring it relates to the <insert name of organisation> Business Continuity Plan.

Disaster Recovery Plan Manager – maintains the Plan on behalf of the SIRO ensuring that testing is undertaken. A post ***shall*** *be allocated for this role.*

Information Asset Owners (IAOs) and Business Owners – ensure that the requirements from the Disaster Recovery planning are adequately considered and documented for all information assets of which they have ownership; and, enable the recovery to be enacted.

Line Managers – ensure that staff follow the <insert name of organisation> Disaster Recovery Plan procedures.

Chief Information Security Officer (CISO) – management of disaster recovery procedures relating to IT and information security.

App 4.10.2 Training and Awareness

Personnel who are required to undertake specific technical and functional roles associated with disaster recovery ***shall*** *be trained and formally qualified to complete this specialist function.*

All <insert name of organisation> staff, including third parties, ***shall*** *be made aware of the requirements of the <insert name of organisation> Disaster Recovery Plan and its Procedures.*

App 4.10.3 Management and Implementation

The Disaster Recovery Policy and the resulting Disaster Recovery Plan ***shall*** *be reviewed and re-issued annually or upon identification of a change in procedure or lesson learnt.*

The effectiveness of the Policy and Plan ***shall*** *be monitored through audits and tests (external and internal) and from lessons learnt during any business continuity activity.*

App 4.10.4 Testing

On behalf of the SIRO the Disaster Recovery Plan Manager ***shall*** *coordinate and manage testing which* ***should*** *follow the below levels and is recommended to be at least annually at each level:*

Table Top

Walkthrough

Real-time Live Test

APP 4.11 SOCIAL MEDIA POLICY

Social media are considered to be *IT based technologies (desktop, laptop, tablet and smartphone) that allow the creating and sharing of information, ideas, career interests and other forms of expression via virtual communities and* networks.

Social media includes, but is not limited to:

Facebook

WhatsApp

Messenger

Tumblr

Instagram

Pinterest

LinkedIn

Snapchat

Twitter

YouTube.

App 4.11.1 Social Media Activity

Only social media sites that have been authorised and enabled by <insert name of organisation> IT Service operations for users ***shall*** *be accessed via <insert name of organisation> IT systems, including via <insert name of organisation> issued smartphones.*

When accessing social media, including personal accounts, for personal use on <insert name of organisation> IT systems the following principles ***shall*** *be followed by users:*

Excessive personal use of the social media during working hours ***shall*** *be forbidden and contraventions to this* ***may*** *lead to disciplinary action.*

Social media ***shall*** *only be used for personal activities; it is not for use for the transmission, storage or discussion of any NHS or other UK Government information.*

Social media ***shall*** *be used in a manner that does not bring <insert name of organisation> or the wider NHS into disrepute or harm or tarnish its image or reputation through offensive, inappropriate or derogatory remarks.*

Where a <insert name of organisation> role is authorised to use social media for their responsibilities (e.g. use of Twitter, Facebook and YouTube) this shall be in accordance with the role requirements and as outlined in the job description.

Users using social media (for personal and corporate use) ***shall*** *be forbidden from:*

Breaching data protections laws or patient confidentiality.

Publishing images or text that might be considered as harassment or are discriminatory, offensive or abusive. This includes the promotion of discrimination based on factors such as race, sex, religion, nationality, disability, sexual orientation or age.

Publishing images or text that might be considered threatening, abusive, hateful or inflammatory, which constitutes an invasion of privacy, or causes annoyance, inconvenience or needless anxiety or which promotes violence.

Doing anything that may be considered discriminatory against, libellous or bullying and/or harassment of, any individual.

Infringing any copyright, database right or trade mark of any other person or organisation including posting copyrighted information in a way that violates the copyright of that information.

Publishing images or text that advocate, promote or assist in any unlawful act or any illegal activity.

Introducing or promoting the use of any form of computer virus or malware.

Deliberately impersonating any person, or misrepresenting your identity or affiliation with any person.

Breaching the terms of service of the social network.

Promoting messages for party political purposes or for campaigning organisations.

Promoting personal financial interests or commercial ventures to secure personal advantage.

Providing links to websites of a violent, obscene or offensive nature or which contain any content that can be construed as violating any of the above guidelines.

Making any discriminatory, disparaging, defamatory or harassing comments or otherwise engaging in any conduct prohibited by the <insert name of organisation>'s policies.

Making slanderous, defamatory, false, obscene, indecent, lewd, pornographic, violent, abusive, insulting, threatening or harassing images or comments.

APP 4.12 MOBILE AND REMOTE WORKING POLICY

App 4.12.1 Physical Security of Information and Systems

*Users **shall** ensure that confidential information is not removed from site without prior approval and authorisation from management.*

*Users **shall** ensure that mobile systems or devices are not used outside <insert name of organisation> premises without prior approval and authorisation from management.*

*Mobile equipment **shall** be stored securely when not in use in and out of <insert name of organisation> premises.*

Confidential information **shall** be protected to the appropriate level at all times.

Mobile systems, devices or information **shall** be transported securely and kept with the individual at all times.

Remote locations **shall** be secure to work in, i.e. not overlooked by unauthorised persons.

Sensitive matters **shall** not be worked on in public places.

Sensitive conversations or those involving the Company **shall** not be carried out in public. Secure email **should** be used or wait until you are back in <insert name of organisation> premises if possible.

*If left unattended in semi-controlled areas such as conference centres or customer offices, laptops **shall** be shut down and locked to a fixed point using a physical lock available from IT support.*

*Confidential Information **shall** be brought back to <insert name of organisation> premises for secure disposal.*

*Precautions **shall** be taken to protect assets against opportunist theft.*

*Mobile systems, devices or information **shall** never be left unattended in airport lounges, hotel lobbies, vehicles and similar areas as these areas are insecure.*

*Mobile systems, devices or information **shall** be shut down and physically locked down or locked away when left in the office overnight.*

*Mobile systems, devices or information **shall** never be left in parked cars, unless unavoidable and for the minimum amount of time, completely invisible from outside the vehicle and protected from extreme temperatures.*

*Mobile systems, devices or information **shall** not be checked in as hold luggage when travelling, but treated as hand or cabin luggage at all times.*

*Users **shall** ensure that unauthorised persons (friends, family, associates, etc.) do not gain access to mobile systems, devices or information in their charge.*

*Any loss, theft, misplacement or unauthorised access of systems, devices or information **shall** be reported immediately to <insert name of organisation> management.*

App 4.12.2 Technical Security of Information and Systems

Files containing confidential information data ***shall*** *be adequately protected e.g. encrypted and password protected in accordance with <insert name of organisation> encryption policy.*

All removable media ***shall*** *be virus checked prior to use.*

Mobile devices ***shall*** *have security options enabled, such as a pin numbers or a password.*

Automatic lock outs ***shall*** *be enabled when IT equipment is left unattended.*

Users ***shall*** *ensure that Virus protection software or any other security measures put in place on devices are never disabled or bypassed.*

Users ***shall*** *ensure that confidential information is stored on mobile systems or devices unless it is protected with <insert name of organisation> approved encryption, and it is absolutely necessary to do so.*

Staff ***shall*** *ensure that privately owned mobile systems or devices are not used for official <insert name of organisation> business.*

Users ***shall*** *ensure that unauthorised software is not installed on any mobile system or device in their charge.*

Index

[*all references are to paragraph number*]